MARRIAGE AND DEATH NOTICES

from the

Southern Christian Advocate.

Volume II: 1861-1867

I0094115

by Brent H. Holcomb, C. A. L. S.

Southern Historical Press, Inc.
Greenville, South Carolina

Please direct all correspondence and orders to:

www.southernhistoricalpress.com
or
SOUTHERN HISTORICAL PRESS, Inc.
PO BOX 1267
375 West Broad Street
Greenville, SC 29601
southernhistoricalpress@gmail.com

ISBN #0-89308-154-X

Printed in the United States of America

TO

MISS KARON MAC SMITH

who has made an inestimable contribution to genealogy by indexing
this and numerous other books and without whose cooperation many
books could not have been published.

INTRODUCTION

This second volume of abstracts from the Southern Christian Advocate covers the period from 1861-1867, the Confederate War and aftermath. Of course, any such volume is useful to genealogists but this period is of particular value because of the paucity of tombstones erected during this time of distress and poverty. Miss Smith, the indexer, has kindly added an index of military units mentioned in this volume. This is a real boon to Civil War buffs, and to genealogists as well.

The Southern Christian Advocate continued into the twentieth century, but so many notices are found, a book covering the entire run of the newspaper would be impractical and too large to bind. However, a third volume will be considered, perhaps only marriages or only obituaries, if reader interest is sufficient and expressed.

Brent H. Holcomb, C. A. L. S.
P. O. Box 21766
Columbia, South Carolina 29221
February 15, 1980

Married in this city, on the 12th inst., by the Rev. Mr.
Southerland, Peter M. Wallace to Miss Catherine A. Mousseau, both
of this city.

By Elder W. M. Verdery, at the late residence of Benj. F.
Latimer, deceased, Hancock co., Miss Julia A. Latimer and Jeptha
M. Cody, M. D. of Covington, Ga.

On Tuesday, 27th Nov., by Rev. West Williams, Mr. G. W. Raysor, of Hardeeville, S. C., to Miss S. Henrietta Mims, daughter
of the late Capt. Thos. Mims, of Charleston Dist., S. C.

Dec. 12th, by Rev. Martin Eaddy, Pinckney Killingworth to
Miss Silvania Smith, all of Williston, S. C.

In Scriven co., on the 16th inst., by Rev. W. Knox, Rev. L.
B. Payne, of the Ga. Conf., to Mrs. Sarah M. Currell, of Scriven
co., Ga.

By Rev. W. C. Bass, on the 4th Dec., at the residence of the
bride's father, Mr. George A. Bivins, of Bibb co., Ga.,to Miss
Tissie Tomlinson, daughter of Dr. Romlinson, of Americus, Ga.

By Rev. N. H. Palmer, on 12th Dec., Mr. James Glen to Miss
Susan Littlejohn, daughter of Rev. A. Littlejohn,all of Nacoochee, Ga.

On the 18th Dec., near Monroe, Ga.,by Rev. George W. Yarbrough,
Dr. James M. Horton of Banks co., Ga.,to Miss Emma O. Mitchell,
of Walton co., Ga.

By Rev. Albert Gray, on the 18th Dec., at Mt. Zion, Hancock
co., Rolin W. Stevens, of Greensboro, Ga. to Miss Mary A., Green
of the former place.

Perry F. Ingrem, late of Bradley co., Ark., was born in Lancaster Dist., S. C. Oct. 17th, 1833, and died at the residence
of his father, in Kershaw Dist., on the 9th of Dec., 1860. He
first settled in Pickens co., Ala., where he married a Miss
Ingram, who lived only about one year after their union. He
then moved to Mississippi, where he married a Miss Pagan, who
died in little over twelve months after their marriage, leaving
an infant which soon followed her to the tomb. He subsequently
moved to Bradley co., Ark., and married Miss Francis F. Brawner,
from whom and an infant only about four months old he is now
taken...   Landy Wood

John Monroe, infant son of Perry F. and Frances L. Ingrem,
aged 4 months, died on the 12th Dec., 1860. Thus the widow is
also motherless....   L. Wood

Issue of January 3, 1861

Married in Talbot co., Ga., Dec. 13th, by Rev. D. T. Holmes,
Mr. J. R. James of Atlanta, Ga. to Miss Susan A. Leonard, of Talbot co.

Died of diphtheria, in Columbia, S. C., on Monday, Dec. 10th,
1860, Frank, son of Charles and Charlotte G. Taylor, aged 3 years,
4 months and 10 days.

In Oct., near Tarversville, Ga., Mary C., youngest child of
Jas. W. and Harriet Ward, in his 13th year....

On 17th Dec., in Jeffersonville, Ga., William Hinton, infant
son of Robert R. and Penelope Wimberly, aged 6 weeks.

Mrs. Mary Ledbetter, daughter of David Verner (a revolution-
ary soldier) and Esther his wife, was born in Abbeville dist.,
S. C., Nov. 13th, 1782. When small, her parents moved to Anderson dist., S. C., in which she lived until nine months previous
to her death. She moved to Hart co., Ga...married to John Ledbetter in 1803, was left a widow in 1831. They raised ten children, seven sons and three daughters....   B. B. Parker, Jr.

1

Nancy C., my wife, died Sept. 8, 1860. She was the daughter of William and Elenor Henderson. was born in Cornersville, Tenn., July 6, 1813....   Goleman Green.
     Mrs. Mary McClerg died Dec. 15th, at the dwelling of Dr. T. Y. Henry, in the 90th year of her age...a native of Va., her maiden name was Red....   D. L. White, Sr.
     Martha E., wife of Dr. M. W. Gray, and daughter of James and H. W. Baskin, of Carroll co., Ga., died at Cave Spring, Ga., the 14th Dec. 1860, in the 21st year of her age....
     Bedford Cade died in Caldwell Parish, La., Nov. 20th, 1860, in the 67th year of his life...born in Wilkes co., Ga., July 6, 1793....   R. Parvin

Issue of January 10, 1861

     Rene W. Armor, died on the 30th Nov., 1860, in Cobb co., Ga., about 54 years of age....
     Mrs. Nancy Hamilton, a native of Wythe co., Va., who had resided in Rutherford, N. C., about 60 years, died at Rutherford on the 4th Dec., in the 85th year of her age....   A. Hamby
     Mrs. Lizzie Polk, wife of Levi E. Polk, Esq., of Macon co., Ga., died while on a visit to her mother's, Mrs. Howard, in Lexington Dist., S. C., Nov. 9th, 1860, aged 29 years and 24 days...joined the Evangelical Lutheran Church in 1853, moved with her husband to Macon co., Ga., in Dec. 1859. There being no Lutheran Church convenient, she united with the M. E. Church at Oglethorpe...left husband and four interesting children....
     Miss Susan H. Lowman, daughter of Mr. Wm. Lowman, Sr. of Barbour Co., Ala., died on the 11th Nov., 1860, at the residence of Mr. A. A. Person, near Enon, Ala., aged 22 years and one month ....
     Miss Julia Ann Moore, of Catawba co., N. C., died on 3rd Nov., in her 20th year....
     Mrs. Sarah E. Dews, wife of Bethel Dews, died in Grahamville, S. C., on 10th Dec., 1860....
     Mrs. Mattie Kirkland, wife of Mr. Murray Kirkland, died 21st Dec., in Fairfield, S. C....   J. W. Puett
     Mrs. Charlotte Smith, died 26th Dec., 1860, in Fairfield, S. C., in the 74th year of her age....   J. W. Puett

Issue of January 17, 1861

     Married by Rev. A. Davis, Nov. 28th, Capt. Francis Broward to Miss Mary Demine, all of Hamilton co., Fla.
     On 1st Jan. 1861, in Suwannee co., Fla., by Rev. Joshua Caraway, Samuel Mitchell, of Hillsborough co., Fla., to Miss Jane C. Urquhart, of the former county.
     On 20th Dec., by Dr. E. C. Ragsdale, Samuel Meares, of Greenville, to Miss Eliza Nash, of Laurens Dist., S. C.
     Jan. 2d, 1861, by Rev. Lewis M. Hamer, Charles T. McRae, to Miss Janett Meekins, all of Marlboro Dist., S. C.
     In the Methodist Church, Sumter, by Rev. F. M. Morgan, Rev. J. Litle McGregor of the S. C. Conf., to Miss Eliza Jane, daughter of Rev. Jesse Morgan, of Sumter.
     By Rev. M. M. Boyd, on 27th Dec., Rev. Wm. B. Currie, of the S. C. Conf., to Miss Martha Glymph, of Newberry.
     In Schley co., Ga., at the residence of her uncle, John N. Hudson, on the 27th ult., by Rev. Wyatt R. Singleton, Mr. Hiram H. Mott to Miss Jane E. Hudson, both of Macon co., Ga.
     By Rev. Geo. C. Clarke, at the house of Peter Corbin, Taylor co., Ga., Mr. Wm. J. Pollard, of Augusta, to Miss Isabella C. Corbin, of said county.

By Rev. H. V. Mulkey, on 23d Dec., T. T. Garland to Miss Martha J. Fuller, all of Barbour co., Ala.

By Rev. L. M. Little, on 29th Nov., Mr. S. B. Jordon of Williamsburg, to Miss Susan Pipkin, of Georgetown Dist., S. C.

By Rev. L. M. Little, on 20th Dec., Mr. Julius Gamble to Miss Martha J. Graham, all of Williamsburg, S. C.

On 25th Dec., by Rev. R. N. Cotter, Mr. Stephen H. McArther to Miss Nancy Pitman, all of Telfair co., Ga.

By Rev. W. A. Gamewell, Dec. 19th, near Columbia, Edward Lomas to Ella Douglass, of Richland Dist.

On Dec. 30th, at the residence of John C. Turner, by Rev. J. W. Yarbrough, Mr. E. J. Bond to Miss Mollie E. Nail, all of DeKalb co., Ga.

By Rev. T. A. Pharr, on 23d Dec., Mr. C. R. Hames of Cherokee co., Ga., to Miss Mary A. Thomas, of cobb co., Ga.

By Rev. Geo. C. Clarke, Mr. Joseph Dasher to Miss Sallie E. Harris, both of Fort Valley, Ga.

On the 18th Dec., by Rev. A. J. Cauthen, Mr. James McDow, of Lancaster, to Miss Malissa Crane, of Fishing Creek, Chester Dist., S. C.

In Wilmington, on the 20th inst., by Rev. Jos. H. Wheeler, Rev. Jos. Wheeler, of the N. C. Conf., to Miss Mattie, eldest daughter of Wm. Sutton, Esq. of Wilmington.

On 10th Jan., 1861, by Rev. R. B. Lester, Dr. Edward Hatcher to Miss Augusta V. Churchill, both of Burke co., Ga.

In Hardeeville, S. C., Dec. 27th, by Rev. M. L. Banks, Rev. Jno. W. McRoy of the S. C. Conf., to Miss Amelia J. Coburn, eldest daughter of Rev. Jno. R. Coburn, of the S. C. Conf.

On Sunday morning, 6th inst., by Rev. J. T. Turner, Rev. J. T. Payne to Miss Roxie E., eldest daughter of John Reddick, all of Weston, Webster co., Ga.

In New Orleans, Dec. 25th, 1860, by Rev. J. R. Walker, Maj. A. Jackson, of Texas to Mrs. S. C. Brownlee, of S. C.

Mrs. Caroline Louise Van Epps, daughter of Gen. Nicholas and Mrs. Judith Howard, of Columbus, Ga., and wife of A. C. Van Epps, Esq., of Chattanooga, Tenn., died on 21st December...E. F. Sevier

Wm. D. Meetze, died in Graniteville, S. C., Sept. 2d, 1860, in the 37th year of his age....

Sarah Jane, daughter of Dougal and Sarah Calhoun, of Marlboro Dist., S. C., was born Nov. 7th, 1860, and died Dec. 22d, 1860 ....   Lewis M. Hamer.

Lemuel Glymph died in Newberry Dist., S. C., Dec. 5th, 1860, in his 66th year....   W. Bowman

Miss Julia Joy, eldest daughter of Rev. Miles Joy, died in Darlington Dist., Dec. 4th, 1860, in the 17th year of her age....

Benjamin Kemp Hurt died Dec. 31, 1860, at the residence of Joel E. Hurt, Esq.,near Columbus, Ga., aged 21 years and 3 months ....

Mary Ann, wife of John W. W. Snead, and daughter of Rev. John B. Davies, was born in Chatham co., Ga., Nov. 10th, 1827, and died in Milledgeville, Ga., Dec. 19th, 1860....

Mrs. Martha J. Reid, wife of Mr. James L. Reid, died near Eatonton, Ga., on 28th Nov., 1860, aged 46 years...left husband, and six children....   C. W. Key

Miss Mattie N., daughter of Roland Bivins, and Nancy Bivins, deceased, died in Bibb co., Ga., on 14th Dec., 1860, aged 20 years and 16 days....   C. W. Smith

James S.Strickland was born on the 7th May, 1835, was married to Sarah Haymans, 24th Feb., 1853, died 9th Oct., 1860.... since that time his wife and infant daughter have followed him to the same grave-yard....

Sister Strickland died 23d November in the 29th year of her age....

James Emory, a promising son of Rev. Anderson R. and Mary Ann Lovejoy, was born 20th Feb. 1847, and died 11th December 1860, aged 13 years and 21 days....

Martha Ann Grier, fourth daughter of Moses and Sarah Grier, died in Coosa co., Ala., Oct. 23d 1860, in her 36th year...in early infancy she was baptized by the late Rev. Isaac Grier, D. D., a relative and well known minister of the A. R. P. Church...
                                                        A. B. Elliott.
Miss Fannie E. Yarbrough, daughter of Mr. S. H. and Mrs. S. K. Yarbrough died in Pike co., Ga., Dec. 16th, 1860, aged 18 years
....

Tallulah Clayton, only daughter of R. W. and Carrie E. Hart, died in Sparta, Hancock co., Dec. 12th, aged 9 years, 25 days....

Mrs. Margaret G. Besser, was born in Charleston, S. C., in 1811, where she lived until 1840 when she removed to Dahlonega, Ga., where she died 25th Dec., aged 49 years....

Mrs. Sarah Mann, wife of Jesse Mann, died in Harelson co., Ga., Nov. 8, in her 63d year....

Nicholas M. Bradley, was born in Oglethorpe co., Ga., June 13th, 1807, and died in Clay co., Fla., Dec. 22d, 1860....
                                                        H. F. Smith
Tribute of Respect to Adolphus J. Orr, by Thomasville station, Fla. Conf....

Issue of January 24, 1861

Married in Hardeville, 11th Jan, by Rev. J. R. Coburn, Mr. J. P. Singleton of Georgetown, S. C., to Miss E. C. Coburn, second daughter of Rev. J. R. Coburn.

On the 15th inst., in Eatonton, Ga., by Rev. A. M. Wynn, Dr. G. W. Andrews to Miss Ellen G. Harwell.

On the 18th Dec., by Rev. A. R. Lovejoy, Madison Freeman to Miss Amanda Crum, all of Merriwether co., Ga.

James M. Calhoun of Atlanta on the 18th Dec., to Mrs. Amelia A. Holt, of Thomaston, Ga.

On 3d January, by Rev. A. B. Stephens, Dr. C. G. Stephens of Blackville, S. C. to Mrs. Janie Barns, of Orangeburg, S. C.

Alexander Johnson, son of Rev. Russell W. Johnson, died at Spier's Turn Out, Jefferson co., Ga., Dec. 20th, 1860, aged about 16 years....

Mrs. Sarah Bird, died near Taylor's Creek, Ga., Dec. 12th, 1860, in her 74th year. She was married to Capt. James Bird in 1805, and left a widow with six small children in 1819.... W. M. Watts

Mrs. Mary P. Danner, relict of William T. Danner, died in Beaufort, S. C., Dec. 25th, 1860, in her 43d year....

Samuel S. Lockhart, son of John and Sarah A. Lockhart, died near Griffin, Ga., 1st Nov., 1860, in the 18th year of his age
....

Mrs. Nancy Lewis died in Greene co., Ga., Jan 7th, 1861, in her 75th year....left four children....

Susan Swicord was born June 9th, 1792, and died in Decatur co., Ga., Nov. 27th, 1860, in her 69th year....

Issue of January 31, 1861

Married on 10th January, at the house of Mr. Tradewell, by Rev. A. B. Stephens, Mr. Daniel Zeiglar to Miss Jane Lary, all of Orangeburg, S. C.

On 15th January, by Rev. A. B. Stephens, Hon. Donald Rowe Barton to Miss Julia Augusta Rowe, all of Orangeburg.

By Rev. Albert Gray, on 14th January, at White Plains, Ga., Mr. Albert Jernigan to Mrs. Henrietta M. Shaffer, both of the former place.

In Upson co., on 19th Dec., 1860, by Rev. W. F. Cook, Mr.
R. S. Lockets, of Culloden, Ga., to Miss Julia H. Kendall, daughter of the late Dr. Kendall, of Upson.

On 20th December, by A. D. Eason, Esq., J. P. R. Siken to Miss
Victoria Fletcher, all of Tattnall co., Ga.

On 10th Jan. 1861, by Rev. W. F. Cook, John M. Stubbs, Esq.
of Macon, Ga., to Miss Ella Tucker, daughter of Dr. Nathan Tucker,
of Laurens co., Ga.

In Beaufort Dist., at the residence of Mrs. C. W. Thomson,
by Rev. J. W. Kelly, Mr. W. W. Daniel of Savannah, to Miss
Rebecca S. Deloach, of the former District.

on 20th Dec., by Rev. John M. Smith, Mr. Thos K. Watts, and
Mary L. Baker, all of Fulton co., Ga.

By C. A. Crowell, January 9th, 1861, Mr. Milton C. Jackson,
of Calhoun, Gordon co., to Miss Emily Milican, of Cass co., Ga.

On the 22d inst., by the Rev. Thomas T. Christian, Robert G.
Gorce of Newberry Dist., S. C., and Miss Fannie E. Johnson, of
LaGrange, Ga.

In Dallas co., Ala., on the 9th inst., at the residence of
the bride's father, by the Rev. David M. Reeves, Capt. Seaborn
J. Soffold, of Madison, Ga., to Miss Maggie Molette, eldest
daughter of Mr. John W. Molette.

On Jan. 16th, by Rev. S. H. Browne, Rev. A. H. Harmon, of
the S. C. Conf., to Miss Martha Medley, daughter of Joseph Medley, Esq. of Anson co., N. C.

On 30th Dec., by Joseph K. Rishe, S. H. Langdale to Miss
Victoria A. Smith, all of Colleton Dist., S. C.

Jan. 15th, by Rev. J. B. McGehee, Mr. A. J. Barrow, of Jones,
to Miss Mary F. Pound, of Putnam co., Ga.

Died at White Plains, Ga., Dec. 25th, Alice Magnolia, daughter of T. T. and Mary A. Eason, aged 2 years and 9 months.

In Macon, Ga., Jan. 2d, Emma E., infant daughter of Rev.
W. W. and Mrs. Georgia V. Oslin.

Miss Keziah Arthur, daughter of the late Hargrove Arthur,
Esq., died Dec. 13th, at her residence near Granby....

Fanny R., youngest daughter of Daniel L. and Rebecca Trussel,
of Talbot co., Ga., was born Jan. 16th, 1841, and died after a
protracted illness, Jan. 11th, 1861....

Rev. Philemon Murray, a local preacher in the Cooper river
circuit, died in the 36th year of his age....

Mrs. Nancy Lee (formerly Mrs. Turner) died in Henry co., Ga.,
31st December, in her 54th year....   W. W. Hardy

Rev. Richard Godfrey was born in Charleston, S. C., and died
9th Jan., 1861, in his 53d year....

Sarah M. Ren, daughter of G. G. and Mrs. N. C. Heath, was
born Nov. 4, 1832, and died in Chester Dist., Dec. 8th, 1860....

Sarah Ann C. Robertson, was born 26th May, 1834, and died
Jan. 12th, 1861....

Issue of February 7, 1861

Married on the 29th of January, by Rev. W. H. Ellison, D. D.,
Rev. Jesse Wood of the Ala Conf., to Miss Alice Tison, daughter
of Rev. James G. Tison, of Glennville, Ala.

On the 29th of January, by Rev. L. M. Hamer, Dr. J. S. Stoney
to Miss Laura A. Allen, all of Allendale, S. C.

On the 3d of January, by Rev. L. J. Crum, Dr. Wm. Murray,
of Colleton Dist., to Miss Eugenia E. Bowman, of Orangeburg
Dist., S. C.

Mrs. Elizabeth A. Brown, daughter of the late S. G. and Mrs.
A. B. DeVeaux, and wife of Rev. Manning Brown, of the S. C.
conf. died near Pineville, Dec. 17th, 1860, in the 30th year of
her age. (elong eulogy).

5

James W. Smith, died in Warren co., Ga., on 2d January, 1861, aged about 80 years...born in Southampton co., Va., In 1811 he settled where he has lived until his death...raised ten children ...Since that on 21st January, another daughter Mrs. Emily T. Felts has joined him in heaven. She was the wife of L. F. Felts, and died in the 44th year of her age....   W. A. Florence

Wm. H. Rainy was born in Anderson Dist., S. C., 10th July 1834 and died 7th Nov 1860....

Priscilla M., wife of W. S. Gregory, Esq. and daughter of Rev. Ambrose Ray of Miss., died Nov. 29th, 1860, near Belmont, Union Dist., S. C., in the 36th year of her age...Colin Murchison.

Miss Ellen S. Templeton died at the residence of Dr. W. E. Hall, near Rocky Mount, S. C., on the 3d Dec., ...W. J. Templeton

Mrs. Mary E. Johnson, daughter of Thos. E. and Martha Zuber, was born in Oglethorpe co., Ga., died Dec. 22nd, 1860, near Floyd Springs, Floyd co., in her 19th year...   R. H. Jones

Mary, daughter of Gen. H. H. and Louisa Kinard, of Newberry S. C., died Jan. 8th, 1861, in the 9th year of her age...
                                            W. A. McSwain.

Tribute of Respect to John U. V. Wilson by Faldosta Circuit, Fla. Conf....

Issue of February 14, 1861

Married in Lynchburg, S. C., on the 9th Jan., by Rev. Colin Murchison, W. W. Spencer, Esq. of Cheraw, S. C. to Miss Ella J. eldest daughter of Rev. Kenneth Murchison, deceased.

At. Powell & Fant's Hotel, Unionville, S.C., on Thursday evening, 24th Jan., by Rev. Colin Murchison, Mr. Preston Fant, of Mississippi, to Miss Attilla Fant, of the former place.

By Rev. Josiah Barker, at Spring Hill, Marengo co., Ala., Jan. 16th, 1861, Mr. Jno. W. Deanes to Miss Jane Elizabeth Pegues.

In Macon, Ga., Feb. 6th, 1861, by Rev. R. B. Lester, James W. Lester, of Cobb co., Ga., to Miss Hattie E. Smith of Warrenton, Ga.

On the 3rd Jan., by Rev. L. Cannon, Mr. Elisha Driggers to Miss Caroline Hilton, both of St. James', Goose Creek.

On Jan. 20, by Rev. L. Cannon, Mr. Thos Huff to Mrs. Sarah Huff, both of St. James's, Goose Creek.

On Feb. 7th, by Rev. Geo. C. Clarke, Mr. Wm. T. Alford, of Macon, to Miss Larua N. McArthur of Bibb co., Ga.

On 24th Jan., at the residence of Rev. G. T. Spearman, by Rev. A. C. Mixon, Mr. Samuel S. Blackwell to Miss May Spearman; all of Jasper co., Ga.

Jan. 3d, by Rev. Geo. G. N. McDonell, Mr. Joseph H. White to Miss Sallie R. Redding, all of Monroe co., Ga.

On 31st Jan by Rev. J. M. Smith, Jeremiah T. Gilbert to Miss Sarah M. Perkerson, all of Fulton co., Ga.

William D. Starr, son of Benjamin and Charlotte Starr, was born Jan. 6th, 1821, and died Nov. 14th, 1860...   N. Miller

Hubert B. Gaither, son of Dr. Henry and Sarah Gaither, was born in Newton co., Ga., Aug. 6th, 1836, and died at his father's residence, Oxford, Ga., Jan. 13th, 1861....   J. R. Thomas

Miss Amanda Floyd was born Nov. 18th, 1837, and died near Sandersville, Ga., Jan. 26th, 1861....   W. S. Turner

Sarah A. Griffith, wife of Rev. James Griffith, died in Butler, Ga., on the 13th December, aged 27....   G. W. Persons

John S. Johnson, brother to sister Griffith, died at the same place, on 19th December, in his 24th year   G. W. P.

Mary Abaline, daughter of Keelin D., and Sarah H. Kearce, of Barnwell Dist., S. C., was born January 17th, 1853, and died January 28th, 1861....

6

Tribute of Respect to Bro. T. J. Holton, editor of the N.
C. Whig, by Charlotte station....

Issue of February 21, 1861

Married on 28th Jan., by Rev. J. S. Connor, Mr. Wm. K. Blake,
President of Spartanburg Female College, to Miss Mariana Gregg,
daughter of Mr. and Mrs. Lewis Jones, of Edgefield, S. C.
On 24th Jan., by Rev. V. A. Sharp, Mr. J. D. Masters, to Miss
Sarah M., eldest daughter of W. A. Lesley, all of Pickens.
On Jan. 17th, 1861, by Rev. J. T. Turner, Henry J. Fillingim
to Mrs. M. Millen, both of Randolph co., Ga.
On 24th ult., by Rev. A. B. Stephens, Mr. J. Wesley Crum, of
Orangeburg, to Miss Rebecca Hartzog, of Barnwell, S. C.
On 17th Jan., 1861, by Rev. R. H. Waters, at the house of
the bride's father, Mr. Jas. M. Langford, to Miss Elliott Hollings-
worth, all of Henry co., Ga.
On 6th Feb., by Rev. D. W. Seale, Maj. Wm. F. Deschamps to
Miss H. E. Law, all of Sumter Dist., S. C.
Died in St. Stephen's Parish, S. C., on the 16th Jan., 1861,
Lovey A. M. Orvin, daughter of N. W. and M. M. Orvin, aged 4 years,
6 months and 13 days.
Miss Kittie Tooke, daughter of Joseph Tooke, Esq., of Hayne-
ville, Houston co., Ga., died at the residence of Rev. John W.
Burke, inMacon, Ga.,on Monday the 4th inst., at 8 A. M...in the
Senior Class of the Wesleyan Female College...
Rev. George Washington Dansby died at the house of Daniel
Scott, Esq., in Alachua co., Fla., in his 34th year...a student
at Cokesbury, in the year 1843...   Samuel Leard
Mrs. Susan White died in Anson co., N. C., Nov. 1860, in the
84th year of her age....   William Hutto

Issue of February 28, 1861

Married on Thursday 7th inst., at Greenwood, by Rev. W. C. Mc-
Swain, Dr. E. T. McSwain, to Miss Julia Hackett, all of Abbeville
Dist., S. C.
By C. A. Moore, on the 12th inst., Mr. Jas. Mason, of Laurens
co., to Miss C. W. Walker, of the same co.
On the 18th inst., by Rev. W. C. Power, Mr. Columbua R. Aber-
crombie, of Perry co., Ala., to Miss Wincy A. Dunlap, of Anson
co., N. C.
By Rev. T. B. Harven, on 12th inst., Mr. J. B. Jones to Miss
J. J. Patrick, both of Oglethorpe co., Ga.
By Rev. Henry J. Evans, on the 5th Feb., Thomas Brown, of
Henry co., and Amanda Ivey, of Newton co., Ga.
By Joseph T. Webb, J. P. on the 29th Jan. 1861, at Mrs.
Elizabeth Joyce's, Mr. Geo. W. Pike, to Miss Alice E. Joyce, all
of Brooks co., Ga.
On the 14th Feb., by Rev. Smith Davenport, Dr. Augustus V.
Ball to Miss Argent W. L. West, all of Randolph co., Ga.
On 9th Feb., by Rev. J. Austen, Rev. J. S. Strange to Miss
Florence Wilson, all of Effingham co., Ga.
On 30th ult., by Rev. E. W. Thompson, Mr. J. S. Ivy, of Stan-
ly co., N. C. to Miss Mary E., eldest daughter of Mr. allison Dry.
On the 12th inst., by Rev. E. W. Thompson, Mr. Thomas Eagle
to Miss Jane E. Patterson, second daughter of J. A. Patterson,
all of Concord, N. C.
On the 14th inst., by Rev. C. A. Fulwood, Mr. Thomas Leigh,
to Miss Mary F. Brewster, all of Coweta co., Ga.
On the 19th inst., in Clay co., Fla., by Rev. H. T. Lewis,
Mr. David Long to Miss Isabella Wingate.

On the 7th inst., by Rev. R. E. McGinty, Dr. Henry Q. Harper, to Wilkes co., Ga., to Miss Cassie M. Stone, of Warren co., Ga.

On Feb. 14th, by Rev. H. J. Hunter, Mr. Alexander McLeod, of Orion, Ala., to Miss Carrie Mahone, of Millville, Butler co., Ala.

On the 24th Jan., 1861, by Rev. R. B. Lester,Mr. John B. Wolfe, of Dublin, Ga., to Miss Mary Douglass, of Alexander, Ga.

On 20th Feb., 1861, by Rev. R. B. Lester, Mr. William A. Wilkins, of Louisville, Ga.,to Miss Ann E. M. Carswell, of Burke co., Ga.

In Lumpkin, Ga.,Feb. 17th, 1861, by Rev. D. D. Cox., Dr. Jas. R. Barnum, of Savannah, Ga., to Miss Floretta S. Boynton, of Lumpkin, Ga.

Died on the 17th Feb., Lucy David, infant daughter of Rev. L. M. Hamer, of the S. C. Conf, aged 11 months and 25 days.

In Albany, Ga.,Feb. 13th, Anna Dell, infant daughter of Jos. H. and Frances E. McClellan, aged 8 months and 16 days.

Mrs. Tesie J. Godfrey, wife of Dr. T. J. Godfrey, and daughter of Samuel F. and Martha E. Frink, died in Hamilton co., Fla., Dec. 14th, 1860, aged 19 years, and 8 months....   R. H. Howren

Mrs. Martha Smalley, daughter of D. G. And Phebe Colvin, and wife of Ferdinand Smalley, died in Columbia co., Ga., Feb. 1st, in her 24th year....   J. M. Austin

Frances E. Hearn was born 14th Sept., 1790, and died Jan. 24th, 1861, in her 71st year....

Ralph Lemaster died in Chambers co., Ala., at about 80 years of age....   Thomas H. Whitby.

Issue of March 7, 1861

Married on 20th Feb., by Rev. G. H. Pattillo, Mr. George H. Davis, of Butler, Ga., to Miss Mary E. Bryant, of Talbotton, Ga.

On 17th Feb., by Rev. W. G. Booth, Mr. Z. H. Caldwell to Miss H. E. Sturdevant, all of Taylor co., Ga.

On Feb. 21st, by Rev. A. J. Doan, Mr. S. S. Griffith to Miss C. A. L. Johnson, both of Butler, Ga.

By Rev. J. M. Smith, Feb. 19, 1861, at the house of Jas. H. Wilson, Campbell co., Ga., William H. Ferguson, to Miss Nancy L. Wilson.

In Jones co., Ga., Feb. 19th, by Rev. J. H. McGehee, Mr. John B. Moore to Miss Christian Blow.

By Rev. L. G. R. Wiggins, on the 18th Jan., 1861, at the residence of Mr. Alvis Stafford, father of the bride, Mr. A. J. Blalock, of Pike co., Ga., to Miss Henrietta F. Stafford, of Upson co., Ga.

On the 28th Feb., by Rev. L. T. Mizell, Dr. Robert R. Murry, of Watkinsville, Ga., to Miss Josephine E. C. Lindley, of Powder Springs, Ga.

Mrs. Sally Smith died at the residence of her son-in-law, in Fayette co., Ga., Dec. 26th, 1860, in her 80th year...born in Va., emigrated with her father, Wm. Mitchell, to Clarke co., Ga., was married to Miles Smith in 1805. She has a large circle of relatives in various states...All her living children were with at the time of her death....

Henry Holman died at his residence in Barnwell Dist., S. C., on the 29th of Dec., 1860, in his 60th year....

Mr. John T. Scott was born and reared in Williamsburg, S. C., where he lived a highly respected and useful man...purchased land in Arkansas and set out on 25th Nov. with his family and servants for their new home....died 23d Dec., in his 58th year....

Martha Jane Hutto, daughter of H. J. M. and Lydia Hutto, of Thomas co., Ga., was born Jan. 26th, 1842, and died Feb. 13th, 1861 ....Mrs. Eady V. Smith, wife of Rev. James R. Smith was born in Henry co., Ga., Feb. 25th and died in Decatur, Ga., Feb. 6th, 1860

Mrs. Sarah A. Barton, wife of Dr. Barton, Jr. of Richmond
co., Ga., died Jan. 31st, 1861, aged 18 years and 7 months.
leaves a husband....
    Mrs. Elizabeth Ann Box died in St. Peter's Parish, S. C., Jan.
4th, 1861, in her 40th year....
    Martin Y. Arnold, youngest son of Benjamin F. and Catharine
Norman, formerly of Laurens Dist., now of Carroll co., Ga., died
on 29th Jan., 1861, in his 11th year....   J. R. Hood

Issue of March 14, 1861

    Mrs. Mary Harris died in Greenville, Ga., Feb. 19th, 1861, the
daughter of Richard Sasnett, and was born in Edgecomb co., N. C.
Dec. 8th, 1795. About the year 1799, her father emigrated to
Hancock co., Ga., In 1818, married Henry Harris. In 1832, they
left Hancock and settled in Merriwether co....   W. J. Sasnett
    George M. Condrey was born in Barnwell Dist., S. C., Oct.
28th, 1814, and lived several of his last years at Adamsville,
Fla....   C. W. Parker
    Mrs. Mary A. Stein, wife of Capt. John F. Stein, was born in
New York Sept. 24th, 1813, and died in Charleston, S. C., Dec.
24th, 1860....
    Mrs. Sarah P. McGowen, wife of H. N. McGowen, and daughter of
the late John D. and Sarah Brown, of Columbia, S. C., was born Oct.
13, 1816, and died Jan. 16, 1861...left husband and four children
....
    Matthew L. Crawford, son of Thomas and Thirza Crawford, died
in Walton co., Ga., Feb 17, 1861, aged about 21 years and 6 months
....
    Mrs. Sarah E. wife of Thos. J. Shepherd, and daughter of Mr.
John and Catharine Bedsole, of Barbour co., Ala., was born in
Muscogee co., Ga., and died in the vicinity of Cotton Valley,
Macon co., Ala., Feb. 17th, 1861....   Abel Tatom
    Charles W. McCall was born Sept. 25th, 1827, and died in
Tatnal co., Ga, Jan. 3d, 1861...left wife and children...
                                                W. J. Jordan
    Tribute of Respect by Fairfield Circuit, to Dr. George Wash-
ington Dansby local preacher....

Issue of March 21, 1861

    Married by the Rev. W. A. Montgomery, on the 6th inst., at
the house of Mr. Albert Z. Barclay , near Greenwood, Jackson co.,
Fla., Dr. Samuel W. Anthony to Miss Marion H. Snipes.
    January 10th, by Rev. S. F. Pilley, Rev. B. G. Fleming, of
the Ala. Conf., to Miss Virginia Walker, of Covington co., Ala.
    By Rev. W. Ivy, on 12th March, Mr. I. B. Robinson to Miss
Julia Ann Asbury, daughter of Rev. Henry Asbury, all of Lincoln
co., N. C.
    In Thomasville, Ga., on March 7th, 1861, Lyman A. Sermons,
Esq. and Mary J. Griffin, daughter of Rev. W. W. Griffin.
    On the 12th inst., by the Rev. Arminius Wright, Mr. Jas. T.
Redding of DeSoto Parish, La., to Miss M. Bibb Haraway, of Colum-
bus, Ga.
    on the 5th inst., by Rev. J. J. Morgan, Mr. Wilson A. Gilles-
pie, to Miss Mary C. Cheek, all of Heard co., Ga.
    On the 26th Feb., by W. R. Branham, Mr. Isham H. Branham of
Floyd co., Ga., to Miss Mollie Mathews, only daughter of Dr. Wm.
A. Mathews, of Ft. Valley, Ga.
    By Rev. W. Hutto, on the 10th Jan., Mr. Wm. D. Connor to Miss
Laura Stokes, both of Colleton, S. C.
    Feb. 27th, in Burke co., Ga., by Rev. J. W. McGehee, Capt.
J. M. Folson of Twiggs co., Ga., to Miss M. M. Roberts, of the

former place.

Feb 28th, by Rev. W. P. Mouzon, Rev. L. B. Varn of Colleton, to Miss A. K. Matilda Rich, of Charleston.

By Rev. W. H. Thomas, on the 27th Feb., 1861, in Blakely, Early co., Ga.,at the residence of his mother, Mr. Edward S. Powers, to Miss Queen Ann Vester Allbriten, both of Ala.

Died on 10th Feb. 1861, Harriet Ann, daughter of Geo. and Melbry A. Kittrell, of Orangeburg Dist., S. C., aged 12 years and 3 months.

Margaret Emeline, only daughter of M. and W. Klutts, died at ___ Jan. 19th, 1861, in the 4th year of her age.

On Round O., on the 12st Feb., Sarah Elizabeth, daughter of A. E. and Caroline Simmons, aged 4 years, 11 months and 7 days.

Mrs. C. A. Lewis, wife of Rev. H. T. Lewis, died in Middleburg Fla., Feb. 23d, in the 34th year of her age. She was born in St. Tamany Parish, La...married to Rev. H. T. Lewis, in Marion co., Miss., Sept. 18th, 1847....   E. P. Wilson

William Maxwell Martin, son of William and Margaret Martin, heads of the Columbia Female College, died on 21st of Feb., in the city of Columbia, S. C., in the 24th year of his age. His immediate ancestry in the maternal line were from Dumfrieshire, Scotland....   A. B. Longstreet.

Mrs. Basheba Lampley, wife of Jacob Lamplet, died on 6th Feb. 1861, in Anson co., N. C., near White's Store, in her 48th year ....

Dr. Lemuel Keebler died at Purysburg, S. C., ___ 1861, in the __ year of his age....   John W. McRoy.

Mrs. Lucy Ann Warnock, wife of Simeon Warnock, Esq., died at the residence of her fahter in Emanuel co., Ga.,Feb. 7th, 1861, in the 25th year of her age....   J. M. Stokes

Mrs. Martha T., wife of Wingfield Wright, died in Warren co., Ga.,Feb. 8th, 1861, in the 50th year of her age....R. W. Hubert

Mrs. Sarah C. Ward, wife of P. W. Ward, and daughter of James and Nancy Nicholson, of Iredell co., N. C. and sister to the Rev. D. B. Nicholson, of the N. C. Conf., died at Vanwert, Ga., Feb. 12th, 1861, in her 36th year....

Issue of March 28, 1861

Married on 7th Feb., by Rev. John Inabinet, Mr. John Culler, of Lexington Dist., to Miss Caroline E. Stabler, of Orangeburg Dist., S. C.

by Rev. John Inabinet, on 14th March, Mr. Ephraim H. Graves, of Pike co., Ala., to Miss M. C. Rucker, of Orangeburg Dist., S. C.

In Troup co., Ga., on 24th Feb., by Rev. W. H. C. Cone, Mr. Jeremiah Jackson to Miss Palmfra F. Norwood, daughter of Mr. A. P. Norwood.

In Columbua, Ga., on 12th inst., by Rev. Arminius Wright, Mr. James T. Redding, of La., to Miss Martha Bibb, daughter of Mr. R. S. Hardaway, of Columbus, Ga.

In Brooks co., Ga., at the residence of Col. James Young, on the 10th inst.,by Rev. O. L. Smith, Sanford T. Kingsberry, Esq. to Miss Janie M. Smith.

On 7th inst., by Rev. J. B. McGehee, Mr. Wm. F. Killen to Miss Mattie P. Lane, daughter of Saunders Lane, Esq., of Houston co., Ga.

On 20th March at the house of J. W. Rosser, Esq., by Rev. J. L. Stewart, Mr. F. S. Treadwell to Miss Frances Rosser, all of Conyers, Ga.

By Rev. J. T. Turner, Jan. 17th, 1861, Mr. H. J. Fillingim to Mrs. Mary V. Miller, both of Randolph co., Ga.

Mrs. Mary Barco died in Marion co., Fla., Dec. 23d, 1860, aged about 61 years.-.a native of Camden co., Ga., and joined the Church when quite young...married to David Barco in 1816, and moved to Florida about the beginning of the Indian war...her only daughter is the wife of Rev. J. T. Stockton, of the Fla. Conf....

Jno. C. Ley

Mrs. Mary J. E. Addy, wife of Mr. M. L. Addy, of Coweta co., Ga., and daughter of A. Gray, died in Griffin, Ga., March 3d, 1861, in her 23d year....   Wm. A. Rogers

Mrs. Elizabeth Lake, wife of Abraham Lake, was born in Greene co., Ga., in 1793, and died, in Forsyth, Ga., Feb. 18th, 1861, in the 69th year of her age...leaves an aged companion of well night four score years, and a large family of descendants nearly 70....

Geo. G. N. MacD.

Mrs. Margaret Guire, died in Mecklenburg, N. C., on the 18th of Jan, in the 55th year of her age....

Adie E., wife of James A. Hall, and daughter of Dr. Thomas F. Green, of Milledgeville, Ga., died in Charleston, on Tuesday the 5th of March, aged 29 years....

Edmund M. Pendleton, Jr., died in Sparta, Ga., March 12th, 1861....

Georgia Ann Elizabeth, daughter of Dr. C. R. and Elizabeth J. Moore, died in Weston, Ga., Feb. 24, 1861, in her 11th year...

Mrs. Sophronia A. Small, wife of Dr. W. F. Small, died in Georgetown, S. C., March.11th, 1861, in the 35th year of her age...

Tribute of Respect to Whitman C. Hill by Georgia Annual Conf.

Issue of April 4, 1861

Married on the 7th March, by Rev. F. A. Johnson, Mr. Jonathan C. Blitch to Miss Cynthia Geiger, of Duval co., Fla.

By the Rev. C. B. Webborn on 25th inst., Mr. E. W. Bond, of Whitefiled co., Ga., to Miss Mary L. McClain of Murry co., Ga.

By Rev. H. J. Adams, in Milledgeville, Ga., on March 14th, Adolphes F. Bayne and Mary J. Jenkins.

Also, on the 27th, C. J. Wellborn and Sarah M. Candler.

By the Rev. John F. Berry, on the 5th instant, Mr. William Clank to Miss Mary Price, all of Darien, Ga.

By Rev. A. Gray, at White Plains, Ga., March 23d, Mr. Randolph Tappan to Miss Eliza Ely, both of the former place.

On 19th March, by Rev. J. Ledbetter, Rev. John P. Guest, of the Ga. Conf., to Miss Letty A. Pearman, of Hart co., Ga., and Mr. Laureston H. Price of Pickens co., Ala., to Miss Margaret L. Pearman.

On 20th of March, by Rev. Wm. J. Jordan, near Reidsville, Ga., Mr. George J. Merriman to Miss Victoria Adamson, daughter of Dr. H. W. Adamson, all of Tattnall co., Ga.

January 29th, by Rev. James W. Shores, Mr. A. M. Wing to Miss Mary E. DuBose, all of Jackson, Clarke co., Ala.

Feb. 21st, by Rev. James W. Shores, Mr. R. M. McKinley to Miss Rebecca P. Wright, all of Clarke co., Ala.

March 18th, by Rev. James W. Shores, Mr. Wm. T. Jones, of Suggsville, Ala., to Miss Maria L. Ulmer, of Clarksville, Ala.

Died on Round O., March 18th, 1861, Catharine E., only daughter of A. E. And Caroline E. Simmons, aged 6 years, 5 months and 3 days.

Fannie Adella, infant daughter of Asbury H. and Frances H. Steagall, in Rusk co., Texas, March 1st, aged 6 months and 1 day.

Mrs. Eliza Dawson, wife of Hugh B. Dawson, and daughter of the late Dr. A. H. and Mrs. Elvira Flewellen, died in Wynnton, on the 23d of March aged 24 years....

Rev. Dr. Thomas W. Ellis died inValdosta, Ga., Feb. 27th, 1861, being 56 years of age....   P. P. Smith
Elizabeth R., wife of Col. Edward Stoudenmire, and daughter of Henry Whetstone, was born in Orangeburg Dist., S. C., March 25th, 1811, and died in Autaugaville, Autauga co., Ala., March 8th, 1861....   Wm. H. Armstrong.
Mrs. Ann Rakestraw, was born April 9th, 1807, and died March 10th 1861....
George Whisnant died on 3d January, in his 37th year....
                                                            A. P. Avant
Mrs. Elizabeth Murrel was born in Brunswick co., N. C., in 1802, removed in 1837 to Horry Dist., S. C.,where she died Feb. 17, 1861....   W. Bowman
Tribute of Respect to Rev. James Gamble, a local preacher of Vienna Circuit, Ga. Conf....

Issue of April 11, 1861

Mrs. Elizabeth A. Crump died in Augusta, Ga., March 13th, 1861, in the 69th year of her age....
Allen T. Meacham was born in Mecklenburg co., Va., May 6th, 1810, was married to Mrs. Clara Leach, Jan. 6th, 1854, and died in Cobb co., Ga., Feb. 5th, 1861...in 1850 or 51 came to the neighborhood of Smyrna, Cobb co....   S. J. Bellah
Eliza Vass died March 6th, 1861, in her 46th year...quite young in Putnam co., Ga.,joined the Missionary Baptists....left husband and children....   M. Penwell
Mrs. Mary Virginia, wife of John R. Daniell, was born in Sussex co., Va., and died in Mecklenburg co., N. C., on the 18th March, aged 24 years....
Mrs. Lucy Jane Wadsworth, wife of Mr. John C. Wadsworth, Jr., and daughter of Mr. Albert and Mrs. Ann Evans, died at the residence of her father in Chesterfield Dist., on 18th March, in her 24th year....
Mrs. Mary E. DuPont, daughter of the late Col. R. A. L. and Mrs. E. A. Atkinson, of Macon, Ga., was born in Louisville, Ga., April 30th, 1836...married to Joseph H. DuPont, Esq., Dec. 16th, 1858, and died near Quincy, Fla., March 24, th 1861....
                                                          A. T. Woldridge
Tribute of Respect by Madison Lodge, A. F. M. to Rev. M. H. Hebbard....

Issue of April 18, 1861

Married on 14th March, Francis L. Gallaway, Esq., to Miss Susan J. Hughes, daughter of Capt. John Hughes, all of Orange co., Fla.
On the 28th March, 1861, by Rev. E. T. McGehee, Mr. S. T. Lofley to Miss T. M. Harvey, all of Houston co., Ga.
By Rev. H. J. Hunter, Mr. Augustus J. Hamil, of Barnesville, Ga., to Miss Elizabeth J. Flowers, of Butler co., Ala.
On 3rd April, at the Parsonage in New Port, Fla., by Rev. S. A. McCook, Robt. Alexander, of Wakuila co., Fla., and Miss Mahala Freeman, of the former place.
March 21st, at the residence of S. Dupuies, Esq., near Flemington, Fla., by Rev. H. F. Smith, Alexander P. Price, to Miss Frances Penelope Dupiuse.
Bro. James Z. Dismuke died near Talbotton, Ga.,23d March, aged 60 years and 5 months. He was born in Hancock co., Ga., 17th Oct 1810, and shortly thereafter his parents removed to Putnam co., Ga., where he was raised and lived until 1829, when he moved to Harris co., Ga....   Geo. H. Patillo.

Mary A. E. S., daughter of Jordan H. and Mary Harvard, was born April 20th, 1841, and died in Dooly co., Ga., Jan. 10th, 1861....

Mrs. Nancy Kramer died in Milledgeville, Ga., on the 1st of March 1861, in the 75th year of her age....   F. L. Brantly.

Alfred M. Carpenter was born 29th June, 1798, and died in Pickens Dist., 22 March 1861....

Mrs. Mary, widow of Rev. John Christian, died in Montgomery co., N. C., 27th Feb. 1861, at the residence of Dr. Montgomery, in her 84th year....

Mary J. Garrison, wife of Lovick P. Garrison and daughter of John and Sarah Black was born Dec. 1, 1841, and died on 25th March 1861....left two little children.

Mrs. Maria A. Laval died in Georgetown, S. C., March 27th, within a day of the 73d anniversary of her birth....

Mary A. V., wife of A. C. Green, and daughter of Rev. McC. and N. C. Purifoy, died in Butler co., Ala., March 8th, 1861, in the 26th year of her age....   John D. Worrell.

Mrs. Beulah Ann Cramer, died in Charleston, S. C., on 23d Feb. 1861, aged 65 years and 3 days....

Robert Anderson a native of Charleston, S. C., died in said city, Feb. 2, 1861, in the 67th year of his age....T. R. Walsh

Mrs. Susan W. Stukes, wife of Mr. Joseph Stukes, was born May 20th, 1810, and died in Manning, S. C., Feb. 7th, 1861....
                                                        W. Smith

Mrs. Ruth Newton, wife of Willis Newton, died Feb. 4th, 1861, in the 72d year of her age....   W. A. McSwain

Sister Eliza Gibson was born Dec. 26th, 1786, and died March 18th, 1861...died at the residence of brother Jno. G. Solomons, St. Peter's Parish, S. C.   J. W. Kelly

Issue of April 25, 1861

Married by Rev. S. G. Chiles, on the 28th of Feb., 1861, Mr. Richard Harris to Miss C. A. Groover, daughter of the late Mr. Josiah and Nancy Groover, all of Brooks co., Ga.

On the 20th of March, by Rev. S. G. Chiles, Mr. Wm. A. Blackburn to Miss Sarah Gelser. Also at the same time and place, Mr. J. B. W. Cobb, to Miss Harriet Gelser, daughters of Mr. G. W. Gelser, all of Jefferson co., Fla.

By the Rev. J. D. Anthony, on the evening of the 9th of April, at the residence of Col. Dumas (Father of the bride) in Alpine, Ga., Charles E. Price and Jennie E. Dumas.

On the 31st March, by Rev. Wm. Mood, Mr. Micajah Hutson and Miss Georgianna Sheppard, all of Beaufort Dist., S. C.

In Culloden, Monroe co., April 4th, by Rev. Wesley F. Smith, Mr. James H. Smith and Miss Julia H. Cook.

On 4th April, by Rev. Manning Brown, at the residence of the bride's father, Gen. Wm. J. Taylor to Mrs. Agnes Harton, daughter of Mr. Andrew Wallace, all of Columbia, S. C.

On Sunday 14 inst., by Rev. T. R. Walsh, Mr. W. J. Smith of this city, to Miss Frances Hardcastle, formerly of Savannah, Ga.

On the 16th April 1861, by the Rev. J. Rush, Mr. A. N. Johnson of Harris co., Ga., to Miss May A. Jones of Troup co., Ga.

In Richmond co., Ga., April 16th, 1861, at the residence of Col. John F. Lawson, by Rev. W. H. Potter, Col. Edward F. Lawson, of Burke co., Ga. to Miss L. A. Martin of the former place.

On April 17th, by Rev. J. Blakely Smith, Wm. B. Berry to Hibernia L. Dougherty, both of Newnan, Ga.

On 16th inst., by Rev. John H. Harris, Col. Robert M. Young, of LaGrange, Ga.,to Mrs. Sue E. Pitts, of Hamilton, Ga.

On 16th inst., by Rev. Geo. W. Fagg, Dr. Robert H. Butler, of Leon co., Fla., to Mrs. Louisa J. Parham of Decatur co., Ga.

13

At the house of the bride's father, Mr. John S. Brook, April 12th 1861, by Rev. H. J. Hunter, Mr. John J. Flowers, of Greenville, Ala., to Miss P. Kate Brook, of Butler co., Ala.

April 4, by Rev. B. J. Johnson, Hon. William W. Woodruff to Miss Nancy J. Galloway, both of Orange co., Fla. "Due West Telescope" please copy.

In the Methodist E. Church, Gainsville, Ga., on 3rd inst., by the Rev. R. W. Bigham, Walter S.Brewster, Esq. of Charleston, S. C., and Miss Susan W. Banks of Gainsville, Ga.

Died April 4th, 1861, near Oak Bowery, in Chambers co., Ala., Daniel Pierce, son of Daniel P. and Ann Hightower, aged 2 years, 10 months and 28 days.

Near Summerville, S. C., Feb. 13th, Anna Jane, only daughter of John W. and Anna Jane Lemacks, aged 11 months and 28 days.

Hepzibah S. Ramsey (widow of the late Judge Isaac Ramsey) died at Mt. Vernon, Columbia co., Ga., aged 61 years.... H. J. Adams

Julia C. Eberhart, daughter of Rev. John A. Hurst, died in Fredonia, Chambers co., Ala., Dec. 25th, 1860, aged 21 years, 4 months. She was married to J. L. Eberhart in 1857, and left a widow in 1859....

John A. Sessions eldest son of E. and M. Sessions, was born in Lee co., Ga., Dec. 31st, 1837, and died in Starkville, Ga., March 30th, 1861....

Antoinette T. Erwin, wife of Capt. James B. Erwin, and daughter of James Simms, of Chambers co., Ala., died in West Point, Ga., March 29th, 1861...born in Hancock co., Ga., March 24, 1834 ...leaves husband and children....   Wm. A. Simmons

Issue of May 2, 1861

Married on 24th inst., by Rev. T. R. Walsh, Joseph McLaughlin, Esq., of Anson, N. C., to Miss S. A. Walsh, of this city.

By Rev. Geo. G. N. MacDonell near Forsyth, Ga., April 18th, 1861, Judge D. F. Walker to Miss Sallie L. Banks, all of Monroe co., Ga.

By Rev. Geo. G. N. MacDonell, in Forsyth, Ga., April 23, Mr. Wm. F. Gibson of Macon co., Ga., to Miss Sarah E. Dews, of Forsyth, Ga.

Died in Barnesville, Ga., on the morning of the 18th inst., Willie Howard, son of X. C. and E. M. Fryer, aged 18 months.

Maj. Isaac Nathans was born in Philadelphia, Pa., Jan. 10th, 1783, and died in Quincy, Fla., April 10th, 1861....
                                              A. J. Wooldridge

Thomas McCully died in Chester, April 5th, aged 32 years....

Mrs. Elizabeth Cordelia, wife of Daniel S. Johnson, daughter of Jeremiah Hamilton, of S. C., died in Chickasaw co., Miss., April 15th, 1861, aged 29 years....   A. C. Allen

James Westbrook died at the residence of his uncle, B. C. Jackson, in Hamilton co., Fla., April 10th, 1861, aged 29 years...
                                              Chas. P. Murdock

Tribute of Respect to Rev. Dr. Thos W. Ellis, by Valdosta circuit, Fla. Conf....

Issue of May 9, 1861

Married on 1st May, by Rev. W. S. Turner, Mr.Benj. T. Castellaw, to Miss Martha O. Scarborough, both of Sandersville, Ga.

On 14th April by Rev. Wm. G. Booth, Mr. John C. Barfield, to Mrs. Frances M. Bustian, all of Taylor co., Ga.

On 25th April, by Rev. Chas R. Jewett, Mr. W. W. Owen, to Miss Eliza Ann, daughter of Mr. James Willis, all of Talbot co., Ga.

In Preston, Webster co., Ga., on 16th April, by Rev. Jas. G. M. Ball, Mr. George W. Peddy, of Perry, Houston co, Ga., to Miss

Elizabeth J. Dukes, of the former place.

On April 4th, in Sumter co., near Adamsville, by Rev. H. F. Smith, Mr. N. B. McLin, of Newnam, Fla., to Miss L. A. McNair, of Sumter co., Fla.

On 14th April in the M. E. Church at Ocala, Fla., by Rev. H. F. Smith, Mr. Sylvester Rivers, to Miss Rebecca M. White, all of Ocala, Fla.

Died in Forsyth co., Ga., on 30th Dec., 1860, William Alonzo, son of E. and M. Mashburn, aged 4 years, 2 months and 19 days.

In Savannah, on 19th April, Lewis Eugene, only child of Rev. F. B. and M. E. Davies, aged 15 months.

Mrs. Virginia Caroline Moorman, wife of Hon. Robert Moorman, died 17th March 1861. She had been married about 12 years, and was in the 32d year of her age...adopted a child of Brother Moorman's by a former marriage....   W. A. McSwain

Mrs. Nancy S. Willingham, wife of Mr. Isaac Willingham, was born in Lincoln co., Ga., Nov. 1st, 1799, moved to Coosa co., Ala., in 1851 and died April 14th, 1861.....   E. S. Smith

Edmund H. Jackson, died in Monroe co., Ga., on the 16th April 1861, in his 39th year....

-William C. Workman died in Camden, S. C., March 1st, 1861, in the 58th year of his age....left widow and five children.
                                                    R. J. Boyd.

Daniel Dantzler, Sr. of Orangeburg Dist., died 21st March, in his 67th year....   D. W. Seale

Mrs. Christiana Bull, wife of David Bull, died in St. Matthews Parish, S. C., on the 19th April aged 56 years....William Hutto.

Cecil Clare, daughter of Job D. and Martha A. Gibson, was born in Decatur co., Ga., May 31st, 1848, and died April 10th, 1861....

Wiley Kent died in Houston co., Ga., on 2d April 1861, in the 61st year of his age...left wife and daughter....

J. D. Gorden, a local preacher of the M. E. Church, was born June 14th, 1811, and died 15th April in Clay co., Geo....

Tribute of Respect to Bro. James Z. Dismukes by Talbotton station, Ga. Conf....

Issue of May 16, 1861

Married near Wadesboro, on 30th April, by Rev. James W. Wheeler, of the N. C. Conf., Mr. James P. Richardson, to Miss Annie E., daughter of Mr. S. V. Simmons, both of Anson co., N. C.

In LaGrange, Ga. on 31st ult., by Rev. C. W. Key, Mr. Wm. H. Russell, of Augusta, Ga., to Miss Marianna B. Pullen of the former place.

In Thomas co., Ga., at the residence of Mr. Benjamin McIntosh, on the 5th inst., by Rev. Cape. Raiford, Rev. Leroy C. Lesley, of Tampa, Fla., to Miss Jane Sandwich of the former place.

Died in this city, on 6th May, 1861, Sarah Pelzer, 4th daugh= ter of L. C. And Ann F. Loyal, in her 2nd year.

In Taylor co., Ga., March 28th, 1861, Zachariah S., son of Wade H. and Lydia S. Helms, aged 3 years, 10 months and 22 days.

Mrs. Mary F. Tradewell, daughter of Mr. H. Toomer, of Wilmington, N. C., and wife of Mr. F. A. Tradewell, was born Jan. 12th, 1798, and died in Columbia, S. C., March 3d, 1861.... W. A. Gamewell

Daniel Evans, son of Daniel and Mary Evans, formerlyof Burke Co., Ga., was born Aug. 19th, 1798, and died in Walker co., Ga., April 12th, 1861....leaves widow and five children....
                                                    Charles T. Evans

Mrs. Virginia P. Walker, consort of Col. Alexander C. Walker, died inRichmond co., Ga., April 24th, in her 46th year....

Mrs. Penelope, wife of W. R. STewart, and daughter of Wm. and Elizabeth Sims, died in Sumter co., Ga., 22d April, 1861, in

the 34th year of her age...the wife of a near and dear kinsman...
                                                    T. H. S.
    Mrs. Catherine Frierson, wife of John Frierson, and daughter
of Benjamin and Mary A. Lavender, died near Lynchburg, S. C.,
April 27th, 1861, in the 54th year of her age...   W. H. Smith
    Mr. William Rain, died in Trader's Hill, Ga., March 25th,
1861, in his 59th year....

Issue of May 23, 1861

    Married on 24th April by Rev. D. D. Cox, Mr. Martin Burke to
Miss Mary Williams, both of Lumpkin, Ga.
    In Savannah, Ga., May 7th, 1861, by Rev. W. H. Potter, Rev.
Thos. H. Jordan, of the Ga. Conf., to Miss Camilla A. Saussy, of
the above place.
    By Rev. W. H. Thomas, on 8th May, Dr. Wm. P. Chapman to Miss
Ann E., daughter of Capt. Mean,s both of Colquitt, Ga.
    On 6th May, by Rev. B. W. Whilden, J. M. Frierson, of Sumter,
to Mattie A., daughter of Jesse Garland, of White Plain, Chester-
field Dist., S. C.
    On Thursday evening, April 25th, by Rev. T. A. Carruth, Dr.
James A. Williams and Mrs. Florida A. Standley, all of Newnansville,
Fla.
    On Wednesday, May 1st, by Rev. T. A. Carruth, Mr. G. S. M.
Huggins, to Miss Lydia Downing, all of Alachua co., Fla.
    At Macon, Ga., on 30th April, by Rev. David Wills, Robt. H.
Johnson, of Floyd co., to Mrs. B. A. Dickens, of Marianna, Fla.
    Died Harry, infant son of Wm. and Julia Monroe, of Quincy,
Fla., was born March 13th, 1861, and died May 3d,1861.
    Mrs. Eliza J. Martin, wife of Rev. C. P. B. Martin, and
daughter of Jordan and Maria Rees, died at the residence of her
father, April 10th, 1861, in her 38th year....
    Miss Sarah Josephine, eldest daughter of Reddick and Milicent
Graddick, of Barnesville, Ga., died on 21st April, in her 19th
year....
    Died in Effingham co., on the 27th of April, Laura, the wife
of Dr. A. P. Longstreet, and only daughter of Dr. Ayer, leaving
four children....
    Mrs. Sarah Mallery, wife of the late Lewis Mallery, died in
Charleston, May 8th, aged 70 years. She was a native of Sauga-
tuck, Conn., and for the past 32 years a resident of this city
and a member of the Cumberland St. Church....Sam'l A. Nelson.
    William Fussell was born in Duplin county, N. C., Jan. 11th,
1798, and died in Coffee co., Ga., April 17th, 1861. He moved to
Irwin county, Ga., about 35 years ago, and settled on the Ocmul-
gee River...   F. M. Wilson.
    Mrs. Elizabeth Welbourn, wife of P. L. Welbourn, died in
Chickasawhatchie, Terrell co., Ga., April 8th, 1861, in her 32d
year...left husband and nine children....

Issue of May 30, 1861

    Married at the residence of Rev. W. F. Conlye, Tatnal co., Ga.,
on the 25th April, by Rev. D. R. McWilliams, Murial M. M. Sikes
to Sarah A. Conley, both of Tatnal co., Ga.
    By Rev. C. A. Crowell, Mar 28th, Mr. T. S. Strickland, second
son of Rev. J. Strickland, of the Ga. Conf., to Miss L. C. Ellis,
all of Gordon co., Ga.
    On the 16th May, by Rev. H. J. Hunter, Mr. D. A. Rutledge of
Millville, Butler co., Ala., to Mrs. S. M. Reddock, formerly of
the Reddock Springs, Ala.
    On the 14th inst., by Rev. I. S. Connor, at Mr. A. Walker's,
Mr. S. M. Williams to Mrs. C. Freeman, all of Edgefield Dist., S.C.

James Shuptrine was born in Wilkes co., Ga., and died in
Thomaston, Ga.,May 4th, 1861, in the 54th year of his age....
                                                    W. Knox.
    Miss Ann E. Hanna, was born Sept. 21st, 1839, and died May
1st, 1861....   W. S. Black
    C. D. F. Evans, wife of Richard Evans, Jr., died in Orange-
burg Dist., April 13, 1861, in the 24th year of her age....
                                                D. W. Seale.
    Sallie B. Tucker died at the residence of her mother, Mrs.
M. H. Tucker, in Midway, Ga., on 27th April, aged 16 years....

Issue of June 6, 1861

    Married on 23d May, by Rev. V. A. Sharpe, Mr. Charles Kay
of Anderson Dist., to Miss Charlotte Miller, of Pendleton, S.
C.
    On 21st May, at the residence of Mrs. McGuires, by Rev. L.
B. Payne, Rev. J. F. Berry, of the Ga. Conf.,to Miss Susie M.
Shelman, of Darien, Ga.
    On 22d May, by Rev. W. L. Pegues, Mr. H. C. Dickinson to
S. Fraser Hay, daughter of Dr. L. S. Hay, all of Barnwell Dist.,
S. C.
    In Jones co., Ga., May 23d, by Rev. J. B. McGehee, Mr. Fran-
cis Marion Adams to Miss Elizabeth Jarrel.
    May 21st, by R. A. Conner, Rev. Walter Ewing Johnston to
Miss Emily Frances Winter, all of Richmond co., Ga.
    Nicholas Morgan was born May 3d, 1782, in Mecklenburg co.,
Va., and died May 13th, 1861, in Jackson co., Fla. When he was
about 15 years old, his father moved to Wilkes co., Ga., where
about a year afterwards he joined the M. E. Church. When 25
years of age, moved to Morgan co., where the next year he mar-
ired Miss Elizabeth Clay...later removed to Monroe co., Harris
co....left nine children....   W. A. Montgomery.
    Col. J. N. Ramsey, of Columbus, Ga., now the commanding Col.
of the first Ga. Regiment, stationed near Pensacola, Fla., was
a few days since called from the tented field to the chamber
of death. His little Ada, died 20th May... J. M. Campbell
    Samuel F. Brandon, sonof John and Martha Brandon, was born
in Marshall co., Miss., Feb. 10th, 1844, and died in Hillsboro
co., Fla., on 5th May 1861....two brothers Wesley and Robert....
    Mrs. Rachel R. Stevenson, widow of the late Capt. Daniel
Stevenson, of Philadelphia, was born in Kent co., Md., April
28th, 1807 and died in Louisville, Ga. April 12th, 1861....
    Huger, son of John J. Bunch, was born in Orangeburg Dist.,
S. C., March 14th, 1847, and died in Calchou co., Ga.,May 17th,
1861....   John J. Sessions
    Stephen G. Pettus, Sr., died in Washington, Ga., April 25th,
1861, in his 74th year...born in Hanover co., Va., Jan. 11th,
1788....

Issue of June 13, 1861

    Married on the 29th May, by Rev. L. M. Hamer, Mr. P. H.
Tison, of St. Peter's, to Miss Sallie Allen, Allendale, S. C.
    In Thomas co., Ga., on 29th May, at the residence of the
bride, by Rev. Capel Raiford, Mr. Charles J. Rice to Mrs. Mary
A. McKinnon, all of Thomas co.
    By Rev. H. J. Hunter, at LibertyChapel, on Sabbath morning,
June 2d, 1861, Mr. Joshua W. Evans to Miss Anthony, formerly
of Georgia, but now all of Butler co., Ala.
    By Rev. H. V. Mulkey, Mr. T. J. Cobb to Miss Nancy Wright,
all of Barbour co., Ala.

Dr. Alanson Saltmarsh, died near Cahaba, Dallas co., Ala.,
on May 13th, 1861...born in Greene co., N. Y. on 8th Oct. 1794.
He came to Alabama in earlymanhood, and settled first at Ft.
Claiborne in 1819...married a near relative of the late Vice-
President King...office of Register of the U. S. Land Office at
Cahaba....

Mrs. Martha Elizabeth Easterling, wife of Rev. W. F. Easterling, of the Fla Conf., died May 18th, 1861, at Newton, Ga., in
her 23d year....

Mrs. Narcissa Bell died on the 4th May 1861, aged 60 years
....

Col. Harvey Phillips, formerly of Chambers co., died at
Monroeville, Ala., Feb. 14th, 1861, aged about 37 years....

Dr. Wm. A. Albert died in Mecklenburg co., N. C., May 22d,
aged 63 years....

Mrs. Sarah Long, wife of Mr. William D. Long, of St. Mary's,
Ga., and daughter of Mr. and Mrs. John Stevens, of Columbia, S.
C., died in Columbia, May 24th, in his 31st year...left two
little ones....   W. A. Gamewell

Rev. Gospero Sweet Jr., was born in Marion Dist., S. C.,and
died May 9th, 1861, in the 56th year of his age....

Issue of June 20, 1861

Married in Atlanta, Ga.,at Trinity Church, on the 28th of May,
by Rev. T. F. Pierce, Mr. James McAllen Pace, of Covington, to
Miss Leonora Hugh Haralson, of LaGrange.

On Thursday, May 9, 1861, by the Rev. George W. Moore, Mr.
Thomas C. Cox, to Miss Sarah E. Anderson, all of St. Thomas'
Parish.

At the residence of Mr. James J. Coachman, Decatur co., Ga.,
on the evening of the 30th ult., by Rev. Jos. Law, Dr. Leonidas
Crews, to Miss Helen Coachman.

By Rev. W. B. Miller, May 24th, Mr. G. N. Bell of Sumter co.,
Fla., to Miss S. R. BEnnett, daughter of William Bennett, of
Volusia co., Fla.

On May 30th, by Rev. W. A. Clarke in Fairfield Dist., S. C.
Mr. Richard Kearney, of Columbia, S. C. to Miss Sallie J. A.
Crumpton, daughter of J. A. Crumpton, Esq.

On June 4th, by Rev. C. A. Drowell, Mr. B. D. Clarke, and
Miss Mary R. Barrett, all of Grodon co., Ga.

In Sandersville, Ga., on the evening of the 21st ult., by
Rev. Dr. James R. Smith, Mr. C. R. Pringle, of Carnesville, Ga.,
to Miss Nora G. Brantely, only child of Maj. Harris Brantley,
of the former place.

Died in Colleton Dist., S. C., Mary Eliza, infant daughter
of Wm. and Eliza J. Stokes, aged 13 months and 20 days.

Nancy Dawkins died at her residence in Union Dist., S. C., on
the 26th May, in the 84th year of her age.

Miss Laura Fisher died at Irwinton, Ga., on the 13th April
in the 22d year of her age....   W. S. Turner

Burwell Blanton was born in Dinwiddie co., Va., Nov. 1st,
1762, and died in Cleaveland co., N. C., May 14th, 1861, being
nearly, 99 years of age....a cousin of the Rev. Benjamin Blanton
of the Ga. Conf. While my grandfather was very young, his
father George Blanton removed from the province of Va. to that
of S. C., within the limits of what is now York District. After
residing here a few years he again removed and settled within
the bounds of N. C., in that portion which became Rutherford
co., but much later still became Cleaveland co., N. C. Soon
after the Rev., he married Margaret Bridges, and settled on
Beaver Dam Creek...by two marriages had twelve children....
Israel P. Hughes.

18

Frances Ann Elizabeth, second daughter of Capt. James Dawkins, (dec'd) and Mrs. F. S. Dawkins, was born in Union Dist.,
S. C., Nov. 12th, 1829, and died at the residence of her brother-
in-law, Mr. Henry in Elberton, Ga.,April 20th, 1861...
                                                  Susan N. Connor
    Dr. Elias Sinclair (formerly of Anson co., N. C.) died in
Kemper co., Miss., May 10th,1861, in the 63d year of his age...
a travelling preacher in the S. C. Conf....   Francis Walker
    Mrs. Elizabeth Espy died near Carrollton, Ga., on 21st April,
in her 63d year....   Wm. Timmons.
    Ann Deloach, daughter of L. B. and Ann Varn, died May 2d,
1861, in her 15th year, in Colleton Dist., S. C...L. B. Varn
    Mrs. Barbary Lawson, wife of Col. A. J. Lawson, died in
Burke co., Ga.,on 26th May, while talking with her only daughter,
son and husband....   Tilman Douglas
    Capt. J. W. Moore, Cokesbury Dist., S. C., died May 1, 1861,
aged 50 years and 4 months.....   Jas. F. Smith
    Mrs. Jane V., wife of Dr. W. F. Harllee, died in Anson co.,
N. C., May 27th, 1861, in the 34th year of her age....
                                            Aug. W. Walker

Issue of June 27, 1861

    Married on 18th June 1861, by the Rev. Charles B. Murdock,
Mr. R. W. Adams, and Miss Sophia J. Broward, all of Hamilton co.,
Fla.
    At Ansonville, N. C., on June 18th, by Rev. Aug. W. Walker,
Mr. William G. Wright, of Darlington Dist., S. C., to Miss
Amanda M. Tyson of Ansonville, N. C.
    In the Church at Alston's, Telfair co., Ga., on the 2d June,
Mr. John B. Coffee to Miss Marcilla Griffin, of Gwinett co., Ga.
    On the 29th May, by Rev. W. J. McCormick, Mr. A. A. Maulden,
formerly of Lowndesville, Abbeville Dist., S. C., to Miss Rebecca
Crain, formerly of Chester Dist., S. C., now all of Gainesville,
Alachua co., Fla.
    In Greensboro', Ala., on the 12th June, by Rev. Dr. Wadsworth,
Dr. Frances M. Peterson, to Miss Margaret Jane Sledge, daughter
of Dr. Alex. Sledge.
    Died in Buena Vista, Ga.,May 25th, 1861, Loula Rebecca, in-
fant daughter of John T. and Rebecca A. Mathis, aged 8 months and
18 days.
    At Marietta, Greenville Dist., S. C., June 12th, Willie R.,
only son of Robert and Elizabeth Stone, aged 4 yeras and 9 days.
    Mrs. Mary H., wife of James T. Daniel, died in Columbus,
Ga., May 7, 1861, in the 24th year of her age....
    Mrs. Lucy Tarrant, relict of the Rev. John Tarrant of the
S. C. Conf., died May 8th, 1861, at the residence of Bro. James
Plunkett, in Wadesboro, N. C....
    John Webber died in Shelby, N. C., June 7th, in his 66th
year....   J. T. Nelson
    Richard Lovell Edgeworth, sen., nephew of Maria Edgeworth,
was born in Anson co., N. C.,Nov. 4th, 1793, and died in Chesterfield dist., S. C., June 3rd, 1861....
    Alexander Cassady was bron in Chesterfield dist., S. C., Feb.
1795, and died at Lawrenceville, Ala., May 14th, 1861...moved to
Henry Co., Ala., in 1833....   John W. Solomon
    Mrs. Mary Gay, wife of Jacob M. Gay, and daughter of John and
Elizbaeth Hudson, was born in Lawrence co., Ga.,Nov. 24th, 1814,
and died in Macon co., April 29th, 1861, in her 47th year....
                                         Jno. N. Hudson
    Rachel Jordan, wife of Jesse Jordan and daughter of Solomon
and Nancy Bird, of Edgefield dist., S. C.,died in DeKalb co.,
Ga., 31st of May last, in the 72d year of her life....

Mrs. Sarah E. Parks was born Sept. 9, 1828, married to Dr.
Rich. M. Parks, Sept. 9, 1845, and died in Lawrenceville, Ga.,
May 28, 1861....left husband and two small children....W. W. Oslin

Wm. Brantly born in Columbus co., N. C., Feb. 1796, died
near Ocala Marion co., Fla., May 24th, 1861, leaving a widow
and five children....   Wm. T. Harrison

Mrs. Ann W. M. Hines was born in Lawrence co., Ga., Dec. 16,
1805, and mvoed to decatur co., Ga.,1830, died April 8, 1861....
left four children, two are in the Confederate Army....
                                                     W. M. Kennedy.

Mrs. Emily Amanda Spencer, wife of Wm. S. Spencer, died in
Tampa, Fla., on the 3d June, aged 44 years....

Issue of July 4, 1861

Married in Clinton, Jones co., Ga.,June 19th, by Rev. J. B.
McGehee, A. S. Hamilton, Capt. of the Floyd Sharp Shooters, to
Miss Sallie, daughter of the late Dr. Bowen.

On 24th June, by the Rev. Isaac J. Tatom, Mr. Wm. G. Meriwether, to Miss Eliza L. Barnett, all of Montgomery co., Ala.

On the 11th of June, by Rev. W. W. Jones, Rev. J. W. Abernathy of S. C. Conf., to Miss Martha A. Ray, of Mecklenburg co.,
N. C.

In Tampa, Fla., June 13th, by Rev. R. M. Burgess, Lieut. R.
L. Simms of Covington, Ga., to Miss Lucy H. Branch, daughter of
Rev. Dr. F. Branch.

In Concord, N. C., on the 20th inst.,by Rev. E. M. Thompson,
Mr. T. L. Rice to Miss Marana v., second daughter of J. L. Bundy,
Esq.

In Carrollton, Ga., June 20, by Rev. J. Blakely Smith, Mr.
John W. Stansell to Miss Mary S. Mandeville, all of Carrollton,
Ga.

On June 18th, by the Rev. John Woods, Rev. George R. Park,
of Catoosa co., to Miss Maggie C. Porter, of Lawrenceville, Ga.,
daughter of Rev. H. H. Porter, of Ringgold circuit.

Died on the 23d June, William, son of W. M. and Mary O'Neal,
aged about 1 year and 4 months.

On the 25th June, Langdon Cheves, son of James Y. and Jennett E. Calhoun, aged 1 year, 5 months and 8 days.

Laura, eldest daughter of George W. and Mary Bucnh, of Calhoun co., Ga.,died June 6th, 1821, aged 6 years, 2 months and
12 days.

Charles Winter was born in London, near Lambeth, 24th April
1807. At ten years of age his parents emigrated to America, -
and settled near Pendleton, S. C.....died 19th of May....
                                                     F. O. Dannelly

Mrs. Amanda M., wife of M. W. Rasbury, and daughter of D.
H. Witcher, deceased, died in Atlanta, June 18th, in her 20th
year....   J. C. Simmons

Mrs. Jane Hill died near Timmonsville, S. C., May 29th, 1861,
aged 23 years...joined the Baptist Church about 4 years ago...
leaves husband, mother, seven brothers and sisters....
                                                     John W. McRoy

Dr. George W. Palmer died in Washington, Ga., June 7th,
1861...the death of Bro. Pettus, his father-in-law....

Mrs. Abigail R. Anders died in York Dist., May 10th, 1861,
in the 41st year of her age....Samuel A. Roper

Mrs. Susan Hendrix died at my residence in Henry co., Ga.,
in the 85th year of her age. She was born in Fairfield Dist.,
S. C., in April 1777, and died June 4th, 1861....
                                                     John H. Smith.

Issue of July 11, 1861

Married on 26th June, by Rev. G. S. Spearman, Rev. Walton
F. Holland of the Ga. Conf., to Miss Sarah Binford, of Jasper
co., Ga.
        In Coffee co., Ga., June 18th, 1861, by Rev. F. M. Wilson,
Mr. Geo. W. Smith to Mrs. Mary A. McLean, both of Coffee co.,
Ga.
        On June 27th, 1861, by Rev. A. J. Hunter, Mr. H. R. Shines
of Butler, and Miss Drucilla Herlong of Lowndes co., Ala.
(Died)--Macon, Ga., on the 5th inst., Sallie R.,daughter of W.
T. and Annie E. Morgan, aged five monts and ten days.
        Died on typhoid fever, in Tatnal co., Ga., on the 26th May
last, Francis Asbury, infant son of L. A. H. and Martha S. M.
Tippins, aged 1 year and 4 months.
        Agnes E., daughter of John W. and Margaret S. Gardin, died
in McDowell co., N. C., June 21st, aged 3 years and 15 days.
        Mr. Michael M. Eason died near Reidsville, Tatnal co., Ga.,
June 15th, 1861, in his 56th year....   Daniel Sikes
        The Rev. H. W. Adamson died near Reidsville, Ga.,on 23d
April 1861...born in London, 22d Nov 1811, reared by pious parents, both members of the Presbyterian Church...in his 21st year
he married in his native land and came to New York perhaps in
1833....
        Dan'l Horton died May 9th, 1861, near Gillisonville, S. C.,
aged 64 years....   J. W. Kelly
        Martha C., wife of Wm. Wood, daughter of Joseph Garlington,
late of Oglethorpe co., Ga., was born March 23d, 1822, and died
at Snapping Shoals, Ga., May 7th, 1861....   J. W. Reynolds
        Mrs. M. R. Richbourg died in Clarendon Dist., S. C., May
21st, 1861, in her 55th year....   left family of 8 children
wife of Bro. S. C. Richbourg....   M. Puckett
        Asbury B. Johnson, son of T. M. Johnson, died May 18th,
1861, at South Butler co., Ala...born July 12th, 1841....
                                        John B. Warren.
        Mrs. E. A. Williams, wife of J. J. Williams, and daughter of
M. M. and S. L. Tillman, died at her mother's residence, in
Alachua co., Fla., June 11th, 1861, in the 32d year of her age
...joined the M. E. Church in Lancaster Dist., S. C.....
        Mrs. Mary Ann, wife of Dennis Colson, Esq., died in Chatta-
hoochie, Fla., on 7th June, 1861, in her 41st year....
        Mrs. Sarah Groves, relict of Joseph Groves, of Abbeville
Dist., S. C., died on the 18th June, 1861, in her 83d year...
daughter of James and Gilley Alston, born in N. C., removed
while young to Elbert Co., Ga.,where she married Mr. Joseph
Groves in 1797. They raised eight children, seven of whom still
survive....
        Tribute of Respect to Joseph Francis Hough who died 24th
June 1861, in Monroe, N. C.....
        Wm. T. Wingate died in Nassau co., Fla., May 14th, 1861, in
his 27th year....triubte of Respect by Mt. Vernon Sunday School
....

Issue of July 18, 1861

Married at the house of the bride, by Rev. A. B. Stephens,
Dr. J. D. Kleckly to Mrs. H. L. Jennings, all of Orangeburg, S.C.
        Died in Macon, Ga., on the 5th inst., Sallie R., daughter of
W. T. and Annie E. Morgan, aged 5 months and 10 days.
        In Effingham co., Ga., on 23d June, 1861, at the residence
of J. F. Berry, John D. Berry, aged 33 years, 8 months and 16
days.

Near Centre, Ala., June 21st, Agnes Mary, infant daughter of Dr. Jno. P. and Mrs. A. M. Ralls, aged 17 months.

The Rev. Levi W. Jarrell, son of John and Elizabeth Jarrell, was born in Jones co., Ga., and died on the 28th June, in Ft. Valley, Ga., aged 27 years....   T. B. Russell

Elizabeth Seago was born March 10th, 1794, was married to William Seago June 4th, 1816, and died in Houston co., Ga., April 8th, 1861....

Mrs. Mary Whetstone, daughter of the late Jacob and Mary Hook, and wife of Absalom Whetstone died in Orangeburg Dist., in the 61st year of her age....left eight children....   A. B. Stephens

Mr. Adam Holman died in St. Matthews Parish, Orangeburg Dist., S. C., on 18th April, in the 59th year of his age...
                                        A. B. Stephens

Coke Browne, son of J. M. and L. L. Browne, was mortally wounded by the accidental discharge of a gun in Clarksville, Ga., on April 25th, aged 18 years, 7 months and 13 days...my nephew
                                        Sidi H. Browne.

Rev. Joseph T. Edwards died of comsumption, May 28th, 1861, at Newton Factory, Ga., born in Abbeville Dist., S. C., Sept. 2d, 1810...his parents, Robt. L. and Isabella Edwards, moved to Elbert co., Ga., when he was quite a boy....

Mrs. Margaret A. wife of Mr. Garrettson W. James, and daughter of Mr. Duncan McMillan, died in Williamsburg Dist., S. C., June 8th, 1861, in her 25th year...joined the Presbyterian church about 16, married in her 21st year..joined the M. E. Church... left two little ones....

Mrs. Jane Dyall, wife of Judge Joseph Dyall, died in Suwannee co., Fla., on 21st June 1861, aged about 50 years....
                                        John J. Taylor

Felix W. House, died in Twiggs co., Ga.,on 17th May, 1861, a native of S. C., but for several years a resident of Habersham co., Ga.,where he married and lived until last fall when he removed to Twiggs co....   A. M. Thigpen

Wm. M. Lewis was born in Warren co., Ga.,and died at Midway co., Ga., in his 46th year....   R. W. Hubert

Miss Mary Barnett died in Appling co., Ga., May 25th, 1861, in the 80th year of her age....her brother, Rev. Thomas Barnett ....   J. W. Mills

Mrs. Vicie Johnson, wife of J. R. Johnson, died in Appling co., Ga., April 12th, 1861, in the 27th year of her age....
                                        J. W. Mills

Mr. Daniel Horton died in St. Luke's Parish, S. C., May 9th, 1861, in the 65th year of his age....

John Thompson died in Richland Dist., S. C.,May 13th, 1861, in his 87th year....   J. L. Shuford

Tribute of Respect to James Shuptrine....

Issue of July 25, 1861

Married in Colquitt, Ga.,on 30th June, by Rev. W. H. Thomas, John S. Hopkins to Miss Louisa H. Means.

Rebecca Cobb, wife of the Hon. and Rev. Howell Cobb, of Houston co., Ga., died on 17th June. Her only child, Mrs. Dr. Culler....   John W. Talley

Mr. Wm. A. Ross died at Bailey Springs, Ala., July 8th, 1861...resided in Macon, Ga., where he had lived from early childhood...a native of N. C., came to Ga. when but 7 years old....

Sister Elizabeth F. Simmons, consort of the Rev. John C. Simmons, of the Ga. Conf., was the daughter of Wm. and Elizabeth C. Smith, of Cumberland co., Va., and was born 4th April 1814....
                                        A. Means

22

Mrs. Rebecca K. Ingrem, wife of Capt. James M. Ingrem, died
in Lancaster Dist., S. C., June 27th, 1861, aged 33 years, 1 month
and 27 days...left two small children....   L. Wood
   Rev. Whitman C. Hill was born in 1790...his wife was the
daughter of Rev. Isaac Smith...died 5th Feb., 1861....John W.
Talley
   Mrs. Della M. Cook, wife of W. D. Cook, died near Bennettsville, S. C., June 11th, in her 23d year...left an orphan when
but a child...married in 1853....
   John Daily was born in 1802, and died near McDonough, Ga.,
25th June 1861, in early manhood he came from Elbert to Henry
Co....
   Bro. James Gulley was born March 13, 1800, and died at Snow
Hill, Wilcox co., Ala., June 30th, 1861....   W. H. Wild
   Augusta Foscue was born in Jones co., N. C., March 21st,
1793. In 1816 he was married to Miss Mary Sanderson, and in
1817 moved to Clark co., Ala. In 1834 his wife died leaving
several children. His second wife was Miss Hetty Hatch, by whom
he had two chilren....   John D. Fisher
   Mrs. Fatha Stevens, widow of Elijah Stevens, late of Bibb
co., was born in Warren co., Ga., on 22d April 1787, and died at
the house of Mr. Wm. Oslin, at Oak Bowery, Ala., June 21st, 1861,
aged 84 years and 2 months....   E. B. Norton
   Mrs. Elizabeth Ham died in Elbert co., Ga.,on 26th June, in
her 91st year...born in Va., and moved to this country 70 years
ago....   J. H. Grogan.
   Ann Bradford died in Columbus, Ga., July 8, 1861, aged 85
years....
   Mrs. Zadah Heustis died near Bennettsville, S. C., June 4th,
1861....left a husband and four children....ThomasCook.
   Mrs. Mary E. Haff, wife of William W. Haff, and daughter of
John and Mary Jane McMichael, was born in Talbot co., Ga., Nov.
15th, 1831, and died at her father's residence in Marion co.,
Ga., June 17th, 1861....
   Tribute of Respect to William K. Oliver by Socapatory circuit,
Ala Conf....

Issue of August 1, 1861

   Married by Rev. L. B. Giles on 11th July, Mr. Charles F.
Heirs, of S. C., to Miss Martha T. Paxton, of Charlton co., Ga.
   By the same on 16th of July, Mr. Gary Nongazer, to Miss Isa-
bella H. Wright, all of Charlton co., Ga.
   In Quitman, Brooks co., Ga., July 16th, by Rev. O. L. Smith,
Mr. Clayton Groover and Miss Florida Burney.
   In Brooks co., Ga., July 21st, by Rev. O. L. Smith, Mr. Ran-
dolph Avera, and Mrs. Mary Jane McElvin.
   In Talbot co., Ga., on the 18th inst., by Rev. Chas. R. Jew-
ett, Mr. John E. Fuller, and Miss Palatine L., daughter of Jno.
W. Dozier, Esq., all of Talbot co., Ga.
   In Tuskegee, Ala., June 6th, 1861, by the Rev. M. S. Andrews,
W. C. Torrance, to Cornelia A. Bascom, all of Tuskegee, Ala.
   Died at Senora (sic) Coweta co., Ga., June 17th, 1861, Alice
only daughter of John M. and C. M. Stallings, and grand daughter
of the Rev. Ivey F. Steagall, deceased, formerly of the Ga. Conf.
in her 2d year.
   Emma Stoll, infant daughter of W. J. and Mrs. Susan Davis,
died in Marion Dist., July 3d, 1861, aged 18 months.
   C. Fulwood, son of Thos. and Sarah Rogers, died June 25th,
1861, in Burke co., Ga.,in the 2d year of his age.
   Mrs. Mary Ann H. Mott died in Columbus, Ga., July 3d, 1861...
born in Milledgeville, April 1806, married to R. L. mott, who
still lives....   L. Pierce

Capt. James Abercrombie died at Pensacola, July 2d, 1861...
born in Hancock co., Ga., but spent most of his manhood days in
Alabama...moved to Fla. from Russell co., Ala., within the last
two years....   L. Pierce
Annie C. Snead, daughter of Rev. T. Snead, was born in
Milledgeville, Ga.,April 12th, 1831, and died near the same place
June 2d, 1861....
Esther Eliza, daughter of Henry R. and Labana Priester, was
born Sept. 15th, 1837, and died July 2d, 1861....L. M. Hamer
Mrs. Mary E. Elkins, wife of Willis Elkins, Esq., died in
concord, N. C., June 20th, 1861, in her 35th year....
David Liston died in Colleton Dist., S. C., May 10th, 1861,
in his 60th year....
William Masterman was born in London, England, Oct. 29, 1831
...removing to America, he commenced business in Charleston...
removed to Spartanburg....   Jas. Stacy
Miss Cynthia A. Sills was born March 29th, 1840 in Columbia,
co., Ga., and died July 9th, 1861, in Jackson co., Fla., to which
county her father, Wm. Sills, removed when she was in her 16th
year....   W. A. Montgomery.
Mrs. Artelia Tutt, wife of J. V. Tutt, and daughter of Philip
F. and Mary R. Beazley, died in Sumter co., Ala., May 13th, 1861,
aged 32 years and 14 days....   Geo. F. Ellis
Mrs. Nancy Stackhouse, daughter of John and Martha Roper,
died in Marion Dist., S. C., June 10th, in her 17th year....
                                                       W. L. Pegues
Bro. P. Clemens died at his residence in Williamsburg Dist.,
S. C....

Issue of August 8, 1861

Married on 16th July, in Augusta, Ga.,by Rev. W.F. McCook,
Rev. T. S. T. Hopkins to Miss Emliy Gibson, both of Augusta, Ga.
On July 28th, at 8 o'clock, A. M. by Rev. W. A. Florence,
Mr. Lewis F. Felts to Miss Susan Trimble, both of Warren co.,
Ga.
By Rev. Morgan Bellah, July 18th, William S. Middlebrooks,
to Miss Nancy Josephina Stephens, all of Upson co., Ga.
By Rev. Morgan Bellah, July 29th, 1861, Mr. David S. Hodo, of
Warren co., Ga.,to Martha B. Shehee of Barnesville, Ga.
By Rev. Jos. S. Key, in Athens, Ga.,on 23d July, Hon. Asbury
Hull to Mrs. Maria Cook.
In Athens, Ga., on 22d July,by Rev. Jos. S. Key, Capt. Jepter-
son Lamar, of Covington, to Miss MaryAnn Lamar, of the former
place.
In Athens, Ga.,. on 29th July, by Rev. Jos. S. Key, Mr. Lamar
Cobb to Miss Ann Olivia Newton.
Died at Pineoplis, St. John's Berkeley, on Tuesday, 22d
inst., Eliza Henrietta, aged 3 years and 6 months--daughter of
Harlock H. and Margt. F. Harvey.
In Elijay, Gilmer co., Ga., July 13th, 1861, Salina Frances,
daughter of Levi M. and Priscilla J. Greer, aged 3 years.
In Gwinnett co., Ga., of consumption, on 26th June, 1861,
Madison L. Lenoir, aged 25 years and 7 months.
Mrs. Caroline L. Moore, wife of P. E. Moore, Esq., and daugh-
ter of the late George Applegate, of Grand Fulf, Miss., died in
Athens, Ga.,May 28th, aged 30 years...married in 1847....
Jesse Sanders died in Duval co., Fla., June 10th, 1861...
born in Wilmington, N. C.,in 1782, and in 1822, emigrated to Fla.,
and settled in St. Augustine....

Married July 18th, 1861, by Rev. J. M. Richardson, Thos. J.
Simmons to Miss Nancy G. King, both of Whitfield co, Ga.
OnJuly 25th, by Rev. W. S. Williams, Joseph H. Banks, Esq.,
to Miss Mary L. young, daughter of Robert Young, of Hall co., Ga.
By Rev. I. Austin, George H. Mallette to Miss Julia H. Ams-
dorff, all of Effingham co., Ga.
Died Walter D., son of James D. and S. A. Sauls, was born
June 12, 1858, and died in Quincy, Fla., June 5th, 1861.
Willie, infant son of James D. and S. A. Sauls, was born
Dec. 24th, 1859, and died June 18th, 1861, in Quincy, Fla.
In Cheraw, S. C., on 27th July, Lilly Victoria, infant daugh-
ter of Alonzo A. and Cynthia T. Vanderford, aged 1 year, 2 months
and 19 days.
In Atlanta, July 17th, 1861, Paul Haygood, infant son of Rev.
A. G. and Mrs. M. G. Haygood, of the Ga. Conf., aged 16 months.
Mary S. Thomas, wife of Rev. E. L. Thomas, formerly of Oxford,
Ga., the daughter of Mr. Hogue, of Oglethorpe (now Taliafero co.),
Ga., married Aug. 14th, 1806, died 12th June 1861....A. Means.
Mrs. Mollie H. Hill, wife of P. B. Hill, Esq., of Newnan, died
on the 24th June, in the 29th year of her age...the youngest child
of the late Mr. Clarke Taylor, of Oglethorpe co., Ga. Her mother
survivies....   Chas. A. Fulwood
Mrs. Mary Elizabeth McGehee DeJarnett, wife of Dr. John T.
DeJarnett, died in Eatonton, Ga., in her 23d year....
Allen A. Beall died in Putnam co., Ga., on 15th June 1861,
in the 46th year of his age....leaves a wife and 8 children...
                                            W. G. Allen
Mrs. Mary Harrison, widow of James Harrison, Sr. died in
Edgefield Dist., S. C., April 20th, 1861, in the 75th year of
her age....
Mary A., wife of Judge P. M. Williams, was born in Charleston,
S. C., Dec. 11th, 1812, died in Lowndesboro', Ala., on 27th July
1861....   Wm. A. McCarty.
Sarah Freeman Reid, relict of Judge J. B. Reid, and daughter
of Rev. Benjamin Blanton, died in Griffin, Ga.,on 4th July, in
the 51st year of her age....   Chas. W. Thomas
Robert T. Owen, eldest son of Hon. A. F. and Mrs. E. L.
Owen, of Talbotton, Ga.,was born in Charleston, S. C., 1840, and
died at Ft. Morgan, Ala., aged 20 years....
David Clarke Kirkland died July 1st, 1861, at Centerville,
Fairfax co., Ga. aged 24 years...son of D. B. Kirkland, Esq. of
Fairfield Dist., S. C., and a volunteer in the 1st Regt. S. C.
V. in Va.....   J. W. Puett
Mrs. Anne R. Houghton, widow of the late Col. Joshua Houghton,
was born in Va. on the 22d Jan 1776, and died at her residence,
in Greene co., Ga., on 13th June 1861....
Reuben W. Westbrook was born in Franklin co., Ga., Nov. 15th,
1809, and died in Cherokee co., Ga., July 11th, 1861....
Greenville Simmons, a native of Hancock co., for several years
Cashier in the State Bank, died 28th July in his 55th year....
                                            W. H. Potter
Tribute of Respect to Van Leonard, by St. Paul's M. E. Church,
Columbus, Ga....
Tribute of Respect to J. L. Williams, by Marion-Street Sunday
School....

Issue of August 22, 1861

Married on Sunday, August 4th, 1861, by the Rev. I. L. Cotton,
A. Sternes, Esq. of Columbia, S. C., to Mrs. J. K. Lowman, of
Eufaula, Ala.

On 18th July, by Rev. W. A. Houck, Mr. J. F. Baxter, to Miss Sallie O. Livingston, both of Orangeburg Dist., S. C.

By Rev. T. S. L. Harwell, August 4th, 1861, Mr. Mills C. Brinson, to Miss Mary E. Ingram, all of Scriven co., Ga.

Died in Columbus, Ga.,on the 8th instant, in the 2d year of his age, George Harwell, infant son of Rev. H. H. Parks, of the Ga. Conf.

Mrs. Sallie L. Wright, daughter of John W. and Letitia Greer, and wife of Rev. Arminius Wright, of the Ga. Conf., was born in Monroe co., Ga., August 17th, 1834, and died in Columbus, Ga., July 22d, 1861...in early infancy she was left an orphan...reared by her uncle. (long account and eulogy).

Rev. Absalom Ogletree died in Monroe co., Ga., July 20th, 1861....

Samuel G. Swindle was born on the 31st Dec., 1841, and died near Norfolk, at Camp Jackson, Va., July 14th, 1861...member of the LaGrange Light Guards, 4th Regt. Ga. Volunteers....

Mrs. Elizabeth Adaline Seale, wife of Rev. D. W. Seale of the S. C. Conf., and daughter of J. and Ann Law, of Sumter Dist., died July 15th, at the residence of Mr. Robert J. Moorer, of Cypress circuit, in her 39th year....

Martha Jane North, daughter of Perry and Letha Dye, was born Sept. 14th, 1838, and died at her father's residence in York Dist., S. C., August 9th, 1861....   John W. North

Hartwell McCrary, late of Spartanburg, S. C., was born July 29th, 1839...in 5th S.C. Regt.   Jas. Stacy.

Miss Mary Louisa Warren, second daughter of W. S. And Helen M. Warren died in Tallapoosa, Ala., August 1, of consumption....

Reuben Tyler was born in Oglethorpe co., Ga., and in his 16th year removed to the northern portion of Elbert, now Hart co., and died 12th June, 1861,at the residence of Rev. B. Parker, in his 70th year....   H. Tyler

Mrs. Martha A. Mixon, wife of A. E. Mixon, died in Dallas Co., Aug 2d, in her 39th year....   T. Moody

Frances Permelia, daughter of Wm. and Mary Sills (the latter deceased) was born in Columbia co., Ga., May 24th, 1841, and died in Jackson co., Fla., Aug 2d, 1861....   W. A. Montgomery

Samuel Dubose was born in Darlington Dist., S. C., came to Ala., in 1819, and died near Pineville, in Monroe co., June 30th, 1861, being 79 years of age....   W. K. Norton

Mrs. Hannah Eliza Andrew, widow of the Rev. Jos. B. Andrew, of the Ga. Conf., and daughter of Zachariah and Nancy Timmons, of Glynn co., Ga.,was born March 11, 1808, and died at the residence of her son-in-law, Capt. E. M. Mallette, in Camden co., July 20th, 1861....

Tribute of Respect by Sumter mission, Fla conf., to George M. Condry....

Issue of August 29, 1861

Married on 25th July, by Robt. A. Carson, Mr. Zechariah Mathus to Miss Mary Mills, of Troy, LaFayette co., Fla.

Mrs. Mary McGinnis, died at the residence of her mother, Mrs. Sarah Aken, in Monroe co., Ga.,on 16th July 1861, in her 36th year....   R. W. Dixon

Mrs. Margaret Edwards, wife of Louis Edwards, died in Spartanburg Dist., S. C. on 22d July in the 38th year of her age....
          T. J. Clyde

Col. Van Leonard died in Wynnton, near Columbus, Ga., Aug. 2d, 1861, aged 71 years....

Mr. Theodore Sturdivant died in Charlotte, N. C., on 29th May, in his 22d year....

Mrs. Elizabeth Brown died in Camden co., Ga., June 29, 1861,
aged 65 years...brought up in Baldwin co., and immediately after
her marriage removed to this county....   R. H. Howren.
     Mrs. Minerva Jolley, wife of Clarke Jolley, and daughter of
Rev. Thomas and Sarah Cook, was born Dec. 7th, 1832, and died at
Indian Springs, Ga.,Aug. 3d, 1861....   John W. Reynolds
     Mrs. Charity Stephens, wife of Solomon Stephens, died in
Heard co., Ga., July 19th, in the 35th year of her age...joined
the Presbyterian church, but upon her marriage joined the M. E.
Church....leaves a hsuband and five children....J. J. Morgan
     Dr. John C. Gibson died in Monticello, Ga., June 16th, 1861.
He was born in York Dist., S. C., May 27th, 1785, In 1809 removed
to this place....
     Eliza Lawton, wife of Jas. J. McMillan, and daughter of Samuel
and Martha Newbold, was born in Charleston, S. C., and died in
Aiken on Saturday night, the 27th July, aged 23 years and 8
months....
     William Harberson, died in St. Geroges Parish, Aug. 2d, 1861
....   D. C. Appleby
     James. F. D. Culver, son of J. G. Culver, died on the 3rd
July, near Culverton, Hancock co., Ga., at about 18 years of age
....
     Geo. T. Stovall, fell in the great battle of Manassas Plains,
a member of "Rome Light Guards." 8th Ga. Regt.... J. W. Hinton
Tribute of Respect to him by Sunday School of M. E. Church, Rome,
Ga.

Issue of September 5, 1861

     Married by Rev. Martin Eaddy, Dr. Wm. F. Higgins to Ann E.
Conley daughter of Allen Conley, Esq., all of McDowell co., N. C.
     By Rev. J. W. Farmer, on 7th July, Mr. M. M. Mattox, to Miss
Rebecca E. Hill, all of Liberty co., Ga.
     At the residence of Mr. Wm. H. Kennedy, in Alachua co., Fla.,
August 15th, by Rev. T. A. Carruth, Dr. Samuel D. Smoke, of
Providence, Fla., to Miss Lizzie Sealy, of Alachua.
     By Rev. Wm. B. Neal, Aug. 22d, 1861, Mr. Sterling H. Pitts
to Miss Sarah Nelms, all of Russell co., Ala.
     By Rev. W. H. Thomas, on the 21st August, Mr. Cicero Crooks,
of Ala., to Miss Sarah A. Leath, of Early co., Ga.
     Died in Lowndes co., Ga., on 4th August, William Alston, aged
15 months, son of Archibald and Elizabeth Ann McIntyre.
     Rev. Thomas Dougherty was born in Charleston, Mass., of
Irish parents, about the year 1821, and died at Memphis, Tenn., at
about 40 years of age...his mother was a zealous Roman Catholic....
     Mrs. Sena Galloway was born July 5th, 1801, in Darlington
Dist., and died June 18th, 1861, aged 59 years, 11 months and 13
days...the daughter of Arthur and Juday Pipkin, and was married
to Mr. Enoch Galloway, Dec. 24th, 1827....
     Margaret E., wife of Charles M. Sudduth, and daughter of Noah
and E. H. Spainhour was born Jan. 30th, 1839, was married Sept.
3d, 1856, and died in Lenoir, N. C., July 31st, 1861....
                                              John Watts
     Mrs. Sarah E. Sibley, wife of W. C. Wibley, was born in Meck-
lenburg co., N. C., Oct. 6th, 1815, and died in Taylor co., Ga.,
Aug. 15th, 1861....   A. J. Dean
     Clisby G. Cobb was born in Burke co., N. C., July 30th, 1808,
and died in Caldwell co., N. C., July 18th, 1861.... J. W. Ruby
     James Theodore Daracott was born in Abbeville Dist., S. C.,
in the year 1832 and died Aug. 15th, 1861, at Culpepper, Va.
joined Capt. Shanklin's Co., Col. Sloan's Regt...leaves a wife
and one child....

Mrs. Mary P. Kilpatrick died in Rutherford co., N. C., July
8th, 1861, in the 69th year of her age, and in the 55th year of
her church membership....   A. Hamby
      Mrs. Sarah E. Beall, wife of Thomas Beall, private in Spalding
Grays, near Norfolk, Va., died in Griffin, Ga., July 19th....
      The parents of Joseph Harrell moved to the vicinity of Ft.
Valley, Houston co., Ga., from N. C., in the year 1830, bringing
their three children, Joseph, Charity and Sarah...until 23d Aug
when he died in his 65th year....none ever married...M. L. Green
      Judge John Sturdivant was born in N. C., and died in Taylor
co., Ga., June 29th, 1861, in the 64th year....   A. J. Dean
      Harriet Lyons, who was born in Columbia co., died in LaFayette
co., Fla., June 14th, 1861....
      Mrs. M. A. Wells died in Clarendon Dist., S. C., on 7th Aug.
She has left 5 orphan children....   A. C. Wells

Issue of September 12, 1861

      Married by Rev. W. A. Montgomery, Aug. 29th, Henry J. Robin-
son to Miss Antoinette Bowls, daughter of H. H. Bowles, all of
Jackson co., Fla.
      On Sept. 3d, 1861, by Rev. T. S. L. Harwell, Mr. Thos Young
to Miss Laura M. Williams, all of Bullock co., Ga.
      In Baldwin co., Ga., Sept. 3d, by Rev. J. B. McGehee, Mr. J.
W. Bouner to Miss Kate N. Webb
      Aug 28th, 1861, in Walker co., Ga., by Rev. J. W. Brady, Rev.
Jas. H. Thomas to Miss Sarah A. Lowery.
      On 5th Sept., 1861, by Rev. John M. Smith, Samuel G. Pegg, of
Ala., to Miss Elizabeth P. Avery, of Fulton co., Ga.
      Mrs. Charlotte Green Miller, wife of Rev. J. Wesley Miller,
of the S. C. Conf., and daughter of William and Jane F. Wilson
of Georgetown District, died in Charleston, July 10th, 1861, aged
28 years....
      Frederick Foster Page, only son of Dr. George H. and Mrs.
Nancy Page, died near Preston Academy, in Coweta co., Ga., on 13th
Aug., in the 22d year of his age...a student at Emory College....
                                              Luther M. Smith
      Thomas W. Snyder was born Feb. 17th, 1829, in Greenville Dist.,
S. C. After he left school he emigrated to Mississippi, where
he remained until the fall of 1860...returned to his father's
house and died July 13th, 1861....
      Lucy D., youngest daughter of E. V. and D. R. Collier, died
in Caddo Parish, La., July 21, 1861, in the 11th year of her age
...also at the same place, August 6, Mrs. D. R. Collier, mother
of the above, formerly of Oglethorpe co., Ga., in the 56th year
of her age....
      Robert Raymond, son of Capt. Wm. H. and Mary A. Rousseau, died
at Camp Magnolia, near Pensacola, on the 25th June, in the 21st
year of his age....
      Posey Brooks was born Nov. 4th, 1801, and died July 15th,
1861, in the 60th year of his age, in Russell co., Ala....leaves
wife and nine children....   William B. Neal
      Mrs. Rebecca C. Chambers, widow of the late John M. Chambers,
died in Cherokee co., Aug. 17th,in her 41st year....
      Richard William Lenox, printer, was born in Charleston, S. C.,
July 30, 1838, died Aug. 17th,1861....
      Elizabeth Z. McFaddin, wife of John J. McFaddin, died on 20th
August, in Clarendon Dist., S. C.,in the 30th year of her age....
      Daniel F. H. Martin, son of S. R. Martin, of Fairfield Dist.,
S. C., died on the 19th Aug., 1861, in the 18th year of his age
....   J. W. Puett
      Miss Margaret Ann Drusilla, daughter of Mr. and Mrs. A. S. D.
Murray, died in Colleton Dist., S. C.,on the 24th ult., aged 23

years and 3 months....   William Hutto
     Susan P. Barco, wife of Thomas Barco, died in Marion co.,
Fla., on 14th June 1861..born 12th Feb. 1841, in Pike co., Ala,
the daughter of James F. and Matilda M. Allen....
                                          Jas. T. Stockton
     James E. Allen died in Hernando co., Fla., Aug. 19th 1861,
born in Elbert co., Ga.,Dec. 25th, 1808....   W. L. Murphy
     Tribute of Respect by Crystal River Mission at Magnolia
to James E. Allen....

Issue of September 19, 1861

     Mrs. Nancy S. Tarver, mother of the late Hon. Walter Colquitt,
died in LaGrange, Ga., on 23d August, in the 82nd year of her age
...her maiden name was Holt, and she was the last surviving member
of a large family....   C. W. Key
     Henry Harrison Avery, youngest son of Jas. Avery, Esq., of
Burke co., N. C., died at Yorktown, Va., aged 21 years....
     The Rev. S. E. Randolph of the Lowndes Volunteers, 12th Ga.
Regt., died at Camp Alleghany, Va., Aug. 29th, 1861, about 28
years of Age, and a native of Tennessee....   Wesley P. Pledger
     Seaborn Hargroves, died at the residence of his mother, in
Jackson co., Ga.,Aug. 13th, 1861, in his 32d year....
     Alice A. Canady, daughter of Seabrook P. and Ann J. Canady,
was born Sept. 12th, 1848, and died Aug. 12th, 1861....
     Tribute of Respect to Julia Potter....

Issue of September 26, 1861

     Married on the 17th inst., by Rev. William Hutto, Mr. David
Bull to Miss Elizabeth M. Byrd, all of Orangeburg, S. C.
     On the 18th inst., by Rev. D. J. Myrick, Col. James W. Harris,
of Cartersville, Cass co., Ga., to Miss Julia Florence Candler,
of Villa Rica, Carroll co., Ga.
     Died in Calhoun, Gordon co., Ga.,on 2d Sept., Hannah Altoe(?),
only daughter of Z. T. and Elizabeth Gray, aged 2 years and 4
months.
     Near Fort Mill, Aug. 22d, Ann Lucinda, infant daughter of J.
H. and M. E. Allen, aged 6 months and 21 days.
     In Georgetown, S.C., Sept. 10th, Salina Jane, daughter of
Alex. J. and M. L. Cox, in the 3d year of her age.
     On 21st Aug., Alice Ann Eliza, daughter of Mr. and Mrs. Henry
Caskins, formerly of Charleston, aged 7 years, 5 months and 27
days. Also, on 22d Aug., Martin Simms and on 23d Julia Emiline,
twin children of the same, aged about 4 years and 6 months.
Also on the 24th Aug, their only surviving John Henry, aged 2
years, 7 months and 14 days, all of country fever.
     Coe, infant son of Mr. and Mrs. J. R. Harris, of Quincy, Fla.,
was born Dec. 15th, 1860, and died Aug. 30, 1861.
     Clara Morton, died on Tuesday, 17th inst.,at the Wesleyan
Female College, Macon, Ga., little daughter of Rev. J. M. and
Mary A. Bonnell, aged 3 years.
     The Rev. A. H. Harmon, of the S. C. conf., died at the resi-
dence of Capt. J. M. Ingrem, in Lancaster Dist., S. C., on Tuesday
night, the 20th Aug 1861, in the 39th year of his age...the son
of Mr. Peter Harmon, of Cleveland co., N. C....early in the
present year, he married Miss Martha Medley, of Anson co., N. C.
(long account and eulogy).   Landy Wood
     Rev. Girard George Washington DuPre was born in Greenville,
S. C., Nov. 24th, 1837...buried beside his mother in Greenville
....   Sidi H. Browne
     Berrien Oliver, died on the 4th inst., in Wakulla co., Fla.,
in the 60th year of his age, leaving a widow and several children...

born in Edgefield Dist., S. C., he was carried at an early age, an orphan to Elbert co., Ga., until he removed to Russell co., Ala., in 1840...

Bro. Thomas Hardeman died in Vineville, Ga., on the 11th ult., born in Oglethorpe co., Ga., April 15, 1797.... J. E. Evans

Mr. Calvin Carpenter, of Alexander, Burke co., Ga., died at the Indian Springs, on the 14th ultimo, at the age of about 45 years...a member of the Baptist Church, but attended with his wife, the M. E. Church....

John P. Smith, Sen., was born inOrangeburg Dist., S. C., July 9, 1806, and died in Lexington Dist., Aug. 31, 1861, in the 56th year of his age....

Mrs. Sarah Williams, wife of A. Williams, died near Union Springs, Ala.,on the 31st Aug, in the 66th year of her age...born in Hancock co., Ga., and moved to this State some 8 years ago....
Jesse Wood

Mr. James Ward, of Burke co., Ga., died 30th ultimo, at the age of about 60 years....   Tilman Douglas.

David Locket Peek, son of William W. Peek, Esq., of Cedartown, and son-in-law of Major Wooley, of Cass co., Ga.,died on the 19th August, at Gordonsville, Va....

William J. Parris died of typhoid fever in the hospital at Warrington, Fla., on 30th Aug., in his 40th year. He was a native of Ga., I believe of Oglethorpe co.....

Jasper E. Heath died on 4th Sept., at the residence of his father, in Burke co., Ga., aged 23 years....

Robert D. Alston died Sept. 3d in his 27th year....
Tribute of Respect to L. W. Jarrell....by Ft. Valley Conf....

Issue of October 3, 1861

Married on 25th September, 1861, by the Rev. J. L. Stevens, Mr. J. Swann, to Miss Elizabeth Roper, of Conyers, Ga.

Died in Sparta, Hancock co., Ga.,on 17th instant, Agnes Irene, infant daughter of H. W. and Sarah P. Forbes, aged 1 year and 10 months.

Little Sallie, daughter of Samuel and Nancy Browne, (Broadway, S. C.) was born May 19th, 1853, and died 18th Sept. 1861.

In Charleston, on 29th July 1861, Mrs. Pamelia S. T. Adair, wife of Captain William F. Adair, aged 21 years, 5 months and 25 days, leaving a babe 25 hours old, who died when it was 1 month and 2 days old.

Dr. Alexander Sledge was born in Haligax co., N. C., in 1787, and died near Greensboro, Ala., Aug. 12th, 1861...in 1813 removed to Jones co., N. C., and in 1817 married Winifred Lane. In 1821 came to LaGranga, Ala....   E. Wadsworth

Mrs. Mary Crews was born in Kershaw Dist., S. C., April 11, 1796, removed to Jones co., Ga., with her parents in 1811, in 1815 was married to Arthur Crews, Esq. She came to Barbour co. (then Pike co), Ala., in 1822....

Mrs. Naomi Wylley, wife of W. C. Wylley, died at the residence of her son, at the Isle of Hope, Chatham co., Ga., in her 73d year ....   Jas. E. Godfrey

Mrs. Catharine Reese, the surviving consort of Dr. Joseph Reese, deceased, died in Florence, Stewart co., August 13th, 1861, aged 61 years, 6 months and 27 days...born in Washington co., Ga ....

Mrs. M. S. Lucas, youngest child of pious parents, Robert and Elizabeth Jones, was born in Granville co., N. C., Nov. 9th, 1825, married Mr. H. G. Lucas, April 15th, 1851, and died on 23d July in Marlbor' Dist., S. C....

Nancy McCornell died in Cherokee co., Ga., August 20th, 1861 born in Franklin co., Ga., Aug. 2, 1813, daughter of Maxfield H.

and Sarah Pain, and was married to Joseph McCornell, 16 April
1840....
    Penelope F. Price, wife of Mr. A. P. Price and daughter of
D. S. Dupuis, died inMarion co., Fla., on 11th August, in the
20th year of her age...born in Beaufort Dist., S. C....
                                                    Jno. C. Ley
    Mrs. Rebecca Pillsbury, the oldest Methodist in Columbia,
was born near Eutaw Springs, St. John's Parish, S. C., in 1778,
and died in Columbia, 20th Sept. 1861...Her grand-parents by the
name of Mouzon, were refugees from France...married to Samuel
Pillsbury in Charleston....   Wm. Martin
    Mrs. Ellen Ashley, wife of Alexander Ashley, died on 17th
Sept., in Telfair co., Ga.....   Alex. Ashley.
    Joshua R. Simmons was born in Rutherford co., N. C., July
14th, 1811, and died at Cave Spring, Floyd co., Ga.,July 16th,
1861....   J. J. Singleton

Issue of October 10, 1861

    Married by Rev. J. W. Puett, on the 19th of September, in
Fairfield Dist., S. C., Mr. Geo. Glover of Chester, to Miss
Elizabeth, daughter of Samuel Mundle, Esq.
    By Rev. J. W. Puett, on 26th Sept., in Richland Dist., S. C.
Hilliard G. Souter, of Clayton co., Ga., to Miss Jane C. Ruff.
    On 22d Sept., at Munden's chapel, by Rev. Isaac Munden, Mr.
Hezekiah Tucker of Jefferson co., Fla., to Miss`Anna Mary
Braddock, of Nassau co., Fla.
    Died at Concord, Conacuh co., Ala., Mary Ann, daughter of J.
O. and Martha A.Sellers, July 25th, 1861, aged 5 years, 6 months
and 2 days.
    Mrs. Emily McLellan Dannelly, wife of Dr. F. O. Dannelly, was
born in Portland, Maine, April 6, 1823, and died in Greenville,
Ga., April 11th, 1861....
    Bartley C. Williams, died in the bounds of Sumter Mission, E.
Fla., on 10th July 1861, in the 78th year of his age...born in S.
C., in 1783, soon after his birth, his parents moved to Ga.,
and settled on the Ogechee river....
    James Augustus Jones, son of S. S. Jones, of Hart co., Ga.,
and member of the 15th Ga. Regt., died at Manassas Junction, on
25th July 1861, in his 24th year....
    Miss Gertrude Snider, daughter of the late Benmamin Snider,
died in the city of Savannah, Sept. 19th, 1861, in her 17th year
....
    Mrs. Frances A. Smith, wife of Rev. Alfred B. Smith, formerly
a member of the Ga. Conf., now a local preacher of Burke co.,
Ga., died on the 17th Sept., aged 41 years....   Tilman Douglas
    Dr. John Thompson, died in Thomaston, Ga.,on 8th of Sept.,
in the 42d year of his age....   W. Knox
    Sergt. Wm. H. Hargrove, of Oglethorpe co., Ga., died in
Gloucester co., Va., Sept. 14th, 1861, in his 22d year....
    Samuel Lofton, son of William Lofton, of Lowndes co., Ga.,
and nephew of Mrs. A. Peurifoy, died at Camp Bartow, Va., Sept.
8th, 1861....   A. Peurifoy.
    S. G. R., son of Henry W. and Louraney P. Walton, died at
Fairfax station, Va.,on 7th of Sept.,1861, in the 22d year...
a native of Monroe co., Ga., moved from thence to Alabama....
    Mr. D. H. Mason died on 25th Aug, from a woudn received July
21st, at the battle of Manassas Plains....   C. A. Moore
    Sydney Ann Feath, wife of Washington Feath, died at the
residence of her mother, in Burke co., Ga.,in her 22d year...leaves
two small children, and a husband....

Died on South Santee, St. James' parish, Oct. 7th, 1861, Susannah Miller, infant daughter of J. D. and M. A. Green, aged 5 months and 9 days.

In Newton, N. C., at her grand-father's, Rev. J. W. Broomfield, Oct. 4th, 1861, Idora, only daughter of Mrs. Sophronia Houser, aged 6 years, 10 months and 23 days.

At the residence of the Rev. J. Rufus Felder, in Perry, Houston co., Ga., on Sunday afternoon, Sept. 22nd, John McPherson, infant son of Hamblin R. and Catharine A. Felder, aged 12 months, 23 days.

In Colleton, on 26th Aug, "Little Bella" only daughter of Dr. James and Mrs. Mary Stephens, aged 2 years, 5 months.

Neighbor D. Lesesne, of Williamsburg, S. C., died Aug. 29th, at the residence of Dr. Williams, Montrose, Va., aged 30 years... private in "Manning Guard"....

Mrs. James Culloden Johnson, was born in Dec., 5th, 1837, in Monroe co., Ga.,resided several years, in Butler, Ga.,and died in Petersburg, Va., Sept. 27th, on his way home from Yorktown....
A. J. Dean

Zaccheus Butler Gatewood, son of John C. and Elizabeth W. Gatewood, was born in Putnam co., Ga., Oct. 10th, 1842, and died at Staunton, Va., Sept. 18th, 1861....

Sergt. Donald Cameron McCaskill of the "Davis Rifles" aged 17 years, died at Camp Bartown, Pochahontas co., Va.,on 20th Sept....son of M. and E. A. McCaskin, born in Houston co., Ga., Sept. 26th, 1844....   M. J. McK.

Mrs. Ann Elliott, daughter of James Babcock, who was one of the patriots of the Revolution of 1776, was born in Scriven co., Ga., Feb. 16th, 1788, and died in Columbia co., Fla., aged 73 years, 5 months and 4 days...in early life married Richard Rabourn, of Scriven co., Ga., soon after which they removed to the west, where Mr. Rabourn died, leaving widow and infant daughter ....she married to Mr. Elliot, and returned to Ga., in 1815 or 1816 removed to Fla....   T. A. Carruth.

Mrs. Jane E. Burroughs, wife of B. B. Burroughs, and daughter of Seaborn and Martha Skinner, was born Sept. 1, 1852, and died in Pike co., Ala., Sept. 23d, 1861....   S. I. Kelly

Laura Jane, only child of B. C. Altriend of White Plains, ga., was born Aug. 31, 1838, and died Sept. 26th, 1861....
A. Gray

Mrs. Elizabeth Wadsworth, widow of John Wadsworth, died at Daniel Wadsworth's, her son, in Chesterfield Dist., S. C., August 19, 1861, aged 80 years, 1 month and 7 days....Lewis Scarborough

Susan, wife of William Wynne, and daughter of William and Martha Hinson, late of Burke co., Ga.,died in Wilkinson co., Ga., on 11th August, aged 65 years and 8 months...married to her husband 2 May 1811, has had twenty children...leaves husband 11 children, and 45 grandchildren....

Miss Frances Wynne, daughter of William and Susan Wynne, died in Wilkinson co., Ga., July 17th, 1861, aged 43 years and 3 months....

Mrs. Beneter Davis, daughter of William and Susan Wynne, and widow of Elbert Davis, dec'd, died in Wilkinson co., aged 32 years, 4 months and 12 days, leaving five children....

Francis Marion Nolley, oldest son of Welsey and Jane Nolley, was born in Baldwin co., Ala., on 13th March 1842, and died at Fort Morgan, Ala., on 21st July 1861....

A. P. Livingston, Esq. of St. James, Goose Creek, died August 18th, at Brentville, Va., in the 38th year of his age....

John S. Page, died in Marion Dist., S. C., July 28th, 1861....
J. W. Murray

Ellen P. Williams died in Macon co., Ala., on the 19th Sept.,
1861, daughter of Newnum and Lucy Reynolds, was born in N. C.,
May 3d, 1823, emigrated to Alabama in 1833, and was married to
L. S. Williams, Feb. 14th, 1849...left a husband and five little
children....   A. J. Williams

(No issue October 24, 1861)

Issue of October 31, 1861

Married on 20th inst.,by Rev. A. H. Lester, R. W. Kimbrel,
to Miss Rosana M. Smith, all of Spartanburg Dist., S. C.
By Rev. W. W. Oslin, Oct. 17th, Mr. James W. Johnson, of
Paulding co., Ga., to Miss Parmelia A., eldest daughter of J.
D. Brown, of Gwinnett co., Ga.
Died at her residence in this city, Mrs. Elizabeth M., Moore,
wife of Rev. G. W. Moore of the S. C. Conf, on Oct. 26th.
On Sept. 1st, at the residence of Mrs. Elizabeth Connor, in
St. James Goose Creek parish, Ellen Elizabeth, daughter of W. C.
and F. E. Williams, aged 11 months and 24 days.
In Monroe co., Sept. 16th, 1861, James Barrow, infant son
of John W. and L. P. Dozier, aged 8 months and 19 days.
N. A. Lamar Duncan, of the Sumter Light Guard, 4th Regt.
Ga. Volunteers, and son of Rev. J. P. Duncan of the Ga. Conf.,
died at the Naval Hospital near Portsmouth, Va., Sept. 26th....
Sister Eliza Thomas Williams, of Cokesbury, S. C., died on the
12th inst., and was buried at Tabernacle Church by Rev. W. H.
Lawton...born May 5th, 1799 in Granville, N. C., the daughter
of George and Martha Daniel, married to Thos W. Williams,March 18,
1824 by Rev. L. Q. C. DeYampert....   W. A. McSwain.
Fletcher C. Gradick of Edgefield, S. C., died at Culpepper
C. H., Va., Aug 7th, 1861, aged 22 years, 7th Regt. S. C. V....
Wm. B. Davis died at Heapville, on the 5th inst.,leaving
a wife and four children....   C. McLeod
Mrs. Winifred Ainsworth, the wife of Rev. James T. Ainsworth,
of the Ga. Conf., died in Sandersville, Ga.,Sept. 26th, 1861,
in the 27th year of her age...married in Jan. 1849....
                                          W. S. Turner
Daniel D. Rogers was born in Marion Dist., S. C., Jan. 2d,
1839, joined the M. E. Church and later the Missionary Baptist
Church, died 14th Sept 1861....   J. T. Galloway
Lt. Henry W. Trippe, son of John B. Trippe, Esq., and Mrs.
L. P. Trippe, of Milledgeville, Ga., died at the Stribling
Springs, Augusta co., Va., on 25th Sept., aged 24 years, 5 months,
and 19 days....1st Regt. Ga. Regualrs....
Henry Hay was born in Aberdeen Scotland, and died in Charleston,
S. C., July 24th, 1861, aged about 62 years....
David H. Montgomery died in Fairifeld Dist., S. C., Aug. 31,
1861, aged 41 years...in '58 married to Miss C. E. Watts, and
she died July 15th, and in one week after, John David, their only
child, aged two years....   W. A. Clarke
Mrs. Eugenia Suber, wife of I. H. Suber, Esq., died in
Newberry Dist., S. C., on 27th Aug, in the 44th year of her age
....   J. W. Wightman
Jeptha F. Westbrook died in Cherokee co., Ga.,August 18th,
in the 18th year of his age....
Mrs. Mary J. Westbrook died in Cherokee co., Ga.,August 21st,
in the 26th year of her age...born in Walton co., Ga., and was
the daughter of Anderson D. and Amelia Smith....
Joseph G. Jones died at his residence in Bamberg, Barnwell
Dist., S. C., aged 53 years...born in Chester Dist., in 1809,
and lived there until in 1835 removed to Orangeburg Dist...married
21 Dec 1837 to Mrs. A. Caroline Kitteral....   Wm. Crook

Joseph A. Riley, son of Mr. George Riley, died in Barnwell
Dist., S. C., on 18th July 1861....
Mrs. Catharine Milner, wife of Jonathan P. Milner, daughter
of Jacob Addie, of Coweta, died in Griffin, Ga., on 5th of Oct.,
aged 27 years....
Mrs. Nancy Tally died at the house of her son in Macon co.,
Ala., on Sept. 4th, in the 62d year of her age...born in Green
co., Ga....   Thomas W. Slaughter.
Benjamin S. Murdock, son of Wm. P. and Sarah A. Murdock, was
born in Bulloch co., Ga.,March 8th, 1840, and died in Fairfax,
Va., on the 25th Sept 1861....my brothers Benjamin and James
left their home to join the army in Va.... Charles P. Murdock
Bro. George Alfred Allen died 26th of Sept 1861...a member
of the M. E. Church about 27 years....   W. A. McSwain.
Mary A. R. Rouse, daughter of James B. Rouse and Amy Eubanks
formerly Amy Rouse, was born Jan. 8th, 1847, in Walton co., Fla.,
and died Oct. 8th, 1861, in Macon co., Ga...John N. Hudson
Emma E. V., daughter of Ephraim Weathers, died in St. George's
Parish, on the 29th ult., in her 9th year....
Lucius Bellinger, infant son of John and Rebecca Shider,
died in St. George's Parish, S. C., on the 1st inst., aged 2 years
nad 14 days....
Tribute of Respect to Rev. Columbus W. Howard, by Harris
circuit, Ga. Conf....
Tribute of Respect Rev. D. D. Henry, by Suwannee circuit....

Issue of November 8, 1861

Married on the 29th Oct., by Rev. Geo. C. Clarke, Dr. A. F.
Pharr, of Newton co., to Miss Sue C. Hiley, of Houston co., Ga.
Died in Talbotton, Ga., Oct. 10th, Julia Havis, daughter of
Abner and Julia Turner aged 3 years, and 10 months.
In Union co., N. C., on Tuesday 15th Oct., James Edward,
only son of J. J. M. and Hester C. Heath, aged 11 months and 27
days.
In Taylor co., Ga.,September 29th, Christopher Francis, infant
son of W. H. and C. E. Fickling, aged 1 year and 3 months.
Mrs. Elcey Grinell, wife of Peter Grinell, died in Eatonton,
Ga., Oct. 3d, aged 63 years....
Mrs. Jane B. Evans died in Marion, S. C., on 3d September,
aged 67 years....
John L. Brown was born in N. C., and died at Camp Butler,
near Aiken, S. C., on the 15th Oct., and was buried at the M. E.
Church in Aiken....   E. F. Thwing
George W. Barnes died in Baldwin co., Ga.,17th Aug....
                                          L. Q. Allen
Capt. Alexander McCarty died at an advanced age in Darien,
Ga., Oct. 17th, 1861....   J. F. Berry
Sarah E. Watts was born in Hall co., Ga., Jan. 8th, 1832,
married Bro. Joseph M. Watts, Sept. 1848, died 25th Sept 1861....
                                          J. D. Anthony
Dr. Joseph S. Marshall, of Abbeville Dist., one of the
stewards of the Cokesbury circuit, died Sept. 16th, 1861....
                                          W. A. McSwain
Mrs. Martha R. Johnston, wife of Iredell Johnston, and daugh-
ter of Jacob and Mary Hoffman, was born in Lowndes co., Ala., May
7th, 1826, and died inMacon co., Ala., on the 27th Sept 1861....
                                          F. G. Ferguson
E. M. Underwood died in Fairfax Court House, Va., 18th of
Sept., aged 18 years...   Lewis L. Ledbetter
Roland Bivins, son of Shadrach and Mildred Bivins, was
born in Hancock co., Ga.,Feb. 22, 1801, and died in Bibb co.,

Aug 17th,1861...27th July 1820, he married Nancy S., daughter of
Arthur and Frances Redding....
     Nancy Purvis, wife of Rev. J. B. Purvis, died in Jefferson
co., Ga., Oct. 9th, 1861, aged 34 years....   S. A. Clarke
     Harriet E. Garner, daughter of C. W. Garner, of Darlington
Dist., S. C., died at Hickroy Plain, Ark., July 25, 1861, aged
14 years....   B. G. Johnson
     Eli Lockhart died in Tampa, Fla., Aug. 23d, 1861, aged 32
years....
     Mrs. Sarah Ann, wife of Robert Cunningham, died in Mecklen-
burg, N. C., Sept. 11th, 1861, aged about 26 years...leaves husband and three little children....
     Derrel Harrison, died in Summerfield, Ala., Oct. 13, aged
72 years...a native of S. C., he removed thence to Alabama in
1833...his son B. J. Harrison....   R. K. Hargrove
     Mrs. Henrietta Taysor, wife of G. W.Raysor, and daughter of
the late Thomas and Eliza Mims, died 7th September 1861, aged
20 years....   A. R. Danner
     Wm. J., son of Henry T. and Nancy E. Holt, was born Jan. 3d,
1842, and died Sept 12th, 1861, near Greenwood, Montgomery co.,
Ala....
     Mary B. Holt, sister of William, was born Sept. 15th, 1843,
and died Sept. 8th, 1861....   C. S. Hurt
     John A., son of L. T. and E. G. Barge, died Sept. 16, 1861,
aged 14 years....   J. D. Worrell
     Dr. Enos C. Moyer, died in Talbotton, Ga.,on the 25th Sept.,
aged 55 years....
     Tribute of Respect to Lawrence Augustus Felder who died in
Western Virginia, 12th Sept 1861, in the Confederate army...
by Southern University of Alabama....
     Tribute of Respect to Elim Wilbanks by O'Brian ct., Ala....

Issue of November 14, 1861

     Married by Rev. E. A. H. McGehee, on 15th Oct., in Marion co.,
Ga., Mr. Robert H. Peacock, to Miss Martha C. McMichael.
     On Sept. 11th, by Rev. A. R. Bennick, Mr. Joseph Reid, of
Union co., Ga., to Miss Martha E. Weaver, of Rutherford co., N.
C.
     On the 27th Oct., 1861, in Johnson co., Ga.,by the Rev. James
V. M. Morris, Rev. Charles A. Moore, of the Ga. conf., to Miss
Nancy E. Hicks, youngest daughter of James Hicks.
     Anson McCallum Sperry died Oct. 13th, at the house of Mr.
Palmatary, near Yorktown, Va., aged 18 years...Beauregard Volun-
teers....   Geo. C. Clarke.
     Mrs. Ann Eliza Blakewood, wife of Capt. John S. Blakewood,
and daughter of Mr. Solomon L. Reeves, of Charleston, died 18th
Oct., 1861, in Hardeeville, Beaufort Dist., S. C., in the 40th
year of her age....left husband and ten children....
     Rev. Thomas Hawkins of the Methodist Protestant Church, died
Oct. 4, at Cleveland Tenn...born in Wilkes co., Ga., afterwards
lived in N. C.   J. W. Hinton
     Corinthia A. Mitchell, wife of George W. Mitchell, died in
Crawfordsville, Ga.,on 13th July 1861, in her 27th year...followed
by Little Kate the youngest of the household....
     Samuel B. Coney, son of Rev. James N. Coney, of Gwinnett co.,
Ga., was born Dec. 27th, 1842, died in Richmond, Va., Oct. 17th,
1861...an officer of the "Flint Hill Grays."...   W. W. Oslin
     George M. Taylor was born in York Dist., S. C., Jan. 27th,
1809, and died in Cherokee co., Ga.,aged 52 years....
     Mrs. Margaret J. Grant, daughter of Rev. Samuel Segrist died
on the 15th Oct., in Macon co., Alabama....   William Barrow

Asbury Yarbrough, of the 14th Regt, S. C. F., Co. F., died
at Aiken, Oct. 4th....   W. B. Carson, Chaplain.
    Mrs. Narcissa J. Gillespie, wife of A. M. Gillespie, and
daughter of Joseph and Temperance Gillespie of Lancaster Dist.,
S. C., died in Union Springs, Ala., on the 25th Oct., in her 39th
year, leaving four children....
    Mrs. Jane Chandler, wife of Mr. Elias Chandler, and daughter
of Mr. Ezekiel and Mrs. Isabella Keels was born Sept. 16th, 1827,
and died July 25th, 1861....left a husband and 7 children...
                                                W. H. Smith
    Ezekiel Smith, son of Hopson and Eliza Smith, died in Russell
co., Ala., June 30, 1861, aged 22 years...Annie died in her 17th
year....
    Mrs. Elizabeth Avinger died Oct. 16th, 1861, at the residence
of her eldest son Mr. James Parier, in St. Matthews Parish, Orangeburg Dist., S. C.,in the 69th year of her age....
    J. M. B. Goodbred died in Suwannee co., Fla.,on 27th Aug.,
in the 42d year of his age...Captain of the Columbus Ranger....
                                                J. W. Mills
    A. Thompson, of Henry co., Ga., and member of the 18th Ga.
Regiment, died at Richmond, Va., on the last of Sept. 1861, in
his 22d year....
    James S. Jones son of Dr. James S. and Susan A. Jones, of
Thomson, Ga., was killed on the 9th Oct., on Santa Rosa Island,
Fla., in his 20th year....
    John B. Brown died Oct. 16th, 1861, near Campbellton,
Jackson co., Fla., born in Washington co., Ga., 1789, married in
the year 1810...of fourteen children only two survive....
    George Walker, son of Joel Walker, late of Houston co., Ga.,
died at the house of his father-in-law, in Marshalville, Oct.
15th, in the 43d year of his age...in 1848 married Clara F., daughter of Daniel and C. A. Frederick....   Geo. C. Clarke.
    Mrs. Mary Roland, daughter of David Jackson dec'd of Greene
co., Ga.,was born Aug 16, 1801, married Jan 28th, 1819, and died
10th Oct. 1861....   William Bryan
    Sister Mobly, wife of Brother Byrd Mobly, died in Appling
co., Ga.,on 11th Oct., 1861...born in appling co., in 1828,
married in Oct. 1846....   J. W. Mills
    Josiah Mathews,son of Francis L. Mathews, of Upson co., Ga.,
died on the 19th Oct., aged 15 years....
    Miss Martha Eliza Tennant of Charleston was for upwards of
20 years a member of the M. E. Church...died 19th Oct. 1861...
    Mrs. Patience H. Bradley, wife of Rev. J. M. Bradley (former-
ly of the S. C. Conf.) died in Caddo Parish, La., on the 26th
July 1861....

Issue of November 21, 1861

    Married on the 11th Sept., in Jasper co., Ga.,by Rev. Chas.
R. Jewett, Dr. Goodwin M. Clements, of Baldwin co., and Miss
Rebecca E., daughter of Benj. W. Purifoy sr., of Jasper co.
    At the residence of Mrs. MaryA. Atkinson in Chattooga co.,
Oct. 8th, 1861, by Rev. J. D. Anthony, Mr. Perry Harper, of the
said county and Mrs. Ann R. Jones, of Va.
    On 6th November 1861, by Rev. T. Lanier, Hon. Clem C. Slater,
to Miss Mary Edwards, all of Bryan co., Ga.
    Near Griffin, Ga.,on the 27th Oct., by Rev. G. H. Pattillo,
Dr. Augustus L. Edwards, of Taylor co., Ga., and Mrs. Elizabeth
C. Doyal, of the former place.
    Died in Thomaston, Julia Bethel, infant daughter of Dr. John
and Mrs. Elizabeth Thompson, botn Oct. 23, 1860, died Oct. 17,
1861.

Sallie Pope, daughter of Rev. W. H. Moss, of the Ga. Conf.,
and M. E. Moss, was born Nov. 1, 1860, and died in Caddo Parish,
La., Nov. 1, 1861.

Elliott H. Muse Jr. of LaFayette, Ala., died at the house of
Mrs. J. T. Caldwell, in Pensacola, Fla., on 4th Oct., from a
wound received in the Santa Rosa flight....

Thomas J. Hills, son of Col. Dennis and E. A. Hills, died at
Gordonsville, Ga.,on Jluy 26th, from a wound of the battle at
Manassas, July 21st, aged 21 years, 7 months and 9 days....

Dr. Daniel A. Zimmerman, died at the residence of his father,
the Hon. J. P. Zimmerman, in Darlington Dist., Oct. 25th, 1861,
in the 29th year of his age....   D. J. Simmons

John W. R. Felder died in Barnwell, on 9th Sept., 1861, in
his 37th year..in 1st S. C. Regt....

Mrs. Louisa Elizabeth Lamar was born 31st December 1834,
married to Lavoisier L. Lamar, Dec. 4th, 1859, died on 23d oct.
1861....   G. F. Pierce

Lizzie C., wife of Jacob Robertson, died in Jasper co., Ga.,
in her 26th year, a daughter of the Rev. John Tunnel, dec'd....

Miss Mary Frances, daughter of Dr. John and Mrs. Elizabeth
Thompson, died in Thomaston on 27th Oct., in her 16th year....
                                           W. Knox

William J. Sanders, a native of Ga., died in Camp Davis, Macon
co., Ala., 3rd Nov. 1861, in his 28th year...Capt. Burnett's Co.,
17th Ala. Regt....

Mr. A. H. Palmer of the Evans Guards, 13th Regt., Ga. Volunteers, son of J. A. Palmer, was born 30th Oct 1842, died at White
Sulpher Springs, Va., Oct. 22d, 1861....   J. A. Palmer.

Mrs. Sarah H. Wright, wife of Rev. Stephen Wright, was born
in N .C. and died in Coweta co., Ga., Nov. 2d, 1861, in her 70th
year...married in Greene co., Ga., in 1813....

S. K. Crawley, of the Griffin Light Guards, 5th Ga. Regt, died
in Pensacola, of typhoid fever....   J. A. Crawley.

Mrs. Jane Miles died near Perote, Ala., on 10th Oct., 1861,
aged 64 years...raised a large family....   Robert C. Hayne

Mrs. Ann D. Shuptrine died in Thomaston, on 7th Oct., in the
55th year of her age.....   W. Knox

Wm. A. Sweany was born Dec. 26th, 1789, in Granville co., N.
C., and in 1860 moved to Greene co., Ga., died Oct. 31, 1861....
                                           Hinton Crawford

Tribute of Respect to Rev. Absalom Ogletree by State Conf of
Ga....

Issue of November 28, 1861

Married on 3d Oct., 1861, at De Sota Mound, Orange Grove, by
the Rev. R. W. Burgess, Mr. George P. Washington to Miss L. E.
Youngblood, all of Hillsborough co., Fla.

On 31st Octo., at Bluff Springs, Hernando co., Fla., by the
Rev. R. W. Burgess,Mr. A. Jackson Youngblood to Miss M. E. Stevenson.

By Rev. W. S. Black on 12th Nov., Dr. A. F. O'Bryan, of Walterboro', to Miss Annie M. Reid, of Cheraw, S. C.

By the Rev. W. D. Martin, on the 13th Nov., in Marion Dist.,
Mr. B. Dill to Miss Lydia L. Rogers.

Died in Columbia, S. C., on Thursday evening 7th instant,
Henry Muller, son of R. D. And M. R. Senn, aged 2 years, 1 month
and 7 days.

Elizabeth Ann, wife of Rev. Hartwell Spain, of the S. C. Conf.,
died Oct. 16th, 1861, at the residence of Dr. Thomas Briggs,
Clarendon Dist., S. C., in her 63d year...a native of York Dist.,
where she spent her girlhood....

Benjamin Ward, eldest son of R. H. and Sarah M. Ward, of Greene co., Ga., died Oct. 28th, 1861, at Raleigh C. H., Western Va., in his 19th year...a member of Philips' Legion, Ga. Volunteers....   A. Gray

Mrs. Drusilla Riley, died Aug. 20th, 1861, in Barnwell Dist., S. C., in her 57th year...daughter of Father David Felder....
                                                 W. W. Graham

James Asbury Durant, son of John O. and Abigail H. Durant; of Sumter Dist., S. C., died 14th Oct., 1861, in his 19th year.... in Chicora Guards on Morris Island....

Mrs. Cynthia C. Seale, wife of Jarvis Seale, was born Jan. 19, 1797, and died in Wilkes co., Ga., Sept. 4th, 1861....lived to see 5 children grown....

Mrs. Sarah Simpson, wife of the Rev. James Simpson, of the N. C. Conf., departed this life in Elizabethtown, Balden co., N. C., Oct. 6, 1861. She was a native of Anne Arundel co., Md., was 36 years of age....   Charles F. Deems.

Wm. A. Florence, Jr. died Oct. 13th, at Greensboro', Ga., in the 25th year of his age....

Mrs. Sallie Turner, died on 14th Sept. 1861, in Barnwell Dist., aged about 85 years....

Isaac Culver Edwards, son of James J. and Lucinda Edwards, died at Lawrenceville, Henry co., Ala., Oct. 17th, 1861...born in Putnam co., Ga., Oct. 25th, 1847....   J. W. Solomon

Jno Wesley, son of Washington and Harriet Warner, of Lowndes co., Ala., died Nov 3, 1861, in his 23d year, at Huntsville, Ala., a soldier....

Sarah E. Hay, died in Fairfield Dist., S. C., Oct. 17h, 1861, having been a member of the church 41 years....   J. W. Puett

James Whitman Crumpton, died in Fairfield Dist., S. C., Aug. 21st, 1861, aged 23 years....   J. W. Puett

Mr. Simon Rogers of Upson co., Ga., died at the residence of his son, Dr. C. Rogers, in his 79th year....

Martha Louisa, oldest child of James H. and Indiana A. Barksdale, of Appling co., Ga., was born in Abbeville Dist., S. C., 12th June 1847, and died in Savannah, Ga., on 12th Nov 1861... pupil in Massie school in Savannah....

Issue of December 5, 1861

Mrs. Sophia D., wife of the Rev. Jesse Sinclair, died in Stewart co., Ga.,on the 24th Oct., 1861, in the 60th year of her age....   Jesse Sinclair

Jackson Hathorn died at his residence in Monroe co., Ga., on Saturday the 9th inst., in the 41st year of his age....

Mrs. Cornelia Fielding, died in Gainesville, Ga.,on 29th Oct 1861....

Mrs. Sarah Allen, wife of John B. Allen was born in Ga., Dec. 18th, 1809 and died in Hernando co., Gla., Sept. 14th, 1861, in the 52d year of her age....

Washington Postell Larr, only son of Rev. John Larr, of Orangeburg Dist., S. C.,died at the residence of his father in the 24th year of his age...a member of the Edisto Rifles, 1st Regt. S. C.V: ....

H. H. Brewer was born and raised in Taylor co., Ga.,was about 22 years old, and a member of the Taylor Guards...died August 31, 1861....   A. J. Dean

Jesse L. Brewer was born and raised in Taylor co., Ga., about 19 years old, died Oct. 5th, 1861....

Issue of December 12, 1861

Married at the residence of the bride's father, Nov. 17th,

1861, by Rev. T. R. Barnett, Dr. F. A. Hall of Tatnal co., Ga.,
to Miss Lavana Mobly, of Apling co., Ga.

on the 25th Nov., by the Rev. L. M. Little, the Rev. J. C.
Stoll, of the S. C. Conf., to Miss Mary L. McCullough, of Williamsburg Dist.

By the Rev. W. S. Williams on the 19th Nov., in Forsyth co.,
Ga., Mr. William H. Norman, of S. C., to Miss Lucretia J. Graham,
of the former place.

At the residence of the bride's father, in Saline co., Ark.,
on 31st Oct., by Rev. A. R. Winfield, Rev. Cadesman Porr, of the
Ouachita Conf., to Miss Sallie A. Cooper, formerly of Union Dist.,
S. C.

Nov. 16th, 1861, by Rev. Lewis W. Rast, Matthias Rucker, Esq.
of Lexington Dist., to Miss Elizabeth Rucker, of Orangeburg Dist.

In Fairfield Dist., S. C., on 26th Nov., 1861, by Rev. J. W.
Puett, Mr. Jeremiah Cockerel of Memphis, Tenn. to Miss Jemimah
Cockerel, of the former place.

On the evening of the 20th inst., by the Rev. H. C. Parsons,
Dr. J. W. Burnett to Miss Mary, only daughter of Major P. Richardson, all of Anson.

At the residence of the bride's fahter, near Red Clay, White-
field co., Ga., on Tuesday 26th Nov., by Rev. W. D. Bussy, Dr.
Moses Quinn to Miss Lovonia J., daughter of Wilson Norton, Esq.

In Dale co., Ala., Nov 10th, by the Rev. W. R. Talley, Mr.
Dickson Hallford, to Miss Harriet A. F. Skipper.

By Rev. W. R. Talley, Nov. 17th, 1861, Mr. George Youngblood
to Miss Frances Dougherty, all of Dale co., Ala.

By Rev. J. M. Smith, on 3d Dec., 1861, James H. Wilson and
Miss Mary F. Green, all of Campbell co., Ga.

At the residence of the bride's aunt, Mrs. E. F. Boatwright,
in Columbia co., Ga.,on the 28th Nov., by Rev. J. F. Stockton,
Miss Eliza Jane Bell and Mr. John W. Samuels.

On the 26th of Nov., by Rev. J. W. Puett, Mr. Jerry Cockrell
of Memphis, Tenn. to Miss Mittie E. Cockrell of Fairfield Dist.,
S. C.

Nov. 27th, by Rev. S. H. Browne, Rev. James W. Wheeler, of
the N. C. Conf., to Miss Lucy M., eldest daughter of Mr. James
Plunkett, of Wadesboro', N. C.

By Rev. R. E. Oliver, onthe 1st December, Joseph T. Whitehead,
to Miss Fadora V. Shockley, both of Jackson co., Ga.

By the Rev. Thomas J. Williamson, on the 24th Nov., in Chambers co., Ala., Capt. Jas. H. Erwin of West Point, Ga., to Miss
Josephine, daughter of James Simms, Esq.

Died in Polk co., Fla.,on the 11th Nov., Simon H. Smith, son
of Simon P. and Clarissa Smith, formerly from Tatnal co., Ga.

Perry William, son of W. T. and Mary E. Smoke, was born Sept.
15th, 1857, and died in a few hours from a burn, Oct. 23d, 1861.

Emma M., daughter of John W. and Laura Hibbert, died in
Houston co., Ga., Aug. 12th, aged 17 years and 10 days....
                                                    R. M. Heath

Mrs. Clara Jackson, wife of Edmund Jackson died in Monroe co.,
Ga., Nov. 21st, 1861, in the 70th year of her age...married in
1808....leaving husband and six children....

Mrs. Mary E. Salley, wife of Maj. J. J. Salley, died at her
home in Orangeburg Dist., S. C., Aug. 28th, 1861, in the 49th
year of her age....   A. B. Stephens

Sister Shannon died in Newnan Ga., on the 29th Oct., in her
26th year...husband and two brothers in the Confederate army....
                                          Charles A. Fulwood

J. Wesley Bass Evans, son of Wade and Sarah Evans of Orangeburg Dist., S. C.,died Sept. 13, 1861
in the 20th year of his age....   D. W. Seale

39

J. Edwin Evans, son of Wade and Sarah Evans, of Orangeburg
Dist., S. C., died Sept. 13th, 1861, at Jackson River, Va., in
the 21st year of his age....   D. W. Seale
    James H. Kendrick son fo W. B. Kendrick dec'd and C. E. Ken-
drick, died on 19th Oct., 1861, in Pike co., Ala., in his 22d
year....   C. Hardy
    Mrs. Lucinda Norton, wife of Rev. Ethelbert B. Norton, of the
Ala. Conf., and daughter of Rev. Elias W. and Ann Story, was born
in Fayette co., Ga., Sept. 21st, 1837, married Aug 9th, 1859, and
died Nov. 7th, 1861....   F. G. Ferguson
    Mrs. Jane D. Heath aged 27 years, 11 months and 9 days, died
in Burke co., Ga., on the 18th Nov., left a husband....
    Adam Edgar (better known as Judge Brown) son of Rev. Jos. E.
and Rebecca W. Brown of Sumter Dist., S. C., died Nov. 6, 1861,
in the 21st year of his age, near Manassas in Va....
    Beasor Barrow, died in Dale co., Ala., Oct 22d, 1861, aged
60 years....
    James D. Beckham died in Pike co., Ga.,on 30th Aug, 1861, aged
about 58 years....six of his children preceded him to the grave
....leaves a wife and four children....   C. Hardy
    Elder Wilkerson, died in Macon co., Ala., Oct. 16th, 1861,
born in Putnam co., Ga., Sept. 1795, and was married to Elizabeth
Phillips in 1822 in Jasper co., Ga....
    Mary S. Risher, daughter of Benjamin and M. E. Risher, was
born 24th Feb., 1841, and di-d in Colleton Dist., S. C. 8th Nov
1861....
    Thomas Barron died in Autauga co., Ala., near Prattville,
Oct. 25th, 1861, born in Marland, Dec. 9th, 1777....

Issue of December 19, 1861

    Married on the 19th Nov., by the Rev. J. W. Bates, Mr. John
Rees, to Miss Mary Jane Carlton, all of Panola co., Miss.
    Died in Richland Dist., S. C.,Nov. 17, Ellar Rebecca, infant
daughter of C. G. and J. W. Leitner, aged 4 weeks and 2 days.
    Lt. Peyton Lisby Wade, of the 1st Regt., Ga. Regulars died
at Richmond, Va.,on 16th Nov., 1861....
    Lindsey Garvin Weaver was born Oct. 22d, 1841, in Greenville
Dist., and died Oct. 2d, 1861, near Fairfax Station, Fairfax co.,
Va....
    Rosey C. Ponder, a lovely girl in her 8th year, the daughter
of T. J. and Rebecca B. Ponder, died in Walker co., Ga.,Nov. 13,
1861....   W. K. Neal
    Homer V. M. Prescott of the 25th Reg. Ga., Co. and son of
Benjamin Prescott, of Scriven co., Ga.,died on Tygee Island, Ga.,
Nov 2, aged 18 years and 8 months....
    Mrs. Mary Pennington, died on the 16th ult., near Cotton
Valley, Marion co., Ala., aged 68 years and 5 days...born in
Hancock co., Ga., married to Mr. Pennington of Ga. who died 10
years afterward....
    Rev. Robert Campbell, a local preacher on Darlington ct.,
died 13th of Nov...a native of Va., in early life his parents
moved to N. C., later he removed and settled in Darlington Dist.
...   P. F. Kistler
    Mrs. Harriet R. Still, wife of W. T. Still, died in Mecklen-
burg, N. C., on the 15th of Oct., aged 44 yeras and 5 months....
    Ambrose Hutchinson was born in Virginia, June 12, 1782, and
died in Greene co., Ga., Nov. 18, 1861, in the 80th year of his
age....   W. Bryan
    Mrs. Jane McLeod, relict of the late Dan'l McLeod, died on
7th Nov., in the 60th year of his age, at her residence near
Mechanicsville, Sumter Dist., S.C.....

Sister Ann Daniel,   born in Burke co., Ga.,July 1809, and
died in Jefferson co., Ga., Oct. 19th, 1861....   J. W. McGehee
    John Wm. Schmidt Jones, P. M., Aransas, Texas, died Nov., 14th,
aged 21, ledest son of Wm. H. and C. R. S. Jones of tetanus....
                                        J. H. Frost, Missionary
    Dr. J. H. J. Hook died in St. Matthews Parish, on the 26th
Nov., 1861....
    Tribute of Respect by Laurens circuit, S. C., to. Rev. Hilliard
Judge Glenn....

Issue of December 26, 1861

    Married by Rev. J. M. Smith, on the evening of the 21st Nov.,
1861, Mr. Christopher C. Burk to Miss Jane C. Redwine, all of
Fulton co., Ga.
    By the same on the 27th of August, 1861, Mr. Wm. P. Medlock
and Miss Vilena A. Mason.
    On the 18th December by Rev. Luther M. Smith, Mr. John T.
McLaughlin of Colinsworth Institute, and Miss Mary Fannie Lee,
daughter of Judge Wm. Lee, of Newton co., Ga.
    On 17th Dec., by the Rev. J. M. Smith, in DeKalb co., Ga.,
Adam S. Pool, of Fulton co., to Miss Sallie J. Stubbs, daughter
of James F. Stubbs.
    On 17th of Dec., by the Rev. J. H. Elder, Mr. Joshua H. Mea-
lair, of Spalding co., Ga.,and Miss Ophelia P. Ramsey, of Newton
co., Ga.
    On 20th Nov., near Wadesboro, N. C., by Rev. H. C. Parsons,
Dr. John W. Bennett to Miss Mary S. Richardson, of Anson co.
    On the 8th inst., by Rev. R. J. Sampler, Mr. James S. Felton
of Smith co., Texas, to Miss Julia Langley of Calhoun co., Ala.
    Miss Mary E. Grant was born inMerriwether co., Ga., July 15th,
1843, and died Oct. 28th, 1861....   John K. Leak
    Mr. Enoch Galloway, was born July 27th, 1795, in Darlington
Dist., S. C., where he resided until his death, Nov. 25, 1861...
married to his wife Mrs. Sena Galloway, Dec. 24th, 1817....
                                        A. B. Galloway
    Mrs. Esther Josephine Stokes, wife of M. C. Stokes was born
in Dinwiddie co., Va., Sept. 29th, 1831, removed to Alabama in
1853, and married in June 1854; died Nov. 5th, 1861....
    Alginus N. Salmons, died at the residence of his father in
Atlanta, Ga. 29th Nov., aged 18 years....
    Mrs. Jane McLeod, relict of the late Daniel McLeod, died on
the 7th Nov., in the 60th year of her age, at her residence near
Mechanicsville, Sumter Dist., S. C...left affectionate children
....
    Miss Martha Whitlow, daughter of Mr. Jas. Whitlow, deceased,
formerly of Clarke co., Ala., died at Warrior Stand, Macon co.,
Ga., Nov. 4th, in her 27th year....
    Rev. Abraham Littlejohn was born in Burke co., N. C., Sept.
8, 1790, and died at Nacoochee, Ga.,Nov. 14th, 1861, aged 71
years....
    George Leonidas Heath, a member of the Lancaster Greys, Capt.
Wylie, Co A., 9th Regt. S. C. V., died 19th Nov. 1861, at the
Byrd's Island Hospital, Richmond, Va., aged 24 years, 9 months,
and 18 days....
    John W. Short, died at Camp Bartow, Pacohontas co., Va., in
his 27th year...raised in Macon co., Ga., and a member of the
Davis Rifles....buried in the Village Church-yard....
    Mrs. Harriet R. Stitt, wife of W. T. Stitt, died in Mecklenburg
co., N. C., 15th Oct.,aged 44 years and 8 months...for many years
a member of the Presbyterian Church, later joined the M. E. Church
....

Matthew Dorsey was born in Oglethorpe co., and died at his
residnece in Stewart co., Ga., the 22d Oct. 1861, in the 81st
year of his age....
   Tribute of Respect by Forest Rifles, Coosawhatchie, S. C.,
to A. S. Summers, of Orangeburg, who died from the accidental
discharge of a pistol....
   Dougald McKeller, was born in Scotland, Aug. 15, 1793...came
to America when about 21 years of age, and died near Columbus,
Miss., Nov. 21st, 1861,leaving a widow and child....
   Wm. C., son of John C. Peek, died in his 19th year Nov. 1861
...with Capt. King's Co. of 9th Ga. Regt....   D. Blalock.
   Susan F. Parker died on 12th Nov, 1861, at Winnsboro,S. C.
aged 33 years, 8 months and 17 days....   J. W. Puett
   Henry Williams died at Winnsboro, S. C., on 25th Nov., 1861,
aged about 45 years...left widow and children...J. W. Puett
   L. Dow Byrd, a member of the Webster Confederate Guards, died
at Camp Johnston, near Manassas Va., Oct. 2, 1861...born Sept.
23, 1841....   R. F. Jones

Issue of January 9, 1862 (New Series, Vol. I, No. 1)

   Married by Rev. W. A. Gamewell, at the residence of J. Henry
Dingle, in Sumter, F. A. Tradewell, of Columbia, and Miss Ann
Eliza Dingle, of Clarendon, daughter of the late Adam Dingle, Esq.
   On the 18th of Dec., by the Rev. Geo. C. Clarke, Lt. James
A. Everett and Miss Jose C. Rumph, all of Houston co., Ga.
   By Rev. H. V. Mulkey, on the 17th Dec., 1861, Mr. Ucal Head
to Miss Fannie Sheppard, all of Barbour co., Ala.
   On Dec. 24th, 1861, by Rev. D. C. Appleby, Mr. Garland M.
Yancey, of Chapel Hill, N. C. to Miss Sallie C. Williams, daughter
of Rev. P. A. M. Williams of Colleton Dist., S. C.
   On 26th Dec., 1861, by Rev. J. W. Williams, Mr. Thomas L.
Penn Jr., to Miss Enoree W. Penn, daughter of Hon. T. L. Penn, Sr.
all of Cupeta, Ala.
   Mrs. Martha F. Beall, wife of Col. James M. Beall, and daughter of Maj. George Heard, died in LaGrange, Ga., on the 12th Dec.,
in the 40th year of her age....   C. W. Key
   Mrs. Didama Anderson died on 25th Nov., at the residence of
her son, Dr. E. S. Wimbuch, in LaGrange, Ga., in the 89th year
of her age...among the early pioneers of Methodism in Abbeville
Dist., S. C....   C. W. Key
   Mrs. Nannie M. Kile, daughter of Benjamin Elizabeth Thrower,
now of Atlanta, Ga., was born Feb. 12th, 1832, and died Oct. 23d
1861....
   Mrs. Jane W. Brinson, widow of Jason Brinson, died at the
residence of her son-in-law, Dr. Hill, in Columbia co., Fla.,
Sept. 23d, 1861, aged 63 years, 2 months and 11 days. Her maiden
name was Tyson. She was married in 1826 to Joseph Thomas in Cam-
den co., Ga.,who died in 1829, and in 1836 to Jason Brinson, in
St. Mary's, Ga....   Chas. P. Murdoch.
   Emory Fletcher Arnold, youngest son of the late Rev. Wm.
Arnold, died on 15th Nov., in Eatonton, Ga., in his 25th year....
   George Johnson was born in Va., March 25th, 1815, and died
in Maconco., Ga., Dec. 14th, 1861...joined the Wise Guard in
Western Va....   D. O. Driscoll.
   Miss Sarah E. Anderson was murdered in York Dist., S. C.,
Oct. 28th, 1861, in the 16th year of her age...an orphan living
with her grandfather, William Anderson....   E. A. Faris
   Francis A. Smith, son of Campbell and Margaret R. Smith, of
Rutherford co., N. C., died Oct. 13th, 1861, in the 19th year
of his age...member of the Rutherford Volunteers, 6th Regt. N. C.
Vol's....leaves a widowed mother and brothers and sisters....

Mrs. Caroline Avara was born in Washington co., Ga., and died in Quitman co., Ga., Nov. 13th, in the 36th year of her age ....

Issue of January 16, 1862

Dr. W. L. Manning Austin, late captain in the Hampton Legion, C. S. P. A., died in Greenville Dist., S., C., aged 58 years....
                                                            Wm. T. Capers
The surviving family of our recently departed Bro. Wm. B. Davis are called to mourn the loss of two our of four of the children he left...Wm. Brewington, his youngest son died Dec. 14, 1861, in his 16th year. Selina Ann, his eldest daughter on the 17th of the same month, in her 18th year....   C. McLeod
Mrs. Sallie E., wife of Dr. Wm. L. Phillips, and daughter of Capt. Jesse and Mrs. Emily Smith, was born Aug. 21, 1837, and died in Homer, La., Dec. 10, 1861....   Phil L. Henderson.
Tillman H. Dozier, son of E. A. and L. T. Dozier, of Creek Stand, Macon co., Ala., died near Centerville, Va., on 30th Nov... born 19th Oct., 1839....   George W. Carter
. Robert Peacock was born in Wayne co., N. C., and died Dec. 9th, 1861, in Brooks co., moved to Ga., some 45 years ago....
                                                            M. C. Smith
Waddie Fowler died at Adams' Run, S. C., a mamber of Capt. Perrin's co., of Abbeville. He was born in Union Dist., S. C., Dec. 11th, 1843, and died Dec. 16th, 1861....
Nathan Goren died in Lafayette co., Fla., Oct. 22, 1861... just entered upon the 83d year of his age....   D. L. Kennedy
Mrs. Mary Freeman, wife of the late John Freeman, of Christ Church Parish, S. C., died in Mt. Pleasant, on 6th Dec., in the 56th year of her age...left a daughter and many friends....
Patrick Lynn died in Griffin, Ga., on 2d Nov. 1861, in the 22nd year of his age.
William Marin, died in Raleigh, N. C., on 12th Nov. 1861, in the 19th yearof his age.
John Hughs died in Raleigh, N. C.,Nov. 21st, 1861, in the 20th year of his age.
David J. Hesters, died on 22nd Nov. 1861, in the 19th year of his age.
William Eason died in Richmond, Va., on 21st Dec. 1861, in the 20th year of his age.
Jacob S. Rentz died on the 25th Nov. 1861, in the 23d year of his age.
David Taten died on the 27th Nov., 1861, in the 22nd year of his age.
Moses Tomberlin died in Culpepper, Va., on 25th Nov. 1861, in the 19th year of his age.
Isham Crosby died at Manassas, Va., on 3d Dec. 1861, in the 16th year of his age. The above men joined the Appling Grays in July last....They were all native citizens of Appling Grays.
G. W. L. Nicks died on 26th Dec., 1861, in the 18th year of his age...   Nicks, Taten and Jacob S. Tentz were natives of S. C....
Elizabeth Catharine Bundy, wife of Joshua D. Bundy, and daughter of John L. and Barbara Adams, of Butler co., Ala., was born Nov. 14th, 1845, married 11th Oct. 1860, and died 13th Oct. 1861 ....

Issue of January 23, 1862

Married by Rev. W. Hutto, on the 7th inst., Dr. Peter L. Horne to Miss Mary E. Moorer, all of St. George's Parish, Colleton Dist, S. C.

On the 15th of Dec., 1861, in Walton co., Ga., by Rev. Jos. S. Key, Dr. D. C. Jones of Atlanta, Ga., to Miss Mollie Harris, of Walton.

On 24th December, in Lowndes co., at the residence of the bride's father, by the Rev. N. B. Ousley, Mr. John H. Jones, of Twiggs county, to Miss Mary F. Watts of the former place.

On the 9th Jan. 1862, by ghe Rev. T. E. Wannamaker, Dr. A. N. Wannamaker, to Miss Sarah Pooser, all of Orangeburg, S. C.

On the 7th of January, 1862, by Rev. J. M. Cline, Rev. John Hutchinson, of the S. C. Conf., to Miss Mary Jane, daughter of Capt. Benj. Henry, of Anson co., N. C.

James Joseph M. McGehee, son of Rev. Thos F. and Sarah K. McGehee, was born in Meriwether co., Ga.,June 17th, 1840, and died in Culpepper Hospital, Va.,Nov. 29th, 1861....J. W. McGehee

Emily G. Huggins died on the 19th Nov., 1861, in Athens, Ga., in her 54th year....

Mrs. Epsey Bowdre, wife of Thomas Bowdre, late of Columbia co., Ga., died at Washington, Wilkes co., Ga., on 19th Dec. 1861, in her 76th year....

H. Fletcher Corbit, was born in Sumter Dist., S. C., Dec. 9th, 1830...died 18th October...left wife and infant....

Wm. F. Matthews, son of Rev. W. D. and Rebecca Matthews, of Alabama, died on 7th Dec. last....   W. D. Martin

Rev. Thomas A. Rosamond, was born in Abbeville Dist., S. C., on 5th June, 1787, and died in Yalabusha co., Miss., Nov. 30th, 1861, in his 73d year....

James P. Dixon, son of Turner B. and Mary A. Dixon, of Sumter co., Ga., died in the Hospital at Staunton, Va., on 28th Dec., 1861, in the 21st year of his age....   R. W. Dixon

Ezekiel Carson Brace, a member of the M. E. Church in Cabarrus co., N. C., died Dec. 31, 1861, in the 83rd year of his age...
                                           R. H. Northrop

Mrs. Harriet E. Cade, wife of J. L. Cade, died in Darlington Dist., S. C., Dec.8th, 1841, in her 23rd year....

Miss Ann B. Ferdin, died in Columbia, Jan. 9th, in the 60th year of her age...a native of Charleston, and her mother a member of the Presbyterian Church....

Mrs. Minerva E. How, born in Harris co., Ga., July 1838, married Rev. Benj. How in Enon, Macon co., Ala., in Nov. 1859, and died Nov. 5th, 1861....

Mrs. Jane J. Stewart, wife of Jas. Stewart, Sr. of Sumter co., Ga., died on 26th Oct., 1861, in her 59th year.... S. Anthony

Caswell Mobley died on 14th Nov 1861, in his 62d year...a member of the M. E. CHurch, Lancaster Circuit....

Mrs. Jerusha C. Pye, wife of Beniet Pye, died near Forsyth, Monroe co., Ga., Dec. 11th, 1861, aged 36 years... A. V. Mann

E. F. Millican, son of Lewis and Temperance Millican, was born in Madison co., Ga., Dec. 11th, 1824, whence his father moved to Chattooga co., when he was a small boy....in "Chatooga Volunteers." died 22 november....   J. D. Anthony

Mrs. Martha E. Greer, wife of Wm. B. Greer, died in Richmond co., Ga., Dec. 9th, 1861, in her 21st year....

Rev. Wm. C. Clark died at Ansonville, N. C., Dec. 2, 1861, aged 48 years...traveling minister in the S. C. Conf about 18 years....

Miss Eliza Jane, daughter of George W. and S. A. Hill was born in Cass co., Ga., Sept. 9th, 1845, and died in Dalton, Ga.,Dec. 19th, 1861....   L. D. Palmer

Nathan B. Stephens died 11th Dec., near Darien, Ga., in his 19th year--the youngest of four brothers, the sons of a widowed mother....

Mrs. Agnes Morris died near Sparta, on the 22d Dec. 1861, in the 60th year of her age....

Mr. James Solomon, of Dougherty co., Ga., died at the house of her sister (Mrs. Hartwell) on 29th Dec. 1861.... S. Anthony
Mr. Alexander Walker died in Edgefield Dist., S. C., on 3d Jan., 1862, in the 59th year of his age....

Issue of January 30, 1862

Married by Rev. John M. Smith, on the 16th Jan., 1862, at the house of Mrs. Elizabeth Connelly, in Fulton co., Ga., George J. Beasley, of Fayette co., to Miss Margaret F. Connelly, of Fulton.
On 18th January, 1862, by Rev. George C. Clark, Mr. Charles S. Winn, and Miss Martha Bryan, all of Houston co., Ga.
On 1st Jan. 1862, by Rev. R. N. Cotter, Maj. D. F. McRae to Miss Marion, second daughter of Judge D. McRae.
On 1st Jan., 1862, in Drayton, Dooly co., Ga.,by the Rev. Jno. P. Duncan, Mr. W. R. Stewart, of Sumter co., Ga., to Miss M. Virginia Lott, of Griffin, Ga.
By Rev. T. M. Lynch, on 15th inst., in the M. E. Church, in Prattville, Ala., Mr. George L. Smith to Miss Addie P. Holt.
Dr. D. R. Dunlap was born 6th Oct., 1776, and died in Charlotte, N. C., Dec. 8th, 1861....
Mrs. Martha Braddock died 6th Dec., 1861, in Nassau co., Fla., in her 82d year....   Isaac Munden.
Lt. Henry E. Moore was born in Ga.,6th Novl 1826, and fell mortally wounded on the battle-field at Valley mountain, Va., on 12th Dec...Lwondes Volunteers, 12th Ga. Regt.... N. B. Ousley
Mrs. Maria Whitaker died in Talladega, Ala., on the 10th inst.,aged 65 years...remembered by her TEnnessee friends as the wife and widow of John Saxon, and by her Alabama and Ga. friends as the wife and widow of Joseph J. Whitaker, formerly of Harris co., Ga....leaves two brothers, Rev. John P. Duncan of the Ga. Conf. and myself.   Daniel Duncan
Mark White Sanford, youngest son of Caswell and Mary Sanford, died in the hospital near Yorktown, Va, Nov. 16th, aged 24 years ....

John D. Hardy, son of John P. Hardy, died in the hospital at Columbus, Ky., 28th Dec., 1861, in his 22d year...Jas. W. Hardy
Sumpter W. Tarrant, son of J. B. And E. W. Tarrant of Greenwood, S. C., died at Warrenton, Va.,on 17th Nov., 1861, aged 20 years....
Alfred Jefferson Hammond was born in Anderson Dist., S. C., April 20th, 1831, and died at Manassas, 17th Dec. 1861....
James Madison McCarty died at Camp Bartow, Pocahontas co., Va., Sept. 24th. 1861...born in Macon Ga...Pvt. in the Davis Rifles....
Miss Laura Victoria Jordan, daughter of Henry and Elizabeth Jordan, died at Marietta, Ga.,22d Dec. 1861, in her 20th year....
Mrs. Margaret L. Sally, died at Poplar Spring, in Orangeburg Dist., S. C., in the 74th year of her age, leaving six sons and two daughters....
Mrs. Elizabeth Ann Pardue, only daughter of the late Thomas R. and REbecca McCrary, was born in Greenville Dist., S. C., Sept. 14th, 1842....   James Stacy
Robert B. Woodall was born 6th Feb. 1824, and died 12th Nov 1861, in Talbatton co., Ga.... Nathaniel Athon
David N. McCorkle was born in Catawba co., N. C., Feb. 19th, 1829...joined the company of his brother, Capt. M. L. McCorkle, 13th Regt., N. C. Voluntters....died Jan 9th, 1862...J. A. Sherrill
Rev. James N. Brown was born 25th May 1814, and died Nov. 17th 1861....
William F. Beall died in Dooly co., Ga., on 10th Nov. 1861, aged 35....

45

Married on 1st January 1862, in Wayne co., Ga., by Rev. T.
B. Barnett, the Rev. James D. Maulden, of the Fla. Conf., to
Miss Mary Z. Robison.

George Willis Mogmaugh died near Holmesville, Appling co.,
Ga., Dec. 26th, 1861, aged 7 years, 2 months and 5 days.

John R. Wooding died in the Naval Hospital at Portsmouth,
Va., Jan. 2d, aged 25 years and 1 day...born in Upson co., Ga.,
but at an adult age settled in Savannah....

Cornelius Hendrix died in Milledgeville, Ga., on 27th Dec.,
1862, in the 53d year of his age, and also Elizabeth, his wife,
on 31st Dec...Bro. H. was born in Anderson Dist., S. C....left
son William...

The Rev. Gregg Fulton was born in Grayson co., Va., Nov. 9,
1802...died 16th Sept 1861....   M. S. Fulton

Martha M., wife of Lt. A. C. Edwards, of the Ga. Volunteers,
and daughter of Wm. C. Riddie, Esq., of Washington, Ga., died
on 29th Dec. 1861, in her 30th year....   James B. Smith, M. D.

Mrs. Lillias Potts, wife of William Potts, and daughter of
Robert and Elizabeth Cooksey, was born in Walton co., Ga., May
4th, 1801, and died in Troup co., Ga., Jan. 3d, 1862....

Mrs. Francis Riley was born in Orangeburg Dist., S. C., in
1835, and died Jan 5th, 1862, aged about 27 years.

Mrs. Amanda Foster, wife of Dr. J. M. Foster, and daughter
of Dr. N. B. Powe,, of Chunnengee, died in Union Springs, Ala.,
on 11th Jan., in the 32nd year of her age...leaves husband and
two children....   Jesse Wood

Mrs. Elizabeth F. Bussey, wife of Nathan D. Bussey, and daughter of Ben.j Tutt of Lincoln co., Ga., was born Feb. 1828, married
Dec. 1842, and died in Rome Ga., Dec. 19th, 1861....J. W. Hinton

Richard Walters, son of Seborn and Sarah Walter, died in
Camp Walker, on 8th Jan. 1862, aged 21 years and 3 months....

William H. Smith, a member of the Brown Light Infantry, Ga.
Volunteers, died in Scriven co., Ga.,Jan. 20th, 1862, in his 19th
year....

Mrs. Caroline Murphy died near Sandersville, Ga., on 1st Jan.,
1862, in her 38th year....

E. M. Smith departed this life on 16th of this month, in
the 72nd year of her age....

Tribute of Respect to Rev. P. H. Skeen by Campbellton circuit,
Ga. Conf....

Issue of February 13, 1862

Married by the Rev. P. H. McCook in columbia co., Fla., Capt.
Jacob T. Goodbread to Mrs. Nancy H. Berry, Jan. 8th, 1862.

By Rev. W. R. Bell on 7th Jan., 1862, Mr. Thomas Thompson to
Mrs. E. C. Pendergrass, daughter of Rev. W. J. Parks both of
Banks co., Also by the same, on the 16th, E. A. Shankle, to Miss
Smith of Jackson co., Ga.

On 23d Jan., by the Rev. John H. Harris, the Hon. Anderson G.
Jones, of Harris co., to Miss Zelenia M. Mahone to Talbot co.,
Ga.

Near Zebulon, Pike co., Ga.,on the 29th of January, 1862, by
Mr. Zachariah Sims, J. J. C., Mr. John B. Slaton to Dadeville,
Ala., to Miss Martha F., daughter of James and Martha Beckham.

By Rev. W. A. Montgomery, Jan. 20th, 1862, Wm. H. Logan and
Miss Addie C. Bullock, all of Jackson co., Fla.

Died Jane Elizabeth and John William, youngest children of
David L. and Jane E. laton (sic), the former Oct. 1st, 1861, the
latter, Dec. 15th, 1861, On Dec. 25th, Mary Henrietta, their eldest
daughter....

Dr. Henry Lockhart was born in Hancock co., Ga., Jan. 31st, 1795, and died in Beallwood, near Columbus, Ga., Jan. 16th, 1862 ....

Andrew J. Sims, Esq., died on the 28th Dec., 1861, in Lowndes co., Ala...born near Dead Fall, Abbeville Dist., S. C., Oct. 16, 1817, and removed to Lowndes co. with his parnets in 1832....

Mrs. Martha J. E. Minton, daughter of Randall and Harriet Morgan, grand daughter of Rev. Wm. Sharp, niece of Thos Asbury and Hobson Morgan of the S. C. Conf., was born March 16, 1836, in Merriwether co., Ga., and died at Pinckneyville, Tallapoosa co., Ala., Jan. 2nd, 1862....   R. A. Timmons

J. Gospero Sweet Smith died Oct. 16, 1861, in his 18th year....

Rev. Joseph Puett died at home in the 68th year of his age....
Fletcher Golightly, son of Richard and Harriet Golightly, of Spartanburg Dist., S. C., died near Manassas, Va., 15th Nov. 1861 ....   T. J. Clyde

Dr. John C. Douglass was born in N. C., on 1st Jan. 1827, and died in Louisville, Ala., Nov. 24th, 1861....

Mrs. Rachel Blackburn, relict of Stephen Blackburn was born in Columbia co., Ga., and died in Scriven co., Nov. 4th, 1861, in her 70th year.   Samuel G. Scoover

George Pierce, the youngest son of J. and C. Johnson was born in Bibb co., Ga., Oct. 26th, 1839, and died at Manassas, Va. Nov. 2d, 1861...His brother, William P. Johnson, brought home his remains....

Mrs. Jane E. Slaton, daughter of Benjamin H. and Mary Brown, of Muscogee co., Ga., and wife of David D. Slaton, died in Dec., leaving a husband and four small children....   J. H. Mealing

Miss Sarah E. McFadden, second daughter of Jno. J. McFadden, died at the residence of her grandmother, Mrs. J. M. McFadden, in Clarendon Dist., S. C., in her 14th year....

Mrs. Mary D. Watson, daughter of Nathan and Hannah Shackelford, was born in Georgetown, S. C., and died in Marianna, Fla., Dec. 2d, 1861, in the 60th year of her age....   S. H. Cooper

Issue of February 20, 1862

Married on the 6th instant, by Rev. W. W. Oslin, Mr. Williamson H. Waiter to Miss Amanda A. Nunnelly, all of GWinnett co., Ga.

By Rev. R. N. Cotter, on 6th Feb., Mr. A. Johnson to Miss N. C. McRimon, all of Montgomery co., Ga.

By Rev. John W. Reynolds, Feb. 2d, Mr. Jesse Mason, of Haralson co., Ga., to Mrs. Nancy M. Carter, of Polk co., Ga.

On 6th instant, by Rev. A. L. Smith, Rev. Manning Brown, of the S. C. Conf., to Miss Rebecca Green, daughter of Rev. H. D. Green, of Sumter, S. C.

On the 4th Feb., in Union co., N. C., by Rev. F. Milton Kennedy, W. W. Greer, Sheriff of Mecklenburg co., to Miss M. M. MOrrison.

Died Lula Paul Harbey, born May 28th, 1859, and died near Waukeena, Fla., Jan. 16, 1862, aged 2 years, 7 months and 18 days.

F. A. Ansley of Fort Valley, Ga., died in Savannah, Ga., on 16th Jan., 1862, aged 28 years, born in Crawford co., Ga....

Joseph Billups Jennings was born May 12th, 1841, in Clark co., and raised in Oxford, Ga., by a widow mother, Mrs. Eliza Jennings ....died 29th Sept 1861

Maria S. Beall, wife of Jeremiah Beall, Esq., and daughter of the late Col. Thomas Moughon of Jones co., Ga., died in Milledgeville, Ga., Nov. 25th, 1861, in the 48th year of her age....

Miss Susan E. Rumph, daughter of Mr. David and Mrs. Mary W. Rumph of Randolph co., Ga., died 6th Jan., 1862, aged 17 years, 1 month and 14 days....   J. D. Wade
     Mrs. Margaret H. Colquitt departed this life in Tallapoosa co., Ala., Dec. 31st, in the 43d year of her age...the youngest daughter of James and Margaret Sewell....   W. D. Matthews
     John Wesley Chipley, son of p. S. and Mary Chipley, was born in Abbeville Dist., S. C., Sept. 30th, 1840...member of Hampton Legion....died Dec. 23, 1861....
     M. S. McGee, Com. H., 17th Regt. Ga. Volunteers, died at 3d Ga. Hospital, Richmond, Va., 10th Dec. 1861...died in the 32d year of his age....   F. O. Dannelly
     Mrs. Elenor Collier died in Orangeburg Dist., S. C., on the 26th Nov., in the 39th year of her age....   William Hutto
     Mrs. Sophronia McLean, wife of John McLean was born Feb. 14th, 1834, and died 13th of Dec. 1861, aged 26....   E. F. Gates
     Mrs. Charlotte T. Davis, widow of the late Daniel H. Davis, of Shelby co., died at the residence of her son in Sabine co., Texas, Feb. 3, 1862. She was born Aug. 27, 1813, in Marion Dist., S. C., and married to Daniel H. Davis Sept. 20th, 1832. They moved to Texas and settled in Shelby co., in Feb. 1853....
     J. Wesley Smith, a private from Anson co., in Capt. Liles' co., died on 31st Dec., 1861, at his father's in Richmond co., N. C. also in the same family, a few days after, the youngest sister Sarah, in her 11th year...   W. L. Pegues
     Robert A. Hargrove, youngest son of Major Charles G. Hargrove, died on 23d December last....
     William Hargrove, died at Yorktown, Va., 14th Sept. last....
     Sister Elizabeth Funderburke died in Orangeburg Dist., S. C., Feb. 10th, 1862, in the 51st year of her age....   J. W. Kelly
     Malcom McCranie, son of wiliam and Melvina McCranie, died near Darien, Ga., on the 2d Feb., in his 19th year....
                                        A. D. Patterson
     John P. Wilson, of Meriwether co., Ga., was born Oct. 10th, 1838, and died Jan. 16th, 1862...left wife and little child....
     William B. Airs died on the Black Swamp Circuit, Jan. 8th, 1862, in the 56th year of his age...leaves wife, two sons, and an aged mother....   John R. Stokes
     Tribute of Respect by Richland Circuit, S. C., to David H. Montgomery....

Issue of February 27, 1862

     Married in Bainbridge Ga., at the residence of B. F. Bruton, Esq., on 31st Dec., by the Rev. J. Law, Mr. Theodore R. Warden to Miss Mary Jane Bruton, daughter of Daniel J. Bruton, decd.
     In Fowlston, Decatur co., Ga., in the Methodist Church on 4th inst., by the Rev. J. Law, the Rev. Wm. F. Easterling, of the Fla. Conf., to Miss Mary E. Kern, daughter of A. V. Kern, decd.
     By Rev. Morgan Bellah, on 13th Feb., 1862, Mr. Henry W. Holmes formerly of Barnesville, but now of Sumter co., Ga., and Miss Lucy O. Ellis, daughter of Judge J. Ellis, of Henry co., Ga.
     On 11th Feb. 1862, by Rev. S. H. Cooper, Gustave G. Henslee to Miss Annie M. Lewis, all of Marianna, Fla.
     By the same, on 16th Feb., 1862, John Roch, to Mrs. Lauranna A. Robinson, all of Marianna, Fla.
     On 2d Jan., 1862, in Whitesville, Fla., by Rev. W. K. Turner, the Rev. J. Rast, of the Fla. Conf., to Miss Virginia L. Blitch
     In Irwinton, Ga., on 12th Feb., by Rev. J. W. Burke, Rev. Jas. T. Alsworth, of the Ga. Conf., to Miss Lucinda C. McRaney, of the former place.
     Died in Barnwell Dist., S. C., on 11th inst., Henry Fletcher,

son of Churchwell O. and M. L. Bunch, aged 2 years, 9 months and
14 days.
Mrs. Sophia W. Huson, widow of the late Mr. E. D. Hudson,
died in Warrenton, on 24th January, 1862, in her 44th year....
James Bethel Howren, son of Rev. R. H. and Martha Howren, of
the Fla. Conf., died in camp, at Fernandina, Fa., Feb. 9, 1862,
precisely 24 years of age....   P. P. Smith
John C. Shareouse was born in Effingham co., Ga., Nov. 10th,
1818 and died in Marion co., Fla., Jan. 10th, 1862....H. F. Smith
Susanna W. C. Syfrett, daughter of Jacob E. B. And Rachel S.
Syfrett, died in Orangeburg Dist., Dec. 17th, 1861, aged 12 years
and 11 months.
Also on Dec. 26th, 1861, their daughter Ellen J. C. Syfrett,
aged 2 years and 8 months.
Also on Jan. 6th, 1852, their daughter Sophia J. B. Syrfrett,
aged 8 years....
Rev. T. P. Kirton died at the residence of his father, in Hor-
ry Dist., S. C., on 6th Dec., 1861, in his 25th year....
                                                       G. H. Wells
Mrs. Gartha Smith, widow of George Smith, died in Morgan co.,
Ga., Nov. 24th, 1861...born in Maryland....
Reuben W. Blalock, Jr.,son of R. W. and M. E. Blalock, a
member of the Holloway Greys, of Upson co., Ga.,died at Hayneville, Tenn., Dec. 24th, 1861, aged 16 years...buried in the
family burying ground....
Algernon N. Jennings, son of Wm. T. and M. C. Jennings, died
in Greenville, S. C., Dec. 29th, 1861, in the 13th year of his
age..-.
Tribute of Respect to Dr. D. R. Dunlap by Charlotte station
....

Issue of March 6, 1862

Married in Talbotton, Ga., Feb. 21st, by Rev. G. H. Pattillo,
Dr. WM. D. Boyd, of Ala., and Miss Fannie C. Cottingham, of the
former place.
Mrs. Ann T. Greenwood, wife of Thomas B. Greenwood, died in
LaGrange, Ga., on 13th inst., aged 62 years....   C. W. Key
A. S. T. Norwood, of the Southern Rights Guards, 1st Ga.
Regt of Volunetters, son of Lorenzo D. and D. H. Norwood, of
Houston co., Ga., died near Harrisonburg, Va., on 16th Dec., 1861,
in his 17th year....
W. S. Wimpy died Jan. 13th, in the Potomac Army, Va., a member
of the "Miller Rifles", Capt. J. R. Towers, Floyd co., Ga....age
22...   J. W. Hinton
Francis Ann Zachry, daughter of Jefferson Turner, deceased,
and wife of Col. Charles Zachry, died in Herny co., Ga., Dec.
4th, 1861, in her 26th year....   A. Gray
Mrs. Eliza M. Ward was born March 28th, 1802, and died
Jan. 28th, 1862, the widow of Rev. Nicholas Ware, who was a pastor
in the S. C. Conf...leaves seven children a son and six daughters
                                                    L. M. Hamer
Mrs. Jane Butler, wife of Larkin Butler, died in Jackson co.,
Ga., 18th January...81 years of age...left an aged husband and
several children....
William E. Copeland, son of Obadiah and Sarah Copeland, was
born August 31, 1850, and died in Camp near Savannah, Jan. 28th,
1862....   William Bryan

Issue of March 13, 1862

Mrs. Susan Elizabeth Cleveland, was born in Lincolnton, N.C.,
May 3d, 1825...died 14th Feb. 1862...   Jas. Stacy

Mrs. Nancy Monford aged about 70 years, died near Greensboro',
Ga., on the 3d(?) of this month....

Jas. H. Reid, son of James L. Reid, of Eatonton, Ga., was born
May 8th, 1840, and died at Staunton Hospital, Va. 29th Dec., last.
a member of Putnam Light Infantry, 12th Ga. Regt....

Mrs. Amelia B. Jordan was born in Charleston, S. C., Dec. 20th,
1808...died in Eufaula, Ala., Feb. 19th, 1862....Jas. L. Cotten

James Arnold Tally was born April 2d, 1833, and died Nov.
18th, 1861, in Macon co., Ala....   WM. B. Neal

Mr. Eli Corey(?) died Jan. 3d, 1862, in his 30th year, in
LaFayette, Ga., Dec. 15th, 1861....   J. W. Brady

Sarah D. Larkin was born Dec. 23d, 1825, and died near Appling,
Ga., Feb. 9th, 1862....   J. M. Austin

Sister Clementine Rone died 30th of Jan 1862.... W. C. Patterson.

Sister S. Ticer, wife of Rev. Hugh Ticer, died in Warren co.,
Ga., Oct. 24th, 1851, aged 77 years and 20 days....

Issue of March 20, 1862

Eugenia M. Syphrett, daughter of Abraham and Mary Syphrett,
died Jan. 23, 1862, in the 6th year of her age.

Lowvicy Freelove Henry Gilkirson, infant daughter of J. L. and
S. E. Gilkirson, died in Laurens Dist., S. C., March 10th, 1862,
aged 2 years, 1 month and 4 days.

Capt. Frank A. Florence, of the "Robert Defenders" died Dec.
8th, 1861, in Thompson, Ga., in the 29th year of his age.

John W. Stewart, a member of the Winter Guards, Company F.,
17th Regt. Ala. Volunteers, died near Pensacola, Fla., Jan. 3d,
1862, aged 19 years....

Florence Alexander, daughter of S. W. and Celia Hill, died in
Horse cove, Macon co., N. C., 19th Feb. 1862....

Thomas H. Smith died at the residence of W. L. Mason in Laurens co., Ga., on 17th Feb. last....   J. Mason

Issue of March 27, 1862

Married on 23d Jan., by Rev. S. J. Hill, Mr. Alexander Wall
to Miss Ellen Ratcliff.

Also by the same, on 13th of Feb., Mr. D. L. Saylor and Miss
E. O. Beeman.

At Magnolia Springs, Sumter co., Ga., on 24th Nov., by the
Rev. Thomas Stewart, Rev. George L. Johnson, of the Ga. Conf.,
to Miss Emma N. Blalock, daughter of Rev. D. Blalock.

At Lancaster C. H., S. C., on 19th Feb., by Rev. Aug. W.
Walker, Rev. A. N. Wells of the S. C. Conf., to Mrs. Ann D. Tippen,
of the above place.

In Laurens co., Ga., on 2d instant, by Wm. Adams, J. I. C.,
Mr. John M. McNeel and Miss T. Augusta Mason, daughter of Mr.
and Mrs. W. L. Mason, all of said county.

On 27th Feb., near Culverton, by the Rev. Thomas T. Christian,
Mr. Newton A. Mason and Miss Fanny Latimar.

Also, by the same, in Sparta, on 10th March, Mr. James B.
Knox and Mrs. Julia A. Skipton.

On the 27th of Feb., by Rev. R. A. Conner, Mr. Oliver G.
Tarver, of Burke co., to Mrs. Marcellia Tinley, of Richmond co.,
Ga.

February 4th, by Rev. W. A. Hemingway, Mr. Pinckney Nesmith,
of Williamsburg, and Miss Maggie, daughter of Hugh Thompson, Esq.
of Georgetown.

On the 20th of Feb. 1862, by J. W. Puett, Marton(?) A. Helms,
of Union co., N. C., to Miss Mary Harden, of Monroe, N. C.

In Green co., Ga., on 25th Feb., by Rev. W. J. Cotter, Mr. Wm. Rowland to Mrs. W. Newton.

Adolphus S. Rutherford died in Montgomery, Ala., on his way home....held the clerkship of the Superior Court of Muscogee county, at the time of his death....   L. Pierce

Mrs. S. A. C. Benett, wife of W. R. Benett, and daughter of Andrew J. Macky, died in Lancaster Dist., S. C., Feb. 16th, 1862, in the 29th year of her age.... C. E. Land

Mr. Rowland Mahone was born Sept. 27th, 1786, and died in Talbot co., Ga., August 29th, 1859. His wife Mrs. Eliza Mahone was born Sept. 18th, 1794,a nd died at the same place, Dec. 1, 1861....

Mrs. Mary Medlin died Jan. 9th, 1862, about 70 years of age ....   L. M. Hamer

Mrs. A. B. Stubbs was born June 17th, 1802, and died March 8th 1862....   James B. Campbell

Mrs. Rachel Anna Dixon,wife of Rev. John Lee Dixon, and daughter of Mr. and Mrs. Samuel Staley, of Orangeburg, died in Columbia, March 18th, 1862, aged nearly 25 years, leaving an infant daughter about nine months old....

. Darley B. Riley, fourth son of George Riley, was born Nov. 18th, 1832, and died 26th Nov. 1861....

D. L. Trussell, of Talbot co., Ga., died on 12th of March, aged 57 years....

Mrs. Amelia B. Glisson, wife of E. C. Glisson, died in Burke co., Ga., Feb. 23d, 1862, aged 58 years and 3 months....
                                                    C. M. Smith

Catharine Ware, daughter of Rev. Nicholas and Eliza M. Ware, died Feb. 7th, 1862, in her 21st year....   L. M. Hamer

Joseph Travis Walker died at Warren Springs' Hospital, Va., on the 23d Jan., after an illness of 26 days....

(No issue April 3, 1862)

Issue of April 10, 1862 (place of publication moved to Augusta,Ga.)

Married in Oglethorpe co., Ga., on the 25th ult., by Rev. J. W. Burke, Asa Holt, Esq., of Macon, Ga., to Miss Nora M. Burke, formerly of Athens, Ga.

On Thursday, 20th March, by Rev. J. T. Kilgo, Rev. J. W. North, of the S. C. Conf., to Miss Cynthia J., second daughter of J. R. and Mary G. Wells, of Cleveland, N. C.

Died in Columbia, S. C., March 5, 1862, Charles Edwin, only son of R. F. and S. E. Miller, aged 1 year, nine months, and 25 days.

At Blackmingo, S. C., James Samuels, son of James F. and Margaret E. Carraway, Nov. 14, 1861, aged 6 years, 1 month and 23 days.

Mrs. J. K. Armstrong, formerly Miss Lucy Jane Bondurant, was born April 5th, 1824, in Buckingham co., Va., and died in Marion Ala., March 8th, 1862...in early life left an orphan....
                                                    A. H. Mitchell

Mrs. Elizabeth Leonard died in Spartanburg dist., S. C., on 4th March, in the 55th year of her age...in early life united with Nazareth Presbyterian Church, until she moved her membership to Antioch Church...left eight children, 6 grandchildren....

Henry M. LeVert died Jan. 22d, 1862, at the residence of his aunt, Mrs. M. B. Skillern, near Pulaski, Tenn...born and reared in Green co., Ala., was 32 years and 6 months old...son of Rev. E. V. LeVert...a citizen of Mississippi....   Wellborn Mooney.

James B. Ogilvie was born in Oglethorpe co., Ga., March 31, 1829, was married to Lucy J. Dunn, April 1, 1854, to Emily T. Moore

51

Feb. 7, 1854, and died in Caddo Parish, La., Dec. 4, 1861....
    Lt. Jas. S. Tindal of the Santee Guerillas died at Camp
Reynolds, S. C., Feb. 23d, 1872, in the 45th year of his age....
                                                M. Puckett
    Mrs. Argent Fralix, widow of the late Hiram Fralix, died in
Colleton Dist., S. C., on the 1st of March, 1862, in the 48th year
of her age....left ten children....
    Mattie R. Johnson, wife of Dr. J. C. Johnson, and daughter
of B. and C. M. Holleman, died at the house of her father, in
Houston co., Ga., Feb. 22nd 1862, aged 16 years and 3 months...
on 25th Nov. 1860 she was married....   Geo. C. Clarke.
    Wm. O. Stanford, son of D. P. and M. H. Stanford, died near
Thomson, Ga., on 9th Feb., in the 19th year of his age....a member of the Thomson Guards, 10th Ga. Regt....
    Mrs. Eliza Ann Elam, wife of Samuel C. Elam, Esq., died at
Americus, Ga., Jan. 11th, 1862, in the 38th year of her age....
born in Mt. Zion, Hancock co., Ga., and was the youngest daughter,
save one, of the late Rev. Micajah Thomas....
    Paul Spigener, died on the 20th Feb., in Orangeburg Dist.,
S. C., in the 17th year of his age....
    Mrs. Evelina B. F. Jones, widow of Thos. B. Jones, dec'd.,
was the daughter of Robt. and Susan B. Wynne, of Franklin co.,
N. C., born Jan. 11th, 1815, died at Kings Ferry, Ga., on 24th
Feb. 1862...married 2d June 1825....   W. H. Thomas
    James C. Lankford of the Dekalb, Murphy Guards, died on 4th
January...son of Curtis C. and Catharine Lankford, of Gwinnett
co., Ga....
    R. A. Vinson, died Nov. 4th, 1861, in Crawford co., Ga., in
the 43d year of his age....
    Tribute of Respect to Daniel L. Turssell, a member of the
Centreville circuit, in Talbot co., Ga., who died March 12, 1862
in the 57th year of his age....

Issue of April 17, 1862

    Rev. James Leroy Carruth died in Fernandina, Jan. 9th, aged
19 years, 6 months and 12 days...his brother Rev. T. A. Carruth
....   J. W. Mills
    Rev. John L. Newby, of the N. C. Conf., was born in Pascotank
(sic) co., N. C., April 6, 1818, and 16th Feb. 1848 married Miss
Octabia Moosly, and died in Fayetteville, N. C., March 11th, 1862
...
    Dr. Turner Hunt Perry, son of Rev. Dow Perry, was born Feb.
19, 1832, in Harris co., Ga., in Dec. 1860, he accompanied his
parents from Alabama to Attala co., Miss....   J. D. Shaw
    Capt. D. T. Patterson, son of Archibald and Mary Patterson,
was born in Elizabethtown, Bladen co., N. C.,Oct. 26th, 1812,
removed to Tallapoosa co., Ala., in 1841, thence to Attala co.
in 1855....   Dow Perry
    Mrs. Frances A. Culver, wife of the Rev. Levin E. Culver,
died near Troyp, Pike co., Fla., on 22d March, 1862, aged 59
years...born in Hancock co., Ga....
    Mrs. Mary H. Beall died in Wilkes co., Ga., on 19th Jan.,
1862, in the 72d year of her age...was left a widow in early
life and the mother of five children....
    Mrs. Lucretia Steedman, wife of Anderson Steedman, died in
Lexington Dist., S. C., 13th March, 1862, in her 49th year....
                                                D. W. Seale
    Sarah Frances Johnson, wife of M. W. Johnson, daughter of
Wm. H. White, of Rome, whose death is noticed below, died March
15th, near Rome Ga...in her 32d year, leaving an aged monther
to mourn the loss of her husband and only child, and leaving

to her care four children....   J. W. Hinton
      Rev. John A. Sermon, son of Nathan and Lucretia Sermon, died
in Comack co., Ala., Feb. 11, 1862, in the 32d year of her age....
                                                H. J. Hunter
      W. Wilkins Brooks died in Columbus, Ga.,on the 29th ult.,
in the 24th year of his age....
      Abel Barge was born in Fayetteville, N. C., and died in Wil-
cox co., Ala., Dec. 28th, 1861, aged 82 years... D. S. McDonald
      Mrs. Elizabeth Cox, formerly of Morgaon co., more recently
of Greene co., but for the last year of Talbot co., Ga., died
April 3d, aged 83 years....   H. P. Pitchford
      Tribute of Respect to Wm. H. White by Methodist Sunday School,
Rome Ga., aged 65 years....

Issue of April 24, 1862

      Married on 1st April by the Rev. H. J. Hunter, Mr. William
Wilkins, of South Butler, to Miss Mart A. McCormick, of the same
place.
      On 23d March, by Rev. W. Williams, Mr. James B. Tally, to
Miss Telitha Baker, all of Macon co., Ala.
      On 5th March, 1862, by Rev. A. J. Cauthen, Mr. J. R. DeLoach
of Barnwell District, and Miss M. E. Cockrell of Fairfield Dist.,
S. C.
      On 16th April by Rev. A. J. Stokes, Dr. Samuel N. Kennerly
to Miss Julia H. Culler, all of Orangeburg District.
      Roxanna Cornelia, eldest daughter of Robert and Hester A.
Stewart died on the 4th March 1862, aged 9 years 6 months and 9
days.
      Benjamin Boon, infant son of Carter C. and Malinda T. Porter
died on the 8th March 1862, aged 16 days.
      On 29th March in Madison, Ga., Dolly Blythe, infant daughter
of Rev. B. W. and C. E. Brigham, aged 6 months.
      At Buena Vista, Greenville District, S. C., on Tuesday, 15th
instant, Thomas Philip, only child of Rev. A. H. and S. J. Lester
of the S. C. Conf, aged 18 months, lacking 2 days.
      Sgt. Wm. Capers Stitt, of the 14th Ala Regt, died at Frederick-
burg, Va., Jan. 10th, 1862, in the 25th year of his age...the only
son of pious parents....   M. C. Turrentine
      Dabney H. Jones son of Rev. Dabney P. and Mary W. Jones, died
March 29th, 1862....one weeks after, the daughter-in-law, Mrs.
Julia Jones....within the last 15 or 16 years they have buried
9 or 10 children, all having lived to mature years....
      Sallie A. Story, wife of S. G. Story, and Allen Craige decd.,
died in Augusta, Ga., on 12th of Feb., 1862, in the 29th year of
her age....
      Mr. Lucius C. Wilks, son of B. M. Wilks, Esq., died on 27th
March in LaGrange, Ga., aged 21 years....
      Dora P. Green, wife of Robert W. Green, was born 19th April
1837, and died in Upson co., Ga., 5th April 1862....
      Mrs. Elizabeth Towns died in Cobb co., Ga., on 22d Jan., in
the 63d year of her age...born and raised in Spartanburg Dist.,
S. C., but for many years lived in Greenville Dist., where she
married Mr. Peter Towns...removed to Madison co., Ga....
                                                Jennie Towns
      Lucy A. Gore, wife of Henry Gore, jun., and daughter of
Josiah B. and Nancy H. Scott, was born Dec. 5th, 1834, and died
March 16th, 1842....   Jas. D. Anthony
      William H. Sheppard was born in Barbour co., Ala., 1836,
and died at Fort Morgan, Feb. 7th, 1862....
      Mary Mary Gorley died in Greene co., Ga., aged 68 years....
Richard E. Burke, long a resident of Athens, Ga., died 4th March

in Oglethorpe co...a native of Ireland, and about 76 years of age. He was raised in the Catholic faith...in 1824 joined the M. E. Church.

Issue of May 1, 1862

Married April 20th, 1862, by Rev. G. C. Andrews, Mr. Wm. R. Durham and Miss Julia M. Crenshaw, eldest daughter of Rev. David Crenshaw, of the Ga. Conf.

In Union co., N. C., by J. W. Puett, on 1st April, Mr. A. J. Price, to Emily J. Hooie.

Also by the same, on 3d of April, Dr. Daniel McC. Smith to Elizabeth J. Cuthbertson.

By Rev. W. A. Montgomery at Greenwood, Fla., April 8th, 1862, Wm. F. Snelling and Miss Carrie M. Watts.

April 8th, by the Rev. R. A. Connor, at the residence of Col. A. C. Walker, Mr. Wm. E. Walker, and Miss Elenora Evans, all of Richmond co., Ga.

Willie Washington, eldest son of James T. and Catharine Kilgo died at Laurens C. H., S. C., April 15th, 1862, aged 4 years, 3 months and 10 days.

Father George Riley died 30th Dec., 1861, in Barnwell Dist., in his 78th year....

John Riley, a son of George and Drusilla Riley, died in his 23d year....

Thomas W. Davis, a member of the Quitman Guards, 1st Regt. Ga. Volunteers, died near Winchester, Va., on 18th Feb....

William J. Smith, eldest son of A. H. and E. L. Smith, was born in Green co., Ga., Nov. 13th, 1834, and died at Cumberland Gap., Tenn., March 26th, 1862...leaves mother, three brothers, and three sisters....

Mrs. Julia A., wife of col. Joseph M. Clarke, died in St. John's, Berkley, on the 6th April in the 28th year of her age ...a few days before, her little Belle, aged 8 months....only child of Arnold and Bolicent Harvey, of St. John's Parish....

Issue of May 9, 1862

Married at Irwinton, Ga., on 1st May, by Rev. J. T. Ainsworth, Lt. Wm. K. Methvin to Miss Julia Chambers.

On 20th April, in Macon co., Ala., by Rev. A. J. Williams, Mr. James Cash to Miss Fannie McDaniel.

Rev. Henry C. Ware was born in Augusta, Ga., April 30th, 1820, and died in Elberton, Ga., April 2d, 1862....   John Henry Grogan

Dr. Robert D. Sinclair, died in Macon, Ga., April 23d, in the 27th year of his age....   W. C. Bass

Capt. John Ray died in Catawba co., N. C., on the 21st April 1862, aged 38 years, 2 months and 17 days...Capt. of a Co. in 1st Bttn. N. C. Vol's....

Ann E. Huff, wife of D. M. F. Huff, died in Orangeburg Dist., S. C., April 11th, 1862, aged 26 years, 11 months and 19 days..-.

Mrs. Nancy Little, wife of Bro. G. S. Little, died in Catawba Co., N. C., April 9th, 1862, aged 58 years, 6 months and 8 days ....

Mrs. Rebecca Lewis, wife of Theophilus Lewis, died near Dalton, Ga., 20th Feb., 1862....   J. Lewis

Issue of May 15, 1862

Married May 6th, by Rev. J. O. A. Clark, Rev. Charles M. Smith, of the Ga. Conf., and Miss Florence M. Harris, daughter of Mr. Benjamin Harris, of Richmond co., Ga.

In Taylor county, on the 6th inst., by Rev. G. W. Persons,
Rev. Dr. J. Griffith to Miss Eva C. Bryant.
    On the 30th April, by Rev. J. J. Seely, Dr. W. M. Hicks, to
Miss Ann Lang, of Suwannee co., E. Fla.
    On 1st April 1862, by Rev. H. J. Hunter, Mr. Wm. W. Mims,
of South Butler, Ala., to Miss Mary A. E. McCormock, of the same
place.
    Mrs. Martha A. Weeks, daughter of Judge Wm. and Mrs. S.
Stallings, and wife of Mr. W. J. Weekes, died inTalbotton, Ga.,
April 13th, 1862, aged 32 years, 1 months and 17 days....
    Mr. A. D. Johnson died on Beech Branch, S. C., 2d April, in
the 29th year of his age....
    Mrs. Mary Moorer, died February 4th, 1862, at the residence
of her son, J. R. Moorer, in St. Matthews Parish, S. C., at about
86 years of age....
    John C. Turner died in DeKalb co., Ga., 3d March , 1862, in
the 87th year of his age...born in N. C., when a young man, he
moved to Warren co., Ga....Eight children are left....
                                                J. T. Turner
    Mrs. Elizabeth D. Pollard died in Wetumpka, Ala., on the 25th
of March 1862, in the 23d year of her age....   John D. Fisher
    Mrs. Margaret Weatherly, wife of T. C. Weatherly, and daughter
of Jeremiah and Elizabeth Waters, was born July 3d, 1820, and
died April 13th, 1862, being a member of the M. E. Church at
Bennettsville, S. C....   T. R. Waller
    Louis Gray of the 34th Regt. N. C. Volunteers, was born May
11th, 1811, and died March 8th, 1862....   W. W. Jones
    Mrs. Deborah Ann Frances Moore was born in Crawford co., Ga.,
Jan. 20th, 1828, married to Mr. John Moore, Dec. 10th, 1846, and
moved to Snow Hill, Wilcox co., Ala...died April 20th, 1862, left
husband and four children....   D. S. McDonald.
    James T. Harris, son of h. H. and Emily Harris, was born in
Harris co., Ga.,June 7th, 1838, and died in Newton co., Ga.,
April 22d, 1862....   Morgan Bellah
    Gen. Samuel R. Pyles died near Newnansville, Fla., on 8th
April aged 47 years....   Geo. Watson
    Corporal John S. Ward of Greene co., Ga. Vols., died at
Goldsboro, N. C., 21st April in the 35th year of his age....
    James Pope Martin, son of the Rev. W. D. and Martha P. Martin,
of Merriwether co., Ga.,was born 2d Jan 1842, and died in Richmond
Va., 23d March 1862...Co. D., 8th Ga. Regt.... Wm. M. Crumley
    Tribute of Respect to Wilds Kolb, by Madison Sta., Ga. Conf.
Tribute of Respect to Dr. Henry Lockhart by St. Paul's charge,
Columbus Dist....
    Tribute of Respect to Wm. G. Varn who died 4th Nov. 1861, in
S. C.....

Issue of May 22, 1862

    Bro. Moses Banks was, the writer believes, a native of Gilmer
co., Ga...co. F. 4th Ga. Bttn....
    The Rev. Paul Johnson was born 22d April 1789, and died in
Brooks co., Ga., 8th March 1862...licensed to exhort in Colleton
Dist., S. C., and removed to Lowndes co., Ga., in July , 1837....
    Mr. Barnabus Melton, son of John W. and Mrs. L. Melton, died
in the Hospital at Goldsboro, N. C., 10th March 1862, in the 27th
year of his age....
    Robt. B. Wright, eldest son of C. C. and Rebecca Wright, of
Newton co., Ga., a member of the 19th Ga. Regt, Co. A., died at
Ashland Station, Va., on 24th April 1862, in the 22d year of his
age....
    Stephen F. Marshall of Talbot co., Ga.,died 5th March 1862,
aged 28 years....

Joseph Durrance was born in N. C., Dec. 23d, 1782, and died
in South Fla., March 29th, 1862, from disease of the heart....
E. H. Giles
Thomas J. Bridges, of Harris co., Ga., died April 16th,
aged 28 years....
Mrs. Sarah Cunningham, widow of the late Albert W. Cunning-
ham, died in Decatur co., Ga., April 20th, 1862, in the 82d year
of her age....
Mrs. Jane E. Bouknight died in Alachua co., Fla., on 5th
April, in the 32d year of her age...maiden name was Mitchell,
a native of Edgefield Dist., S. C....   Jno. C. Ley
Jas. R. Buchannan, youngest son of John R. and C. N. Buchanan,
deceased, died in Richmond, Va., March 17th, in the 24th year of
his age....
James L. Cooper, son of Dr. J. A. Cooper, and last brother of
Rev. L. W. Cooper, late of the Fla. Conf., died in Micanopy, on
the 9th April in the 35th year of his age....   Jno. C. Ley
William H. Forbes, Surgeon of the 27th Ga. Regt, C. S. A.,
died in Skidaway Island, near Savannah, Ga.,March 12th, 1862....

Issue of May 29, 1862

Married on 8th May, by Rev. Sanford Leake, Mr. William D. Ley,
of Fannin co., Ga.,to Miss Naomi A. Hyatt, of Cherokee co.
By Rev. R. H. Howren, Mr. A. J. Groover, to Miss M. J. McKenon
April 24th, all of Brooks co., Ga.
By Rev. W. A. Gamewell, Samuel C. Wolf, R. B. Agent, and Miss
Hester Ann Green, all of Columbia, S. C.
On 20th April, by Rev. J. K. Glover, Mr. William A. Willey, to
Miss Annie Hall, of Leon co., Fla.
On 7th May, at Bainbridge, Ga.,by Rev. F. A. Branch, Dr. Hor-
ace M. Granniss to Miss Fannie A., daughter of Wm. C. Dickinson.
On 22d May 1862, by the Rev. J. L. Stewart, William M. Christ-
ian, to Miss Emily H. S. Branna, Conyers, Ga.
May 20th, by Rev. Charles M. Smith, Rev. Alfred B. Smith, and
Miss Malissa Godbee, all of Burke co, Ga.
Died at Abbeville C. H., S. C., Sallie White, daughter of
Rev. A. G. and Mrs. C. F. Stacy, aged 1 year, 4 months, and 27
days.
Miss Julia S., daughter of Rev. John C. Simmons, was born in
Eatonton, July 12th, 1842, and died in Thomaston, Ga., April 22d,
1862....
Hilliard McKendree Derrick was born in Lexington Dist., S. C.,
Oct. 2d, 1816, and died at his brother-in-laws (J. Alford) in
Montgomery co., Ala., April 4th, 1862....   D. Derrick
Rev. John B. Werlin, died at his father-in-law's, A. A.
Edgars, May 7, 1862, in about the 35th year of his age....
H. J. Hunter
Mr. Mc. F. Mullins, died in the Hospital at Richmond, Va.,
May 3d, in about his 23d year....
M. D. Mullins, brother of the above, and a few years younger,
died a few days before....   A. J. Dean
Henry B. Hix, son of Davis and Mrs. Hix, was born in Randolph
co., N. C., March 16th, 1832, removed to Chattooga co., Ga., with
his parents...Feb. 24th, 1853 married to Mary A. A. Millican...
died in Hospital in Richmond, Va.,on 20th April....
J. D. Anthony
Thomas B. West, son of R. S. and Elizabeth West, died near
Hardeeville, S. C., on 19th March in the 20th year of his age...
joined St. George's Volunteers in July last....
Mrs. Ann Eliza, wife of Dr. J. A. Hays, of Union Springs,
Ala., and daughter of Dr. John H. and Sarah A. Thomas, of Russell

56

co., Ala., died at her father's residence the 27th April 1862....
      Albertus Parks, son of James and Jane R. Parks, a member of
Co. A., 7th Regt., Ga. Vols, fell at Yorktown, April 16th, aged
about 18 years....
      Mrs. Effy McRae, widow of the late Alexander B. McRae, died
8th May 1852, in Telfair co., Ga., in her 68th year....
                                                    M. H. McRae
      Mrs. H. C. Castles died April 30th, 1862, in Fairfield Dist.,
S. C., in her 32d year....
      Dr. Richard B. G. McRee died at the residence of his father-
in-law, Maj. Charles Hargroves, in Oglethorpe co., Ga., 15th
April 1862....
      James J. Barnes died in Leon co., Fla., 20th April 1862, in
the 58th year of his age....   S. R. Weaver
      Sister Eleanor Howad, a native of Hancock, but long a native
(sic!) of Monroe co., Ga.,died 1st May 1862, in the 69th year
of her age....   J. E. Evans
      Mrs. Martha R. L. Roberson, daughter of Rev. J. H. and Martha
G. Wilkins, was born March 7th, 1841, married to James W. Roberson, Oct. 25th, 1859, and died April 27th, 1862, at the residence
of her father in Lowndes co., Ga....
      ˙Mr. George P. Paschal a recruit to 9th Reg.- Ga. Vols, and
died in the Hospital at Richmond, Va.,May 15th, 1862, in his 17th
year....
      Tribute of Respect by Enon circuit, Ala Conf., to Rev. John
W. Norton....

Issue of June 5, 1862

      Married on May 27th, by Rev. W. C. D. Pe-ry, Lt. Wm. T. Sad-
dler of the Sumter Flying Artillery, and Miss T. C. Green of Lee
Co., Ga.
      By Rev. Dr. Sherwood, on 29th May, in Monroe co., Ga., Mr.
J. P. Milner to Miss Eliza L. M. English.
      By the Rev. A. Sidney Link, in York Dist., S. C., Mr. Fergu-
son H. Barber to Miss Mary Elizabeth, daughter of J. J. Watson,
Esq., May 29th, 1862.
      On 28th May, at St. Luke's Church, Columbua, Ga., by Rev. H.
H. Parks, Mr. U. B. Hargold of Americus, Ga., to Miss Mary E.
Fogle, daughter of Dr. J. Fogle.
      Died Eliza Estelle only daughter of J. Dunklin and C. T.
Sullivan, died on 23d May 1862.
      In Forsyth, Ga., May 9th, 1862, Jimmie Glenn, son of Rev. W.
F. and Mrs. L. J. Cook, aged 3 years, 5 months and 12 days.
      On 28th May, little Louis, son of Wm. L. and E. C. Pou....
Mrs. Ann S. Capers, was born in Marion Dist., S. C., June 6,
1792, and died at Ocean Springs, Miss., on 14th March, 1862, the
daughter of Rev. Thomas and Mrs. Elizabeth Humphries, and was
married to my venerable father, Rev. Gabriel Capers, Dec. 24th,
1809....   Sue Capers
      David G. Slappey, a member of the Governor's Guards, 3rd Ga.
Regt., was born August 8th, 1842, and died April 30th, 1862, in
Portsmouth, Va....   T. B. Russell.
      Felder D. Houser,son of Capt. D. and Mrs. Ada L. Houser, of
Orangeburg Dist., S. C., was born 25th July 1840, and died 19th
April 1862....   W. H. Fleming
      Mrs. Martha Myrick, daughter of the late Stith Parham, and
widow of Goodwin Myrick, senior died in Baldwin co., Ga., on 13th
May, aged 71 years, 4 months and 25 days....
      Reuben S. Willingham died in Lincolnton, Ga.,on 10th May, in
his 39th year....
      Asa E. Sherwood, of Macon, Ga.,fell at the recent battle of

McDowell, Western Va., on 8th day of May, aged 20 years, 5 months and 3 days....   J. W. Burke
    Luther T. Easley was born in Walton co., Ga., and died in the hospital at Lynchburg, Va., 14th March 1862, aged 25 years....
    Wm. L. P. Matthews, son of J. F. and Letty Matthews, died in Knoxville, Tenn., April 27th, 1862...born in Lincolnco., Ga., Jan. 29th, 1841....
    Miss Ellen Almira, daughter of Mr. and Mrs. Jacob Utsey, died in St. George's Parish, Colleton Dist., on 23d April, having just entered her 15th year....   Wm. Hutto
    Thomas Wesley Entrickan, son of Thomas and Sarah Entrickan, was born in Coweta co., Ga., Oct. 5th, 1837, and died at Columbus, Ky., 27th April 1862....   David Stripling
    George W. Hines,senior, a native of Georgia, died in Tallahas-see, Fla.,on 1st April, in the 57th year of his age....

Issue of June 12, 1862

    Mrs. Catharine Nelson, died at the residence of Mr. James B. Williams, of Effingham co., Ga., on 22d of May, aged 79 years and 4 months...left at an early age an orphan....
    Mrs. Mary A. Hardee was born in Nassau co., Fla., 8th Jan., 1802, and died May 20, 1862. Her maiden name was Berry. She was married to Thos. E. Hardee, brother to Gen. Hardee of the Confederate Army, in 1818...in 1829(?), he met with a violent death while a citizen of St. Mary's, Ga, leaving a widow and nine children....   B. J. Johnston
    Geo. W. Ray, was born in Columbia co., May 10th, 1802, and died in Warren co., Ga., April 26th, 1802...
    Mrs. Alzina Speir, widow of James Speir, died near Thomaston, Upson co., Ga., on the 21st of March,1862, in the 56th year of her age....
    Mrs. Eugenia E. Murray, wife of Dr. William Murray, died in Orangeburg Dist., S. C.,in the 21st year of her age....
                                                    Wm. Hutto
    Mrs. D. F. Moore, wife of John Moore, Esq., died at Snow Hill, Ala....   T. Moody
    Wm. S. Ravens died in Sumter co., Ga., in the 42d year of his age.....   S. Anthony
    Rev. David Brendel, was born in Lincoln co., N. C., Feb. 1st, 1797, and died in Catawba co., March 22, 1862, in his 66th year
.....   A. R. Bennick
    Mrs. Elizabeth Carson the wife of Bro. Peter Carson, died at Midway, Barnwell Dist., S. C., in the 61st year of her life....
                                                L. Bellinger   -
    Ellis Taylor died at Camp Elliott, Beaufort Dist., S. C., May 18th, 1862, in the 44th year of his age.... left wife and two children....

Issue of June 19, 1862

    Married June 5th, at the residence of the bride's father, Dr. C. Rogers, near Thomaston, Ga., by President James L. Pierce, Mr. Horace T. Shaw, of Madison, to Miss Sallie R. Rogers.
    on May 22d, 1862, by Rev. M. L. Banks, D. A. Gasque, to Mary E. Boineau, both of Colleton Dist., S. C.
    Died Robert T. Pleasant Palmer, son of J. A. and Emily G. Palmer May 10th, 1862, aged 10 years, 11 months and 10 days....
    Mrs. Frances Edgar was a native of Mecklenburg co., N. C., and was born in 1784...her maiden name was Walker. When quite a child, her family removed to Asheville, to Buncombe county.... married Adam Edgar in 1801, when she removed with her husband to

Columbia...died 24th May last....
    Mrs. Sarah Tompkins died 5th May, at the residence of Irby H.
Scott, Esq. in Putnam co., Ga., in the 81st year of her age....
    Benjamin Franklin Backstrom, son of J. G. and L. B. Backstrom
was killed May 31st, in the recent battle near Richmond, Va., in
the 29th year of his age...an elder brother James died in camp....
    Rev. Johnson Frost died in West Point, Ga., May 6th, 1862, in
the 76th year of his age...born in N. C., and emigrated to Ga.
early in life....   E. P. Birch
    Martha Eugenia, eldest daughter of Rev. J. F. Norman, died
in Union District, S. C., May 11th, 1862, aged 14 years, 7 months
and 21 days....   Colin Murchsion
    Thomas Wesley Smith died in the Hospital in Richmond, Va.,
on 23d May 1862, aged 22 years, 4 months and 1 day...son of Rev.
Burgess Smith of Elbert co., widely known....
    Mrs. Rebecca Harn, wife of Mr. William Harn, died near New-
nansville, Fla.,on 28th April 1862, and within three weeks of
the death of her brother, Gen. Sam'l R. Pyles....
    William M. Meriwether son of Esq. and Mrs. W. B. Meriwether,
was one of the first company that left Abbeville Dist. for the
war.... aged 24 years, 4 months and 10 days....
    Mrs. Rebecca Royal born in Burke co., Ga., April 10th, 1777,
and died April 21st, 1862....
    Mr. Joseph W. Howell, eldest son of Joseph M. and S. A. Howell,
died in Lowndes co., Ga., April 29th, in his 20th year....
                                                  N. B. Ousley
    Mrs. Elizabeth Freeman, wife of John Freeman, died in Wilkin-
son co., Ga., 25th May at about 59 years of age....

Issue of June 26, 1862

    Married in Talbot co., Ga., on the 19th inst., by Rev. Charles
J. Jewett, Rev. S. D. Clements, (Lt. C. S. A.), and Miss M. Kate
daughter of Wm. T. Hollmes, of Talbot co.
    On 1st May, 1862, by Rev. J. M. Bridges, Capt. James Denning,
to Miss Julia Dalrymple, all of Marion Co., Fla.
    Mrs. Nancy Neil was born in Newberry Dist., 4th August, 1801
and died in Laurens Dist., 22nd March 1862, in the 61st year of
her age...born and raised in a Presbyterian family....
    Thomas P. Mullinix, a son of the late Rev. Wm. G. Mullinix,
and a member of Capt. E. Smith's company of Ga. Volunteers, from
Forsyth county, Ga., was born in Pickens Dist., S. C., Feb. 8th,
1838, and was killed in the battle of Roanoke Island....
    Wiley M. White died at Ocala Fla., May 15th, 1862, in his 54th
year...a Georgian, but a citizen of Fla. for some years...
on the same day his little grand-daughter Leonora Augusta Rivers,
died aged 3 months and 23 days.
    On the 25th of the same month, at the same place, Joseph P.
White, son of Bro. White died....   H. F. Smith
    Mrs. Jane F. E. Stivender, daughter of Absalom and Mary
Whitestone, died 29th May 1862, in Orangeburg Dist, in the 29th
year of her age...her children (two in number) preceded her....
                                               A. J. Stokes
    Mrs. Missouri T. Heath, wife of R. A. Heath, died on Comsump-
tion in Washington, Ga., June 12th, 1862...born June 6th, 1829
and was the daughter of John M. Madison(?) of Hancock co., Ga.
....   R. W. Hubert
    James E. Thomas died May 23d, 1862, at Camp Winder near Rich-
mond, Va....   W. E. Cameron, Chaplain 26th Regt. Ala Vols.
    Fannie C. Williams, youngest daughter of C. W. and E. S.
Williams, died May 21st, 1852, aged about 7 years and 9 months....
    Mrs. Kizzina B. Feaster, daughter of John B. Pickett of Fair-
field Dist., S. C., and wife of John M. Feaster, died near

Micanopy, Alachua co., Fla., 29th April, aged about 54 years....
    Mrs. Margaret C. Gifford was born March 16th, 1828, in
Jasper co., Ga., and died in Garard, Ala., May 29th, 1862...
leaves 7 children and a husband....
    Thomas H. Harden was born in Chester Dist., S. C., August
5th, 1838, and died at Beiglers Mills Hospital, Va., April 14th,
1862...Hammock Guards, Marion co., Fla. 1st Fla. Regt, Col. Ward
....   H. F. Smith
    John Davidson died in Harris co., Ga.,on 29th May, 1862, in
the 71st year of his age....left a large family of children and
a wife....

Issue of July 3, 1862

    James Marshall Smith, eldest son of Samuel and Jane H. Smith,
of Anson co., N. C., was born April 9th, 1830, and died at his
father's residence on 26th May 1862....   B. G. Jones
    Dr. J. T. Gaddy, late of Milledgeville, Ga. and formerly of
Marion Dist., S. C., died on the 26th ult., in the 31st year of
his age....
    Giles H. Griswold was born in Jones cl., Ga., Jan. 14th, 1821,
and died in Columbus, May 19th, 1862....
    William W. Russell was born in Gwinnett co., Ga., June 19th,
1831, and died in Cumberland Gap., Tenn, June 11th, 1862...married
to Miss Mary Ann Vaughn, in 1852, who died in 1856, and married
again to my eldest sister in Nov. 1858....   Wesley P. Pledger
    Robert M. McKinley was born in Abbeville Dist.', S. C., August
25th, 1790, and died in Clarke co., Ala., May 25ht, 1862....
                                                James W. Shores
    Joel T. Geiger, son of Wm. Geiger, was born Sept. 16, 1839,
in Lexington Dist., S. C., and died at Bartow's Mills, Va., April
17th, 1862....
    Mrs. Mary C. Weber was born May 1st, 1824, and died May 17th,
1862....   W. A. Hodges
    Sgt. T. J. Ormsby, son of Eben and Clara T. Ormsby, was born
at Fortville, Jones co., Ga., May 28th, 1828, married Miss Hannah
Hale in Prattville, Jan. 5th, 1854, and died in the Hospital at
Corinth, May 9th, 1862....
    James E. Williams, son of Rev. P. A. Williams, of the S. C.
Conf., died on 18th May...died in camp at Brahamville, S. C....
    William P. Conner was born Dec. 20th, 1839, and died May 21,
1862, in one of the Hospitals in Richmond, Va.... J. M. Austin

Issue of July 10, 1862

    Married June 17th, 1862, by Rev. John Inabinet, Mr. Daniel F.
Spigener, of St. Matthews, to Miss Glamvenia E. Rast, of Lexington
District.
    Died on the 19th June, Henry Shuford Clarke, in the 5th year
of his age, at Lexington C. H., eldest son of Rev. William A.
Clarke of the S. C. Conf....
    Mrs. Catharine Maner, relict of the late Maj. John S. Maner,
died in Black Swamp, S. C., May 27th, at the residence of her son-
in-law, Maj. W. J. Lawton, in the 68th year of her age....
    James William Wimbish was born in Elbert co., Ga., Jan. 29th,
1840, and was killed in the battle near Richmond, May 21st, 1862
....   James W. Shores
    Edmond Pain Rylander, son of Rev. Wm. J. and Harriet Rylander,
was born 3d Nov. 1862, in Columbus, Ga., and died near Helicon,
Ala., May 26th, 1862....   A. J. Coleman
    Joseph Travis Speed, son of W. O. and Margaret Speed- was
born May 21st, 1809, and died in the hospital, at Mobile, Ala.,
June 2d, 1862...member of Jones co., Coleman's Regt....

60

Bro. Durrela R. Hunt died in Wakulla co., Fla., on 18th June, 1862, aged about 45...born in Monroe co., Ga., moved to Lee co., Ga., about 1840....

Mrs. Sarah Asbury Holleyman, late of Augusta, Ga., died in Spartanburg, S. C., June 13th, 1862...daughter of Rev. George Clark of the S. C. Conf....born Feb. 22, 1804....   James Stacy

Mrs. Elizabeth Thurman, wife of William Thurman, senr., was born in N. C., in 1790, and died near Atlanta, Ga., March 28, 1862, in the 73d year of her age....   Geo. G. N. MacD.

Tinsley T. Crymes, son of Rev. W. M. Crymes, died in the hospital at Charlottesville, Va., 18th April last, aged 29 years and 6 months....

Mrs. Blancky Morison was born 17th Feb. 1800, in Morgan co., Ga., and died in Berrien co., Ga., 15th, May 1862....Aaron W. Harris.

Robert Kendall, eldest son of Thomas W. and Eliza P. Kendall of Anson co., N. C., died 24th May last, aged 13 years, 6 months and 8 days....   H. G. Jones

John C. Young, son of Rev. I. F. Young, of Habersham co., Ga., died on 22d June, at Hardeeville, S. C., aged 28 years.... member of Habersham Volunteers, co. C., Phillips' Legion....

Dr. John F. Trippe, of the Lowndes Vols., 12th Ga., Regt., died in Staunton, Va., 6th June, from a wound received in the battle at McDowell, on 8th May....

Jonathan Hager died in Carroll co., Ga., May 30th, 1862, in his 52d year...a member of the Presbyterian Church, joined M. E. Church in 1854...left wife, four daughters a son....James Baskin

Miss Emily Mears, died May 28th, 1862, at her father's residence in Colleton Dist., S. C., in the 32d year of her age...

Alexander G. Bullock died in Monroe, Ga., June 16th, 1862, in the 25th year of his age....

Issue of July 17, 1862

Married at Indiantown, Williamsburg Dist., S. C., on Thursday 19th June, by Rev. J. W. Murray, Rev. Thomas Mitchell of S. C. Conf., and Miss Rett Williams, daughter of Dr. Charles Williams, of Georgetown, S. C.

On 17th June, by Rev. John Inabinet, Miss Glovenia Rast to Mr. Daniel Spigner, at the residence of Rev. L. W. Rast, of Lexington Dist., S. C.

Capt. Richard T. Davis of the Putnam Light Infantry, 12th Ga. Regt, died 21st May 1862, in the battle of McDowell, aged 37 years....

Thomas James Parsons, of Lynchburg, S. C., a member of col. Jenkins' Regt., Palmetto Sharp Shooters, died in the S. C. Hospital, Richmond, Va., Jun 1st, 1862...left widow and children....

James Plunket died near Wadesboro', N. C., May 8th, 1862 ....tribute of Respect....

Charles W. Bridges, son of Rev J. W. Bridges, and Bethany Bridges, was born in Floyd co., Ga.,July 30th, 1845, and died at Corinth, Miss., May 2nd....   E. L. King

Mrs. Caroline L. Rast, wife of Frederick M. Rast and daughter of Rev. John Larr, aged 28 years, 6 months and 8 days, died in Lexington Dist., S. C., May 22nd 1862....   John Inabinet

Mrs. F. A. Blalock, my precious wife, daughter of Rev. G. C. S. and Mrs. M. H. Johnson, now of Thomasville, Ga., died in Atlanta., Ga., 26th May 1862, 3½ days after the birth and 2 days after the death of her first born child..born in Leon co., Fla., on 25 Oct. 1833....   D. Blalock

Mrs. Sarah H. Haynes, wife of Wm. A. Haynes, and eldest daughter of James and Elizabeth Gouedy(?), was born Jan. 11, 1840, and

died in Atlanta, Ga., June 8th, 1862....   Geo. G. N. MacD.
     Robert R. E. Roberts, son of Rev. D. Roberts of the Fla.
Conf., and N. H. Roberts, deceased, died in the hospital in
Tallahassee, Fla., June 18th, 1862, aged 19 years....
                                             Chas. P. Murdock
     Mrs. Catharine Jones, wife of Lt. John E. Jones died in Tus-
kegee, Ala., 6th June 1862, in the 23d year of her age....
     Miss Amanda Littlejohn, daughter of John and Catharine Little-
john, died in Polk co., N. C., June 2, 1862, in her 22d year....
     Miss Elenor Motteray, daughter of J. M. and Esther Cox, died
in Burke co., Ga., 6th June 1862, in her 18th year....
     Mr. James White, late of Charleston, died in his 68th year,
2nd June, at Lynchburg, S. C., where he and his family were refugees from the city....   H. A. C. Walker
     Jas. Henry Sewell died in Merriwether co., Ga., June 22, 1862,
aged 24 years....   J. J. Morgan
     Tribute of Respect to David L. White, a member of Gadsden
Quarterly Conference....

Issue of July 24, 1862

     Married on the 19th June, Mr. Henry Ceans and Miss Mary
Daganhart, both of Tampa, Fla.
     Died at Athens, Ga., July 18th, 1862, John Mann, youngest
child of Rev. J. O. A. Clark and Amanda A. Clark, aged 8 months
and 7 days.
     Mrs. Lucy Aurelia Evans, wife of Capt. John W. Evan,s of
Bainbridge, Ga., died at the residence of her father, Maj. Wm. A.
Beck, in Murray co., Ga., June 5th, 1862, aged 33 years lacking
4 days.
     Miss Mary A. Brame, daughter of Mr. Henry Brame, of Marengo
co., Ala., died at the residence of her brother, William Brame,
Jasper co., Miss., on 18th June 1862, in the 19th year of his age
....
     William Capers Round, my second son,of the 1st Regt. of
Rifles, S. C. V., was killed in the late battle near Richmond, on
27th June, aged 20 years....   G. H. Round
     Mrs. Mary Amelia Mustin, wife of Mr.Charles E. Mustin, late
of Augusta, now of Madison, Ga., died in the latter place on 14th
June 1862...daughter of Burrel Lathrope....   W. M. Crumley
     George Barton Stone, son of Barron W. Stone, Esq., of Mont-
geromy, Ala., died in Richmond, Va., 9th June; on Sat. 31st May
received wounds at the battle near Richmond...barely 25 years of
age....
     Mrs. Elizabeth Rhodus, died in Abbeville Dist., S. C., April
29th, 1862, at the residence of her son, W. S. Headwright, in her
80th year...a native of Charleston, S. C., and for 50 years a
member of the Presbyterian Church in that city....
     John J. Murphy, of Company E., 1st Regt., S. C. V. Cavalry,
and son of Mrs. Mary Syfrett of Orangeburg Dist., S. C., died at
Adams Run Hospital, Colleton Dist., S. C., on Friday, the 27th
June in his 23d year....
     George Robert Perrin Cosper, son of the late Rev. George H.
Cosper, died at Camp Selma, Ala., June 23, 1862, in his 30th
year....   N. Trimble
     Robert T. Collier, of Pike co., Ga., died on 29th June, at
Battery Harrison, near Savannah, in the 24th year of his age....
                                             J. M. Greene
     Mrs. Matilda, wife of Rev. A. J. Green, died in Colleton,
S. C., June 22d, 1862, in the 41st year of her age...
                                             H. A. C. Walker
     William P. M. Strickland, son of Rev. John Strickland of the
Ga. Conf., died at Knoxville, Tenn., June 3d, 1862, aged about

23 years.:..   T. S. L. Harwell

James Edward Davis, son of Mrs. Orpha Floyd, born in Charleston Dist., S. C., July 5th, 1840, one of the Appling Grays, Co. I., 27th Regt., Ga. Volunteers, died on or about the 15th of April, 1862, at the hospital, Gordonville, Va....

Daniel Green, a member of the M. E. Church, South, died on 26th June, in Rabun co., Ga., born in Pickens Dist., S. C., on 21st April 1808....

Mr. Jared H. Wood, died at Augusta, Ga., on the 7th inst., in the 23d year of his age....   Geo. F. Pierce

Rev. George W. Stokes was born in Colleton, April 16th, 1831, and died in Barnwell, June 22d, 1862.... H. A. C. Walker

Mrs. Martha Ann Barker died in Brooks co., Ga., May 16, 1862, aged 68 years...born and reared in Robertson (sic) co., N. C., moved to Ga. about 40 years ago....   J. J Giles

Marshall Leard Legrand, son of Mrs. F. G. Legrand, of Camden, S. C., died in Virginia, June 7th, 1862, in his 17th year....

Mrs. Martha A. C. Short, wife of John R. Short and daughter of John and Elizabeth Rush, was born 25th April 1838, and her husband being in the army, died at her father's residence, 29th June 1862....   George Watts

Lt. Wesley B. Mills, of the 15th Ala. Regt. (Col. Canty) was killed June 28th, in Virginia, in the 29th year of his age....

Meredith Driggers, a resident of Union Springs, Ala., died at Petersburg, Va., in the 37th year of his age....died 27th June 1862...left a wife....

John T. Carpenter, son of Jas. L. and Jane S. Carpenter, died in Baldwin co., Ga., 11th July, in the 20th year of his age....

W. H. A. Richbourg, second son of J. A. and E. H. Richbourg, of Sumter Dist., S. C.,was born March 23rd, 1828...died 16th ult. at his father's residence...left a wife, three helpless orphans, an aged father and mother, and give brothers....J. A. Richbourg.

W___ Eidson, died near Green Wood, Montgomery co., Ala., June 2d, 1862, born in Edgefield Dist., S. C., and was about 53 years old....left wife and seven children....   C. S. Hurt

David Gilbert, son of Henry W. and Mary A. Long, was born in Fairfield Dist., S. C.,Sept. 23d, 1852, and died in Marion co., Fla., July 6, 1862....

Bro. Thos. Downing, died in Pike co., Ala., May 31st, 1862, born in N. C....

Mr. C. W. Danner, son of Rev. A. R. and M. A. T. Danner, died 13th July 1862, aged 23 years....

Tribute of Respect to W. W. East by Yorkville Station, S. C. Conf....

Tribute of Respect to Col. Robert A. Smith by Macon Station, Ga. Conf....

Issue of July 31, 1862

Married July 9th, by Rev. M. L. Banks, Capt. Wm. K. Lane, C. S. A., to Miss Mary J. Kittles, only daughter of R. N. Kittles, of Prince Williams Parish, S. C.

By Rev. John Calvin Johnson, on 2d July 1862, Dr. John L. Callahan to Miss Ann Osburn, all of Clarke Co., Ga.

By Rev. John Calvin Johnson, on 17th June 1862, Dr. Thos. D. Hutchinson, to Miss Mary Jane M'Ree, both of Oglethorpe co., Ga.

Died John Warnock Hodnett, son of Dr. Wm. H. Hodnett, Asst. Surgeon, 12th Ga. Regt., and Mrs. Martha Hodnett, born March 19, 1858, died June 19th, 1862, aged 4 years and 3 months.

John W. Samuels died last of May 1862, near Knoxville, Tenn., in his 24th year....   R. W. Dixon

Jas. D. Samuels, brother to the above, died on 7th June, in Lincoln co., Ga., in his 26th year...

Mrs. S. C. Appleby, wife of Capt. W. P. Appleby and daughter
of Mr. Jesse and Mrs. Salena Dubrier, died on the 4th inst., at
the residence of Rev. D. C. Appleby, in St. George's Parish, in
her 24th year....

Mrs. Nancy Redwine, wife of Jacob Redwine and daughter of
John and Charlotte Tremble, was born in Franklin co., Ga., in
1791, married to Bro. R. on 24th Feb. 1815, removed to Fulton
co., where she died 10th June 1862....   D. Blalock

Thomas N. Clarke, aged 18, fell inbattle on 27th June, near
Richmond, son of Rev. Geo. Clarke, of the Ga. Conf....
                                                 T. B. Russell

James T. Penny died June 5th, 1842, in one of the hospitals
in Richmond...Orr's Regt, S. C. V...two brothers were with him
when he died....

Rev. Andrew Hood died in Buena Vista, Ga., June 28th, 1862,
aged 74 years...began in Primitive Baptist Church....W. H. Merritt

Mr. C. A. Hinson, eldest son of James Hinson, of Coffee co.,
Ga., a member of the 20th Ga. Regt, Co. H., died at Richmond,
6th May, in his 20th year....   R. W. Flournoy

Rev. Joseph B. Key, son of Henry H. and Anna Key, was born in
Harris co., Ga., and died in Stewart co., Ga.,May 27h, 1862....
                                                 S. Key

John Augustin Adams, a member of the Lawrenceville Blues, Capt.
Mattox, fell before Richmond, on Tuesday, July 1st, in his 22d
year....

Lt. John W. Reaves, of the Johnson Guards, 14th Regt, Ga.
Volunteers, fell in the battle field at Ellyson's Mills, below
Richmond, Va., on 26th ult., in the 39th year of his age, buried
at Watkinsville, Clark co., Ga.,on 12th July 1862....

Wiley H. DuBose, aged 28 years, a member of the Irwin Artillery, from Wilkes co., was killed before Richmond....T. F. Pierce

Rev. Philip H. Pickett, died in Chester Dist, S. C., on the
12th inst., in the 51st year of his age...in the S. C. Conf for
2 years, and travelled the Darlington and Black River circuits....
our sister, Mrs. S. A. Simmons, wife of Rev. Wm. Simmons, who is
a chaplain in the Conf. Army, She lived in Bayou Sarat, which is
in the hands of Yankees as I understand....

James P. Holloway was born March 6, 1842, died at Richmond,
Va., July 6th, 1862....

Wm. T. R. Abernethy was born March 6, 1839, killed in the
battle near Seven Pines, Va., on 30th June, 1862....J. Watts

Zaccheus Downing Golightly, of the Palmetto Sharpshooters, son
of Richard and Harriet Golightly, was born Dec. 17, 1841, and fell
at Yorktown, May 6th, 1862....

John T. McGlon, son of David and Sarah McGlon, was born in
Chattahoochee, co., Ga., June 12th, 1842, and died in Richmond,
July 7th, 1862....   R. F. Williamson

Jerome T. Stanford, eldest son of David and Martha H. Stanford, was born Jan. 28th, 1835, and died in Columbia co., Ga.,
June 27th, 1862...teaching for last 5 years in Smith co., Texas....

John Tompkins (a member of Co. K, 14th Regt. S. C. V. of
Edgefield Dist.,S. C.), was wounded at the battle of Gains' Farm
on 27th June 1862....

Benjamin Drake Robertson, Sr. son of Rev. John Robertson, fell
wounded in the battle of Richmond, Va., and died in his 25th year
....

William Melton, son of John W. and Mrs. L. Melton, died in
the Hospital, at Raleigh, N. C., May 30th, about 20 years of age
....

James C. P. Martin, a son of Mrs. M. A. and James Martin, of
Williamsburg Dist., S. C.,died at Canton, Miss., on 27th May
1862, in his 27th year...Co. E., 10th Regt., S. C. V.....

Mrs. Ellen Frances Jones, wife of Mr. Sam'l A. Jones, died
on the Newberry co., S. C., 24th May 1862, in the 35th year of
her age....
James J. Washington was born in Culloden, Ga., and died in
Coweta, Ga., 7th July 1862, in the 27th year of his age....
                                                    J. T. Wright
James Moore, a member of the Confederate Volunteers, of Mon-
roe co., Ga., was killed near Richmond, Va.,27th June 1862....
James W. Green died in Houston, Fla., May 26th, born in Jones
co., Ga....
In Memoriam. Lt. Thomas S. Jones and William Moore, at
Fort Valley, Ga....
Bro. William Moore, was a private in the Henderson Rangers,
45th Ga. Regt...about 32 years of age....
Tribute of Respect to Robert A. Smith, by Mulberry St. Sunday
School....

Issue of August 7, 1862

Married in Colleton Dist., S. C., on Tuesday evening, July
22nd, 1862, by the Rev. J. W. Miller, Mr. William Riley, of
Charleston, to Miss Mary Ann Wiggins, of the former place.
By D. R. McWilliams, July 17th, 1862, in Effingham co., Ga.,
Mr. Sherrod N. Zetthour to Miss Irena N. Nease.
Died Jesse Benjamin Duffey, in Augusta, Ga.,July 27th, 1862,
aged 14 months and 9 days.
Waterman Glover Bass, son of the late Rev. Henry and Amelia
M. Bass, was born Nov. 7th, 1828, and killed at Malvern's Hill,
near Richmond, Va., July 1st, 1862....(long eulogy and account).
Lt. N. F. Reinhart, son of L. W. and Jane Reinhart of Chero-
kee co., Ga., was born Jan. 1, 1833, wounded in the head 21st
May, before Richmond....
Sgt. George L. Reinhart, brother to the above, was born Apr.
19th, 1844, died at his father's house, on 16th June....P. H.
Brewster.
Lt. James M. Chambers, second son of Col. James M. Chambers,
of Columbus, Ga., died at Columbus, Miss., on 22d June 1862, aged
27 years....
Capt. D. B. Henry was killed in the battle near Richmond, Va.,
June 26th....
Mrs. Priscilla Chavous, wife of John Chavous, died in Richmond
co., Ga., May 20th, 1862, in the 58th year of her age....
Bro. John W. W. Snead, son of the Rev. Tilman Snead, was killed
in battle, 25th June....
Leonard J. Nease died at Camp near Savanah, June 10th, 1862,
only son of Frederick J. and Rosannah A. Nease, aged 18 years....
Benjamin T. Rogers, son of Henry Rogers, of Putnam co., Ga.,
died near Griffin, Ga.,about the 1st of May last....
Rufus W. Rogers, son of the same, died in Richmond, Va., on
22d June in his 23d year....
Alex. G. Rogers, son of the same, died at Warrenton, Va.,
Dec. 10th, 1861, in his 25th year....
Sgt. Beaufort Simpson Buzhardt, son of David H. and Mary M.
Buzhardt, was born in Newberry Dist., S. C.,26th Dec. 1838...fell
29th June....
Sgt. Wm. A. Fair, son of Peter Fair, Esq.,of Milledgeville,
Ga., died 30th June near Richmond, Va., in the 22d year of his
age....
Andrew Monroe Pickens, son of Robt. and Nancy Pickens, of
Anderson Dist., S. C., died in one of the hospitals in Richmond,
May 17th, 1862, in the 23d year of his age....   V. A. Sharpe
Mary R. Pinner (whose maiden name was Lawrence) relict of
Joseph Pinner, was born in Northampton co., N. C., in Sept. 1784,

and died in Jackson co., Fla., July 22d, 1862....W. A. Montgomery

Thomas J. Gibson, son of Silvanus Gibson, was born in Upson co., Ga., Feb. 9th, 1839, died in hospital at Lauderdale Springs, Ala., June 23d....

Wm.J. Hunt, eldest son of Goodwin and Elizabeth Hunt, of Spalding co., Ga., a private in Co. J., 13th Ga. Regt, fell in battle near Richmond....   F. B. Dismukes

William Brewer, died on 12th July 1862, in the Hospital at Augusta, Geo., in his 18th year...born in Chesterfield Dist., S. C....

Joseph W. Davidson, son of Drury Davidson, of Stewart co., Ga., died of wounds from the recent battle nearRichmond, in his 19th year....

J. T. S. Johnson of the Rome Light Guards, 8th Ga. Regt., fell in the 3d days' battle near Richmond, June 28th....

William Gregg Hard, died in Graniteville, S. C., on the morning of the 11th inst., having nearly attained his 7th year, 5th and twin son of B. C. Hard, of Graniteville....

James W. Garrison, son of S. and R. Garrison died 22nd July 1862, in his 30th year....   Samuel Garrison

Tribute of Respect to Lt. Hope H. Roberts, who feel on 26th June....

Tribute of Respect by M. E. S. School, Griffin, Ga., to Anna Maxwell....

Issue of August 14, 1862

Capt. Robert L. Mays of the Tuskegee Light Infantry, was killed at the head of his company June 1st, in the battle of Seven Pines...born in Dallas co., Ala., May 16, 1862(sic). M. S. Andrews.

Watson Clarke, son of Rev. and Mrs. M. Puckett, died at Summerville, S. C., June 11th, 1862, in his 13th year.

Mrs. M. A. Green, wife of R. P. Green died in Scriven co., Ga., on 11th July 1862, in her 29th year. T. B. L.

Mrs. Harriet Turrentine died July 26, 1862, in the 65th year of her age...born and raised in Columbia co.

Mrs. Olivia C. M. Inabnit, wife of Rev. John Inabnit and daughter of Lewis and Dallas Zeigler, died 25 July, in her 39th year. J. W. Kelly.

Mrs. Caroline R. Rowe, youngest daughter of John and Margaret Staley, of Orangeburg Dist., S. C., born 16 March 1817, died in Issequena co., Miss., 26 June 1862. W. J. Rowe.

John Spearman, of the 44th Ga. Regt., born 31 Aug 1823, died at Central Railroad Depot Hospital, Richmond, 9 July 1862.

William H. Southall was born in Wilcox co., Ala., Sept. 15, 1835, died in Richmond, Va.,May 31, 1852...left without a father in early infancy. His mother married James Kirk senr....

Edward M. Ward died at the 1st Ga. Hospital, Richmond, J. W. Talley.

Mrs. Sarah Ford, wife of Joseph Ford, sen., died in Floyd co., Ga. 21 July in her 56th year.

Rev. Ezekiel Ellis was born in S. C. and died in Clark co., Ala., June 17, 1862, aged about 72 years...married three times, father of 18 children.

Samuel T. D. Martin, son of Pleasant L. and Mary Martin, was born 25 Dec 1849 in Perry co., Ala., died in Clarke co., Ala., July 10, 1862.

Miss Frances Goodwin, youngest daughter of the late Joseph and Mrs. Eleanor Goodwin died near Lawrenceville, Ga.,July 21, aged about 20 years. R. M. P.

Cyrus A. Barkly died in Anson co., N. C., on 7 July aged 27 years...soldied in the 43d N. C. Regt. J. D. CArpenter.

66

John R.Barkley died in Anson co., N. C. 9 July 1862, aged
nearly 19 years. J. D. Carpenter.
Lt. Samuel G. B. Odom of the Bibb Greys was killed on 27th
June, in his 32d year....
David R. Odom of the Beauregard Volunteers, killed on the
27th June, in his 22nd year. Isaiah L. Avant.
Henry Nimrod Hurt, of the carter guards, son of Joel Hurt, decd.
of Hurtville, Russell co.,Ala., died at Tupelo Miss, July 15, in
his 23d year.
Dr. R. H. J. Hunt of the 14th Ala. Regt. fell near Richmond,
on 27th June, in his 30th year... L. C. W.
William L. Evans, son of John and Susan Evans, was born in Ware
co., Miss.,June 28, 1835, died in the Marine Hospital, Mobile, Ala.,
June 16, 1862...
Serg't. Claiborne C. McKinney born March 7, 1830, died July 20
1862...my brother.... J. B. C. McKinney.
Capt. Perry C. Carr, co A, 27th Ga., Regt., died in Richmond,
Va., June 13, in his 48th year... A.J. Dean.
John M. Smith was born Oct. 2, 1828, died July 19, 1862.
Nathaniel J. Smith was born Jan. 24, 1830, died July 12, 1862...
brothers. J.H.C. McKinney.
Robert C. Newell born in Abbeville Dist., S. C.,Sept. 5, 1823,
died in Lauderdale Springs, Miss., June 25, 1862.
Joshua A. Baggett born Aug. 6, 1823, in Walton co., Ga., died
at Lauderdale Springs, Miss., July 6, 1862.
Lt. Edwin S. Gwinnett of Capt. Haney's cavalry company, Floyd
co., Ga.,died June 28, in his 25th year....
John T. Nash, second son of J. and S. Nash, of DeKalb co., Ga.,
died inthe Hospital at Charlottesville, Va., May 7, 1862, in his
24th year.
Mrs. Sarah C. Patterson, wife of Archibald Patterson, and
daughter of Clairborn and Sarah Buckner, was born in Baldwin co.,
Ga., Oct. 20, 1839, and died at her father's residence, near
Tallassee, Ala., June 29, 1862...her husband in the Conf. army.
Mr. J. F. Passmore, died in the Hospital Petersburg, Va.,
June 26, in his 28th year...born in Jones co., Ga., moved to
Harris co., Ga.
Bro. Asa DuBose, formerly of Barbour co., Ala., died in Early
co., Ga., 27 July 1862, aged about 70.
Winfred Moore born 1811, died in Marengo co., Ala...

Issue of August 21, 1862

Married on 19th inst. by Rev. J. P. Duncan, at the residence
of Col. J. D. Lester, Dooly co., Judge J. T. B. Turner of Florence
Stewart co., to Mrs. Sarah S. Wright, of Hancock co.
In Berrien co., Ga., Aug. 10, by the Rev. John H. Wilkins,
Capt. Jonathan D. Knight, of the Berrien Minute Guards, to Miss
Emily E. Brandon.
Died in Talladega co., Ala., John W. Depuree, son of Rev. J.
N. and M. E. Dupree, aged 4 years, 2 months and 4 days.
11th July, William Kelly Boland, aged 1 year 6 months and 4
days, only child of Rev. Jeremiah M. Boland of the ALA. Conf.,
and Sarah E. Boland.
Lt. Virgil P. Shewmake, only son of Judge Joseph A. and Mrs.
Caroline Shewmake, of Alexander, Burke co., Ga., died in Richmond,
Va., July 20, 1862... R. B. Lester.
B. F. Leitner, 2nd son of Col. Geo. and Mrs. C. D. Leitner,
formerly of Fairfield Dist., S. C.,now of Alachua co., Fla., a
member of his brother's, Capt. Qm. Z. Leitner's Co., died 14th
July, in Manchester, near Richmond, aged 21 years... F. C. Johnson
Charles G. Thomas of Lowndesboro Beauregards, son of George
and Mary Thomas, died in his 22nd year....

Albert Olin Treadwell of Co. C. 6th Ala. Regt, died near Richmond, Va., 10th June 1862....

George Felix Lewis, son of Rev. Josiah and Elizabeth Lewis, was born July 10, 1837, and killed May 31, 1862.

Lt. Joseph Babcock of the Cahaba Rifles, 5th Ala. Regt, died 27th June.

Mr. James Nicholson died in Decatur co., Ga., July 16, in the 65th year of his age.

Mrs. Margaret R. Page, was born in Abbeville Dist., S. C.,Nov. 17, 1803, and died July 14, 1863, in Kemper co, Miss. Her maiden name was Ward.

Mr. Henry Washington Page, died at his father's residence, in Kemper Co., Miss., on 23d June, aged 23 years.

Joseph Manning Austin died July 28th, in his 23d year. Oliver Burr Hillard, son of W. H. and Louisa M. Hillard, was born in Charleston, S. C., and died on 29th July, his 20th year.

Senus H. Clark was born in N. C. Dec. 8, 1801, where he was raised mostly in orphanage, and in early life came to Twiggs co., Ga., where he was married to Miss Elizabeth Barton in 1827, died in Sumter co.,Ga., July 1, 1862....

Mrs. Martha Alley was the daughter of Robert and Sarah Poston, of Iredell co., N. C., where she was born June 23, 1787, married to W. W. Alley, Jan. 10, 1811, and died in Habersham co., Ga., May 15, 1862...Her parents were Presbyterians and members of "Center Church."

Mrs. Lucretia M. Betsill, wife of Joel Betsill, and daughter of Samuel and Anna Pearson, died near Cross Keys', Union Dist., S. C., May 23, in her 40th year...

James F. Brown was a native of Burke co., but for years a citizen of Savannah...died 24th June last....

William B., son of Rev. Smith Davenport, 47th Regt. Ga. Vols., died at Oglethorpe Barracks, Savannah, Aug. 11, in his 20th year.

William D. Coombs, pvt 8th Ga. Regt., died in Richmond, July 26th, in the 37th year of his age...

Sgt. W. W. Gregg, of Marion, S. C., was killed near Richmond, in the battle of Gaines Mills, 27th June.

Mrs. Martha M. Boyt, wife of J. D. Boyt, died at the residence of her father, Alexander McAfee, in Forsyth co., Ga., July 4, in her 24th year.

Mrs. Margaret M. Wright, wife of John M. Wright, died in Walton co., Ga., July 28, in the 34th year of her age.

Joseph M. Nicks died near Covington, Ga., June 19, 1862, in the 42d year of his age...

James W. Finley, son of T. B. and Mary Finley, 13th Miss. Regt, from Lauderdale co., Miss., was killed 1st July, in his 25th year.

Sophronia A. I. J. Langford, wife of C. C. Langford, died in Warren co., Ga., 22d July, in her 25th year.

Mr. Pierce S. Prickett was born in Mrogan co., Ga., 8th Nov. 1832, died in Huey Hospital, Atlanta, 8th July.

W. H. Saxon, 1st Regt. Ga. Cavalry, son of Lewis and Caroline Saxon, died in Bartow co., Ga., July 1st, aged nearly 24 years.

Isaac Sullivant died in a hospital at Richmond, Va., July 14, in his 21st year, from Anson co., N. C.

Sarah A. Shell, widow of C. C. Shell, died in Fayetteville, Ga., July 25th, aged 43 years. 8 months ago C. C. Shell died.

Caroline Busbey, daughter of Rev. Marady Busbey, died in Shelby co., Ala., 18th July 1862, in her 48th year.

Rev. Lewis Mallard, of Decatur co., Ga., died May 15th, in his 56th year.

Henry M. Cranford, only son of Rev. Henry Cranford of the Ga. Conf., died in the Winder Hospital, Richmond, on the 16th May.

Issue of August 28, 1862

Married on August 17th by Rev. A. Gray, W. G. Turner, of Henry co., Ga., to Miss Lucy A. Zachry, of Newton co., Ga.

Died on 10th inst., in Lafayette, Ala., in the 10th month of her age, Annie E., infant of Dr. J. W. and Mrs. H. E. Oslin.

In Hamilton, Aug. 17th, Ellen Benit, infant of Dr. R. A. and M. E. Smith, of Russel co., Ala., aged about 2 years.

Col. Lewis Rumph died Aug. 8th, 1862, in Houston co., Ga., in his 70th year...a native of Orangeburg Dist., S. C., and a son of Gen. Jacob Rumph, one of the Whigs of the Revolution.

Lt. Samuel B. Adams, eldest son of Rev. David Adams was killed at Seven Pines, May 31, 1862. a native of Strawberry Plains, Tenn, but a resident of n. C. for 18 months. Maggie E. Adams.

Ann Talbot, daughter of Wm. E. and Eliza Philips, was born in Williamson co., Tenn., S pt. 25, 1817, whence they removed in her early infancy to Madison co., Ala., married to John A.Fox, Oct. 1, 1833...died in Carroll co., Miss., July 19, 1862, mother of 8 children.

Lt. James A. Jordan, of 14th Ga. Regt, died in Richmond Va., on 31st ult., in his 29th year.

John J. Cook was born near Camden, S. C., Feb. 10, 1796, and died inJackson, Butts co., Ga., July 6, 1862.left wife and children.

Shadrach Holmes aws born Nov. 15, 1825, and died July 6, at the 4th Ga. Hospital in Richmond, June 28, 1862.

Lt. William J. Jones of Talbotton, Ga., died in Richmond, July 9th, aged 22 years.

Thos Herbert, eldest son of Hugh T. and Valeria E. McDonald, and grandson of Richard J. and Ann Bryan of Dallas co., Ala., and great grandson of Henry Ulmer and Richard Bryan of Colleton Dist., S. C., was born July 5, 1838, and was killed 29th June near Richmond.

Alexander W. Davis was born March 9, 1828, in Dallas co., Ala., and died March 18, 1862, in Stevenson, Ala. In 1854, lost his father...married Helen E. McDonald in 1860....

Wm. M. Haughton of Harris co., Ga., died 28th July, aged 47 years.

James Asbury Harris was born in Gwinnett co., Ga., May 21, 1831, and died in the hospital at Richmond, July 27, 1862.

Wm. H. Fuller, Orderly Sgt. of Talbot Vols, 27th Ga. Regt., was born in Warren co., Ga., Sept. 6, 1833, and was killed 31st May 1862.

Sgt. James Rufus Leak of 7th Regt. Ga. Vols., was born in Newton co., Ga., July 2, 1830, and died before Richmond, July 1st.

Benjamin Arnold Leak of 42d Ga. Regt., was born in Newton co., Ga., Aug. 26, 1844, and died in the hospital at Morristown, Tenn., July 11th, 1862.

Rev. J. L. Peeples was born 5th July, 1820, died 17th July 1862, in the hospital at Savannah.

Solomon A. Waters son of Mr. E. D. and Mrs. Ann Waters, of Bainbridge, Ga., was wounded in the battle of Gaines' Mills and died in Richmond, July 19th, in his 21st year.

John H. Mealing, was born Nov. 11, 1824, and died at Noxubee co., Miss., June 23, 1862....

Joseph W., son of James and Rachel Willis, was born Jan. 9, 1837, in Montgomery co., Ala., and died Oct. 28, 1861, near Auburn, Macon co., in service since 15th August.

Benjamin F., son of James and Rachel Willis born in Montgomery co., Ala., Jan. 10, 1841, and died in Conecuh co., Ala., June 10, 1862.

69

James R., son of James and Rachel Willis, was born March 21, 1844, and died July 3, 1862.

Isaac S. Barnett was born in Ala., April 1, 1840, and died July 22, 1862.

James W. Bonner, eldest son of Rev. E. P. Bonner was born May 1834, died July 15, from wounds recd. in battle.

Rolin W. Stevens, son of Toliver and Amanda Stevens, was born 7th May, 1835 in Putnam co., Ga., and was killed 1st July near Richmond....

John Thomas Smith of Marion co., Ga., died at Richmond, July 23d, of a wound, in his 24th year.

Zimmerman J. DuBose of 21st S. C. Regt, died in Darlington Dist., S. C., 17 July 1862.

Wm. Edward Box, of St. Peter's Parish, Beaufort Dist., S. C., died on 27th June last, before Richmond.

Mark A. Beall, of 48th Ga. Vols., son of James and Melinda Beall of Monroe co., Ga., died at Richmond, 14th July, aged 26.

Wesley A. Holbrook was born Feb. 25, 1839, died in Atlanta, 5th June 1862.

Mary Holbrook the mother of the above was born Dec. 8, 1801, and died in Cherokee co., Ga., July 17th, 1862.

Russel A. Holbrook was born Sep. 3, 1830, and died in Hospital inAtlanta, 15th June 1862.

Mrs. Carrie E. Holt, wife of Dr. William H. Holt, and daughter of Mrs. Mary E. Fort, died inStewart co., Ga.

Sgt. John H. Pearson, son of Saml Pearson and member of Putnam Volts., 44th Ga. Regt, died in Richmond, July 11th...

William V. Lazenby of 22d Ga. Regt, was born Dec. 7, 1842, and died August 18, 1862.

William L. Solomon, my brother, of 37th Regt. Ala. Vols., was born in Talbot co., Ga., Feb. 8, 1838, died at Tupelo, Miss., June 22d, 1862. John W. Solomon.

Mrs. Mary Haynes, wife of Ezekiel Haynes, was born in Maryland Sept. 10, 1776, and died in Lowndes co., Ala., July 7, 1862.

Joseph B. Coper, Jr. was born in Wilkes co., Ga., Aug. 27, 1827, and died in Hospital, Richmond, on 1st June 1862.

W. R. A. Kinney, 34th Ala. Regt., died at Tupelo, Miss., 22nd June, 1862, in his 21st year.

Jacob B. Bouknight, 1st Lt. of Co. M., 7th Regt. S. C. V., son of Wm. Bouknight was born in Edgefield Dist., April 17, 1835, died in Columbian Hotel in Richmond, 24th July of wounds....

Miss Ashia Jane Page was born April 10, 1834, and died in Kemper co., Miss., Aug. 4, 1862.

Henry J. Perry of Co. H, 45th Ala. Regt, son of Getson and Louisa Perry, died at Tupelo, Miss.27th June, in his 28th year. born in Baldwin co., Ga....

Lemuel Reynolds, 45th Ala. Regt, son of Newman and Lucy Reynolds, died at Tupelo Miss., 5th July, in his 35th year...born in Anson co., N. C.

Capt. Thomas N. Martin of Black Mingo Riflemen, 10th Regt. S. C. V., son of M. A. and James Martin, was born in Williamsburg Dist., S. C., died at Macon, Miss., 11th May, in his 24th year.

Tribute of Respect by James L. Varnes, prvt., formerly of S. C., but afterwards of Berrien co., Ga., died 29th July, in his 26th year by Co. A., Milton Battalion of Partisan Rangers.

Issue of September 4, 1862

Mrs. Mary R. Salmons, daughter of the late William Freeman, of Griffin Ga., and wife of Rev. L. S. Salmons died in Atlanta, Ga., July 29, 1862, in the 34th year of her age....

Rev. Francis Thomason was born 8th Dec., 1810, in Laurens Dist., S. C., and died in Greenville Dist., 29th July 1862....

Mrs. Eliza S. Powell was born March 28, 1807, in Brunswick
co., Va., married Nov. 18, 1829 at Marquis D. Powell, removed to
Ga., in 1845, and died in Sparta, Ga., Jule 23, 1862....
   William N. Powell, Hancock co., Ga., youngest son of Mrs.
Eliza S. Powell, was born March 19, 1840, and died at Berkville,
Va., Aug. 19, 1862....
   Mrs. E. A. Mobley, formerly Mrs. Wessinger, was born in
Richmond, Va., July 27, 1830, and died in Orangeburg, S. C., June
21, 1862...
   Daniel Kirton died in Williamsburg, S. C., on 17th August,
in his 71st year.
   Samuel A. Todd, son of Rev. A. Todd, died in Bartow co.,
near Cartersville, Ga., July 25th, in his 19th year.
   Mrs. Elizabeth Jackson, wife of Turner Jackson, died in great
peace, in Hamilton co., Fla., Aug. 6, 1862, in the 54th year of
her age...married to her surviving husband in Dec. 1829, in S. C.,
and came to Fla., in 1846...
   Miss Emma E. H. McIver, daughter of Alexander and Elizabeth
McIver, was born Dec. 29, 1845, and died at the residence of her
grandmother, Mrs. Mitchell, in Gadsden co., Fla., July 31, 1862.
   Mrs. Theresa McLean, daughter of John and Patience Newsom,
was born in Marion Dist., S. C., April 13th, 1795, and died in
Watikeenah, Fla., July 16, 1862.
   Wm. P. Green, son of T. J. and Mary A. Green died in Richmond,
on 19th July in his 22d year
   Everet Morton of Jones co., Ga., died in Richmond, Va., in
July, aged 23 years.
   James L. Varn, youngest son of Wm. G. Varn of Lowndes co.,
Ga. was born in Colleton Dist., S. C., 16 May 1835, and died
in Hospital below Savannah, July 29, in his 28th year.
   Lorenzo Dow Ridgeway, son of James E. and Elizabeth Ridgeway,
died in the Hospital at Staunton, Va., on 1st Aug, in his 23d
year.
   Lt. E. A. Smith, son of Stoddard W. and Augusta B. Smith born
in Warrenton, Ga., June 4, 1837, and died in Richmond, Va., Aug.
16, 1862....
   Duke H. Scott was born in Hancock co., Ga., July 7, 1836,
and died Aug. 15, 1862, at the home of his brother, Thomas G.
Scott, in Culloden, Ga.
   Gambrell McPherson, second son of Benj. H. and Destimony
Douthit, of Anderson Dist., S. C., died in the Hospital near
Richmond, Aug. 2, in his 22d year.
   James R. R. Doggett, of 12th Regt. N. C. Troops, died July
16, in the Hospital near Richmond, in his 29th year....
   Mr. Henry J. Moorer, died 9th Aug. at the Hospital, Atlanta,
Ga., in his 23d year...a native of Lowndes co., Ala. His remains
rest in Orangeburg Dist., S. C., where his family now resides.
   Mr. Jas. D. Brown of 38th Ga. Regt., son of Mr. Ebenezer
Brown, of Jefferson co., Ga., died inStaunton, Va., 9th Aug, in
his 21st year.
   Thomas Agerton, son of Alfred Agerton was born in Chesterfield
Dist., S. C., aged about 20 years, died at the Hospital, Ports-
mouth, Va.

Issue of September 11, 1862

   Married at the residence of Jacob S. Depass, in Camden, S. C.,
on 4th Aug., by Rev. Mr. Brown, Mr. Victor Mangat, to Miss Eliza
A. DePass, all of the above place.
   August 28, 1862, by Rev. Henry Evans at his residence in
Walker co., Ga., Mr. James A. Evans to Miss Susan Ann, daughter
of John Patton of Knoxville, Tenn.

On August 14, by Rev. M. L. Banks, Mr. James A. Copeland to Miss Martha E. Marvin, both of Prince Williams, S. C.

Died at Ringgold, Ga. on 22nd Jan., James Foster, only son of James H. and Julia D. Willy, in the 10th yearof his age.

In Talbot co., Ga., at the residence of Mr. Solomon J. Marshall, on 17th Aug., Virginia Watts, infant daughter of Rev. E. S. and Sarah S. Tyner, aged 6 months.

David Hill, in his 6th year, Willis Spence, in his 2d year, sons of Rev. Robert J. and Matilda C. Hodges, died in Sumter co., Ga., 12th and 28th of August.

Rev. G. L. Crosby died at Brookhaven,Lawrence co., Miss., on 4th July, in the 54th year of his age....

Orrah A. Norwood of 7th S. C. Regt., died in Richmond, 28th July, in his 22nd year...son of Nathaniel and Mary Norwood, of Abbeville Dist., S. C.

Mrs. Ann L. Houser wife of Capt. David Houser, of Orangeburg Dist., S. C., was born 29 April 1799, and died 6th July 1862. son-in-law, Capt. S. J. Reed, died from battle of Secessionville.

Mary Rebecca, wife of Rev. William H. Flemming, of the S. C. Conf., died in Walterboro, S. C., Aug. 18, 1862, daughter of Capt. David and Mrs. A. L. Houser, born in Orangeburg Dist., Oct. 1, 1833.

Lt. Wm. T. Cobb of 48th Regt. Ga. Vol., died in Butler, Ga., July 23, 1862, in his 40th year.

Julia H. McRae, daughter of John C. and Jane McRae, died in Knoxville, Tenn., Aug. 18, 1862.

Sgt. Maj. Johnson of 35th Regt. Ga. Vol., died in the 37th year of his age, at the residence of Col. Garnett, near Richmond, on 21st June.

Mrs. Lille W. Wells, daughter of the late John Weber, Esq., of Shelby, N. C., wife of Rev. G. H. Wells, of the S. C. Conf., died Aug. 25th, 1862.

Wesley A. Gober pvt. in Clarke Co. Rigles, was born Oct. 18, 1818, died near Richmond, Va., July 13, 1862, buried in Watkinsville, Ga., July 22nd, 1862.

Dr. John G.Rowland died on 18th Aug., in Greene co., Ga... native of Greene Co...

John W. Edwards of 39th Ala. Regt, died at Okolona Hospital, Miss., July 8, in his 17th year....

Charles H. and William M., sons of Rev. Dr. Powers, decd., members of Co. A. 9th Ala. Regt, have died...

Virginia A. Brown, wife of Rev. T. A. Brown, died in the city of Griffin, July 19, in her 26th year...

Martha G. Harris, daughter of Wm. Harvey, and widow of Rev. West Harris was born in Madison co., Ga., raised in Oglethorpe co., died in Hamilton, Ga., 24th Aug., at the residence of her son, Rev. J. H. Harris, of the Ga. Conf., in the 65th year of her age....

Dr. Charles R. Law died near Chattanooga, 26th Aug., aged 28 years...

Thomas Allen son of Bryant and Caroline Allen was born in Jasper co., Ga., on 11th Nov., 1836, married Miss Eliza J. McCowan in 1858, and moved to Monroe co., Ga., in the fall of 1860. died at Richmond 8 Aug 1862.

William Threadgill died near Uchee, Russell co., Ala., 28th August, in the 82d year of his age....

Miss Virginia P. Leggette, daughter of J. N. and S. A. Leggette, was born in Britton's Neck, Marion Dist., S. C.,on 19 Feb 1830, and died Aug 13, 1862, in Franklin co., Miss....

William H. McGlaun, eldest son of John and Nancy McGlaun, was born June 20, 1834, and died at Quitman, Miss., Aug. 17, 1862, in Capt. Clayton's, co., 29th Regt. Ala. Vols.

R. H. Harper of Henry co., Ga., fell in the battle before
Richmond, 28th June, in his 39th year....
John D. Cornutt of Floyd co., Ga., co. G. 22d Regt, died at
Poplar Lawn Hospital, Petersburg, Va., Aug. 16, aged 21 years,
3 months and 4 days.
O. G. Stafford, eldest son of E. and L. Stafford, 55th Ga.
Regt., died at Empire Hospital, 6th August.
Hamilton Lafayette Jones died in Kemper co., Miss., in his
23d year.
Rebecca Adaline Jones, his sister died on 21st July, in her
27th year.
Martha Eliza Jones, who died on 22nd July in the 29th year
of her age.
Sarah Elizabeth Skinner, a married sister, was next called
...Her husband was in the Confederate army....
Mrs. Ellen Ann Dennis, wife of Major George E. Dennis died
in Jefferson co., Fla., Aug. 1, 1862, aged 52 years...formerly
of Wilmington, N. C....

Issue of September 18, 1862

Gabriel R. Thomas, of Eatonton, Ga. died on 13th August, in
his 62d year...leaves wife and a number of children.
Rev. D. M. Keith was born in Merriwether co., April 3, 1828,
and died in Gordon co., Ga., on 1st July 1862...
Charles Bancroft Sr. died August 19, 1862, at Enterprise,
Miss., in the 63d year of his age...born in Boston, Mass., but
for the last 30 years resided in Mobile, Ala...
Charles E. W. Gerry, Co. I, 2d Fla. Vols., son of the late
Rev. John L. Gerry, of Hamilton co., Fla., died in Chimborazo
Hospital, 11th July, aged 22 years....
Davis Hix, of Chatooga co., Ga., who was born March 5th, 1830
in Randolph co., N. C., and died in Richmond, Aug. 8, 1862,
married in 1851 Nancy E. Hill, who is left wife five little chil-
dren... J. D. Anthony.
Thomas M. Langston was born Aug. 15, 1831, and died at Camp
Winder, Va., June 28, 1862.
Robert E. Langston was born Dec. 15, 1829, and died in the
La. Hospital, Richmond, Va., July 13, 1862...left wife and four
small children.
John T. Smith, son of Silas and Jane Smith, was born Nov.
3, 1839, in Gilmer co., Ga., and died a short time since at Chattanooga, Tenn.
Samuel F. Smith, only brother of the above, was born Aug.
2, 1841, and died at Bean's Station, Aug. 20, 1862...
Lt. J. T. Greenwood, son of Thomas Greenwood, of LaGrange
was killed in the battle of Gaines' Mills, July 27, in his 22d
year...14th Ala. Regt.
Edwin N. Richbourg, son of Simeon C. and Martha R. Richbourg,
was born in Clarendon Dist., S. C.,Sept. 17, and died May 31,
from wounds received at the battle of "Seven Pines."
William Baugh, of Warrior Stand, Ala., of the 45th Ala. Vols.,
died at Tupelo, Miss., in July last, in the 41st year of his age.
David Dougherty Legg, of the 11th Ga. Regt, son of Layton and
Eliza M. Legg, was born June 14, 1842 ... and was married to
Miss Lidy Matilda Jones, June 8, 1861(death date not given).
D. Horace Lee of the 45th Ga. Regt, son of J. S. Lee, Craw-
ford co., Ga., was born April 11, 1843, and died 30th last July.
Henry Clay Snow, youngest son of John P. and Susan R. Snow,
died in Walton co., Ga., Aug. 8, 1862, in his 21st year...
G. W. Conine, of the 14th Ala. Regt., died in Danville, Va.,
on 21st July, in his 21st year...

Married by Rev. B. C. Franklin, Sept. 9th, at Dartsville, Ga., Mr. J. J. Newton to Miss Mary E. Pritchard.

In Columbia, S. C., on the 4th inst., by the Rev. W. A. Gamewell, Rev. J. Lee Dixon to Miss Mary Jane, eldest daughter of the late John G. Bowman, Esq.

By the Rev. P. L. Herman (S S C), on 2d Sept., Mr. W. T. Warlick, son of Rev. David Warlick of Catawba co., N. C., to Miss M. E. Warlick, of Cleaveland co., N. C.

By Rev. S. H. Browne, Sept. 4, Mr. C. M. Ritchie of Newberry, to Miss Sallie V. Cromer of Abbeville Dist., S. C.

In Perry, Houston co., by Rev. Howell Cobb, on 16th Sept., Rev. John H. Leak, of the Ga. Conf., now on the Newnan station, and Miss Alice R. Culler, of the former place.

In Aberdeen, Miss., 26th ult., Mr. Pat Hamilton, of Waverly, Miss., to Miss Sarah Felix Paine, eldest daughter of Bishop Paine.

At the Presbyterian Church, Milledgeville, 8th Sept., by the Rev. C. W. Lane, Major Stephen F. Miller, associate editor of the Southern Recorded, to Miss Jane J. Windsor, of Charleston, S. C.

Died Louisa Caroline Varn, daughter of Mr. and Mrs. Isaac Varn, 9th Sept. 1862, aged 12 years, 4 months and 6 days.

Also Henry Dufford Varn, son of Mr. and Mrs. Isaac Varn, died 9th Sept., aged 13 years, 5 months and 3 weeks.

In Opelika, Ala., on 22d ult., Grune Williamson, eldest child of Wm. B. and Anna M. Page, aged 2 years and 20 days.

In Walton co., Ga., 7th Sept., John P. Snow, only son of John W. and S. A. C. Snow, aged 8 months and 10 days.

Charles Fletcher, son of Rev. Wm. and Mary Park, was born July 26, 1855, and died in Dawson, Terrell co., Ga., Sept. 12.

Clarissa Eugene Harben, second daughter of Rev. T. B. and Clarissa Harben, died 13th Sept., aged 6 years, 1 month and 21 days.

Oliver R. Phelps was born Aug. 4, 1830, and died in Forsyth, Ga., July 18, 1862....

Sister A. F. Hill, wife of J. O. D. Hill, aged 41 years, died June 19th, 1862...She first married John Young, and in 1859, Bro. Hill.

William C. Robinson, son of Rev. W. C. Robinson, was killed in battle near Richmond on 27th June, in the 22d year of his age.

Wm. A. Barker, son of Rev. Geo. W. and Tempe E. Barker, was born Nov. 14, 1834 in Wilkinson co., Ga, and was killed in the battle before Richmond, June 27th, 1862.

John E. Barker, son of the same, was born in Dooly co., Ga., Jan. 12, 1837, and died in the army in Miss, July 12th, 1862.

Geo. T. Barker, brother to the above was born in Barbour co., Ala., Nov. 8, 1841, and died in hospital at Greenville, Ala., Aug. 29, 1862.

Thomas D. Simons of the "Anson Guards" 14th NC Regt., was born in Montgomery co., NC, Sept. 13, 1842, and died 14th July 1862.

James H. Dye was born in Augusta, Ga., June 5th, 1829, and died in the same place, July 29th, 1862, in the 34th year of his age.

Mrs. Ann Parrish, daughter of the late Hope Hull Slatter, of Mobile, Ala., and consort of Wm. DeForest Holly, Esq., died in Clinton, Jones co., Ga., in the 43d year of her age.

Lt. David Marshall Miller, son of Dr. J. W. T. Miller, of Shelby, N. C. was killed in front of Richmond, July 1st, nearly 22 years of age.

James Polk Harden, son of A. T. Harden, died August 10, 1862, near Shelby, N. C., nearly 18 years of age.

Mrs. Eliza J. Hardaway, wife of Thomas J. Hardaway, was born in Warren co., March 29, 1817, and died in Pike co., Sept. 10, 1862.

Sgt. Lorenzo Newton Byars, eldest son of P. H. and Sarah Byars, was born 6th April 1840, and died at the Soldier's Relief Hospital, Charleston, SC, 14th July.

James J. Ricks, of 14th Regt. Ala. Vols., was born 22d July, 1839 in Chambers co., Ala., and died 2nd July 1862, near Richmond.

John M. Manning, died July 15th, 1862, of a wound received at Seven Pines, son of Maulding B. Manning...in the 23d year of his age.

Mrs. Ann Rebecca Reeves, wife of Solomon L. Reeves, died at Summerville, SC June 29, 1862, in the 60th year of her age.

Sgt. Thos. J. Pickens, son of Robert and Nancy Pickens of Anderson Dist., S. C., was born Feb. 13, 1841, and died at the Wayside Hospital in Columbia, SC July 30th, 1862.

John B.Chadwick, son of J. R. and Tamar Chadwick, late of Brunswick, N. C., was born August 16, 1842, and died at Brookville, MS, June 24, 1862....

William J. McKinzie, second son of Duncan and Mary McKinzie, of Monroe co., Ala., died June 2, 1862, aged 19 years...

Joseph G. Padrick was born in Tallahassee, Fla., on 2d Nov., 1840, and died in Richmond, Va., in the Hospital on 2 July 1862.

Mr. Young F. Stroud died near Bean's Station, East Tenn., Aug. 28th, 1862, in his 33d year...left wife and children.

Issue of October 2, 1862

Married on 16th Sept., by Rev. B. F. Breedlove, Rev. R. F. Williamson, of the Ga. Conf., to Miss M. E. Green, of Schley co., Ga.

On Tuesday morning, 16th inst.,by Rev. G. G. Norman, Col. John C. Fanning, and Miss Marcia A. Gartrell, both of Wilkes co., Ga.

Died on 9th Sept., 1862, Mary, infant daughter of Mr. John Dunn and Sarah Ann, his wife, of St. Helena Parish, La.

At Charleston, Sept. 27, 1862, Francis Asbury Mood, Jr., the only son of Rev. F. A. and S. R.Mood, aged 2 years, 9 months and 2 days.

On 17th Sept., Robert Fletcher, infant son of R. O. and V. D. Moreland, of Crantville, Coweta co., Ga.

My brother, Lt. Col. E. H. Miller, 34th NC Regt, fell on the battle-field, near Germantown, Sept. 1, 1862...a resident of Unionville, SC....Jno. F. Miller.

John T. Willhite of the 45th Regt. Ala. Vols., died at Tupelo, Miss., Aug. 7, in his 26th year....

E. L. P. Bull, son of Eliza and Middleton Bull, died 11th Sept. in St. Matthews Parish, SC, in his 19th year....

Henry Lewis Dudley, son of Edward and Mary H. F. Dudley, was born Nov. 29, 1841, in Lowndes co., Ala., and died in hospital near Richmond, July 1, 1862....

Mrs. Martha Hurt, widow of the late Col. Joel Hurt, of Ala., died 3 July, at the residence of Maj. James Freeman, of Gordon co., Ga., aged 73 years....

Capt. Apollo Forrester was born in England and brought by his parents to American when five years old, and fell in battle, 28th August, near Manassas, being a little over 23 years of age. He was an only son and one of two children....

Dr. John G. Parham was born in Greenville co., Va.,Nov. 5th, 1800...emigrated to Miss. and settled near Vicksburg, in 1830, then removed to New Orleans and to St. Helena Parish, where he died 25th June 1862, in his 62d year.

Sgt. J. N. Wilson died in Putnam co., Ga., July 27th, aged
21 years 5 months and 23 days....
Mrs. Missouri Hamer, wife of John H. Hamer of Marion Dist.,
S. C., was born Sept. 1, 1842, and died Sept. 8, 1862, married
Nov. 11, 1859....
Mrs. Anna Hart, wife of Thos Hart died in Greene co., Ga.,
on 31st August, aged 76 years...raised by Presbyterian parents.
Rev. John F. Thrasher died in Clark co., Ga., Aug. 22, in his
33d year....
Thos J. Watts, son of Jos. M. Watts, was born March 12, 1842
and fell June 29th near Richmond.
Robert Williams died in Columbia co., Ga., July 18th, aged
31 years.
William Henry Kimbrough of Harris co., Ga., son of Henry C.
and Mary A. Kimbrough was born May 24, 1827, and died at Lynch-
burg, Va., 9 Aug. 1862....
William C. Cunningham, of 22d Regt. Ga. Vols., eldest son of
J. S. and Willy C. Cunningham, was born in Cass co., Ga., Jan.
7,1843 died in Richmond, July 14, 1862....
Mrs. Margaret Price, consort of Gen. John C. Price, died on
21st Aug., born in Limestone co., Ala., Jan. 7, 1819, daughter
of Col. Wm. Hodges, married Sept. 4, 1834, moved to Marion county,
Ala., then to Lowndes co., in 1859....
Wm. F. Garrison, son of P. G. Garrison of Carrollton, Ga., 19th
Regt. Ga. Vols., was in the battle of Seven Pines, and on 31st
May was reported missing, in his 20th year.... .
Wiley J. Baggett, son of Alfred Baggett of Gwinnett co., was
born in Gwinnett co., Oct.28, 1842, and died in the Hospital,
Richmond, about 9th July last....
Mrs. Eliza C. Randle, of Lowndes co., Miss., died 16th June,
born Jan. 31, 1824, married to Henry Randle, Oct. 11, 1842.
C. H. Ranlett, died at Aiken, S. C., Aug. 18, 1862, aged 46
years and 4 months...native of Freedom, Maine, but for 15 years,
resident of the above named place...leaves four children.
Mrs L. J. Walker, wife of Charles J. Walker, died on 2d inst.,
in Richland Dist., S. C., in the 35th year of her age....
Peter James Daniel Jayroe died at the residence of Mr. James
M. Rogers, his brother-in-law, of Sampit, Georgetown Dist., S. C.,
July 28, 1862, in his 27th year....
Colemon V. Hammet, son of Moses and L. Hammet, of Spartanburg
Dist., S. C., was born Feb. 7, 1846, and died in Hospital in
va., Aug. 26, 1862...
Mrs. Nonie L. Newsome, daughter of Col. Wm. Ragland, died
Aug. 28, 1862, in her 22d year....
Tribute of Respect by Lawrenceville Ct., to William Baugh ·
who died near Lawrenceville, Gwinnett co., Ga., Aug. 27, in his
71st year...born in Laurens Dist., S. C., March 8, 1792, removed
at an early age of Jackson co., Ga. In his 24th year married to
Miss Elizabeth Lindsey, and she died...in Oct 1839, married to
Elizabeth Henderson of Jackson co....raised 16 children....

Issue of October 9, 1862

Died Joseph Wesley Beauregard son of Edward and Mrs. Caroline
Easterling, died in Orangeburg Dist., S. C., on 29th June, aged
1 year, 3 months and 15 days.
Sgt. Wm. Nixon McCaskill of the 12th Ga. Regt, eldest son of
Murdock and E. A. McCaskill was born in Houston co., Ga., Jan.
29, 1843, and on 6th April at the battle of Cedar Run the sa-
crifice was redeemed....
Col. John Aaron, a native of Barnwell Dist., S. C., born 12th
May 1800, and died 16th Sept. 1862. His father died when he was
young...

Sister Polly Wllace, wife of Bland Wallace of Marion co., Ga.,
and daughter of John and Mary James, died Aug. 28, 1862...born
in N. C. in 1805, grew up and married in that state. In 1831,
they came to Ga.
Sgt. Horace A. McSwain, son of Rev. W. A. and Elizabeth Mc-
Swain, was born Dec. 9, 1843...killed 20th Aug. at Manassas.
Lt. Thomas J. Murray of St. Georges Parish, Colleton Dist.,
S. C., was born 5th April 1852, and died on 6th Sept. 1862.
D. H. Gillespie was born Jan. 26, 1820, and died at Lauder-
dale Springs Hospital, Aug. 3, 1862....
Mrs. Salina Catharine Littlejohn, wife of John Littlejohn,
died in Polk co., N. C., July 3, 1862....
Mrs. Emily A. Harper, daughter of Lewis and Mary Redwine,
died in Carroll co., Ga., in her 44th year....
Mr. Anderson Johnson of Laurens Dist., S. C., died 17th Sept.
1862, in his 53d year....
L. A. Haslam, of Beauregard vols., 6th Ga., Regt., missing
in action 27th June....
Sgt. George Pickett Tucker, son of Rev. Geo. B. Tucker, of
Union Dist., S. C., died at Warrenton, Va., Sept. 9th, in his
22d year....
·Col. James P. Hunt a native of S. C., for 5 or 6 years a
resident of Fla., died in Chattanooga, Sept. 2nd, Col. 4th Fla.
Regt.
Queen A. M. Parker, eldest daughter of James B. and Georgi-
anna Smith, of Tatnall co., Ga., was born July 6th, 1846,
and died Aug. 10, 1862, in her 17th year....
Mrs. Mary Mendenhall, relict of Dr. Wm. Mendenhall, was born
in Chesterfield Dist., S. C., June 25, 1757, and died Aug. 14,
1862, at Ansonville, N. C....
Lt. J. A. J. Peacock of Reidsville, Ga., was born June 21,
1826, died 1st June last....
Wm. Franklin Anderson was born in Anderson Dist., S. C.,
March 18, 1839, and died at Orange C. H., Va., Aug. 11, 1862...
George Olin Anderson was born March 4, 1841, and died July
20, 1862 in Va.
Frances Irvin Easterling, died in Orangeburg Dist., S. C.,
9th July in his 15th year....
Mrs. Ellen L., wife of Capt. R. W. Bonner, died in Clinton,
Ga., Sept. 15, aged 32 years...
Mrs. Margaret Carn, wife of David L. Carn, died near Cen-
treville, Leon co., Fla., Sept. 20, 1862, aged 61 years....
James Monroe Smith died at Richmond, Va., 6th Aug, in his
22nd year...wounded in battle.
Tribute of Respect by Reuven L. Tyler, Jr. a member of the
Quarterly Conf. of Carnesville Ct., Ga., who died July 2, in the
41st year of his age....
Tribute of Respect by Trinity Circuit, Fla. Conf.to James
Nicholson.

Issue of October 16, 1862

Mrs. Ann Moore, wife of Rev. James Moore of Abbeville C. H.,
S. C., and mother of Rev. H. D. Moore of S. C. Conf., was a na-
tive of Liverpool, England. Her mother was a Roman Catholic.
They landed at Norfolk, Va., and from thence removed to Charles-
ton.... A. G. Stacy.
Mary Julia, wife of J. R. Herrin, was born in N. C., whence
her parents moved to Pike co., Ala., in 1853, died 9th Aug., 1862.
In 1848 she married J. R. Herrin....
Mrs. Harriet Sutton, wife of Wm. Sutton, Esq., died in Wil-
mington, N. C., Sept. 24, 1862, in the 47th year of her age....

John K. Moore, son of Jason and Mary A. Moore, was born in Lee co., Ga., May 31st, 1841, and died 29th July 1862...

Osborne G. Johnson, son of Rev. Wm. B. and Mrs. M. A. Johnson was born in Jefferson co., Miss., Jan. 1, 1843, and died near Richmond, Va.,on Friday, June 27, 1862....

Mrs. Sarah R. McDaniel, daughter of James and Susan B. Gillespie, was born in Brunswick co., N. C., July 1822, died near Cave Spring, Ga., Sept. 27, 1862...In 1850 married to Rev. P. W. McDaniel, then a member of the S. C. Conf...

John Wesley McCoy, was born July 8, 1827, in Sumter Dist., S. C. and fell 30th June, near Richmond, Va. and died the next day...

Edward McCoy was born Jan. 1, 1826, and died Aug. 25, 1862, a soldier in Confederate service in Charleston, S. C.

Samuel Capers Traywick of 23d Regt. N. C. Troops, died 29th July at camp near Richmond, Va., in his 20th year...tribute of respect by   Ansonville ct....

Robert D. Gibbs, eldest son of John and Eliza A. Gibbs, was born Sept. 8, 1843, and killed in battle, 27th June last at Richmond, Va.

Mrs. Eliza A. Gibbs, wife of John Gibbs was born in Spartanburg Dist., S. C., April 4, 1823, and died in Cherokee co., Ga., Aug. 31, 1862...

Mrs. Elenda P. Harvey, daughter of Robert and Nancy Martin, of Forsyth co., Ga., wife of Ezekiel P. Harvey, was born in Buncombe co., N. C., and died in Gwinnett co., Ga., 23d Sept. 1862, in her 49th year....

Col. James R. Bryan, son of James R. and Mary Bryan, was born in Jones co., N. C, Jan. 17, 1822, and died near Jefferson, Marengo co., Ala., Aug. 14, 1862, in his 41st year....

Zachariah C. Finley was born 2nd Sept. 1843, and died 4th June 1862, near Richmond....Orr's S. C. V.

Thomas Wesley Finley was born 1st March, 1836, and died near Richmond, 24th July 1862...Orr's Regt, S. C. V.

Mrs. Martha E. Dawson, wife of Philip H. Dawson, and daughter of Lewis H. and Amy Lynch, was born 12th April 1804, in Brunswick co., Va., married Jan. 29th, 1823, and died in Putnam co., Ga., June 20, 1862...

Mrs. Elizabeth J. Abbott, wife of J. U. Abbott, died Sept. 26th, in Autauga co., Ala., in the 33d year of her age.

Robert Lemuel Pearson was born in Marlboro Dist., S. C., May 5, 1841, died in Va., Sept. 26, 1862...

James Barr, son of Wm. J. and Harriet Barr, died near Chattanooga, Tenn. on 28th Aug., 1862, in his 18th year....

Mrs. Lucy King died in Griffin, Ga., July 21, 1862, in her 66th year...a native of Brunswick co., Va., maiden name was Clayton. In 1820 married to the late Nathaniel King, and these two, with an only daughter, settled in Merriwether co., Ga.

John C. Hagans, of 53d Regt, Ga. vols., was born May 18, 1838, and was killed at Sharpsvurg, Md., Sept. 17, 1862.

Thomas D. L. F. Johnson, my youngest brother on my mother's side, fell at the battle of Gaines' Mill, before Richmond, Va. born in Sept. 1837... B. L. Johnson.

Penelope Hartsell, daughter of Micajah and Nancy Barkley, was born July 17th, 1840, married to Rev. John C. Hartsell, May 8, 1862, and died in Anson co., NC, Sept. 12, 1862...

James M. Lackey, was born 1833, and died in the Hospital at Chattanooga, Tenn., Aug. 6, 1862.

Andrew J. Hancock was born 1837, and died Aug. 14, 1862, in the Hospital at Chattanooga, Tenn....

Owen H. R. Carden was born 1820, and died in the Hospital at Atlanta, Ga., in July, 1862.

Rev. Thomas Legg died at his residence in Pike co., Ga., on
14th July, 1862 in his 76th year...born and reared in Prince
William co., Va., emigrated to Ga. when a young man....
    Augustus Baxter Richburg, a member of Hampton's Legion, was
born in Clarendon Dist., S.C., Oct. 19, 1827, and was mortally
wounded May 31st, 1862....
    Mrs. Elizabeth Collins died in Marion Dist., S. C. (no date
given).
    James H. Ragan was born Dec. 8, 1830, and died in Rusk co.,
Texas, June 14, 1862...
    R. M. Williams of 19th Ga. Regt. died in Richmond, Va., July
21, 1862....
    Robert Charles Harlee, son of Robert and Susan Harlee, died
in Marion Dist., S. C., aged 6 years...
    James McLeod, son of Alexander and Susan McLeod was born in
Montgomery co., NC, and died at Chattanooga, Aug. 12, 1862, in
his 30th year...emigrated to Pike co., Ala. where he was a
school teacher.
    Tribute to Three Deceased Chaplains, by Greenville ct., Ala.
Conf. to William Franklin Herlong who died July 26, 1862; James
Tillery, who died Sept. 9, 1862; and Isham Morris, who died Sept.
16, 1862....

Issue of October 23, 1862

    Married in Talbot co., Ga., Oct. 2d, by Rev. G. H. Patillo,
Capt. W. A. Davis of the 46th Ga. Regt. and Miss F. E. Brown.
    At the residence of Rev. G. W. Persons, Fort Valley, and by
him on the morning of the 9th inst., Rev. and Hon. Howell Cobb
of Perry, Houston co., Ga., to Miss Mary C. Rumph, late of Fla.
    By Rev. Aug. W. Walker, of S C Conf., on 25th Sept., Capt.
James M Ingram, of Kershaw Dist., S. C., to Miss S. Z. Horton,
of Lancaster Dist., S. C.
    By the same, on 2d inst., Mr. Andrew Cauthen to Miss Eliza-
beth Bell.
    On 25th Sept., by Rev. L. M. Little, Lt. Henry Ham to Miss
Rosa Huett, all of Darlington Dist., S. C.
    In Midway, Baldwin co., Ga., on 30th ult., by Rev. H. J. Adams,
John N. Gilmore, Esq. of Washington co., and Miss Laura C.,
daughter of the late Harper Tucker.
    At Richland, Stuart co., Ga., Sept. 12, 1862, by Rev. L. J.
Davies, Dr. L. A. Purvis to Miss Martha E. Snelling.
    In Manning, S. C., on 9th inst., by Rev. Wm. W. Mood, Mr.
Elias E. Dickson of Darlington and Miss Mary M. Plowden, daugh-
ter of the late Samuel E. Plouden of Clarendon Dist., S. C.
    At Gainstown, Ala., Sept. 23d, by Rev. James W. Shores, Mr.
L. M. Sullivan to Miss Maria Lou Smith.
    In Oxford, Ga., on Wed. evening, 1st Oct., by Rev. W. R.
Graham, W. J. Young(?) of the 29th Gert. Ga. Vols., to Miss
Sudie A. Smith, daughter of Dr. O. G. Smith.
    On 3d Oct., by Rev. A. J. Cauthen G. H. Parker and Miss Mat-
tie Andrews, all of Fairfield Dist.,S. C.
    By Rev. W. B. Neal, Sept. 25, 1862, Mr. Turner L. Green to
Miss Martha G. Cox, near Loacapek(?), Ala.
    John William, son of John M. and Carrie Branham, was born
Dec. 12, 1859, and died Sept. 22, 1862.
    In Barnwell Dist., S. C., Sept. 29, 1862, Mary Georjean,
eldest daughter of John and Mavina M. Whetstone, aged 15 months
and 23 days.
    At Rural Retreat, Barnwell Dist.,S. C., Sept., 26, 1862, Mary
Elizabeth, infant daughter of J. Henson and Mary E. Jones(?),
aged 19 months and _ days.

On 17th Oct., Frances E., infant daughter of Wm and T. A. Puden, of Fair Grove Parish, N. C., aged 3 years, 8 months and 11 days.

In St. Helena Parish, La., 24th August 1862, Lula Elizabeth N---, daughter of Dr. McDuffie and Sarah Jane Blanchard, and grand-daughter of Rev. T. H. Whitty, of the Ala. Conf., aged 1 years 2 months and 6 days.

On Sept. 25, Nannie Stewart, aged 7 years, daughter of J. D. and Mary Stewart.

On Oct. 3d, Joseph Stewart, son of J. D. and Mary Stewart, aged 5 years.

In Decatur co., Ga., on 20th Sept., Priscilla Neill Gardner, eldest daughter of Rev. S. and Emma Gardner, aged just 4 years.

In St. Matthew's Parish, SC, Sept 27, 1862, John Thomas, aged 9 years, 6 months, and 5 days; and in a few hours, Tommy Sarah, aged 4 years, 7 months and 19 days, children of W. A. and V. Shuler.

In Monroe co., Ga., Oct. 5, 1862, Julia Agnes, only daughter of John R. and Fannie M. Ralls, aged 2 years 2 months and 15 days.

In Monroe co., Ga., Aug. 18, Josiah Garland son of Josiah and Mollie E. Jordan, aged 3 years 4 months and 5 days.

Charles Wesley Pooser, son of Jacob H. and Eliza R. Pooser, late of Orangeburg Dist., S. C., now of Jackson co., Fla., fell at Sharpsburg, MD., Sept. 17, 1862, and died the next day...born near Branchville, SC, 24 Nov 1842....

Mrs. Mary J. Ellison, wife of John P. Ellison and daughter of Rev. W. W. Robison, of the Ga. Conf., died near Enon, Ala., on 30th Sept., in the 22d year of her age....

Banes P. Shaw, only son of Capt. James Shaw, decd, and Mrs. M. D. Shaw, of Columbus Vols., was killed at Manassas, Aug. 30, 1862, aged 22 years.

John C. Gwindle died at Richmond, Va., 25 June, in his 23d year.

Mrs. Eliza Jane Key, wife of Thomas Key, died in Jonesboro, Clayton, Ga., on 21st Sept., in the 22d or 23d year of her age.

Miss Anna L. Woodruff died in her 16th year at the Tuskegee Female College, daughter of Dr. and Mrs. M. Woodruff of Beallwood, near Columbus, Ga....

Charles W. Harrison, son of Hartwell and Mary A. Harrison of Warrior Stand, Ala., 45th Ala. Regt., died near Chattanooga Tenn., Aug. 29, 1862, aged 21 years.

Cicero T. Wells, son of Joseph and Adelasa Wells, was born in Clark co., Ga., Jan. 30, 1828...moved to Pike co., in Jan., 1851, died in Richmond, Va., Sept. 6, 1862....

Bushrod Page was born Feb. 18, 1819, married to Miss Georgia A. Paty in 1853, and died Sept. 26, 1862, in Cobb co., Ga.

Sister Mary L. Coombs, widow of John S.Coombs, of Augusta, Ga., and eldest daughter of Rev. Lewis Myers, decd., died in Atlanta, Ga., 2d August 1862...

Lovick P. Dozier was born in Columbia co., Ga., Feb. 6, 1838 ...died Sept. 1st.

Pleasant H. McDonald of 6th Regt Ala. Vols, son of James McDonald, Henry co., Ala., fell mortally wounded on 31st May....

Malcom Johnson died in Appling co., Ga., August 15, 1862, in his 68th year....

John W. Black, son of J. W. and E. Black was born in Elbert co., Ga., April 1836, and fell at the battle of Manassas 29th August.

Frances Augustus Hightower, of 22d Ala Regt, son of A. W. and Sarah F. Hightower, was born in Macon co., Ala., Nov. 27, 1843 and died in Hospital at Macon, Miss., June 30.

James D. Felder died in the battle of Manassas.

James McKinley Dorris, son of James and Elizabeth Dorris, was born in Coweta co., Ga., Oct. 22, 1844, and died in the Montgomery Hospital, June 17, 1862.

A. B. Hobbs of 22d Ga. Regt., was born Nov. 28, 1842, and died Sept. 9, 1862....

Edward T. Brinson of Reidsville, Ga., was born March 17, 1845, and died August 14, 1862, in Staunton Hospital, Va.

Lt. Jasper N. Hawthron, of Pickens Dist., S. C., was killed in battle June 30th, near Richmond, Va., aged 32 years.

Mrs. Charlotte Mauldin, wife of Laban Mauldin, died near Pickensville, S. C., Sept. 18, aged 72 years.

Tribute of Respect to Wiley Monroe Whitely, member of Mt. Zion Sabbath School, Russell co., Ala.

Tribute of Respect by Laurens Ct., to Rev. Addison P. Martin of the S. C. Conf....

Issue of October 30, 1862

Married on Oct. 16th, by Rev. R. N. Cotter, Maj. W. H. Mann, 54th Regt. Ga. Vols., to Miss L. Joanna Ryals, of Montgomery co.; Ga.

On Oct 16th, by Rev. Albert Gray, Samuel E. Dailey of Henry co., Ga., to Miss Mary E. Stillwell, of Spaulding co., Ga.

Died in Rockingham, Richmond co., NC, Sept. 22, 1862, John Leak son of R. L. And H. P. Steele, aged 1 year, 5 months and 9 days.

At the residence of Rev. Joshua Bowdon, Gordon co., Ga., on 10th Oct., Pickett, son of Stephen and Ann F. Sikes, aged 2 years and 9 months.

In LaGrange, Ga., on 24th August, Susie Marietta, infant daughter of Mr. Wm. A and M E Pullen, aged 11 months.

Joseph A. Smith, son of Rev. Henry A. and Mrs. Hephziba E. Smith died Sept. 23d, in Lexington Dist., S. C.

On Sept. 5th, 1862, Rebecca, daughter of N S and S C Connelly, aged 2 years, 8 months and 8 days....

Oct. 5th, Benjamin C., son of Sophia C and N S Connelly, aged 4 years and 11 months and 10 days.

Mrs. Sarah Chandler Wilson, wife of L. M. Wilson, died in Summerville, Ala., on 6th Oct., in the 41st year of her age.

Mr. Charles D. Pullen, of the firm of Pullen and Cox, died in LaGrange, Ga., on the 10th inst., in the 47th year of his age. He was a native of Giles co, Tenn., but a citizen of this place from the year 1835.

Mrs. Temperance Mims was born Aug. 21, 17 1, in Warren co., Ga., and died in Bibb co., July 31, 1862...

Miss Mary Emily Virginia DuPre, youngest daughter of C. P. and E. M. DuPre, formerly of Pendleton, late of Abbeville Dist., died 18th Sept., aged 20 years and 27 days.

Susan Buddington, daughter of James M.N. and Mary Elizabeth Gardner, died 2d August, aged 9 years and 11 months.

Mary Elizabeth Gardner, wife of James M. N. Gardner died near Centreville, Leon co., Fla., 22 Sept. 1862. She was born June, 1824...

Mrs. Mary Ann Burns, widow of Thos Burns sr., died Sept. 4, 1862, in Scriven co., Ga., aged 58 years....

Cpl. Josephus Delamar and Prvts. Thomas Tees Dunaway and Thomas Perkins, of 31st Regt Ga. Vols., all from Stewart co., died on the battlefield of Cold Harbor, 27th June 1862. Josephus Delamar was the eldest son of Thomas and Mary Ann Delamar, in the 18th year of his age....

Mr. Samuel D. W. Tompkins, of Muscogee co., Ga., of 40th Regt.

Ga., son of Mr. John Y. Tompkins, died in the Roper Hospital, Charleston, S. C. in his 22d year.

Miss Annie Susan Anderson, youngest daughter of the late Robert Anderson, of Charleston, S. C. died 20th July, at the temporary residence of her brother in Williamsburg Dist., S. C., in her 29th year.

Rev. Stephen Wright was born in Somerset co., Md., March 17, 1798, and died in Coweta co., Ga., Oct. 6, 1862. He was raised in Hancock co., Ga... D. J. Wright.

Newton B. McLin of Newnansville, Fla., of 1st Fla. Battn, died 31st August, in his 27th year near the Arsenal in Chattahoochee...born in Tenn., but a resident of Fla. for several years.

Mrs. Sarah Glymph died 4th Oct., in the Newberry ct., S. C. Conf., in her 55th year...

William S. Patrick, son of A. W. and Mrs. R. A. Patrick, of St. George's Parish, Colleton Dist., S. C., died on the 7th inst., in the hospital at Hardeeville, S. C. in his 23d year...

Francis Davidson Littlejohn, son of John and Catharine Littlejohn was born in Polk co., N. C., Jan. 24, 1839, died in Richmond Va., July --, 1862.

Rev. S. B. Treadaway, of Floyd co., Ga., member of 22d Ga. Regt., fell at the battle of Manassas, Aug. 30.

Wm. A. Pullen born Aug. 14, 1844, and died near Richmond, Va., August 10, 1862.

James Parnell was born Oct. 14, 1838, and died in the hospital at Tallahassee, July 4, 1862...left wife and children.

John L. Thomason died in York Dist., S. C., in his 20th year ...Mecklenburg Beauregards, N. C. V.

Higdan Corley died in Talbot co., Ga., Sept. 25, in his 67th year....

Mrs. Caroline R. Danner, died at Graham's Turn Out, on 16th Oct., aged 22 years...

Wm. Miles Boggs, son of Elijah and Jane Boggs, was born Nov. 14, 1841, and died at Richmond, Va., 18th Sept. 1862.

Mrs. Mary Ann Westwood was born in England, Feb. 22, 1792, and died in Harris co., Ga...raised in the Episcopal Church....

S. O. Cowen, of Coweta Co., Ga., son-in-law, of Wm. and Ellen Neill, 53d Ga. Regt, died on 17th Sept...left wife and children.

Robert Kenny Sr. died Oct. 6, 1862, in Edgefield Dist., S. C. born in Antrim co., Ireland, 8 March 1782, and emigrated to America in 1791...

Brother Gober died 15th Sept., in his 40th year...left wife and six children.

Thomas J. Wolf, son of Samson and Mary Wolf of Mecklenburg co., N. C., died in the Hospital, near Richmond, on 30th July, in his 19th year.

John B. Ellis, son of Henry and Caroline Ellis of Jasper co., Ga., died in Richmond, Va., Aug. 12, 1862, aged 22 years.

Tribute of Respect by Franklin ct., to Dr. W. O. Redwine, who died Sept. 30, 1862.

Tribute of Respect to Col. J. Felix Walker, of 18th Regt. S. C. V,, who was wounded Aug. 30, and survived 11 days....

Tribute of Respect to Rev. N. B. Powell by Chunnenggee Ct., Ala. Conf.

Issue of Nov. 6, 1862

Married on 22d Oct., by Rev. Wm. W. Mood, Mr. R. Warren Burgess and Miss Martha E., daughter of Capt. Joseph Stukes, all of Clarendon Dist., S. C.

On 28th Oct., by Rev. Wm. W. Mood, Mr. John W. Hodge and Miss Harriet Eugenia, daughter of Mr. Robert L. McLeod, all of Clarendon Dist., S. C.

On 16th Oct., by Rev. E. G. Murrah, of Ga. Conf., Mr. I. B.
N. Cochran to Miss Annie J. Davis, all of Oglethorpe co., Ga.
Died in Rome, Ga., Oct. 24th, Edgar W. Hinton, son of Rev.
J. W. and S. C. Hinton, aged 7 years and nearly 3 months.
Capt. James G. Rogers was born in Darien, Ga., April 20,
1827...moved to Macon, Ga....killed in service...left wife and
nine children.
Rev. George R. Edwards was born Sept. 22, 1807, and died
Aug. 19, 1862....
Dr. F.Marion Tucker, son of S. W. And L. Tucker was born
Nov. 2, 1828, married to Miss Ada M. Nisbet, 2d Dec. 1852, a
brother of J. Wofford Tucker, Esq. fell instantly in the Manassas
struggle, aged nearly 34 years.
Mrs. M. C. Sullivan, wife of W. D. Sullivan, and daughter of
Rev. J. G. and Mary Humbert, died at Tumbling Shoals, Laurens,
S. C., 30th Sept., in her 23d year....
Lt. R. J. Dandridge, 11th Regt. S. C. V. died at McPherson-
ville, S. C. Sept. 24, in his 21st year...
Dr. Thomas P. Haddock was born in Caswell co., N. C. and
died in Macon, Ga., the 19th Oct.
Sgt. Edward H. Darby of the Caroline Light Inf. Vols., was
killed on 29th Aug., in the 21st year of his age...
John Seay died near Camp Randolph, August 6, 1862, in the
35th year of his age....
Robert L. Anthony, was born in Gwinnett co., Ga., July 22,
1828, and died at Cave Spring, Ga., Aug. 22, 1862.
Aaron S. Spivy, of 17th Ala. Regt, eldest son of Aaron and
Elizabeth Spivy, died 9 Oct. 1862, in Coosa co., Ala., aged about
19 years.
James Thomas Smith, son of Joseph D. Smith, of Warren co.,
Ga., died near Richmond, Va., Aug. 29, 1862, in his 21st year.
Mrs. Priscilla Holman, daughter of Mr. David Felder died on
13th Oct., inBarnwell Dist., S. C., in the 61st year of her age.
Sister Matilda Stevens, wife of Henry Stevens, was born in
Green co., Ga., Aug. --, 1823, and died in Whiting, Baldwin co.,
Ga., Sept. 30, 1862...
Lt. Col. E. O. Shelton of the 51st Regt, Tenn. Vols., died
in Mobile, Ala., Aug. 4, 1862, in his 33d year...
Green Evin Glisson, son of E. C. Glisson, of Burke co., Ga.,
was born Feb. 4, 1842, and died 5th Sept... E. C. Glisson.
Miss Rebecca Karnes was born near Wilmington, N. C. and
died at the house of Milton Smith, Esq., near Georgetown, Ga.,
Oct. 13, 1862, in her 77th year...Mr. S., the only relatives
she had perhaps in this State.
John McKindrick Sears, son of John L. and E. M. Sears, died
Sept. 29, 1862, in his 14th year....
Tribute of Respect by Sparta Sabbath School to Robert P.
Jordan, killed in the battle of Sharpsburg.

Issue of November 13, 1862

Married in Tuskaloosa, Ala., Oct. 20th, 1862, by the Rev. Dr.
Summers, Mr. Henry S. Merritt of Columbus, Mi., to Miss Henrietta
Hargrove, of Tuskaloosa.
In Winston co., Ala., Oct. 24, by the Rev. Dr. Summers, the
Rev. William Edward Mabry, of the Ala. Conf., son of Rev. Dr.
Mabry, formerly of the S. C. Conf., to Miss Sarah Rusk Calhoun
DeGraffenreid, of Winston co., Ala.
By Rev. S. H. J. Sistrunk, Nov. 4, 1862, Dr. A. C. Simmons of
Monroe co., Ga. to Miss S. C., daughter of James and Ann E.
Turrentine, of Houston co., Ga.
On Sunday morning, Nov. 2d, by Rev. T. M. Lynch, in the M. E.
Church at Prattville, Ala., Lt. M. E. Pratt, C S A to Miss Julia

A. Smith.

Lt. Coleman C. Brown of Newton co., Ga. was killed instantly in the Sharpsburg battle, Sept. 17, 1862....

Mrs. Catherine Watts, wife of Rev. Hope Watts, died near Cave Spring, Ga., Oct. 15, 1862, in the 74th year of her age.

Lt. A. W. Cameron, 8th Regt. S. C. V., died on 26th Aug., aged 21 years.

H. Stacy Hammond, son of Col. and Mrs. E. Hammond, of Anderson, S. C., was killed on the plains of Manassas, 30th Aug. 1862, being nears 27 years of age.

Joseph T. Albert of 22d Ga. Regt, fell at the battle of Manassas, Aug. 30, 1862....

Mathis M. Vaught died in Madison co., Fla., Sept. 11, 1862, aged 29 years...called to mourn the loss of two companions, Miss Sallie and Bettie Tooke, and was married to the third, Miss Antonia Tillman about two years ago...left wife and two children.

Saml Leard Jr., eldest son of Rev. Samuel Leard of the S. C. Conf., died at the Parsonage, near Brighton, St. Peters Parish, Beaufort Dist., S. C., on 30th Oct....

Wm. Franklin, son of Rev. Daniel and Sarah E. Hurlong, died near Chattanooga, on 26th July, 1862, in his 35th year....

J. D. Short, son of Nathan and Nancy Short, was killed 28th Aug. at Manassas...from Marion co.

Mary Narcissa, only child of W. D. And Jane A. Diskey, died on 28th Oct., in Greenville Dist., S. C., in his 17th year...

A. M. Mewborn, son of Thomas and Frances Mewborn, of 42d Ga., died at Bean Station, Tenn., Oct. 29, 1862....

William C. Murdock son of Wm. P. and Sarah A. Murdock, was born in Bulloch co., Ga., Nov. 19, 1834, and died in the hospital in Richmond,Va. Sept. 20, 1862.... Chas. P. Murdock

J. Franklin Rape, of Tallapoosa co., Ala., died in his 22nd year....

Lt. Alexander H. Barnett, son of Wm. Barnett, of Russell co., Ala., was born July 6th, 1832, in Leaksville, Rockingham co., N. C. and died inOpelike, Ala., Sept. 20, 1862.

Perry Butler Austin, youngest son of Dr. Thomas C. and Mrs. Mary James Austin, of Gilan, Greenville Dist., S. C.,died on 20th Oct., 1862, in his 21st year.

Ratio E. Shepard, son of Daniel and Mahala Shepard, died in Sept. 1862, in Escambia co., Fla., in his 24th year...

W. F. Mily, of Barnesville Dist., died Sept. 18, 1862, in the 30th year of his age.

Issue of November 20, 1862

Married in Tuscaloosa, Ala. Nov 9, 1862, by the Rev. Dr. Summers, Mr. W. H. Sanborn, of Greensboro', Ala., to Miss Mary Emma Lowndes, of Tuskaloosa.

Died in Brundridge, Ala., on 20th Sept., little Kate Malone, youngest daughter of G. Y. and T. E. Malone, aged 2 years, 5 months and 5 days; and on the 25th Sept., her sister Sallie, aged 4 years and 11 months...the only children of their parents.

In Atlanta, Ga., Nov. 11, Loulie Pierce, youngest child of Rev. Geo. N. and Margaret R. MacDonnall.

On Oct. 22, Mary Josephine, eldest daughter of Joseph H. and Cornelia J. Harris, aged 2 years 2 months and 20 days.

In Augusta, Ga., Nov. 13, 1862, Sarah Frances, wife of C. Canning.

Rev. Benjamin Huger Capers, son of Maj. Wm. Capers was born in Sumter Dist., S. C., Oct. 24, 1805; in Feb. '31, married Miss Rebecca Greaves...father-in-law, Mr. Francis Greaves...died 17th Sept.

Susan A. C. Bodie, wife of Rev. Jesse P. Bodie, and daughter
of Rev. H. C. and Mary Herlong, died on 30th Oct., in her 33d
year.   J. S. C.
    Lt. Hugh B. Dawson, son of Dr. Thos H. Dawson, is dead...
Daniel Butler Bird of Jefferson co., Fla., was born at Edgefield
C. H., S. C., June 24, 1828, and was killed in the battle of
Perryville, 8th Oct....
    John A .Davis died in the army of Va., near Winchester on
15th Oct., in the 23d year of his age....
    Mrs. Mary V. Hamilton, wife of Mr. John H. Hamilton, died
near Columbus, Ga., on the 24th Oct.,in the 26th year of her
age....
    Andrew Taylor Arline was born 17th Jan., 1824, wounded, and
lived till 29th June....
    Wm. F. Bass, son of Ingram Bass was born in Hancock co, Ga.,
Jan. 25, 1840, and died Oct 1, 1862....
    Andrew Augustus Henderson was born in Jackson co., Ga., 18th
Nov. 1845. In his infancy his parents removed to Tempa, Fla.,
where he was read...died at Frankfort, Ky., 22d Sept....
    Mrs. Elizabeth Starke was born Dec. 23d, 1792, and died at
the home of G. A. B. Dozier, in Harris co., Ga., Oct. 26, 1862.
She was buried by a brother, Rev. Richard Dozier.
    C. W. Powell, son of G. W. and Mary Powell, died at his resi-
dence near Bovina, on 20th Sept., 1862....left wife and three
little boys.
    Charles Richards, son of William and Catharine Downing, late
of Columbus, Miss., born Feb. 15, 1835, fell in battle before
Mumfordsville, Ky., Sept. 14, 1862....
    Hannah Manila, wife of J. C. Rawls and daughter of Rev. Jesse
and Hannah Ellis, died Oct. 29, aged 30 years, 6 months and 1
day.
    Joel A. H. Alfriend, was born Aug. 15, 1829, and died 12th
Oct. 1862....
    Mr. Samuel Frink sen., died inBrunswick co., N. C.,on Nov. 3,
aged 76 years, 2 months and 1 day....

Issue of November 27, 1862

    Married in Caddo Parish, La., May 27, 1862, by Rev. D. McFar-
lin, Dr. W. W. Mitchell to Miss S. J. Bradley, daughter of Rev.
J. M. Bradley, formerly of the S. C. Conf.
    On 23d Oct, by the Rev. Wm. D. Martin, Mr. Joseph B. Jackson
to Miss Louisa M. Park, daughter of Dr.(?) A. Park, of Merriwether co., Ga.
    Oct 23, 1862, Capt. J. T. Baggett(?) to Miss Eliza A. Griffin,
all of Paulding co., Ga.
    Rev. John B. Warren died inButler co., Ala., aged about 36
years...born in Monroe co., Alabama....
    Jeptha H. Warren, 42d Ala. Vols., died at Columbus Hospital,
aged about 33 years...born in Monroe co., Ala.
    Mrs. Sarah A. V. Hayes, wife of Howard A. Hayes, and daughter
of Henry and Mary Walker, late of Greene co., Ga., died in Lexington, Ga., on August 29, in the 27th year of her age.
    Mrs. Louisa Frances McLean, wife of John C. McLean, died in
Barnesville, Ga., on 13 Oct. 1862, in the 34th year of her age.
    Capt. C. D. Pearson, son of Samuel and Lucinda Pearson, of
44th Ga. Regt., was killed at Sharpsburg, Sept. 17, in the 38th
year of his age...left wife and 4 little children.
    Lt. Col. Thomas C. Watkins, of 22d Regt. S. C. V., was born
in Anderson Dist., S. C., Nov. 1, 1825, killed in battle of
Boonsboro, Md., Sept. 14, 1862.
    Mrs. Susan Emma Griffin, wife of Thomas Griffin, and daughter
of M. C. and R. A. Shields, died in Midway, Barbour co., Ala.,

Oct. 16, 1862, in the 22d year of her age, born in Putnam co.,
Ga...left infant daughter.

James E. Land of York Dist., S. C., killed at Manassas, Aug.
30, 1862, in his 31st year.

Joseph H. McClesky, oldest son of Dr. G. L. McClesky, born
Nov. 2, 1842, and died near Malvern Hill, below Richmond, July 1.

John W. Hollingsworth born in Madison co., Miss., Nov. 22,
1834, died in Richmond, Aug. 27, 1862.

John B. Carpenter of Madison co., Miss., 18th Miss Regt.,
died in Richmond, May 10, 1862.

Henry Carpenter bro. of John B., died at Lynchburg, May 18,
in his 18th year.

Mrs. Virginia C. Jackson, wife of W. W. Jackson, and daughter
of Kinchen Thweatt, died in Culloden, Ga., Oct. 1, in her 28th year

Tribute of Respect to John F. Thrasher by Watkinsville ct.,
Ga. conf.

Issue of December 4, 1862

Married Nov. 26th, by Rev. Paul Derrick, Mr. John D. Keitt
and Miss Texas C. Wolfe, all of St. Matthews Parish, S. C.

Nov. 17th, at the residence of Col. A. J. Lane, near Sparta,
by Rev. Thomas T. Christian, Mr. James Bass and Miss Elizabeth
Buckner.

Nov. 20th, 1862, by Rev. C. E. Land, Mr. W. S. Horton, and
Miss J. E. O. V. Hunter, all of Lancaster dist., S. C.

Mrs. Elizabeth O. Cunningham, was born in Claiborne co.,
Ala., on 7th Dec. 1828, and died on 8th Nov. 1862....

Sgt. Truman E. Kellogg, 19th Regt. Ga. Vols, son of Mr.
George and Caroline Kellogg, of Coal Mountain, Forsyth co., Ga.,
was born Nov. 4, 1841...fell at Manassas 26th Aug.

W. W. Morris, son of Thomas and Elizabeth Morris, a member
of the Washington Reflemen, 7th La. Regt., died in Hospital near
Richmond, Va....

Eliza H. Hankins, wife of Dr. Summerfield Hankins, died at
Cook's Hammock, Sept. 30, in her 29th year....

Dr. John Gay died in Coweta co., Ga., on the 4th inst., in
the 37th year of his age...

Wm. J. Donald was born in Abbeville Dist., S. C., Aug. 13,
and died in Bartow co., Ga., at the residence of his father-in-
law, G. H. Gilreath, Oct. 25, 1862...left wife and three children.

Mrs. Emma G., wife of Dr. David P. Hines and daughter of Jno.
S. Coombs, late of Augusta, Ga., decd., died inBainbridge, Ga.,
on 1-Oct., in her 31st year...born in or near Augusta...

John Lucius Bellinger, son of James G. and Laura M. Varn,
was born Feb. 25th, 1851, and died Nov. 19, 1862....

Bro. Asa McLendon of the 9th Ga. Regt. died inWinchester,
Va., Oct. 20, 1862, aged 37 years.

Sgt. Wm. P. McCluer of Capt. Cox's Co., S. C. V., born in
Anderson Dist., S. C., June 9, 1832, and was killed in the battle
of Manassas, Aug. 30, 1862.

Sister Amey Smith was born in Va., Sept. 9, 1799, married
to Bro. Wm. D. Smith 10 Sept 1817, and died in Jackson co., Ga.,
Oct. 2, 1862....

Wm. Dailey, died at Windsor Hospital, Richmond, June 22,
in his 32d year....left wife and five small children.

Miss Mary L. C. Punch, daughter of Wm. F. and Mary Punch,
died Oct. 29, in her 13th year....

Jas. H. Tyler, son of Acy J. and Mary A. Tyler, was born in
Harris co., Ga., May 8, 1840, and died at the Mountain Hospital
in Tenn., 1 Aug 1862.

James M. Winchester of Capt. Turner's co., N. C. Vols., was
killed in the battle of Sharpsburg, Md., on 17 Sept. 1862....

Georgia Anna, eldest daughter of Rev. E. A. and Mrs. A. A.
Flowers died near Clinton, La., June 22, 1862, aged 12 years.

Thomas A. Faison, son of George S. and Eleanor A. Faison, died July 24, at Chattanooga, in the service.
Maj. James Harvey Dingle, Jr. was a native of Clarendon dist., S. C., Hampton Legion, S. C. V.....
Tribute of Respect to Maj. H. Dingle, Jr., who fell at the battle of Sharpsburg.
Tribute of Respect to Dr. Wm. C. Ware, of Starksville Mission, Lee co., Ga.,who was killed in Va., Aug. 28, 1862....
Tribute of Respect to Joseph a. Barlow, Esq., who died July 10, in the 42d year of his age....

Issue of December 11, 1862

Died in Orangeburg Dist., S. C., Nov. 17, 1862, Theophilus D. W. Baxter, son of D. H. and A. C. Baxter, aged 2 years, 10 months and a few days.
Whitefoord Andrew Smith, only son of the Rev. Dr. Whitefoord and Mrs.Eliza C. Smith was born in Wilmington, N. C. where his father was then stationed, on 25 July 1844...fell at Manassas Sat., Aug. 30....
Richard Ragin King, son of William and Mary M. King of Clarendon Dist., S. C., died in the hospital at Winchester, Va., on 11th Oct.,in the 27th year of his age...
Leigh H. Westcott, of Quincy, Fla., was born in Tallahassee, Fla., Feb. 10, 1842, and fell a martyr Sept. 17, 1862....
Mrs. Mary Atkinson was born in Darlington Dist., S. C.,Nov. 27, 1801, married to Thomas Atkinson, Esq., 4 Jan 1821, died 9 Nov 1862...
Arthur Sanford was born April 8, 1826, and died at Lauderdale Springs...left wife and 4 children, the eldest of shom, Martha Ann has since died, Nov. 10, aged about 18 years....
Francis J. Sanford, born June 19, 1832, and died Sept. 2, 1862...34th Regt. Ala. Vols.
John Morgan Sanford, son of John and Bethena Sanford, died 30th Oct. 1862, aged 8 years, 5 months and 15 days.
Sister Eliza C. Barton, relict of Thomas Barton, Orange Parish, S. C., died on 18th Nov., 1862, in the 65th year of her age... J. W. Kelly.
My brother, Samuel Parks Read, was born Jan. 24, 1830, and died Nov. 29, 1862.... W. T. R(ead).
John E. Pearson was born March 18, 1831...died 30 Sept 1862.
Clinton R. Evans, son of Rev. Uriah Evans, was born in Talladega co., Ala., Jan. 4, 1843...killed by accident at or near Cleveland, Tenn., Nov. 4, 1862....
John M. Hays died in Winchester, Va., Oct. 4, 1862, aged 22 years, 8 months and 2 dasy...native of Houston co., Ga., Co. E. 8d Ga. Vols....
Frances Catharine, youngest daughter of Col. David and Mrs. Nancy Hoke, was born Aug. 23, 1847, and died in Greenville, S. C., Nov. 20, 1862...
Mrs. Sarah Chapman, of Pickens Dist., S. C., died Oct. 31, 1862, in the 54th year of her age...left children.
Archibald Maulden died in Abbeville Dist., S. C.,Sept. 15, in his 56th year....
David Keller died near Abbeville C. H., S.·C., Sept. 26....
Cpl. Thomas H. Stutts of Co. G., 11th Regt. S. C. V., died at Hardeeville, Nov. 6, 1862, aged 17 years and 9 months.
W. H. Cason, son of W. B. And Parthenia Cason, 14th Regt. S. C. V., was killed Aug. 29, 1862, at Manassas, aged 19 years, 3 months and 3 days...
Judge Catlett Campbell of Merriwether co., Ga.,died Aug. 30, 1862...born Sept. 15, 1797....

Married on the 2d inst., near Walhalla, S. C., by the Rev. Fletcher Smith, Rev. P. M. Morgan, of the S. C. Conf., to Miss Mary V. Dickson, daughter of Capt. A. Dickson.

On the 6th of Nov., by the Rev. W. R. Bell, the Rev. Britton Sanders of the Ga. Conf., to Miss Sarah E. Daniel of Madison co., Ga.

By the Rev. T. J. Rutledge, Mr. Charles H. Greene to Miss Mattie Thompson, both of Union Springs, Ala., on the 25th Nov., 1862.

Died in Crawfordville, Ga.,on Tuesday the 9th inst., Charles B., only son of David F. and Mary E. Irving, aged 1 year, 5 months and 20 days.

Joseph Maner Lawton Senr., departed this life on the 5th inst., at his residence in St. Peter's Parish, Beaufort Dist...born in 1800...

C. S. Thomason son of Robert Thomason, died in Greenville Dist., S. C.,on the 11th Nov., in the 23d year of his age... Hampton's Legion....

S. S. Lever, son of John and Nancy Lever of Richland Dist., S. C., died in the hospital at Columbia, Nov. 10, 1862, in his 42d year...24th Regt. S. C. V.

Miss Eliza H. Branch died at the residence of her mother, in the 26th year of her age....

Wm. J. A. Gibson, a private of Co. F., 12th Regt. S. C. V., died 12th Nov., at the Chimborazo Hospital, from wound at Sharpsburg, Md., 17th Oct, in the 25th year of his age...

Emma Caroline Jones, only daughter of John H. and Leonora T. Jones, died on 20th Oct., aged 6 years, 4 months and 11 days.

David Cowper died at Columbia, S. C., born Aug. 31, 1827... left wife and six children.

Mary Jane Andrews was born April 28, 1854, and died Nov. 2, 1862....

D. T. M. Shields died Nov. 7, 1862, aged 27 years...in the service one year.

Robt Randolph Gilbert was born in South Carolina, April 7, 1807, moved to Putnam co., Ga., and then to Russell co., Ala., where he died Nov. 13, 1862....

W. R. Thomas, son of Rev. J. P. Thomas, of Fayette co., Ala., born in Blount co., Ala., Oct. 2, 1834....died 7th of August.

Maynie, oldest child of Mary T. and P. F. Stevens, died in Oxford, Ga., 9th Nov.,aged 6 years and 9 months.

John W. Lumpkin, son of John and Sallie Lumpkin, died at Tazewell, Tenn., on 27th Sept., 1862...born in Jones co., Ga., in 1829...moved to Pike co., Ala...left wife and two little children.

Nathan B. Robertson, son of James and Hester Ann Robertson, died 27th June from wound in the battles before Richmond.

Caroline Josephine, daughter of Capt. Arnold and Sarah Catharine Parlor, died at the residence of her father, in the upper part of Charleston Dist., 25th Sept., 1862, in the 8th year of her age.

Brother Joseph P. Smith died Nov. 5, 1862...born in Anson co., N. C., but for some years past a citizen of Spartanburg....

Maj. Harvey Wheat was born in Columbia co., Ga.,in 1786, and died Oct. 2, 1862....

Tribute of Respect to Major Harvey Wheat by Lincolnton Ct., Ga.

Tribute of Respect to 2d Lt. C. E. Coner, who died Sept. 27, by Co. C., 35th Ga. Regt....

Tribute of Respect to Hugh B. Dawson, from Columbus, Ga.

Issue of December 25, 1862

Married in Columbia, S. C., on the morning of Dec. 11, by Rev. W. A. Gamewell, Major William M. Gist of Union Dist., to Miss Mollie S. Black of Columbia.

By Rev. R. B. Lester, Dec. 10, 1862, Mr. James M. Rowland to Miss Victoria Burton, all of Burke co., Ga.

Died Ashley H. son of C. C. and James Griffin, born May 5, 1858, died Dec. 3, 1862.

Mrs. Eliza Jane Thweat died in Enon, Ala., 30th Nov., 1862, born in Jacksonville, Ala., Dec. 5, 1837, married to Mr. Fletcher G. Thweatt on 15 Nov 1859...daughter of Mrs. M. A. Brown, a widowed sister of Rev. Thos. P. Crymes, of the Ala. Conf....

Rev. P. M. Huckabee of Fannin co., Ga., son of Joseph and Delilah Huckabee, was born in N. C., Feb. 23, 1831...died in Hospital in Richmond....

Joel H. Legg was born in Wayne co., Ky., Jan. 17, 1827, and died Oct. 18, 1862..married to Miss Elizabeth Wilbanks, Sept. 3, 1857, wounded 13 Aug 1862 and died thereafter....

Eugene Summerfield Dickson was born in Covington, Ga., 9th Sept. 1843, died in Nicholasville, Ky. Nov. 16, 1862....

Armour James Carpenter died at Manassas, Ga. (sic), 12th Nov. 1862, in the 21st year of his age....

John M. Sexton, a citizen of Gwinnett co., Ga.,and in 42d Regt. Ga. Vols, died at Bean's Station, Tenn., 4th Nov., in the 40th year of his age....

Mrs. Margaret Neill, wife of Thomas Neill, and daughter of Isom and Nancy Dean, and widow of Shadrach East, died in Laurens Dist., S. C.,Oct. 18, 1862, aged 50 years 5 months and 3 days... married 16th Oct., last, and died 18th.

George F. Byrd fell in the last battle at Manassas, aged 19 years and 2 days...

Mrs. Ann Wright was born in Baldwin co., 12th Oct., 1808, and died in Thomasville, Ga.,18th Sept. 1862....

Mrs. Elleighimare, daughter of Wesley and Elizabeth King, of Wilkinson co., Ga., died on 9th ult., in the 18th year of her age....

Issue of January 1, 1863

Married by Rev. Atticus G. Haygood, in Trinity Church, Atlanta, Wed., Dec. 17, Mr. James B. Garrison to Miss Isabella Thomas, daughter of the late Rev. T. L. Thomas, of this place.

In Atlanta, Ga.,Dec. 23, by Rev. L. Lawshe, Mr. A. R. Watson, of Leesburg, Va., to Miss F. A. Latimer, of Atlanta, Ga.

In St. Paul's Church, Columbus, Ga., Dec. 4, by Dr. L. Pierce, Rev. Arminius Wright, of the Ga. Conf., to Mrs. Amelia Taft.

In Perry, Ga.,Dec. 18, at the residence of John M. Giles, Esq., by Rev. W. H. J. Sistrunk, Mr. H. B. Laseure to Miss Ann J. Jenkins.

At Fort Valley, Ga., Dec. 9, by Rev. T. B. Russell, Mr. W. E. Brown to Miss Emma Hollingshead.

On 8th Dec.,by Rev. W. S. Black, Mr. W. A. C. Doggett, of Spartanburg, to Miss Sallie A.Moore, of Cheraw, S. C.

Issue of January 8, 1863

Died in Bennettsville, on 18th Oct., little Franky, son of Mrs. C. C. Douglass and the late A. H. Douglas, aged 2 years and 5 mos.

The Rev. Sidney Myers Smith, son of Rev: John M. and Nancy Smith, was born in Franklin co., Ga., April 22, 1818, and died

Savannah, Ga., Nov., 4, 1862... P. P. Smith.

Mrs. Martha Ann Hill, wife of Major James M. Hill, of Chambers co., Ala., died on 25th Nov.,in the 46th year of her age...

Thomas Preston Samford, younger son of the Rev. Thos. Samford, formerly of the Ga. Conf., now residing in Marshall, Texas, born in 1837, in LaGrange, Ga...1st Texas Regt., died 11th Oct. 1862 in Sharpsburg.... Wm. F. Samford.

Nicholas J. Drake, eldest son of Dr. John C. and Mary A. Drake, born in Thomaston, Ga., May 11, 1840, died Nov. 8, 1862.

Mr. T. S. Chandler, Capt. Brand's co., 6th S. C. Regt., son of Mrs. M. E. Chandler, of Williamsburg Dist., S. C., aged 26 years, died 27th Sept., from battle of South Mountain.

George Southwell, son of Simeon and Hester A. Tyner, of Butler co., Ala., was born inEffingham co., Ga.,24th March 1834, died about the middle of Sept., 1862.

Wm. E. Hightower, son of Daniel P. Hightower, was born in Chambers co., Ala., Feb. 3, 1846, and died Sept. 22, 1862 in Warrenton, Va....

Mrs. Rachel Dry, relict of the late Daniel Dry, of Cabarras co., N. C., died 19th Dec., in the 72d year of her age....

Thomas Baker Irvine, son of William and Eliza Irvine, of Oxford, Ga., was born in Jackson, Butts co., 4th May, 1839, and fell in the battle of Crampton's Pass, Sept. 14, in his 23d year.

Sgt. James F. Williams of Capt. Langford's Co., 6th Fla. Regt., son of Roland Williams, was born in Madison co., Fla., and died in the hospital at Mumforsville, Ky., Sept. 30, 1862, in his 21st year.

Mrs. Mary R. Harris, wife of E. S. Harris senr., died in LaGrange, Ga.,7th Dec. 1862, in her 68th year...

Mrs. Sarah Maria Ingerville, daughter of Mr. and Mrs. Daniel Mickler, was born in Camden co., Ga., July 10, 1838, and died in Suwannee co., Fla., Oct. 29, 1862...

Lt. Thos J. Henderson of 43d Ga. Regt., died at Stone Mtn., Ga., 8th Oct., 1862, in his 22nd year.

Leonard Chapman Tart, son of James and J. G. Tart, was born in Marion Dist., S. C., 20th Oct., 1840....

John Hebbard Mickler son of Daniel Mickler, was born March 23, 1835 in Camden co., Ga., and died at his father's house, in Suwanee co., Fla., Nov. 26, 1862...

Mrs. Artemesia Mullins, wife of Dr. J. C. Mullins, died Oct. 11, 1862, at her father's Mr. Deberry, Marion dist., S. c., aged 27 years.

Matthew F.Miller died in Talbot Valley, Ga...on Dec. 13, '62, in the 67th year of his age....

Francis M. Biggers was born in York dist., S. C.,in 1817, - and died in Muscogee co., Ga...left wife and seven children.

Mrs. Eliza J. Landrum, wife of brother L. L. Landrum, and daughter of Thos. J. and Mary Green, was born Dec. 4, 1838, and died in Fairburn, Campbell co., Ga., Dec. 5, 1862...married 9th Jan. 1861...

Sgt. David J. Wallis, of 38th Ga. Regt, aged 29 years, died from a wound at Manassas....

Capt. David A. Lee was born in Walton co., Ga., Jan. 1841, and died in Oxford, Sept. 7, 1862....

Benj. W. Wells in 13th S. C. Regt, died in the Winder Hospital, Richmond, Oct. 29, in his 26th year....

C. W. Brannan was born Nov.6, 1842, and died Dec. 6, 1862, Lynchburg, Va...born in Spartanburg dist., S. C....

George McKinley, son of Martin B. Dye, was born in Suggsville, Ala., April 18, 1848, and died in Clarke co., Ala.,Nov. 23, 1862.

Jas. L. Eaton son of Mr. and Mrs. Eaton of Euharlee, Ga., fell in the battle of Fredericksburg....

Lucy A. Wadsworth, daughter of B. and S. B. Conine, was born in Greene co., Ga., and died 17th Nov., at Tallapoosa co., Ala.

Susan C. Caruthers, wife of Freeman W. Caruthers, and daughter of Washington and Rebecca Rogers, died 16th Dec., 1862....

John Murphy, died in Hamilton, Harris co., Ga., Nov. 29, 1862, in the 64th year of his age....

Issue of January 15, 1863

Married on the 1st Jan., in Lancaster District, S. C., by Rev. J. W. Puett, Rev. J. L. Stoudemire of the S. C. Conf., to Miss Betty E. Coffee, of the above district.

On the 4th inst., by Rev. Wm. W. Mood, Capt. Thomas J. China, of S. C. V. to Miss Sarah Ann, daughter of Mr. James D. Gordon, of Williamsburg Dist., S. C.

By Rev. J. W. Yarbrough on 4th Jan., Lt. B. A. Grist of Marietta, Ga., to Miss Elizabeth A. King, of Atlanta, Ga.

In Columbus, Miss., 18th Dec., by Rev. P. P. Neely, Capt. Nathaniel D. Cross, C. S. A., to Miss Martha, daughter of Dunstan Banks, Esq.

By the same, Surgeon Charles S W Price, C. S. A., to Miss Mollie Dowse, daughter of Col. George H. Harris.

At Cheraw, S. C., on Sept. 18, 1862, by Rev. E. W. Thompson, Mr. Joseph Henry Cadien, to Miss Margaret Covington.

At Cheraw, S. C., Oct. 2, 1862, by Rev. Charles Taylor, Mr. John J. Pickard to Miss Mary Jane, daughter of Mr. Joseph Cadien.

In Marlboro District, S. C., Jan.,5, 1863, by Rev. Charles Taylor, Dr. James Patterson of Williamsburg District, to Miss Rebecca E., daughter of Henry Easterling, Esq.

On 9th inst., by Rev. C. A. Fulwood, Capt. Jacob W. Caracker, of C. S. A., to Miss Elizabeth Bayne, of Baldwin co., Ga.

At Bellwood, Upson co., Ga., 6th Jan., by Rev. W. R. Branham, Miss Lula W. Kendall, to James H. Rogers.

Died in Monroe co., N. C., Dec. 21, 1862, William Hayden, son of D. F. And Susan Hayden, aged 9 years.

Also, on December 24th, Ira Jane, daughter of the above parents, aged 2 years.

In Thomasville, Ga., Dec. 2, 1862, Auston G. Holloway, aged 9 years, 5 months and 8 days.

Also of the same fever, on 17th Dec., 1862, Robert M. Holloway, aged 3 years, 8 months and 23 days, both sons of David J. and Sarah A. Holloway.

Little Willie Shields, daughter of A. J. And Eliza Shields, of Noxubee co., Miss., died on 1st Jan., 1863, aged 2 years, 4 months and 6 days.

Mr. Charles Henry Equen died on 8th Dec., 1862, near Vicksburg, Miss., in his 21st year.

Also, Mr. Joseph Daniel Equen his brother at his late home, Judge Hoover's, near Summit, Miss., in his 18th year.

Mrs. Eliza, wife of James G. Stone, died in Burke co., Ga., Nov. 13, 1862, in her 49th year....

Mrs. Sarah Jane Powers, wife of Rev. William Ira Powers, was born in Wayne co., Ky., May 1st, 1833...died 16 Nov 1862.

Mrs. Sarah Frances Canning, youngest daughter of the late Charles Canning, died in Augusta, Ga., Nov. 13, 1862...when about 18 years old, she came to Charleston, where she married....

Charles Fletcher Williams, son of Elijah and Martha J. Williams, and grandson of the late Rev. Charles F. and Amelia Patillo, was born in Haynesville, Ga.,and died at Frederick City, Md., Oct., 2, 1862, of wounds from Sharpsburg...8th Ga. Vols....

Aaron Birdett Asbill of Edgefield Dist., S. C., on 25th Oct., 1862, near Knosville, Tenn., in his 34th year...10th Regt. S.C.V.

91

E. Madison Waldrop died at Murfreesboro, Tenn. Nov. 9, 1862, from
Polk Co., N. C. His brother Thomas H. Waldrop, fell in battle
1st July 1862....
     Miss Arabella Davis, died in Gwinnett co., Ga.,9 Nov. 1862,
in the 42d year of his age... W. W. Oslin.
     Mrs. Theodocia Boineau died 6th of Dec., 1862...left husband
and child.
     John Derrick was born in Lexington Dist., S. C., moved to Ala.
in 1831, and died in Montgomery co., Ala., Dec. 12, 1862, nearly
80 years of age... D. Derrick.
     Woodson Ligon, son of Mrs. Permelia Ligon of Bartow co., Ga.,
died in Va., while on a march in December, from Port Royal to
Fredericksburg....
     Mrs. Sarah Rumph, wife of Christopher Rumph, of St. George's
Parish, Colleton Dist., S. C., was born Jan. 11, 1803, and died
at the residence of her daughter, Mrs. West, Cuthbert, Ga., Jan.
1, 1863.
     John H. Townsend son of P. H. and Cicilly Townsend died at
London, Tenn., Nov. 28, 1862, in his 21st year...
     Willis Hall died in Sparta, Ga., Dec. 1, 1862, aged 12 years.
Peyton Ward Sr. was born in Va., August 1, 1796, and died in
Baldwin co., Ga., Dec. 18, 1862...
     John L. Boyd, 10th Ga. Regt, son of James and Milia Boyd,
of Fayette co., Ga., died at 2d Ga. Hospital, Richmond, 30th Nov.
1862, in his 21st year....
     Laura Dunn eldest daughter of H. V. and Mary Dunn, died near
Clinton, La., on Dec. 7, 1862, aged about 17 years....
     Matthew E. Hobbs, of 5th Ga. REgt, died Nov. 6, in Tenn.,
aged about 24.
     Mrs. Sarah J. Thomas died in Columbia co., Ga., Nov. 30,
1862 at about 16 years of age.
     Tribute of Respect by Sabbath School, Perry, Ga., to John
Shellman Talley....

Issue of January 22, 1863

     Married in Shelby, N. C., Dec. 18, 1862, by the Rev. O. A.
Darby, Mr. Lawrence Moore of York Dist., to Miss Mary Miller,
daughter of Dr. W. J. T. Miller, of the former place.
     On the 4th of December, by the Rev. D. W. Scale, at the bride's
Uncle, Mr. John Fork of Lexington Dist., to Miss Julia Hook,
of Orangeburg Dist.
     In Troup co., Ga., Dec. 18, 1862, by Rev. J. A. Palmer, Mr.
Richard Lyons, of Polk co., Ga. to Miss Mary E. Harwell, daughter
of W. J. Harwell.
     On Jan. 8,1863, by Rev. E. S. Smith, Capt. John C. McKenzie
of the 10th Ala. Regt. to Miss Eliza F. Parks, of Fayetteville,
Alabama.
     In Atlanta, Ga., on Dec. 30th, 1862, by Rev. H. H. Parks, Mr.
Robert Wallace to Miss Anna L. Patch, all of this place.
     By the same, on Jan. 7th, 1862, in Trinity M. E. Church,
Mr. Patrick H. Wade to Miss Josephine Thrower, all of this place.
     On 7th Dec., 1862, by Rev. H. C. Parsons, Dr. H. W. Robinson,
of the Anson Guard, 14th N. C. Troops, to Miss E. Kate Smith,
daughter of Col. W. G. Smith, of Ansonville, N. C.
     Died Little James Manson Glass, son of Capt. Glass, Co. E.,
53d Ga., and grandson of Rev. J. E. Evans, at his grandfather's
in Macon, Ga.,Jan. 9, 1862, aged 2 years and 5 months.
     In Tuskaloosa co., Ala., James Sharper Gregory and Harriet
Florence Rosa Gregory, children of Rev. J. T. M. Gregory.
     Mary Fair Spence, my mother, died in Pleasant Hill, Lowndes
co., Ala., Jan. 1, 1862...born in Abbeville Dist., S. C., March
22, 1793, daughter of Archibald and Mary McMullen...moved to

Pickens co., Ala., and from thence to Kemper co., Miss....J. A. S.
Mrs. Rebecca Brown, wife of Rev. Manning Brown, of the S. C.
Conf., and daughter of Rev. H. D. Green of Sumter Dist., S. C.,
born July 12, 1834, married Feb. 6, 1862, and died Dec. 27, 1862.
Rev. Henry Holmes Brown was born in Washington co., Fla., and
at an early age moved with his parents to Jackson co., where he
died 22d Dec. 1862, in his 28th year....
George T. Weathersbee was born in Jasper co., Ga., 19th Aug.,
1839...died in Savannah, 25th Dec. 1862, 1st Ga. Regt....
John N. Halliday was born in Jones co., Ga., in 1812, moved
to Montgomery co., Ala., in 1829, and died on 21st Dec., 1862.
George W. Waller died Dec. 30, 1862, in Pike co., Ga., in
his 49th year....53d Ga. Vols.
Susan Matilda Hay, daughter of Wm. F. and Susan J. Hay, was
born in Tishomingo, Miss, and died 5th Jan. in her 18th year
at the residence of brother John Patterson near Stylesboro, Bartow co., Ga....
Miss S. E. Smith was born Oct. 5, 1842, and died Oct. 28,
1862...daughter of Rev. W. R. Smith, and Mrs. E. Smith of Marlboro Dist., S. C...
Lt. W. J. Solomon of Co. B. 14th Regt, of Wilkinson co., Ga.,
killed at the battle of Fredericksburg on 13th Dec....Gordon,
Ga.

Issue of January 29, 1863

Married on 14th Jan., by Rev. Morgan Bellah, Mr. John T.
Chambers, C. S. A., to Miss Mary J. Chambles, of Barnsville, Ga.
By Rev. C. A. Moore, on 1st Jan., Mr. J. J. L. Smith of
Wilkinson co., to Miss S. E. J. Snell of Johnson co.
By Rev. J. W. Abernath, Dec. 20th, 1862, Mr. J. B. Squiers of
the 30th Regt. N. C. Vols., to Miss M. A. Stevens, all of Meck-
lenburg, N. C.
Capt. Walter S. Brewster died near Fredericksburg on 14th
Dec., 1862, in the 30th year of his age...born in Maine, 3d April
1833. On the death of his parents, an uncle, then residing in
Charleston, took him in....
Rev. Stephen Ellis was born March 25, 1784 in Pendleton Dist.,
S. C., and removed to Cass co., Ga., 1838....
Capt. W. F. Jones of 22d Regt Ga. Vols., my brother, has
fallen...six brothers, son of Rev. S. G. Jones of Chambers co.,
Ala., volunteered and joined the 22d Regt. Ga. Vols. Wesley was
one of these...died in Baltimore, Oct. 25, 1862, from wounds at
Sharpsburg, on 17th Sept...R. H. Jones.
Clement Fletcher Maddox son of Rev. P. N. Maddux, was born
near Warrenton, Ga., May 18, 1836, and was killed at Fredericks-
burg, Va., 13th Dec. 1862...
Rev. Obadiah C. Gibson a native of Warren co., Ga., died in
Griffin, Dec. 29, 1862, aged 53 years....
Wilbur Fisk Leight, son of Rev. Dr. Leigh of Floyd co., Ga.,
died in his 27th year, at Warrenton, Va., on 25th Sept. last
from wounds at Manassas....
William John Gramling was born August 21, 1836, died near
Culpepper C. H., Va., Dec. 1, 1862....
Marcus Gramling, his brother, six years younger died in
Winchester, Va., 17th Oct., 1862.
Henry E. Townsend of 8th Regt. S. C. V., died in Winder
Hospital, Richmond, on 3d Dec., in his 22d year...
Sister Jane E. Ruff died Nov. 19, 1862, in Richland Dist.,
S. C., in his 58th year...About 18 years ago, lost her husband,
D. H. Ruff, Esq., left her with nine children.
Mrs. Margaret, relict of Edward Hays, died on 16th Dec.,
in Barnwell Dist., in the 68th year of her age...leaves five

children....

Mrs. Mary Gregory, was born in N. C., May 4, 1801, and married to Louis Gregory, Oct. 7, 1824, moved to Florida soon after, and died Jan. 9, 1863, in her 62d year... A. Davis.

Mrs. Jane Calhoun Linton, wife of Rev. Thos. Linton, of Madison co., Fla., died 23d Nov 1862, aged 56 years and 10 months. born in Abbeville Dist., S. C., Jan. 1806, married Jan. 1831, and soon after moved to Fla....

Dr. A. O. Walker was born Nov. 9, 1820, and died January 10, 1863....

Mrs. Sidney N. Buckner died in Hancock co., on 10th Jan., in her 39th year....

Nathaniel Breedlove, died in Hancock co., Ga., at his son-in-law;s, Michael Butler, Jan. 15, 1863, in his 63 year...born in Prince Edward co., Va., and moved to Ga. when quite young. J. V. M. M.

Issue of February 5, 1863

Married on 6th January 1863, by the Rev. David Nolan, Mr. W. N. Dickson of Henry co., Ga., to Miss C. A. Y. Starr, of Spaulding co., Ga.

In Macon, Ga.,on the 25th Jan., by Rev. T. T. Christian, James R. Collins, of Milledgeville, and Mary Griss, of Macon, Ga.

On January 18th, at Sunny Level, Tallapoosa co., Ala., by Rev. W. D. Matthews, Mr. James Young to Miss Julia J. B., daughter of Judge Randel Morgan, of Harris co., Ga.

On 15th Jan., by Rev. J. Hammond, Mr. John Sighler, aged 71 years to Miss Narcissa Morris, aged 51 years, all of Lexington District.

Died in Gilmer co., Ga., Jan. 15, 1863, Hellena Emogene, daughter of D. E. And Priscilla An Slagle, aged 4 years, 5 months and 16 days.

Died in Manning, S. C., on 14th instant, Willie Edward, aged 15 months and Dora Alice on the 24th, aged 3 years and 4 months and 2 days, children of Lazarus W. and Mary M. Bell

James H. Southall was a native of Gates co., N. C., the son of a Methodist preacher in the Va. Conf...For many years, he has been a well known resident of Columbus, Miss... J. J. H.

Mrs. Elizabeth Kennedy, wife of James Kennedy, Esq.,died in Greene co., Ala., on 20th Dec. 1862, in her 55th year...born in Abbeville Dist., S.C., and removed with her parents to the neighborhood of her late residence in 1818. In 1824 married to James Kennedy... J. J. H.

Sgt. Thos Elijah Dawkins, youngest son of Capt. James and Mrs. F. S. Dawkins of Union Dist., S. C., was born Jan. 1, 1839, and was killed at Sharpsburg....

Robert Augustus Brooks, son of Dr. J. D. and Maria T. Brooks, of Belleview, Talbot co., Ga., a member of 7th Regt. Ga. Vols, died in Farmville, Va., in his 21st year....

Norphlet Mizell, Sgt. Major of the 33d Ala Regit. fell wounded in the battle of Murfreesboro, and died the next day Jan. 1, 1863. born in Stewart co., Tenn, and was, I think, in his 19th year... W. J. Sasnett.

Henry Clark was born in Lancaster Dist., S. C., and died in Anderson District, S. C., Oct. 25th, 1862, in his 62d year....

Mrs. Nancy Freeman, widow of Foster Freeman was born in N. C., August 20th, 1782, and died November 3, 1862, at the residence of her son, Francis A. Freeman, inSpaulding co., Ga., in the 81st year of her age...In August 1809, married to Foster Freeman. W. M. Blanton.

John E.Sappington of Troup co., Ga., died in one of the Hospitals in Richmond, Va., in his 21st year.... R. W. Dixon.

Fordham McKewn, Palmetto Sharpshooters of Orangeburg, S. C.,
died Dec. 14, 1862, at his post... J. H. J.
Mrs. Elizabeth M. Greene, wife of Robert T. Greene, and
eldest daughter of Wm. Perry, late of Merriwether co., Ga., died
in Clay co., Ga., 16th Jan. 1863, in her 63d year... James M. N.
Low.
Zadoc T. Timmons, was born Nov. 17, 1811, and died at Montezuma, Ga., Dec. 21, 1862... W. S. Turner.
Middleton J. K. Murray, was born May 5, 1841, died July 12,
1862...died at his father's in Charleston Dist.
Joel Asbury Murray was born Dec. 3, 1845, and died Aug. 23,
1862. These were both sons of Arnold Murray who had nine sons.
J. W. Abernathy.

Issue of February 12, 1863

Married in Perry, Ga., Feb. 6th, 1863, by Rev. George C.
Clarke, Mr. J. F. Hook of Orangeburg District, S. C. to Miss
M. C. Houser, daughter of L. M. Houser, of the former place.
In Cotton Valley, Ala., on 1st Feb., by Rev. A. Tatom, Miss
E. M. Davis and Iredell Johnston.
In Augusta, Ga., at Asbury, on 8th Feb., by Rev. D. D. Cox,
Mr. James W. Johnson and Miss Harriet E. Eply.
Also by the same, on 5th Feb., Mr. Benjamin Daniel and Miss
Letitia Tice, all of Augusta, Ga.
In Athens, Ga., Jan. 13th, by Rev. H. J. Adams, Dr. Clifford
A. Stiles, of Savannah, and Miss Anna Wyley, daughter of the late
Major N. A. Adams.
In Augusta, Ga., Feb. 5th, 1863, by Rev. A. J. Huntington,
Mr. C. Thomas Craig to Miss Agnes E. Rose, both of Charleston,
S. C.
Died in Greene co., Ga., Nov. 30, 1862, Mary Adaline, aged
4 years 3 months and 14 days, children of Dr. John W.and Sallie
Wright.
Brother A. P. Peavy was born 14 May 1833...died 8 th Nov
1862....
James C. Pelot of 7th Fla. Regt., son of Col. Jno. C. Pelot,
of Fla., died Sept. 6th, 1862, at Rock Castle Ford, Ky., in his
33d year.
James W. Smith of Lexington Dist., S. C., died in Richmond,
in his 23d year....
Sister Sarah S. Shockley died at her father's residence in
Covington, Ga., Dec. 30, 1862...married not quite three years,
left a husband and an infant child only a few weeks old... W. J.
Parks.
S. H. S. Starr died in Oxford, Ga., on 21st instant, in his
30th year....
W. H. A. Davenport, Orderly Sgt. 25th Ga. Regt, died at
Lynchburg, Va., Dec. 31....
Dr. Newdaygate Augustus Moreland was born in Jones co., Ga.,
Oct. 13, 1822, and died in Corinth, Heard co., Ga., Dec. 25, 1862,
leaving a widow and five children.
His sister Mrs. Mary Tucker Miller, relict of Joseph Miller,
decd., was born in Jones co., Oct. 30, 1820, and died in Corinth
Dec. 31, 1862, leaving seven children...
They were the children of the Rev. Isaac Tucker and Mrs.
Penelope Moreland.
Her youngest son Joseph Newdaygate Miller followed her to
the tomb in less than three weeks. He died Jan.16, 1863....
Berry L. Holliday, eldest son of D. N. and Levina Holliday,
was born in Chambers co., Ala., 2nd Nov. 1840...died 31st Oct.
1862. C. S. J.

Mrs. Sarah May, relict of John May, late of Camden co., died 7th Jan., 1862, near Valdosta, Lowndes co., Ga., in her 71st year.

Rev. Ephraim Pennington died in Campbell co., Ga., on 23rd Dec. 1862, in his 71st year...leaves a widow and several daughters, all married, some in Georgia, some in Texas, and three sons, one in the army from Texas and two from Ga. D. P. Jones.

Rev. William Wommack Hendrick was born in Va., Dec. 17, 1788, settled in Talladega co., Ala., in 1837, and died Jan. 17, 1863.

George A. Smith, son of Alex. and Judith Smith, of Houston co., Ga., died Nov. 28, 1862, in his 21st year... G. C. Clarke.

Capt. John Fletcher Vinson was born in Crawford co., Ga., Dec. 6, 1829, where he died Jan. 12, 1863... W. J. S.

Mrs. Frances R. Johnson, wife of Capt. Abner Johnson, and daughter of James R. and Martha G. Pickett, was born in Fairfield Dist., S. C., July 16, 1814, and died at Ocala, Marion co., Fla., Jan. 25, 1863....left husband and children. H. F. Smith.

Jacob Moses Varner was born in Beaufort Dist., S. C., May 30th, 1798, and died in Marion co., Fla., Jan. 18, 1863. H. F. Smith.

N. D. Halley of Buena Vista Guards, 2d Ga. Regt, son of Benjamin and Rebecca Halley died at Wilmington, NC, of wounds, aged 22 years.

Samuel W. Grant was born in Columbia co., Ala., 9th Nov., 1842, and died at Perryville, Ky...

Mrs. Martha Samantha Flynt, daughter of Beniah and Cuzziah Pye, and wife of Franklin Flynt, was born 11th April 1841, and died at her father's residence, Monroe co., Ga., 15 Jan 1863.

Jas. M. Pearson, son of Thomas G. and Susan H. Pearson, was born in Heard co., Ga., and died in Danville, Va., Nov. 9, 1862, in his 24th year... W. D. Matthews.

Miss Alice C. Richbourg, eldest daughter of F. R. and M. A. Richbourg, of Clarendon Dist., S. C., died Dec. 16, 1862, in her 18th year...

Dennis McClendon was for 24 years a member of the M. E. Church, South.... Geo. C. Clarke.

Mrs. Matilda A. Pennington, wife of Wm. B. Pennington, and daughter of Wm. and Elizabeth Davenport, died inCampbell co., Ga., Jan. 3, 1863, in her 39th year...

Mrs. Mary Harmon died in Abbeville, S. C., 1st Nov. 1862, at about 80 years of age....

Tribute of Respect by Trinity conf., Atlanta, to Bro. Green B. Haygood, who died 24 Dec 1862....

Issue of February 19, 1863

Married by Rev. W. A. Clarke, on the 8th inst., in the Methodist Church, at Lexington C. H.., Lt. Alfred J. Norris, of the State Military Academy, to Miss Mary J. Fox, of Lexington, S. C.

By Rev. H. H. Parks, in Atlanta, Ga., Feb. 8th, James M. Knapp and Miss Julia T. Alexander.

By the same, Feb. 8th, Wm. Wimbly, Confederate Army, and Miss Elory Ann C. Watts.

By the same, Geo. W. Martin, Confederate Army, and Miss Sallie M. Davis, January 28th.

Died on January 13, 1863, David Thomas, infant son of Rev. Wm. and Mrs. M. A. Carson, aged 13 months.

In Greenwood, Fla., Benjamin Hill Robinson, only child of H. J. and S. A. Robinson, aged 3 months and 18 days.

In Milledgeville, Ga., on 9th inst., James, youngest son of Mrs. Adda M. and Hon. James Jackson, aged 1 year and 7 months.

Cpl. J. H. Allison died in Marion Dist., S. C., on Jan. 27th, in his 38th year... G. H. Wells.

Mrs. H. M. Mitchell, wife of Dr. R. V. Mitchell, was born June 22, 1836, and died at Mt.Meigs, Ala., Jan. 22, 1863...reared in LaFayette, Ala....

Henry Little, son of Rev. John J. and Eliza Little was born in Harris co., Ga., Jan. 3rd, 1845, and died in Richmond, Va., Jan. 16, 1863... D. D. Cox.

Mrs. Martha J. E. Fields, daughter of Major E. C. Eggleston, of Columbus, Miss., was born in Rutherford county, Tenn., March 29, 1835, married to Dr. B. F. Fields, in 1852, and passed from earth Jan. 26, 1863....

Mr. Samuel Woodruff was born in Surry co., N. C., and died Jan. 26th, 1863, near Silver Creek, Floyd co., Ga., aged 70 years....While his father was lying a corpse in the house, his son M. Woodruff died, aged 30(?) years... John W. Reynolds.

Mrs. Sarah E. Durrell, wife of Richard J. D. Durrell, and youngest daughter of Charity and James Banks, Senr., decd., of Elbert co., Ga., died on 9th Dec....

Seaborn C. O'Neill was born Sept. 6, 1833, and died Nov. 4th, 1857. Wm. D. O'Neil was born Sept. 12, 1832, and died Oct. 27, 1862. Andrew W. O'Neil was born Sept. 9, 1847, and died Jan. 26, 1863... Julia Ann O'Neil their mother was born Oct. 1810, and died Jan. 11, 1863....

Sgt. John T. Sherwood fell wounded at the battle of Fredericksburg, Dec. 13, 1862, in his 22d year....

S. W. Myrick was born in Warren co., Ga., in 1802, and died in Schley co., Ga.,in his 61st year.... B. F. Breedlove.

Mrs. Mary A. Hooker was born Sept. 3d, 1810, married August 1, 1830, to Capt. Wm. B. Hooker...died near Brooksville, Fla., 2d January, 1863..left husband and children....

Wm. Blanton was born in Lincoln co., Ga., and died in Talbot co., Dec. 11, 1862, in his 65th year....

Mrs. Sarah Parker, wife of G. H. Parker was born May 12, 1827, in Dooly co., Ga.,and died Feb. 1, 1863, in Henry co., Ala... joined the Baptist Church in 1846, and joined the M. E. Church in July 1861... John D.Clark.

Wm. A. Chandalier, of Fayette co., Ga., son of Wyatt and Ellen Chandalier, died on 25th Jan., 1863 at Howard's Grove Hospital, Richmond, Va.,in his 22d year....

George A. Griffin, son of Lewis and E. G. Griffin, died in the hospital at Hardeeville, in his 25th year....

Basil S. Braswell of Co. A., 38th Ga. Regt., was born in Anderson Dist., S. C., on March, 1838, and died at the hospital at Richmond, Va....

Issue of February 26, 1863

Married on 27th January, 1863, by Rev. A. M. Chrietzberg, Capt. T. E. Raysor, C. S. A., to Miss Bellzona Bowyer, all of St. Georges, S. C.

On 18th, near Eatonton, Ga., by Rev. Geo. G. N. MacDonell, Mr. Wm. M. Tucker of Midway, Ga., to Miss Elvira E. Reid, eldest daughter of James L. Reid, esq., of Eatonton, Ga.

February 17th, by Rev. G. W. F. Price, Mr. Nich L. Redd, of columbus, Ga., to Miss Rebecca Catharine, eldest daughter of Rev. F. G. Ferguson, of Tuskegee, Ala.

Died on Feb. 4th, 1863, Willie D. Little, son of Dnaiel and Mary Little, aged 2 years, 2 months and 7 days.

Mrs. Sarah E. Davis, daughter of Mr. Sam'l Marvin, and wife of Mr. Franklin Davis, died in Summerville, S. C.,Nov. 24th, 1862, aged 35 years... J. W. M.

Thomas M. Mason, aged 23 years, was wounded in the battle of Sharpsburg, and died on 25th October last....

Mrs. Rebecca Payne, wife of the late Col. R. Payne, died at Blackville, S. C., Nov. 1862, in the 53d year of her age... G. H. G.

Mrs. Harriet Bowdre Phinizy, wife of Mr. Ferdinand Phinizy, and daughter of Mr. Hays Bowdre, formerly of Augusta, Ga., died in Athens, Ga., on 7th February 1863... A. Means.

Miss Sallie Hacknett Newell, daughter of Mrs. and Mr. Isaac Newell, of Milledgeville, Ga., died 24th Jan. 1863, in her 22d year... C. A. Fulwood.

Mrs. Mary Ann, wife of Wm. T. Cole, of Newnan, Ga., died in Merriwether co., Ga., Feb., 2, 1863, aged 30 years and 6 months. joined the Baptist Church, in 1858, joined the M. E. Church.

Joseph W. Cook was born in Abbeville Dis., S. C., Jan. 1, 1802, married his first wife Rhoda Morris, August 4, 1825, his second wife, Caroline Jones, Dec. 24, 1854, and died in Richmond, Va., Nov. 16, 1862, in his 61st year...

Jas. O. Andrew Stewart, son of Matthew and Priscilla Stewart, was born in Newton co., Ga., in 1830...died Dec. 4, 1862...

Mims J. Baker, son of Col. R. A. and Mrs. N. E. Baker, of Summerfield, Dallas co., Ala., died in his 15th year, Jan. 30, 1863. R. H. Rivers

Mrs. Mary Margaret Smith, wife of Dr. Southwood Smith, and youngest daughter of Mr. and Mrs. Reuben Tyson, of St. Peter's Parish, Beaufort Dist., died on 14th Feb., in the 19th year of her age, and the third of her married life...

Sgt. Wm. B. Wofford, son of Maj. Harvey Wofford, 3rd S. C. Regt., was born in Spartanburg Dist., Jan. 31, 1826...died 26th January 1863... H. A. C. W.

Saml. U. Phifer, son of McCullum and Harriet C. Phifer, died at Atlanta, Ga., on 8th Nov., 1862, in his 22nd year....

Miss Francenia E. Shuler, daughter of Francis Carn, of Orange Parish, and wife of Mr. Lewis Shuler, died on 17th Jan., 1863, aged 22 years and 6 months... A. M. C.

George J. Crawford, of St. James' Goose Creek Parish, S. C., died in Winchester, Va., at a private residence, on 12th Nov. 1862, aged 24 years... M. C. C.

Nancy Elmore Houck, wife of Joseph Houck, was born in Laurens Dist., S. C., and died in Greensboro', Ala., 1st Feb., 1863, in her 59th year...removed with her mother, Judith Williams, to Autauga co., Ala., in 1819...leaves a large family of children.

Marcus Newton, only son of the late Rev. Smith C. and Harriet E. Quillian, died inDalton, Ga., Jan. 9, 1863, aged 8 years and 6 days.

Wm. A. McCord, was born in Lincoln co., Ga., and was killed in the battle of Murfreesboro', Tenn., Dec. 31, 1862...left wife in Pontotoc co., Miss.

Ella Hearn, daughter of Rev. A. C. and Mrs. E. J. Ramsey, was born Jan. 24, 1859, and died Nov. 27, 1862....

Issue of March 5, 1863

Died Walter Henry Steele Starr, infant son of the late S. H. S. Starr, died at Oxford, Ga., 24th February, aged 5 months and 20 days.

William Edwin, son of F. D. and P. C. Graham of Pomaria, died 4th Jan., aged 3 years, 9 months and 3 days.

Died in Terrell county, Ga., Feb. 4th, L. A. M. Edwards, in her 9th year, daughter of Thomas and Matilda Edwards.

Josiah W. Hill died January 12th, 1863, in Carroll co., Miss., aged 55 years....

J. Woods Hill, youngest son of Josiah W., and Sarah Hill, died in Carroll co., Miss., Jan. 24, 1863, in his 16th year....

George Wesley Hudson was born in Franklin co., Ga., July 16, 1794, and died in Clarke co., Ga., Jan. 27th, 1863....

John Shuly, of 15th Regt. S. C. V., died at his father's residence in Lexington Dist., S. C., Dec. 27th, 1862, in his 28th year... W. A. C.

Mrs. Gillie Ann Byrd, wife of Wm. Byrd, and daughter of Mr. and Mrs. C. Baker, died near Columbus, Russell co., Ala., 4th Feb., in her 26th year...

Jas. D. Wright, Esq., was born July 14th, 1804, and died Dec. 16th, 1862... M. A. McKibben.

Darius R. Weems was born in Franklin co., Ga., Sept. 2, 1811, and died in Forsyth co, Ga. Dec. 5, 1862.

Benjamin Cicero Weems, son of the above, died in Forsyth co., Ga., Jan. 18, 1863, aged 19 years and 14 days. W. D. Bently.

Shelldrake Brown was born in Lincoln co., Ga., Sept. 16, 1820, and fell in battle near Fredericksburg, Va.

Robert Brown, his brother, was born in Lincoln co., Ga., March 6, 1830, and died on consumption, Dec. 4, 1862....

Benjamin T. Turner, third son of James R. and Mary A. Turner, was born Sept. 28, 1838, in Jones co., Ga., died at Guinea Station, Va., January 2, 1863.

Lt. Ezekiel Pickens Miller of 17th Regt. Miss Vols., son of M. T. and L. E. Miller was born Nov. 9, 1838, in Anderson Dist., S. C., fell mortally wounded at Fredericksubrg, Va.,on 11th Dec., 1862, and survived but a few moments.

William Thomas Miller, of 17th Regt. Miss Vols., brother of the above, was born 23d July 1830, in Anderson Dist., S. C., and died in the Chimboraso Hospital, Richmond Va.

Lt. Wm. R. Mayfield, of 42nd Ga. Regt., fell in the battle of Vicksburg, 29th Dec., 1862, aged about 26 years.

Robeson G. Weaver son of Rev. John C. Weaver, formerly of Va., now of Ala., and brother of Rev. Shelton R. Weaver of the Fla. Conf., died in Sumter co., Fla., Jan. 9, 1863, in his 42d year....

Seaborn Covington, died in Barnesville, Ga., Dec. 13, 1862, aged 60 years.

Sgt. Charles Betts McInnis of Union co., N. C., 48th N. C. Regt, died near Fredericksburg, Va., 18th Dec. 1862, aged 26 years.

Mary F. and Martha M., daughters of Samuel and Martha Newbold, formerly of Charleston, were returning to their residence in Wilmington, accompanied by their mother, when the car was thrown from the track, and they were killed, Nov. 26, 1862....

Martha Cartwright, relict of John Cartwright, died near Halston's in Green co., Ga., on 17th Feb., in her 89th year....

Lt. Jas. Hollingsworth of 3d Regt, S. C. V., was born in Laurens Dist., Feb. 12th, 1831, and was killed Dec. 14, 1862, in the battle at Fredericksburg....

Nathaniel R. Patterson, died in Sumter, Feb. 5, 1863, in his 25th year....Hampton's Legion.

Robert Evans Clark, son of Charles and Mrs. Sarah Clark was born in Burke co., Ga., joined Co. A., 3rd Regt., Ga. Vol., was killed at Sharpsburg, in Md., in his 25th year.

Corp. Henry C. McKinzie of Co. C. 3rd Regt. Ga. Vols., died at the residence of his father, in Lee co., Ga.,on 23d Jan., of wounds from the battle of Malvern Hill, aged about 21 years.

Mis Elizabeth Webb Barge was born in Ga., Dec. 25th, 1802, and died in Butler co., Ala., Dec. 14, 1862....

John A. Tyler, son of A. J. and M. A. Tyler of Marion co., Ga., was born in Harris co., Ga., May 3d, 1833, and died in Wilson Hospital, N. C., Oct. 8, 1862...

J. D. Smith, of Reidsville, Ga., was born May, 1833, and died Sept. 29th, 1862....

Tribute of Respect by 27th Regt. Ga. Vols., to Capt. Pe-ry C. Can, who died of fever, in Richmond, Va.

Issue of March 12, 1863

Married on 11th Jan., by Rev. S. G. Chiles, Dr. B. F. Treadwell, to Miss Eleanor Raysor, daughter of Col. J. M. Raysor, all of Jefferson co., Fla.

On 15th Feb.,by Rev. E. G. Murrah, Lt. James F. Sullivan, of 4th Ga. Regt., to Miss Jennie A. Law, of Hall co., Ga.

On 17th Feb.,by Rev. N. D. Morehouse, Capt. John N. Wilcox, to Mrs. Lucretia G. Hutchins, all of Burke co., Ga.

On the evening of the 4th inst., in the M. E. Church, by Rev. W. C. Bass, Capt. Edward P. Bowdre, of the 1st Ga. Regulars, and Miss Mary M., daughter of J. B. Ross, Esq., of Macon, Ga.

Died Lydia Eliza King Feb. 6, 1863, in Sampit, Georgetown Dist., S. C.,in his 13th year.

Miss Eliza L. Stubbs daughter of the late Peter Stubbs, Esq., was born Dec. 27, 1838 and died Feb. 18, 1863, in Macon, Ga.

John W. Hoyel of 41st Miss Regt., was born 28th Dec. 1839, and joined the M. E. Church in Texas, 1858, and was married to Miss Marsha Gale, May 1861, and died 8th July 1862, at his father's in Pontotoc co., Miss. A. J. S.

D. H. Hoyel, of 41st Miss Regt., a younger brother, was born 14th August 1842, and died at Shelbyville, Tenn., Dec. 1862.

James F. Montgomery, eldest son of Mr. and Mrs. Green Montgomery, died of wounds received at Murfreesboro, on 1st Jan., 1863...

Wm. Nevis was born in Early co., Ga., June 26, 1843, and died of wounds received in the battle of Murfreesboro, Jan. 3, 1863...

Dr. Samuel G. Cloud was born in Adams co., Miss., Aug. 17, 1792, and died 20th Dec. 1862, in Franklin Parish, La., aged 70 years... N. L. Green.

James J. Milhous died near Bamberg, S. C., Jan. 28th, 1863, in his 71st year....

J. C. Milhous died Jan. 10, 1863, in the General Hospital, Richmond, in his 26th year.

Also at his father's, near Bamberg, S. C., Casper P. Milhous, in his 20th year....

Mrs. Elizabeth Wilkinson, daughter of Jas. and Sarah Pulliam, and wife of William H. Wilkinson, was born in Franklin co., Ga., Sept. 29th, 1793, and died in Walton co., Ga., 23d Feb 1863...

Noel Norwood was born in Darlington Dist., S. C. 12th May 1786, removed to Miss. in 1807, and to East Feliciana Parish, La., in 1819, where he died 12th Jan. 1863. In May, 1806, he was married to Elizabeth, daughter of John and Ann Hodges. His cnildren, to the third and fourth generation were all around him. H. T. Lewis.

Corporal David B. McCord, Co. G. 42d Regt, Ga. Vols., was killed in the battle of Viskburg, Dec. 29th, 1862, in his 21st year... John E. Sentell.

Miss Jane C. Huff died in Bibb co., Ga., 11th Feb. 1863, in her 19th year.... W. G. Allen.

Wm. F. Richardson, was born in 1806 in Marion Dist., S. C., and died Feb. 13th, in his 55th year... J. M. C.

Wm. D. Jordan of Colleton Dist., S. C., died Dec. 1862, aged 89 years... M. L. Banks.

Mrs. Mary Adams was born in North Carolina in 1784. Her father removed to Franklin co., Ga., when she was quite young. In 1805 she was married to Absalom Adams, and died 13th Feb. 1863.

Sgt. H. C. Browning of the Schley Guards, 5th Ga. Regt., was born in Montgomery co., Ga., 1837, and died in the hospital at

Bridgeport, Ala., in his 26th year... B. F. Breedlove.
R. C. Lester was born in Boston, Mass., Jan. 11, 1799, and
died at Sweet Water, Tenn., on his wasy home from Knoxville, Dec.
26, 1862...one of the first settlers of Quincy, Fla....
Adaline Hearn, daughter of Rev. Thomas T. and Tabitha Hearn,
was born in Campbell co., Ga., on Feb. 2, 1862(sic), aged 19.
T. Garrison, son of the late Rev. Levi Garrison, was born
25th March, 1819, served in S. C. and Va. in Col. Moore's Regt.
left wife and children.
Mrs. Harriet Neal, daughter of Jacob and Catherine Turnipseed,
and wife of P. T. Neal, Esq., died in Pickens co., Ala., 8th
Jan. 1863...born in Fairfield Dist., S. C.,20th Jan., 1818, and
removed to Alabama in 1836....
Fannie Scott Spearman, daughter of Edmund and Martha Spearman,
died Jan. 20th in her 6th year....
Wm. A. T. Turrentine, son of Daniel C. and Caroline E. Turrentine, of Gadsden, Ala., died at Richmond, Va., in his 22d year.
Benjamin M. Scott of Co. B., 24th Ga. Regt., died at Howard's
Grove Hospital, at Richmond, Va.,in his 22nd year, on 21st Jan.
last....

Issue of March 19, 1863

Married near Sharon, Miss., Feb. 12, 1863, by Rev. H. H. Montgomery, J. C. Richards, Esq., and Miss Laura H. Devine.
By Rev. R. H. Harwell, Feb. 18th, Dr. R. W. Oliver to Miss
Mary Lovett, all of Scriven co., Ga.
Died in Henry co., Ga.,Jan. 14, 1863, Mirabeau Demetrius, son
of William R. and Alletha P. Henry, aged 4 years and 30 days.
in Cuthbert, Ga., during the months of Jan. and Feb., the
two youngest children of Rev. R. B. And Marah Antoinette Stewart,
one a daughter named Martha Ann, in her 3d year, and the other
an infant son, without a name, in his 6th month.
In Madison co., Miss. little Nellie Lambuth, daughter of the
Rev. J. W. Lambuth, Missionary of the M. E. Church, South, in
China. She was born in Shanghai, May 6, 1857, and died March 2,
1863.
Bro. Joseph D. White was born in Montgomery co., Ala., Dec.
1829, and died of consumption in Montgomery, on 28th Feb. 1863.
J. W. Jordan.
Mrs. Martha S. Dickinson, daughter of John G.and Ellen Smith,
was born in Marion Dist., S. C.,Nov. 16, 1819, and moved to
Ala. with her parents in 1839, married to Rev. A. S. Dickinson,
of the Ala. Conf., Jan. 13, 1835, and died in Barbour co., Ala.,
3rd Feb. 1863....
Lt. Wiley J. Bridges of 19th Ga. Regt., died in Coweta co.,
Ga., 10th Feb. 1863, in his 23rd year.... F. W. B.
Pvt. Aaron Owen Lee 34th Regt. N. C. Troops, died in hospital
at Guineas Station, Va., Jan. 27th, in his 21st year....
Mr. John Wesley Stansell, son of Rev. Levi Stansell, died near
Oxford, Ga.,on 19th Feb., in his 27th year... A. Means.
Pvt. A. McCorkle of 9th Ga. Bat., was born in Lincoln co.,
Ga., and was killed at Murfreesboro, Tenn., Dec. 21, 1862, aged
34 years...married Miss S. R. Skinner of Columbia co., Ga....
John Franklin Martin, of Ray Gaurd, 34th Ga. Regt., was born
in Crawford co., Ga., March 19, 1840, and died in the same co.,
Jan. 17th, 1863, aged 23 years....
John P. Ward, son of Uriah and Frances Ward of Putnam co.,
died in ths hospital near Savannah, Ga.,on Feb.26th, in his 21st
year... M. W. Arnold.
Jas. B. Wilbanks, was born Aug. 22d, 1868, and died in Richmond, Va., Feb. 3, 1863... J. R. S.

Mrs. Susan Elizabeth Hines, youngest daughter of the late
Col. Wm. Harrison, and wife of Joseph M. HInes, Esq.,died at
White Hall, Washington co., on 19th Feb., in her 39th year....
     Lt. Wm. Partin, of Reidsville, Ga., died 18th Feb. 1863...
Mrs. Martha Eliza Hood, wife of Martin D. Hodd, daughter of Jas.
G. and Ann E. Cotton, died on 21st Jan., in Harris co., Ga...
     Lt. Wm. R. Mayfield, of Walton co., Ga., 42d Ga. Regt., fell
killed instantly at Vicksburg, Miss., on 29th Dec. 1862, in his
35th year....
     Sister Margaret Homes, wife of Wm. Homes, of Horry Dist., S.
C., died 29th January, at about 42 years of age... J. A. Wood.
     Lida Alston, daughter of Jas. Y. and Martha Alston, was born
Aug. 11, 1852, and died at McKinley, Ala.,on 15th Feb., 1863...
J. C. Huckabee.
     Gussie E., daughter of Wm. C. and Elizabeth Wimberly, died
near Centreville, Talbot co., on 5th Feb. in her 11th year...
     Miss Mary J.Willingham, eldest daughter of Julia A.Willingham,
died in Linco-nton, Ga., on 14th Feb. 1863, in her 14th year.
G. L. W. Anthony.
     Mrs. Emily V. Patrick born and reared in Marion co., Ga., died
Feb. 12, 1863, in her 30th year...member of the Baptist Church.
     Tribute of Respect by Black Swamp Circuit, to Joseph Maner
Lawton....

Issue of March 26, 1863

     Israel Smith died in Liberty co., Ga., Dec. 23, 1863, aged
48 years.... J. W. Turner.
     Mrs. Ann M. Lin was born in Wilkes co., Ga., 1792, died in
Augusta, Feb. 4th, 1860, in her 73d year...J. T. Lin.
     Mrs. Lucy A. N., wife of David Baughn, was born April 7,
1836 and died Feb. 9th... J. R. Thomas.
     Miss Nancy Elizabeth, daughter of Rev. Joseph and Nancy Ray,
of Telfair co., Ga., was born in '44, and died in December....
     Thomas J. Smith of 2nd Ga. Cavalry, only son of Mr. George
W. Smith, deceased, and Mrs. Mary M., now Mrs. Hawkins, was born
January 16, 1845, and died in Bedford co., Tenn., Jan. 28, 1863.
     James W. Penn Co. G., 37th Regt. Ala. Voluntters, son of
Thomas L. Penn, Sr. of Cusseta, Ala. was born 11th August 1836,
and died 15th Nov. 1862....
     Miss Margaret G. Biddenback, daughter of J. and M. Biddenback
of Effingham co., Ga., died Feb. 15th, 1863, in her 18th year.
     William Capers Holmes, of Pike co., Ga., 3d Ga. Battn., died
near Shelbyville, Tenn., Feb. 16, in his 19th year....
     Lt. H. H. Clarke, 8th Ga. Regt, was born in York Dist., S. C.,
July 13, 1835, and died at his father's in Anderson Dist., S. C.,
Jan. 1863....
     John McInnis, of Stanley co., N. C. was born in Richmond co.,
N. C., died on 12th Jan. 1863, aged 58 years and 5 months....
     Tuttle H. Moreland, of Waddells Artillery, was born in Russell
co., Ala., and died at Chattanooga, Tenn., 4th Dec., 1862, in his
31st year....
     Thomas Benton Rayfield, son of Daniel and Louisa Rayfield,
of Coosa co., Ala., Stewart's Cavalry, was born in Bibb co., Ala.,
killed near Laurel Mills, Va., 10 Nov 1863, aged 22 years.
     Emma A. Granniss, daughter of E. C. and B. E. Granniss, died
in Macon, Ga., March 1863, in her 14th year....
     Elizabeth, second daughter of Dr. R. and Mrs. Elizabeth Tho-
mas, was born in Camden co., Ga., Nov. 27, 1851, and died near
White Springs, Hamilton co., Fla., Feb. 20, 1863....
     James Warren, a native of Louisiana and pvt. in Capt. Hayden's
Co., La. Vol., died near Murfreesboro, Tenn., on the 31st Dec.,
1862, aged about 37 years....

Daniel J. Willis of 16th Ala. Regt., son of James and Rachel Willis, was born in Montgomery co., Ala., Dec. 16, 1835, and died at Triune, Tenn., Dec. 19, 1862.... J. O. Sellers.

Joseph Hays of Butler co., Ala., Capt. Green's Co., 18th Ala. Regt., adopted son of Esther Hays, died at the hospital in Okolona, Miss, in his 23d year.... J. O. Sellers.

James Tart was born Jan. 18, 1797, in Marion Dist., S. C., and died March 2, 1863... M. A. McK.

Dr. Willis Fore was born July 10, 1816, and died in Marion Dist., S. C., Dec. 15, 1862... M. A. McK.

Miss Winna B. Sealy died at the residence of her brother, in Tuscaloosa co., Ala., aged 57 years, 6 months and 17 dahs....

Issue of April 2, 1863

Married on the evening of the 10th inst.,by Rev. P. L. Herman, Mr. Landon Tucker of Edgefield, S. C. to Miss Rebecca L. Cantelou, of Lincoln, Ga.

On 5th March, near Black Hawk, Carro-1 co., Miss., by Rev. Dr. Stewart, Mr. Wm. S. Hitt to Miss F. Florence Moore, of Paris, Tenn.

March 8th, 1863, by Rev. L. L. Ledbetter, Rev. J. M. Stokes, Chaplain of 3d Ga. Vols., to Miss C. Louisa Heath, of Burke co., Ga.

Died in Butler co., Ala., March 12th, Henry McTieire, only son of John T. and Elizabeth A. Harris, aged 2 years and 4 months. In Butler co., Ala., March 22nd, Mary Willie, only child of William C. and Sallie S. McTyeire, aged 18 months.

Edward Phillips was born July 17, 1836, and died in Winnsboro, S. C., April 17, 1863... A. J. Cauthen.

Sgt. Asbury S. Johnson was born in Troup co., Ga., 25th July 1835, and died in Calton, Ga., 30th Dec. 1862....84th Ga. Regt. W. M. D. Bond.

Elizabeth A., wife of Joseph Speer died in Fayette co., Ga., March 4th, 1868, aged 60 years.... left 13 children. F. W. B.

Francis Marion Bobo was born in Spartanburg District, S. C., June 5, 1826, and died in Fayette co., Ala., March 3, 1863... Lewis Bobo.

Thomas Crawford, of 2d Ga. Cavalry, died in the Academy Hospital at Chattanooga, March 6, 1863...born Dec. 1, 1836, in Duplin co., N. C...At an early age his parents removed to Marion, Ga. on June 12, 1860 married to Mary Park... W. B. Merritt.

Sister W. M. Ivy died in Sumter co., Ala., on 4th March, 1863, aged 20 years... W. Spillman.

W. H. Robuck of 49th Ga. Regt. died near Guinea Station, Va., 10th March 1863... J. R. Mobley.

Alexander McIver died March 3, 1863, in Gadsden co., Fla., aged 58 years...member of St. Joseph's M. E. Church... G. W. Pratt.

Albert Maximillian Padget of 7th Regt. S. C. V., son of M. M. and M. Padget, was born in Edgefield Dist., S. C., March 4, 1844...died Jan. 3, 1863, at Frederick City...

A. C. Wooten, 49th Ga. Regt, died in Winchseter, Va... J. M. Mobley.

Sister M. A. Carr was a native of N. C., married to Col. J. W. Leonard in 1809, moved to Fla., in 1828, married to Mr. Jacob Carr in 1830, and died 31st Jan. 1863, in her 70th year... S. P. Richardson.

Rev. William R. Gappen died in Fannin co., Ga., on 22d Dec., 1862, aged 54 years...born in Charleston, S. C... A. C. C.

Wm. A. Cameron of bht 3d Ga. Regt. died near Fredericksburg, Va., March 10, 1863, in his 22d year...

Mrs. Mary Pruitt wife of Turner F. Pruitt, formerly of Talbot co., Ga., died in Coosa co., Ala., March 1, 1862(sic)...
left husband and three small children at home and five sons in the army of the Confederacy....

C. C. Collins of 57th Ga. Regt, born in Wilkinson co., Ga., July 20, 1841, died near Vicksburg, Feb. 20, 1863...

Sister Phebe Stevenson, was born in Newberry Dist., S. C., and died in her 70th year on 27th Feb. 1863... W. D.

Tribute of Respect to Andrew Wallace, by Washington St. Charge, Columbia, S. C.

Issue of April 9, 1863

John Groves Pearson son of Thos G. and Susan H. Pearson was born in Centreville, Talbot co., Ga., April 13, 1835, and died in Richmond, Va. 12th Feb. 1863... Willis D. Matthews.

Jo Emma C., wife of Peter Vaught, Jr., died 30th Jan. 1863, aged 22 years and 7 days... D. J. McMillan.

Mrs. Elizabeth Holloway, wife of Dr. Z. Holloway died in West Point, Ga., on 22d March, 1863, in her 66th year... R. H. Dixon.

Mrs. Catharine Hubbard(?) Thomas, only daughter of James and Elizabeth Dowdell born in Va., 21st Dec 1793, an orphan at 13 years of age, with seven brothers older...on 23d Sept 1828, married to Wm. C. Thomas. On 24th Feb. 1863, died at Oakland, in Chambers co., Ala... Wm. F. Samford.

Mrs. Elizabeth Wester, wife of Benjamin Wester was born in Green co., Ga., Aug. 28, 1795, and died in Chambers co., Ala., Feb. 18, 1863... S. Harwell.

John Jackson born in Brunswick co., Va., died on 11th March 1863 at the residence of Mr. L. Ragland in Henry co., Ga., in his 92d year...

Mrs. Matilda E. Rodd was born in Laurens Dist., S. C., Nov. 8, 1824, and died in St. Clair co., Ala., at the house of her brother, F. M. Waite, Feb. 10, 1863...left husband and three children. T. Moody.

Eugenia D. Smart, daughter of Asa D. and Charlotte H. Smart died recently in Decatur co., Ga., aged 18 years....

John W. Groomes, eldest son of Benj. and Lucy Groomes, was born in Tatnall co., Ga., 20th Oct. 1837, and died in one of the hospitals in Richmond, Va., 18th Feb. 1863... W. J. Jordan.

Rev. Moses G. Pruitt died Feb. 18, 1863, in his 25th year. died in Hospital in Atlanta, Ga....

Lulie, daughter of Rev. J. M. and Mrs. M. A. Bonnell, died in Macon, Ga., March 25t,h 1863, aged 10 years and 2 months...:

Rev. Dennis Glisson of 3d Ga. Vols., died in Burke co., Ga., Feb. 26th, 1863, aged 27 years....

Miss Ellen Augusta Young, daughter of W. H. Young, Esq., died in Columbus, Ga., Jan. 25th, 1863...

John W. Hodnett of 45th Ga. Regt., son of Wm. and Caroline Hodnett, died near Middletonw, Va.... J. A. P.

Mary A. E. Crowley, daughter of Tyse H. and Martha Smithwick, was born in Cherokee co., Ga., March 2d, 1845...married to Seaborn Crowley, Aug 22, 1862, and died in Cherokee co., Ga.,Jan. 17, 1863....

Rev. William P. Arrowood was born March 1, 1837...died near Fredericksburg, some time in Feb. 1863....

Mrs. Charlotte Cassady, wife of Wm. Cassady, died in Sumpter ct., Fla., aged 55 years... W. C. W.

Dr. Bird B. Meacham was born in Union Dist., S. C.,April 6th, 1821, and died near Bristol, Liberty co., Fla., March 21, 1863.

Mrs. Sarah A. Marbut, daughter of Wesley and Mary Beaswell, and wife of D. P. Marbut died in DeKalb co., Ga., Jan. 9, 1863,

aged 27 years.
Tribute of Respect to Rev. Alexander McIver.
Tribute of Respect by Bryan ct., Ga. Conf. to Rev. W. S. Baker.
Married on 2d April by Rev. George C. Clarke, Mr. Derrill H.
Culler and Miss Mary Melissa, daughter of L. M. Houser, all of
Perry, Ga.

Issue of April 16, 1863

Wm. Fletcher Smith of 45th Ga. Regt., son of Rev. Wesley F.
and Louisa J. Smith died in Culloden, Ga., 24th March 1863, aged
19 years.
Bro. Ephraim M. Greenlee died in McDowell co., N. C., on 5th
of March, in his 80th year... J. S. E.
Pvt. Green H. Peavy of 56th Ga. Vols., was born in Meriwether
co., Ga., and died at Cumberland Gap, Tenn., March 27, 1863,
in his 32d year.
Miss Elizabeth A. J. Randle died in Burke co., Ga., 18th Jan.,
1863, in his 64th year....
E. F. Mellard, 28th Regt. Miss Vol. was killed on 24th March.
George Washington Peace died at Longhorn Hospital, Lynchburg,
Va.', Jan. 18, 1863, aged 31 years....
Mrs. Eleanor Peace, a member of the Baptist Church, died at
the residence of her nephew, G. W. Peace, decd., on 17th March
1863, aged 76 years, 7 months and 13 days. J. H. C. McKinney.
Albert E. Slate, son of Joseph and Elizabeth A. Slate, was
born in Buncombe co., N. C., May 27th, 1836...died 14th Jan....
Mrs. Elizabeth Thomas, wife of Dr. Robert Thomas and eldest
daughter of Isaac and Mrs. Caroline Lang, of Camden co., Ga.,
was born Jan. 26, 1837, and died 28th March near White Springs,
Hamilton co., Fla.   J. M.
James Henry Collins of Chesterfield Dist., died near the
Blackwater River in Southampton co., Va., on 22d Jan., in his
28th year....
Mrs. Hannah Mallard died 23d Dec. 1862, in her 68th year....
Miss Susan, eldest daughter of Mr. R. and L. A. Dilworth, of
Union Point, Green co., Ga., died on 18th Feb. in her 15th
year.
Benj. C. Duncan, son of Matthew Duncan, of Graniteville, 7th
S. C. V., died in Richmond, aged 17 years...
Rev. John Majors Smith died in Fulton co., Ga., 21st March
1863, in the 74th year of his age....
Rev. Jasper K. Harper, a member of the Rio Grande Conf., aged
24 years, died 19th Jan. 1863, in Gonzales co., Texas....
Capt. James T. Gray died in Griffin, Ga., on March 30th...
Samuel Cornelius Ingraham of Ben Hill Infantry, died near Fre-
dericksburg, on the 14th Feb.
Rev. Isaac Ellis, son of Rev. Stephen and Phebe Ellis was
born in Pickens Dist., S. C., May 10, 1821, and died 11th March
1863....
N. Smith Howard of 45th Ala. Regt, son of Major James and
Tabitha Howard was born in Autauga co., Ala., Sept. 22, 1823,
fell mortally wounded in Murfreesboro, Dec. 11, 1863, and died
Jan. 8, 1863.
Tribute of Respect by Darlington ct., S. C. Conf. to Rev.
J. F. A. Elliott, who died on Morris Island, Jan. 27th...
Tribute of Respect to Rev. Jno K. Leak by Quarterly Conf. of
Cuthbert....
Married by Rev. H. H. Parks, 7th inst., O. A. Caldwell to
Miss Carrie E. Birdsong, all of Macon, Ga.
Died in Atlanta, April 4th, aged 15 months, Pauline, only
surviving child of Rev. Atticus G. and Mary F. Haygood, of the
Ga. Conf.

Mrs. Cynthia W. Nobles, wife of James A.Nobles, and only
remaining daughter of the late Capt. Bartlett Brown, died on 27th
March, 1863, near Speedwel, Barnwell Dist., S. C., aged 63 years.

Frances Albert Speer, son of Rev. Alexander Speer, died in
Richmond, Va., 17th March, 1863, in his 21st year...6th Ga. Regt.
T. B. Russell.

William H. Black son of Joshua S. F. And M. W. Black died
Feb. 26th, 1863, aged 18 years and 6 months.

Marcellus A. Black died March 17th, aged 4 years and 9 months.
Susan E. P. Black died March 25th, aged 14 years and 6 months.

Mr. John Frazier, a native of Ireland, of Capt. Mabry's co.,
19th Ga. Regt, fell before Fredericksburg, Dec. 13th, 1862, in
his 30th year... A. Means.

Miss Lucretia A. Morgan, died in Effingham co., Ga.,Jan. 9th,
1863, in her 21st year....

Mrs. Hattie E. Hines, wife of James T. Hines and daughter of
Wm. Donalson, was born March 1, 1810, and died April 2, 1863...
F. A. Branch.

T. W. Moore Jr. of Co. F., 6th Regt. S. C. V., son of Dr. T.
W. Moore, of Chester Dist., S. C.,died in Petersburg, Va., March
10, 1863, in his 22d year... J. O. H.

Miss Princey, daughter of James and Elizabeth Coleman, was
born March 15, 1803, and died March 1, 1863

Sister Elizabeth Blount, of Warren co., Ga., was born Sept.
25, 1760, and died having been 60 years a member of the M. E.
Church.

A. D. Cleveland, Sgt. 27th Regt. La. Vols., died at Vicksburg, 9th Feb. 1863, aged about 32 years....

Thomas Christian was born in Lunenburg co., Va., March 7th,
1791, and died in Chattahoochee co., Ga., March 28h, 1863...
R. F. Williamson.

Mrs. Jane Elizabeth Barker, daughter of Richard and Susan
Payne and wife of Rev. Josiah Barker, of the Ala. Conf., was
born in Culpepper co., Va., 1828, and died in Dayton, Ala., April
4, 1863...

Isaac Betts, Sr., was born August 18, 1793, married May 18,
1813, to Miss Mary Dawson and lived in Hancock, Jasper and Jackson
cos., Ga., until 1819, when he removed to Consouh co., Ala...

Asa Clarke Walker died 23 Feb 1863, in the hospital in Georgetown, S. C., in his 30th year...left a fond mother....

Rev. Wm. Crapps, local preacher, died March 25, on Sampit,
Georgetown Dist., S. C....

Tribute of Respect to John H. Burton who died March 2, 1863,
by White Plains ct., Ala. Conf....

Married in Augusta, on 4th April, by Rev. D. D. Cox, Mr. John
Rugden to Miss Elizabeth Wiley.

By the same, on 13th April, Mr. William T. Coxe to Miss Kate
E. Little.

On 8th April, at the residence of D. A. Horn, Thomas county,
Ga., by Rev. C. Raiford, Mr. Daniel McIntosh to Miss Lucy Ellen
McLeod, both of said county.

On 25th ult., by Rev. W. J. Cotter, Mr. Charles Howel, of
Milton co., to Miss Addie Park, of Green co.

Died in Talbotton, on 26th ult., Carrie, youngst daughter of
Dr. W. G. And Mrs. M. A. Little, aged 3 years and 3 days.

In Atala co., Miss., Feb. 20th, 1863, James Wiley, son of
Ezekiel J. and Elizabeth T. Bridges, aged 7 years 1 month and
2 days.

On 19th April, Henry Charles, son of Wm. K. and Phebe E.
Turner, aged 3 years, 3 months and 7 days.

Mrs. Mary J. King, wife of William H. King, and daughter of
Mr. Robert and Patience Lowery, of Jefferson co., Ga., died in
Webster co., Ga., on 15th April 1863, in her 47th year...member
of the Baptist Church. James G. M. Hale.

Jesse A. Bailey, 43d Regt. Ga. Vols., son of Mary A. Bailey,
of Newborn, Newton co., Ga., was born March 24, 1844, and died
in the Hospital at Vicksburg, Miss., Jan. 13th, 1863...

Catherine E. Davis, wife of Archibald Davis, Esq., died near
Rome, Ga., February 7th, in her 42d year....

Eusebius Cooper, second son of Frank and Arabella C. Nisbet,
of Russell co., Ala. died at the mansion of Mr. and Mrs. George
Cook, in Atlanta, Ga., 16th April 1863, aged 18 years....

Miss Carrie A. E. Handy, was born 30th March 1829, and died
in Henry co., Ga., 19th March, 1863....

Mrs. Jennie A. Green, daughter of B. F. Harris, Esq., died
in Richmond co., Ga.,on 5th Feb., in her 30th year...an affectionate husband preceded her to the grave....

Elizabeth R. Howell, was born in N. C., Sept. 14, 1805, and
died in Talladega, Ala., Feb. 4, 1863.

Isaac N. Thompson, son of Jeremiah and Polly Thompson, was
born January 16, 1837, and died in the Hospital in Orange Court
House, Va., on 23d April 1863.

Jethro Thompson, brother of the above was born November 17,
1834, and died May 16, 1863, in Richmond Va....

Miss Sarah A. Mills, daughter of Benjamin G. and Elizabeth
W. Mills, of Marion, Fla., was born in Brunswick co., N. C.,
Nov. 6, 1846, and died March 17, 1863....

Richard Asbury Ford, son of J. S. and Jane Ford, was born
in Rutherford, N. C., Oct. 15h, 1818, and died in Shelbyville,
Tenn., March 30,1863....

Rev. Alexander McBryde was born June 23, 1816, in Marlborough
Dist., S. C., died Dec. 13, 1862, in the cars between Montgomery
and Mobile, on his way home from the Ala. Conf....

Mrs. Elizabeth Skipper, wife of J. B. Skipper, Sr. of Horry
Dist., S. C., died March 7, 1863, aged 66 years...

William Epps, died in Williamsburg Dist., S. C., Jan. 28th,
1863....

Joseph F. D. Richbourg, youngest son of Isaac A. and E. H.
Richbourg, was born 22d Oct. 1843, died 19th Jan. 1863...

Mrs. Davis, wife of Henry Davis, and daughter of James
Palmer, died 27th March, near Albemarle, N. C., in her 38th year,
leaving a husband and nine children....

Miss Anna Pamelia, youngest daughter of Mr. Wm. V. and Mrs.
Ann McGehee, died in Harris co., Ga., March 16, aged 24 years....

Mrs. L. E. Gasque, wife of J. W. Gasque, died in Georgetown
Dist., Feb. 14, 1863, aged 23 years....

George R. Dawson, son of Samuel C. and A. C. Dawson was born
Jan. 13, 1842, and died March 10, 1863....

Willie M. Horne(?) was born in Warren co., Ga., Oct. 23,
1835, and died in Richmond, Va.,April 24, 1863....

Issue of May 7, 1863

Rev. Aquillla Leatherwood was born in Burke co., N. C., Jan.
30, 1786, and died Dec. 19, 1862, in Jefferson co., Ala., in
his 76th year... R. Philips.

Capt. Thomas Seay, son of John and Sarah Seay, was born in
Jackson co., Ga., April 12, 1834, married Dec. 26, 1860, and
fell mortally wounded at Murfreesboro', Dec. 31, 1862....

Catharine Bowen, wife of J. R. Bowen, and daughter of Charles
and Elizabeth Christian, died in Gordon co, Ga., April 15, 1863....

John Clemens, formerly a resident of S. C., died in Telfair
co., Ga., on 26th January, 1863, in his 63d year... G. S. Johnson
Anna Elizabeth, daughter of Ransom and Susan Jeter of Lowndes
co., Ala., was born Jan. 27, 1854, and died Feb. 1, 1863....
Also their next oldest son, Dowe Perry, born Sept. 20, 1850,
died March 17, 1863....
Dr. James A. Cooper, the father of the late Rev. T. W. Cooper,
of the Fla. Conf., died in Micanopy, Fla., on the 24th March,
in his 67th year...His wife died many years ago, leaving him a
large family. These, one by one, have all preceded him to the
grave, except two daughters.... John C. Ley.
Rev. Thomas L. Smith died in Catoosa, Ga., on 28th March,
1863, in the 3_th year of his age.... J. P. Bailey
Mrs. Elizabeth Smith, wife of Rev. Anthony Smith, died in
Catoosa co., Ga., on March 8, 1863....left husband and children.
Wm. A. Reife(?), was born in Fairfield Dist., S. C., March
3, 1833, and died at London, Tenn., March 24, 1863, in his 31st
year....
James H. Jones, son of James and Celia Jones, was born Aug
29, 1832, and was killed in the battle of Perryville, Ky....
Joel H. Smith died in Tenn, 8th Jan., in his 19th year....
7th Fla. Regt.
Married on 24th March, by Rev. A. Dickerson, Rev. J. O. A.
Cook, Chaplain 2d Ga. Bttn., to Miss Ella C., daughter of Thomas
G. Frazier, of Alabama.
In Clayton co., Ga., April 7, 1863, by the Rev. __ B. Powell,
Mr. T. L. Roberds to Miss J. T. Wesley, both of said county.

Issue of May 14, 1863

Mr. Henry Augustus Young, second son of Edward B. and Ann F.
Young, of Eufaula, Ala., was killed in the Railroad accident on
Chunkey river, Miss., Feb. 19, 1863, in his 27th year...on 5th
June 1860 married to Miss Maria McRae of Barbour co....
Mrs. Sarah J. Workman, widow of the late Wm. C. Workman, of
Camden, S. C., and daughter of the late Rev. James Jenkins, of
the S. C. Conf., was born May 5, 1812, married Dec. 29, 1831, and
died Feb. 16, 1863....
Mrs. Elizabeth J. McDaniel, wife of T. T. McDaniel and daugh-
ter of Jabish and Elizabeth Townsend, was born in S. C., Dec.
27, 1824. married 9th Feb. 1843, moved to Fla., in 1845, where
she died 14th Feb.1863, leaving a husband and eight children....
Mrs. Elizabeth Brewer was born February 21, 1793, and died
Feb. 17, 1863, M. B.
Mrs. Mary E. Loftin, wife of John D. Loftin, formerly a mem-
ber of the Ala. Conf., and only daughter of James and Eliza Mc-
Queen, died 31st March 1863, in Montgomery co., Ala....
Thomas L. Turner, son of Samuel and Rebecca Turner, of 18th
Ala. Regt, Co. G., died in Jefferson co., Ala. 7th Feb., 1863,
aged 23 years....
John H. Williamson, of Jackson co., Ga., died in the Hospital
at Winchester, Va. in his 61st year....
Lt. Y. J. King died in East Tenn., born in Mullins Cove, 1824.
settled in Coosa co., Ala....
Mrs. Mary Jane Chambers, wife of Josiah Chambers died near
Jonesboro, Ga., April 1, 1863, in her 46th year, leaving a hus-
band, and aged mother and ten children.... J. B. Powell.
Tilmon H. Moore died at Tunnelhill, Ga., April 17, 1863 in
his 50th year... J. P. Bailey.
Dr. Joseph G. Jenkins, son of the late Rev. James Jenkins,
of the S. C. Conf., was born in Sumter Dist., S. C., Feb. 17, 1818,
died near Gainesville, Fla., leaves a wife and children.

William Henry Sharp died in Jonesboro', Ga., April 10th, 1863, in his 49th year, leaving a wife and five children.

Maj. Alfred Hammond, died inElberton, Ga.,Feb. 6, 1863, in the 69th year of his age... A. T. Akerman.

J. S. King, son of B. S. and Fenton King was born in Upson co., Ga., in 1842...died in the army....

Augustus F. Eubanks of 48th Ala. Vols. was born 30th March 1830, and died 11th Feb. 1863, in Hospital, in Dalton, Ga.

Mrs. Rebecca N. Jones, wife of S. N. Jones, Esq. of Union Springs, Ala., and daughter of David and Rebecca Grier, of Washington co., Ga., was born Feb. 18, 1830, and died April 30, 1863.

Aaron Varn Senr. died Jan. 23, 1863, in St. Bartholomew's parish, S. C., in his 73d year... M. L. Banks.

Jacob A. Herlong was born 19 Jan 1837, and died Feb. 3, 1863. leaves a wife and three children.

Mr. D. N. Page, of 8th S. C. Regt., died at Camp Winder Hospital, on 25th April 1863....

Rev. Bartlett Thomason was born in S. C., and died April 7, 1863, in Walker co., Ga., in his 73rd year...joined the Baptist Church. He with his wife Mary (who died 12 years ago) joined M. E. church....

James Driskell , 18th Regt. Miss Vols., died on 21st April.

Ella, daughter of Wm. H. and M. L. Huff, was born in Wilcox co., Ala., June 10, 1849, and died Feb. 26, 1863....

Married in Thomaston, Ga., on 21st ult., by Rev. W. C. Bass, Col. Geo. P. Harrison Jr. of 52d Regt. Ga. Vols. and Miss Fannie M., eldest daughter of Dr. John Drake, of Thomaston.

Died on 2d instant, James Kendall, son of Prof. J. L. and C. K. Wright, of Trinity College, N. C., aged 5 years and 6 months.

Issue of May 12, 1863

Mrs. Catharine L. Gayle, wife of A. J. Gayle, was born Dec. 4, 1844, and joined the M. E. Church in Pontotoc, Miss. On 14th March 1863, she was cruelly murdered by a negro woman...in her 19th year.

M. B. Freeman, of 41st Ga. Regt. of Merriwether co., was born Dec. 20th, 1829, and died at Harrodsburg, Ky., from a wound at the battle of Perryville....

R. P. Smith, son of the late Rev. Burgess Smith, was born May 30, 1842, and died inElbert co., Ga., April 20, 1863.

Rev. Steven Vanvoris was born in Albany, N. Y. 16th Oct. 1818, and settled in Miss in his 21st year...died in Confederate service....

Mrs. Elizabeth M. Sherrard, daughter of A. and M. Carraway, died in Lafayette co., Fla., on 21st Feb., 1863, aged 27 years. left four children.

Pvt. James Johnston of 32d Ga. Regt, died in the Hospital at Savannah, Ga., May 2, 1863....

Thomas J. Powers, eldest son of Jasper and Ann Powers, of Capt. Franc's co., was born in Calhoun co., Ala., Dec. 1837, and died at Vicksburg, Miss., on 24th Feb. 1863....

Mr. Bryant Clower, died in Auburn, Ala., on April 17, 1863, in his 52d year....

William A. Winford, son of Alex. J. Winfield, was born 31st Oct. 1842, in Lebanon, Tenn, and died near Suffolk, 28th April 1863....

Emma Stokes died May 2d, in his 14th year, near Louisville, Ala...daughter of Major Henry and Martha A. Stokes, formerly of S. C.

Sgt. Rialdo Downer, of McNair Rifles, 33rd Miss. Vols., son of Mrs. C. M. Downer, died of wounds from the battle of Shiloh, at Forest Home, Miss....

T. J. Dunlap, 41st Ga. Regt, was born April 9, 1836, and died in Jackson, Miss., Jan. 22, 1863....

Mrs. Charlotte J. Paisely, died March, 25, 1863, aged 60 years....

Tribute of Respect to Dr. John P. Zimmerman, by Darlington Station, S. C. Conf.

Tribute of Respect to Rev. William D. Ross who died at Winder Hospital, Va., Aug. 8, 1862, a member of Isabella Mission, Quarterly Conf....

Married by Chaplain S. M. Cherry, 1st Ga. Regt., May 5th, 1863, Dr. Edward A. Norton of Cornersville, Tenn., formerly of Eufaula, ala., late Surgeon 4th Texas Regt., to Miss Bettie E. Siglar(?) of Giles co., Tenn.

On 8th inst., by Rev. James E. Morrison at the residence of the bride, Major R. Richardson to Mrs. Julia B. Leak, all of Anson co., N. C.

By Rev. W. R. Talley, May 3d, Mr. Nicholas A. Bowles to Miss Mary E. Sparks, all of Jackson co., Fla.

In Demopolis, Ala., May 7, 1863, by Rev. H. A. M. Henderson, Rev. C. W. Miller, of Kentucky Conf., to Miss Virginia Markham, of Demopolis.

On 7th inst., in Autaugaville, Ala., by Rev. A. J. Briggs, Mr. Ellis A. Mixon, of Dallas co., and Miss Lavinia E. Waugh.

Issue of May 28, 1863

Mrs. Matilda Eggleston, wife of Major E. C. Eggleston, sheriff of Lowndes co., Miss., died near Columbus, May 11th, 1863... born in Williamson co., Tenn., June 12th, 1816....

Miss Julia Lyle, daughter of C. B. Lyle, Esq., died in Athens, Ga., on the 24th ult., aged 13 years....

R. W. Sparks, youngest son of Rev. Giles P. Sparks, formerly of the Alabama Conference, was killed on the 3d May, 1863, in the battle of Chancellorsville, in his 19th year....

Mrs. Louisa J. Ellenwood, died in Monticello, Fla., March 18, 1863...born July 5th, 1834... A. J. W.

Mrs. Jane Bailey, wife of Wm. Bailey, dec'd formerly of Oglethorpe co., died in Coweta co., Ga., on the 2nd May, in the 74th year of her age... G. E. Smith.

Jacob Gamewell Hill, of 32nd Regt. N. C. T., and son of the Rev. Jacob Hill, of Catawba co, N. C., died in camp, near Kingston, N. C., on May 12th, 1863, in his 19th year....

Emma (Parker) McCard, about 16 years and two months old, died in Griffin, Ga, on April 6, 1863...reared by brother and sister C. W. Parker....

Mrs. Lucy P. Larrabee, wife of Rev. B. F. Larrabee, President of Columbus (Miss.) Female Institute, died April 30, 1863, in her 37th year... Phil P. Neely

Sackie J., wife of Wm. Skisson, and second daughter of Sallie and J. K. Thompson, was born in Macon co., Ala., March 25, 1846, and died in Newton co., Miss., March 13th, 1863... J. J. W. Smith.

W. H. Cox of Empire State Guards, Upson co., died in the Hospital at Savannah, on 1st May 1863, in her 34th year...a kind husband, indulgent father...left wife and six children. F. B. D.

Jesse Collier died April 26th, 1863, in his 56th year...
Joseph H. Storey, son of Rev. Wm. H. and Elizabeth Storey, was born April 19, 1845....

Sister Abigail Martin died inAbbeville Dist., S. C., on 10th May 1863 at more than 80 years of age...leaves three children....

Tribute of Respect by Long Cane and Bethel circuits, Ga., to Rev. George T. Hodnett, who died near Fredericksubrg, Va., on 8th April....

Tribute of Respect from Frederick's Hall, Va., to L. A. Norwood,
C. H, 94th Ga. Regt, who died in his 23d year....
Lucy J. Carry, only daughter of H. P. and S. Holcombe, of
Chattahoochee co., Ga., died May 13th, aged 7 months and 17 days.

Issue of June 4, 1863

My grandfather, Thomas Turner was born in Worcester co., Md.,
Aug. 21, 1774, removed to Ga. in 1798 or 9, settled in Hancock
co., and in 1828, removed to Putnam where he died...
Sgt. John T. Bass Co. B., 2nd Batt Ga. Vols., died 14th May
1863...
Mrs. Frances L. Willingham, died near Greensboro, Mi., March
9, 1863... W. H. Armstrong.
Mrs. P. A. Evans was born May 21, 1834, and died in Macon co.,
Ga., April 20, 1863....
Mr. Simpson Evans died of wounds received at Fredericksburg,
Feb. 14, 1863, aged 34 years....
Mrs. Sarah T. Lander, wife of Hon. Wm. Lander, died in
Lincolnton, N. C., April 1, 1863...left husband in children.
John Love died in Chambers co., Ala., April 1, 1863, aged
about 73 years...joined M. E. Church in Putnam co., Ga., about
1822....
Rev. John B. Wallace died May 13, 1863, in his 50th year...
born in Wilkes co., Ga., in 1813, in 1842 settled in Union Par-
ish, La.... G. M. W.
Calvin J. Branham was born in Wake co., N. C., Nov. 9, 1864,
and died at his brother's, near Hamilton, Harris co., Ga., May
11th, 1863....
George W. Newby of 15th Regt. S. C. V. died at Petersburg,
Va., March 7th, 1863, aged 24....
Miss Sallie Gantt Whitaker, second daughter of the late James
A. Whitaker died in Russell co., Ala., May 13th, 1863, in her
12th year....
Thos. A. Berry, son of Nathan and Eliza Berry of Twiggs co.,
Ga., fell in the battle near Chancellorsville, May 3, 1863, in
his 19th year....
John M. Morrison was born April 28, 1844, and died in Hospi-
tal at Wilmington, Feb. 25, in his 18th year....
Mrs. Barbara Haigler, relict of the late Maj. David Haigler,
of S. C., died in Randolph co., Ga., May 8, in her 67 year...
originally a member of the Lutheran Church....
Mrs. Margaret E. Hall, wife of Rev. Willis Hall was born in
Telfair co., Ga., and died 16th, May 1863...
Tribute of Respect to Rev. Thompson Green(?)...Villata Ct.,
Ala. Conf....
Married on the 24th inst.,by Rev. Thomas T. Christian, Rev.
James L. Neese and Miss Cecilia J. Dorsett, all of Macon, Ga.
May 24th, by Rev. M. L. Banks, Mr. Henry E. Stephens and
Miss Amanda M. Spell, both of St. Bartholomews, S. C.
April 22d, at Monticello, S. C., by Rev. A. J. Cauthen, Mr.
J. R. Dellbery and Miss Rebecca Dawkins.
Died 16th May, in Richland Dist., S. C., John H., infant son
of Capt. J. H. and L. A. Kinsler, aged 1 year and 8 months.

Issue of June 11, 1863

The Rev. James Theus Munds, of Columbia, S. C.,died 11th
of May 1863, aged 34 years. He lost his father in infancy... W.
T. C.
Mrs. Mary A. Kimbrough, died on the April 22d, 1863...daughter
of David and Sarah Rosser of Putnam co., Ga., born May 3, 1813,
married to Mr. H. C. Kimbrough in March, 1833... L. G. R. W.

111

John F. Keenson, of Savannah, Ga., was born June 22, 1843, wounded in first Manassas, and again at Gaines's Mill....

Elijah P. Lowman was stricken at the last battle near Fredericksburg....

Richard Lang was born in Camden co., Ga., Nov. 27, 1798, married in 1822, and died in Jefferson co., Fla., May 4, 1863... C.P. Murdock.

Dr. Benjamin Garrett died April 12th, 1863, aged 33 years... 2nd Ga. Cavalry... S. L. Hamilton.

John Evans Lykes was born in Richland Dist., S. C., Dec. 1797, and died March 5th, 1863...leaves wife and eight children. J. B. Stone.

Benjamin Hays died in Jackson co., Fla., May 22d, 1863, in his 69th year...a native of N. C., and in early life removed to Jackson co....

Josephine R. Rogers, wife of J. Rufus Rogers, died in Burke co., Ga., April 16th, 1863, in her 23d year, leaving a husband and four (two step) children...

J. Simpson Young died in the Federal Hospital in Frederick City, Md., Oct. 1, 1862. He was a native of Union Dist., S. C., a private in Co. A., 13th Regt. S. C. V. He was wounded on the 14th of Sept., lived 13 years... Colin Murchison.

Married on 27th May, by N. D. Murchison, Mr. H. H. C. McRoan of Jackson co., Ga., to Miss Elizabeth C. Robinson, of Burke co., Ga.

On 26th May, by Rev. J. H. Littlejohn, Rev. Thomas A. Brown, of Barnesville, Ga., to Miss Cynthia D. Askins, of Monroe co., Ga.

On 26th May, by Rev. G. H. Patillo, Capt. John B. McDowell, and Miss Nannie P. Daniel, both of Talbot co., Ga.

In Marengo co., Ala., on 20th May, by Rev. J. M. Boland, Dillard Thomas of Harris co., Ga.,to Mrs. Sarah M. Jackson.

Died at Grove Station, May 26th, 1863, Sallie Eloise Whitfield, daughter of J. and E. M. Westfield, aged 1 year 2 months and 3 days.

Issue of June 18, 1863

Miss Mary G. Mixon died on 24th April at the residence of her father, Elijah Mixon, Oxford, Ga., in her 37th year....

James Robertson, died March 30th, 1863, in his 66th year, in Pickens Dist., S. C...left wife and nine children.

Mary Ann E. Turnipseed was born in Columbia co., Ga., Dec. 3, 1833, and died in Marion co., Fla., near Ocala, March 30, 1863.

George M. Keisl of Charleston, S. C., died in Columbia, April 19th, in his 53d year... J. T. W.

D. Duncan Williams of Escambie co., Fla., died at the Breckinridge Hospital, Tullahoma, Tenn., on 6th April, 1863, in the 26th year of his age....

Mrs. Mary M. Wilson, wife of Robt. C. Wilson, of Talladega co., Ala., was born April 25th, 1806, and died May 20, 1863...

Mrs. Antoinette Broughton, died in Madison, Ga., March 17, 1863....

Bro. Charles Kennon, son of Dr. Kennon, died at Westville, Ala., April 27, in her 23d year....

Henry Clay Palmer, died May 3, 1863, killed in the battle of Chancellorsville...born Feb. 12, 1843....

Rev. Tilman Douglas died on May 28th, 1863...settled in Burke co., Ga.... L. L. Ledbetter.

Mrs. Isoline Amanda Due, wife of Mr. A. J. Due, died in Wetumpka, Ala., April 21, 1863, aged 23 years....

Tribute of Respect to Lt. F. E. Ross, Lt. R. S. Fletcher, Cpl. R. C. Dukes, Pvt. John N. Miles, James Spruill, and T. J.

Morris, all of Co. B., Cobb's Legion...
   Tribute of Respect by Quarterly conf. of Newnansville, Fla.,
to Rev. Peyton P. Smith....
   Married in Washington co., on the 4th inst., by Rev. H. D.
Murphy, Mr. Joseph J. Bradley of Macon, and Miss Anna E. Murphy,
of the former place.
   June 5th, by the Rev. George C. Clarke, Mr. J. F. Barrett,
of Houston co., to Miss Martha C. Price of Perry, Ga.
   On 7th June 1863, by Rev. A. W. Harris, A. D. Patterson to
Miss Mary J. Bryan, all of Berrien co., Ga.
   By Rev. O. L. Smith, in Brooks co., Ga., May 28th, Mr. James
Miles Hunter, and Miss E. F. Lake, of Magnolia, N. C.
   By Rev. O. L. Smith, in Brooke co., Ga., May 31st, Sgt.
J. B. R. Stanley and Miss Winneford Brown.
   In Bishopville, S. C., May 28th, 1863, by Rev. Aug. W. Walker,
Dr. M. C. Wallace of Darlington, S. C. to Miss Nancy O. Stuckey,
of Bishopville, S. C.
   Died on 20th May, James Louis, only child of John and Janette
Howell.
   On 28th May, A. T. F., youngest son of J. A. and W. B. McHan,
18 months old.
   Louis Franklin, son of Abraham and Elizabeth Thomas, died at
Fowistown, Ga., on 26th May, aged 4 years and 10 months.
   In Barnesville, Ga., June 8th, Julia, daughter of Rev. D. T.
and M. T. Holmes, aged 6 months and 26 days.
   In Spartanburg, S. C., June 6th, 1863, Julius Houser, son of
Rev. W. H. Fleming, in the 8th year of his age.

Issue of June 25, 1863

   Mrs. Fannie Ransom, wife of Rev. Richard F. Ransom, of the
Tenn. Conf, died June 5th, near Rome, Ga., in her 34th year....
   My Mother-in-law, Mrs. Jane Marion, relict of the late Nathaniel Marion, was born in Charleston Dist., S. C., married
there, early removed to Abbeville Dist., and with her husband
united with the M. E. Church about 50 years ago...died at Cokesbury, S. C., May 21, 1863, aged 83 years. G. H. Round.
   Rev. John P. Guest died inRichmond, Va., 1st April 1863, in
his 26th year....
   Henry C. Brown, the eldest son of Mr. G. Brown, was born
2d Sept. 1844 in Oak Bowery, Ala...3d May 1863 fell on the battle
field near Chancellorsville....
   Sherrod C. W. F. Campbell, son of Dr. C. E. F. W. Campbell,
of Jasper co., Ga., was born Aug. 12, 1841, and fell on the battle
field at Chancellorsville, May 3, 1863...
   Daniel Lawrence died at his mother's residence near Griffin,
Ga., on 24th May, 1863, in his 37th year....
   Wm. W. Scott died 29th March, 1863...born Abbeville Dist.,
S. C., Nov. 7, 1831...left wife and family.
   Dr. Edward V. Munro, died in Lee co., Ga., on 12th June, in
his 54th year...leaves an only daughter, and aged mother....
   Benjamin F. McKay died in Covington, Ga., April 17th, 1863...
born in S. C., April 11, 1819, resided in Covington a number of
years....
   J. W. Whitlow, of 48th Ala. Regt., son of James and Elizabeth
Whitlow, formerly of Clark co., Ga.,was born Dec. 6, 1837, and
died in Foard Hospital, Ga., March 20th, 1863....
   Richard Daniel Maddox, eldest son of George W. Maddox, of
Chambers co., Ala., was born in Merriwether co., Ga., 2d March
1840...found dead on 21st May 1863...
   Josiah R. Padgett died in Auburn, Ala., May 7, 1863. born
in Milledgeville, Ga., 1808...left wife and five children.

J. R. Hodnett of 5th Regt. Ga. Vols. was born in Merriwether co., Ga., Sept. 16, 1840, and died in Richmond, Va.,May 17th, 1863....

Bro. Starling E. Powers, father of John B.and Wm. J. Powers, members of the Ala. Conf., died at the residence of his son-in-law, Rev. Allen Weems, in Cherokee co., Ala., 27th May 1863...born in Union Dist., S. C., 15th March 1798... C. L. Dobbs.

Lt. J. Willis Moore of Newton co., Miss., 6th Regt. Miss. Vols,, died at Mrs. Henry's, near Fort Gibson, Miss., May 31, 1863...aged 19 years 9 months and 4 days.

Maggie Jane, daughter of Henry and Rebecca Stillings, of Columbia, S. C., died March 18th, 1863, aged 9 years, 5 months and 17 days....

Andrew H. Newton of 22d Ga. Regt., son of R. H. and E. H. Newton, died inSpottsylvania co., Va...

Mrs. Susan C. Stansell, wife of William A.Stansell, and daughter of Nathan and Elizabeth Passmoer, was born in Jones co., Ga., Nov. 13, 1836, in Harris co., Ga., March 12, 1863....

Lorenzo D. Williams, son of L. D. and M. Williams, died 28th March, 1863, in his 18th year....

Lawrence Wilson Barge, son of Mr. Lewis T. and Mrs. E. Barge, died in Wilcox co., Ala., March 5th, 1863, in his 13th year....

Joseph Day, was born August 17, 1811, and died May 9, 1863.... Saml. W. Harris.

Married at the residence of Leonard Chapin, Esq., in Spartanburg, S. C.,on Wed. evening, June 10th, by Rev. A. M. Shipp, D. D., President of Wofford College, F. G. DeFontaine, and Georgia W. Moore, of Charleston, daughter of Rev. G. W. Moore, of the S. C. Conf.

On 11th June, 1863, at Aiken, S. C., by Rev. Edward F. Thwing, ot the S. C. Conf., Mr. William H. Joiner of Atlanta, Ga., to Miss Katharine O. Merritt, of Prattville, Ala.

On the 9th of June, 1863, by Rev. J. B. Stone, Rev. J. W. Peavy, of the Ala. Conf., to Miss Sallie Sartor, all of Monroe co., Miss.

By Rev. A. Johnson on 7th June, Dr. William B. Rich to Miss Eugenia C. Stewart, all of Jasper, Fla.

Died Laura Alice Buntyn, daughter of W. D. And S. A. B. Buntyn, May 25th, in Butler co., Ala., aged 5 years, 1 month and 26 days.

Issue of July 2, 1863

Sgt. Wm. Wade Simpson, son of John Wells Simpson, was born in Lawrenceville, S. C., and was killed at South Mountain, Md., 14th Sept. 1862...joined Co. D. of James' Batt., on his 17th birthday...

Mrs. Jane Goss, wife of Wm. Goss of Unionville, S. C., died June 5, 1863, in her 68th(?) year... H. A. C. Walker.

Wm. W. Pearson, was born in Putnam co., June 9, 1826, married Miss Ann M. Morton in 1857, and was killed at Chancellorsville, May 5, 1863... A. M. Thigpen.

John Ross Langford was born in Columbia co., Ga., July 18, 1863...died at Frederic city, Md., May 16, 1863...not a member of the church.

John Gilbert, of 24th Ala. Regt, was born in Clarke co., Ala., July 31st, 1841, and died in Chattanooga, Tenn., May 30, 1863....

Thomas E. Hyer, died on the 6th March, 1863, near Covington, Ga., in his 46th year...left wife and nine children....

R. A. Sikes died at Bristol, Tenn., March 2, 1863, in his 28th year....

William S. Harm was born February 9, 1836...died on board a steamer as a prisoner of war on his way to Vicksburg to be exchanged...married to Miss Rosa D. Livingston of Jacksonville, Fla., in 1859....

James C. Little, son of Daniel and Mary Little, died May 18, 1863...24th Regt. S. C. V...

Lysias Stackhouse was born April 10, 1813, and died May 7, 1863....

John G. Lovett died near Orrville, Ala., June 3, 1863, aged nearly 63 years....

Sister Margaret S. Frasure, died at the residence of her mother, in St. Peter's Parish, S. C., in her 28th year...

Mrs. Sarah E. A. Lee, wife of Dr. J. C. Lee, died in Walker co., Ga., 26th April 1863, in her 43d year....

James Cicero Hammett was born in Franklin co., Ga., on 24th Feb., 1832, and died in the hospital at Tallahassee, Fla., 1st May 1863....

Married on Tuesday evening the 9th inst., by Rev. H. W. Hilliard, Mr. Albert A. Beall and Miss Savannah Spears, all of this city.

In Augusta, Ga., on 3rd May, by Rev. D. D. Cox, Mr. William Glover and Miss Frances Buffington.

By the same, in Augusta, Ga., on 18th inst., Mr. Robert C. Hampton and Miss Mary J. Miller.

In Americus, Ga., on 18th inst., by Rev. R. V. Lester, Dr. William W. Barlow and Miss Elizabeth Gaither.

On the 9th inst., near Palmetto, Ga., by Rev. Atticus G. Haygood, A. B. Lathane, Esq. of McMin co., Tenn., and Miss Phoebe Brooks, of Coweta co., GA.

Issue of July 9, 1863

Dr. J. Benson Wise died on 7th May, in his 31st year, near McMinnville, Tenn....

Mrs. Maria Vaughn, wife of Edward B. Vaughn, was born in Mecklenburg co., Va., 1802, married Mr. V. in 1826 and died in Tuskaloosa, Ala., June 16, 1863...mother of eight children, two of whom preceded her to the grave....

Mrs. L. M. House, was born Oct. 31, 1833(?) and died June 11, 1863...Early in life, joined the Baptist Church. In Nov. 1836 married to R. E. House, Esq...left one daughter.

Orderly Sgt. B. F. Session, second son of Rev. J. J. and Mary S. was born in Lee co., Ga., August 1, 1835, and died in Fredericksburg....

Thomas Frink was born in Columbia Co., N. C. 1816...left N. C. and moved to Martin co., E. Fla....left widow and five children...

Henry H. Hay, son of W. P. Hay of Bartow co., Ga., died June 18th, 1863, aged 17 years and 7 months...entered the 28th Miss. Regt. with his uncle....

Bro. Henderson A. Cope was born near Raleigh, N. C., Aug. 18, 1817, and died in Washington co., Ala., May 26th, 1863....

Bro. Thomas Cope was born in Wake co., N. C. May 7, 1831, removed to Ala. in 1851, and died in the hospital at Tunnell Hill, Ga., May 1, 1863....left wife and three children.

Augustua J. Bell was born in Burke co., Ga., June 26th, 1817, and died in Decatur co., Ga., May 2nd, 1863....

John L. Rowell and Henry M. Rowell, sons of Henry and Elizabeth Rowell of Tallapoosa co., Ala.; the former died at Shelbyville, Tenn., April 10, 1863, in his 22d year; the latter died in Chattanooga, Tenn., April 29, 1863, in his 19th year-...

Lt. W. H. Turner of Fulton co., Ga., died in Albany, Ga., 20th June....

Mrs. Rebecca Fields, was born in Franklin co., Ga., Jan. 9, 1809 and died in Autaugaville, Ala., June 24th, 1863....

Mrs. J. Eliza Arline, wife of Jesse Arline, was born in
Edgcomb, N. C., Jan. 6th, 1808, and died in Decatur co., Ga.,
April 14th, 1863....
Robert Caldwell died at Tampa, Fla., June 12th, 1863....
Thomas Miers, son of Joseph J. and Susan Miers, of Macon co.,
Ala., and member of Co. C., 38th Regt. Ala. Vols., died near
Wartrace,Tenn., May 20th, 1863, aged 19 years and 26 days....
James Baily, son of Mrs. Ann Isbell, was born in Kershaw
Dist., S. C., and died at Adams' Run, May 25th, 1863....
John W. Fields, of Eufaula, Ala., Died at Clinton, Tenn.,
April 24, 1863, aged 19 years....
Charles Wesley Lengley, son of Rev. Wm. A. Langley, of Autau-
ga co., Ala., died in Chattanooga, Tenn., April 13th, 1863, aged
20 years and 31 days....
Sister Nancy Stewart died in Talbot co., Ga., May 30th, 1863,
in the 78th year of her life...born in Lincoln co., Ga., daughter
of Nehemiah Dunn, and wife of Earley Stewart decd....
Martha Antoinette, daughter of Rev. John L. and Julia Ann
Stewart, died at Conyers, Ga., June 19th, 1863, in her 11th year
....
John Vine Neill was born in Laurens Dist., S. C., and died
29th April 1863, at hospital, Richmond, Va.
Edward H. Greer, of 19th Regt. S. C. V., died at Guthries-
ville, S. C., Feb. 9, 1863, aged 18 years and a few days.
Married by Rev. J. H. Williams, June 14th, 1863, Mr. T. G.
Norwood to Miss Elizabeth A. Carter, all of Lowndes co., Ga.
By the Rev. J. F. Berry, June 22d, 1863, Mr. Henry M. Brown,
of Butler, Ga.,to Miss Dora A. Boyd, of Talbot co.
By Rev. W. P. Miller, at the house of the bride's sister, Mrs.
Durr, on 16th June, Mr. John M. Sigrest, of Macon co., Ga., to
Miss Susan J. Barbow, of Dale co., Ala.
On 25th June, at the residence of the late Peter Corbin, in
Taylor co., Ga., by the Rev. G. H. Patillo, Mr. Wm. H. Carpenter,
of Crawford county, and Miss Ella H. Gray.
In Charleston District, on 3d June, by Rev. T. L. Siffey, Mr.
Joseph R. Crawford to Miss Martha V. Owens.
Also, at the same time and place, Mr. H. Hamilton Murray to
Miss Sarah E. Owens.
On 28th June, by Rev. Thomas F. Pierce, Capt. James H. Alex-
ander and Miss Sarah J. Irvin, all of Washington, Ga.
In Lumpkin, Ga., on 26th June, by Rev. R. B. Lester, Rev.
John C. Simmons to Mrs. Sarah M. Sibley.
Died in Lexington District, S. C., June 13th, 1863, Christina
Derrick Shuler, daughter of J. H. and ___ Shuler, aged 1 year,
3 months and 16 days.
At the residence of her grandfather, T. H. Audas, Sparta, Ga.,
June 24th, Amanda Clifton, daughter of Rev. James S. and Mrs.
S. J. Lane of Talladega, Ala.
Lora Bird Murray, only daughter of James B. N. And N. A. M.,
died in Terrell co., Ga., May 12th, in her 3d year.

Issue of July 16, 1863

Holm Sturdivant was born April 4th, 1813, and died near
Wadesboro, Anson co., N. C., May 23, 1863, leaving a wife and
two children....
James Sawyer of Lexington Dist., S. C., died June 12th, 1863,
aged about 40 years...member of the Baptist Church in early life.
Mrs. Ann T. Whitfield was born March 15, 1850, and died
in LaGrange, Ga.,May 21st, 1863...she was left a widow with a
large family of children....
John H., son of Rev. Daniel and Sarah E. Herlong, of Lowndes
co., Ala., died at Fort Gaines,near Mobile, Ala., on 8th April,

in his 39th year....

Thos. Sandford Shuford, of Cleveland co., N. C., was killed in his 28th year, at the battle of Chancellorsville, May 3, 1863 ...34th Regt. N. C. T.

James T. Redding, son of Rowland and Sarah Redding, was born in Monroe co., Ga., Jan. 22, 1842...12th Ga. Regt...fell on 2d May last....

William Turpin Hardy, only son of R. B. and Caroline Hardy, of Anderson Dist., S. C., was born Dec. 7th, 1840, and was killed Sunday, May 3, at Chancellorsville....

Mrs. Lucy Hill died in Wetumpka, Ala., June 27th, 1863, in her 71st year...

Miss Susan H. Curtis, died in Pike co., Ga., on 20th April, 1863, aged 23 years....

Sgt. Henry W. Brooks of 14th Rgt. Ala. Vols., eldest son of Capt. Henry Brooks...died at Richmond, Va., 22nd May in his 19th year....

James W. Witherington was born Nov. 23, 1833, married to Miss Sarah A. Saxon, Dec. 17, 1855, and died at Winder's Hospital, Richmond, Va., June 13, 1863....

Mrs. Susan D. Kilgore, died on 3d May 1863...left six children ...her father, Dr. Robert Giles, of Anderson Dist., S. C., where she died....

N. J. Griffin, of 6th Regt. Ga. Vols. fell at Chancellorsville, Va., May 2, 1863....

My two brothers, Wm. A. and Isaac E. Pace fell on the 16th May at Edward's Station, Miss. Wm. A. Pace was 21 years of age in March. Isaac E. Pace was not a member of the church....Jno. A. Pace.

John B. Barrow, son of E. E. Barrow, of Dale co., Ala., died at Oak Grove Hospital....

Henry H. Banks of Pike co., Ga., died at Hamilton's Station, Va., in the 23d year of his age....

Wallie B., son of Co. John L. and Mrs. Addie Woodward died in Culloden, Ga., June 20th, born June 6th, 1848(?)....

Married by Rev. J. M. Dickey, July 6th, 1863, Mr. H. A. Hayes to Mrs. Susan C. Landrum, both of Lexington, Oglethorpe co., Ga.

Died Missouri Isabella, daughter of Reuben and Naomi Jordan, in Calhoun co., Ga., May 25, 1863, aged 4 years, 3 months and 1 day.

In Macon,Ga., on the morning of July 1st, George John Snider, in the 4th year of his age, only son of James J. and Eliza R. Snider.

Issue of July 23, 1863

Capt. John Lamberth, of 16th Regt. Tenn. Vols., aged 24 years and 6 months, son of John Lamberth, Esq., of Tallapoosa co., Ala ...fell at battle of Perryville.

George Madison Houser was born May 6, 1838, and died at his father's residence, in St. Stephens Parish, S. C., June 21, 1863.

Col. D. B. Creech died June 13, 1863, in his 53d(?) year... married in 1835 in Montgomery co., Ga., removed to Dale Co., Ala. in 1854...son-in-law, J. D. McRae...left wife, three sons and five daughters... W. P. Miller.

Rev. Wm. Beverly Chandler was born in DeKalb co., Ga., Sept. 20th, 1837, and died near Fredericksburg, Va., May 31, 1863....

Charles Carter, died at Green Hill, Stewart co., Ga., June 20th, 1863, in his 34th year....

James L. Taylor, died at his residence in Rutherford co., N. C., Jan. 29th, 1863, in the 52d year of his age.

Also Eliza E. Taylor, his wife died May 21, 1863, aged 55 years.... A. Hamby.

Mrs. Sallie Pullig, wife of P. Pullig, Esq., was born Dec. 12, 1792, and died in Fairfield Dist., S. C., June 2, 1863... left aged husband and many relatives.

Thomas M. Clyde, father of Rev. T. J. Clyde of the S. C. Conf., died in Pickens Dist., S. C., June 30th, 1863, in the 65th or 66th year of his age....

Wm. Sitton was born April 18th, 1785, and died in Anderson Dist., S. C., April 18, 1863....

Sarah Bassett was born in Philadelphia in 1790, and died in Mobile, Ala., June 20th, 1863....

Sgt. James D. McRae of 54th Ala. Regt. died in Montgomery, Ala., May 30th, 1863, in his 40th year...left wife and three children....

William James Moore, son of Rev. William Moore, of Chesterfield Dist., S. C., 1st Regt. S. C. V., died at home on July 6, 1863, in his 20th year....

Tribute of Respect by Ceneva ct., Ga. Conf. to Calvin J. Brannan.

Tribute of Respect by Atlanta ct., Ga. Conf. to Revs. John M. Smith and Jas. Mangum.

Married in Jones co., Ga., at the residence of John Williams, Esq., July 8th, by the Rev. Wm. S. Turner, Skelton Napier, Jr. and Mrs. Issie R. Lawrence.

On 5th inst., by Rev. T. R. Barnett, John Eubanks, of Putnam co., Fla., to Miss Amanda Smith, of Clay co., Fla.

Near Tallassee, Ala., on 12th inst., by Rev. M. E. Butt, Mr. F. M. Osbourne, of Montgomery co., to Miss S. J. Taylor, of Tallapoosa co., Ala.

On July 16th, in Alexander, Burke co., Ga., by Rev. W. H. Potter, William T. Revill of Meriwether co., Ga., to Miss Alice A., eldest daughter of Rev. L. L. Ledbetter, of the Ga. Conf.

Died Mary Sallie Kirsh, only child of William M. and H. Oliver Kirsh, in Barnwell Dist., May 15, 1863, aged 1 year, 6 months and 2 weeks.

In Eatonton, Ga., May 24th, Eddie Benjamin, youngest son of Berrien and Mary Rice, aged 1 year and 10 months.

Issue of July 30, 1863

John D. Newell, son of Johnson and Martha Newell was born in Abbeville Dist., S. C., and died in Tallapoosa co., Ala., May 19, 1863, aged 26 years....

Maj. James Lane was born in Green co., Ga., Dec. 22nd, 1795, and died in Cave Spring, Ga., July 17, 1863...

W. H. Noell of Co. B., 32d Ga. Regt, oldest son of James W. and Sarah Noell died in the hospital at Savannah, Ga., May 29, 1863....

Mrs. Courtney V., wife of Erastus B. Duncan, of the Tenn. Annual Conf., died June 17, 1863, at the residence of Dr. Robt. Tweedy, Limstone co., Ala...daughter of Jacob Wythe Walker, Esq., and born in Logan co., Ky., April 1, 1815.

Miss Nannie B., her daughter was born in Washington co., Ark., Nov. 4, 1845, and died April 23, 1863... Welborn Mooney.

Capt. Peter V. Guerry fell dead at the battle of Gains Mills, June 27, 1862...born in Ga. in 1815, came to Ala., in 1853, married Mrs. Mary Guerry in 1854, lived in Tuskegee...Macon co., Ala., where his widow now resides... E. J. Hamell.

Bro. Josiah Matthews of Talbot co., Ga., died July 8, 1863, in the 78th year of his age, and 52d year of his membership in the M. E. Church...born in Halifax co., N. C.,married in Baldwin co., Ga....his son (the Doctor).... H. P. Pitchford.

Jacob Wright was born in Newberry Dist., S. C.,June 19, 1805, and died in Edgefield Dist., S. C.,7th May 1863....

Mrs. Ann Register was born in Colleton Dist., S. C., and died in Greenwood, Fla., June 14th, 1863, being about 70 years old....

Mrs. Mary Frances Graham, wife of Dr. Isaac W. Graham of Williamsburg Dist., S. C., died June 21, 1863, at the residence of her brother-in-law W. H. Scott, in Gadsden co., Fla., in her 24th year.

John Brownlee was born Sept. 17, 1806, and died June 6, 1863. R. C. Oliver.

Mrs. Nancy Gillespie, wife of P. H. Gillespie, died in Carroll co., Ga.,July 5, 1863, aged 57 years... B.E.L. Timmons.

Sarah R. Copeland was born Jan. 17, 1813, and died July 12th, 1863...left husband and five children.

James W. Evans, of 6th Ala. Regt. was born in Clarke co., Miss., April 21, 1843, and was killed at the battle of Chancellorsville, May 3, 1863....

Grandmother Barker, mother of Rev. G. W. Barker died July 8, 1863, at the residence of her son , in Barbour co., Ala. born in Rockingham co., N. C.,in March 1781... Jesse Wood.

Thomas R. Cain was born in Gadsden co., Fla., May 6, 1836, died a prisoner in Bardstown, Ky., 39th Regt. Ala. Vols...

Married on 12th July by Rev. Thomas T. Christian, Mr. Thomas Barr and Miss Sarah Johnson, all of Macon.

By the same on 15th July, Robert Richards of Atlanta, to Miss Mary Craig of Macon.

By the same, on 16th July, Henry Pool and Miss M A E Sessions, all of Macon.

July 7th, by Rev. C A Crowell, at the residence of Capt. A J Weems, Capt. J. M. Powers, of the 18th Ga. Regt., to Miss Emma W. Davis, of Anderson Dist., S. C.,

In Macon, Ga.,on 21st July, by Rev. Thomas T. Christian, Mr. O H P McClendon, of Cave Spring, Ga., and Mrs. Mary Thomas, of Dublin, Ga.

Died on Sunday, July 5th, at the residence of her Uncle, Col. C. J. Munnerlyn, Ella H., second daughter of Rev. W. M. and Mrs. S. B. Wightman, in the 22d year of her age.

In Union District, S. C., on 10th July, Georgie, infant daughter of Mrs. Anna Holmes, aged 2 years and 4 months.

At the residence of her grandmother, Mrs. R P Sasnett, Sparta, Ga., July 19th, 1863, Alice Henry, daughter of Mr. and Mrs. Frank L. Little, aged 1 year and 8 months.

Issue of August 6, 1863

Mrs. Eliza Phillips of Duval co., Fla., daughter of Albert G. and Margaret Phillips, died June 21, 1863, at the residence of Mr. Brantly, Madison co., Fla., aged 26 years....

Mrs. Mary S. Peurifoy, a native of Charleston, S. C., and daughter of L. H. Mouzon, died 18th June 1863, in her 26th year ...In 1861 she removed to upper S. C....

Mrs. Fannie Margaret, wife of Thos. B. Anderson and only daughter of the Rev. Alexander W. and Mrs. L. W. Walker, died June 5, 1863, in her 25th year at Spartanburg, S. C....

Duncan McMillan died in Marion Dist., S. C., July 7, 1863, aged 59 years...a member of the Presbyterian Church....

Rev. F. A. Johnson of Duval co., Fla., was born Dec. 28, 1821, and died in Richmond Va., March 26, 1863, in his 43d year.

Miss Elizabeth M. Lemmond, died on 21st May, 1863, ...joined the M. E. Church in 1848, in her 16th year... E. A. Lemmond.

Benjamin P. Wood, second son of John J. and Arminda Wood, of Cobb co., Ga., died in Hospital, Richmond, Va., May 3, 1863, in his 19th year...

W. W. White, of 28th Regt. Ala. Vols., died at the Gilmer Hospital, Chattanooga, Tenn., May 11, 1863, in his 25th year....

Rev. Lindsay C. Weaver of the S. C. Conf., was born in Spartanburg Dist., S. C., Nov. 18, 1837, and died at Bishopville, Sumter Dist., Feb. 28, 1863....

Stephen Downey was born in Marengo co., Ala., April 10, 1835, married Rhoda Jane Moore, Nov. 22, 1849, and died in Dalton, Ga., June 24th, 1863....

George J. Miller, son of Rev. W. F. Miller, of the Ala. Conf., was born 28th Nov. 1844 and died near Mobile, Ala., June 28th, 1863, 34th Regt. Ala. Vols....

Elisha Hunter of 43d Ga. Regt. of Gwinnett co., was born Oct. 5, 1833, and died near Knoxville, Tenn....

Mrs. Mary Clements was born Sept. 20, 1787, and died in Telfair co., Ga., 19th May 1863...

Mrs. Rebecca Gardiner, wife of Rev. Thomas Gardiner, dec'd, died in Macon, Ga., on 12th July 1863, in the 72d year of her age....

D. R. Rudasil, 37th Regt. N. C. T., died at the Winder Hospital, in Richmond, Va., on 15th July....

Washington D. Smith, son of James M. and Ruth Smith, of Floyd co., Ga., died at the residence of Mr. Johnson, in Rappahannock co., Va., in his 34th year....

Stephen Rhudy died at the residence of his son, in Floyd co., Ga., in his 74th year....

Mrs. Alice Johnson, daughter of John R. and Alice Lowery, dec'd, of Twiggs co., Ga., died at my house in Thomasville, Ga., on 21st May, in his 31st year....

Thomas Dozier died at the residence of his son in Oglethorpe co., Ga., July 2, in his 87th year...

Wm. W. Worwick, son of W. A. and Mary Ann Worwick, of White co., Ga., fell near Gettysburg, Pa., aged 16 years.

Tribute of Respect by Clayton and Louisville station, Ala. Conf. to Rev. Alexander McLenan.

Married by Rev. R. S. Woodward, in Dallas co., Ala., July 14, Mr. Richard Merriman to Miss Maggie Chestnut.

By Rev. R. S. Woodward, at Centrall Mills, Dallas co., Ala., July 21st, Rev. E. S. Moore to Miss Jennie Hall.

On 1st July, in Leon co., Fla., by Rev. J. O. Branch, Rev. W. . Murphy, of the Fla. Conf., to Miss Laura S. Holland, daughter of Dr. G. N. Holland of said county.

On July 28th, in the Methodist Church, at Traveller's Rest, Macon co., Ga., by Rev. R. B. Lester, Rev. Wm. S. Turner of the Ga. Conf. to Miss Martha A. Harris, third daughter of Wm. Harris, Esq., of Macon county, late of Fort Valley, Ga.

On July 28th, by Rev. John H. C. McKinney, Mr. Samuel McCarter to Miss Ramath A. Ballard, both of Spartanburg Dist., S. C.

By Rev. R. B. Lester, July 28th, 1863, Mr. George W. W. Williams, of Montezuma, to Miss ___ O'Connor, of Macon co., Ga.

On 28th July, by Rev. N. C. Morchouse, Simeon Skinner to Miss Mary Colesuer, all of Burke co., Ga.

Died Dr. William M. Lamkin at Enon, Ala., July 18, 1863, aged 71 years, 4 months and 1 day.

At Swainsboro, Ga., July 23, Sarah Allen Bouchelle, daughter of Dr. L. B. and Sarah E. Bouchelle, aged 1 year, 10 months and 8 days.

Issue of August 13, 1863

Lt. Col. Wm. Terrell Harris, 2d Ga. Regt. of Merriwether co., Ga., fell at Gettysburg, 2d July 1863, aged 33 years...

Mrs. M. A. E. Hardman, wife of W. B. Hardman, Esq., of Atlanta, Ga., was born in Hamburg, S. C., Feb. 14th, 1823, and died in Walton co., Ga., July 11th, 1863...joined M. E. Church in Charleston in her 9th year....

Capt. J. Henry Ellison of 15th Ala. Regt., son of Rev. Dr.
W. H. Ellison, and grandson of the late Bishop Capers, fell at
Gettysburg, 15th July....

Lt. George E. Pooser, of Apalachicola, Fla., 2d Regt. Fla.
Vols., son of Jacob N. and Eliza H. Pooser, formerly of Orange-
burg, S. C., now of Jackson co., Fla., died in Martinsburg, Va.,
July 6, 1863....

Maria E. Yancey, wife of Milton P. S. Yancey, and daughter
of Freeman and Hannah Ellis, died near Auburn, 28th June 1863....

John W. Hays of 37th Regt. Ala. Vols., son of Cadar Hays,
of Henry co., Ala., was born April 2, 1840 and died July 6,
1863, at Vicksburg, Miss....

Thomas Garner was born in Fauquier co., Va., March 28, and
died at the residence of his son, J. T. Garner, in Haralson co.,
Ga., July 3rd, aged 105 years...He was perhaps the oldest man
in Ga....

James H. John of 29th Ala. Vol., born Nov. 17, 1828, and
died in the Hospital at Shelbyville, Tenn., June 17, 1863....

The sabbath school at Bethlehem, Orangeburg ct., records the
death of Eliza R. Dukes, daughter of Abram and Elizabeth Dukes,
who was born July 26, 1832, and died July 3, 1863....

William Flint was born March 1, 1813, and died 23d July 1863,
in his 51st year....

John W. Prator, died in Upson co., July 7, 1863, in his 85th
year...left large family and children and grandchildren.

Wm. A. Padgett was born March 20th, 1834, in Fayette co.,
Ga., being the oldest son of Moses and Rebecca Padgett, and died
May 6th, 1863, in Richmond, Va.

Miss Emma S. Brown died in Baldwin co., Ga., July 9, in her
14th year...

Tribute of Respect by Liberty Chapel, Crystal River ct.,
to brother Thomas Frink.

Married on 15th July, by Rev. B M Calloway, Lt. Thomas H. Dozier of Oglethorpe co., and Miss Hattie Arnold, of Wilkes co.,
Ga.

On August 1st, near Mapleton, S. C., by Rev. P. L. Harman, Mr.
S. G. Thompson of Augusta, Ga., to Miss Susan Ferguson, of Abbeville, S. C.

On 3rd August, by Rev. A. D. Chenault, Mr. George P. Tankers-
ely to Miss Amanda M. Paschall, at Rev. L. Steed's, all of Columbia co., Ga.

Died, Nannie Alberta(?), infant daughter of Dr. A. G. And
S. F. Bennett, of Gadsden, Ala., died on 29th July, being 9 months
and 10 days old.

At Shubutt, Miss., on 19th June, Charles Henderson(?), aged
1 year, 1 month and 3 days.

And on the 4th July, David Edwin, aged 2 years, 5 months and
15 days, both sons of Dr. D. M. and Mary T. Dunlap.

At Wacahoota, Fla., on 21st July, Talitha Ley, daughter of J.
Porter and Drusilla Smith, aged 9 months and 9 days.

Issue of August 20, 1863

Robert M. Davis died near Lowndesville, Abbeville Dist., S.
C., June 17th, in his 63d year....

Miss Frances S. Gray, of Charleston, S. C., died June 27,
1863...

Nancy Ann Carson, wife of William Carson, and mother of Rev.
A. C. Carson, was born in Greenville, Tenn., and died in Fannin
co., Ga., May 23, 1863, aged 72 years...member of the Presbyterian
Church...Mary England.

Mrs. Fannie N., wife of Rev. U. B. Philips, and sister of the Rev. E. T. Nabors, of the Ala. Conf. died near Mt. Pleasant, Ala., July 18, 1863....

Miss Euphrasia C. Rumph of Houston co., Ga., died in Orangeburg Dist., S. C., June 9, 1863....

Mrs. Fanny Mitchell, wife of Hamilton Mitchell, died at Marion C. H., S. C., 1st April...born in the North of Ireland, and was brought up among the Covenanters...came to America in early life, and found a home in Fayetteville, N. C....

Mrs. Mary Taylor died at Thomasville, at her son's, Major Taylor, June 27th, 1863, in her 74th year...born in N. C., moved with her parents to Washington co., Ga., where she married Rev. Andrew Taylor...moved to Leon co., Fla....

Miss Mary A. Wilson, daughter of James and Nancy Wilson, was born in Gwinnett co., Ga., and died on 21st July, 1863, in her 16th year....

Wm. S. Lamberth, 14th Ala. Regt., third son of John and Parmelia Lamberth, of Tallapoosa co., Ala., was born in Carroll co., Ga., Nov. 12, 1843, and fell at Gettysburg, Pa., July 2,1863....

Mrs. Elizabeth Ann Hays, wife of Wilson Hays, Esq., died in Marion Dist., S. C., June 30th...about 33 years of age....

Jesse R. Dungan, died in the Asylum Hospital, Knoxville, 4th August, 1863...Co. F. 25th Ga. Regt....

Mrs. Mary A. Lowman, eldest daughter of Rev. John W. Morton, decd., was born in N. C., and died in Barbour co., Ala., July 21, 1863, in the 40th year of her age....

C. C. Stokes of 13th Miss Regt., son of W. W. and M. F. Stokes, died in Dalton, Ga., July 9, 1863, aged 18 years and 7 months....

Married on 13th August, by Rev. E. G. Murrah, Mr. Walter C. Johnson to Miss Pillond F. Simmons, daughter of C. R. Cimmons, all of Gainesville, Ga.

Died at Manning, S. C., Aug. 9, 1863, Lucy Rogers, daughter of Rev. William W. and Lucy I. Mood, of the S. C. Conf., aged 9 months and 5 days.

Issue of August 27, 1863

Rev. J. H. Montgomery was born in Mecklenburg co., N. C., Dec. 15, 1811, removed to Ala in 1846, and died in Summerfield, Aug. 3, 1863.... James O. Andrew.

Henry Frederick Detouhns, a native of Amsterdam in Holland, died in Georgetown, S. C., July 26th, in his 51st year...came to this twon 30 years ago...intermarriage with the McGinney family. left widow and children.

Mrs. Martha R. Carey, wife of Ebenezer Carey, of Augusta, Ga., died in Thomson, Ga., at the residence of her brother, Rev. J. H. Stockton, in her 43d year....

Allen S. Shell died in Newberry Dist., S. C., in his 66th year. Emma Frances Connor, daughter of Ezra and Mary Connor, died in Orangeburg Dist., S. C., July 12, 1863.... E. J. Connor.

Mrs. Ruth Talmage, wife of Mr. Jas B. Glover, was born in Milledgeville, Nov. 20th, 1842, and died in Marietta, at the residence of her mother, Mrs. E. F. Bostwick, Aug. 9, 1863....

Rev. J. A. W. Johnson, of the Fla. Conf., died at the residence of his brother-in-law, June 20th, 1863, in the 82d year of his age...

Robt. H. Allen died in Marengo co., Ala., July 15, 1863, in the 41st year of his age...a native of Iredell co., N. C...

Tribute of Respect by First Army Corps Northern Va to J. N. Henly Co. D., 7th Ga; D. Hill, Co. C., 8th Ga; S. B. Strong Co. F. 8th; G. W. Aarons, Co. I, 8th; R. L. McCall, Co. G, 8th;

A. W. Budd, Co. G. 8th; H. Arnold, Co. K, 8th, J. W. Moody, Co.
L., 8th; Lt. E. W. Bowen, Co. I, 9th; J. H. Hughes, Co. I, 9th;
J. Edwards, Co. K., 9th, W. E. Edward, Co. K, 9th; J. C. McCullars,
Co. F. 9th; J. W. Mann, Co. D., 9th; T. L. Lyda, Co. B. 9th;
J. M. Oroy, Co. E. 9th; N. Marlow, Co. E., 11th; W. M. Partin,
Co. H, 11th; J. L. Davis, Co. B., 11th; E. O. Sharp, Co. F.,
11th; F. M. Horne, Co. C., 11th....
    Married on 13th August, 1863, by Rev. N. H. Self, Rev. W.
J. Johnson, of Calhoun co., Ala., to Miss Nancy E. Nunally, of
Shelby co., Ala.
    Died, Aaron Walter Nunally, born Oct. _-, 1863, and died
in Shelby co., Ala., Aug. 13th, 1863.
    Died at Black Mingo, S. C., August 8, Lola Gertrude, infant
daughter of M. S. and W. C. Brightman, aged 4 months.

(No issue of September 3, 1863)

Issue of September 10, 1863

    Married in Macon, Ga., on 17th inst., by Rev. Thos. T. Christ-
ian, Mr. John R. Lownds, and Miss Elizabeth Johnson, all of that
city.
    On 19th instant, by Rev. Thomas T. Christian, Mr. John G.
McGulderick and Miss Rosetta K. Jeffers, all of Macon, Ga.
    On 19th August, 1863, by the Rev. R. W. Burgess, Col D. D.
Hankins, of Lafayette co., Fla., to Miss Belle McLeran at Wellborn, Fla.
    On 24th July, 1863, by Rev. W. Williams, Andrew O. Webb to
Miss Laura Baker, both of Duval co., Fla.
    On 19th July, by Rev. W. H. Thomas, Crawford Brown to Miss
Laura Parrish, both of Camden co., Ga.
    In Polk co., N. C., August 13, 1863, by Rev. W. Bowman,
Mr. Robert L. Taylor of Rutherford co., to Miss Lizzie A., daugh-
ter of Mr. Richard Whiteside.
    On 26th August, by Rev. J. D. Fisher, Lt. E. M. Davis, C S A,
to Miss M E Mims, daughter of S Mims, Esq. of Autauga co., Ala.
    On 19th instant, by the bride's father, in Talladega, Kate
Duncan, daughter of Rev. Daniel Duncan, of the Ala. Conf., and
Lt. J. Morgan Smith, of Mobile.
    In Merriwether co., Ga., August 11th, by Rev. J. B. McGehee,
Dr. N. C. Campbell to Miss Mary E. Howard.
    By Rev. J. S. Heard, August 26th, at the Bride's camp, in
clark co., Miss., Rev. John A. Ellis, Army Chaplain and member
of the Tenn. Conf., to Miss S. M. Hamilton, refugee from near
Jackson, Miss.
    By the same, August 25th, Mr. Thomas Jackson of the 37th Ga.
Regt., to Miss Sallie, only daughter of Green H. Rollins, Esq.
    On 27th July in Athens, Ga.,by Rev. Joseph S. Key, Mr. John
A. Cobb, to Miss Lucy Barron, all of Athens.
    By the same, in Columbus, on 22d August, Mr. Lucius Cady and
Mrs. M. L. Armhurst.
    By the same, in Bealwood, near Columbus, on 5th August, Mr.
John M. Dews and Miss Sophronia F. Woodruff.
    By the same, in St. Paul's Church, Columbus, Ga.,on 1st inst.,
Capt. N T N Robinson, of New Orleans, and Miss Susan R. Bethune,
of the former place.
    By Rev. S. J. Kelly, on 16th July, Mr. Stephen Bradley, of
Lowndes to Miss Frances Elizabeth Cornley, of Pike co., Alabama.
    On 23d August, by Rev. J H C McKinney, Mr. James Marcus Rudi-
sail to Miss Parasade King, both of Spartanburg Dist., S. C.
    On 3d September, 1863, by Rev. J. T. Ainsworth, Rev. WM. S.
Baker of the Ga. Conf. to Miss Mary A. Beall, of Irwinton, GA.

Died Bettie Lou Donald, daughter of H. H. and Carrie Donald, of Bartow co., Ga., died 9th August, aged 1 year and 2 days.

In Madison co., Ga., on 28th May, Hugh Blair, infant son of R P and M A Griffith, aged 1 year 19 months and 17 days.

Also, on 30th May, Willie Patton, only surviving child, aged 4 years 4 months and 21 days.

Near, Athens Ga., on 16th July, Minnie F., daughter of W. C. and E. C. Colbert, aged 4 years, 5 months and 24 days.

In Shelby, N. C., August 22d, Mary Rebekah, second daughter of Rev. G W and S R Ivy, of the S. C. Conf., aged 1 year, 4 months and 3 days.

In Bristol, Fla., on 21st July, Mary E., daughter of Rev. A and M E Davis, aged 3 months and 3 days.

In Butler co., March 12th, Henry M. Harris, only son of Elizabeth and John T. Harris, aged 2 years.

In Terrell co., Ga., Nettie, daughter of J. R. and A. H. Knight, aged 3 months and 10 days.

The second and eldest sons of Mr. H. V. McClelland of Jefferson co., Fla., have died. William Wesley at Palmyra Hospital, Va., March 11, aged 17; Rudolphus Henry, aged a little more than 19, on the 5th July, in Maryland....

James B. Bell died in Chesterfield Dist., S. C., on 28th June 1863, in his 52d year. Also on 4th June, Margaret Bell, in her 53d year....

Sister Frances B. Keller, wife of Morgan J. Keller of Shady Grove, St. Matthews Parish, died June 13th, 1863, aged about 40 years....

Sister Margaret Kennerly died on the 25th of June, aged about 82 years.

Bro. Saml. B. Staley died June 19th, near Newhope, Orange Parish, in his 49th year....

Mrs. Sarah McKern was born March 4th, 1781, and died in Athens, Ga., July 30th, 1863....

Mrs. Sarah H. Duncan, wife of Rev. J. P. Duncan, of the Ga. Conf., died in Americus, Ga., on 21st August, in her 46th year.

Mrs. Sarah A. Johnson, daughter of Thomas and Sarah Lancaster, was born in Hancock co., Ga., in 1819, removed to Stuart co., in 1835, married David Johnson, in 1838, and died in Rankin co., Miss., Aug. 4, 1863....

Robert S. Cowles, of Capt. Howard's co., died in Stewart co., Ga., 31st July, aged 32 years....

Cpl. Julis J. Cooper was born in Williamsburg Dist., S. C., July 11, 1838. His parents dying when he was young, he made his home with his brother-in-law, Rev. Jesse F. Smith...died at Ladies Hospital in Columbia.

J. Green Price, of 12th Regt. S. C. V., fell at Gettysburg, July 1, 1863, about 30 years old....

On the same day, G. Wesley Price, died at Howard's Grove, S. C., about 19 years old.

C. Fred Price, died at Adams Run, S. C., June 9, 1863...Three of my brothers are gone... E. A. P.

Mrs. Sarah Bowman, my mother, died in Rutherford co., N. C., the place of her nativity, August 11, 1863, aged about 73 years. She lived a widow more than 40 years....

Mrs. Lucy Allen, wife of Paul H. Allen died at Allendale, S. C., July 23d, 1863, in her 52d year....

John E. Funchess of S. C. V., died at the Wayside Home, Charleston, S. C., June 30th, in his 37th year....born in Orangebrug Dist., S. C....left wife and two little children.

Amos W. Reeves of 22d Batt Ga. was born in Fayette co., Ga., July 7, 1845, and died at Savannah, on 14th August, 1863....

Henry E. Clark, son of Daniel and Eliza Clark, of Macon, Ga., died inRichmond, Va., July 31st, in his 24th year....

Dr. James Smith was born 5th Feb. 1835, and died 7th August. 1863...37th Miss Regt...

Capt. E. Daniel died in Liberty co., Ga., on 28th August, in his 55th year....

Samuel Lovejoy was born in Fairfield Dist., S. C., and died in Tallapoosa co., Ala., aged about 82 years.

Sophia, wife of Samuel Lovejoy, July 25, 1863, aged about 72 years. She was also born in Fairfield Dist., S. C...

Mrs. Rebecca C. Stelling was born in Fairfield Dist., S. C., March 29, 1830, and died in Columbia, July 10, 1863...Oct. 23, 1856, married to J. H. Stelling...William P. Mouzon.

Capt. Augusta Franklin Boyd, 52d Regt. Ga. Vols., son of Wier and Sarah J. Boyd, Dahlonega, Ga., was born in Lumpkin co., Ga., and fell at Baker's Creek, Miss., May 16th, in his 10th year.

Mrs. Alice M. Clark, wife of Rev. W. H. Clarke of Decatur, Ga., died Aug 8th, J. W. Hinton.

Mrs. Sarah Wyatt Minor Johnston, widow of the late Dr. Walter Ewing Johnson, and daughter of the late Freeman Walker died at the residence of her brother, George A. B. Walker, near Augusta, Ga., on 31st July, in her 41st year....

John T. Bently, Esq. was born in Greene co., Ga., in 1787, and died on 1st August, 1863, in his 78th year...one of the first settlers of Henry co., Ga....

A. B. Carter of 15th S. C. V., only son of G. W. and S. B(?) Carter died in the hospital, Lynchburg, Va., on 9th June, 1863, in his 24th year.... George W. Carter.

Sgt. M. A. Hutchens of the Echols Guards, 8th Regt. Ga. Vols. fell at Gettysburg, July 2, 1863....

Thos S. Lipsey was born in Chester Dist., S. C., on 3d of March, 1801, and died in Pickens co., near Carrollton, Ala., 1st July 1863....

Mrs. A. K. Matilda Varn, wife of Rev. L. B. Varn, died in colleton Dist., August 19th, 1863, in the 27th year of her age.

Louisa Brunson, wife of J. J. Brunson, was born April 12th, 181, and died June 14th, 1863. She lived to see two of her sons, Rufus and John go up before her....

Cpl. W. P. Zeigler died July 17, 1863, aged 26 years, 5 months and 4 days.

Rebecca Elizabeth Harrell died at Newton, Baker co., Ga., Aug. 2, 1863, aged 14 years and 5 months.

Lt. John C. Blake of 5th Fla. Regt., was killed near Gettysburg, July 3, 1863....

Tribute of Respect by 24th Ga. Regt. to Wm. W. Worwick, who was killed at Gettysburg, Pa.

Issue of September 17, 1863

David Wesley Neal of 44th Ala. Vols., son of Patrick S. and Catharine Neal of Pickens co., Ala., was born 10 Oct. 1837, and died 3d July 1863, near Gettysburg, Pa. Three of his brothers had previously fallen in the service of their country.

Bro. A. B. Crane of 4th Rgt. Ga. Cavalry, died Aug. 30th, aged 21 eyars....

Maj. R. Dye died Aug. 5, 1863, near Meridian Miss., while returning with his company to S. C....

Mrs. Frances J. Fabian, wife of G. W. Fabian, died on 2d inst., in St. Georges Colleton Dist., S. C.,in her 53d year....

Dr. James Alston Groves, son of John J. and Mary L. Groves, was born in Culloden, Ga., Jan. 17th, 1837, and died in Gettysburg, Pa., while attending the wounded....

Mrs. Tabitha Ritchie Earnest died in Noxubee co., Ms., July 4, 1863, in her 63d year...joined M. E. Church in S. C., in 1830.

Also at the same place, on 25th August, William B., infant
son of William T. and Julia A. Bevill, aged 14 months, the
son of the adopted daughter of Jacob and Tabitha R. Earnest.
Mrs. Lavina McGee died in Campbell co., Ga., June 7, 1863,
in her 44th year...daughter of Rev. John M. Smith and sister of
Rev. P. P. Smith, late of the Fla. Conf....
Benjamin Franklin McDowell, son of Joseph H. and July Ann
McDowell was born in Coweta co., Ga., Nov. 1, 1840, moved to
Texas with his parents in 1857....
Mrs. Nancy Walker was born 19th May 1797, and died 1st of
August 1863....
Wiley Elias Fort died in st. James Santee Parish, on 26th
July last...
Miss Mysia Rogerson of Bethel Church, Williamsburg ct., S. C.
conf. recently died...
Tribute of Respect by 3rd Ala. Regt. to A. A. Wall and M. W.
Rogers of Co. I, killed on battle of Chancellorsville, May 2.
J. M. Chapman of Co. A., Mobile Cadets on 3d May. J. S. Lynch
of Co. L, killed in Gettysburg, 2d July; Baily Holt of Co. C.
killed 2d of May....
Tribute of Respect by Amelia Circuit, Miss Conf. to Thompson
H. Jackson.
Married by Rev. Atticus G. Haygood, on the 1st inst., Rev.
George W. Yarbrough to Miss Mary Boyce Morris, daughter of J. S.
Morris, Esq., Marietta, Ga.
At Gen Mahone's in Talbot co., Ga., Spt. 8, by Rev. G. H.
Patillo, Mr. Wm. Perry, of Columbus, Ga., and Mrs. Catharine
L. Imbey.
Near Elijay, Ga., Sept. 6th, 1863,by Rev. B. B. Quillian,
John M. Watkins and Miss D. S. Dillingham, daughter of John W.
Dillingham, late of Buncombe co., N. C.
Died, Sarah Jane,daughter of John and Martha 1. Elsberry,
born in Lowndes co., Ala., Nov. 11, 1856, died Aug. 17, 1863.
Also, Dunn Rogers Elsberry, their baby boy, was born in
Lowndes co., Ala., Aug. 25, 1861, and died Aug. 8, 1863.
Carrie L., daughter of Thomas J. and Mary A. Middleton, was
born in Lowndes co., Ala., March 26th, 1858, and died Aug. 11,
1863.
At the residence of Rev. C. A. Crowell, Bartow co., Ga., Aug.
26th, Elizabeth Rebecca, infant daughter of Rev. H. D. and Mrs.
C. B. Moore, of S. C., aged 1 year 4 months and 6 days.

Issue of September 24, 1863

J. A. Woodall, of 32d Ga. Regt, oldest son of James D. and
Frances Woodall, was born in Talbot co., Ga., June 26, 1842,
and died at the hospital in Charleston, S. C., Aug. 19, 1863.
Daniel Dantzler, died in St. Matthews, Parish, S. C., Aug. 24,
1863, in his 67th year....
Mrs. Elizabeth Taylor, wife of Rev. Thornton A. Taylor, was
born in Stafford co., Va., Feb. 17, 1796, and died in Noxubee
co., Miss., Aug. 2, 1863... She was the daughter of Jeremiah
Kirk. Her mother's maiden name was Nancy Munroe....
Lt. Wm. T. Belvine of 29th Regt. S. C. V., died near Spring
Hill, Sumter Dist., S. C., 28th August, in his 32d year...
Julius Clement Corbett of 15th Regt. S. C. V., was born in
Sumter Dist., S. C.,May 26th, 1836, and died at Gettysburg, 2d
July last....
Eleanora Mood Corbett, the youngest child of Br. Hampton
Corbett was born Nov. 9, 1852, and died August 22, 1863....
Margaret Hodges, wife of H. B. Hodges, and daughter of Eli
Kennedy decd., died in Bullcoh co., Ga., July 6, 1863, in her
44th year....

126

Mary Simmons, wife of Rev. John Simmons, died in Griffin,
Ga., Sept. 9, 1863, aged 67 years old...a member of the Baptist
Church and for many years the wife of a Baptist preacher....
William S. Murphy was born in N. C., Feb. 27, 1809, and
died in Wankeena, Fla., Aug. 30, 1863....
Rev. D. S. Edwards was born Sept. 1, 1863...killed by light-
ning Aug. 4, 1863....left widow and 13 children.
Major John B. Haney died in Cleveland co., N. C., at the age
of 89 years...born in Hagerstown, Md., but removed from Harrison-
burg, Va., to Lincolnton, N. C., in 1807....wife Sarah Haney,
died in 1844....
Willie Fletcher Buxton, son of William and Sarah Buxton, of
Burke co., Ga., died from a stroke of lightning on 30th Aug,
below Savannah, in his 20th year.
Mrs. Elizabeth Cockran Connor, wife of Dr. P. W. Connor, and
daughter of Gen. G. W. Hudgen, died in Cokesbury, S. C., on 22d
August in the 47th year of her age....
Died, Francis Davie Green, son of J T and L D Green, 11th
Sept., 1863, aged 1 year, 3 months and 2 days.
In this city, on Sunday morning, the 6th instant, Andrew
Wardlaw, infant son of Andrew W. and Elizabeth S. Lewis, aged
1 year 11 months and 24 days.
July 27, Rosa Stevens, infant daughter of George W. C. and
Martha Munroe, aged 1 year, 10 months and 27 days

Issue of October 1, 1863

W. S. Warren was born in Hancock co., Ga., May 30, 1816,
married to Helen M., daughter of Spencer and Susannah Moore, Dec.
13, 1837, and emigrated to Tallapoosa co., Ala., in 1838, and
died Aug. 2, 1863....
Bro. Moses Jones was born in Lincoln co., Ga., Aug. 6, 1809,
and died in Chattahoochee co., Ga., July 5, 1863....
Mrs. Mary Gleton, relict of Joseph Gleton, died at her son-in-
law's, Mr. Taylor, in Worth co., Ga., Aug. 12, 1863, in her
67th year.
William F. Thomason, of 2d S. C. V., died in Greenville Dist.,
S. C. 2d August, 1863, in her 33d year....
Miss Rowena R. F. Johnson, daughter of Rev. Amos and Mrs.
Frances A. Johns died in Warren co., Ga., Sept. 18, 1863, in her
14th year....
Mrs. Arabella M. Cooper died 6th August 1863, in Marengo co.,
Ala., her maiden name was Wood. On 5th Nov, married to Anderson
W. Cooper...left husband and six little children.
W. J. Roach was born in Charlottesville, Va., April 13, 1842,
and moved to Columbia S. C., in Oct. 1860...
Tribute of Respect by "Rutherford Volunteers" Co. G., 18th
Regt. N. C. Troops to Lt. John H. Ford, who fell at Gettysburg,
July 1st....
Married in Cedar Town, Ga., Sept. 2, by Rev. J. T. Norris,
Dej't John O. Waddell, of the 25th Ga. Regt., to Miss Ella C.
Peek, of Cedar Town.
In Sparta, Ga., on 17th inst., by Rev. P. M. Ryburn, Mr.
Sanford D. Massey of Macon, Ga., to Miss Charlotte A. Henry.
On 22d Sept., at McIntyre, Wilkinson co., Ga., by Rev. J. T.
Ainsworth, Robert G. Hyman of Co. F., 3d Ga. Regt. to Miss Mary
McIntyre, of the above place.
On 22d inst., by Rev. H. M. Jones of Montevallo, Mr. Horace
Ware to Miss Mary Harris, both of Columbiana, Ala.
Aug. 12th, 1863, near Tuskaloosa, Ala., by the Rev. Dr. Sum-
mers, the Rev. Wm. N. Lawrence, of Lowndes co., Miss., to Miss

Mary Elizabeth Neal, daughter of Casper Neal, Esq.
In Jefferson co., Ga. 22d inst., by W A Hayles, Mr. William Rollins to Miss Sallie Jones.
Died, in Augusta, on 16th Sept., Maria Louisa, oldest daughter of Charles A and Laura V. sledge, of Sparta, Ga.
In Tuskegee, Ala., June 17, 1863, Sidney Collins, only child of George H. and Mary V. Smith, aged 1 year, 10 months and 17 days.
In Houston co., Ga., on 28th July, Lula L., daughter of David H. and Helen C. Houser, aged 2 years, 3 months and 14 days.
Also, on 13th Sept., her sister Eva T., aged 14 months and 10 days.
Thomas Henry, infant son of Rev. George C. and Martha H. Clarke, died on 21st Sept., aged 1 year, 2 months and 11 days.
In Pleasant Hill, Desoto Parish, La., June 23d, Edgar Lewellyn, infant son of A M And Sallie Freeman Chapman, aged 19 months and 14 days.
In Griffin, Ga., 3d Sept., 1863, Eliza Blodget, daughter of S C and E R Mitchell, aged 2 years 11 months and 10 days.

Issue of October 8, 1863

Mrs. Catharine A. Hannah, wife of J. D. B. Hanna, died at Black Mingo, S. C., on 14th August 1863...left husband and children.
Nathan Johnston was born March 3, 1810, and died in Choctaw co., Ala., Aug. 11, 1863....
John H. Walker son of the late Rev. W. W. Walker, of Abbeville Dist., S. C., was killed at Gettysburg, July 1st, 1863...
Randolph Mitchell was wounded in a skirmish on the Rappahannock on 6th June, died 17th August, aged 22 years...of Barbour co...
Dr. Irvin P. Hendrix, of Co. I, Col. Adams' Cavalry, was born 16th Dec., 1830, in Monroe co., late a resident of Marengo co., died near Vernon, Miss July 16, 1863...
Miss Sarah Ann Little, daughter of R. W. and Sarah Little was born in Cheraw, S. C., Sept. 20th, 1829, and died in Bennettsville, S. C., Aug. 21, 1863....
Mrs. Eliza J. Kearney died near Vernon, Miss., on 29th Aug. 1863, aged -8 years....
Julius M. Leach of 8th Regt. S. C. V., was killed at Gettysburg, July 3, aged 22 years and 25 days.
William M. Cooper, of Co. H. 11th Ga. Regt was born Feb. 3, 1842, and was killed at Gettysburg, July 2, 1863.
David Leitner died in Richland Dist., S. C.,on 17th Aug., in his 67th year...
Wm. Sealy was born in Greenville Dist., S. C., Sept. 8, 1823, and died at Lauderdale Springs, Miss., July 23, 1863...16th Regt. S. C. V.
Charles Clyde, brother of Rev. T. J. Clyde of the S. C. Conf. was wounded at Gettysburg, and died there July 26th, 1863, in his 21st year...
Tribute of Respect by Auburn Station to F. G. Freeman, who died in Tuskegee, Ala., on 2d inst (Sept.)
Married on the evening of the 24th Sept., in Autauga co., by Rev. Andrew J. Briggs, Mr. Robert H. King of Dallas co., and Miss Maria Z. Taylor.
By Rev. S. H. Browne, Sept. 25th, Rev. P. L. Herman of the S. C. Conf. to Miss Frances Jay, daughter of Tyrn Jay, of Abbeville Dist., S. C.
Died in Warsaw, Ala., Sept. 16th, Mary Narcissa, second daughter of Wm. H. and Mary D. Gill, aged 1 year and 12 days.

Near Canton, Ga., Sept. 23, 1863, Paul Brewster, the only son of the Rev. W. F. And Sarah Holland, aged 8 months and 14 days.

James B. Pearce was born Jan. 4, 1855, and died Sept. 4, 1863....

John Leverman, son of Charles A. and Laura V. Sledge, died in Sparta, Ga., Sept. 20th, 1863, aged 5 years and 7 months.

Issue of October 15, 1863

Mrs. Charlotte O'Neal, widow of Dr. Charles O'Neal, died at my residence in Orangeburg Dist., S. C., Sept. 2, 1863, in her 77th year....Lark O'Neal.

Alfred George Marchman was born Nov. 11, 1824, and married to Miss Susan Amanda Wells of Troup co., Ga., in 1844, and died Sept. 19, 1863....

Mrs. Julia, wife of Col. Donald R. Barton, of Orangeburg Dist., died on 2d Sept., 1863...a member of the Presbyterian Church....

Sarah Cook, widow of Rev. Thomas Cook, was born in Greene co., Ga., Jan. 7, 1798, married to Rev. Thoams Cook, July 7, 1814, and died in Butts co., Ga., Sept. 6, 1863....

W. T. Connor, of Co. I, 23d S. C. Regt, died ---- aged 27 years

Mrs. Sophronai Harris, wife of James H. Harris, decd., died at Warrior Stand, Macon co., Ala., Sept. 6, 1863, in her 38th year.

Married on 7th Sept., 1863,by Rev. W. M. Wilson, Rev. G. H. Wells of the S. C. Conf., and Mrs. Fannie M. Lester, of Georgetown, S. C.

By the same on 15th August, Mr. Thomas Durant and Miss Susan A. Clarke, both of Georgetown Dist., S. C.

On the 17th of September, 1863, by Rev. W.H. Thomas, Rev. William Williams of the Fla. Conf., to Miss Martha Geiger, of Duval co., Fla.

In this city, on 5th inst., by Rev. Thomas T. Christian, Mr. William Springer of Macon, to Miss Ellen M. Scott, of Milledgeville, Ga.

On 8th inst., by Rev. Thomas T. Christian, Mr. Virgil A. Krepps, of Virginia, and Miss Mosie A. Russell, of Macon, Ga.

William Mouzon Crocker, son of T B and A H Crocker, was born May 12, 1863, and died Sept. 22, 1863.

In Macon, Ga., Sept. 29th, William Elias Gilpin, aged 15 years, 8 months.

Sue Tekoa Connor, eldest daughter of Rev. J S and Miriam L. Connor, of the S C Conf., died in Pineville, S. C., Oct. 1, 1863, aged 5 years, 1 month and 20 days.

Louisa Augusta, youngest daughter of G. M. and Sarah J. McDonald, died near Tilton, Ga., July 2, 1863, aged 13 months and 13 days.

Issue of October 22, 1863

Rev. James Moore was born in Charleston, S. C., Dec. 24, 1798, and died in Abbeville, Sept. 23d, 1863...his father died when he was quite young...married in Charleston to Miss Ann Fisher.

Mrs. Mary Caroline Motley, daughter of Rev. Ebenezer and Mary Hearn, was born in Dallas co., Ala., July 21, 1830, died near Allenton, Wilcox co., Spet. 4, 1863....

Dr. Charles F. Dandridge was born in Henry co., Va., and died in Panola, Miss., from an accidental pistol shot, Sept. 2, 1863, in his 54th year....

Mrs. Ellen G. Andrew, daughter of Thomas B. and Elizabeth C. Harwell, and wife of Dr. Wm. G. Andrews, died in Eatonton, Ga., Sept. 10, 1863, on her 20th birthday.

Her sister Lucy F., wife of Dr. John Andrews, died also in Eatonton, Oct. 7, 1863, in her 22d year...

Mrs. Timney P. Phillips, was born in Morgan co., Ga., Dec. 14, 1805, was first married to Mr. Warren of Hancock co., Ga., and after his decease to Mr. John Phillips, now decd., and moved to Macon co., Ala., where she died Sept. 2, 1863....

Mary James fourth child of H. J. and E. E. Agee was born in Anson co., N. C., and died in Smith co., Miss., 12th Sept., 1863.

Col. Jno. M. Raysor was born in colleton Dist., S. C., May 23, 1812, and died Sept. 10, 1863...served two years in the S. C. Legislature....

Alfred William Walker, a member of the Jefferson Rifles, Fla. Regt., son of David and Rebecca Walker, was born Dec. 8, 1838, and died Sept. 30th, 1863.

Michael Walker, his brother of the same Regt., was born Nov. 8, 1829, and died (date not given).

James Walker, another brother, was born July 8, 1844, member of 5th Fla. Regt....

Mrs. George A. J. Black, wife of Dr. R. C. Black died in Americus, Ga., Sept. 11, 1863, aged 27 years and 6 months.

Robert McBride Boring, son of Rev. Isaac Boring, formerly of the Ga. Conf., died at the Confederate hospital, near Gettysburg, 23 July 1863, in his 21st year....

Zaccheus C. Galoway of 33d Regt., A. V. C., died near Georgianna, Butler co., Ala., on 8th Sept 1863....

J. P. Randall, 14th S. C. Troops, was wounded near Hagerstown, Md., and died at Camp Winder, Aug. 7, 1863....

Miss Sallie J. West, daughter of Judge T. D. and C. F. West, of Macon co., Ala., died on 15th Aug., aged 21 years....

Frances Asbury Miles was born April 29, 1826, and died Sept. 30th, 1863...

Mrs. Mary A., wife of A. J. Beckham, died in Atlanta, Ga., Aug. 6, 1863, in her 27th year....

John Carroll of Thomas co., Ga., 20th Ga. Regt, died in Augusta, on 2d Oct, aged 18 years....

Married on 18th inst., by Rev. F. E. Manson, Rev. B. J. Johnson of the Ga. Conf. to Miss M. F. Arnold, daughter of Elijah B. Arnold, of Henry co., Ga.

On 19th July by Rev. J. A. Pace, Mr. Wm. McGown, and Mrs. Nancy Fields, of Daleville, Ala.

Sept. 30th, died in Camden, S. C., Mary Mansfield, only child of Dr. and Mrs. D. L. DeSaussure, aged 5 years 5 months and 19 days.

Sept 6th, Charles Joel, youngest child and only son of Ann L. and Theodore Jungher....

Issue of October 29, 1863

Rev. Washington Ford, son of Rev. John Ford, was born in Marion co., Miss., Feb. 13, 1810...left widow and children.

Robert Roberson was born in N. C., July 20, 1807 and died in Jefferson co., Ga., Sept. 10, 1863....

Mrs. John N. Birch, died in the city of Columbus, Ga., on 18th Sept., 1863, aged 28 years...born in Talbotton...married Miss M. S. Snider in 1856.

John Thomas Reeves of 18th Regt. Ala. Vols., was mortally wounded at Chickamauga, and reached Salem on the way to his widowed mother's, Jefferson co., Ala...died in his 19th year.

Martha M. Reeves, his sister died on 24th Aug., in her 14th year....

130

Mrs. Margaret Ring was born on 1st Dec., 1791, married to E. F. Ring, on 4th Feb. 1813, and died in Perry co., Ala., on 25th Sept., 1863...

Major George W. Ross of 2nd Battn. Ga. Vols, was born 22nd Nov. 1825, near Macon, Ga., and died 2nd August, 1863 from wounds received at Gettysburg...left little son.

Mrs. Margaret Prentice, wife of James Prentice, died Sept. 25, 1863...

Louisa A. Carpenter, daughter of John D. and Eppes G. Carpenter, died at Manassas, Ga., Sept. 6, 1863, in her 20th year...

W. E. Felder oc 2nd S. C. Regt., fell at Gettysburg, in the 19th year of his age....

Mrs. Zilpah Williams was born Sept. 12, 1793, and died in Wilcox co., Ala., Sept. 29th, 1863...

Mrs. Lucinda Pearson, wife of Judge Samuel Pearson, was born in Hancock co., Ga., returning home on 27th Sept., from a visit to a sick relative, was thrown from her buggy and died in Eaton-ton, Ga., Sept. 27, in her 61st year....

Sgt. E. P. Sharpe, son of James Sharpe, and son-in-law of Rev. Jos. Chambers of 11th Ga. Vols, was born in Buncombe co., N. C., 5th Nov., 1840, and died on 4th July, aged 22 years.

Mrs. Sarah Berry, wife of James A. Smith, and daughter of Col. Elbert Lewis, died at Oglethorpe, Ga., Oct. 11, 1863, at about 18 years of age...

Mrs. Nannette Shaw, widow of the late Thos. L. Shaw, of George-town, S. C., died at Marion, S. C., on 25th Aug., 1863, in her 54th year...a native of Georgetown Dist., trained in the P. E. Church....

John F. McCollough died in the Hospital at Gettysburg, Pa., in Aug. 1863, aged 27 years.

R. L. Adams, 12th Regt. N. C. V. was killed at Gettysburg, in the 35th year of his age....

Bro. R. W. Rykard was born Sept. 20, 1838, and died in Madi-son co., Fla., Aug. 21, 1863....

Angus Morrison was born in Richmond co., N. C., and died in Wakulla, Fla., aged 56 years.

Mrs. Julia A. Sellers of Beaufort Dist., S. C., died Aug. 16, 1863, in her 63d year....left daughter and son-in-law....

John B. Valentine, died Sept. 23d, in Aberdeen, Miss., at the residence of Dr. John L. Tindle, in his 46th year....

T. B. Gardner was born Oct. 1837, and died from wounds at Gettysburg, 20th July 1863...

David S. Fralix of 11th Regt. S. C. V., died in Charleston, S. C., on 18th Oct., of typhus.

Major D. M. McLeod, aged 30, member of M. E. Church on Ben-nettsville ct., S. C. Conf. fell at Gettysburg...

Tribute of Respect to Capt. E. Daniel, by Hinesville ct., Ga. Conf.

Tribute of Respect by Robert Dickins, by Greensboro, Demopolis and Mt. Vernon, Ala....

Married in Beallwood, near Columbus, Ga., on the 14th inst., by Rev. Joseph S. Key, Hon. Josephus Echols and Miss Rowena M. Lockhart.

In Decatur co., Ga.,on 7th inst.,by the Rev. B. S. Brockett, Sgt. Henry A. Carr, Co. "A" 27th Ga. Volunteers, to Miss Mary A. Martin.

Died, Aug. 31, 1863, Charles Edwin Smith, aged 5 years 7 months and 18 days.

Albert Houghton, son of Co. John A.and Mary V. Jones, of Scottsville, Ala., Aug. 12, 1863, at his grandfather's, in Wilcox co., Aged 4 years and 6 months.

Issue of November 5, 1863

Rev. Alonzo F. Gill 44th Regt. Tenn. Vols., son of Rev. Wm.
A. and E. F. Gill was born in Lincoln co.,Tenn. Oct. 23, 1841,
and killed at Chickamauga, Ga., Sept. 19, 1863....
Jacob Little was born in Cabarars co., N. C. 1794, and died
in Harris co., Ga., Oct. 7, 1863... D. D. Cox.
Col. Peyton H. Colquitt was wounded at Chickamauga, Sept.
19, and died the next morning....
Rev. Robert Adams died on 29th Aug 1863, at the residence of
his son-in-law, Wm. Hope, Tuskegee, Ala., in his 71st year...
Born in Charleston, S. C.
Mrs. Margaret King was born 1st Dec. 1791, married to E. F.
King, 4th Feb. 1813, and died in Perry co., Ala., 25th Sept.,
1863...
Sgt. Robert Power Bryce eldest son of Mr. and Mrs. Robert
Bryce of Columbia, S. C., born 25th Dec. 1842...killed at Chicka-
mauga, Sept. 20....
Mrs. Jennie Henry died in Newnan, Ga., Sept. 6, 1863, in her
23d year....
Lt. John B. McArthur of Montgomery co., Ga., was born 18--
and fell at Chickamauga....
Miss Ann Eliza Just, daughter of Rev. James and Eliza Rus-
sell decd., was born in Charleston, S. C., and died in Columbia,
S. C., 24th Oct. 1863, aged 45 years...
Capt. Joseph E. Helvenstein, of 4th Ga. Regt, fell 17th
Sept. in his 38th year...McLemore's Cove, Walker co., Ga.
Mrs. Sarah Ann Hill, daughter of Henry and Elizabeth Howell,
born July 25, 1837, and died at her father's, Tallapoosa co.,
Ala., Aug. 8, 1863....
William L. Kendall was born Nov. 3, 1822, and died in camp at
Savannah, Sept. 14, 1863....
Married in Meriwether co., Ga.,on the morning of the 27th
of Oct., by Rev. J. B. McGehee, Mr. John E. Moss to Miss Mary J.
Underwood.
By Rev. Robert A. Connor, Mr. William A. Tompkins to Miss
Emma M. Hayles, daughter of Rev. William A. Hayles, all of
Jefferson co., Ga.
On 15th Oct., by Rev. T. T. Mangham, Rev. Moses E. Butt,
of the Ala. Conf., and Miss Jerucia J. Reedy, of Wetumpka, Ala.
Died at Mapleton, Abbeville Dist., S. C., Sept. 17th and 18th
Martha E. and Mary S., daughters of Henry and Frances Barret, the
former aged 10 years and 16 days, the latter 5 years 7 months and
29 days.
In Eatonton, Ga., Oct. 20th, Reid DeJarnette Norris, only
child of John T. and Ella Norris, aged 18 months.

Issue of November 12, 1863

Mrs. Mary B., wife of Dr. John C. Taylor, a native of S. C.,
died in Forkland, Ala., Sept. 29, 1863...
Capt. Samford W. Glass of Covington , Ga., son of Manson
Glass and son-in-law, of Rev. J. E. Evans, died 5th July 1863,
from wounds at Gettysburg.
Samuel Hawkins, of 41st Ala. Vols., died on the 7th Nov.,
at Murfreesboro, Tenn., aged about 32 years.
Lt. Aaron Hawkins of 41st Ala. Vols., was killed 20th Sept.,
1863, at Chickamauga, aged about 26 years...These brothers....
William Thomas Powers, was killed at Chickamauga, Sept. 20,
1863, in his 21st year.
Bro. Thos. S. Powers, father of the above, died Nov. 1st, 1863
in his 68th year....

Cpl Joseph Hutchinson, of 36th Ala. Regt., son of Rev. J. J. Hutchinson, of the Ala. Conf. was mortally wounded at Chickamauga, and died Sept. 22nd in his 21st year....

Mrs. Elizabeth, wife of Eli McFall, of Liberty co. Ga., died Oct. 4, 1863, aged 61 years... T. S. L. Harwell.

Wiley H. Ellis was born in Green co., Ga.,and died near Nixburg, coosa co., Ala., 3dr Oct 1863, a son of Nathan and Mary Ellis....

Wm. M. Johnson, died in Gadsden co., Fla., on 17th Aug., aged 25 years....

John W. M. Hile was killed at Chickamauga, Sept. 20th, 1863; born December 31, 1826...Evan Nicholson.

Mr. Josiah Rogers formerly of Hancock, Ga.,died in Jasper co., Miss., on 20th Sept., 1863, aged 75 years...for some time resided near DeSoto, Clarke co., Miss...

Tribute of Respect by Conf. of Montgomery, Ala., to Rev. F. G. Ferguson.

Married Oct. 20th, by Rev. Wm. A. McCarty, Mr. A. M. Glenn and Miss Louisa H. Thompson, all of Glennville, Ala.

On 5th Nov., by Rev. R. A. Connor, John Winter to Miss Indiana H. Dove, all of Richmond co., Ga.

Near Eatonton, Ga., Nov. 5th, 1863, by Rev. Geo. G. N. Mac-Donell, Mr. F. Milton Little to Miss Anna R. Reid.

Died in Eatonton, Ga., Oct. 18, Mary Mitford Russell, daughter of the late James A. and Mary J. Russell, aged 8 years and 10 months.

Willie M., daughter of Matilda and Henry Thomas, died July 22, aged 2 years, 8 months and 23 days in Calhoun co., Ga.

In Calhoun co., Ga., August 13, George Ann V. E., daughter of Naomi and Reuben Jordan, aged 3 years, 11 months and 15 days.

Richard Venable, infant son of Rev. L. F. and A. R. Dowdell, on 16th Oct., aged 1 year, 1 month and 6 days.

Issue of November 19, 1863

Miss Mary Lou Burge, daughter of Thomas and Mary Burge, decd., died at the residence of her step-mother, Mrs. D. S. Burge, in Newton co., Ga....

Mrs. Mary S. Coleman, daughter of John H. and Mary Walpole, died in Guntersville, Ala., in the 33d year of her age...born and raised in Huntsville, Ala...

Capt. Thomas J. Warren, late Editor of the Camden Journal, fell at Gettysburg....

Elmoe Marion, son of B. M. Grier, Esq., died Sept. 9, in Topsaw, Georgetown Dist., S. C., aged 25 years.

Edward Osgood, son of Rev. L. A. Grier, died Oct. 8th, at the same place, in his 19th year.

Miss Margaret Skinner, daughter of Rev. L. A. Grier, died on the 13th Oct., aged 20 years and 3 months....

Lt. J. B. Holloway, of 25th N. C. Regt., died July 2, 1863, from wounds at Gettysburg, in his 29th year....

Sister Mary Ann Meriwether, wife of T. M. Meriwether, daughter of Zaccheus Price, formerly of Newton co., Ga., now of Marion co., Fla., was born 7 Aug 1825, and was married 18 Dec. 1862, and died in Newton co., Sept. 20th, 1863....

Silas M. Grubbs died in Webster co., Ga., Oct. 4th...born in S. C., Jan. 27, 1819...came to Ga., and married Susan M. Birch.

Emma May, youngest daughter of Rev. D. W. and Mrs. A. A. Calhoun, died in Augusta, Ga., Oct. 20th, 1863, aged 9 years, 5 months and 18 days...

John Henry Gary, died Oct. 25th, 1863...

Miss Elizabeth Compsey died near Aiken, S. C., Sept. 2, 1863.

Mrs. Louisiana Winbush, wife of M. M. Wimbush, daughter of
J. C. and A. C. Rodgers, of Jasper co., Ga., died Sept. 24,
1863, in her 42d year....
Tribute of Respect by 6th Ala. Regt to B. Turbeville, Co. E.,
who died at Grace Church, Va.,May 1863; F. T. G. Walker, Co. G.,
who died at Williamsport, Md.,June 19, 1863; S. W. C. Weston;
N. M. Carter, Co. M.; J. B. Colquit, Co. G., who fell at Gettys-
burg, Pa., July 1; also Lt. Henry King, Co. F, who fell at War-
renton Springs, Oct. 12, 1863....
Married by Rev. A. M. Chrietaberg, in St. George's Parish,
S. C., 20th Oct., Mr. Davie A. McIntosh to Miss Isabella A. Hill.
In St. George's Parish, 4th Nov., 1863, by Rev. A. M. Chrietz-
berg, Mr. T. D. Bird, to Miss Elizabeth Harrison, both of Colleton
Dist., S. C.
By Rev. S. H. J. Sistrunk, on 5th Nov., at the residence of
Mr. John H. King, Mr. F. Marion King to Miss MaryE. Gilbert,
both of Houston co., Ga.
On the 11th inst., by Rev. W. C. Bass, Abner T. Holt, Esq.,
of Bibb co., to Miss Fannie M. Searcy, eldest daughter of Dr.
Daniel Searcy, of Monroe co., Ga.
Died Oct. 14, 1863, in Spartanburg Dist.,S. C., Lulie F.
Anderson, daughter of Lt. John M. and H. Lizzie Anderson, aged 1
year, 11 months and 2 days.

Issue of November 26, 1863

Floyd Crocket Bostwick of Co. D., 2nd Regt. Ga. Vols., died
at Atlanta of wound received at Chickamauga, 4th Nov., 1863, in
his 24th year. He was an only son and brother...
Edmond S. Harris, Sr., of LaGrange Ga., died Oct. 31, 1863,
while absent from home on a visit to his children in Alabama. He
was born in Hancock co., Ga., Oct. 24, 1786...
James M. Davis died at Creek Stand, Ala., Aug. 8, in his
55th year...
Mrs. Nancy Branman was born in N. C., Jan. 1784, and died in
Harris co., Ga., Oct. 27th, 1863, in her 89th year....
I. M. Ward of 4th La. Bat., was born Oct. 27, 1844, died at
Greensboro, Ga., Nov. 11, 1863....
William D. Shine was born in Ala., and had attained his 80th
year...mortally wounded by a minnie ball on 15th May...
E. T. Lumpkin, son of John Mars and Sallie Low Lumpkin,
was born in Talbot co., Ga.,1802, and removed to Columbus, Ga...
removed to Macon co., Ala., thence to Tallapoosa co., leaves
a wife and two lovely children...
Sister Margaret E. Boatright, formerly Mrs. Whetstone, of
St. Matthew's Parish, S. C., died Aug. 28, aged 68 years....
Mrs. Elizabeth Culpepper, wife of Joel Culpepper, was born in
1798, and joined the Baptist, afterwards the M. E. Church...died
August 20, 1863...
Wm. Samford Lassiter, only child of Rev. C. S. D. Lassier, of
the Ala. Conf. died in Vicksburg, in May 1863, nearly 10 years
old....
Jasper N. Copeland of Greensboro, Ga., died Nov. 17th, aged
50 years.
Leon Henry, aged 4 years, son of Dr. A. A. and R. A. Jernigan,
of Green co., Ga.,died Nov. 15th.
In Sandersville, on 11th Nov., 1863, little Willie Benjamin,
eldest son of Capt. and Mrs. S. B. Jones, aged 2 years and 3
months.
on 4th and 6th Nov., in Greensboro, Ga., Margaret Jane aged
1 year 8 mos. and 3 days, and Nancy Elizabeth, aged 3 years, 10
months and 14 days, children of Philip B. and Nancy T. Robinson.

Issue of December 3, 1863

Mrs. Sallie Leake died in Cartersville, Ga., Nov. 4, 1863, aged 64 years, 9 months and 20 days...

Major Wm. Winstell, died inTallapoosa co., Ala., Sept. 2, 1863, in the 57th year of his age....

Capt. James S. Watkins was the son of Lorenzo Watkins of Summer co., Tenn...born March, 1841....

Samuel E. Smith was born March 28, 1842, and died in hospital Savannah, Ga., Oct. 5th, 1863...

Thomas A. Norwood, youngest son of Maj. W. C. and Eliza Norwood, aged 18 years, 3 months and 4 days, 1st Ga. Cavalry, was killed at Philadelphia, Tenn., 28th Oct., 1863...

Theodore S. Hance, of Laurens, S. C., died, aged about 18 on the battle field of Chickamauga...the last of three sons of fond parents, 3d Regt. S. C. V.

Mrs. Sarah A.Owens, wife of Capt. James W. Owens, Timmonsville, S. C., died on 5th Nov., aged 41 years, _ months and 25 days... widow of Maj. Samuel Blackwell, of Darlington Dist., and a member of the Baptist Church at the time of her last marriage...

William T. Henning, son of Joseph R. Hennings of Madison co., Tenn., 9th Tenn Regt., died Nov. 2, 1863, at the Fair Ground Hospital, Atlanta, from wounds at Chickamauga.

Lt. C. S. Patillo, of 1st Ga. Sharpshooters, died at his mother's residence in Marietta, Ga.,on 13th Nov, two days before completing his 22d year....

Mrs. Catharine M. Henry died on 20th of Oct. last,in her 48th year, Baldwin co., Ga...

Mrs. Samantha R. Story died in Warren co., Oct. 20, 1863, in her 38th year....

Married on the 19th Nov., by Elder E. J. Van Hoose, at the residence of Mr. E. W. Johnson, Col. Wm. B. Hall and Miss Sallie S. Johnson, all of Pike co., Ala.

On 10th Nov., by Rev. W. R. McHan, Lt. G. W. Cox and Miss E. A. Wells, at the house of E. R. Cox., Esq.

In Augusta, Ga.,by Rev. D. D. Cox, Oct. 14, Mr. Jackson T. McCook and Miss Martha Jane Cobb.

By the same, Nov. 13, 1863, Mr. Wise Widener and Miss Elizabeth Moore.

By the same, Nov. 19th, 1863, Mr. James Scarborough of Augusta, and Miss Patience Lassiter, of Burke co., Ga.

Died Lucy Ann Persons, wife of Dr. J T Persons, at her residence in Macon co., Ala., on 3th Nov.

Charles Hamet, son of Rev. S. H. and A. M. Browne, died in Cokesbury, A. S., Nov. 27, 1863, aged 5 years 3 months and 5 days.

In Hawkinsville, Pulaski co., Ga., Sep. 2, Arthur Milton, only son of Horace B. and Anna L. Heath, aged 3 years, 7 months and 11 days.

At the same place, Oct. 1, Mary Louisa, infant daughter of Otis E. and Rosetta M. Heath, aged 1 year 3 months and 7 days.

Little Maria Elizabeth, infant daughter of John T. and Mary C. Body was born March 13, 1862, in Pontotoc co., Miss., and died Sept. 2nd, 1863, ad the residence of her grandmother, Mrs. M. B. Cameron, in Pickens co., Ala., aged 3 years 5 months and 18 days.

Issue of December 10, 1863

Married near Cleveland, Ga., on 15th Nov., by Rev. Mr. Richardson, Rev. Dr. Wm. M. Wightman, Chancellor of the Southern University, to Miss Maria D., daughter of John Davies, Esq., late of Macon, Miss.

In Talbotton, Ga., Dec. 3, by Rev. G. H. Patillo, Maj. James

Gardner, of 27th Ga. Regt, and Miss M. Virginia, daughter of
Thos. Person, Esq.

Issue of December 17, 1863

Lt. W. M. Wilcox, of the 8th Ark. Regt., fell mortally woun-
ded on the 10th of Sept., at Chickamauga...a native of N. C.,
born 8th Dec. 1837, emigrated to Miss. where he married Miss
Sallie M. Shearer, of Okolona, Miss., in 1860...
Mrs. Unity Bryan, widow of Wiley Bryan, and daughter of
Wm. Johnson, was born in Green co., Ga., in Oct. 1794, and died
at the house of her daughter, Mrs. Barnett, in Opelika, Ala., Oct.
24, 1863...
Fannie, wife of J. W. Clarke, was born Nov. 10, 1836, married
Nov. 17, 1858, and died near Pendleton, S. C., Oct. 26, 1863.
Mrs. Elizabeth Moore, wife of Eli(?) Moore and daughter of
Edward H. and Margaret Alderman, was born in Damerara, S. A.,
April 24th, 1824...When quite young removed with her parents to
New York, six years after to Marianna, Fla., where she died Oct.
10, 1863....
Martha E., daughter of John J. and Jane E. Epperson, died
in Cherokee co., Ga., Oct. 20, 1863, in the 17th year of her age.
Nathan Watson was born in Monroe co., Ala., 14th Jan. 1821,
and died in Marianna, Fla.,Oct. 15, 1863....
James Gowdy, died in Houston co., Ga., on 21st Sept., 1863,
in the 65th year of his age....
Mother Bryan was born in Craven co., N. C., 1793, removed to
Fla., in 1832, and died in Marianna, Fla., Oct. 2, 1863....
J. B. Godley died on 25th Oct., 1863, in Colleton Dist.,
S. C...
Thomas J. son of Rev. James Wooddy, decd., and member of
29th Ga. Regt died in Miss., 9th Sept., at the Newton Hospital.
J. T. Ivy, 53d N. C. Regt., and from Stanly co., N. C. died
Aug. 1, 1863, on a steamer between Fort Delaware and City Point.
Married on the 5th inst., by Rev. R. V. Mulkey, the Rev.
Henry P. Waugh of the Holston Cof., to Mrs. Mary A. Procter, of
Barbour co., Ala.
On the 8th Dec., 1863, by Rev. D. D. Cox, Rev. Jesse P. Bodie
of Edgefield Dist., S. C. to Miss Martha Sego, of Richmond co.,
Ga.
On 10th Dec., at the residence of the bride's mother, in
Williamsburg Dst., S. C., by Rev. S. C. James, Rev. F. Gamewell
Puckett to Miss S. Snow Johnson.
On 26th Nov., near Dalton, by Rev. J. M. Richardson, Col. J.
W. Avery of the 4th Ga. Cavalry, to Miss Sallie H. Morris,
daughter of Judge Morris of Whitfield co.

Issue of December 24, 1863

Married on Dec. 2, 1863, by Rev. Charles Taylor, at the residence of the bride's father, Ella, daughter of Maj. James Boggan,
to Mr. Henry Buchanan, all of Anson co., N. C.
By Rev. B. R. Searcy, in Griffin, Ga., Wm. Hogg, to Marg't
E. Stearns.

(No issue of December 31, 1863)

Issue of January 7, 1864

Married on 11th Dec., in Sumter, S. C., by the Rev. Bishop
G. F. Pierce, D. D., Mr. J. R. Daniel, and Miss Lizzie R. Boyd,
all of N. C.

On Dec. 22, by Rev. Wm. H. Fleming, Hon. D. Houser, of St. Matthews, to Miss E. Vernelle Felder, eldest daughter of Edwin Felder, of Sumter Dist., S. C.

By Rev. Albert Gray, December 15th, in Crawford co., Ga., Samuel T. Coleman, of Macon, Ga., and Miss Aurelia A. Hilsman, of the former place.

By Rev. Albert Gray, Dec. 17, at Culloden, Ga., Jas H. Gray of Taylor co., Ga., and Miss Helen O. Walker, fo the former place.

In Eatonton, Ga., Dec. 15, 1863, by Rev. Geo. G. N. MacDonell, Mr. Charles M. Wiley, of Macon, Ga., to Miss Sarah Juliet Reid, of Eatonton

In Augusta, Ga., Dec. 13th, by Rev. D. D. Cox, Mr. Wm. J. Murphey, and Miss Judith Stevenson.

By the same, Dec. 17, 1863, Mr. John Sheehan, and Miss Hepsey Cason.

By the same, Dec. 24, Mr. David Butler and Miss Nancy Cheely.

By the same, Dec. 24, Mr. Jas. J. Nichols, and Miss Mary Watkins.

On the 10th Dec., by Rev. W. M. Watts, Capt. Wm. e. Carswell, of the 3d Ga. Regt., to Miss Anna T. Chapman, near Jeffersonville, Ga.

On 17th Dec., by Rev. J. B. Gaines, Mr. Dilmus R. Williams, of Jackson co., Ga., to Miss Ann R. Crag, of Lawrenceville, Ga.

On 14th Dec., by Rev. S. H. Sistrunk, Mr. Robt E. Hess of Houston co., to Miss Martha, daughter of Joseph E. Tooke, of Haynesville, Ga.

At Middleburg, E. Fla., on 15th Nov., by the Rev. A. Graham, Rev. D. L. Branning, of 2d Fla. Cav., to Miss Jennie A. Hudington, of Webster, E. Fla.

On 21st Nov., by Rev. A M Wynn, Mr. John W. Lake, of Forsyth, to Miss Mary Jane Godfrey, of Savannah, Ga.

On the 18th Nov., by the Rev. J. M. Boland, in Marengo co., Ala., Capt. T. C. Elliott, and Miss Fredonia M. Carter.

Died Dec. 13, in Augusta, Ga., Josiah Haden, youngest child of Rev. J. O. A. Clark and Amanda A. Clark, aged 5 months and 27 days.

In Iredel co., N. C., on 3d Nov., in her 13th year, Izaphiar Clementine, eldest daughter of J R and M C Cunningham, of Mecklenburg co., N. C.

Near Greenwood, Fla., Oct. 2, Little Florence, youngest child of Amos and Mary Hays, aged 1 year, 9 months and 15 days.

in Terrell co., Ga., Nov. 11, Thomas F. Jones, second son of W T and Mary A T Jones, aged 3 years, 10 months and 9 days.

in Newberry Dist., S. C., Sept. 19, 1863, Martha Jane, eldest daughter of James A. and Sophia E. Henry, in the 5th year of her age.

Rev. Charles Mouzon Smith, son of Robert S. Smith of Washington, Ga, was born in Charleston, S. C., June 7, 1841, and died in Richmond co., Ga., Oct. 6, 1863.

John P. Nall died near Lowndesboro', Ala., Oct. 9, 1863, aged 64 years....

Gen. William Hopkins was born in Kershaw Dist., S. C., 8th April 1805, and died in Richland Dist., S. C., Nov. 7, 1863....

Mrs. Mary Pamelia DeGraffenreid, wife of Lt. Marshall DeGraffenreid, and daughter of B. F. and M. A. Ross, died in Macon, Ga., Nov. 25th, 1863, in the 23d year of her age.

Pleasant Stovall died in Athens, Ga., 29th Nov. 1863, aged 70 years...born in Virginia, but his life from early infancy was spent in Ga....

Mrs. Mary Phillips wife of Mr. William Phillips, was born in Hillsboro', N. C., August 22, 1806, and was drowned in the canal, at Augusta Ga., Dec. 1, 1863...member of St. John's Methodist Church in Augusta.

Sister Martha Turner, wife of Rev. Joseph T. Turner, of the
Ga. Conf., died in Lumpkin, Ga., Nov. 4, 1863, in her 48th year.
Rev. W. E. Lucy was born May 2, 1824, and died August 22,
1863...
William M. Connor died near Eufaula, Ala., at the home of his
brother-in-law, on 23d August, 1863, in his 23d year....
Capt. J. Milton Townsend, son of Rev. Joel W. Townsend, of
the S. C. Conf., was born March 28, 1836, and fell at Chickamauga,
20th Sept....
Mrs. Susan Maron Collins, wife of David Collins, and sister
of Rev. Thomas L. Dansler, of the Ala. Conf., died 5th Nov., near
Greenwood, Fla., being about 58 years old....
Joshua L. Spears, son of Caleb W. and Mary Spears, was born
in Jasper co., Ga., 7th Feb. 1841, and died from a wound at
Chickamauga, Oct. 28, 1863.
John H. Spears, his brother, was born 13th Oct., 1843, and
died at Suffolk, Va., 23d March, 1863....
Thomas Potts was born in Jackson co., Ga., March 8, 1809, and
died in Newnan, Nov. 28, 1863...
Samuel W. Williams, 47th Regt., Ga. Vol., died in Breckenridge
Div. Hospital, Miss., in his 41st year....
Matilda A. Smith, daughter of Rev. C. and Margaret R. Smith,
of Rutherford co., N. C., died Nov. 7, 1863, in her 26th year.
Francis Monroe Robison, son of Mr. and Mrs. N. A. Robison,
18th Ala. Regt, was slain at Chickamauga, 19th Sept 1863.
Wm. E. F. Spruill fell wounded at Chickamauga, Sept. 21, 1863,
in his 21st year.
Mr. Archie Gunn, of Open Pond, Ala., was born June 12, 1835,
and died Sept. 25th, 1863, from a wound received at Chickamauga.
Rev. B. C. McCurry died near Dallas, Ga., on Nov. 12th, 1863.
George W. Bunch, son of Levi and Sealy Bunch, was born April
8, 1832, and died Dec. 13, 1863, in Terrill co., Ga.
C. G. Wesley, third son of Joseph T. and Margaret H. Tally,
was born Sept. 9, 1845, and died at the Battle of Colliersville,
Miss., at the house of Mr. Jasper Jones, in Tulahoma, Marshall
co., Miss., being 18 years 1 month and 17 days old....
Sgt. Stephen M. Crosby, of 54th Ga. Regt fell on Morris Island,
on 9th Sept 1863....
Tribute of Respect by Rev. Goodman Bethea who was born in
Marion Dist.,S. C., July 2, 1798, and died in Conecuh co., Ala.,
Sept. 22, 1863.

Issue of January 14, 1864

Married by Rev. D. D. Cox, Rev. Julius T. Curtis, of the Ga.
Conf., to Mrs. Lou Belle Applewhite,of Augusta, Ga.
At Farmerville, Meriwether co., Ga., by Rev. Thos F. McGehee,
Mr. Joseph W. White, recently of Lexington, Ky., to Miss Sarah
A. Clayton, of the former place.
On 3d Dec., by Rev. J. D. W. Crook, Mr. T. B. Shuler, of
Charleston Dist., and Miss Olivia C. Shuler, of Orangeburg Dist.
On Dec. 22, 1863, by Rev. Dr. J. B. Powell, at the residence
of the bride's father, Warner, daughter of Mr. J. O. Hill, of
Grantville, to Mr. Thos D. Johnson, of Jonesboro, Ga.
On 22d Dec., by Rv. Samuel H. Smiht, Pvt. C. R. Browning of
Colquitt co., Ga., and Miss Frances A. Jones of Orange co., Va.
On 26th Dec., 1863, by Rev. J. P. DEPass, Rev. J. J. Workman,
of the S. C. Conf., to Miss Mary Anna, daughter of Dr. James M.
Sullivan, of Greenville Dist., S. C.
By Rev. J. R. Littlejohn, on 31st Dec. 1863, Capt. Wright M.
Carter, of the 4th Ga. Bttn. to Miss Mary A. Drake, of Culloden,
Ga.
In Tuskaloosa, Ala., Dec. 30, 1863, John E. Hall, M. D. of

Maryland, Surgeon in the Confederate Army, to Miss Virginia, daughter of James Guild, M. D. of Tuskaloosa.

Mrs. Samantha Miller, wife of John Miller was born in Marion Dist., S. C., May 28, 1802, and died 3d Sept...

My Mother, Mrs. Mary Reed, was born in Pendleton co., Va., 22d Dec. 1791, and died 13th Nov. 1863, at Natchez, Miss...
Thomas Reed.

Capt. Richard N. Moore, son of Alfred and Sarah Moore, and grandson of Rev. James King, died Oct. 24, 1863, near Fort Deposit, Lownds co., Ala., from a wound at Chickamauga, in his 34th year....

My Sister, Manie J. Durant, died near Marion Village, S. C., Dec. 7, 1863, aged 14 years, 5 months and 20 days...Virginia.

Charles B. Wilkins, son of Rev. John S. and Martha G. Wilkins, of Lowndes co., Ga., died in Hospital, at Cartersville, Ga., on 31st Oct., aged 19 years and 16 days.

Sister Martha A. McKiben, daughter of J. D. and Mary Stewart, was born May 30, 1838, and died in Talladega co., Ala., Dec. 26, 1863....

Zachariah Russell, son of William and Elizabeth Russell, was born in Wayne co., Miss., April 30, 1841, and on 16th of July, a prisoner in Vicksburg.

Mrs. Eliza F. Dorman, wife of L. P. Dorman, Esq., of Americus, Ga., died on 18th Dec. 1863.

John Thomas Jackson, second son of Mrs.Sarah Gains, and stepson of Doc. Gaines, Esq., of Sumter co., Ga., was killed by accident, in his 8th year....

Issue of January 21, 1864

Married by Rev. Thos B. Lanier, Jan. 7, 1864, Mr. Robert A. Rowland to Miss Matt J. Wooding, of Burke co., Ga.

By Rev. Saml Woodbery, on 7th Jan. at the residence of Maj. M. M. Johnston, Sgt. W. W. McGriff to Miss Mary F. Johnston.

By Rev. L. F. Dowdell, on 21st Oct 1863, Dr. Thomas, of Tuskegee, to Miss Mattie Benson, of Macon co., Ala.

By Rev. L. F. Dowdell, on 23d Dec. 1863, Mr. Wm. C. Martin, of Tuskegee, to Mrs. Sallie Mitchell, of Creek Stand, Ala.

By Rev. Chas R Jewett, on 13th inst., in Griffin, Maj. A. B. Smith, C. S. A., to Miss Ophelia, daughter of Mr. E. R. Goodrich, of Griffin, Ga.

By Rev. W. J. Cotter, near Perry, Ga. on 7th Jan., Mr. W. A. Haynes, fo Miss Lizzie C. Gouedy.

By Rev . D. T. Holmes, on 12th inst.,Cap. Allison, Spear, of the 2nd Fla. Regt, to Miss Mary J..A. Davenport, of Pike co., Ga.

Daniel Fairchild, was born on Edisto Island, S. C., 15th of March, 1809, and died in Spartanburg, S. C., 22d Nov. 1863, in his 54th year...his parents, Robert A. and Theodora Fairchild....

Dr. Bobert Clayton Gerry, son of the late Rev. Jno. L. Gerry, died in Hamilton co., Fla., on 20th Novl 1863, aged 27 years....

Dr. John B. Kendle, died in Talbotton, Ga., 31st Dec. 1863, in his 40th year.

Mrs. Elizabeth Bell was born in Jackson co., Ga., and died in Calhoun co., Ala., Nov. 3, 1863, in her 53d year. Her maiden name was Hampton.

B. M. Thompson, son of W. C. and Martha Thompson died at Union Springs, Ala., Dec. 31, 1863, in her 23d year....

Mrs. Mary Dozier, wife of Thomas J. Dozier, died in Talbotton, Ga., on 23d Dec., in her 60th year...

Diogenes W. Grodick of Alachua co., Fla., died in the Hospital in Richmond, Va...2d Fla. Regt...

Dr. Hamlet Goudelock was born Aug. 6, 1863, and died in Union

Dist., S. C., Dec. 13, 1863...member of the M. E. Church more than
30 years.

Issue of January 28, 1864

    Married by J. T. Webb, J. P. on 31st Dec., 1863, at the resi-
dence of A. J. Varn, Berrien co., Ga., James Hurins of 26th Ga.
Regt., to Miss Lovina Varn, of said co.
    By Rev. G L W Anthony, on 17th Jan. 1864, in Lincoln co.,
Ga., Mr. J R Bullard to Miss Susan W Samuels.
    By Rev J D Cameron, on Dec. 22, Rev. H. H. Kavanaugh of the
Ala. Conf., to Miss Anna M. Kinbrough, of Green co., Ala.
    By Rev D J McMillan, on 17th inst., at Bucksville, Mr. L F
Sarvis to Mrs M J Bell.
    By Rev J P Morrell on 13th Jan at her father's residence near
Brighton, Beaufort Dist., S C to Miss Julia A Stokes to Major
Joseph Hamilton of Phillips' Ga. Legion.
    By Rev. John Calvin Johnson in Clark co., Ga.,on 22nd Dec.,
Mr. Robert D Dickens to Miss Mollie M Langford.
    By the same, on 29th Dec. Mr. John M. Gunn to Miss Pamelia
E Ward.
    By the same, on 21st Jan., Mr. George McMunnally of Co. C.,
44th Regt., Ga Vols., to Miss Vatavia A. P. Stephenson.
    On Dec 3, by Rev. J. M. Boland, in Marengo co., Ala., Miss
Mary Rogers to Dr. J M G Luther, of 21st Regt Ala. Vols.
    On Dec 23d, by Rev. Wm. Houser, Chaplina of the 48th Ga. Regt.,
Ezekiel T. Mallory of N. Brunswick, British America, to Miss
Caroline A.,only surviving daughter of Arthur Rudd Cheatham, Esq.
of Jefferson co., Ga.
    On 12th inst., by Rev P M Ryburn, Mr. B H Wrigley to Miss Lucy
M. Knott, both of Macon, Ga.
    On the 22nd inst., by Rev. P M Ryburn, Mr. J. H. Shaw C S A
to Miss Willie M. Banks of Forsyth, Ga.
    On 14th Jan., by Rev. James Cohen, J. O. Terrell, Ajt. of
19th S. C. Regt, to Miss Elizabeth A., youngest daughter of the
late Dr. Manning Austin, of Greenville Dist., S. C.
    Capt. Thos. O. Byrd, of 4th Miss Regt, died on 23d July 1863,
in Vicksburg....
    J. B. G. Mellard was born April 6, 1810, in Orangeburg Dist.,
S. C., and died at the residence of Mr. Farrior, his brother-in-
law, near Fort Gaines, Ga. Dec. 5, 1863....
    Alexander Pope, died Jan. 1, 1863, in Washington, Wilkes co.,
Ga., in the 78th year of his age....
    Mrs. Mary Thompson, wife of Joseph R. Thompson, was born July
27, 1792, and died at Cumming, Ga., Dec. 16, 1863....
    Elizabeth A. Weems, wife of A J Weems, of Bartow co., Ga.,
died Jan. 8, 1863, in her 49th year....
    Nathaniel Allen Ogilby, youngest son of Dr. H. J. and Mrs.
S. A. Ogleby, was born in Madison, Ga., Oct. 24, 1843, and died
in Atlanta, Ga., Dec. 5, 1863....
    Samuel M. Pennington, son of W B R and N J Pennington, of
Morgan co., Ga., was born Aug. 12, 1836, and died Jan 4, 1864,
in his 19th year....
    Samuel D. Johnson died from measles while in Virginia...
The father, Bro. J. B. Johnson, brought him home....
    Franklin P. Johnson was slain at Sharpsburg...
    John Wesley Johnson, fell at Chickamauga....
    Eliza, wife of S. T. Viele, was born Feb. 21, 1824, in Han-
cock co., Ga., and died at Centreville, Talbot co., Ga., Jan. 18,
1864....
    Geo. B. Rorie was born in Washington, Wilkes co., Ga., Nov.
21, 1821, and died in the General Hospital at Macon...
    R. R. Stephens, son of Reuben Stephens of Colleton dist., S.

C., died at his father's residence, Jan. 6, 1864, aged 20 years, lacking 3 days....

Mrs. Annie E. Morris was born Oct. 17, 1848, in Baltimore Md., and died Dec. 11, 1863, near Marietta Ga....

Mrs. Eveline A. Allen, wife of Rev. James W. Allen and daughter of Hon. Wm. J. Rhodes, died in Richmond co., Ga., Dec. 31, aged 34.

Milton M. Mellette born Sept. 2, 1834, died in hospital in Charleston, S. C.

Issue of February 4, 1864

Married near West Point, Ga., by Rev. R. W. Dixon, Jan. 26, Mr. J. W. L. Little of Harris co., Ga., to Miss A. E. Erwin, of Troup co., Ga.

By Rev. Andrew J. Briggs, on 27th Jan., 1863, at the residence of T. J. Motley, Mr. O H Tyus and Miss R P Shackelford, all of Autauga co., Ala.

Died at the residence of S. J. Kidd, Coosa, Ala., on 12th Oct., 1863, Lillie Jane, daughter of Rev. B. F. And Mrs. E. A. Blow, aged 10(?) months and 1 day.

Sister Susan E. Taylor was born July 9, 1827, married to Maj. Geo. W. Taylor, Dec. 19, 1833, and died Jan. 2, 1864...

Sister Rosa A. Turnbull wife of Lt. S. A. Turnbull, died in Monticello, Fla., Jan. 4, 1864, in the 26th year of her age... left a child.

Mrs. Margaret Lipsey, died at the residence of her son, Timothy R. Lipsey, Esq., in Chester dist., S. C., and in the 89th year of her age...about 60 years a widow of an itinerant preacher ...

Virginia Ingraham, eldest child of Hon J. J. and E. J. Ingraham, died in Manning, S. C., Dec. 19, 1863, in her 20th year....

John Wesley Powers, died Nov. 27, 1863, in his 32d year, of a wound received near Knoxville, Tenn.

Mrs. Nancy Roberts, died in Selma, Ala., aged 62 years...

Mrs. Elizabeth Gruber died on Jan. 16, 1864, at the residence of her son, George H. Burber, in Hampstead, in her 70th year....

H. T. Houston, of Randolph co., Ala., and a member of Co. G. 22nd Ala. Regt, died Nov. 30th, from a wound received at Chickamauga....

Mrs. Susannah Richbourg, widow of Nathaniel Richbourg, died in Clarendon Dist., S. C., on 26th Dec., 1863, in her 87th year....

Mrs. Mary M. Lard, wife of Arch. E. Lard, died in Newton co., Ga., Dec. 29, 1863, in the 46th year of her age....

Mrs. Elizabeth Lard, sister-in-law of the above, died on the Saturday night previous, and on the following day, a son of Bro. Lard, also aged 26(?) years....

W. F. Walton, of 37th Ala. Regt son of Manning and Charlotte Walton, of Chambers co., Ala., died at Dalton, Ga., 15th Dec. 1863....

Issue of February 11, 1864

Married in Charleston, S. C., on the 4th February, 1863, by Rev. Aldrich, Mr. John Radcliffe Doughty to Miss Carrie M. Ferira, both of the above place.

In Augusta, Ga.,Feb. 2, 1864, by Rev. D. D. Cox, Mr. Ferdinand Rahner to Miss Anna Castleberry.

By the same, Feb. 4, 1864, Mr. Charles W. Nichols to Miss Martha Bennett.

On 26th Jan., by Rev. T. J. Rutledge, Col. Anderson W. Redding, of Chattahoochie, co., Ga., to Mrs. Jane Rutledge, of Harris co., Ga.

On 28th Jan., by Rev. H. Andrews, Mr. W. F. Harris of Liberty
co., to Miss F. M. Thurman, formerly of Mobile, Ala.

In Marietta, Ga., Jan 28th, by Rev. F. H. Pattillo, Mr. J. H.
Brumet, to Mrs. E. F. Bostwick.

By Rev. W R Talley, on 26th Jan., Lt. Jas. W. Dickson C S A,
to Miss Mary A. Gray, all of Greenwood, Fla.

Also, at the Parsonage in Greenwood, Fla., Jan. 29, Mr.
William F. Dickson to Miss Sallie E. Powers.

By Rev. T. B. Russell, Feb. 1, 1863, in Marshallville, Ga.,
Miss Maggie Ophelia Speight, to Mr. Liews O. Niles of Griffin,
Ga.

On Jan. 31st, by Rev. M. W. Arnold, Col. J. N. Forrest of
Atlanta, to Miss Sallie C. Apple of Greensboro, Ga.

Lt. W. H. Watkins of 43d Regt. Ala. Vols. was born Feb.
18, 1841, and died on the battle field of Chickamauga, Sept. 20,
1863.

Pattie J. Watkins, his wife, and daughter of Rev. N. A. Cra-
vnes, of La. Conf., was born Oct. 4, 1843, and died in Marengo
co., Ala., Oct. 14, 1863.

Lena Watkins, their only child, was born Nov. 16, 1862, and
died Oct. 2, 1863.

Capt. M. G. McWilliams was born in Greenville, Ga., May 7,
1844, in Wetumpka, Ala., Jan. 10, 1864.

Mrs. Malinda Davis, wife of Larkin H. Davis, in her 45th
year...born March 1, 1819...

Seaborn Haughton of Hamilton, Harris co., Ga., of Howard's
Bttn., died at the General Hospital at Columbus, Ga., Dec. 14,
1863....

Daniel R. Varn, of 47th Ga. Regt, was born in Barnwell Dist.,
S. C., Jan. 16, 1817, and died in Appling co., Ga., Nov. 1, 1863.

Miss D. Emmaline Pickens was born Oct. 6, 1845, and died
Jan. 14, 1864...

John Wesley Aaron was born in Bedford co., Tenn., March 28,
1828, and came to Ala. in 1843...died at the Hammond General
Hospital, Point Lookout, Md., in Oct. or Nov. 1863....

Pvt. Martin B. Stanley, 24th Regt. Ala. Vols., born March
18, 1827, and died in the Hospital in Ringgold, Ga., March,
1863...married to Miss Sarah J. Lambert March 18, 1855...left
a wife and four children.

Sgt. James M. Williams 22d Ga. Regt, died on 21st Oct., 1863,
from a wound received at Gettysburg....

Sister Sarah Barton, wife of Dr. Barton, of Burke co., died
18th Jan., 1864, in her 49th year....

Moses D. Harris was born Jan. 22, 1828, and died in Mill Town,
Berrien co., Ga., Dec. 15, 1863

Tribute of Respect to Bro. Wm. C. Dickson, by Greenwood ct.,
Ala. Conf, and who died 28th Dec. 1863....

Issue of February 18, 1864

Sgt. John E. Jones of 38th Miss. Vols., was wounded at Vicksburg, on 29th June, and died the next day, in his 21st year....

James Milton Sistrunk, died on the 11th of Jan., 1864, at
Dalton, Ga., aged 18 years...son of Rev. Saml. H. J. Sistrunk of
Houston co., Ga....

Mrs. Martha C. Carver was born Oct. 14, 1829, and died Jan.
26, 1864. In 1852, she became the wife of Rev. R. D. Carver,
a member of the Ala. Conf....

Mrs. Elizabeth Gregory died in Gadsden co., Fla., Jan. 16,
1864, aged 65 years, 6 months and 17 days...born in Onslow co.,
N. C., where she was raised and married Jesse Gregory....left
six children, 51 grandchildren, and 6 great grandchildren...

Robin M. Duffey, 6th Regt. S. C. V., died at Black Water, Va., aged 22 years...a member of one of the first companies that left Chester....

Seaborn J. Johnson died near Cave Spring, Floyd co., Ga., on 7th Dec., 1863, in his 68th year....

Jannie Gable died in Marietta, Ga., on 13th Jan., aged nearly 12 years

Ida Isadora, eldest daughter of J. F. M. and Mary Michau, died 18th Jan., in her 18th year....

Issue of February 25, 1864

Married on 14th Jan., at T. L. Dukes, inFairfield by Rev. D. W. Seale, Sgt. S. H. Duke of 7th S. C. Vols., to Miss A. G. Loman, of Columbia, S. C.

On 31st Jan., at the residence of the bride, by Rev. J. J. Morgan, Mr. J. Harmon Morgan, of the State Troops to Mrs. Henrietta Blitch, of Effingham co., Ga.

At Pleasant Grove Church, on 23d Jan., by Rev. C. C. Calloway, Rev. A. N. Sikes, of the Ala. Conf., to Mrs. Sarah C. Croute, of Bibb co.

On 28th Jan., at Jamestown, Ga., by Rev. L. R. Redding, Mr. William H. Richardson, of Society Hill, Ala., to Miss Virginia E. Jones, youngest daughter of the late Moses Jones, dec'd, of the former place.

On 9th Feb., by Rev. Anson West, Lt. A. C. Lawrence, of Lowndes co., Miss., to Miss M. N. Mason, of Wilcox co., Ala.

By Rev. H. H. Parks, in Atlanta, Ga., on 4th Feb., Stephen F. Smith, son of the late Rev. Burgess Smith, to Miss Anna G. Bailey.

By the same, in Newton co., Ga.,on 10th Feb.,Lewis S. Salmons, of Atlanta, Ga., to Miss Mary Alexander.

By the same in Atlanta, on 11th Feb. Dr. Wm Judge, of Alabama, to Miss M. F. Blackburn, of Atlanta.

At the Dist. Parsonage, in Marion, S. C., Jan 3, 1864, by Rev. T. R. Walsh, Rev. J. H. Tart of the S. C. Conf. to Miss S. Bird, of Marion Dist.

By the same, on 7th Feb., Mr. Jehu Gasque to Mrs. E. M. Allison, both of Marion Dist., S. C.

At the residence of Mr. Boswell, Eufaula, Ala., by Rev. Jos. B. Cottrell, on 4th Feb., Mr. John S. Lee, Jr., of Fort Valley, Ga., to Miss Laura V. Lowman.

By Rev. F. A. Branch, on 4th Feb.,Mr. Jas. T. Hines of Decatur co., Ga., to Miss Martin A. Smith, daughter of Mr. Benjamin Smith, of Quincy, Fla.

Jan. 19th, 1854, by Rev. James M. N. Low, Mr. Robt T.Green, to Mrs. Tempa Ann Singletary, second daughter of Danfet Singleton, all of Clay co., Ga.

By Rev. John W. Reynolds, Feb. 11th, Maj. A. R. Williams, to Miss Julia E. Grimes, second daughter of Judge Grimes, all of Franklin, Ga.

In Hamburg, S. C., Feb. 16th, by Rev. D. D. Cox, Mr. Robert H. Langford to Miss Sarah T. Hall, all of Augusta, Ga.

Died William Capers Mitchel, son of McKendree and Sue P. Mitchell, near Leesville, S. C., Nov. 15, 1863, aged 3 years and 5 months.

Hester Lurany Elizabeth Hicks, infant daughter of Mr T. M. and Sister E. M. Hicks, was born 19th July 1861, and died Feb. 11th, 1864...

In Monticello, Ga., on 31st Jan. 1864, Clara E., only daughter of J. F. and Georgia E. Mixon, aged 4 years 9 months and 21 days.

Col. James Wimberly of Muscogee co., Ga., died Feb. 9, 1864,
in the 73d year of his age....
Mrs. Mary Ann Myrick, wife of Benj. H. Myrick, and daughter
of John and Lucretia Edmondson, died at the residence of her mother, Jan. 9, 1863, in her 40th year....
Rev. J. D. Mann was born in Cumberland co., N. C., March,
1799. In 1823 he was married to Miss Mary J. Jernigan, of Powel-
ton, Hancock co., Ga...removed to Aberdeen, Miss., where he died
Dec. 16, 1863...a Methodist minister for 40 years.
Cpl. W. S. Dunning, son of Capt. Jas. Dunning, was born in
Darlington Dist., S. C., Sept. 29th, 1832, and was married to
Miss Ann Calding, of Marion co., Fla., Aug. 29, 1855...killed at
the battle of Missionary Ridge, Nov. 25, 1863....

Issue of March 3, 1864

Married on 18th Feb., by Rev. N. D. Moorehouse, Charles M.
Modiset of Burke co., Ga., to Miss Sarah H. Gregory, of Jefferson
co., Ga.
In Monroe, Walton co., Ga., on 11th inst., by Rev. C. D. Davis,
Capt. H. B. Landers, of Co. F. 6th and 7th consolidated Regts.
Ark., to Miss Lou M. Patillo, of the former place.
On 11th inst., by Rev. C. A. Moore, Lt. T. J. Jordan, Co. F.
3rd Ga. Regt., to Miss Sally J. Clay, all of Williamson, Ga.
By Rev. R. F. Williamson, on 16th Feb., at the residence of
the bride's father, Mr. Joseph T. Jipsom, of Columbus Ga., to
Mrs. Elizabeth J. Patrick, of Marion co., Ga.
On the morning of the 26th Feb., by Rev. J. A. Mood, W. Din-
kins of Clarendon, S. C., to Miss Maria J. Easterling, of
Georgetown, S. C.
By Rev. W. G. Allen, at the residence of Mrs. Lewis, Perry,
Ga., on the 23d Feb. Lt. James R. Rice of Southern Rights Bat-
tery, to Miss Anna Fay.
By Rev. J. H. Grogan, on 11th Feb., at the residence of Dr.
Walton, in Wilkes co., Ga., Mr. S. H. Wynn to Miss E. Danforth.
Miss Ella, daughter of Col. Charles and Adaline Strong, of
Newton co., Ga., died 24th Jan. 1864.
Sgt. W. B. Kilpatrick son of G. L. and M. N. Kilpatrick,
died in Columbus, Ga. Feb. 1, 1863, in his 19th year....
Mrs. Margaret Stripling, wife of James B. Stripling, died
in Tatnall co., Ga., Nov. 30, 1863, in the 64th year of her age.
Mary J. C. Johnson, daughter of William and Mary Johnson,
died in Clarendon Dist., S. C., Dec. 26, 1863, in her 23rd year.
Bro. J. R. Daniel died in Mecklenburg co., N. C., Dec. 24,
1863, in his 37 year.
Mrs. Rebecca A.Benbow, wife of W. W. Benbow, and daughter
of William and Ann Hilton, died in Clarendon Dist., S. C., Nov.
29, 1863, in her 37th year....
Mrs. Rebecca D. Williams, wife of Rev. J. W. Williams, was
born in Monroe co., Ga., Sept. 18, 1829...died Dec. 1, 1863,
in Orion, Ala....member of the Baptist Church....
James Meriwether Hull, son of Asbury Hull, died in Athens,
Ga., Feb. 8, 1864, in his 26th year...leaving a wife and two
children.
Mrs. Rebecca A. Nicholson, wife of J. M. Nicholson, of La-
place, Macon co., Ala., died on 22d Jan., 1863, in her 31st year.
W. G. Green was born Feb. 1813, in Colleton Dist., S. C.,
and died Dec. 16, 1863....
Mrs. Sarah R. Duke, wife of Benj. Duke, died in Troup co.,
Ga., Feb. 2nd, 1864, in her 21st year....
Frederick A. Potter, of Charleston, S. C., died in his 17th
year, Nov. 25, 1863....

Houston Taylor Owens of Randolph co., Ala., 22nd Ala. Regt., died Nov. 30th, 1863, at the field Hospital, of a wound at Chicka-mauga....

Sister Patsy James, wife of Absolom James died Jan. 29, 1864, near Magnolia Church, Dale co., Ala., aged 44 years....left husband and 9 children.

Mary A. Cloud, third daughter of J. B. and Margaret Cloud, of Fairfield Dist., S. C., died Nov. 19, 1863, in her 16th year.

Ellen, daughter of J. A. and Rebecca David, died in Green-ville, S. C., Jan. 26, in the 10th year of her age....

Mrs. Elizabeth Strother, was born 1st Jan. 1795, in Wilkes co., Ga., and died in Orion, Ala., 1st Dec. 1863....

Issue of March 10, 1864

Married in West Point, Ga., Dec. 6, 1863, by Rev. R. W. Dixon, Capt. A. F. Zachry, of C S A, Bluffton, Ala., to Miss A. A. Lanier, of West Point, Ga.

In West Point, Ga., Jan. 12, 1864, by Rev. F. W. Dixon, Mr. L. M. Boohardt, of Fairfield, S. C., to Miss J. R. Harrington, of West Point, Ga.

In West Point, Ga., Feb. 16, 1864, by Rev. R. W. Dixon, Mr. E. K. Wilson of Nashville, Tenn., to Miss Mollie Reed, of West Point, Ga.

In Troup co., Ga., Feb. 25, 1864, by Rev. R. W. Dixon, Mr. W. O. Dansby, of LaGrange, Ga., and C S A, to Miss Martha H. Sappoington, of Troup co., Ga.,

On 24th Feb., by Rev. S. R. J. Sistrunk, Mr. Joseph A. Adams, to Miss Amamda P. Kent, both of Houston co., Ga.

At the residence of Mrs. Sarah Maner, near Robertville, St. Peter's Parish, Beaufort, S. C., on 18th Feb. by Rev. Arthur Wigfall, of Grahamville, Rev. Samuel Leard, of the S. C. Conf. to Miss Margaretta Agnes Clark, of said Parish.

On Feb. 23d, 1863, by Rev. W. R. Foote, Mr. Thomas R. Drake, of Thomaston, Ga., to Miss Laura R. Charlton, of Green co., Ga.

By Rev. O. Eaddy, on 17th Feb., 1864, Dr. McLane McFarland, of Chesterfield Dist., to Miss Lizzie Wright, of Darlington.

On the 25th Feb., in Pike co., Ga.,by Rv. D. T. Holmes, Mr. M Pryor, to Miss Cynthia E. Driver.

Died in Greenwood, Fla., Feb. 7, 1863, Little Hur Elizabeth Cravy, only daughter of Sister Eliza Cravy, a widow, aged 5 years, 5 months and 15 days.

On the 6th Jan., 1863, ine infant son of Peter W. and Harriet Gilliam, of Newberry Dist., aged nine days.

Mrs. Behethland Bird was born Feb. 26, 1798, in S. C., and died near Monticello, Fla., Jan. 30th, 1863, in the 71st year of her age....

Wiley M. Harnage of 47th Ga. Vols., died in the Hospital at Kingston, Ga., on 9th Jan., 1864, aged 38 years....

Lt. Richard Chapman died in his 36th year, from wounds received at Blue Springs, Tenn....

Jason Moore, son of James and Lydia Moore, decd.,of Jones co., Ga., was born Jan. 17, 1800, and died in Lee co., Ga.,29th Dec., 1863...

Mrs. MaryA. Moore, wife of Jason Moore, and daughter of Ed-ward and Sarah Sessions, was born Sept. 17, 1811, in Williamsburg S. C...died 22nd Feb 1864...left children. Lizzie J. Moore

Michael Oliver Taysor was born April 13, 1837, in Colleton Dist., S. C., and died Jan. 27, 1864, at the residence of his uncle, Alfred Raysor, in Jefferson co., Fla...in 1859, married Sarah J. Johnson....

Miss Mattie Lamar, daughter of Harmony and Martha Lamar died at her mother's, near Auburn, Ala., Jan. 21, 1864, in her 20th year....

Dr. James A. Jordan of Jefferson co., Ga., was killed at Gettysburg, July 1, 1863, in his 25th year....

Mrs. Sarah Perdue, of Aiken, S. C., died Feb. 24, 1864, aged 66 years...

Mrs. Sarah A. Brookins, wife of Maj. Haywood Brookins, died in Sandersville, Ga., on the 20th Feb., in her 35th year....

Mrs. Celia Jones, wife of James Jones died in Troup co., Ga., Feb. 16, 1864, in her 68th year....

Masalon M. Melson was born in Morgan co., Ga.,and died in Talbot co., Ga.,on 16th Feb.,1863, in his 37th year....

Mrs. Elizabeth Hill, wife of John Hill, died in Troup co., Ga., Feb. 13, 1863, aged 72 years of age....

Mrs. Jane H. Smith, consort of Saml. Smith, Esq., died in Anson co., N. C., 5th Feb. 1864....

Mrs. Martha Byers, died in Pickens co., Ala., 3rd Dec. 1863. She was a native of Virginia...wife of Seth Byers, to whom she was married in 1818, in Jasper co., Ga...77 years of age....

A. McIntyre, died in Lowndes co., Ga., on 28th Nov., 1863, in his 46th year....

Sister Laura Humel Bradley, wife of Jethro Bradley, died in Micanukie, Fla., Jan. 5, 1864, aged 36 years....

Issue of March 17, 1864

Mrs. Martha Ann George...granddaughter of Rev. T. Langsby of England. Her father, Rev. John Cox, also a minister of the M. E. Church...died 24th Feb 1864, having reached the age of 61....

Mrs. Mary T. Brown, was born in Chester Dist., S. C., Aug. 31, 1795, married to Mr. John Brown, Jan 6., 1811, removed to Lancaster Dist., S. C., where she died 20th Feb. 1864....

Dr. John C. Sullivan, of Greenville Dist., S. C., died on 14th Feb., in his 71st year....

James M. Herndon, a member of Co. K. 1st Ala. Regt, was born in Tuskaloosa co., August 26, 1834, and died July 16, 1863.

Mr. John Patterson died near Stilesboro, Bartow co., Ga., 20th Jan., aged 53 years...born in Henry co., Va....

Samuel Clark was born Aug. 29, 1801, and died in Montgomery co., Ga.,Jan. 2, 1863, in his 63d year...

Mrs. R. Ann Helvenstein, wife of the late Capt. Jos. E. Helvenstein, who was killed 17 Sept 1863, died in Whitfield co., 12th Dec., 1863, in her 27th year....

A. E. Magruder Drake, sixth son of Rev. R. M. Drake was born at Magnolia Springs, Jefferson co., Miss., Sept. 21, 1843, and died in Augusta, Ga., Dec. 2d, 1863....

The Rev. and Hon. Howell Cobb died near Perry, Houston co., Ga., on the 15th of Feb., 1864, aged 59 years....

Mrs. Sarah W. S. Chinn, the wife of Judge Chinn, died at Harrodsburg, Ky., Feb. 8th, 1864...daughter of Mark Hardin, a Rev. soldier, and one of the pioneers of Kentucky....

Mrs. Caroline M. C. Burnett, wife of W. M. Burnett, and daughter of Rev. A. Ray, decd., died in Madison, Ga.,Feb. 27, 1864, in her 44th year....

Pvt. E. A. McAndrews, 18th Regt. Ga. Vols., died at the Distributing Hospital, Richmond, Va.,Sept. 26, 1863, aged 26 years.

Lucy M. Stewart, daughter of George and L. E. K. Stewart, was born Aug. 19, 1853, and died in Anderson Dist., S. C., Dec. 26, 1863....

Jacob Ketle Golightly, was born in Spartanburg Dist., S. C., and died in the Atlanta Hospital, Nov. 27, 1864.

Issue of March 24, 1864

Married on 8th March, by Rev. Alex. M. Thigpen, Col. John T.
Low of the 6th Ga. Regt., to Miss Lizzie A. Johnson, of Lexington, Ga.

By Rev. W. J. Jordan, on 21st Jan., Mr. P. H. Mattox, to Miss
Mary S. Mattox, all of Tatnall co., Ga.

On 24th ult., by Rev. W. C. Page, Mr. Edwin S. Castlen, of
Monroe co., Ga. to Miss Mattie A. Harison, eldest daughter of Dr.
Gabriel Harrison, lateof Macon,Ga.

By Rev. R. W. Flournoy, on 3d March, in Madison co., Fla.,
Rev. W. A. McLain, of the Fla. Conf., to Miss Emma C. Breadwell,
of said co.

On 3rd March, at the residence of Mrs. Watson, Sumter, S. C.,
by Rev. Henry D. Moore, D. Alfred J. China, Surgeon C S A, to
Miss Mary H. E. Anderson, of Sumter.

Dr. Edwin H. Perry was born Feb. 29th, 1816, and died Jan.
31, 1864, in Newborn, Newton co., Ga....

Dr. Daniel M. Rogers, died in Bishopville, S. C., Feb. 18,
1863, in his 27th year...Capt. Depass' Co., Light Artillery....
left wife and children.

Mrs. Mary Lucinda Fore, wife of H. J. Fore, died in Marion
Dist., S. C., Feb. 17, 1864, in her 82d year....

Mrs. Mary K. Miller, wife of Mr. David Miller, died in Rutherford co., N. C. on 12th Feb. 1854, in her 65th year....

Mrs. Levy N. Bennett, wife of Rev. Eli Bennett, of the Ga.
conf., died in Newton co., Ga.,11th Feb. 1864, in her 70th year.
daughter of Mr. Benjamin and Mrs. Peggy Bowles, of N. C....

Mrs. Mary Falkenberg was born in Chester dist., S. C., 1780,
and died in Kershaw Dist., S. C., Feb. 20, 1864, in her 84th
year....

J. D. Bundy, son of William and Achea Bundy, of Marlboro'
Dist., s. C., died on 14th Feb.,1864, in his 32d year....

James B. Pou of Jasper co., Ga., of 6th Ga. Regt., was mortally wounded Feb. 20th, at Ocean Pond...and died in the hospital
at Lake City, Fla.

B. B. Haralson died in Chambers co., Ala., Feb. 6, 1864,
aged 47 years....

John O. Hill was born in Anderson co., N. C.(sic), 10th
April 1820...his father moved to Chambers co., Ala...taken
prisoner at Chickamauga, killed by the falling of a gallery....

Mrs. Jane E. Burt, wife of W. W. Burt of Salem, Russell co.,
Ala., died 23d Feb. 1864, in her 48th year....

Miss Susan B.Cauthen, was born in York Dist., March 8, 1835,
died in Lancaster Dist., S. C., Feb. 29, 1863, in her 29th year.

Mrs. Rachel Ervin died in Coweta co., Ga., on 21st Jan., 1864,
in her 60th year.....

Wm. B. Copeland was born in Green co., Ga., in 1796, and died
in Harris co., Ga., March 4th, 1864, in his 68th year....

Harrison McLarin was born near Petersburg, Va.,May 16, 1795,
and died in Campbell co., Ga.,on 31st Dec., 1863....

Mrs M. J. T. Morris, wife of Mr. Simeon W. Morris, and daughter of Rev. Wm. Brockinton, was born Oct. 6, 1821, and died March
1st, 1864....

John Thos. Wright, son of Rev. John C.and Virginia L.
Wright, of Coweta co., Ga., died Feb. 6, 1864....

Mrs. Frances Ann Herbert died at the residence of her husband,
Mr. R. G. Herbert, in Macon co., Alabama, on 26th Feb....

D. A. F. Summers, Esq., 2d Regt. S. C. Artillery, died in
Hospital, James Island, S. C., Feb. 3, 1863, in his 37th year.

Judge Stephen B. Marshall was born in Warren co., Ga., March
14, 1798, While he was yet a child, his parents removed to Putnam
co...died 8th Feb. 1864....

Tribute of Respect by Rev. Howell Cobb who died near Perry, Ga., 15th Feb. 1864, in the 69th year of his age, by Perry ct.

Tribute of Respect by Miss Emma A. Martin, by Sabbath School at Sparta, Ga.

Tribute of Respect to A. Gunn, who fell at the battle of Chickamauga, by Woodville circuit, Ala. Conf.

Issue of March 31, 1864

Married on 3rd March, by Rev. W. A. Rogers, Capt. Geo. S. Niles C S A, to Miss Alice E.Andrews, daughter of Jacob Andrews, of Griffin, Ga.

On 3d March, by Rev. J. L. Lupo, Mr. Wm. H. Nance, of Marshall co., Ky., to Miss Lucy A. Miller, of Campbell co., Ga.

On the 18th Feb., 1863, at St. Peter's Church, by Rev. W. J. Morcock, Dr. Southwood Smith, to Miss Martha, eldest daughter of Hon. W. G. Roberds, all of Beaufort Dist., S. C.

In Eatonton, Ga., Feb. 4, 1864, by Rev. Geo. G. N. MacDonell, Capt. Matthew H. Talbot, C. S. A., to Miss Mollie E. Reid, eldest daughter of Co. H. S. Reid, of Eatonton.

On 3rd Feb., in Whitney, Calhoun co., Ga., Dr. J. E. Blocker, Asst Surgeon of the 4th Ga. Regt, to Miss Lavonia Beekam.

In Vineville, Ga., on the 16th ult., by Rev. G. G. Smith, at the residence of R. F. Ousley, Mr. J. J. Hurt of LaFayette co., Miss., to Miss Mary Newda Ousley, of Vineville.

In Pike co., Ga., on the 18th inst., by Rev. P. N. Maddux, Mr. Thomas B. Lyon, of 37th Ga. Regt, to Miss Talitha Reid, daughter of Mr. J. W. Reid.

By Rev. C. A. Mitchell, on 18th March, Mr. David W. Alexander, of Taylor, co., to Mrs. Sophronia McNeal, of Macon co., Ga.

By Rev. Blakely Smith, on the 23rd March, at the residence of M. L. Green, Esq., near Fort Valley, Rev. R. Afton Holland, of the Ga. Conf., to Miss T H. Everett, of Houston co., Ga.

On 17th by Rev. F. A. Branch, Capt. S. M. H. Byrd. of Cedar Valley, Ga., to Miss Anna W., second daughter of Dr. John G. Pettus, of Jefferson co., Fla.

By Rev. R. H. Howren, on 23d Feb., Mr. Walter Joiner, of the Army, to Miss Janie Sharpe, daughter of Rev. Hamilton Sharpe, of Lowndes co., Ga.

By Rev. E. G. Porter, Chap. 18th Miss Reg., on 10th March, near Dalton, Ga.,Mr. John E. Holloway, of 7th Miss Regt., to Miss Maggie E. Meek.

Died Mary Elizabeth, eldest daughter of Mrs. Emeline Pursley, born 22nd June 1855, died Nov. 11, 1863.

W---Doughty Dick, son of Mr. W. G. and Mrs. F. E. Dick, was born 7th Feb. 1859, and died in Barnwell, Feb. 6, 1864.

Julia Alsada, infant daughter of G. G. and G. E. Perude, died in Aiken, S. C., March 11, 1864, aged 2 months and 15 days.

In West Point, Ga.,Jan. 12, 1864, Lou Ella Clifford, eldest child of Leroy and Angie Wilkerson, aged 4 years, 6 months and 19 days.

Oscar Hamilton, son of Mrs. John A. Ellis, (late Mrs. Sigismunda M. Hamilton) of Banks co., Miss., died March 3, 1864, at the residence of his step-father in Butler co., Ala., aged7 years na d 6 months....

Rev. James F. Wilson was born in Marlboro' Dist., S. C., Feb. 4, 1838, died in Darlington Dist., Jan. 18, 1864....

Mrs. Bettie Louisiana Kenan, wife of Uriah T. Kenan, Esq., died at the residence of her father, Henry B. Holcombe, Esq., near Richmond, Dallas co., Ala., on 1st March, 1864, in the 30th year of her age....

Major Wm. Merriwether Chatfield, diest 17th Feb. 1864, son of Rev. G. W. Chatfield, born in Greenville, Merriwether co.,

Ga., on 19 Sept 1856(sic)....

James Wade Murray, of Montgomery, Ala., died 27th Dec, 1863, of a wound at Bean's Station....

Wm. M. McCutchen, died in Troup co., Ga.,March 4, 1864, in his 54th year....

Rev. James A. Rogers was born in Putnam co., Ga., Feb. 16h, 1832, and died in Polk co., Ga., Dec. 19, 1863...the 5th brother that has died in Confederate service.

Norman McRanny was born in Scotland on the Isle of sky, and died in Wilkinson co., Ga., Nov. 25, 1863, in his 73d year....

Catharine McRanny, was born in Roberson co., N. C., and died in Wilkinson co., Ga.,Sept. 3, 1863....in her 72d year....

Mrs. Rebecca R. Akers, daughter of the late Archibald Turner, and wife of John Akers, senr., died at LaGrange, Troup co., Ga., Dec. 22, 1863, born in Green co., Ga.,April 25, 1810....

Orderly Sgt. E. J. N. Moore, 51st Ga. Vols., son of Jason and MaryA. Moore, was born Dec. 15, 1844, in Lee co., Ga...died at Gordonsville, Va.

Mrs. Caroline Spann, wife of Rev. Toliver Spann, died Dec. 21, 1863, in her 42d year...left husband and six chidlren.

Rev. James Dodson, died in Union co., Ga.,Jan. 3, 1864, aged about 46 years....

Tribute of Respect by Palmetto Guards to Lt. Wm. H. Johnson, who fell 20th Feb. 1864....

Tribute of Respect to J. R. Daniel, Steward of Pineville ct., S. C. Conf....died Dec. 24, 1863.....

Issue of April 7, 1864

Married, March 22, by the Rev. Angus Dowling, Mr. J H S Menifee to Miss Emily E McNeil of Montgomery co., Ala.

March 1st, 1864, at the residence of Mrs. L. J. Goodwyn, by Rev. Hardie Brown, Mr. Anson W. cooper, to Miss Mary E. Smith, all of Marengo co., Ala.

In Eufaula, Ala., by Rev. Jos B. Cottrell, on the   of March Lt. Col. Edward Badger of the 4th Fla. Regt. to Miss Matilda Level, daughter of the late Rev. Dr. Level, of the Miss Conf.

March 23, 1864, in Colleton Dist.,S. C.,by Rev. M. L. Banks, Mr. Chas. J. Owens to Mrs. Rebecca Lightsey.

By Rev. J. C. Simmons, in Randolph co., Ga., 19th March, Mr. Green A. Bull to Miss Martha Emma Ward, daughter of Jackson Ward.

At Wesley Chapel, Columbus, Ga.,on 30th March by Rev. J. T. Ainsworth, Macajah F. cooper to Miss Lucinda E. Harris.

On 17th March, near Mt. Hilliard, Ala., by Rev. J. W. Hightower, Mr. Henry Nash of the 18th Ala. Regt., to Miss Martha Moore, of Pike co., Ala.

Died in Sumter, S. C., Feb. 24, 1864, little Lola Porter, daughter of J. W. and Mrs. Emma E. Craig, aged 2 years, 10 months, and 24 days.

Mrs. Emily B. Long, wife of Felix G. Long was born in Halifax co., N. C., Dec. 1, 1822, and died in Jackson co., Fla., March 2, 1864....

Sgt. H. R. West of 25th Ala. Regt. was born in Shelby co., Ala., Feb. 16, 1838, and died at Chattanooga, Tenn., Dec. 12, 1863, of a wound received at Missionary Ridge, Nov. 25....

Sister Frances Merriwether, wife of James Merriwether, died in Coweta co., Ga.,7th Feb. in her 70th year....

Lt. W. H. McMurray, of 50th Ga. Vols., was killed at Knoxville, Tenn., in the charge on the fort, 29th Nov. 1863, in his 31st year....

William Henry Gray, son of Matthew M. Gray, decd., and Caroline A. Mays, was born near Hamburg, S. C., March 20, 1844....

Sister Elizabeth Anne McCrary, wife of Rev. P. R. McCrary, of the Ala. Conf., died in Dallas co., Ala., on the 10th Feb., in her 46th year...daughter of Alexander and Melinda Awtry...

Mrs. Joanna Bourn, widow of the late Mr. John Bourn, of Georgetown Dist., S. C., died Jan. 2, 1864, in her 52d year....

Elizabeth, widow of Thomas House, decd., was born in N. C., in 1787, and died in Stewart co., Ga., Dec. 9, 1863....

Miss Margaret E. Felder, daughter of E. D. and Caroline Felder, of Lodebar, Sumter Dist., S. C.,died Feb. 18, 1864, in her 26th year....

Mrs. Mary H. Sawyer, died in Williamsburg Dist., S. C., on 15th March, 1863, in her 21st year....

Jas. Padgett of Colleton Dist., S. C., died near Dalton, Ga., Dec. 1863, from a wound received at Chickamauga....

Issue of April 14, 1864

Married on Wednesday 23rd March, by Rev. L. M. Hamer, Mr. Charles Anderson to Miss Julia Register,both of Darlington Dist.

On Thursday 31st March, by Rev. L. M. Hamer, Dr. John E. Ellis, to Miss Mary C., daughter of Mr. Hardy M. Parrott, all of Darlington Dist., S. C.

In Augusta, Ga., March 24th, by Rev. D. D. Cox, Mr. Alexander Baker to Mrs. Margaret Watson.

By the same, March 30, 1864, Mr. William M. Stevens, to Miss Jesse Josephine Young.

Died on the morning of the 18th of March, Jane M., beloved child of N. M. and S. B. Salley, aged 18 months and 16 days.

William T. Capers, son of Wm. S. And Mary E. Bellune, died in Georgetown, S. C.,19th March 1864, aged 3 years 1 month and 7 days.

Mrs. Ann H. Jones was a member of the M. E. Church Russell-ville, Franklin co., Ala., for 42 years...wife of Wm. S. Jones ...died on 22d Jan 1863, in the 64th yearof her age.

Mrs. Caroline E. Read, widow of Parks Read, and daughter of Mr. and Mrs. J. B. Zachry, was born Dec. 21, 1833, married in 1853 and died in Newton co., Ga., 20th March 1864.

Miss Ella C. Sinclair, daughter of the Rev. Jesse Sinclair, of Stewart co., Ga., died at the residence of Dr. L. Bankston, Early co., Ga., Feb. 29th, 1863, in her 21st year....

James M. Hockenhull was born in Forsyth co., Ga., Jan. 2, 1843.. in Nov. 1863 from wound at Knoxville....died 5th Dec. 1863, from a wound at New Market, Tenn....

Emanuel Golson, father of the late Lewis P. Golson, of the Ala. Conf. died 22d March in his 78th year....

Elisha M. K. McClutchen was born Nov. 7, 1806, and died March 17, 1864....

Benj. T. Judkins, was born in Sussex co., Va., April 16, 1813, and died in Augusta Ga., March 16, 1864....left large family.

Bro. James R. Talley died in Macon co., Ala., Feb 3, in his 65th year...left children, one a member of the Ala. Conf.

Reuben C. Bridges, of Harris co., Ga., of 37th Ga. Regt., was born in Green co., Ga.,March 27th, 1845....died at Ocean Pond, Fla.

Mrs. Martha A.,wife of Patrick Murphy, died March 10, 1864, in Coosa co., Ala., aged 35 years, left husband and three child-ren....

John W. Spear, of 2nd Ga. Regt, died Dec. 20th, 1863, near Morristown, Tenn....

Francis Miller was born April 3, 1795, and died in Butts co., Ga., 28th, Jan. 1864....

Married in Augusta, Ga., April 9, 1864, by Rev. H. J. Adams,
Dr. Jno T. Marable C S A, to Miss Ernestine, daughter of the late
Gen. Acee of Miss.

In Augusta, on 14th April, by Rev. H.J. Adams, Mr. George E.
Dendy of Charlotte, N. C. to Miss Hattie B. Hopkins, of the former place.

In Madison, Ga., March 9th, by Rev. Dr. A. Means, Capt. C. H.
Sanders, C S A, to Miss Celeste Broughton, only daughter of
J. A. Broughton of Madison.

In Houston co., Ga., on 6th April by Rev. E. A. H. McGehee,
Sgt. David H. Brown to Miss Mary F. Riley.

On 7th April, by Rev. P. M. Ryburn, in Forsyth, Ga., Capt.
Jas. T. Martin, of Ala., to Mrs. Mary F. Farrabee, of Galveston,
Texas.

On 9th April 1864, by Rev. John Calvin Johnson, Sgt. John W.
Edwards of Troup Artillery, Ga., to Miss Arthanetta H. Ward, of
clarke co., Ga.

In Tuskaloosa, Ala., Feb. 25, 1864, by Rev. Dr. Summers, Mr.
Charles Hines, to Miss Cornelia, daughter of Mr. Theodore Smith,
of Tuskaloosa, Ala.

At Campbellton, April 12th, 1863,by Rev. J. L. Lupo, Mr. E.
D. Cheshire, of Bartow co., Ga.,to Miss Mary L. Beavers, of
Campbellton, Ga.

On the 16th inst., by J. W. Godkin, Esq., at the residence
of John F. Winter,of Greene co., Ga., Mr. Martin Markwalter,
of C S A, to Miss MaryAnn E. Winter.

Died in Greenville, S. C., Capt. John F. Stein, aged 59
years, 10 months and 15 days.

March 30th, 1863, in Williamsburg Dist., S. C., Louisa James,
daughter of Dr. James M. and Mrs. M. Anna Burgess, aged 1 year,
1 month and 3 days.

Rev. Amos Davis was born in Bulloch co., Ga.,June, 1829,
and died in Waukeenah, Fla., March 16, 1864...In May, 1858,
married to Miss Mary E., daughter of Rev. D. Roberts, of the
same conf....

Mrs. Elizabeth Wier, relict of Rev. Wm. Wier, decd., died at
Enterprise, Miss., on 10th March, born in Abbeville Dist., S. C.,
May 5, 1798, married May 12, 1818....

Roger L. Whigham, only son of his widowed mother, Mrs.
Caroline M. Whigham, of Jefferson co., Ga., died at Augusta, Ga.
Feb. 1864, aged 18 years....

Mrs. Sarah Kinsler, was born in 1780 in the midst of the
Revolution, died April 4, 1864....

Mrs. Jane Delilah Davis, wife of Jas. H. Davis, died in
Mecklenburg, N. C., Feb. 17, 1864, in her 54th year....

Nathaniel Bailey was a native of Maryland, but removed to
Wilkes co., Ga., when a lad of 10, poor and an orphan...died in
Columbia co.,in his 78th year....

Rev. Wm. J. Simpson of Houston co., Ga., died 9th March in
his 29th year....

Mrs. Susannah Lack, wife of Rev. Abner Lack died at Forest,
Miss., Jan. 24, 1864, aged nearly 78 years....

Thomas Lester was born in Guilford co., N. C. In 1851, he
moved to Macon co., Ala., where he died in his 78th year....

Angus McRea of 4th S. C. Cavalry was born in Marlboro Dist.,
S. C., and died at McPhersonville HOspital, near Pocotaligo, S.
C., in his 89th year....

Mrs. Dorothy Hill died in Warren co., Ga., at the residence
of her son, in the 79th year of her age...born in Southampton
co., Va., and in early life came with her parents to Ga., where
she married and had several children....

Mrs. Mary Jordan, wife of Rev. John Jordan, of Lee co., and daughter of Richard M. Stewart, decd., was born in Marion co., Ga., Jan. 5, 1840, and died Feb. 9, 1864....

William Rufus Willingham, 38th Regt. Ala. Vols., died in Fayette co., March 2, 1863, in his 31st year....

Thomas Duke Freeman, son of H. H. and E. W. Freeman, died 9th March 1864, in his 12th year....

Isaac H. Royal was born in Burke and moved in early life to Houston co., Ga...died 27th March, in his 89th year...leaving a wife and children.

Sgt. Lewis P. Miles of 35th Ga. Regt. died at Staunton, Va., on 15th Jan., 1864, aged 21 years....

Mary L., wife of James C. Thomas, died near Bennettsville, S. C., March 13th, 1864, aged 64 years....

Mrs. Mary Beddingfeld was born Jan. 11, 1785, and died 26th March 1864...left children and grandchildren.

Hattie Shand Herbert, eldest daughter of Rev. Thos. G. and H. S. Herbert, was born 26th May 1855, and died in Abbeville Dist., S. C., March 26, 1864....

Tribute of Respect by Rev. Wm. Dm Martin who died in the 56th year of his age, by Greenville ct....

Issue of April 28, 1864

J. Melvin Epting, a son of John and Margaret Epting, was born in Lexington Dist., S. C., on 24th Sept., 1842, and died at Pt. Lookout, Md., 7 Jan 1864....

Bryan Dallas, of 28th Ala. Regt., was born in Sumter co., Ala., Jan. 28th, 1842....(date of death not given)

Miss Ellen F. Dutton daughter of S. S. and E. R. Dutton, was born Sept. 16, 1844, and died in Anson co., N. C., March 31, 1864.

Ginnie, eldest daughter of Robt. C. and Caroline Jenkins, died in Eatonton, Ga., March 25, 1864, in her 15th year...

James G. Neal, son of Wm. and Elena Neal, was born Oct. 3, 1822, and died 6th April 1864....

Mrs. Fannie Holloway, wife of Peter Holloway, died in Upson co., Ga., March 2, 1864, in her 25th year...

Rev. Leroy B. Giles, son of William A. Giles was born in S. C., July 20, 1834, and died in Marion co., Fla., Jan. 20, 1864.

Tribute of Respect by Ocala Conf. to Rev. L. B. Giles.

Mrs. Lucinda S. Edwards, wife of J. J. Edwards, was born in Hancock co., Ga., and died at Lawrenceville, Ala. on 29th Feb. in her 40th year....

Robt. G. Moore, son of Greene and Eliza Moore, of Greene co., Ga., died March 2d, in his 20th year....

B. L. Smith, of 32d Ga. Regt, died March 1, 1863, from wounds at Ocean Pond, Fla.

Mother Elizabeth Shines was born May 30th, 1790, and died in Butler co., Ala., Feb. 1, 1864....

Bro. C. C. White, of 69th Regt. Ala. Vols., was born in Montgomery, Ala., in 1833...died at Morristown, Tenn., Jan. 28, 1864.

Mrs. Joanna Ward, wife of Dr. T. A. Ward, of Burke co., Ga., and daughter of E. C. Glisson, died Feb. 17, 1864....

Miss Margaret B. Aughtry was born 25th Dec. 1808, and died 18th Jan. 1864...left three brothers and three sisters....

Mr. T. B. Butler, was born in Scriven co., Ga., Nov. 29, 1806, and died in Burke co., Ga., April 7th, 1864....

Lt. J. O. Andrew, 30th Ga. Regt, died in Elbert co., Ga....

J. M. Chapman, son of T. K. and E. W. Chapman, of Dale co., Ala., was wounded at Chancellorsville, and died shortly thereafter....

John A. Shine died March 16, 1864, in the 60th year of his age...

Tribute of Respect by 18th Regt. Tenn. Vols. to R. A. Cole,
who died 28th Dec., at Rock Island, Ill.
Tribute of Respect to Rev. A. M. Grantham, by Lawrenceville
circuit, Ala. Conf.

Issue of May 5, 1864

Mrs. Mary Morgan, daughter of Eliab and Ann Kingman, and
relict of Rev. Asbury Morgan, formerly of the S. C. Conf., died
at the residence of her son-in-law, Rev. J. Blakely Smith, in
Newnan, Ga., April 12, 1864....
Elizabeth A. Crawford, wife of Mr.Thos. C. Crawford, and
daughter of Capt. J. B. and Mrs. F. E. Morgan, of Charleston,
S. C., was born 5th August 1841, and died in Marion Dist., S. C.,
16th April 1864....
Mr. L. G. Sutton of Albany, Ga., was taken sick while on a
trip to the West on business, and died 18th Feb. 1864, at the
house of Mr. Stephen Sikes, in Montgomery, Ala., in his 49th year.
Susan Matilda, eldest daughter of the late Hugh Archer, Sr.,
was born in Beaufort Dist., S. C., in Aug. 1822, and died in
Tallahassee, Fla., March 4, 1864....
Rev. David C. Appleby died in St. George's Parish, Colleton
Dist., S. C.,March 10, 1864, while on a visit to his sons in the
army of Tenn., aged 56 years....
Mrs.Susan J. Murger was born in Scriven co., Ga.,July 13,
1816, and died Dec. 29, 1863....
Matthew Stewart died in Newton co., Ga., had passed his three
score years on earth....
Hugh McLaughlin, son of Archibald J. McLaughlin of Darlington
Dist., S. C., died in the 1st S. C. Hospital, near Charleston,
April 14, 1864, aged about 18 years.
Mrs. Letty N. McBride, wife of Mr. Henry McBride, and daugh-
ter of Rev. John Foust, formerly of the Ala. Conf., was born in
Blount co., Ala., Nov. 6, 1831, and died at the house of her
mother, in Shelby co., Ala., March 23d, 1864....
My father, Jas. B. Talley was born in Green co., Ga., 18
Aug 1800, and died in Macon co., Ala., 5th Feb. 1864...mother
and three of the children have crossed the flood. Wm. R. Talley.
John Rusk, died in Marion co., Ga., on 29th Feb.,1864, aged
about 62 years....
H. A. Martin, daughter of John and Jemima Martin, was born in
Abbeville Dist., S. C., May 4, 1832, and died near Waverly, Ala.,
March 7, 1864....
Mrs. Elizabeth R. West was born Oct. 23, 1800, and died 20th
March 1864, in her 64th year.....
Helen T., wife of Dr. H. H. Robinson, of Bladen co., died in
Statesville, N. C., aged 46 years...
Mrs. Julia Dunning, wife of Capt. James Dunning, of Marion
co., Fla., died 19th Jan. 1864, in her 27th year....
Henry Costine died near Walterboro, S. C., on Wed. evening,
March 23, 1864, in his 66th year....
Rev. J. J. Wannamaker, died in St. Bartholomew's Parish, S. C.,
on the 23rd Feb. 1864, aged 68 years.
Tribute of Respect by Sandersville ct., Ga. Conf., to
Henry Heath and Danl. Harris....
Sgt. Thos. W. Clements, son of Bishop Clements, of Merriwether
co., Ga., died from wounds in the battle of Gettysburg, in his
23d year....

Issue of May 12, 1864

Married in Griffin, Ga., on 14th inst.,by Rev. Chas. R.
Jewett, Mr. J. Thos Ware of Atlanta, to Miss W. T. Lockett, of

In Marietta, Ga., March 31st, at the residence of Mrs. Waters, by Rev. G. H. Patillo, Mr. J. T. Orman, of Tenn., to Miss Mattie Harris, of the former place.

In Houston co., Ga., April 6th, by Rev. W. G. Allen, Mr. Thomas Lane, of the Southern Rights Battery, to Miss Martha Logan, of said county.

By Rev. S. E. Weaver, on 13th April, E J S Lee to Miss Anna T. Blocker at Stephen Blocker's, the bride's father, all of Clay co.

In Elberton, Ga., 14 April, by Rev. James M. Austin, Mr. John T McCarty to Miss M G G Harper.

Also, by the same, April 19th, Lt. Robert M. Heard, to Miss Louisa H. Jones, all of Elberton, Ga.

On 14th inst., by Rev. A J Briggs, Lt. Jno F. Bond to Miss Fannie Brown, of Autauga co., Ala.

In Anderson Dist., S. C., April 6, by Rev. S. H. Browne, W. T. Browne, oc Fo K, Hampton Legion, to Miss Frances E Carpenter.

On 27th April, at the residence of W. H. Austin, in Greenville Dist., S. C., by Rev. A. H. Lester, Rev. Wm.H. Fleming of the S. C. Conf. to Mrs. R. Carrie Gilreath, third daughter of Dr. W. L. M Austin, decd.

By Rev. A. J. Cauthen, on April 28th, Mr. J. S. Cureton, Capt. Foster's, S. C. Cavalry, to Miss Fannie, eldest daughter of D W and Mrs. Amanda Brown, all of Lancasterville, S. C.

On 21st April, by Rev. G. T. Spearman, Mr. Thaddeus P. Shy, to Miss Mary An Benford, all of Jasper co, Ga.

Also, by the same, at the same time, Mr. Francis A. Leverett, of Jasper to Miss Mary Ella Wyatt, of Newton co., Ga.

In Montgomery co., Ala., April 26, by Rev. Angus Dowling, Mr. A. C. Butler, of the 1st Ala. Cavalry, to Miss N. C. Rylander, daughter of Rev. W. J. Rylander, formerly of Ga.

At Warrior Stand, Ala., April 27, 1864, by Rev. L. F. Dowdell, Mr. Calvin Philpot, of Ga. to Miss Fannie E. Moore, of Macon co., Ala.

In Forsyth co., Ga., April 28th, 1864, by Rev. G. Hughes, Sgt. James M. Hughes, to Miss Nancy E. Parks, daughter of Rev. James W. Parks, of Forsyth co., Ga.

Died, Feb. 29th, 1864, Annie Lou, infant daughter of Rev. J. E. Penny, of the S. C. Conf. and MRs. S. M. Penny, aged two weeks.

Wm. Pinckney Hay was born in Rockingham co., N. C., May 22, 1820, moved to Tishamongo co., Miss, and settled in Bartow co., Ga., where he died March 4, 1864....

Mrs. Ariadne Alexander, wife of William Alexander, and daughter of the late Capt. Henry Crowell, was born Sept. 26, 1826, and died at Oswichee, Russell co., Ala., March 13, 1863....

Dr. Cornelius Trawick died at Georgetown, Copiah co., Miss., on March 28th, 1863, in his 57th year....

Mrs. Edmund Jackson died in Monroe co., Ga.,March 25, 1864, in the 78th year of his age....

Mrs. Miriam Permelia Powell died at her brother-in-law's, near Summerville, Ga.,on 10th Feb. 1864, in her 23d year....

S. W. Hatch, died in Jeffersonville, Twiggs co., Ga., April, 1864, in the 43d year of his age...a native of Maine, came some yars ago....

John T. Lominack, son of Thomas K. Lominack died near Russellville, Tenn., Feb. 13, 1864, at the Varioloid Hospital...born in York Dist., S. C., 16th Sept., 1845....left father and mother, and an only sister.

Miss Cornelia, eldest daughter of Mr. and Mrs. Murdock McCaskill, of Marshallville, Ga., died on Friday, 15th April 1864....

Unity Jefcoat, wife of Rev. J. Jefcoat, was born in S. C., Dec. 7, 1788, married Bro. Jefcoat in 1810, and died in Pike co.,

Ala., about 1st March, 1864...She was 54 years a wife, 52 years a mother....

Mrs. Maria Lassiter, widow of A H Lassiter, Esq., was born March 14th, 1842, married to Mr. Lassiter in 1858, and died March 10, 1864....

Mrs. Ann C. Berry, wife of John B. Berry, and youngest daughter of Benjamin Kennedy, died in Effingham co., Springfield ct., Ga., on 2d April 1863, in her 43d year....

Mrs. Eliza English, was born in Warren co., Ga.,June 30th, 1822, and died April 21, 1864....

Wm. G. Smith, Jr. was born Jan. 5, 1822, in Jasper co., Ga., and died April 11th, 1864....

Wm. B. Pennell was born in Cartwright, co., N. C., and died in Lawrenceville, Ala., on 26th Nov. 1863, aged 72 years....

Mrs. Martha H. Zachry, wife of Maj. Lewis Hzachry, died in Newton co., Ga.,April 13, 1864, aged 56 years...born in Columbia co., Ga., maiden name was Barden....

Mrs. Susan H. Dozier was born in Warren co., Ga., 1806, and died in Clopton, Ala., Feb. 18, 1864....

Martha L. Gelzer, eldest daughter of N. and L. Gelzer (former dec'd), died March 20, aged 11 years, 1 month and 13 days.

Bro. Jas. L. Carpenter, died near Stilesboro', Bartow Co., Ga...left wife and children.

Tribute of Respect by M. E. Church in Charleston, S. C., to Rev. John Mood who died 29th March, 1864, in the 73d year of his age...four sons in S. C. Conf....

Tribute of Respect by Ebenezer Church, Monroe co., Ga., to L. B. Alexander....

Issue of May 19, 1864

Married on 7th inst., by Rev. C. A. Fulwood, Lt. J. P. Baldwin, C S A, to Miss M Lizzie Walton of Milledgeville, Ga.

On April 14th, by Rev. J. R. Littlejohn, Mr. Wm. H. Willis, C S A, to Miss Fannie E. Dumas, of Barnesville, Ga.

On May 10, in Augusta, Ga., by Rev. J. T. Lin, Wm. T. Garrison to Miss Anna Carpenter.

Also, in the same city, May 12th, by Rev. J. T. Lin, Capt. Wm. C. Walters of Maryland, to Miss Anna M. sheridan, of Charleston, S. C.

In Tatnall co., Ga., 5th May, by Rev. R. A. Conner, Capt. P. H. Ward, of Augusta, to Miss Maggie Stripling, of the former place.

Eliza Caldwell Kenner, daughter of the late James L. Kenner, of Newberry Dist., S. C., died in Columbia, April 10, 1864, aged 24 years...the only child of a widowed mother....

R. Thomson Roberds, Agt. of the 50th Ga. Regt., in the 30th year of his age, died a prisoner, at or near Knoxville, Tenn... Born and educated in St. Peter's Parish, Beaufort Dist., S. C.

Rev. James M. Gains was born Nov. 18th, 1808, married to Miss Mary Anderson, Dec. 22, 1826, and died in Cobb co., Ga., March 27, 1864...remains conveyed to Mt. Bethel Church....

Miss Nannie was the oldest daughter of Bro. Edward and Sister Eliza Curtis of Springhill, Marengo co., Ala., in her 16th year.

Isaac B. Williamson, Esq., died in Pike co., Ga., on 27th Feb., 1864, aged 76 years, and 1 day....

James Harris died at his residence in Morgan co., Ga., Jan. 21st, in his 70th eyar...a native of Va., but in early life removed to Ga....

Willie B. Gerry died at Point Lookout, Md., on 6th Feb., 1864, aged al most 19 years, a prisoner of war....

M. J. Milam of Henry co., Tenn, 5th Regt. Tenn Vols., died in the enemy hand in hist 21st year....

155

Sallie, aged 12, and Cares(?), aged 7 years, daughters of Thomas H. and MaryR. Owen, of Jonesboro, Ala., died a few weeks of each other....

John Christopher Graham of Clarendon Dist., S. C., died April 2, 1864, aged 72 years....

Mrs. Mary Bowen, wife of Dr. J. H. Bowen, died in Clinton, Ga., Wed. 20th April 1864, in her 64th year....

Mrs. Mary D., wife of Dr. S. N. Ferguson, and daughter of Rev. F. D. and M. S. Poyas, died in Pickensville, Ala., March 13, 1864...born in Charleston, Nov. 20, 1824....

Rev. John Henderson, died at the residence of his son, Capt. J. J. Henderson, in Irwin co., Ga.,April 7, 1864, in his 66th year....

Miss Elizabeth T. Johnson, daughter of Stephen Johnson, decd., was born in Dooly co., Ga., 28th Jan. 1832, and died on 31st March 1863, at the residence of her mother, in Taylor co., Ga.

Margaret L. Printice, daughter of Zachariah and Nancy Printice, was born Dec. 14, 1856, and died inShelby co., Ala., April 26, 1864....

Robt. B. Collins, died at the residence of his mother in Cobb co., Ga., April 10, 1864....

John Thomas Turner, eldest son of Rev. J. A. Turner, of Monroe co., Ga.,died in Macon, Ga., Jan. 31, 1864, aged 17 years.

Issue of May 26, 1864

Married in Augusta, on 18th May, by Rev. H. J. Adams, Wm. F. Peck, of Atlanta, Ga., to Miss Charlotte J. Ellis of Augusta, Ga.

Also, by the same, on 19th May, Daniel M. Mongin of Richmond co., to Miss Louisa M. Antony, of Augusta, Ga.

In Augusta, Ga., April 7, 1864, by Rev. D. D. Cox, Mr. William Hatherly to Miss Virginia C. Walker.

Also, by the same, April 27th, 1864, Mr. M. M. Walker to Miss Harriet E. Hardman.

Also, by the same, May 16, 1864, Mr. Wellington Evans to Miss Enith McCook.

Also, by the same, May 17, 1864, Mr. William H. Marshall to Miss Maria Murray.

May 10, by Rev. J. W. Hinton, Mr. Benier Pye, of Forsyth, Ga., to Miss S J W Nunnally, of Pike co., Ga.

May 12, in Oglethorpe co., Ga.,by Rev. W. P. Pattillo, Rev. E. G. Murrah, of the Ga.Conf. to Miss Ellia C. Maxwell.

In Richmond co., Ga.,May 12th, by Rev. R. A. Conner, Mr. Robert M. Smith of 5th Ga. Cavalry, to Miss Emma F. Dove, of the former place.

On 14th April, in Milton co., Ga.,by Rev. G. Hughes, Lt. Joseph L.Moore, of Forsyth co., Ga.,to Miss Sarah L. Rogers, daughter of Rev. William Rogers, of the former place.

May 11, by Rev. J. W. Rush, Mr. Wm. B. DeVampert, of Green co., Ala., to Miss Emma Portis, daughter of Col J W Portis, of Suggsville, Ala.

Robert Bryce, son of Rev. Thos G and H. S. Herbert, was born Nov 8, 1861, and died April 25, 1864.

Mr. Charles W. Cary died at Chunnenuggee Ridge, Ala., March 29, 1864, in his 36th year....

Sister R. A. Felkel was born in S. C., and died March 2, 1864, in her 59th year....

Mrs. Dorothy W. Palmer died March 7th, at the residence of the writer, in her 69th year... F. A. R.

Alston McNinch, a member of Co. A., 6th Regt. S. C. Cavalry, died at the hospital at Adams Run, S. C., May 4, 1864....

Aaron B. Varn, of Co. F. Appling Rangers, 47th Ga. Regt., was born in Barnwell Dist., S. C. and died at Atlanta, Ga., aged 28 years...

Mrs. Elizabeth Wilson, widow of the late Jenkins Wilson, of Jasper co., Ga., died in Troup co., Ga.,on 25th March, in her 87th year....

Wm. Newton Crawford, was born Nov. 30, 1832, and was baptized in infancy by Rev. Mr. Carlisle, a Presbyterian minister, joined M. E. Church in his 18th year....died March 24th, 1864, aged 31 years, 3 months and 24 days.

Sarah Ann Lazenby, wife of Richard S. Lazenby, died in Warren co., Ga., April 10, 1864, in her 68th year....

Mrs. Wilhelmina Floyd died in Watkinsville, Clark co., Ga., on Sunday, 24th April 1864, aged upwards of 80 years....

Mrs. Mary E. Tennehill died at her residence in Macon co., Ala., on 12th April 1864, aged 52 years....

Tribute of Respect to Mr. D. H. Haynie, 6th and 9th Regts. Tenn...died 1st May.

Tribute of Respect by Quarterly Conf. at St. George's, to Rev. D. C. Appleby.

Issue of June 2, 1864

Married on Thursday evening, 12th, May, by Rev. Thos Mitchell, Maj. M. A. Dunham to Miss Maggie, daughter of Gen. Wm. Evans, all of Marion, S. C.

By Rev. T. B. Lanier, on 18th May, the Rev. Norman D. Morehouse, of the Ga. conf. to Miss Amanda A. Rahn, of Whitesville, Effingham co.,Ga.

Died, Martha Bertha Rebecca, second youngest daughter of James B. and Martha M. Neal, April 17, 1864, in the 4th year of her age.

Charles Herbert, son of Rev. E. J. T. and Mrs. M. A. Blake, died 24th May, in Taliahas co., Fla., aged 7 months and 8 days.

Mary Susan, infant daughter of Rev. D. T. And Martha T. Holmes, died May 1, 1864, aged 6 weeks.

Mrs. Lucy Maddux, died at her residence near Eatonton, Ga., May 31, 1864, in her 71st year....

Mrs. Esther Perdrian, died in Sumter Dist., S. C., March 13, 1864, in the 73d year of her age....

Mrs. Caroline V. Blake, wife of Dr. J. C. Blake, died in Columbiana, Ala., May 6, 1864....

Wm. T. Lemmond was born April 5, 1791, and died near Oak Grove, Union co., N. C., Feb. 29, 1864, having reached the age of 82 years, 10 months and 15 days....

Mrs. Mary L. Starr, wife of John H. Starr born 15th April, and died in Spaulding co., Ga., on 14th March, 1864....

Mrs. Mary S. Hudson, daughter of Thomas and Frances Norris, died in Baker co., Ga., 25th March, 1864, in her 23rd year....

Mrs. Charlotte U. Sturzennegger, relict of the late John Sturzenneger, Esq., died March 7th, on Beach Island, Edgefield Dist., S. C.,in her 81st year....

Mrs. Charlotte Panton, daughter of Mrs. Sturzenegger, and wife of James S. Panton, Esq., died on 4th April, in the same vicinity, in her 47th year...left husband and children....

Mrs. Susan R. Rutledge, wife of R. K. Rutledge, died in Clarendon Dist., S. C., May 8, 1864, in her 39th year....

Eliza A. M. Little was born in Harris co., Ga.,Jan. 30, 1849, and died in Sparta, May 7, 1864....buried by the side of brother Henry....

Col. John Thompson Green was born in Sumter Dist., S. C., Feb. 15, 1825, died near Bishopville, S. C., May 3, 1864....

Joshua G. Taylor was born in Laurens co., Ga., Nov. 12, 1821 and died at Lake City, Fla., April 7, 1864...left wife and six children....

Mrs. Ann Maria Boughman, was born April 22, 1782, and died while on a visit to her friends in Richland Dist., April 27, 1864, aged 82 years....

Martha Conine, widow of Richard Conine, was born in S. C., died in Tallapoosa co., Ala., 17th May, 1863, in her 78th year. left children and grandchildren.

Oliver P. Cox, of Upson co., 32nd Ga. Regt was killed in the battle of Ocean Pond.

Mrs. Sarah Howell was born in Edgefield Dist., S. C., in 1813, married to Josiah Howell, 1833, and died in Tallapoosa co., April 18, 1864....

Lottie H. A., daughter of Mr. and Mrs. James M. Ingram, died aged 8 years and 7 months.

Tribute of Respect by Gaston ct., Alabama Conf., to Benj. H. Thompson.

Tribute of Respect by same to William A. Lummnus, about 50 years of age....

Tribute of Respect by Carnesville circuit, Madison co., Ga., to Silas W. Kay....

Issue of June 9, 1864

Married in Columbia co., Ga., on the 19th of May, by Rev. J. R. Grogan, Mr. S. F. Thomas, of Richmond co., to Miss Mary O. Bacon, of Columbia co., Ga.

Mrs. Josephine Evans, wife of A. B. Evans, and oldest daughter of Seaborn and Elizabeth McMichael, was born in Green co., Ga., Nov. 4, 1827, and died in Stewart co., Ga., May 26, 1864... left husband and six children.

Sgt. Joseph W. Evans was born in Ware co., Miss., Dec. 27, 1828...died from wound received Sept. 20....

Sister Louisa Lamar McGehee died in Summerfield, Ala., on 27th May, wife of Abenr McGehee, to whom she was married in 1832.

Freeman F. M. Hooker of Orangeburg Dist., S. C., died on 20th May, in her 25th year near Spotsylvania C. H....

His brother, David Hooker of the same regt. was killed upon the same battlefield a few days before.

Mrs. Mary Kenney, died at her son-in-law's, H. T. Wright, Esq., in Edgefield Dist., S. C.,April 3, 1864, aged 79 years....

Mary Warren died in Sumter co., Ga.,May 22, 1864, in her 68th year....

Mrs. Catharine E. Wade, wife of Rev. Daniel F. Wade, was born Sept. 30, 1837, in Orangeburg Dist., S. C.,and died May 24, 1864, in Fort Valley, Ga.

Sarah Short was born in Columbia co., Ga., 1805, and died in Marion co., Ga.,March 13, 1864....

Tribute of Respect by Albany Station, Fla. Conf., to L. G. Sutton, who died in Montgomery, Ala. Feb. 18, 1864....

Issue of June 16, 1864

Married in Augusta, Ga., May 25th, 1864, by Rev. D. D. Cox, Mr. P. Emmett to Miss Candes Scroggins.

By Rev. John Calvin Johnson, in Morgan co., Ga., on 7th June, Col. John W. Evans of 64th Regt., Ga. Vols., to Mrs. Ann Olivia Lenoir, daughter of Basil H. Overby, Esq., deceased.

Mrs. Rebecca Douglass was born in Edgefield Dist., S. C., Aug. 14, 1787, removed with her parents E. and F. Tilman, to Ga. while but a child, and married to J. Douglass, decd., in May 1803...died in Gwinnett co., Ga.,March 20, 1864....

Sgt. Wm. Decatur McKinstey of 6th S. C. Vols., Fairfield
Dist., S. C., died on the battlefield near Spotsylvania, C. H.,
Va., May 12, 1864...in the 23d year of his age.

Capt. James W. Owens, 21st Regt. S. C. V., was wounded in
the battle near Drewry's Bluff, May 14, 1864, and died in the
Officer's Hospital, No. 4 Richmond, Va.,May 13, 1864, in his 45th
year...left five sons....

Rev. Dr. Robert M. Carter died on 6th May, 1864, in his 51st
year....

Sarah E., wife of Capt. Charles J. Jenkins, C. S. A., and
only daughter of Joseph Thomas, Esq.,died near White Springs,
Hamilton co., Fla.,May 25, 1864....

Lt. Edward P. Hendree, son of Dr. George R. and Mrs. Cornelia
Hendree was born in Clarke co., Ga., July 21, 1844, and fell at
the head of the Sharpshooters of 61st Ala. Regt, May 5, 1864,
in Virginia.

Mrs. Laura A. Ransom, wife of Lt. W. J. Ransom, and a member
of the Presbyterian Church, died in Newnan, Ga.,on 28th May,
1864, in her 30th year....

Thomas J. Thompson of 24th Ga. Regt. Ga. Vols., died 12th
May....

Eugene, son of William and M. J. Powell, of Decatur, Ga.,
was born Nov. 22, 1855, and died May 21, 1864....

Henry Harrison Clark, son of Charles and Sarah Clark of
Burke co., was born May 26, 1841, and died May 10, 1864....

Henry Clay Cato, died in Houston, E. Fla., May 29th, 1864, in
his 12th year....

Thos. Winchester died in Monroe co., N. C., April 22, 1864,
in the 91st year of his age....

Tribute of Respect to Rev. Geraldus King who died in Perry,
Ga., March 29, 1864, aged 62 years....

Issue of June 23, 1864

Married on the 24th of May, by Rev. L. B. Varn, Rev. J. J.
Snow of the S. C. Conf., to Miss M. C. Varn of Colleton Dist.,
S. C.

On 30th May, by Rev. C. A. Moore, Rev. Wm. F. Roberts, of the
Fla. Conf. to Miss Mary C. Tarply of Irwinton, Ga.

At the residence of the bride's uncle, by Rev. T. H. Stout,
on the evening of the 14th inst., Capt. J. Berrien Oliver, of
Columbus, Ga., to Bella, daughter of the late Hon A C S Alexander,
of Early co., Ga.

In Chambers co., Ala., by Rev. R. W. Dixon, on 16th June,
Mr. Henry Doolittle, to Miss Fannie Chappell, all of Chambers
co., Ala.

At Middleburg, Fla., June 3rd, 1864, by Rev. J. Rast, Mr.
W. K. Roberts to Mrs. S. A. Smith, widow of Dr. Smith of Ga.,
both of Dooly co., Ga.

Cecilia Pauline, infant daughter of Rev. Jas. W. and Sarah
C. W. Wightman, died in Lexington Dist., S. C., on 7th June,
aged 1 year and 19 days.

Mary Virginia, infant daughter of Rev. J. L. and Mrs. M. J.
Dixon, died in Columbia, S. C.,on the 12th inst., aged 10 months
and 21 days.

Sallie Barnes Davis, daughter of L. D. and Georgia B. Davis,
died May 31st, aged 3 years 6 months and 5 days.

Willie, aged 7 years and Josephus aged 5 years, sons of
Luke H. and MaryE. Taylor, died in May, 1864.

Tallulah Jane, daughter of Jas. W. and Sarah J. Gant, died
in Marietta, Ga., June 15th, aged 2 years 9 months and 13 days.

Jefferson Adams died in Eatonton, Ga., on 21st of May, 1864,
in the 41st year of his age...born in Hancock co., Ga., and while

as an orphan boy was removed by his uncle, the Hon. Irby Hudson, decd., to Eatonton, Ga...

Mr. Robt J. Sessions of Terrell co., Ga., and 12th Ga. Regt., fell on first day of the Wilderness battle, in his 23d year. William, the eldest and first was almost mortally wounded in 1862 at Beverly Ford, and still suffers. Benjamin, the second son, was killed at Chancellorsville.

Mrs. Sarah Ann Coleman, daughter of Joseph and Mary M. Toland, and wife of Rev. A. J. Coleman, of the Ala. Conf., died on 4th June 1864, at DeKalb, Kemper co., Miss., aged 32 years, 3 months and 12 days.

Bro. T. J. Thompson, 24th Ga. Regt., was killed near Spottsylvania C. H. Va., Thursday 16th May 1864.

Lt. P. C. Allen of 15th Regt. S. C. V., was born in Barnwell Dist., S. C., and died in hospital at Lynchburg, Va.,on 16th May 1864....

Capt. H. H. Smith, was killed in the battle of the Wilderness, 6th May...

Miss Mary Margaret Matthews, daughter of J. T. and A. J. Matthews, was born in Fairfield Dist., S. C., May 27, 1847, and died May 27, 1864, in Columbia, S. C...

Mrs. Permelia R. Brickett died inAlexander, Ga., in the 42d year of her age....

T. M. Shannon and J. O. Langston,members of Co. C., 36th Ga. Regt. fell in the battle of Spottsylvania. C. H., May 12, 1864....

Issue of June 30, 1864

Married May 26, by Rev. J. L. Williams, R. D.Nixon to Mrs. M. A. Bowen, both of Liberty Co., Fla.

At the residence of Mrs. S. Scsnyers, on 22nd inst., by Dr. L. B. Bouchelle, Mr. N. W. Martin of Co. G. 32d Regt. Ga. Vols., to Miss Lucy Cowart, of Emanuel co., Ga.

Died on the 11th inst.,Anna Esther, infant daughter of Dr. and Mrs. Geo. S. Pelzer, aged 4 months and 2 weeks.

Miss Amanda J. GArrett, daughter of H. W. and Sarah Garrett, was born April 29, 1834, in Edgecombe co., N. C. and died at the residence of R. F. Shelton, Esq., in Greene co., Ala., May 30, 1864....

Sgt. James J. Morel, 1st Ga. Bttn., son of B. J. and Susan Morel, was born Feb. 6, 1844, and died in Effingham co., Ga., March 31, 1864....

Mrs. Carrie A. Sappington, a member of St. Paul's Church, Columbus, Ga.,died May 17, 1863, aged 34 years and 6 months... daughter of Rev. I.N. Craven of Ga.Conf....

Lt. Wm. N. Swift, of 34th Ga. Regt. Vols., was born in Franklin co., Ga., and died a prisoner of war at Johnson's Island, Lake Erie, Jan. 1, 1864, aged 29 years....

Mrs. Sarah J., wife of H. L. Faulk and daughter of Bennett and Mary Bizzell, was born in S. C., Jan. 14, 1823, and died in Barbour co., Ala., Arpil 24, 1864....

Mrs. E. R. Wilson, died June 10, 1864, at the residence of her son, Hon. B. H. Wilson, near Greenville, S. C., in the 75th year of her age....

Mr. Samuel B. DeWitt, of 21st S. C. V.,was wounded 14th May, near Drewry's Bluff, and died in Richmond, Va., June 8, 1864, in his 35th year....

Rev. Robert A. Ellis fell wounded at Spottsylvania C. H., 12th May, 1864, in his 24th year....

Emory Summerfield Fleming, only child of Allen and Elizabeth Fleming of Barbour co., Ala., and 39th Regt. Ala., died in his 19th year at Gilmer hospital, Marietta, Ga....

160

George N. Hughes, was born in Mecklinburg, N. C., Feb. 23, 1784, and emigrated to Western N. C...left children.

Dr. Joseph T. Jay, son of Tyre and Catharine Jay, died in Abbeville Dist., S. C., May 29, 1863, in his 27th year.

Rev. James Darby died in Duval co., Fla., at the residence of Mr. Allen Geiger, aged 67 years...born in Union Dist., S. C., removed to Abbeville Dist., in 1827, where he remained until 1857, when he came to Fla....

Mrs. Sarah S. Redford, died in Sumter, S. C., May 17, 1864, in the 61st year of her age....

Elijah Martin, 42d Ga., died (no date given)....

Edward E. Brewer, died in Macon Ga.,on 10th June, aged 36 years and 6 days...Confederate soldier.

Tribute of Respect to Lt. Col. J. D. McLennan, 59th Regt. Ala. Vols., on 16th May....

Issue of July 7, 1864

Married by Rev. J. D. Anthony in the Church at Sandersville, Ga., June 9th, C. T. Bayne, of Baldwin co., to Miss Peronia Smith, daughter of Roy J. T. Smith of the Ga. Conf.

Died, Tallulah Jane, daughter of James and and Sarah J. Gant, in Marietta, Ga., June 13th, aged 2 years 9 months and 13 days.

Sarah Alice, daughter of the same, June 24, aged 1 year and 24 days.

Maj. Pinckney B. Bird was born in Jefferson co., Fla., Jan. 2, 1834, and died June 5, 1864, in one of the battles before Richmond....

Mrs. Sarah E.Moreland died in Hogansville, Ga., June 12, 1864, in her 74th year...born in Charleston, S. C...

Col. J. A. Easley, died in the 84th year of his age, April 15, 1864, at the residence of his son, W. H. Easley, of Pickens Dist., S. C....

Wm. B. Buchanan died at the house of the Rev. Mr. Foster,a Baptist minister, residing near Tuscaloosa, Ala., June 7, 1864... 1st Miss. Rangers...left a widow at Tipley, Mi., and eight chil= dren.

W. M. Minbush aged 21 years 9 months was killed in Va., in the battle of May 10, 1864...

Cicero B. Corbin was born in Crawford co., Ga., July 24, 1844, and fell in the battle at Spottsylvania, May 5.

W. Teal, son of Robt and Hester Teal, was born in Henry co., Ala., Feb.1, 1823...killed May 14, 1864.

J. J. Bryant, 6th Ga. Regt, was mortally wounded in the battle near Drewrys Bluff, 16th May, and died about a week afterwards in Hospital, Richmond, Va.

Mr. George Turner, a native of S. C., but for the last year a resident of Fla., died in Marion co., Fla...leaves two sons, both in the army.

Wm. N. Harris 6th Ga. Regt., son of Rev. Isaac C. Harris, was killed at Cold Harbor, June 1, 1864...

Tribute of Respect by Rev. William C. Kirkland by Greenville ct., S. C. Conf...died on March 31, aged 50 years 3 months and 25 days.

Issue of July 14, 1864

Married on 29th June, in Laurens Village, S. C., by Rev. A. H. Lester, Mr. B. F. Hutchings to Miss Nannie L. Lester, both of Greenville Dist.

Mrs. Emily Savage, wife of P. A. Savage, died in Mobile, May 12, 1864, aged 52...maiden name was JAmeson, born in Barren

co., Ky...
     Mrs. Sarah M. Billups, wife of Maj. John Billups, was reared
in Athens, Ga., eldest daughter of Jacob Phinizy, married in
Feb. 1846...died June 1, 1864, in the 38th year of her age....
     Americus Washington Hammond, of Entledge Mounted Rifles,
S. C. V., son of William and Lucy Hammond, late of Whitfield
co., Ga.,died on 12th June, 1863, at the residence of Col. E.
F. Keen, in Pittsylvania co., Va.,in his 19th year.... W. Hammond.
     Mrs. E. A. Brunson, wife of W. L. Brunson, and granddaughter
of Richard Bradford, died in Sumter, S. C., May 18, aged 63
years....
     Sgt. Wm. James Dixon of Richland Dist., 6th S. C. V., was
born Feb. 14, 1841, and was killed May 6, 1864, in the battle
of the Wilderness.
     Julia McSwain, wife of Dr. E. T. McSwain, Surgeon C S A,
deid 25th June 1864... W. A. McSwain.
     Mrs. Sallie Cassady, wife of Rev. John Cassady, of the Ala.
Conf., and daughter of J. J. Edwards, was born in Putnam co.,
Ga., and died at Lawrenceville, Ala., on 7th June, in the 23d
year of her age....
     Mrs. Susan M. Brewster was born in Pendleton Dist., S. C.,
25th Nov 1829, joined the Baptist Church in 1853, married to
Rev. P. H. Brewster of Cherokee co., Ga., the following autumn,
and died in Gainesville, Ga., June 20, 1864....
     Cpl. Z. Jones 11th Regt. S. C. V. fell at Gaines' Mill, Va.,
June 3, 1864....
     Bro. James Major died in Pickens Dist., S. C., 16th March,
1864, in his 70th year....
     Wm. M. Howard, eldest son of John and Lucinda Howard, was
born in Tuskegee, Ala., March 1, 1836, and was killed at Spottsylvania C. H., May 12, 1864....
     Mrs. Mary S. Redding, wife of Col. Wm. Redding, died in Grif-
fin, Ga., on 18th June, in the 31st year of age...
     Rev. George R. Wright, a minister of the M. E. Church, and
Ga. Conf., was born 13th Aug., 1804, in Orangeburg Dist., S. C.,
and died in Effingham, Ga., 6th May 1864....
     Mrs. Sophia A.Godfrey, died June 22, 1864, at Camden, S. C.,
in the 75th year of age...native of Marlborough Dist., S. C., but
for many years resided in Union co., N. C., and a few years in
this place.
     Bro. Leonidas B. Alexander died in Monroe co., Ga., 1st
March, 1864, at 44 years of age...born in Elbert co., Ga....
     Tribute of Respect to Charles W. Cary, by Chunnenugee Station,
Ala.
     Tribute of Respect to Dr. Richard M. Fryer by Louisville -
Station, Ala. Conf....

Issue of July 21, 1864

     Sgt. R. H. Loving, son of Rev. R. G. Loving, of the Mo.
Conf., 2d and 6th Missouri Regt. Inf., was killed July 3, 1864,
at the battle near Marietta, Ga.
     My father, Sankey T. Johnson, died in Tallapoosa co., Ala.,
April 19, 1864, in his 64th year. His youngest son, Dr. E. T.
F. Johnson, was killed in Va., on 5th May. A. H. Johnson.
     Braly Oates, late of Charlotte, N. C., died in Ocala, Fla.,
in the 63d year of his age....left two children.
     Seymour Smith of 20th Batt. Ga. Cavalry, eldest son of Rev.
O. L. Smith, D. D., of Echole co., Ga., was killed 12th June,
in his 20th year....
     Lt. R. M. Freeman, of 61st Regt. Ala. Vols., was killed
near Rome, Ga., May 17, 1864....

Wm. Hodrett died near Long Cane, Troup co., Ga.,in his 70th year...

Miss Joanna B. Kennedy, daughter of the late Rev. Mr. Kennedy, of the Fla. Conf. died in Tuskaloosa, Ala., June 26, 1864....

Mrs. Josephine C. Wilson, eldest daughterof Rev. Charles and Nancy Kelley, was born Oct. 19, 1836 in Anson co., N. C., and died May 6, 1864, in Kemper co., Miss...

Sister Martha M., wife of brother Joseph Sanford, of Baldwin co., Ga., was bor June 26, 1820, and died June 16, 1864....

Mrs. Elizabeth, wife of Dr. Thomas V. Godfrey, was born in Trenton, N. C., 31 Aug 1798, and died in Marianna, Fla., 19th April 1864....

Julian C. Borom, of Hardaway Artillery, was born Feb. 25, 1843, in Macon co., Ala., died in Charlottesville Hospital, Va., April 15, 1864....

Thomas Jefferson McRae, son of Norman and Susannah McRae, died at the residence of Alexander Love, near Quincy, Fla., in his 24th year....

George D. Herman of Co. C., 28th Regt. N. C. Vols., was born in Catawba co., N. C., April 15, 1838, and died in the battle of the Wilderness May 5, 1864...

Lt. Wm. P. McMurray, son of John and Berinthea McMurray, of Carrollton, Miss., and nephew of Gen. Featherston, was born Aug. 29, 1839, and died in Richmond, May 29, 1864....

Elizabeth J. Blantern, daughter of William and Nancy Spear, of Newton co., Ga.,died June 29, 1863...

John W. Hutchison was born Dec. 12, 1829, and was killed in battle, May 5th, 1864.

Mr. Theodore S. Smith, died in Tuskaloosa, Ala., June 26th, 1864...born in S. C., Jan. 2, 1811, removed to Tuskaloosa when 9 years of age, married Miss Charlotte Roberts, May 12, 1841.

J. Wesley Wright of 7th S. C. Regt., a native of Edgefield Dist., S. C.,was killed in the battle of the Wilderness, May 6, 1864, in her 25th year...

Father Wm. Young of Smyrna Church, Abbeville ct., S. C. Conf., died in his 78th year....

Mrs. Mary Bouknight died in Edgefield Dist., S. C.,at the residence of her son-in-law, Mr. Russell Eidson, March 10, 1864, in her 78th year....

Mrs. Sarah E. Roberts, wife of Rancis Roberts, and daughter of James and Nancy Passmore of Harris co., Ga.,died May 26, 1864, in her 18th year....

Mrs. Jane W. McDow was born Aug. 2, 1815, and died May 18th, 1864, at Summerfield, Ala., in her 49th year...

Sgt. Preston S. Gilder of Co. E., 40th Ala. Regt., was born in Choctaw co., Ala., and was killed near Resaca, Ga., 15th May, 1864, in his 21st year...

Miss Ann C. Byrd, was born Feb. 16, 1820, in Orangeburg Dist., S. C., and died 10th June, 1864....

Mrs. Elizabeth Vaughan, died in Grooverville, Ga.,March 23, 1864, in the 52d year of her age....

Abner Reeves died in Pike co., Ga.,April 22, 1864, in his 32d year....

Cpl. J. B. Campbell of 45th Ala. Regt. was killed 13th June 1864....

Aaron F. Lazenby was born April 18th, 1846, and was killed in Virginia, near Richmond, June 26, 1864....

Issue of July 28, 1864

Married in St. Peter's Church, Robertville, S. C., on June 28, by Rev. Richard Johnson, Jno. W. Heidt, Esq.,of Savannah, Ga., to Miss Eliza Agnes, eldest daughter of Dr. Wm. B. Villard, of the former place.

By Rev. E. L. King on the July 6, Sgt. J. W. F. King of Co.
C., 2nd Fla. Cavalry, to Miss Gattie Campbell, all of Alachua
co., Fla.

In Montgomery co., Ala., July 12th, by Rev. A. Dowling, Mr.
Washington Lawrence, to Miss Harriet A.E. Rylander, daughter of
Rev. Wm. S. Rylander, formerly of Columbus, Ga.

By Rev. R. A. Connor, on 18th inst.,at the residence of L. S.
Catlin, Richmond co., Ga.,Mr. Mortimer H. Williams of Savannah,
to Miss Martha W. Williams, of Richmond county.

On THursday evening, 21st inst.,by Rev. J. Lee Dixon, Mr.
James W. Henry, of Columbia, S. C.,to Miss M. Victoria Dixon,
of Richland Dist., S. C.

On the evening of Tuesday 7th July,by Rev. J. A. Mood, at
the residence of the bride, Mr. Paul Allen to Mrs. Z. Z. Allen,
all of Barnwell Dist., S. C.

By Rev. J. L. Lupo, July 5th, 1864, Warren D.Payne, of Atlanta
Ga., to Miss M. L. Miller of Campbell co., Ga.

In Augusta, Ga.,July 20, 1864, by Rev. D. D. Cox, Mr. Henry
Daniel to Miss Drusilla Castelberry.

Died in Whitesville, Ga., July 2d, Willie Dean Jones, son of
Rev. R. F. And P. W. Jones, aged 8 months and 27 days.

Rev. John Emory Rylander, Major 10th Ga. Batt., was born
Sept. 15, 1836...(no date of death given)....tribute of respect
to Rev. J. E. Rylander who was killed on 2d June....

Robt. Asbury Herring, 9th Ga. Regt, died at Warrenton, Va.,
Sept. 1861.

Henry Hamilton Herring, 1st Regt.Fla. Cavalry, died of disease....

John Wesley Herring 1st Fla. Cavalry was killed at Chickamauga, Sept. 1864.

Daniel Bird Herring, 3d Fla. Regt, died on 9th March, 1864,
Thus of five brothers, sons of William and Caroline Herring, of
Columbia Co., Fla., four have died.

Mary E., daughter of Mr. and Mrs. J. T. Montfort, died in
Butler, Ga., June 9, 1864, in her 14th year....

Wm. Herron of 1st Regt. Ala. Cavalry, was born 11th July
1861, and died on 21st near Marietta, Ga.....

Lt. Geo. W. Bedell of Greenville, Ala., 1st Ala. Cavalry,
was killed on June 20, 1864.

Mrs. Anna Simpson was born in Laurens Dist., S. C., Aug. 1,
1770, married to James A. Simpson and settled in Shelby co.,
Ala., in 1820, where she died May 27, 1864...joined the Presbyterian Church....

Mrs. Mary A. E. Hutchison, wife of P. W. Hutchinson, Jr.,
died in Athens, Ga., July 4, 1864.....

Lt. W. R. Barineau, of Decatur co., Ga., was born July 30,
1833, and was killed at Wilderness Run, May 6, 1864.

Ost. J. S. Barineau, was born Jan 27, 1838, and was killed
in the battle of Cold Harbor, June 3, 1864.

Pvt. John M. Jones of Co. D., 46th Regt. Ga. Vols., fell
wounded near Marietta, Ga., on 20th June, and died 23d June 1864.

James Vanse was born in Marion Dist., S. C., May 19, 1827,
and died 6th April 1864....

Mrs. Isabella P. Teague, daughter of Thomas and Mary Crews,
and wife of J. M. Teague, of Ga., died at Laurens C. H., S. C.,
in her 37th year....

W. O. Rahn of 54th Ga. Regt, was born in Effingham co., Ga.,
1st Dec. 1818 and died June 20, 1864, near the place where he was
raised.

Mrs. E. T. Tyler, daughter of John and Elizabeth Wilkerson,
died in Marion co., Ga., in her 24th year...wife of Wm. Tyler.

John E. Livingston, of 3rd Ga. Regt., was killed May 10, 1864, near Spottsylvania C. H., about 27 years of age...Newton co., Ga.

Capt. Jas. P. Ardrey of Mecklenburg co., N. C., 49th N. C. Regt., was mortally wounded near Drewry's Bluff, on 14th May....

Lt. C. H. Lambert fell on 6th May , in the battle of the Wilderness, in his 22d year....

Lst. Lt. Wm. H. Johnson of 64th Regt. Ala. Vols., was born Nov. 20, 1835, fell near Cassville, Ga., May 14.

Pvt. J. L. Johnson, brother of the above, was born Dec. 1, 1831, fell near New Hope Church 29th of May....

Wm. G. McQueen, was born 29th May 1838, and died May 3, 1864, in Coosa co., Ala...left mother and step-father.

Pvt. John R. Slaughter of 31st Ala. Regt. died at the Empire Hospital, Atlanta, Ga., in his 46th year....

Jas S. Shumate, of Butler Guards, 2d S. C. V., was born in Greenville Dist., S. C. Oct. 14, 1834....died 17th June.

Mrs. Mary Sturdivant, widow of the late Hon John Sturdivant died near Butler co., April 29, 1864, in her 64th year.

Mrs. Caroline Bryant, wife of R. M. Bryant, died in Butler, Ga., May 22, 1864, in her 49th year....

Miss Mary E. Montfort, daughter of J. E. and Elizabeth Montfort, died inButler, Ga., June 9, 1864, in her 14th year....

Mrs. Susan L. Stevens, was born in Granville co., N. C., and died at the residence of her son-in-law, T. C. Brewer, in Camden Ala., June 26, 1864, in her 71st year...About 1815 married to Rev. Dr. Thomas Cottrell, and became the mother of 10 children, eight of them still living, three of them ministers in the M. E. Church. about 1840, married Hon. Louis Stevens of Greensboro. Four years later she again became a widow....

Capt. Robert Alexander Chambers, son of Col. James M. Chambers, died at his father's residence, near Columbus, Ga., 18th June 1864, in his 25th year....

Walton Ware was born Feb. 14, 1811, and died in Tallapoosa co., Ala., Feb. 18, 1864, aged 58 years....

Mrs. Laura M. Turner, wife of James Turner, and daughter of Walton and Lucinda M. Ware,was born April 6, 1844, and died in Tallapoosa co., Ala., in her 20th year.

Camilla Thomas, daughter of Walton and Lucinda M. Ware, was born May 27, 1846, and died April 7, 1864...

Cornelia A., daughter of Walton and Lucinda M. Ware was born April 18, 1848, and died Feb. 16, 1864, the youngest child.

Edwin Ernest Padget, of Capt. J. J. Gregg's Cavalry, second son of Mahlon M. and Mary M. Padget, was born in Edgefield Dist., S. C., Oct. 18, 1845, and was killed at Trevillian's Station, Va., June 12, 1864....

Issue of August 4, 1864

Married on July 26, by Rev. N. K. Melton, Mr. Langa to Miss Adaline Brackens, both of Greenville Dist., S. C.

On July 26, in Orange Parish, S. C., by Rev. A. J. Stokes, Rev. R. Benson Tarrant of the S. C. Conf. to Miss Maggie Argoe.

On July 20, by Rev. John Calvin Johnson, Gen. John W. Stroud, to Miss Martha S. Jackson, all of Clarke co., Ga.

On July 17, by Rev. John Calvin Johnson, Mr. Jesse E. Butler, to Mrs. Almeida Jones, all of Clarke co., Ga.

In Macon, Ga., on Sunday, July 24, died Henry Blake, second son of Rev. W. C. And Mrs. A. O. Bass, aged 2 years, 3 months and 18 days.

In Columbus, Ga., July 10, of Robert Laney, son of Camden and Susan E. Evans, aged 2 years and 9 months.

In Butts co., Ga., July 13th, Ella Buttrell, daughter of Asa

and Lucy Buttrell, after two week's illnes....
    Mrs. Mary W. Wilson, wife of Rev. Charles Wilson of the S.
C. Conf., died at the Parsonage of St. Georges ct., June 3, 1863
(sic)...daughter of George Pooser of Orangeburg....
    Joseph T. Medlin, was born Sept. 25, 1819, and was killed in
assisting to arrest a deserter, July 18, 1864....
    Capt. Augustus M. Jones, of 17th Ga. Regt., was killed near
Petersburg, Va., 16 July 1864, in his 23d year...born in Burke
co., but moved to Webster co., Ga....
    Mrs. Mary W. Martin, wife of Rev. O. Martin, died in Monroe
co., Miss., aged 51...born in York Dist., S. C....
    Miss Carrie Richards died in Talboton, Ga., 18th June in her
21st year....
    Rev. Wm. B. Moorman died in Laurens co., Ga., on 23d June,
leaving many to mourn his loss....
    Francis D. Baxter of 11th Regt. S. C. V., was killed on 12th
May, at Swift Creek Bridge, a few miles from Petersburg, Va.,
aged 22 years....
    John H. Payne of 51st Ala. Cavalry, fell mortally wounded
on 20th June, and died in Marietta, Ga., on 24th...born in 1829
....
    Henry M. LIfford, 6th Regt. S. C. V., aged 21 years, was
illed at Taylorsville, Va....
    Lt. Nathan Bookter of Richland Dist., S. C., aged 23 was
killed in Virginia....
    Mary Ann, wife of Andrew G. LaTaste, and daughter of the late
Nathan Napier, was born in Edgefield Dist., S. C.,on 11th Oct.,
1833, and died at Adamsville, Sumter co., Fla., on 29th June....
    Bro. P. T. Thompson of 1st Ga. Regt, died 24th June in Fair
Ground Hospital, No. 1., Atlanta, Ga....
    Pvt. Sanders F. Griffith 2d Regt. Artillery, died 13th July
1864, from a wound received at James' Island, S. C., in his 22d
year....
    Bro. A. J. Strickland of Dale co., Ala., was killed at
Drewry's Bluff, Va., May 16, 1864, aged 22 years.
    Mr. George H. Toungblood, of Dale co., Ala., died at Marietta,
Ga., aged 22 years....
    Miss Eliza Catharine Bowen was born Jan. 1841, and died June
19, 1864....
    Alpheus Hood of 2d Regt. Ga. State Troops, only son of
R. F. and F. Hood, of Pike co., Ga., died in Griffin, Ga., in his
19th year....
    Tribute of Respect by Gist's Brigade to
L. W. Outzs died on 30th May, aged 35 years
T. Grassel 24the S. C. V. wounded on 16th May and died a short-
time after, in hospital at Atlanta, aged 31 or 32, a member of
the Baptist Church.
M. Hyatt, 24th S. C. V., died near Kennesaw Mtn., 22d June 1864,
aged 36 years, member of the Baptist Church
Sgt. John H. Lewis, 24th S. C. V., fell at his post near Kennesaw
Mtn., 2nd July in the 24th year of his age...member of the Epis-
copal Church.
Lt. John Warren a member of the M. E. Church, died July 2, aged
23.
Robert B. Persons, 46th Ga. Vols., a member of the Missionary
Baptist Church, fell 4th July near Smyrna Church.
Pvt. David W. Seay fell near Kennesaw Mtn, aged 32
Pvt. John H. Short of 64th Ga. Vols., died 21st June, aged 29
Pvt. H. L. Spann of 46th Ga. Vols., fell on 20th June, aged 29
Henry L. Smith, 46th Ga. Rgt. fell 20th June, aged 24.
John M. Jones 46th Ga. Vols. died in Atlanta Ga. on 23d June
1864....
Wm. H. Stansell of 46th Ga. Vols. was killed on the 20th June, in

his 27th year.
Cpl. Chas Blanton, 46th Ga. Vols. fell on 20th June, aged 28
Sgt. G. W. Mullens of 46th Regt. Gal. Vols. fell 20th June
His brother, T. J. Mullens, of same, died 7th July.
H. V. Killian, pvt. 24th S. C. V., killed near Marietta, Ga., on
20th June....
    Tribute of Respect by Weston Ct., Webster co., Ga., to
H. S. Chamberlin, who died 28th May last....

Issue of August 11, 1864

    Married by Rev. Isaac Munden, at the residence of Rev. Wm. A.
McDonald, Mr.Thoams H. Miller, of Ware co., Ga., to Miss Rebecca
Grovenstine Flood, refugee from St. Marys, Ga.
    Lt. Sidney T. Farmer, 38th Ga. Regt. of Jefferson co., Ga.,
was killed at Spotsylvania C. H., Va., on 10th May 1864, in his
23d year....
    Sgt. Jacob E. Rast of 25th Regt. S. C. v., born 25th Sept.,
1840, was killed on 7th May...
    J. Marshall Dantzler, son of Dr. Lewis and Mrs. Mary Dantzler,
of St. Matthews, S. C. was killed by a sharpshooter near Petersburg, on 20th May....
    John W. Myers, son of Lewis and Sophia Myers, of St. Matthews,
.S C., was killed in the battle of Port Walthall, on 7th May
last, in his 22nd year....
    Wm. H. Bedgood oc 28th Ga. Regt, son of Cyrus Bedgood, of
Washington co., Ga., was killed south of James River, May 20,
1864....
    Mr. T. J. Fralix, of 11th Regt. S.C. V., was born May 16,
1815, and was killed June 27th, nearly 50 years of age...
    Mary Adeline, daughter of William and Lavisa Cameron, was born
in Tatnal co., Ga., Feb. 12, 1821, died in Stockton, Clinch co.,
Ga., June 19, 1864....
    Mrs. Nancy M. Bigby, wife of G. M. Bogby, was born July 25,
1827, and died in Abbeville Dist., S. C., May 21, 1864.
    Rev. William McGee was born in Abbeville Dist., S. C., Oct.
24, 1797, married to Miss Asenath Rice, April 30, 1818, joined
the Baptist Church in 1820...died in Anderson Dist., S. C., June
22, 1864.
    Tribute of Respect to Rev. H. F. Smith by Ocala ct., Fla.
Conf....

Issue of August 18, 1864

    Married on the 28th July, by Rev. T. Alonzo Harris, Col.
Thomas J. Heard of Elberton, Ga., to Mrs. E. T. Arnold, of
Abbeville Dist., S. C.
    July 28, 1864, by Rev. A. P. Silliman, Rev. C. M. Hutton,
Chaplain of 36 Ala., Army of Tenn., to Miss E. Jennie Gordon,
daughter of Saml. 0. and Ann Gordon, of Greene co., Ala.
    In Newberry Dist., S. C., on 28th July 1864, by Rev. M. A.
Connolly, the Rev. J. Emory Watson, of the S. C. Conf. to Miss
Lovenia N. Richie.
    On July 1864, at the residence of Col. Gee's, Decatur co.,
Ga., by Rev. M. R. Fielding, Mr. W. B. Braswell, to Miss Almira
Carlisle, all of Decatur co., Ga.
    In Athens, Ga., July 21st, by Rev. A. Wright, Rev. W. P.
Pattillo to Miss Sallie E. Chase.
    July 7th, by Rev. D. T. Holmes, John T. Beckham to Miss
Louisa Faucett, all of Pike co., Ga.
    On 2nd August, by Rev. J. T. Ainsworth, Thos. J. Jackson,
Local Editor of the Columbus Times, to Mrs. Virginia Miller, all
of Columbus, Ga.

In Columbus, Miss., by Rev. Philip F. Neely, on Thurs., July 14th, Judge Stephen A. Brown to Miss Mary G., daughter of Rev. George Shaeffer.

On 21st inst.,by Rev. W. W. Leake, at the residence of Capt. D. C. Mims, of Baker co., Mr. W. W. Turner, of Terrel co., Ga., to Miss J. M. Tull, of Baker co., Ga.

Died at Lawrenceville, Ala., on 24th July, Iva Carolina, infant daughter of Mrs. Sallie E. and Rev. J. C. Holmes, aged 17 months and 19 days.

In Randolph co., Ala., July 20th, 1864, Mollie E. L., daughter of Rev. James M. and Elizabeth G. Towles, aged 2 years, 11 months and 28 days.

In Blackville, S. C., on the 3rd inst., Lawrence, infant son of Mr. and Mrs. Samuel Bell, aged 7 weeks.

In Lexington District, S. C., August 6, 1864, Mary Elizabeth, second daughter of J. R. and R. C. Shuler, aged 8 months and 8 days.

Mrs. Susan R. Wiggins, wife of Rev. L. G. R. Wiggins, and daughter of Judge L. Q. C. Lamar, late of Milledgeville, died on 23d May in Muscogee co., Ga....

Capt. Joseph T. Hearn, A. A. Gen. of Granbury's Brigade, Army of Tenn., son of Reb. Ebenezer and Mrs. Mary Hearn, decd., was born in Dallas co., Ala., May 12, 1837. In 1859 went to Galveston, Texas...body brought to Camden, Wilcox co., Ala., and buried in the family grave yard.

Mrs. Elizabeth Dickson died in Hancock co., Ga., at the residence of her son, Mr.1David Dickson, on 5th August, in the 87th year of her age....

Mrs. Mary Ann Fendry, wife of Saml. Fendry, of Newton, Baker co., Ga., and sister of Rev. S. P. Richardson, of the Fla. Conf., was born Sept. 4, 1837, and died June 8th, 1864....

Mrs. Harriet A. S. Kennedy, wife of W. R. Kennedy, Esq.,died in the 47th year of her age...born in Pitt co., N. C., and was married in 1833...removed to Alabama in 1840....

Ajt. Henry Francis Jones of Cobb's Legion, youngest son of Thomas Jones Sr. of Thomasville, Ga., was born June 19, 1841, and died 11th June 1864....

Aaron Varn, son of James G. Varn of Colleton Dist., S. C., 11th Regt. S. C. V., died at Farmville Hospital, Va., June 24, 1864, in his 19th year....

Sarah A., wife of A. M. Callier, daughter of W. A. and S. A. Stillwell, died 9th June 1864, aged 32 years....

Mrs. Eliza Smith, was born in Edgefield Dist., S. C., Jan. 8th, 1796, and died June 20, 1864, at the residence of Shepherd Spencer, in Pickens co., Ala....

Mrs. Mollie L. Anderson, wife of W. W. Anderson, junr., and daughter of H. Cravens, was born in Tennessee, in 1840, and died in Dawson, Ga., April 6th, 1864....

Joseph A. Majors, of 17th Ala. Regt., was born in Dale co., Ala., 31st August 1845, and died near Atlanta, Ga.,28th July, 1864, in a charge....

W. T. Beall, was born in S. C. 9th March 1809, and died in Dawson, Ga., 15th May, 1864, in the 58th year of his age. His parents came to Ga. when he was quite young....

Rev. Thaddeus Pennington died in Monroe co., Ga., July 27, 1864....

Mrs. Cecilia C. Jewell, died in Blackville, S. C., on 21st July, in her 55th year....

Sgt. R. M. Glass, 5th S. C. Cavalry was born Oct. 15, 1829, and was killed June 11th, 1864, near Trevillions Station, Va., in his 42d year....

Cpl. M. L. Dunlap, of Capt Foster's Co., 4th S. C. Cavalry, was wounded May 28th, near Richmond, and died in that city, June

8th, 1864, aged about 22 years.
  Capt. B. T. Davis of 21st Regt., S. C. V.,died 29th May, near
Petersburg, in his 36th year...class-leader and steward in Ches-
terfield ct., S. C. Conf....
  Sgt. D. K. Herbert, of 13th Miss Regt., fell at the Wilderness
on 6th May...member of the Baptist Church....

Issue of August 25, 1864

  Married at Mrs. E. E. Clark's, Montgomery co., Ga., July 13,
1864, by Rev. S. A. Clarke, Mr. D. McMillan to Miss E. A. McRae,
all of Montgomery co., Ga.
  By the Rev. J. H. Wilkins, at China Grove, Lowndes co., Ga.,
Aug. 7, Mr. W. C. Martin to Miss Isabella Peters, both of the a-
bove county.
  On the 19th July, by Rev. W. C. Wigans, W. H. Marsh, of
Georgetown, S. C., to Miss Martha C. Jarman, of Wilmington, N. C.
  Died in Augusta Ga., Aug. 14, Mary Julia, infant daughter of
Rev. D. D. and E. O. Cox, aged 7 months and 14 days.
  Near Jeffersonville, Ga., Aug. 5th, Annie Elvira, only child
of Capt. John H. and Mary F. Jones, aged 1 year and 9 months.
  Wm. H. Young, Jr., 3d son of Wm. H. Young of Columbus, Ga.,
fell mortally wounded 11th June,near Marietta, and expired in
Atlanta on 14th june....
  Gordon Hadden was born in Jefferson co., Ga., March 29, 1807,
and died in Stewart co., Ga., June 2, 1864....
  John W.Tindall of 20th S. C. Regt, died in the hospital, near
Petersburg, Va.,on 1st July, 1864, in his 42d year....
  Nail McMullan of Monroe co., Ga., died on 23d July, 1864, in
his 81st year...a native of Virginia, but was principally reared
in Elbert co.
  Lt. E. F. Hightower, of 54th Ala. Vols., was born April 2d,
1838, and fell mortally wounded 28th July 1864,near Atlanta....
  Mrs. Mary Ann Young, wife of Samuel H. Young, died in Sumter
Dist., S. C., June 25, 1864, in her 45th year....
  Mrs. Mary C. Maddux, wife of Lucius W. Maddux, was born Dec.
2d, 1828, and died in Americus, Ga., Aug. 5, 1864....
  Stephen H. Griffin, died in Pettigrew Hospital, Raleigh, N.
C., 30th July, in the 46th year of his age...4th S. C. Cav....
  Sgt. F. H. Martin of 17th Tenn. Regt., aged 26 years, enlisted
in Tenn...killed 16th May....
  Sgt. John Veal Townsend, son of Rev. Saml. and Mrs. Martha J.
Townsend, of Columbia, S. C., was killed near James River, Va.,
26th July, aged 21 years and 28 days....15th Regt. S. C. V.
  F. M. Alexander of 26th S. C. V., was born July 12, 1838, in
Chesterfield Dist., S. C.,and was killed near Newbern, N. C.,
on 6th May 1864....
  1st Sgt. Daniel M. Livingston, 27th Regt. Ga. Vols. received
a wound near Petersburg, Va., 10th June and lived only a few days.
  Mrs. Caroline T.Sullivan, was born Jan. 8, 1824, and died July
19, 1864....
  Thomas M. Bradley of Lowndes co., Ala., was killed 13th May,
1864, at Spottsylvania C. H., Va.
  Cpl. George J. Hickman of 19th La. Regt. fell on 28th July last.
William T. Ray, son of Rev. Joseph and Nancy Ray of Telfair co.,
was born in 1845, and was wounded at Spottsylvania, died 12th
May....
  Tribute of Respect by Clio Church, S. C. Conf., to Joseph T.
Medlin.
  Tribute of Respect to Zabud Fletcher, by Gadsden circuit....

John Rogers was born in Cabarras co., N. C., August, 1776...
died 23d of last July.

John Grisham Craig of 1st Regt. Ga. Regular Infantry, died
at the Soldiers Relief Hospital, Charleston, S. C., July 21,
1864...born and reared in Pickens Dist., S. C., emigrated to
Whitfield co., Ga., in 1855...fell wounded on 9th July....

Miss Elizabeth E. Adams, daughter of Rev. John M. and Agnes
M. Adams, died in Elbert co., Ga.,26th July 1864, in her 26th year.

Mrs. Catherine Standifer was born in Wilkes co., Ga., and
died in Coweta co., June 28th, 1864, in her 76th year....

Lt. Wm. F. Smoka of 5th Regt. S. C. Cavalry, died in hospital
in Charlottesville, Va., from wound received on 11th or 12th of
June....

Lt. A. S. Womack, 45th Ga. Vols. was killed near Marietta,
15th June 1864, aged 24....

Mrs. Martha Ann Wilcox, daughter of Eliza and the late Maj.
John A. Easley, died in Williamson co., Texas, in her 33d year.

Franklin M. Agerton, eldest son of Alfred and Metty Agerton,
born 12th July 1838, 26th Regt. S. C. V., died before Newbern, on
5th May 1864....

Lt. John Black of 11th S. C. Regt., died in Winder Hospital,
Richmond, Va., July 17th, 1864, in his 22d year...

Wm. H. Jones, received a wound on 16th May last, and died
after a few weeks...left an only child....

Wm. A. Dudley, 5th Ala. Regt. was born March 17, 1833, and
was wounded near Orange C. H., May 5th, and died on 19th June....

Jas. J. Dudley, son of Edward and Mary Dudley, of Lowndes
co., Ala., was born July 11, 1839, fell wounded near Atlanta,
20th July 1864....joined M. E. Church in Davis co., Texas....

Pvt. David S. Ackerman 5th S. C. Cavalry, died in Jackson
Hospital, Richmond, Va.,June 22, 1864, in his 43d year....

Mrs. Mary Jane, wife of Wm. S. Porter, decd., died in Clarke
co., Ala., August 11, 1864....

Miss Emily F. Sessions, died near Brooksville, Miss., July
18, 1864, in her 15th year....

Lewis J. McDonald of 23d Ala. Regt., youngest son of Jason
and Lucinda McDonald, was born August 11, 1844, and died July
2, 1864, in the hospital of Madison, Ga.

Jesse Fletcher O'Briant was born March 12, 1862, and died at
Rev. Mr. Moore's, Macon co., Ala., 34th Ala Regt....

Calipus Asbury O'Briant, his brother was born May 7, 1842,
and died at Benton, Miss., 24th S. C. V.

Hugh Wilson Johnston was born 8th Sept., 1839, and died at
Jackson Hospital, near Richmond, July 31, 1864....

Issue of September 8, 1864

A. Purviance, Sr., died in Camden, Miss., on Aug. 14, 1864,
aged 75 years....born in Cabarras co., N. C., and moved to S. C.
when about 30 years of age...married to Elizabeth P. Schrock...
in Camden, S. C....moved to Jacksonville, Ill., and thence to
Miss....

Charles Morton Younge was drowned on 3d of August 1841, at
Columbus, Miss., son of Rev. James Young, late of Memphis, Tenn.

Lt. John H. Howard of 43d Regt. Ala. Vols. was born in Lenoir
co., N. C., Jan. 13, 1840...fell 11th July 1864.

Miss Matilda McAfee, daughter of E. O. and Emily McAfee of
Cumming, Ga., died in Powellton, Ga., July 19, 1864, aged 12
years and 11 months.

Saml. M. Sandell of 16th Miss Vols., died in hospital at
Richmond, Va., on 26th June, aged 29 years....

Aunt Carter, expired on 26th July 1864, at the age of 73....
Col. Lucius A. Church died in Madison, Fla., 29th June, in his
35th year...
Capt. W. G. Hewitt of S. C. Cavalry was wounded and captured
at Haw's Shop, 28th May, and died in Lincoln Hospital.
Mary Catharine Browne, my niece, daughter of Samuel and Mary
Browne, died in Anderson Dist., S. C.,July 26, 1864, aged 22
years, 11 months... SIDI H. BROWNE.
W J Martin of 4th Miss Cavalry, died at Lee Hospital, Lauder-
dale Springs, Miss., July 24, 1864, aged 36 years.
Cpl. C. W. Terry, Hampton's Legion, S. C. V., killed 13th
June 1864, at Riddle's Shop, Charles City co., Va.
B. F. Roberts was born 29th August 1844, died 13th May 1864.
Cornelius P Sexton was born Nov. 21, 1844, in Spartanburg Dist.,
S. C...died 21st June from effects of a wound....
Sgt. J. C. McDonald departed this life June 15, 1864...born
in Henry co., Va., Jan. 1, 1842, and died in hospital at Gordons-
ville, Va.
Wm. Thompson, of 7th Regt. Ga. Militia, died in Monroe co.,
19th Aug, in the 40th year of his age....
. Charles M. Edwards was born in Orange co., N. C. Oct. 30,
1800, and died in Gilmer co., Ga., May 23, 1864....

Issue of September 15, 1864

Mrs. Eliza Jane Cart, daughter of John and J. Howard was
born in Elbert co., Ga., Sept. 7, 1789, married to Robt. Rutherford, June 22, 1808, married the second time to Edward Cary,
April 25, 1826, and died at Chunnenuggee Ridge, Ala., July 13,
1864....
Samuel James Andrews, of 20th Ga. Bttn., son of Rev. E. Q.
and Margaret Andrews, of Liberty co., Ga., was killed about 50
miles north of Richmond, 11th June 1864, in his 31st year....
Capt. T. W. Bilbro, of 3d Ala. Regt., son of John B. Bilbro,
died May 13, 1864, died of a wound received at Spottsylvania, aged
25 years....
Mrs. Polly Hancock, wife of Richard Hancock, was born in
Franklin co., N. C.,May 12, 1782, and died in Madison co., Ga.,
July 8, 1864,in her 73d year....
Charles P. Hardy of 36th Ga. Regt, was born in Miss., May
1845, killed near Atlanta 20th July 1864....
Oliver S. Johnson son of A. N. Johnson, of Harris co., Ga.,
was born December 16, 1844, and was killed near Atlanta, July 22,
1864....
Francis A. Johnson, was born March 25, 1840, and died June
25, 1864...These brothers belonged to Co. E., 46th Ga. Regt....
Pvt. J. T. Campbell, son of Jeremiah Campbell of Col. Orr's
1st Regt. S. C. V., was born in Marion Dist., S. C., March 15,
1838, and died June 27th, 1864.
Mr. John N. Williams was born 26th Nov., 1838, and died in
Va., July 19, 1864.
Mrs. Jane E. Lawton, wife of J. G. Lawton, died in Beaufort
Dist., S. C., on 26th Aug, 1864, aged 29 years....
Sister Martha R. Hutson, died in Jackson co., Ga., June 30,
1864, in the 61st year of her age...married in her 16th year to
Mr. George W. Hutson...
James Perry Sharpe, of 29th Ga., died at the residence of
his father, in Lowndes co., Ga., 24th Aug 1864...
Lt. William H. Munnerlyn, was killed on 22d July 1864, near
Atlanta, Ga., in his 23d year...10th Regt. S. C. V.
Tribute of Respect to J. O. Davis, Vice Pres. of the Soldiers'
Christian Association at Guyton Hospital....

Issue of September 22, 1864

Married on the 14th Sept., by Dr. E. H. Myers, the Rev. Alfred T. Mann, D. D.,of the Ga. Conf., to Mrs. Frances R. Battay, of Jefferson co., Ga.

In Zollicoffer, Tenn., on the evening of the 11th Aug, by Rev. Dr. Massey, Dr. C. W. Snead, of the 16th Ga. Batt. Cavalry, to Miss Bettie H. Grant, formerly of Virginia.

By Rev. J. C. Harris on 25th inst., at the residence of Mr. M. Flecther, of Webseter co., Ga., Mr. James M. Rogers of 4th Ga. Vols., to Miss Mary E. Martinless, of Webster county.

By Rev. John W. Talley, at the residence of the bride's father, Calhoun co., Ala., at 10 o'clock Sabbath morning, 14th inst., Rev. Robert A. Simmons, of the Montgomery conf., to Miss Sardenia A. Bell.

August 14th, by Rev. Jas. D. Mauldin, Mr. William McRea to Mrs. Rebecca N. George, all of Wake is., Fla.

By the same, Aug. 28th, Mr. C. H. Lee to Miss Harriet L. Ferris, all of New Port, Fla.

In Webster co., Ga., Aug. 28th, by Rev. E. A. H. McGhee, Mr. William B. Stewart of Sumter co., Ga, to Mrs. Martha A. Cox.

August 28th, by Rev. O. L. Smith, Rev. Thomas L. Lanier, of Scriven co., to Miss Clara A. S. Smith, of Brooks co., Ga.

Maggie J. Killingsworth died July 5th, 1864, aged 2 years, 1 month and 3 days.

In Liberty co., Ga., Stuart, only child of Dr. J. P. and Mrs. Mary J. Mell, on 5th August, in his third year.

In Lowndes co., Ga., August 28th, Elithia Ann, only child of S. W. R. and M. J. McClendon, aged 1 year 2 months and 17 days.

August 26th, 1864, Wm. A., infant son of Rev. R. P. and S. M. Franks, aged 1 year and 29 days.

Near Davidson College, N. C.,on 9th August, Gussie, only daughter of A. M. Gillespie, aged 9 years and 20 days.

Thomas Clarke, son of Mrs. E. and Major D. L. Hoyle, died August 15, in Pontotoc, Miss., aged 2 years.

Lt. Wm. R. Ross of 56th Ga. and son of the late W. A. Ross of Macon, Ga...19 years of age.

Wm. Charles Redding, son of Col. Wm. C. Redding, of Monroe co., Ga.,was bor Oct. 25, 1831, and died June 22, 1864....

Caroline Sophia, wife of Barton W. Stone of Montgomery co., Ala., died 3d Sept., 1864...daughter of late Rev. Henry Whetstone, and was born in Autauga co., Ala., 8th April 1823....

Lt. John A. Harrison of 13th Ala. Regt., was born in Butler co., Ala., April 29, 1840...28th July 1864, mortally wounded.

Capt. Milton Butterfield of Union Springs, Ala., was born in Niagara co., Western New York, removed to Ala. twenty years ago...On 22nd August 1863, received a mortal wound in front of Atlanta....

Mrs. Martha Lane, wife of Rev. Richard Q. Lane, decd.,died near Warrior Stand, Ala.,July 28th, 1864, in the 66th year of her age,....

John L. Breeden was born Oct. 3, 1840, and was killed in arresting a deserter July 18, 1864....

Wm. Henson, 4th Regt. Fla. Vols., Army of Tenn., died 23d May, aged 18 years.

Thomas H. Smith, of 45th Ala. Regt. was born April 14, 1822, and was mortally wounded at Atlanta, August 2d, and died Aug. 14, at West Point.

Camden Evans of 45th Ala. Regt. was wounded at Atlanta, and died in Columbus, Ga., 7th August, aged 26 years...son of the late Rev. Josiah Evans of Ga. Conf....

Sgt. Sebron N. Williams of 46th Ga. Regt, was born May 25, 1835, and died July 6, 1863, in the Marietta Hospital, near Atlanta

Elizabeth C.Bundrick, daughter of Mrs. Susannah Bundrick, was born Jan. 30, 1859, and died August 14, 1864....

Issue of September 29, 1864

Married Sept. 13, '64, by Rev. Wm. T. Capres, George Reynolds Capers to Miss Sallie Hane, eldest daughter of the late David B. Witherspoon all of Columbia, S. C.

Near Eatonton, Ga., Sept. 13, 1864, by Rev. Geo. G. N. Mc-Donell, Capt. Seaborn R. Lawrence, C S A, to Miss Sarah Pearson, of Putnam co.

On 6th Sept., by Rev. J. W. Crider, the Rev. Jas. B. Campbell, of S. C. Conf. to Mrs. E. E. Davis, daughter of the late Wm. F. and E. M. Richardson, of Marion District.

At the residence of Mr. Wm. Powell, in Decatur co., Ga., Sept. 8, 1864, by Rev. Dr. A. J. Woldridge, Mr. James A. Varner to Miss Sallie R. Donelson, of said county.

Died at the house of Mr. L. M. Houser, near Perry, Tuesday Aug. 30, 1864, Mary E., only child of Derrille H. and H. Melissa Culler, aged 7 months and 13 days.

In Forstyh, Ga., on 9th inst., Julia A., youngest child of Rev. W. J. And Mrs. R. COtter, aged 22 months.

Lt. J. J. David fell near Atlanta on 22d July last, in his 22d year....

Mrs. Elizabeth Washington was born in Virginia, Sept. 3, 1768, and died in Baldwin co., Ga., 10th Sept. 1864, aged 95 years...daughter of Charles Hammond, who removed to S. C. and settled near Augusta, about the commencement of the Revolution. In 1789 married to moved to Wilkes co., Ga.

Edmund Murphy Clark of Burke co., Ga., was born July 27, 1827, and died in the hospital at Milledgeville, August 31,1864.

Mary Ann Clark, second daughter of Dr. S. B. and Mrs. Martha R. Clark, was born Jan. 21, 1848, and died Sept. 4, 1864....

Maj. J. B. Hunter, late of Marion Dist., S. C., of 4th S. C. Cavalry, was born Jan. 1823...killed instantly (no date).

Mrs. Irene M. Thompson died in Charleston Dist., S. C., on 15th August, 1864, in her 27th year...married to Mr. Daniel Thompson of Orangeburg Dist., S. C., on 14th Dec., 1854....

Lewis F. Rush of 25th Regt. S. C. V., was mortally wounded near Petersburg, Va.,June 5, 1864, and died the next day, in his 21st year....

Robt. P. McEvoy, died in Macon Ga., Aug. 17, 1864, in his 38th year... His father died when he was quite young....

Cpl. J. R. Kennedy, 25th S. C. V., was killed on 16 May, 1864, in his 38th year....

Jas. M. Reynolds, was born in 1829, died at Lynchburg, Va. 21st June....

Leroy Carvoso, son of Rev. D. W. Perry was born in Macon co., Ala., March 28, 1845, killed July 22, 1864, near Atlanta.

Henry Lane, youngest son of Martha and Rev. Richard Q. Lane, decd., was killed before Atlanta, Ga.,July 20, 1864....

N. H. McInnis, of 6th Regt. S. C. V., fell 22d June, 1864....

Mrs. Anna H. Weaver, wife of Mr. William T. Weaver, wife of Mr. William T.Weaver, now in the Conf. service in Va., died in Thomaston, Ga., on 6th Sept. 1864...daughter of Mr. and Mrs. Pence, of Richmond, Va...married 29th Oct. 1863.

Lt. J. W. Culpepper, of 8th Regt. Ga. Vols., son of G. W. Culpepper, of Merriwether co., Ga., was killed Aug. 16, 1864, at Fussel's Mill, Va.

Tribute of Respect by Oxford and Covington Station, to Rev.
Wilbur Fisk Yarbrough, son of our beloved pastor J. W. Yarbrough,
who has fallen near Front Royal, Va.

Issue of October 6, 1864

Married in Augusta, Ga., Sept. 1, by Rev. D. D. Cox, Mr.
Thomas Farrow, to Miss Susan Jackson.
By the same, Sept. 13, 1864, Mr. James A. Morris, to Miss
Alice Stacey.
Near Whitesville, Harris co., Ga., Sept. 18, 1864, by Rev. R.
W. Dixon, Mr. Wm. C. Cotton, to Miss Mary E. Godwin, all of
Harris co., Ga.
At Oak Hill, near Arcola, St. Helena Parish, La., on the
30th August, by Rev. J. W. McNeal, the Rev. Charles F. Evans,
of New Orleans, Chaplain of the Trans-Miss Army, to Miss Laura
Pauline, eldest daughter of Col. R. M. Ellis.
Died Alonzo H. Love, eldest son of H. C. and R. S. Love, of
Russell co., Ala., was born on 25th Sept. 1837, and died on 2
Sept. 1864.
Mrs. Mary S. Sykes, wife of Mr. S. A. Sykes, was born in
Northampton co., N. C., and died in Aberdeen, Miss., Sept.
5h, 1864...left an orphan, she was reared by an aunt....
Harriet Pope Hall, daughter of Maj. Danl Hall, died in Ogle-
thorpe co., Ga., Aug. 2nd, in her 25th year.
Josiah T. Hall, son of Maj. Danl Hall, died in Athens, Ga.,
in his 39th year.
Maj. Danl Hall, died in Oglethorpe co., Ga., Sept. 18, being
64 years old....
John M. Breedlove son of Rev. John H. Breedlove, of Arkansas,
formerly of Georgia, was killed at the battle of the Wilderness,
5th May, 1864. My brother.... B. F. Breedlove.
Capt. Joseph J. McRee, commanding 3d Regt. Ga. Vols., fell
at Petersburg, Va., on 30th July 1864....
Lt. Joseph Wiley Brooks, son of Dr. J. D. and Mrs. T. M.
Brooks, of Bellevue, Ga., was born April 23d, 1847, and died at
the house of Mr. Joel Reese, Jr., in Schley co., Ga., Sept. 5,
1864....
Miss Lizzie D., daughter of the Rev. Charles R. Jewett, of
Ga. Conf., died in Griffin, Ga., on 29th Aug 1864, in her 15th
year....
Henry Heard of 2d Batt. Ga. Sharpshooters, son of Mrs. E.
Heard and grandson of Mrs. Hannah Thompson, of Augusta, Ga.,
died in hospital at Barnesville, 26th Aug, in his 26th year....
Lt. N. Wellborn Grantham of 59th Regt. Ala. Vols. was killed
29th June, near Marietta Ga.
Mr. Stephen T. Townes, of 12th Regt. T. V., was killed Sept.
3, 1864, in the 27th year of his age....
Mrs. Mary Sessions, wife of Rev. John Sessions, was born
24th May, 1812, and died in Terrill co., Ga., 14th Aug 1864....
Mrs. M. J. Cumming, wife of E. Cumming, Esq., and daughter
of E. C. and M. C. Vinson, was born in Hancock co., Ga., Fev.
2, 1832, and died at the residence of her mother, near Milledge-
ville, Ga., April 17, 1864.
Mrs. Mary E. English, was born 1830, and died inBrooks co.,
Ga., July 22, 1864....
Oliver Goudelock was born Sept. 7, 1846, and died 22d June
1864.
Eugene Wilber Fisk Hardy of Co. F., 24th Regt. S. C. V., was
born in Abbeville Dist., S. C., 29th Feb. 1839, and killed in
front of Atlanta, 17th August 1864....
Elizabeth R. Williams, died on 4th Sept., 1864, in Dahlonega,
Ga., in the 73d year of her age...daughter of Richard Sappington,

formerly of Wilkes co., Ga., and at the time of her death, wife
of Wm. R. Williams, with whom she had lived 35 years.

Francis A. Dawkins, of Jefferson co., Fla., aged about
84 years, a son of Wm. and Jane Dawkins, of Jefferson co., Ga.,
died August 9, 1864...in 1826 removed to Leon co., Fla....

Israel Townsend of 4th Fla. Batt. was born Nov. 21, 1828, and
died at his house in Madison co., Fla., Sept. 2, 1864...

Also his son, Samuel A. Townsend, was born Jan. 13, 1845,
and died in the Seabrook Hospital, Richmond, Va., Aug. 23, 1845.

Mrs. Eliza P. Baggs, daughter of Drury and Catharine Ridgeway,
decd., was born in Elbert co., Ga., May 18, 1814, and died in
Whitesville, Harris co., Ga., Sept. 14, 1864....

Wm. J. Green, 24th S. C. Regt., fell wounded on 20th July
near Atlanta, in his 26th year....

Mrs. Cynthia D. Brown, wife of Rev. T. A. Brown, died in Upson co., Ga., Sept. 2, 1864....

Isabella H. Williams, wife of Rev. John L. Williams, of Fla.
Conf., died in Bristol, Fla., July 13, 1864....

Wm. Starr Anderson, son of George and Ann Anderson, of Farm-
ington, Ga., died in Jackson Hospital, near Richmond, 7th July,
in the 25th year of his age.

Mary Ann Gillespie, was born in Conecuh co., Ala., in 1825,
married to Robert Gillespie, in 1843, and died in Sumter co.,
Ala., 15 August 1864.

Jas. D. Lane, my brother-in-law, of Houston co., Ga., fell on
the banks of the Chattahoochee, July 6, 1864... J. B. McGehee.

Mrs. Mattie B., wife of Dr. G. A. Harley, and a native of
Lowndesboro, Ala., died at Orangeburg, S. C., April 27, 1864,
aged 23 years.

James Frederick, only son of Dr. C. A. and Mattie B. Harley,
died at Orangeburg, S. C., April 11, 1864, aged 23 months, 3
weeks and 2 days.

Elizabeth Martha, only child of Dr. C. A. Harley, died at
Orangeburg, S. C., Sept. 12th, 1864, aged 5 months and 2 days.

Mrs. Rachel O'Neall, wife of Rev. L. O'Neall, died in Orangeburg Dist., S. C., 5th Aug, 1864, in her 74th year....

Miss Matilda C. Freeman, daughter of Anderson and S. Freeman,
was born in Upson co., Ga., Nov. 27, 1833, and died in Lowndes
co., Ala., Aug. 26, 1864....

Issue of October 13, 1864

Married by Rev. J. M. Austin,Sept. 22, Mr. T. L. Smith, of
Morgan co., Ga. to Miss Laura H. Carpenter, of Elbert co.

On the 25th Sept., by Rev. R. E. Watkins, the Rev. J. Lee,
to Miss M. L. A. Mathis, both of Worth co., Ga.

Died near Whitesville, Ga., Sept. 22, 1864, James F. son of
J. F. and N. C. Speer, 2 years and 6 months old.

In Greensboro, Ga., Oct. 1, 1864, James Ogilby, eldest son
of Rev. W. C. and Mrs. A. Q. Bass, aged 6 years 5 months and 18
days.

Mrs. Malvina Tignor died in Grayton, Dooly co., Ga., Sept.
20, 1864, in her 35th year...left an orphan at an early age.
brought up by Frederick Green, Esq.,and his wife....

Rev. Jesse Sinclair was born in 1794, and died in Stewart co.,
Ga., July 19, 1864. (long account).

Lt. Thomas J. Carpenter of Genl Morgan's command, was born
in Elbert co., Ga., June 7th, 1840, and died June 13th, 1864,
at the house of Mr. Alberti, near Lexington, Ky.

Mrs. Mary Elizabeth Flournoy, wife of S. Josiah Flournoy,
and eldest daughter of Washington and Sarah Toney, all of Barbour co., Ala., died 25th Sept., in her 34th year..leaving two
infant children....

John Easterling Walker, eldest son of the Rev. Charles S. Walker (S. C. Conf)., was born Oct. 13, 1842, and was killed near Petersburg, Va., July 21, 1864....

Mrs. Henry Seibles was born Aug. 31, 1797, and died in Lexington Dist., S. C., Sept. 8th, 1864....wife and mother.

Edward C. Spann was born in Sumter Dist., S. C., May 15th, 1832, and died near Columbia, S. C., 28th Aug. 1864....

N. M. Stoudenmire, 3d Ala Regt., was born Oct. 14, 1840, and was killed at Spottsylvania, Va., 9th May 1864.

Lt. J. L. Wilkerson, 3d Ala. Regt, was born Dec. 31, 1843, and was killed at Spotsylvania, Va., May 12, 1864.

Jas. T. DeJarnette, in the 18th year of his age, was mortally wounded at Spotsylvania, and died 15th May...

P. G. Golson of 1st Ala. Regt was born 5th June, 1830, and was killed at Atlanta, Ga., on 28th July 1864....

Joseph A. B. Rylander, son of M. F. Rylander, and brother of Maj. Rylander, was killed in Virginia, born 13th Aug 1846, died 21st Aug, 1864.....

John Melson, 45th Ga. Regt Vols., son of W. P. and Della V. Melson, was born Sept. 25, 1829, and died near Atlanta, Aug. 7.

Magdalene Herlong, wife of Rev. H. C. Herlong, and daughter of the late John Minick, died on 12th Sept., in her 60th year.

Pvt. George W. Shelton of 2nd Miss Cavalry died 31st Sept., 1864, at Macon, Ga., in his 19th year.

Pvt. Stephen P. Hooker, of 7th Regt. Fla. Vols., of Manatee co., Fla., died ____ of pneumonia...left wife and two children.

John B.Martin, of 20th Ga. Battn., died at the hospital in Salisbury, N. C., Aug. 11, aged 41 years.

Mrs. Charlotte S. W. Nichols, wife of D. D. Nichols, and daughter of Eli and Catharine Lawler was born in Madison co., Ala., March 28, 1824, and married in Sumter co., Ala., Dec. 18, 1844, died in Coahoma co., Miss., Sept. 18, 1864.

Jas. A. Mann of 14th Regt. S. C. V., was born Aug. 3, 1831, and died June 6, 1864...left wife and child.

Robt. N. Shepard, 4th Fla. Regt., son of Rev. Zachariah Shepard, of Suwanee co., Fla., died at Rock Island, June 19, 1864, in his 22d year.

Martha A. P. Burnett, wife of Daniel Burnett, of Madison co., Fla., died May 25th, 1864, aged 41 years.

Also Capt. Peeler Burnett, of 3d Fla. Regt, son of Daniel Burnett, died in Miss., aged 20 years.

Also, Martha A. Burnett, died Aug. 16th, aged 11 months and 20 days.

Mr. John A. Collins, of 1st S. C. Rifles, was wounded May 12, and died May 28, 1864....

Issue of October 20, 1864

Married Oct. 5, 1864, by Rev. J. D. W. Crook, Mr. Peter Brunson of Barnwell Dist., to Miss Annie, daughter of B. H. and C. R. Welch, of Charleston, S. C.

On 5th instant, by Rev. J. W. Humbert, Capt. J. B. Humbert, 2d S. C. Artillery, to Miss M. Emma, daughter of Maj. Geo. H. Pooser, all of Orangeburg Dist., S. C.

In West Point, Ga., Oct. 4, 1864, by Rev. S. W. Dixon, Col. Saml S. Clarke, Agent Ga. Relief and Hospital Association, of Macon, Ga., to Miss Amanda B. Forest, of Heard co., Ga.

In West Point, Ga. Oct. 9, 1864, by Rev. R. W. Dixon, Mr. L. M. Harris, to Miss Anna M. Anderson, all of West Point, GA.

In Early co., Ga., Oct. 4th, by Rev. S. R. Weaver, R. J. F. Grist, to Miss Martha E. Cook, eldest daughter of Mrs. Sarah E. Cook.

Died in Winnsboro, S. C., August __, 1864, Mary D. Cauthen,

youngest child of M. and Mrs. J. C. Hall, aged 14 months.

Sister Catharine Leslie, was born in Chesterfield Dist., S. C. (her maiden name was Campbell), and died at Deactur, Newton co., Miss., August 4, 1864....

Mrs. Hessie Mildred Cooper, wife of Rev. Chas P. Cooper, and daughter of Col. Wm. H. and the late Mrs. Mildred L. Jackson, of Athens, Ga., died Sept. 26, at Newnansville, Fla., aged 37 years and 4 months; and their three children died at the same place: Wm Henry, aged 5 years and 4 months, on Sept. 22; Robert Harrison, aged about 3 years and 6 months, on Sept. 23; and Mildred Lewis, aged 6 years and 7 months on Sept. 25th....

Mrs. Susan E. Davidson, wife of Mr. J. C. Davidson, and eldest daughter of Rev. E.D. Cottrill, was born near Holly Springs, Miss.,on 17th Feb. 1838, and died at Bluff Springs, Fla. 7th Sept., 1864....

Mrs. Lucy J., wife of James Wall, died in Chester Dist., S. C., June 10th, 1864, in her 26th year.... Her little Willie died Aug. 19, 1864, aged about 4 years.

Sgt. Angus G. Calegun, of 15th La. Regt, was killed at Jonesboro', Ga., Aug. 31, 1864....

Rev. Wm. M. Graham, son of R. T. and E. Graham, of Cass co., Ga. died 16th Sept., 1864, at the General Hospital, Summerville, S. C., of a wound received at Fort Sumter, S. C., in his 34th year....

George L. Scott was son of David Scott, of Alachua ct., killed 11th Sept., near Petersburg....

Mrs.Julia A. Rhodes was born March 5th, 1815, in Beaufort Dist., S. C.,and removed with her parents to Fla., in 1827. In 1837, she was married to Mr. John H. Rhodes...died 21st Sept.

Sgt. J. L. Sherrod of 48th Regt. Ga. Vols., was born in Jefferson co., Ga., July 7, 1828...killed near Petersburg, 30th July 1864....

Lt. J. A. Sarvis 16th S. C. V., was killed before Atlanta, July 28th, 1864.

Capt. Reuben L. F. Richbourg of 19th S. C. Regt., son of Rev. J. S. Richbourg, was born 21st Jan. 1826, and died in Macon, Ga., Aug. 1864....

James Woodman of 21st S. C. V., died Oct. 1, 1864.

Capt. D. S. Wadsworth of Chesterfield Dist., S. C., died on 14th July 1864, in his 28th year in the General Hospital, Richmond.

John F. Bell, son of A. and M. E. Bell, was born in Stewart co., Ga., 1845, and killed at Jonesboro, Ga.,Aug. 31, 1864....

John W., son of H. A. and Sarah Cope, was born in N. C., Dec. 17, 1844, and died in Washington co., Ala., July 31, 1864.

Morgan B. Avant of Orangeburg Dist., S. C., 2d Artillery, S. C. V. died on 27th August, 1864, in his 39th year....

Mrs. Nancy B. McCullers, wife of Jordan B. McCullers was born in Pike co., Ga., March 16, 1824, and died in Baker co., Ga., August 19th, 1864...left husband and chidlren.

Capt. Calvin Logue, 22d Ga. Regt. was killed on 16th August, in his 40th year...

Dr. J. L. Crump, of 2nd Ga. M., was born in Emanuel Co., Ga., March 4, 1837, and died near Macon,Ga., 13th Sept., 1864....

Jas. W. Robertson, of 12th Ga. Regt, was killed 9th May, near Spotsylvania C. H., in his 27th year....

Mary J., wife of Thomas Cope, decd., died in Washington co., Ala., August 27, 1864...daughter of W. F. and Rachel Smith, of N. C. leaves three orphan children.

Miss Sarah Nelson Corby, of Micanopy, Fla., sister of Orrison Corby, of Augusta, Ga., was born in Hanover co., Va., and died at Kaolin, S. C., 18 August 1864, in her 73d year.

John D. Carroll was born in Chester Dist., S. C., 27 Feb 1839 and died in Orangeburg Dist., 9th Sept. 1864

Issue of October 27, 1864

Col. Wylie P. Hill, of Wilkes co., Ga.,died on 10th Sept.,
aged 45 years...left wife and children.
Miss Clara B. Clifton, daughter of Dr. A. S. and Mrs. C. A.
Clifton, died in Columbia, her native city, Sept. 7, 1864, in
her 25th year....
Sgt. Jas. McCalley Pooser, of 10th Fla. Regt., eldest son of
Adkinson and Sarah Pooser, of Alachua co., Fla., was born in
Orangeburg Dist., S. C., Dec. 17, 1833...married to Miss Mary
M. Barton, April 6, 1856, removed to Fla. in 1859, where on 17th
May 1862, he volunteered...died Sept 13, 1864.
Miss Sallie A. Massey died on 14th Sept., 1864, in Yorkville,
S. C. at her home.
Sgt. J. Wm. Rhaney, of Cobb's Legion, was born Jan. 7, 1842,
and died Aug. 26, 1864.
Corpl. D. S. Smyly, of 4th Regt. S. C. Cavalry, fell mortally
wounded, at Hawe's Shop, near Richmond, May 28th, and died May
30th....
John Murchison was born in Moore co., N. C., July 31, 1838,
and came to Crawford co., Ga., died June 25, 1864....
Sgt. J. P. Broom, son of B. F. Froom of Macon co., Ala., was
born Jan. 20, 1845, and was killed at Petersburg, Va.,Sept. 10,
1864.
Benjamin N. Wade, 2nd son of Isaac and Elizabeth Wade, aged
about 22 years, was killed 13th Aug 1864, near Atlanta, Ga.
Mrs. Phebe H. Lloyd was born near Coosawhatchie, Beaufort
Dist., S. C., Dec. 1804, and died on 25th Sept 1864, in her
60th year....
M. A. Hall, son of W. A. Hall of Wilkinson co., Ga., was
killed at Petersburg, Va.,on 30th July 1864.
R. B. Long was born in Russell co., Va., Jan. 29, 1807, in
1844 moved to Franklin co., and then to Gainesville, Sumter co.,
Ala....died 24th Sept.
Capt. G. M. Grimes, of Barnwell Dist., S. C.,was born May
24, 1832, and died 1st Oct. 1844....
Mrs. Victoria E. R. Rowland, died Oct. 5th, 1864, aged 22
years....
Mary Jane Sanders was born in Balden co., N. C., married
Francis C. Waldron, Nov. 17, 1834, and Oct. 6, 1860, Washington
Sanders, and died July 17, 1864, in her 49th year...joined the
Presbyterian Church in 1853.
Mrs. Nancy Elrod, wife of Thos P. Elrod, was born Feb. 28,
1802, and died July 25, 1864, in her 63d year.
Miss Louisa Margaret Shields, eldest daughter of A. J. and
E. Shields, was born in Autauga co., Ala., June 1838, and died
in Noxubee co., Miss., Aug. 27, 1864....
J. M. Hukins, of 17th Regt. Ga. Vols., was killed 15th July
1864, at Petersburg, Va., in his 23d year.
C. J. D. Utsey, of 11th Regt. S. C. V.,son of John and Rose
Ann Utsey, was born Dec. 18, 1841, and died at home 27th Sept.
1864
Tribute of Respect to Aaron Sewell, by Newton Circuit....

Issue of November 3, 1864

Married in Savannah, Ga.,on 5th Oct., by Rev. A. M. Wynn, Mr.
H. Harris Sasnett, of Spartan, Ga., to Miss Mary E., daughter of
the late S. J. M. Cubbedge, of the former place.
By Rev. N. K. Melton, Mr. Wm. Satterfield, of Spartanburg
Dist., to Mrs. Martha J. Christopher, of Greenville Dist., in
Bethel Church, Greenville Dist.,S. C., Oct. 16.
On 5th Oct.,by Rev. C. E. Land, Mr. Simon Beckham to Miss

Sarah Mobley, all of Lancaster Dist., S. C.

In Troup co., Ga., Oct. 4th, by Rev. J. B. McGehee, Rev. John R. Dearing of the Ga.Conf., to Miss Fannie E. Covin.

Died in Marietta, Ga.,May 17th, Victor Samuel, only child of Victor E. and Eliza A. Manget, aged 11 months.

In Loachapeka, Ala., Oct. 1st, Nettie Viera, daughter of Mr. and Mrs. Sadler, aged 23 months.

On 23rd Sept., 1864, in Troup co., Ga., at the residence of her grandmother Mrs. E. K. Taylor, Maggie Alice, infant daughter of J. T. And Rev. A. Johnson, aged 1 year, 11 months and 10 days.

In Charleston, S. C., on 11th Aug., 1864, Julia Elizabeth, child of Lovick P. and Elizabeth Murray, aged 3 years, 3 months and 4 days.

Mrs. Hariet Love died at the residence of her son-in-law, J. Ware, Esq., in Chambers co., Ala., May 23, 1864, aged about 50 years....

Thomas Crews died at Laurens C. H., S. C., on 19th August last, aged near 70 years...left twenty-four lineal descendants.

Lt. John M. Anderson, 18th S. C. V., was born in Spartanburg Dist., S. C., Sept. 28, 1836, and fell in front of Petersburg, July 30, 1864....

Frank J. Bohannan, a noble young Virginian, died at Lands Ford, Chester Dist., S. C., Aug. --, 1864, aged about 17 years... the youngest child of a widowed mother.

Robert Augustus Hayes died inThomasville, Ga.,on 5th Oct., 14th Aug. 1864, in his 26th year....

Capt. W. P. Strange was born in Anderson Dist., S. C.,July 16th, 1874...died in Jackson Hospital, Richmond, July 9, 1864.

Joseph H. Branch was born in Leon co., Fla., Oct. 15, 1844, and died in Tallahassee, on 13th Aug 1864...the only son of his widowed mother.

G. B. Medlock was wounded in the battle near Richmond, and died 20th Sept., aged 23 years....

Noah Cooper of 6th Regt. Militia, was born March 15, 1811, and died in Hospital at Mimer Station, Aug. 14, 1864....

Capt. W. D. Banks, was born 15th Jan. 1830, joined 39th Ala. Regt., ordered to the Army of Tenn...died August 1, 1864.

Lt. Eugene Banks, was born 23 April 1838, died at Resaca, 15th May 1864.

Watkins Banks, killed 11th August 1864...left four other brothers.

Jas S. Bonner was born in Ga., Jan. 27, 1801, and died Pike co., Ala., Oct. 8, 1864....

Jas. H. Chambers, a refugee from Cotoosa co., Ga., died in Clay co., Oct. 5, 1864, in his 56th year....

Bro. John V. Ozley died in Chambers co., Ala, after a whort illness.

Tribute of Respect to Rev. Thadeus Pennington....by Forsyth ct., Monroe co., Ga.

Issue of November 10, 1864

Married in Augusta, Ga.,on the 2d instant, by Rev. H. J. Adams, Mr. Jas. C. Waite to Miss Lucinda C. Bartlett.

In Oglethorpe co., Ga., on 25th Oct., by Rev. Dr. R. W. Hubert, Miss Sallie Dorough to Mr. John P. Hubert, of Warren co., Ga., and of the 5th Ga. Regt.

On 23d Oct., by Rev. J.H. Zimmerman, W. D. Sullivan of Hampton Legion, to Miss Hattie G., daughter of Rev. J. G. Humbert, all of Laurens Dist., S. C.

In Heapsville, S. C., on 3d Oct.,1864, by Rev. J. L. Sifley, Mr. Geo. W. Whaley to Miss Jane Heape.

Mrs. Harriet L. Clyde, relict of our beloved brother, Thomas M. Clyde (late of Pickens District) and mother of Rev. T. J. Clyde of the S. C. Conf., died Sept. 25, 1864, in her 50th year....

Rev. Wesley F. Parks, son of Rev. W. J. Parks, a local preacher, born Sept. 14, 1841, died July 23, 1864....

Capt. Henry P. Parks, a younger brother, was born July 12, 1837, and died July 21, 1864....

Lt. Frank J. Dickinson, of 57th Regt. Ala. Vols., died in Nomtgoery, Ala., at the Madison Hospital, July 22d, 1864, eldest son of Rev. J. P. Dickinson.

Mrs. Lavinia Carswell, widow of Jas. A. Carswell, late of Jefferson co., Ga., died Oct. 25th, 1864, in her 69th year... left an only brother (Hon. William J. Rhodes), three children....

Gabriel M. Johnson, son of Gideon T. and Mary M. Johnson, of Monroe co., Ga., died on 1st May 1864, in hospital at Richmond. Two years ago he removed to Alabama.

Edmund McGlaun, son of John and Nancy McGlaun, of 39th Regt. Ala. Vols., was born Jan. 11, 1837, in Muscogee co., Ga., and died in Henry co., Ala., June 23, 1864.

Alfred H. Hammond, son of Wm. and Lucy Hammond, late of Whitfield co., Ga. (now refugees) was born 31st March 1833, and died in Anderson Dist., S. C., 16th Oct. 1864....

Wm. H. Bowles, of 6th Fla. Regt, was born March 24, 1842, and wounded at Dallas Ga.,May 25th, and died August 19, 1864.

Jas. H. M. Mosely, of the same Regt.,was born.Jan. 13, 1833, died at the Fair Ground Hospital, Atlanta, 1864.

Reuben Cobb of 2d Fla. Regt. was born April 22, 1844, wounded at Petersburg, Va., Aug. 21, 1864...died August 22d....

James A. Parham was born in Marlborugh Dist., S. C.,Feb. 1829, and was killed 17th July, 1864, near Petersburg.

Joseph Lamberth, son of John and Permelia Lamberth, was born June 5, 1829, and died in prison (Camp Douglass, Ill.) July 27, 1864, aged 35 years.

Mrs. M. E. Carter, wife of Dr. L. D. Carter, died at the residence of her father, L. B. Suffell, in Louisville, Tenn., Aug. 17, 1864....

Andrew J. Peed of 59th Ga. Regt. Vols., was born 29th Dec. 1835....killed Deep Valley, Va.

Tribute of Respect by Socapatoy ct., Montgomery conf., to Wm. E. Young who died in a Northern prison, May 1864, in his 31st year.

Tribute of Respect by Fort Gaines Station, by Bro. Zachariah Spinks, who died in Fort Gaines, Ga., Oct. 20th, 1864, aged 38 years, 4 months and 21 days....

Issue of November 17, 1864

Lt. John P. Duncan, eldest son of the Rev. John F.Duncan, of Ga. Conf., who was killed near Petersburg, Va., Sept. 8, was born 15th May 1842, in Madison, Ga...left father, sisters and brothers.

Wm. Smith Patterson, the only son of Mrs. E. Leverton, and grandson of the Rev. Daniel Button, was born 5th May 1840, fell in Va., 30th Sept. 1864.

Iverson L. Graves died in Newton co., Ga., 29th Oct, 1864, aged 65 years and a few months....

Howard Simpson Bobo, younger son of Simpson and Nancy H. Bobo, was born in Spartanburg, S. C., Sept. 24th, 1846, and was killed in the Deep Bottom engagement, Va., Aug. 16, 1864.

Sgt. Alfred L. Robertson, of 12th Ga. Regt, was born in Talbot co., Ga., mortally wounded on 19th Sept., near Winchester, Va., aged 30 years.

Robt. B. Duval of Richmond co., Ga., 2d Ga. Batt. was born
July 23, 1841, and killed at Jonesboro, Sept. 1, 1864.
Wm. G. Bellamy, aged about 66 years, died on Oct. 14, 1864,
in Horry Dist., S. C.
Rev. Peter W. McDaniel was born in Chester Dist., S. C., in
1828...died July 9, 1864....
Mrs. M. A. H. McCoy, wife of Mr. F. B. McCoy, died in Talbot
co., Ga., on 11th Oct., in her 33rd year....
Danl. Carmichael, son of John M. and Sarah Carmichael, was
born July 11, 1864, died Aug. 14, 1864,in McFerrin Hospital, near
Forsyth, Ga.
I. S. Pace, of Tuskegee Light Infantry, 3d Ala. Regt, died
19th Oct., aged 25 years....
Mrs. Margaret Ann Jernigan, was born 12th Jan. 1845, left an
orphan when only 4 years of age, and her grandfather Jas. Dolvin
brought her up....(no date of death given).
Nathaniel C. Harrison, son of Alexander Harrison, was born
in Putnam co., Ga., Dec. 30th, 1830, 44th Ga. Vols., died Sept.
8th, 1864....
Sarah Davis, second daughter of James E. Heape, died on 9th
Sept., 1864, in Heapeville, S. C.,in her 14th year.
Matthew Saxon was born in Burke co., Ga.,died 17th Sept.,
at the Wayside Home at Millen.
Tribute of Respect by Bellevue ct., Ga. Conf. to James M.
Walker....
Tribute of Respect to Alexander Smith, born Dec. 8, 1805,
and died in Houston co., Ga., Oct. 21, 1864. married Mrs. Judith
Tison, in 1831....
Tribute of Respect to Danl. Hall, by Lexington ct., Ga. Conf.

Issue of November 24, 1864

Married by Rev. G. Hughes, at Gainesville, Ga., Nov. 3, 1864,
Rev. Wesley P. Pledger, Presiding Elder of the Dahlonega Dist.,
Ga. Conf. to Mrs. Susan W. Brewster, daughter of the late Dr.
Banks, of Gainesville, Ga.
By Rev. R. A. Conner, on 9th Nov., Oliver Hardy to Miss
Sarah E. Olive, daughter of Thomas Olive, of Columbia co., Ga.
Died near Shubute, Clarke co., Miss., on 29th Oct.,Ellen Lea,
youngest child of J. T. and M. M. Heard, aged two years and six
months.
Thos D. Kemp of 25th Ga. Vols. was mortally wounded above
Kennesaw Mtn., Ga., 28th May, and died that night, in his 22nd
year.
Sarah Savannah, daughter of James and Sarah Maxwell, died
on 28th ult., at Griffin,Ga.,aged 15 years and 6 months.
Col. Elijah M. Fields, of Clarkesville, Ga., died at Bethany,
Jefferson co., Ga., on 9th Oct., left wife and six children.
Mary Ann Snell, only child of Henry and Carrie Snell, of
Orange Parish, S. C., died 5th Nov. 1864....
Jackson Wilder was born in Georgetown Dist., S. C., and died
at the Jackson Hospital, in Richmond, Va.,on 12th July 1864...
left wife and four children.
Robt. H. Griffin, 2nd Regt. Ga. State Line, was born July 11,
1844, in Merriwether co., Ga., and was wounded near Atlanta, Ga.,
July 20, 1864....
Samuel Witherspoon was born at St. Andrews Bay, Fla., Aug.
28, 1852, and died in Mariana, Fla., Aug. 15, 1864.
Sophronia Witherspoon was born at St. Andrews Bay, Fla., Jan.
27, 1851, and died in Mariana, Fla., Oct. 25, 1864....
Robt. W. McKinen, son of Laughlin and Mary McKinen, of Telfair co., Ga., and grandson of the late Rev. Reddick Pierce,
died in hospital in Richmond, 8th July 1864, aged 18 years, and

4 months.

Mr. Jas. H. Brett, was born in Hartford co., N. C., Jan. 26, 1812, and died Sept. 29th, 1864, from battle of Mariana, Fla.

Mrs. Elizabeth Smith, wife of Rev. Joseph T. Smith, of the Ga. Conf., died at the residence of Rev. Milton C. Smith, in Thomasville, Ga., on 31st Oct., in her 52d year....

Sgt. Wm. F. Thompson 5th S. C. Cavalry, a native of Marion, and resident of Georgetown Dist., S. C., fell on 27th Oct., 1864, near Petersburg, Va.,aged 31 years....

Lt. Charles Wightman Williams son of Judge T. M. Williams, of Lowndesboro, Ala., was born Dec. 15, 1831, and in 1860 moved to Pensacola, Fla...married to Miss Martha ranch Thompson, July 19, 1859...moved to Camden, Ala...another son (Stephen) has fallen.

Mrs. Martha Ann Hunt, daughter of Capt. Lovick P. Thomas, died on 9th Nov., at the residence of her father, in Covington, GA.

Wilson W. D. Williams of 61st Regt. Va. Infantry, son of Dr. James H. and Parthenia Williams, formerly of Norfolk co., Va., but now of Shelby, N. C., was killed near Petersburg, Va., -- 27th, 1864.

L. L. Hook died 11th Sept. 1864, aged 41 years.

Issue of December 1, 1864

Married on Nov. 13, 1864, at the residence of Capt. D. J. McDonald, by Rev. N. B. Ousley, Rev. Isaac Munden of the Fla. Conf., to Miss Alice E. Meeks, of Bainbridge, Ga.

In Columbia, S. C., Oct. 27th, by Rev. Claudius Miller, Rev. L. B. Varn, of Colleton, to Mrs. Mary E. Wilson, of Charleston

On the 3d inst., at the residence of the bride's mother, Mrs. Nancy Bass, by Rev. Jos. S. Key, Mr. J. W. Sappington, to Mrs. Rebecca E. Stanley, all of Columbus, Ga.

At. St. Paul's Church, Columbus, Ga., on the 10th inst., by Jos. S. Key. Col. S. S. Scott, of Richmond, and Miss Mary Lula Hurt, of Columbus, Ga.

Oct. 18, 1864, by Rev. A. J. Dean, Mr. Benjamin H. Williams to Miss Mollie S. Beall, both of Hamilton, Harris co., Ga.

On 10th Nov., in Oglethorpe co., Ga., by Rev. E. G. Murrah, Mr. E. M. Cobb, of Carnesville, Ga.,to Mrs. M. L. Moody, of the former place.

Clarence Deleisline, infant son of Dr. W. J. and Mrs. C. J. Miller, died near Crayton, Barbour co., Ala., Oct. 9, 1864, aged 1 year and 25 days.

Sarah Eleanor, daughter of Jefferson and Mary A. Stokes, was born in Barnwell Dist., S. C.,July 7, 1863, and died Nov. 15, 1864.

Sallie E. McGehee, aged 5 years 10 months and 2 days,and John W. McGehee, aged 4 years and 4 months, children of Mrs. P. A. and Rev. E. A. McGehee, of the Ga. Conf., died Oct. 14th, and Nvo. 2nd, 1864.

Mrs. E. F. Fuller died in Marion Dist., S. C., on 31st Oct., in her 39th year....

Mary C. Clark, daughter of Mr. and Mrs. James W. Clarke, was born July 2, 1855, and died Oct. 14, 1864.

Claudia, eldest daughter of R. R. And M. E. Holmes died in Union Springs, Ala., on 2d Nov., 1864, aged 8 years and 5 months.

Cpl. Eli W. Geiger, 9th Fla. Regt., was killed 1st Nov., 1864, near Petersburg.

John Wright Melson, 45th Ga. Regt, was mortally wounded near Atlanta, Aug. 6, 1864, and died Aug 8th....

Jas. E. Heidt, was born in Macon, Dec. 14, 1838, his parents moved to Savannah...died 30th July....

Rev. Moses Coleman, was born Jan. 16, 1798, died 7th Nov. 1864.

Sgt. John D. Zuber, of 8th Ga. Vols., fell mortally wounded, 7th Oct., and died 14th Oct. at Richmond Va.

1st Lt. J. W. Trussell of 32d Ga. Regt. was killed on 12th Nov., at the commencement of the war he was living in Talbot co., Ga....

Rev. Wm. M. Wilson died 1st Sept. 1864....

Mrs. Nancy Ann Bradbury died in Talbotton, Ga.,Nov. 1st, 1864, in the 60th year of her age...a native of S. C.,but for many years a resident of Decatur, more recently of Atlanta....

Rev. Ira L. Potter was born April 16, 1794, and died in Lumpkin, Ga. Oct. 18, 1864, in his 71st year

Capt. Wm. M. Potter, son of Rev. Ira L. Potter, fell at Monocacy on 9th July 1864....

Saml. H. Hallford, son of Burrell and Nancy A. Hallford, was born in Darlington Dist., s. C., Oct. 18, 1805, and died in Dale co., Ala., Oct. 28th, 1864....

Saml. Jesse Hallford, of 11th Fla. Regt, son of Samuel H. and Zillah Hallford, was born in Dale co., Ala., May 24, 1845, and died in the General Hospital, Petersburg, Va., July 27, 1864.

Matthew Myrick, was born Aug. 11, 1838, and died Oct. 7, 1864, in Schley co., Ga.

Wesley Toomer Davis died at Wadesboro, N. C., Nov. 1, 1864, in his 36th year...born in Randolph co., N. C....

Mrs. Henrietta M. Dibble, only child of Saml. L. Wagner of Charleston, S. C. died on 2d Nov. 1864, in Columbia, S. C., leaving four daughters and three sons....

B. F. Hitch, 35th Ga. Regt. died at Field Infirmary, near Petersburg, Va., 7th.Nov.

Wm. Nathaniel Johnson, 15th S. C. V., was wounded on 8th May, and died on 22nd June....

Lt. D. R. Townes, of 8th Ga. Regt. and son of Col. J. R. Towers, 8th Ga. Regt and grandson of Rev. Wm. Magee, of S. C. was born March 15, 1844, and was killed in battle, Sept. 30, 1864....

R. Calvin Robinson, 17th Regt. S. C. V., died Sept. 16th, 1864, at Rock Hill, S. C., in his 42d year.

Mrs. Lucinda Cochran, widow of C. R. Cochran, died in McNairy co., Tenn., Nov. 8, 1864...born March, 5, 1794, in Edgefield Dist., S. C., daughter of Godfrey and Mary Ann Jones, married in 1817 to Jas. Richardson of Lexington Dist., S. C., who lived 11 years,leaving her a widow, the mother of 6 children, three of whom preceded him to heaven.... W. F. Richardson.

Andrew Govan Rowe, died on 21st Oct., in Orangeburg Dist., S. C., in his 37th year...when a small boy he emigrated with his sister to Miss....

John W. Turner of 50th Ga. Regt. was killed on 19th Oct., near Strasburg, Va.

Dr. C. D. Parks was born in Jasper co., Ga., and moved in 1854 to Fla., and died near Lake City, Nov. 11, 1863, in his 56th year....

Issue of December 8, 1864

Dr. James A. Turner, of Jonesboro, Ga., died in Oct., in the 42d year of his age...son of Rev. James B. Turner, late of the Ga. Conf....

Mrs. Matilda B. Morgan was born in Anderson Dist., S. C.,Feb. 12, 1808, removed to Ala. with her parents in Nov. 1843, was married 1834, and died Aug. 11, 1864....

Tribute of Respect by Conf. to Jas. H. Pitts, who died near Hayneville, Houston co., Ga.,Oct., 8., 1864, in his 37th year....

Tribute of Respect by Yorkville M. E. Sunday School, to Miss Sallie A. Massey.

Issue of December 15, 1864

Married on Thursday, Dec. 1, 1864, by Rev. John W. McRoy, Emanuel T. Pooser, Esq. to Miss Rachel Olivia Inabinet, both of Orangeburg Dist., S. C.

Thomas, youngest son of Dr. Geo. and Sarah Peets, of Pleasant Valley, Miss., was born Sept. 24, 1850, and died Oct. 28, 1864.

Lysander Royston, son of Lysander R. and Mary A. Moore, born June 19, 1863, and died in Lowndes co., Ala., Oct. 13, 1864.

Susannah Jane Lester, wife of Rev. A. H. Lester, of the S. c. Conf., and eldest daughter of N. William and Susan McCullough, of Williamsburg Dist., died in Greenville Dist., S. C., on 31st Oct. 1864, in the 27th year of her age....

Stephen S. Williams, of 3d Regt. Ala. Vols., son of Judge T. M. Williams, of Lowndesboro, Ala., was born in Yorkville, S. C., March 30th, 1838, died in hospital at Gordonsville, Va., on 8th June 1864....

Mrs. Mary A. H. McCoy, daughter of Charles and Sarah Allen, and wife of B. McCoy, died in Talbot co., Ga., 11th Oct., in her 39th year.... Sallie A. E.Greene.

Mrs. Elizabeth Stone, wife of Rev. J. B. Stone, of the Mobile Conf., was born in Abbeville Dist., S. C., Feb. 4th, 1837. Her parents moved to Monroe co., Miss., during her childhood. In 1857, married to an itinerant preacher....died 6th Nov.

Mary A. E. Snell, the only daughter of Mr. H. N. and Mrs. C. J. Snell, was born in Orangeburg Dist., S. C., Dec. 18, 1846, and died 4th Nov. 1864....

Jas. E. Ervin was accidentally killed 4th Nov...born in Lowndes co., Miss., 25th March 1846....

Mrs. Susan E. Woods, wife of Col. Richard Woods, died in Chester Dist., S. C., in her 44th year....

William Thomas Webb, son of Col. John F. Webb, died in Madison co., Fla., 31st Oct. 1864, in his 23d year....

Maj. John W. Hollymon of 5th Fla. Regt. died in Richmond, Va., Oct. 14th, 1864, aged 36 years....

Issue of December 22, 1864

Married by Rev. Atticus G. Haygood, Nov. 30th, in Walton co., Ga., Lt. Wilson, Cobb's Legion, Infantry, and Mrs. Roberta Christopher.

Nov. 17th, 1864, by Rev. S. B. Jones, Miss Fanny H., daughter of Dr. W. C. Norwood, to Lt. J. F. Townsend, all of Cokesbury, S. C.

Died on 17th Nov., Sarah Tillman Green, daughter of William M. and Elizabeth J. Green, aged 4 years, 1 month and 10 days.

At Grove Station, Dec. 3, 1864, an infant son of John and Emma M. Westfield, aged 4 days.

Near Charleston, S. C., Nov. 27th, Henrietta Angelina, infant daughter of Benj. W. and Mary E. Warren, aged 3 months and 18 days.

Dr. S. Wade Douglass, son of Dr. Jno Douglass,of Chester Dist., S. C., died at the Jackson Hospital, Richmond, Va., on 26th Sept., 1864, of a wound received near Petersburg.

John Garland Pettus, eldest son of Dr. John G. Pettus, of Jefferson co., Fla., died in the Federal field hospital at Atlanta, July 24th, 1864, in his 29th year....

Thomas Linton Pettus, second son of Dr. Pettus, was born Nov. 3, 1843,was wounded at Jackson, Miss., July 12th, 1863(sic), and died the next day.

Mrs. Elizabeth Murray, youngest daughter of the late Lewis Mallery, of Charleston, Died at Aiken, S. C., on 4th Dec., at the residence of Mr. Saml. A. Nelson, in her 39th year....

Maj. J. J. Underwood, died NOc. 3, 1864, in Hamilton co., Fla., aged 68 years....left wife, 6 daughters, 2 sons....

Margaret T., wife of Bro. William Stroman, died in Centreville, Fla., Nov. 16th, in her 41st year...left husband and children.

Jno. P. Askew, was born in Baldwin co., Ga., and died in Lawrenceville, Ala.,on 21st Oct.,1864, in the 37th year of his age....leaves an aged mother and many friends.

Mrs. Sarah Quillian, my wife, was born in Jackson co., Ga., Jan. 27, 1815, and died in Gilmer co., Nov. 8, 1864....

Archibald Asbury Mauldin, was born in Abbeville Dist., S. C., Dec. 20, 1833, and was killed at Jonesboro, Aug. 31, 1864.

(No issue December 29, 1864)

Issue of January 5, 1865

Married by Rev. John Calvin Johnson1 on 7th Dec., 1864, Mr. John K. Dossett ot Miss Hepzibah B. Ward, all of Clarke co., Ga.

By Rev. John Calvin Johnson, on 20th Dec., Mr. Moses N. Davenport, of Clarke co., to Mrs. Nancy A. C. Tillman, of Walton co., Ga.

On 21st Dec., by Rev. J. W. Kaigler, at the residence of Dr. D. A. Smith, in Macon co., Mr. Thos. L. Wilcox, of Irwin, to Miss Nancy S. E. Smith, of Henry co., Ga.

In Camden, S. C.,on Christmas day, by Rev. W. A. Gamewell, Mr. Millward W. Heats, to Miss Sarah E. Gamewell.

On 13th Dec., 1864, by Rev. J. R. Gaines, R. H. Allen, of Gwinnett co., Ga., to Miss Emily A. Hardaway, of Morgan co., Ga.

In Spartanburg, S. C., on 16th Nov., last, by Rev. A. W. Walker, Mr. T. H. Anderson of Laurens, to Miss Hattie E., second daughter of the late Rev. C. S. Walker, of S. C. Conf.

On 14th Dec., at the Methodist Parsonage, Tuskegee, Ala., by Rev. B. B. Ross, Rev. J. F. Ellison of the Montgomery conf., to Miss Cornelia Tullis, daughter of Rev. John Tullis, of Macon co., Ala.

On the 21st ultimo, at the residence of Lycurgus Rees, by Rev. a. B. Thrasher, Mr. J. F. Jones to Miss M. F. Neal, all of Columbia co., Ga.

Robert Lee, son of Dr. F. A. and Almira N. Thomas died at Oxford, Ga., Oct. 8, aged 2 years and 3 months.

Mrs. Nancy D. Anderson, wife of James C. Anderosn, decd., died in Clark co., Ga., Sept. 8, 1864, in the 75th year of her age....

Rev. Tilman Ansley died in Dale co., Ala., 2d Oct. 1864, in his 67th year....

Mrs. Mary T., wife of N. M. Barnett, and daughter of Thomas and Eliza M. Merriwether, died at the residence of her father, in Montgomery co., Ala., Nov. 16, 1864...married 16th of May 1861.

(No issue of January 12, 1865)

Issue of January 19, 1865

Married in Morgan co., Dec. 27th, by Rev. D. Kelsey, Mr. James N. Stanton, to Miss Eugenia S. Thompson.

On the 3d inst., by Rev. W. C. Rowland, Rev. Patrick H. Brewster, of Cherokee co., Ga., to Miss Pauline N. Law, daughter of Mrs. Mary Law, of Hall co., Ga.

On 1st Jan., 1865, at the residence of Mr. P. Ramsay, Columbia co., Ga.,the Rev. George Kramer, of the Ga. Conf. to Miss Jenney V. Hill.

In Walhalla,S. C., on 24th Dec.,by Rev. Fletcher Smith, Mr. H. C. Geherks, to Miss Agnes Issertell.

Died in Alexander, Ga.,Anna Forrester,infant daughter of William E. and Margaret E.Lasseter, aged 1 year and 6 months.

William T. Overby, was born in Burnswick co., Va., April 2, 1837, and hung by the enemy near Front Royal, Va., Sept. 23, 1864...7th Ga. Vols.

Lambeth Hopkins, Esq., was a native of Clark co., Ga., and died in Burke co., Ga., Dec. 2, 1864, in the 51st year of his age...member of St. John's M. E. Church.

Mariah A. Barker, died in West Point, Ga., Nov. 31, 1864, aged 15 years.

Cpl. B. B. Fortson, 63d Ga. Vols., eldest son of B. W. and Rebecca H. Fortson, of Wilkes co., Ga., died at Tuscumbia, Ala., 7th Nov., 1864, in his 22d year....

Rev. F. A. Quillian, son of Rev. Jas. Quillian, died in White co., Ga.,Nov. 23, 1864, in the 40th year of his age...left wife and children.

Benjamin H. Stroud of Crawford co., Ga., died in Thomasville Hospital, Dec. 14th....

Mrs. Missouri Lee died on 12th Dec.,at the residence of her parents, Burnt Corn, Ala., aged about 23 years...In April, 1862, she married to Dr. R. A. Lee, C. S. A.

My mother, Margaret West, died 18th Nov., 1864, at the residence of her daughter, Mrs. Eliza Butler, in Dooly co., Ga., aged 70 years....

Jonah M. Venning, Esq., of Charleston, died at Greenville, S. C., Dec. 15, 1864, in the 74th year of his age...member of the Circular (Independent) Church in Charleston....

Issue of January 26, 1865

Married at the residence of Jas. B.Neal, on the 10th inst., by Rev. A. B. Thrasher, Lt. George P. Stovall, to Miss E. A. Neal, all of Columbia co., Ga.

On 4th Jan., by Rev. E. H. Giles, Rev. Oscar A. Myers, of the Fla. Conf., and Miss Mattie E. McCall, of Gainesville, Fla.

By W. P. Pledger, in Athens, Ga.,Lt. J. H. Morgan, to Miss Eugenia H. Goode, late of Atlanta, Ga.

Jan. 15, 1865, by Rev. L. M. Hamer, Jno. W. King, Co. A., 21st S. C. V., to Miss Sallie, daughter of Rev. W. Wilson, of Marlborough Dist., S. C.

By Rev. E. Callaway, Nov. 17, 1864, at Brooksville, Noxubee co., Miss., Miss Sallie H. Dixon, to Dr. W. A. Beard, of Summerfield, Ala.

Miss Louisa H. M. Trippe, only child of Henry M. and Elizabeth M. Trippe, died in Eatonton, Ga., Oct. 26, 1864, in her 19th year....

Bro. John Trammell, an aged and venerable servant of God, died 23d Aug 1864, aged 84 years 5 months and 20 days. He was born in 1780 in ____ S. C., and was the eldest son of Thomas and Mary Trammell. He removed with his father from S. C. to Hancock co., Ga., and thence to Chambers co., Ala., in 1834, where he resided until his death. He was married to Mary Dickinson in 1807....

William Pembroke Sasnett, a native of Hancock co., Ga., died on 30th Dec.,1864, in Sparta, in the 28th year of his age.... W. J. Sasnett.

Pvt. Hayne H. Zeigler was born in Orangeburg Dist., S. C., March 6, 1844, and died in Woodstock, Va.,Nov. 19, 1864, from a wound in the Valley of Virginia....

Emeline Streeter was born March 1814, in Anson co., N. C.,
and died Dec. 5, 1864....

Sgt. William H. Strother of 27th Ga. Battn. died in a hospital at Guyton Station, near Savannah, Ga.,Oct. 14, 1864, of
typhoid pneumonia, in his 19th year....

Rev. Saml. Lander, Sr. was born in Tipperary, Ireland, on
12th Nov 1792, married to Miss Elizabeth A. Miller on 22d Oct.
1812, came to America in Sept. 1818...died at his home in
Lincolnton, N. C., 17th December 1864...(long eulogy),

Mrs. Eliza Forbes, wife of Gilbert Forbes, was born in
Reading, Conn., was married in Newark, N. J. in 1832, and came
to LaGrange, Ga., the same year...Here she died 8th Dec. in the
54th year of her age....

Freeman Ellis died in Greenville, Ala., Oct. 8, 1864. Only
14 years old, he joined the army last July. Two weeks more and
his widowed mother was childless...son of Rev. J. W. Ellis, decd.
of the Ala. Conf.

William H. Pace, was born in Augusta, Ga., May 29, 1830, and
died in Fort Valley, Ga., Nov. 22d, 1864.

John T. Murphy, only son of Rev. John and Nancy Murphy, of
the Ga. Conf...died in hospital in Summerville, S. C., Jan. 8,
1865. John Murphy.

Esther Ratcliff Curtis, died 6th Nov 1864, in Anson co., N. C.,
in her 40th year....

Issue of February 2, 1865

Lt. J. E. Barnett was born in Leaksville, N. C., 10 Dec.,
1819, and died in Auburn, Ala., 27th Dec. 1864....For a number
of years resided in Ala.

Adam C. Wells was born in Clarendon Dist., S. C., Nov. 3, 1841,
and died in Williamsburg Dist., S. C., Dec. 7, 1864.

Sarah D. Clark wife of Gen. Clark died at Social Circle,
Ga.,Dec. 16, 1864, aged 50 years and a few months....

Mrs. Elizabeth E. West, wife of E. T. West, Esq.,died in
Chesterville, on 3d Dec., 1864, aged 29 years, 3 months and 19
days....

DR. A. J. Gambrough was born 30th Jan 1830, and died 17th
Nov. 1864, in Marion co., Ga....

Lt. Geo W. Fisher 37th Ga. Vols. fell at Franklin, Nov.
30, 1864....

Elizabeth J., youngest child of J. E. and M. A. Stephens,
died in Berrien co., Ga., Oct. 11, 1864, in her 15th year.

Campbell Tison, of Effingham Hussars, 5th Ga. Cavalry, died
Aug. 27, 1864, in ths hospital at LaGrange, Ga., in his 25th
year....

Issue of February 9, 1865

Married on the 20th Jan. 1865, by Rev. D. D. Cox, Rev.
James T. Linn of Augusta', Ga., to Miss Mary F. Pace, of Covington,
Ga.

On 26th Jan., by Rev. E. P. Bonner, Mr. S. B. Slade, of
Nashville, Tenn., to Miss Annie Bynum, of Columbia co., Ga.

In Jefferson co., Ga., on 24th inst.,by Rev. D. R. McWilliams,
Rev. Henry l. Murphy, of the Ga.,Conf. to Mrs. Laura J. Nasworthy,
of Jefferson co.

By Rev. Saml. Smoke, of Jan 24, 1865, Sgt. J. R. Robinson, 10th
Fla. Regt., to Miss Mary Jane Smoke, of Orangeburg Dist., S. C.

In Tuskaloosa, Ala., Dec. 16, 1864, by the Rev. Dr. Summers,
Mr. Thos C. Sexton, to Mrs. Rebecca C. Groce, of Tuskaloosa co.

In Tuskaloosa, Ala., Dec. 29, 1864, by the Rev. Dr. Summers,
Lt. John C. Cade of Dayton, Ala., to Miss Sarah E. Jemison, of

Tuskaloosa.

In Tuskaloosa, Ala., Jan. 2, 1865, by the Rev. Dr. Summers, Capt. William Battle Fort, of Columbus, Miss., to Miss Sallie B., youngest daughter of the late Governor Collier, of Tuskaloosa.

On the 17th Jan. 1865, by Rev. T. A. Harris, Mr. Henry C. Fears of Madison, and Miss Mary E. Hebbard, of Elbert.

Died at the Parsonage, Bennettsville, S. C., Jan. 18, 1865, John Dilman, son of Rev. J. A. and A. C. Porter, 7 weeks old. Also, Jan. 21st, Mrs. Isabella St. Clair Porter, in her 74th year.

In Orangeburg Dist., S. C., on Sunday evening, Nov. 13, Emily Collins Albergotti, youngest daughter of Thos W. and Margaretta Albergotti, aged 4 years, 10 months and 29 days.

Col. W. J. Josey died in Albany, Ga., on 19th Dec., 1864, aged 36 years...for many years a citizen of Griffin, Ga.

Miss Abby Rush, fifth daughter of John and Elizabeth Rush, was born 12th Feb. 1844, and died 13th Dec. 1864, in Marion co., Ga...left mother, brothers and sisters.

Robt. H. Stafford of 12th Regt. Ala.. Vols. was born Sept. 24, 1842, and was killed at Cedar Creek, Va., Oct. 19, 1864.

Mrs. Hannah Peninah Dunlap, relict of Geo. Dunlap, died near Cedar Hill, Anson co., N. C., 25th Dec. 1864, in the 68th year of her age....

Mrs. Susannah Jane Traywick, died near White's Church, Anson co., N. C., Jan. 13, 1865, in her 28th year.... husband and two children.

Mrs. Matilda C McCay died in Tuscaloosa, Ala., Nov. 15, 1864, daughter of Marmaduke and Agnes Williams, born in Madison co., Ja.n 5, 1812, removed to Tuscaloosa in 1818....

Dr. Wm. A. Thomson, son of Dr. Matthew and Mrs. Arabella Thomson, was born Feb. 10, 1829, married Oct. 28, 1856, to Miss Susan Loftin, sister of Rev. John D. Loftin, died near Rocky Mount, in Montgomery co., Ala., Oct. 19th 1864.

Thos H. Rawlins was born in Gwinnett co., Ga., and died in Franklin co., Ala. 12th Sept., 1864, aged 27 years....

Issue of February 16, 1865

Mary Emily, wife of Rev. E. W. Story, of the Montgomery Conf., and daughter of Archibald and Mary Patterson, was born in Elizabethtown, N. C., July 12, 1815, and died in Macon co., Ala., Dec. 13, 1864....left husband and three children.

Mrs. Margaret Jones died in Camden, S. C., in her 79th year, Jan. 7, 1865. Her granddaughter Rachel B. Joy preceded her to a better world, Oct. 18, 1864, in her 20th year....

An elder sister, Elizabeth T., wife of Capt. Adam Team, also died in the same year, March 27th, in her 25th year...daughters of the late Rev. Jno. R. and Sarah A. Joy of Camden.

Mrs. Elizabeth C. Tison, wife of K. P. Tison, of Grffin, died Sept. 14, 1864, in the 68th year of her age...

Hon. Geo. S. Hooper died on 23d Nov. 1864, in the 64th year of his age..lived in Chester Dist., S. C., about 20 years. In 1855 he removed to Catawba co., N. C...member of the Legislature from Catawba co., N. C.

Rev. Jos Roy, of Telfair co., Ga., died 1st Nov., 1864, in the 65th year of his age....leave a large family.

Tribute of Respect to Joel Hamiter, by Enon Ct., Ala. Conf. Married in Montgomery, Ala., by Rev. Dr. McTyeire, on 12th Jan., Rev. J. W. Jordan of the Montgomery Conf. to Mrs. E. L. McCarter.

On 31st Jan. 1865, by Rev. W.H. Evans, Dr. W. W. Davenport, to Miss Sideny Tiller, all of Oglethorpe co., Ga.

On 25th Jan., by Rev. J. J. Seally, Rev. J. E. Dodd, of Thomasville, Ga., to Mrs. A. E. Pyles, of Alachua co., E. Fla.

Issue of February 23, 1865

Mrs. Judith Howard, widow of Gen. Nicholas Howard, died at the house of her son-in-law, E. H. Muse, in LaFayette, Ala., on 24th Jan., in the 72d year of age....

Lt. W. H. N. Murphy, son of S. Z. and M. A. E. Murphy, was born in Charleston, S. C., March 28, 1844, moved to Savannah, Ga., in 1851...died 6th Jan. 1865.

Elizabeth P. Phillips, eldest daughter of Gen. Wm. Phillips, died at the residence of her grand father, Dr. George D. Phillips, in Habersham co., on 22d Jan., 1865, aged 12 years and 11 months.

Dr. Saml. B. Clarke, a native of Burke co., Ga., died in Brothersville, Ga.,on 1st Feb. 1865, in the 53d year of his age.

Married at the residence of Wm. P. Robinson, in Mecklenburg co., N. C., on 31st Jan., by Rev. T. Z. Johnston, Capt. Wm. E. Ardry, Co. E. 30th N. C. T., to Miss Mag M. Robinson.

On 22d Jan. 1865, by Rev. E. G. Richards, Mr. Thomas A. Stevens, to Miss Mary J., second daughter of the Rev. N. C. Barber, of Chambers co., Ala.

Issue of March 2, 1865

Mrs. Cherry Bethune, relict of John Bethune, who departed this life in Columbus, Ga.,on 11th Oct. 1861, aged 91 years--died on 24th Dec. 1864, in Clayton, Ala., in the 81st year of her age....

Robert L. Rivesr, son of James H. and Harriet C. Rivers, was born in Pike co., Ga., Nov. 28, 1843, and died a prisoner at Elmira, N. Y., Sept. 20, 1864...13th Ga. Regt.

Anderson W. Moore, 31st Regt. Ga. Vols. son of James and Mary A. Moore, was born in Randolph co., Ga., Oct. 6, 1836...died Nov. 24, 1864....the last male member of his family...left three sisters.

Wm. James Duskin, son of j. L. B. and Mary Duskin, of 2d Regt. Ga. Vols., was born April 2, 1844, and died at his father's Oct. 23, 1864....leaves parents, brothers and sisters.

Henry T. Sherman, was born Dec.19, 1829, and died Dec. 21, 1864... tribute of respect from Lumpkin, Ga.

Tribute of Respect by Weston Ct., to J. H. Reddick....
Married on the 8th Feb., in Columbia co., by Rev. R. J. Harwell, Mr. C. G. Welborn to Miss Mary A. Young.

Issue of March 9, 1865

Wm. B. S. Gilmer for many yaers a citizen of Chambers co., Ala., and for the last few years a resident of LaFayette, died on 5th Jan., 1865, in the 69th year of his age....(long eulogy)

Lt. James J. Norman, 15th Ga. Regt., was born in Elbert co., Ga., and killed in the engagement of Fort Harrison, near Richmond, on Sept. 29, 1864, in the 23d year of his age....

Miss Mollie J. Moore, daughter of Dr. and Theresa Moore, died near Wattior Stand, Ala., Feb. 6, 1865....

Hon. J. H. Johnson, Senator form the 36th Dist., of Ga., died at his residence in Coweta co., Nov. 13, 1864, in the 57th year of his age....

Mrs. Elizabeth C. Tison, wife of Dr. K. P. Tison, died in Griffin, Ga.,Sept. 13, 1864, in her 68th year....

Elizabeth E. McBride was born March 20, 1823...died at the residence of her husband in Wilcox co., Ala. (no death date)

J. H. Finley, of Orr's Rifles, was born 3d April 1846, and died 3rd Nov 1864....3rd son of Jos and Matilda Finley.

Issue of March 16, 1865

Privates John and A. S. Durant were the first and third sons of the late Rev. H. H. and Mrs. M. T. Durant. John Durant, Palmetto Sharpshooters died near Darbytown Road, Va., on 8th Oct. 1864. Andrew Soule Durant, Palmetto Sharpshooters, died at Jackson Hospital, Richmond, 2d July 1864, in the 19th year of his age....

Mrs. Sarah Read, relict of the late Hon. Jas. Read was born May 15, 1802, and died in Newton co., Ga., Feb. 17, 1865....

Sgt. Jas W. Sandlin, of 35th Ala. Regt., was born in Lawrence co., Ala., in 1843, and was killed at Franklin, Tenn., Nov. 30th, 1864....

David Swicord died at his residence in Decatur co., Ga., Jan 29, 1865, in the 83d year of his age....

Tribute of Respect to Bro. Iverson L. Graves by Newton ct.

Issue of March 23, 1865

My father,Beverly Allen, was born in Jackson co., Ga., and died in Forsyth co., Ga., 21st Oct. 1864, in his 69th year... W. G. Allen.

Mrs. Rebecca Johnson, was born March 17, 1795, and died March 9, 1865....

Married by Rev. J. Blakely Smith, in Meriwether co., Ga., Feb. 17th, Lt. Curran R. Womble, C. S. A., to Miss India M. Harris of said co.

By Rev. J. Blakely Smith, in Meriwether co., Ga.,Feb. 22, Mr. Robert S. Parham of said co., to Miss Fannie T. Ware of Mississippi.

By Rev. A. J. Dean, Dec. 20th, Mr. C. W. Hines to Miss M. A. Houghton, all of Harris co., GA.

By Rev. A. J. Dean, Feb. 2, Mr. J. F. Sopeland of Hancock co., Ga.,to Miss M. J. Bridges of Harris co., Ga.

By Rev. Mr. Munroe, Jan. 5th, at Mt. Pleasant, Dr. Willoughby Barton of Burke co., Ga., to Miss Anne E. Etter of New Orleans.

By Rev. J. D. Anthony, on Tuesday evening, 7th March, 1865, Thos. N. Mimms and Harriet Missiour Northington, daughter of J. T. Northington, all of Washington, Ga.

On the 1st of March 1865, near Greenville, Ala., by Rev. Jno. A. Ellis, Rev. Wm. H. Morris of the Montgomery conf. to Mrs. E. Cathrine Payne.

Issue of March 30, 1865

Mrs. Francis A. E. Burkhalter, daughter of Judge Travis A. D. Weaver, of Thomaston, Ga., was born 15th Oct. 1830, married to Mr. J. T. Burkhalter,on 16th March, 1854, and died in Buena Vista, Ga., 1st Jan. 1865...mother of five children. (long eulogy).

Capt. Thomas Winston of Troup co., Ga., died 12th Dec., at the age of 84 years...his children of three generations... father of seven children. (long eulogy).

Absalom O. Hardy, of 30th Ga. Regt, and son of Wm. W. and Mary V. Hardy, in his 22d year, fell on 30th Nov., at Franklin, Tenn....

Alexander M. Kimbrough was born Nov. 17, 1837, and died Feb. 4th, 1865....

Nelson Lane, of Houston co., Ga., died __ Jan. 1865 in Conf. service.

Tribute of Respect to Fletcher A. Quillain by Clarkesville circuit, Ga. Conf.

Issue of April 6, 1865

George M. T. Crawford, of Decatur co., Ga., died in the hospital in Augusta, in his 35th year....

Wiley Richard Jones, the only son of W. E. and M. E. Jones, was killed on 6th Feb., 64th Ga. Regt. near Petersburg, Va.

William T. Malone, of the 5th Ga. Cavalry, died in his 42d year, in Waynesboro, Ga.,on 9th Dec.,1864...

Susan A. C. Thrasher wife of Dr. L. G. Anderson, died in Morgan co., March 4th, 1865, in her 40th year....

Died in Columbia co., Ga.,March 3, in her 47th year, Mrs. Martha M. Bonner, wife of Rev. E. P. Bonner....

James P. Passmore, son of brother M. Passmore, of Taylor co., Ga., was born July 4, 1836, and died Oct. 15, 1864 in Point Lookout prison.

Laura J. DeGraffenreid, wife of Capt. C. T. DeGraffenreid, and only daughter of R. H. Wooten, died in Mitchell co., Ga., on the 25th of Feb. 1865, aged 29 years....

Issue of April 13, 1865

Henry Meriwether only son of Thomas M. Meriwether of Newton co., Ga., died in hospital, near Petersburg, Va., on the 6th Feb., in his 18th year....

Emma L. Lamkin died on 10th Feb. in the 26th year of her age...

W. C. Gathright of Oxford, Ga., was born July 18, 1814. At one year old left fatherless, and at four year of age left without a mother...died Feb. 12, 1865....

George W. Watts, son of Rev. George Watts and brother of the Rev. William M. Watts, of the Ga. Conf. was born 10th Feb., 1837, and died at his father's in Marionco., Ga., 9th March 1865...

John F. Stearns son of Rev. Zachariah Stearns died in Talbot co., Ga., Dec. 24, 1864....

Died on 15th Feb., 1865, Mary Nancy Tallulah Talley, youngest child of Rev. W. R. Talley and S. J. Talley of the Montgomery conf. aged 1 year, 7 months and 15 days. in Greenwood, Fla.

Married at Talladega, Ala., on Sunday 12th ult., by Rev. Daniel Duncan, Capt. Richard H. Hays, of 5th Conf. regt., Memphis, Tenn., to Miss Rena, daughter of Rev. D. Duncan, of Montgomery Conf.

Married by Rev. W. R. Talley on the 14th March, 1865, Mr. David Collins to Miss Permelia A. Harden, all of Jackson co., Fla.

(publication ceased until June 29, 1865)

Issue of June 29, 1865

Married on 16th of March, 1865, by Rev. J. M. Lowery, Lt. Thomas M. Freeman to Miss Celia Vanlandingham, of Wilkinson co., Ga.

On the 4th of April, 1865, in Albany, Ga.,by Rev. T. S. L. Harwell, Rev. R. N. Andrews, of the Ga. Conf., to Miss M. Virginia Sutton, of Albany.

In Wilkes co., Ga., on 4th April, by Rev. H. J. Adams, James W. Boyd, of Columbia Co., to Miss Annie E., daughter of B. W. Fortson, Esq.

On the 9th April, by the Rev. M. A. Leak, Mr. J. B. Bryant, to Miss Rebecca E. Turner, all of Henry co., Ga.

Died on 14th March, 1865, G. Mayhorn, Co. B., 55th Ga. Regt., at the residence of C. A. Grasser, Fort Motte, St. Matthews Parish, S. C.

In Washington, Ga., April 8th, Charles Wesley, only son of
Rev. J. M. & Orillia S. Austin, aged 6 months and 12 days.
Sarah Isabella, daughter of Zaccheus and Mary C. Price, and
wife of Dr. Robt. W. Lovett, died on 29th Nov., 1864, in the
27th year of her age....
Osborne Rogers Stewart, only sonof Goerge and Mary Ann Stew-
art, was born on 17th April 1845, and died 16th Jan., 1865, of
wounds received at Franklin, Nov. 30, 1864....
Rev. Thomas Clifft died, at his residence in Brooks (formerly
Lowndes) co., Ga...between 80 and 90 years of age....leaves
children and grandchildren.
Hon. Madison Perry died in Alachua co., Fla., on the 8th
March 1865, in the 52nd year of his age...native of S. C., where
he resided until about 18 years ago, when he removed to Fla.
Mrs. Agnes E. Garrison died at the residence of her brother,
J. G. Faulkn,er of Micanopy, Fla., April 4, 1865.

Issue of August 31, 1865

Died in Macon, Ga., on 27th of June, John Latimer, only son
of Dr. William H. and Mrs. Rebecca A. Felton, formerly of
Cass co., aged about 11 years.
Valinda Balsora Troutman, eldest daughter of M. L. and M. B.
Troutman, died at fort Valley, May 27, 1865, aged 11 year 5
months and 22 days....
Dr. James Myrick died in Montoe co., Ga., July 26, 1865, in
the 78th year of his age...born in Southampton co., Va.,in 1788,
and emigrated to Ga. in 1809....
Alexander W. Robison,fell in the recent attack made upon
Columbus, Ga. He was the son of Rev. W. W. Robison, and in the
17th year of his age....
Thomas Dawson, Threewits, the only son of T. P. F. and Anna
W. Threewits, died in Wynnton, on 10th July, aged 27 years....
David Wright died in columbus, Ga.,June 6, 1865, in his 63d
year....
Mrs. Mattie S. Greene, consort of Maj. Charles H. Greene, and
second daughter of S. C. and M. T. Thompson, died at the residence
of her parents in Union Springs, Ala., on the 13th of August,1865.
Born March 10, 1845...married Nov. 25, 1862.
Tribute of Respect by St. Paul's Church, to J. E. Hurt.

Issue of September 21, 1865

Mrs. Nancy Jones Hurt, wife of George Troup Hurt, and daughter
of the late Dr. Abner H. Flewellen, of Columbus, Ga., died at the
residence of her husband in Russell co., Ala., on the 23d ult.,
aged 34 years....

Issue of October 5, 1865

Married by Rev. G. W. MacDonell, Aug. 10, 1865, Mr. J.
Flournoy Adams, of Eatonton, Ga., to Miss Fannie E. Moore, daughter
of Col. Green Moore, of Greene co., Ga.
By the same, Sept. 7, 1865, Judge Saml Pearson to Miss Fannie
Bedell, all of Putnam co., Ga.
By the same, Sept. 20, 1865, Mr. C. J. DeGraffenreid, of
Mitchell co., Ga., to Miss Julia F. Pearson, daughter of Judge
S. Pearson, of Putnam co.
In Macon, Ga., Sept. 28th, by Rev. J. W. Burke, Mr. Aaron J.
Meeker to Miss Demaris D. Hopkins, all of Macon, Ga.
In Macon, on 26th Sept., by Rev. Charles R. Jewett, Mr.
Dominic Barrett to Miss Mary Sinclair.
Died in Richmond co., Ga.,Aug. 18, 1865, Emily Plympton,

youngest child of Rev. I. S. and Mrs. Emily H. Hopkins, aged 18 months.

Mrs. Elizabeth A. Carlton, wife of James R. Carlton, Athens, Ga., was born 19th Feb. 1802,and died 13th May, 1865...joined Presbyterian Church in 1816...joined M. E. Church directly after her marriage which was 25th day of Nov., 1819....

William J. Thomas was born in Monroe co., Ga.,August 6, 1835, and died in Macon, Ga., August 26, 1865, having just completed his 30th year...married Dec. 20, 1860, to Miss Julia Wright....

Luther C. Peck died at Dawson, Ga., July 11th, 1865, in the 25th year of his age...joined the Baptist Church.

Bro. Richard Brinn was born in Buford co., N. C., Aug. 27, 1796, and died in Macon, Ga., July 26, 1865....

Mrs. Candace Sacrae, died in Macon, Ga.,on 27th inst., aged 78 years....one of the first settlers of Macon.

Issue of October 26, 1865

Married by the Rev. W. J. Cotter, on 5th Oct., W. J. Banks to Miss Mary Williams, all of Monroe co., Ga.

Died in Zebulon, Pike co., Ga., on 3d July, 1865, Jas. O., infant son of Rbot. A. and Rebecca A. Seale, aged 17 months and 29 days.

Mrs. Georgiana Baugh, wife of Col. Robert Baugh, was a native of Edgefield Dist., S. C., born Nov. 12th, 1826, and died in Atlanta, Ga., Sept. 1, 1865...removed with her husband to Ala....

Mrs. Mary Flournoy Schley, wife of Dr. W. K. Schley, died at Columbus, Ga., Wed., Sept. 29, 1865, in the 48th year of her age ...the third of three successive daughters, all of them now gone to the grave. We raised eight children--four sons and four daughters.... L. Pierce.

Martha T. Lupo, wife of Rev. J. L. Lupo, of the Ga. Conf., and daughter of Henry and Mary Leitner, was born in Richland Dist., S. C.,Jan. 19, 1828, and died in Pike co., Ga., Sept. 15, 1865....

Wm. Malthie, Esq., died in Lawrenceville, Ga.,on 24th Sept., in the 82d year of his age...a native of Fairfield, Conn., but for more than 40 years a residence of Lawrenceville....

Issue of November 2, 1865

Mrs. J. L. A. Griswold, died Sept. 2, 1865, at the residence of her son-in-law, Col. J. M. Hill, aged 56 years....

Bro. Wm. Budd was born on the 12th of Sept., 1790, and died in Monticello, Fla., on 29th of June, 1865...native of Charleston, S. C., whence he moved to Fla in 1830....

Issue of November 16, 1865

Mrs. Martha W. Brown, daughter of Benj. and Anna Wharton, of Athens, Ga., formerly of Murfreesboro, Tenn., and wife of Rev. Thos F. Brown of Tenn Conf. was born in Page co., Va., near Luray, Aug. 29, 1843...married Oct. 6, 1859, and died at the home of her brother, Oct. 13, 1865....

Mrs. Martha Alexander wife of Judge Lewis Alexander, died in Tuskegee, Ala., May 25th, 1865...leaves husband and four children.

Issue of November 30, 1865

Married on the 14th Nov., near Newnan, Ga.,by Rev. James Stacy, Rev. W. A. Parks, of the Ga. Conf. and Miss Annie D. Moore.

Also, at the same time, and place, and by the same, Robert
Early of Memphis, Tenn. and Miss Sallie J. Moore.
On Nov. 12th, in Baker co., by Rev. Henry D. Moore, John M.
Bowman, of Macon co., to Miss Julia F. Norris.
Thomas Alston Harris was born in Edgefield Dist., S. C., in
the year 1814. At the age of fifteen he removed to Ga., to
Macon. In 1842, he married a daughter of George Hines....died
15th Sept. ultimo.
The Rev. Wm. J. Sasnett, D. D., departed this life at his
farm in Hancock co., Ga.,on the morning of the 3d Nov., born and
reared in Hancock co.
Mrs. Henrietta Washington Audas, wife of T. S. Audas, Esq.,
died at Sparta, Ga.,Sept. 15, 1865, aged 65 years. She was the
youngest and last child of the venerable Philip Turner, late of
Hancock co....Her nephew, Dr. Sasnett had been designated to
write this obituary....
Margaret E. Cater died on 10th Nov., 1865, in the 17th year
of her age....

Issue of December 7, 1865

Married in Columbus, Ga.,at St. Paul's Church, Nov. 18th, by
the Rev. R. M. Saunders, Mr. Frank N. Graves, of Lumpkin, Ga.,
to Miss Myra J. Norris, of Columbus.
At. St. Paul's Church, Nov. 16th, by the Rev. R. M. Saunders,
Dr. Jas. T. Persons, of Hurtville, Ala., to Miss Jennie Bass,
of Columbus.
At. St. Paul's Church, Nov. 16th, by Rev. R. M. Saunders, Mr.
Jas. H. Conway, to Miss Bertha E. Lawrence, all of Columbus.
Nov. 16th, by the Rev. R. M. Saunders, Mr. W. T. Key, of
Montgomery, Ala., to Miss Mary Smith, of Columbus.
Oct. 31st, by Rev. W. W. Oslin, Mr. O. R. Belcher, Jr. to
Miss Martha L. Slaughter, all of Jasper co., Ga.
Mrs. Hannah L. Wimberly, widow of Col. James Wimberly, lately
decd. of Muscogee co., Ga., died in Columbus, Ga., in her 74th
year....

Issue of December 14, 1865

Married in Bishopville, on the 30th Nov. '65, by Rev. W. W.
Mood, Capt. William J. McLeod, of Lynchburg, S. C., to Miss
Amanda M., daughter of William Rogers, of Bishopville, S. C.
At the same time and place by the Rev. Wm. W. Mood, Mr. Henry
G. Scarborough, and Miss Maria A.,daughter of Mr. William Rogers,
all of Bishopville, S. C.
On the 19th inst., at Flat Shoals, by Rev. Chas. A. Fulwood,
Mr. L. A. Sallee of Arkansas to Miss Julia C. Williams, of Mer-
riwether co., Ga.
On the 22d inst., by Rev. Chas. Fulwood, Mr. John J. Farley,
to Miss S. E. Davis, all of Griffin, Ga.
In Houston co., Ga., on the 8th Nov., by the Rev. Dr. Myers,
Nathan H. Bass, Esq., of Macon, and Miss Valeria Gunn of the
former county.
On the 31st of Oct., 1865, by Rev. James O. Branch, at the
residence of Dr. B. W. Taylor, Junius Turnbull and Miss Willie
Bellamy, all of Monticello, Fla.
Mrs. Mary Ellen Chesnut, wife of Mr. George Chesnut, of
Tenn., and daughter of Dr. John W. and Harriet A. Strother,
died on 19th Nov 1865 at her home in Bainbridge, Ga.
Mrs. Fanny T. Moore died in Athens, Ga.,Sept. 19, 1865.
She had reached her 78th year, surviving her husband, three
married daughters and numerous grand children....

Married on the 7th inst., by Rev. P. M. Ryburn, Mr. B. J.
Hill and Miss Nettie O. Alexander, both of Monroe co., Ga.

On the 7th Dec., by Rev. R. W. Bigham, in Eatonton, Ga.,
Capt. Alex. H. Reid, and Miss Mary A. Rogan, formerly of Knoxville, Tenn.

In Talboton, Ga., Nov. 14th, by Rev. G. H. Patillo, Lt. Robt
A. Mizell and Miss M. S. Dozier.

In Talbotton,Ga.,Nov. 15th, by Rev. G. H. Patillo, Mr. Abner
A. Turner and Miss Carrie E. Jones.

On 6th Dec., by Rev. A. M. Thigpen, Dr. Irby H. Harrison, and
Miss Sallie Parks, daughter of Rev. J. W. Parks, of the Ga. Conf.

On Oct. 10th, by Rev. S. H. J. Sistrunk, Mr. Larkin Stewart,
of Jones co., and Miss Kittie Bryant, of Houston co., Ga.

In Fort Valley, Nov. 31st, by Rev. T. B. Russell, Mr. Henry
C. Harris and Miss Stella Marshall.

In Marshallville, Dec. 12th, by Rev. T. B. Russell, Dr. J. M.
Simmons and Miss Mary E. Slappey.

In Greene co., on Oct. 24th, by Rev. Albert Gray, Dr. R. W.
Lovett of Scriven co., and Miss Marietta A. Smith, of the former
place.

In Newton co., on Nov. 7th, by Rev. Albert Gray, Hardy Treadwell and Miss Mary C. Henry, both of Newton co.

On Nov. 22d, by Rev. W. W. Oslin, Dr. Fleetwood Walker, and
Miss Lucy A. Burney, all of Monticello, Ga.

On Nov. 22d, by Rev. E. H. Henry, C. G. Talmage, of Athens,
and Miss Georgia McDowell, of Jasper co.

On Oct. 29th, by Rev. J. D. W. Crook, at the residence of
S. S. Haigler, in Orangeburg Dist., S. C., L. H. Shuler and Miss
R. A. Dantzler, both of orangeburg Dist.

On Nov. 2, by Rev. J. D. W. Crook, Dr. J. W. Summers and
Miss M. A. Haigler, all of Orangeburg Dist., S. C.

On Oct. 26, by Rev. J. Blakely Smith, John B. Weaver, of
Barnesville, and Miss Mattie C. Carter, of Merriwether county.

Died in Clarendon Dist., S. C., Mary Elizabeth, daughter of
Dr. John L. and Maria J. Dinkins.

Rev. Windsor Graham was born in Richmond county, N. C., but
for many years was a citizen of Jackson co., Ga...died 21st
Jan 1865.

Rev. W. W. Robison was born in Washington co., Nov. 20,
1809. He lost his mother when five years old....leaves a widow
and tow children.

Miss Sarah J. Lin, was born in Wrightsboro, Columbia co.,
Sept. 21, 1826, and died in Augusta, Ga.,June 1, 1865....

Mrs. Mary M. Treadwell, daughter of Wm. and Catharina Ott
died in Eufaula, Ala., on the 6th of Oct., 1865, in the 48th
year of her age....

Mrs. Nancy Thompson, daughter of Rev. Benjamin Haygood, decd.,
died at the residence of her sisiter, Frances Stroud, in Monroe
co., Ga., on 19th ult., in her 84th year....

James S. Stockdale was born in County Down, Ireland, July
18, 1787, emigrated to the U. S. in 1793...died at his house in
Talladega co., Ala., on 24th Nov. 1865.

Cenia Black was born Dec. 4, 1821,and died at Oak Hill, Ga.
Sept. 5, 1865...daughter of Shelby and Rhoda R. Downs...left
husband and six children.

Bro. Ebenezer Tilley was born in N. C. and died in DeKalb
co., Ga. 29th of August...

John E. Smith, son of Lawrence and Caroline Smith, was born
April 18, 1837, and died Oct. 17, 1865, in Pike co., Ga....

Issue of January 5, 1866

Married on the 12th of Dec., by the Rev. Thomas G. Scott,
Maj. John T. Murphey, of Monroe co., Ga., and Miss N. P. Stephens,
daughter of Jesse Stephens, of Upson co., Ga.
On the 20th of Dec., by Rev. James Griffith, at the residence
of F. S. Rucker, Butler, Ga. M. P. Hollis of Calhoun co., Ga.
ON the 14th of Dec., by the Rev. C. A. Mitchell, Mr. S. A.
Baldwin, of Talbot co., Ga., and Miss M. E. Searcy, of Taylor
co., Ga.
By the Rev. H. J. Evans, Dec. 19, 1865, Mr. Wm. W. Shields,
son of Maj. Jos. Shields, and Miss R. Jane Higgins, daughter of
John and Rebecca Higgins, all of Walker co., Ga.
On the 19th Nov., by the Rev. G. W. Yarbrough, Dr. James W.
Herty, of Milledgeville, and Miss Mary Fannie Bonner, daughter
of Oliver Bonner, of Baldwin co., Ga.
Died on the night of the 28th of Nov., David Kendall, son
of the late Dr. David Kendall of Bellwood Farm, Upson co., Ga.
Carrie Will Evans, step-daughter of the Rev. J. M. Dickey of
the Ga. Conf., was born Oct. 12, 1856, and died in Warrenton,
Ga., Nov. 27, 1865, of diptheria.
In Augusta, Ga., John Franklin, eldest son of Rev. John M.
and Ann E. Dickey, aged nearly 6 years.
Myles E. Greene was born Feb. 6th, 1826, and died in Fort
Valley, Ga., Dec. 8th, 65....
William H. Anthony died inColumbia co., Ga., Oct. 25, 1865,
in the 46th year of his age....
Elizabeth McLaughlin was born Oct. 1792, the daughter of
Thomas and Margaret Hall of Oglethorpe...married to George Mc-
Laughlin, Sept. 24, 1818, and died April 27, '65.

Issue of January 12, 1866

Married on the 17th Dec., 1865, at White Sulphur Springs,
Fla. by Rev. W. H. Hunt, Robert L. Wiggins of the Fla. Conf. and
Mary Hardee, daughter of J. N. B. Goodbread, late of Suwannee
county.
On 2nd Nov., by Rev. R. A. Conner, Mr. R. W. Verdery and
Miss Georgia A. Leonard, all of Columbia co., Ga.
In Brooksville, Noxubee co., Miss., Dec. 19, by Rev. Joshua
T. Heard, Rev. Joseph B. Stone of the Mobile Conf. and Miss Mary
B. Koger, of Brooksville.
On Chunnenuggee Ridge, Ala., Dec. 24th, by Rev. F. X. Forster,
Mr. J. R. Herrin and Mrs. Sarah A. Hetur.
In Houston co., Dec. 25th, by Rev. S. H. J. Sistrunk, Mr. W.
D. Morris and Miss Mollie Hogan.
In Houston co., Nov. 30th, by the same, Mr. T. W. Cox, and
Miss Nora E. Singleton.
By Rev. G. C. Clarke, in Fort Valley, Dec. 29th, Mr. W. B.
Dasher and M. J. Walden.
On Dec. 7th, in Hancock co, by Rev. B. F. Breedlove, Junius
W. Branham of Oxford, and Miss Laura Jane, daughter of Rev.
Dr. Wm. J. Sasnett, deceased.
Mrs. Mary A. M. Moore, wife of Col. R. H. Morre, died in
Floyd Springs, Oct. 25, 1865, aged 51 years...born in Columbia
co., Ga., 1814....
Elizabeth J. W., wife of T. S. Hunt and daughter of W. H.
Simmons, died at her father's residence in Pike co.,on the 30th
April in the 39th year of her age....
Josiah Holmes late of Barnesville, Ga., was born about the
year 1790...married about the year 1812....

Issue of January 19, 1866

Married in Houston co., on the 9th Dec., 1865, by Rev. S. R.
J. Sistrunk, Dr. W. F. Gyslop(?) of Arkansas and Miss Eugenia
E. Riley, daughter of the late G. F. And Elizabeth Riley, of
Houston co.

On the same day, by the same, Mr. John G. Woodward and Miss
Sarah E. Morris, all of HOuston co.

By Rev. T. T. Christian, on the 11th inst., Capt. A. O. Gar-
rard, of Columbus, and Miss Anna J. Walker, of Dawson.

At the Parsonage, in Morgan co., Jan. 2, by Rev. D. Kelsey,
Mr. S. Fulton of Monticello, and Miss Georgia R. Kelsey, of Morgan county.

In Muscogee co., on the 19th Dec., 1865, by Rev. A. S. Boyden, Mr. F. D. McLendon, of Merriwether co., and Miss M. E.
Biggers of Muscogee co.

In Muscogee co., at the residnece of the bride's father, Rev.
S. A. Clark on the 26th Dec. 1865, by the Rev. A. S. Boyden, Capt.
David L. Cohen of Pensacola, Fla., and Mrs. Lucy A. McCoy.

On 21st Dec., by the Rev. J. T. Ainsworth, Wm. Bell and Miss
Ellen Fullford, of Buena Vista, Ga.

On 28th Dec., at the house of the bride, by Rev. John A. Reynolds, Mr. John H. Rhodes, and Mrs. Mary J. Malone of Richmond
county.

On the same evening at the residence of the bride's father,
Mr. William W. Tinley, and Miss Elvira J. ----, all of Richmond
county.

On 9th January by same, at Mrs. Elizabeth Evans', Mr.
Whitby H. Rhodes, of Richmond and Mrs. R--- Rheney of Jefferson
co.

Mrs. Julia Robt Rawson, wife of Wm. A. Rawson, died in
Beallwood, near Columbus, Ga., July 31, 1865, aged 47 years...
born in Montague, Mass., subsequently resided in Craftsburg,
Vt., and after her marriage settled in Lumpkin, Ga....

The Rev. Joseph E. Brown died on the 31st July in Sumter
Dist., S. C., in the 57th year of his age....

Mrs. Frances Moore, wife of Mr. Benjamin M. Baldwin, and
daughter of Rev. Thos. and Mrs. Jane Samford, was born in Ga.,
Feb. 7, 1826, and amrried July 31, 1846, emigrated to Texas in
1850, and died near Marshall, Aug. 31, 1865....

Issue of January 26, 1866

Mrs. Mary A. Young, wife of Wm. H. Young, and daughter of
A. L. and Elizabeth Bradley, died -- Nov. 1865....

Miss Mary Rosalie Hardy, daughter of R. Baxter Hardy, was
born June 11th, 1842, and died happily 20th May 1865....

Mr. James Hardy was born in Va., in 1770, and died 27th Jan.,
1865, aged about 95 years...a loving father and grandfather.

Richard Baxter Hardy son of James Hardy, was born 20th Oct.
1812, and died 9th Feb. 1865....

Mrs. Catharine Zimmerman, mother of Rev. John H. Zimmerman,
of the S. C. Conf., lvied to be nearly 75 years old....

Married at Lancaster C. H., S. C. on Jan. 4, by Rev. Charles
Taylor, John Bratton Erwin, Esq., of Yorkville, and Miss Mary
T. Barnes, daughter of the late Col. Dixon Barnes, of Lancaster.

Near Cuthbert, Ga.,on Nov. 30, 1865, by Rev. R. B. L---,
Mr. Samuel --- Neal and Miss Emma Bell.

In Talbot co., on Jan. 9, Dr. Edward Schley of Columbus,
Ga. and Miss Melissa Sparks, of said county.

Issue of February 2, 1866

Mrs. Frances Bonner died in Baldwin co., on the 16th Jan., 1866, in the 75th year of her age....

Married on 26th of Dec., 1865, in Marietta, Ga.,by Rev. J. M. Lowrey, Mr. Devereaux F. McClatchay and Miss Emma K. Lyon.

At George's Station, on 24th Dec., 1865, by Rev. J. A. Mood, Joseph Kennedy, Esq., and Miss Louisa C. George, daughter of Mr. R. E. George, all of Charleston, S. C.

On 28th Dec., 1865, by the same, Mr. Jacob C. Utsey, and Miss Lucy L. Appleby, daughter of the late Rev. D. C. Appleby, all of St. George's Colleton Dist.

On 18th Jan., by the same, Capt. William P. Appleby and Miss Anzly C. Laracy, daughter of Joel B. Laracy, Esq., all of St. George's Colleton Dist.

on the same oocasion, by the same, Mr. P. R. Appleby and Miss Mary R. Laracy, daughter of Joel B. Laracy, Esq., of St. George's S. C.

In Monroe co., Ga.,on 23d Ja.n by Rev. M. A. Maddux, Mr. Wm. Walker and Miss Sarah Jane Zellner, both of said county.

On 31st Dec., 1865, by the Rev. E. H. Henry, Mr. L. Clinton Billingslea, of Atlanta, and Miss Sallie Weaver, of Jasper co.

On 26th Dec., 1865, at the residence of Dr. A. Means, by Rev. W. R. Branham, Mr. James H. Griffin, and Miss Susie C. Mean,s all of Oxford, Ga.

On Jan. 11th, in the Methodist Church, Lumpkin, Ga. by Rev. J. C. Simmons, Mr. Arthur T. Fort and Miss Sarah W. Sibley, of Stewart co., Ga.

Died on 31st of Jan., at his mother's, near Brookville, Miss., Thos J. Koger, aged nine years and five months, son of Rev. T. J. Koger, of the Ala. Conf. who fell at the battle of Perryville.

Issue of February 9, 1866

Mrs. Amelia W. Gresham, wife of G. W.Gresham, Esq., died in Oglethorpe co., Ga., on the 10th of Jan., 1866, in the 66th year of her age....

Mrs. Susan Eubanks, relict of John Eubanks, was born in N. C., July 17, 1795, and died in Montgomery co., Ala., Jan. 12, 1866. Her maiden name was Moore, and her father died when she was only two years old, and the same year her mother moved to Hancock co., Ga., where she was raised and married, in 1813...the mother of 13 children, six sons and seven daughters. Her husband died in 1833....

Bro. James L. Willis was born March 27, 1809, in Columbia co., Ga., and died in Talbot co., Ga., Nov. 19, 1865, in his 54th year ....

Miss Elizabeth Ricer died in Warren co., Ga., Dec. 30, 1865, in her 49th year....

Rev. John S. Henley, for several years a citizen of Banks co., died at his residence in Pontotoc co., Miss., on 15th Dec., in the 64th year of his age. He was a native of Tenn....

Tribute of Respect by Reedy River Ct. to William Adney McSwain, pastor.

Married on Nov. 7th, by Rev. J. W. Shores, Rev. Angus Dowling, of the Montgomery conf. and Miss Laura L. Boswell, granddaughter of Rev. Jno. Boswell, decd.

On Dec. 21, by the same, Dr. Jno. E. Daniel, of Coggee co., Ala., and Miss Eliza J. Teague, of Pike co., Ala.

On Dec. 24th, by the same, Mr. E. D. Atkinson, of Montgomery Ala., and Miss Rebecca L. Butts, of Pike co., Ala.

On Jan. 18th, by the same, Mr. M. W. McKay and Mrs. Harriet Townsend, both of Montgomery co., Ala.

On Jan. 11th, by the same, Mr. M. C. Cooper and Miss J. Texas Farrior, both of Pike co., Ala.

Near Hamilton, Ga.,on the eve of January 30th, by the Rev. A. J. Dean, Seabron N. Jones, Esq., attorney at law, Union Springs, Ala., and Mrs. Mary Francis Houghton.

Near Belvue, Talbot co., Ga., 23d January, 1866, by Rev. R. B. Lester, Dr. James H. Bryan and Miss Fannie E. Holmes, all of said county.

On 30th Jan., 1866, by the same, Mr. Amos C. Boynton, of Panola co., Texas, and Miss Martha B. Fort, of Talbot co., Ga.

On 23d January, by Rev. A. S. Boyden, Mr. Henry C. David, of Harris co., Ga., and Miss Josephine A. Biggers, daughter of L. M. Biggers, Esq. of Muscogee co., Ga.

On 30th Jan., by the same, Mr. Robert S. Crane, of Columbus, Ga., and Miss Margaret J. Biggers, daughter of L. M. Biggers, Esq. of Muscogee co., Ga.

On 23d January, by Rev. W. W. Oslin, Mr. John H. Grimsley, of Nashville, Tenn., and Miss Anna P. Wait, of Bibb co.

Issue of February 16, 1866

Rebecca L. Zant died on 20th Dec., 1865, near Byromville, Dooly co., Ga., in the 55th year of her age....

Miss Mary E. Zant was20 years 2 months and 24 days old at her death, Dec. 5, 1865....

Mrs. Ann Kennon died at the residence of her son-in-law, Col. Robt. H. Moore, of Floyd Springs, Ga.,on 29th Nov. last, in the 75th year of her age....

Mrs. W. Giles, wife of Dr. Robert Giles, and sister of the late Mrs. Eliza T. Williams, of Cokesbury, S. c.,died in Anderson Dist., S. C., in the 73d year of her age...lost two sons during the late war....

Married on the 6th inst, near Macon,by Rev. S. S. Sweet, Mr. Wm. H. Wheaton, of Memphis Tenn., and Miss Martha T. Stubbs.

On the 1st Feb., by Rev. Julius T. Curtis, Mr. J. J. Dickinson, of Pulaski, and Miss Martha Pople of Wilcox.

On the 4th Jan., by Rev. S. A. Pilley, Rev. Anson West of Montgomery Conf. to Miss Sallie B. Kittrell, of Camden, Ala.

On the 1st Feb.,near Talbotton, by Rev. Walter Knox, Mr. Walker G. Camp, of Coweta, Ga. to Miss Sallie E. Maxwell, of Talbot co., Ga.

Willie Asbury, only child of Rev. Julius T. and Lou Belle Curtiss, died in Hawkinsville, Ga., Feb. 3, aged 1 year and 3 days.

Issue of February 23, 1866

Mrs. Julia Mounger, wife of James Elder, Esq., and eldest daughter of the late Major F. C. Heard, died in Mobile, on 2d Dec., in the 43d year of her age....

Mrs. Ella Graham, wife of Rev. Alexander Graham, late of the Fla. Conf., died at Grooverville, Ga., at the residence of her parents, in the 23d year of her age....

Sister Elizabeth J. Livingston, daughter of W. and E. Heath, formerly of Putnam co., Ga.,and wife of Joseph Livingston, of Henry co., Ga., died 5th Dec., 1865, in the 56th year of her age.

Issue of March 2, 1866

Mrs. Elizabeth Shuler died in Lexington Dist., S. C., on 10th Jan., 1866, in the 75th year of her age... She first married

Samuel Kennerly. She was the daughter of Rev. T. Rall...married
second John Shuler, by whom she had tree children. She had four
children by Samuel Kennerly.

Eliza Glenn Read was born Dec. 5, 1843, in Newton co., Ga.,
Jan. 26, 1866....

J. H. More house was born March 14, 1841, and was lost at
sea, about the 20th Oct., last, on the steamer Mount....

Mr. William P. Leak, died near Wadesboro, N. C., Dec. 6,
1865, in the 19th year of his age....

Married on 18th Feb.,in Pike co., Ga., by Rev. P. N. Maddox,
Mr. Joseph M. Cook, of Atlanta, and Miss Anna T. Reid, daughter
of J. Wesley Reid, Esq.

On 20th Feb., in Pike co., by the same, Mr. Thomas A. Smith,
and Miss Josephine A. Shehee, daughter of S. B. Shehee, Esq.

On 14th Feb., 1866, at Bethel, Ga., by Rev. B. C. Franklin,
Mr. Geo. S. Scarlett and Miss Virginis S. Tison, both of Glynn
co., Ga.

By Rev. H. J. Hunter, Mr. K. G. A. Hicks and Mrs. Susan
Jones, all of Butler, Ala.

Issue of March 9, 1866

Married on the 25th Jan. by Rev. J. J. Morgan, Mr. Christopher
C. Johnson to Miss Fannie A. Turner, all of DeKalb co., Ga.

On Sunday morning, Feb. 4th, by the same, Mr. Henry F.
Williams, to Miss Mattie C. Cobb, all of DeKalb co., Ga.

On Wed. evening the 21st Feb., in the Methodist Church, in
Chester, by Rev. Samuel Leard, Rev. Thos Raysor, of the S. C.
Conf., to Miss S. Leard.

On the 16th Jan., 1866, at Nacoochee Valley, Ga., by Rev. F.
G. Hughes, James A. Wily, of Franklin co., Ga., and Miss Mary
M. Williams, daughter of Edwin P. Williams, of White co., Ga.

On the 31st Jan., by Rev. B. J. Baldwin, Mr. Homer S. Bell
to Miss Sallie J. Reddick, daughter of Judge Peter Reddick, all
of Weston, Ga.

On the 21st Feb.,in Milledgeville, Ga., by Rev. G. W. Yarbrough, Mr. Benj. B. Adams of Eatonton, Ga., and Miss Mollie V.
Little, of the former place.

Died on the 27th Feb.,1866, in Madison, Ga., Cobb, infant
and only son of Habersham J. and Florida V. Adams.

Alpheus T. Watson, Hannie his wife...Fannie Worthington, their
little daughter, Wistar, our youngest borther, and Wesley, all
died. (long account).

Mr. Samuel Treadwell was born in Sampson co., N. C., Sept.
5, 1778, and died on 20th August, 1865, at the residence of his
son-in-law, Rev. John P. Margart, in Barbour co., Ala., aged 86
years, 11 months and 24 days....(long eulogy).

Mrs. Anna Elizabeth Smith, wife of Capt. A. G. Smith, and
daughter of Bro. Thos A. and Frances Hightower, died at Fort
Browder, Ala., on 1st Dec. 1865....left husband and children.

Issue of March 16, 1866

Married on Thurs. evening, 1st March in Monroe co., Ga.,by
Rev. Thomas G. Scott, Mr. Richard W. McGinty and Miss Emily M.
Clement, daughter of James R.Clements, Esquire.

On 8th March in Atlanta, Ga., by Rev. Alex. M. Thigpen, Mr.
J. H. Fuller to Miss Lou J. Edwards, daughter of the late Rev.
George Edwards, Chaplain, 23rd Ga. Regt.

On the 7th inst., by Rev. W. C. Bass, Mr. A. F. Clarke, to
Miss Mary D. Brantly, daughter of Maj. T. W. Brantly, all of this
city.

On 21st Feb., by Rev. R. W. Bigham, in Eatonton, Ga., Capt.

Thos L. Wallace, formerly of Knoxville, Tenn., to Miss Susan Lou Harwell.

On 28th Feb, in Sumter Dist., S. C., by Rev. Charles Taylor, Mr. Daniel M. Young to Miss Sarah Jan,e dlest daughter of Mr. Mellard Jenkins, of Richland.

William Jeremiah Sasnett was born in Hancock co., Ga., April 29, 1839...died 3d Nov 1865. (long account).

Rev. William Adney McSwain was born in Montgomery, now Stanley co., N. C., Nov. 5, 1814...married Jan 24, 1844, to Miss Elizabeth Randle...(long account).

Rev. Archibald Peutifoy, M. D. was born 20th July 1798, near Newbern, N. C., and died in Charleston, S. C., 14th Jan., 1866 (long account).

Mrs. Jerusha Simms, widow of the late Richard L. Simms, and third daughter of Allen Bonner of Clarke co., was born 12th Feb. 1808, married and moved to Newton in 1838, and died in Covington, Ga., Jan. 17, 1866....

Mrs. Sarah Young, of Lowndesville, Abbeville Dist., S. C., outlived her three score and ten...

Master Eugene P. Griffin, son of Bro. Joel and Sister E. Griffin, of Oglethorpe, Ga., in his 12th year, was killed by the accidental discharge of a gun....

Bro. Samuel Wilkerson was born in Orange co., N. C., settled in Butts co., Ga.,in 1823, and died 15th Dec. 1865, aged 66 years.

Dr. Thomas F. Wilkerson, son of Samuel Wilkerson, was born May 10, 1840, and died Feb. 19, 1866....

Issue of March 23, 1866

Married on the 16th Jan., 1866, by Rev. F. G. Hughes, Mr. James A. Wyly, of Franklin co., Ga., to Miss Mary M. Williams, of White co., Ga.

On 22d Feb., last by Rev. W. S. Turner, Henry W. Wooding to Mrs. Sarah B. Sharpe, both of Dooly co., Ga.

On the 8th of March, in Lowndes co., Ala., by Rev. J. A. Parker, Mr. C. C. Silkins, of Montgomery, to Miss S. C. Hazzard, of Lowndes co., Ala.

In Scriven co., Feb. 15, 1866, by Rev. J. M. Stokes, Mr. Wm. H. Anderson to Miss Mary V. Sharpe, all of Scriven co., Ga.

In Troup co., Ga., March 8, 1866, by Rev. R. W. Dixon, Mr. R. H. Sledge to Miss E. C. Rutledge, all of Troup co., Ga.

By the same, in Troup co., Ga., March 8th, 1866, Mr. W. C. Hale to Miss M. P. Watts, all of Troup co., Ga.

Died, in Brunswick, Ga., 24th Feb., Miss Jane Amanda Palmer, in her 18th year....

Ada Rembert, daughter of Rev. A. L. and M. J. Smith, of the S. C. Conf. was born Tues. June 16, 1863, and died in Greenwood, S. C., Tues., Oct. 10, 1865.

On Tuesday Dec. 5th, 1865, Holland Paine, the eldest child of brother and sister Smith, in Greenwood, S. C., aged 14 years, 1 month and 16 days....

William H. Rinion, born in Columbia co., Ga.,8th of Jan., 1818, and died in Butler co., Ala., 26th Jan. 1866....

Issue of March 30, 1866

Married in the Methodist Church, Madison, Ga., March 15th, by Rev. H. J. Adams, Lewis P. Rogers, of Kentucky, to Miss Fannie L. Culbert, of Madison.

On the 27th February by Rev. A. G. Dempsey, Mr. Tilley McElroy to Miss Laura Lively, all of DeKalb co., Ga.

In Talbot co., Ga., May 20, 1866, by Rev. T. A. Brown, Dr.
J. A. Hickman, of Clay Village, Ky. to Miss Emma E. Sandiford,
of Eufaula, Ala.
By Rev. Jesse Wood, at the residence of Mr. Stephen Pace,
Miss Ann Pkace, his daughter, to Mr. J. J. Fort, of Cotton Valley,
Ala.
By Rev. J. W. Simmons, March 14, Wm. J. Wilson to Miss Amanda
Miller, all of Hancock co., Ga.
Died, near Bennettsville, S. C. Oct. 2, 1865, in the 35th
year of her age, Mrs. Lucretia Thomas, wife of J. S. Thomas.
Bro. Green Bell, an old and prominent member of the Methodist
Church in Burke co., Ga., died on the night of Feb. 15th, in the
73d year of his age.-..
Died, on the 13th of Feb., in Sumter Dist., S. C., Sarah
Allston Coachman, eldest daughter of E. P. Coachman, of George-
town Dist....

Issue of April 6, 1866

Dr. James Myrick was born in Va., but removed to Ga., in 1809,
spent some time in Baldwin co., where he married Miss Nancy
Flewellyn. (long account).
John F. Hatton was born in Newberry Dist.,S. C., July, 1830.
His father, Robert Hatton, moved from S. C. to Ga. when he was
quite young...died 27th June 1864....
James Snow was born May 31, 1807, died Oct. 8, 1865. In
1830 married his first wife, Susanna Easterling. she died in
1842 leaving four little boys and two daughters...one, Jeremiah,
is a minister in the S. C. Conf. Married Miss A. W. LeGett,
daughter of Rev. James LeGett, in 1844. By her he had six child-
ren....
My sister, Mrs. Mary Martin...member of the Baptist Church...
died in the 86th year of her age...Joseph Holmes.
Married on Wednesday, March 28th, by Rev. Wesley F. Smith,
Rev. George Bright of the Ga. Conf. to Mrs. Sophia A. Jackson,
all of Monroe Co., Ga.
At Creek Stand, March 12th, by Rev. H. B. Cottrell, Mr.
Julius Wicker to Miss Octavia Seegar, all of Macon co., Ala.
On the 22d March, by Rev. Wm. W. Mood, Major Henry H.
Lesesne to Miss Letitia M. Wells, all of Clarendon Dist., S. C.

Issue of April 13, 1866

Married in Atlanta, April 3d, by Rev. Atticus G. Haygood,
Mr. Lee Brown to Miss Mary Eaton.
In Cave Spring, Ga., April 4th, by Rev. A. J. Jarrell, Rev.
Wm. H. Leith of Cahaba--Mobile Conference--to Miss Berta L.
Bynum, of Cave Spring.
On the 12th Dec., in Union Dist., S. C., by Rev. J. E. Wat-
son, Capt. J. D. Jeffries to Miss Harriet E. Littlejohn, daughter
of Jas. Littlejohn, Esq.
On the 23d ult., by Rev. B. J. Johnson, Mr. Turplin Gregory,
of Murray co., Ga., to Miss Susan Terry, daughter of Rev. Jos.
Terry, of Whitfield Co., Ga.
Miss Emma Bostwick, died at the residence of her mother, in
Marietta, Ga. on 25th Feb. 1866....
Mrs. Charlotte A. E. Beall, wife of Col. Erasmus T. Beall,
died in Lumpkin, Ga., Feb. 25, 1866, aged 48 years.
Capt. Geo. W. Moore, formerly Capt. of Co. F. Cobb's Legion,
died at the residence of his father, in Carroll co., Ga.,on 27th
March, in the 25th year of his age....
Mrs. Rebecca White was born in Bladen co., N. C., June 24,
1783, and married Jan. 28,1802, to James B. White, and after his

death to John H. White,in 1821, and died in Macon co., Ala.,
March 21, 1866. Her husband had preceded her some three years.
Samuel Spearman was born in York Dist., S. C.,17th Feb. 1790,
and died in Louisville, 28th Feb. 1866...left aged widow and
several children.
P. V. Perry died near Weston, Ga., on the 21st March 1866,
aged about 55 years....

Issue of April 20, 1866

Married April 8, by Rev. T. S. L. Harwell, Capt. Blair R.
Mayse, to Miss Emma Rivers, all of Sumter co., Ga.
By the same, April 9, Mr. John T. Hamble, of Sumter co., to
MissSarah S. Willbanks, of Webster co., Ga.
On Wednesday, April 4th, in Sumter, S. C., at the residence
of J. Harvey Dingle, Esq., by Rev. Dr. Charles Taylor, Mr. R.
Bloomfield Horton, of Wadesboro, N. C., to Miss Laura A. Tindall,
of Mississippi.
In Springville, Darlington, S. C., the evening of January
18th, by Rev. W. A. Gamewell, Capt. William E. Charles and Miss
Carrie D. Zimmerman.
On the morning of March 25, 1866, by Rev. W. T. Read, Mr.
John W. Read to Miss MaryF. Flowers, all of Newton co., Ga.
In Harris co., Ga., March 29th, 1866, by Rev. R. W. Dixon,
Dr. James M. Hunton, of Dawson, Ga., to Miss Mary E. Huling, of
Harris co., Ga.
On the morning of the 29th March, at the residence of the
bride's mother, in Salem, Ala., by Rev. John A. Pace, Mr. Wm.
Moncreef, of Montgomery, to Miss Elizabeth Dimon.
L. P. Altman died at West Point, Ga., March 2, 1866, in his
20th year....
Rev. Joseph Asbury Hines was born in St. James Goose Creek,
S. C., Sept. 9, 1810, married to Miss Malinda Disher, Oct. 31,
1832, died at his home in Columbia, S. C., March 31, 1866...
buried in Washington Street grave-yard. (long account).
Dr. James D. Young was born Dec. 1, 1830, and died at his
residence in Thomson, Ga.,Jan. 24, 1866. Just one month after
his death, his little Susan, his infant daughter, aged 3 months
and 21 days.
Sister Julia A. H. Ford, was born in Warren co., Ga., April
18, 1825. She was married to Rev. J. C. Ford, Aug. 4, 1842, and
died March 14, 1866, in Atlanta....
Lucy H. Mason was born in N. C., 1792 or '93, moved to Wilcox
co., Ala., in 1817, and died at the residence of Benjamin Williamson, near Camden, Feb. 10, 1866....daughter of Rev. Zedekiah
Ledbetter.

Issue of April 27, 1866

Married on Tuesday evening, 27th March, in Lawrenceville, Ga.,
by Rev. G. L. W. Anthony, Col. Nathan H. Hutchins, son of Judge
Hutchens, to Miss Carrie S. Orr, of the same place.
By Rev. R. H. Howren, April 11, Mr. James T. Smith to Miss
Margaret King, both of Decatur co., Ga.
On the 12th April, by Rev. Wm. C. Power, Major Wm. M. Smith,
of Tennessee, to Miss Alice O., only daughter of James H. Davis,
Esq., of Mecklenburg co., N. C.
Rev. Christian M. Sullivan of the Western Virginia Conf.,
died at his residence in Ashland, Ky. Aug. 3, 1866...(long ac-
count).
Tribute of Respect by Athens Station to Hon. Asbury Hull....
Wm. C. Hall died at his residence in Watkinsville, Ga., 18th
Jan 1866...wound at battle of Griswodlville, Ga...left wife and

two daughters....

<u>Issue of May 4, 1866</u>

Married April 24th, by Rev. T. J. Rutledge, Mr. Jas. A. Bil-
bro, to Miss Frankie Mason, all of Tuskegee, Ala.
On the 24th April 1866, Rev. William H. Thomas of the Fla.
Conf. to Miss Laura M. Baker, of Centre Village, Ga.
In Macon, Ga., on the 1st instant, by Rev. Charles R. Jewett,
Mr. Augustus D. Sharpe, of Greensboro', Ga., to Miss Mary F.,
daughter of Mr. H. L. Jewett, of Macon.
In Gilmer co., March 29, 1866, by Rev. B. B. Quillian, Mr.
Landrum Murray, to Miss Catharine C. Hudson.
In Fannin co., Ga., April 5, 1866, by Rev. J. L. Fowler,
the Rev. B. B. Quillian, of Bilmer co., to Miss Lou Jane Vanzant.
In Brunswick, Ga., April 26th, by Rev. B. C. Franklin, Mr. U.
Dart, Jr., to Miss Angelina McConn.
Died in Monticello, Ga.,on the 9th April, Elizabeth, only
daughter of Joseph P. and Emeline Williams, aged about 14 months.
Evelyn Isolona, youngest daughter of Dr. Thos. S. and W. S.
Mitchell, died in Hamilton, Ga., April 12, 1866, aged 11 months
and 25 days.
Mrs. Mary Ann Forsythe, wife of John J. Forsythe, died in
Macon, Feb. 14, 1866, in the 58th year of her age....
Eliza S. Pope, relict of Rev. Benjamin Pope, deceased, died
in Athens, Ga.,March 23, 1866, in the 60th year of her age....
Charles B. Gable of Marietta, Ga., was killed on Kenesaw
Mountain, near that place, Feb. 14, 1865(sic)....
Mrs. Catharine A. Bunker died at her residence in Madison,
Fla., April 1st, 1866, in the 61st year of her age...All of her
children are members of the Church....
Rev. Luke R. McNamar was born in Dorchester co., Md., Jan.
20, 1837, and died in Talbot co., Ga., April 12, 1866...left
wife and four children.
Victoria Preston, wife of Joseph W. Preston, and daughter of
Wm. C. Leverett, of Jasper co., Ga.,was born 29th Oct., 1845,
married Oct. 31, 1865, and died April 17, 1866....

<u>Issue of May 11, 1866</u>

Married Feb. 16, 1866, by Rev. A. M. Chrietzberg, Mr. George
W. Sturgeon to Miss Alice Betsell.
By the same, Feb. 16, 1866, B. M. Shuler, M. D. to Miss F. E.
Dukes, all of Orangeburg, S. C.
By the same,March 26,1866, James Lalor to Miss Minnie E.
Briggs, of Charleston, S. C.
In Stewart co., Ga., April 27th, by Rev. L. J. Davies, Mr.
B. Randolph Hines to Miss Sallie, daughter of Col. Robert A.
Hardwick, of Stewart co., Ga.
In Lumpkin, Ga., May 2d, by Rev. L. J. Davies, Dr. D. H. Wil-
mot, of Decatur co., Ga., to Miss Carrie V., daughter of Thomas
H. Everette, Esq., of Lumpkin.
Died at the residence of her son, Rev. A. M. Chrietzberg,
Orangeburg Dist., S. C., Mrs. Elizabeth Chrietzberg, aged 86.
Rev. Hilliard Crawford Parsons, of the S. C. Conf., died
in Wadesboro, N. C., January 20th, 1866...born in Sumter Dist.,
S. C., Feb. 28, 1824....(long account).
Mrs. Charlotte M. Trussell, wife of Francis A. Trussell, and
daughter of Jesse and Mahala Davis, and was Aug. 25, 1836, and
died April 11, 1866....
Thomas Eady, died in Auburn, Ala., on the 8th April 1866,
in the 72d year of his age...
Miss E. M. Haley, daughter of Joel and Frances Haley, died

in Cherokee co., Ga., April 6th, 1866, aged 17 years....

Mrs. Virginia A. Fitz, daughter of James and Eliza C. Jennings, formerly of Clark co., Ga., died at Madison station, Ala., on 8th Jan. last...born 2d April 1838....

Tribute of Respect by Mulberry St. M. E. Sunday School to Monroe Chapman....

Tribute of Respect by Waynesboro Circuit, to Green Bell....

Issue of May 18, 1866

Married by Rev. Dr. F. E.Munsen, on 3d May, 1866, Mr. J. W. Hardwick of Newton, to Miss Mattie Ward, daughter of P. Z. Ward, of Henry county.

On the 26th April, at the residence of John Hornady, Macon co., Ga.,by Rev. W. S. Turner, Mr. W. J. Lofley and Miss Mattie S. Simmons.

In Aiken, S. C., on the evening of the 10th inst., at the residence of Mr. S. P. T. Field, by the Rev. John R. Dow, Mr. John B. Hays, of Augusta, Ga.,and Miss MaryF. Dagnall, of Aiken.

On Thursday, May 10th, at the residence of Dr. Reddey, by Rev. P. M. Rybrun, Mr. Nathan B. Ensign and Miss Annie Dyson, all of Forsyth, Monroe co., Ga.

On the 19th ult., by Rev. Wm. Park, Mr. Jno. R. Porter, to Miss Alice L. Jones, daughter of Mr. A. J. Jones, all of Meriwether co., Ga.

James M. Hodnett was born in Newton co., Ga., May 22, 1819, and died in Meriwether co., April 22,1866

Tribute of Respect to Rev. Hilliard C. Parsons by Wadesboro Circuit, S. C. Conf.

Tribute of Respect by Woodville Ct., Montgomery conf., to R. K. Scruggs.

Issue of May 25, 1866

Married on 27th March, by Rev. J. J. Workman, Mr. M. B. Harrison, to Miss Sallie E., third daughter of Dr. J. M. Sullivan, all of Greenville Dist., S. C.

By the same, on the 31st March, Mr. Joseph Smith to Miss Frances Prather, all of Laurens Dist., S. C.

On the 18th January, by Rev. J. R. Little, Mr. Austin Bramlet, to Miss Nannie Nabers, all of Laurens Dist., S. C.

By the same, on 1st Feb.,Mr. R. H. Yeargin to Miss Fannie Wallace, all of Laurens Dist., S. C.

By the same, on the 27th April, in the M. E. Church, Laurensville, Mr. J. W. Cavis to Miss Ella Anderson, all of Laurens Dist., S. C.

In Talbotton, Ga.,on the 15th inst., by Rev. A. Wright, Dr. E. L. bArdwell and Miss Lisa Brown, daughter of Major Thos. A. Brown.

On the 23d March, by Rev. A. R. Lovejoy, Mr. Mathew Estes, to Mollie Sibley, all of Meriwether co., Ga.

In Harris co., Ga., May 16th, 1866, by Rev. R. W. Dixon, Mr. John J. Evans to Miss Mary F. Goodman, all of Harris co., Ga.

On the 9th inst., by Rev. W. M. Crumley, Mr. J. P. Blassingame of Crawford co., to Miss Mattie A. Cherry, of this city.

At the residence of Mr. Blasingim, in Monroe co., on the 3rd May 1866, by Rev. W. G. Allen, Mr. W. W. Lawrence, of Tenn., to Miss Lizzie H. Meanes, of Monroe co., Ga.

Sister Leurena Owen was born in 1784, and died at the residence of her daughter Mrs. Walker, in Mobile, Ala., on 20th April 1863, aged about 79 years.

Rev. Joab Humphries died in Murray co., Ga.,May 17, 1864, born in N. C., Nov. 29, 1810....

Elizabeth G. Carson, wife of Judge Robt. Carson of Texas, was born inEdgefield Dist., S. C.,11 April 1807...10 March 1846, in Talbot co., Ga.,married to Robert Carson, and 6th March 1866 died in Millican, Grimes co., Texas.

George Duffield Rich, a son of Judge G. D. Rice, of Marietta Ga. was wounded near Petersburg, Va., on 1st July 1864, and died 3d July...(long eulogy).

Ophelia F. Veal, daughter of George W. and Eliza Ann Veal, died in Clarke co., Ga., Nov. 2, 1865, in her 16th year.

Tribute of Respect by Marion St. Station, Columbia, S. C. to Rev. Joseph Asbury Hines.

Issue of June 1, 1866

Married by Rev. W. J. Cotter, at Fort Valley, Ga.,on the 23d inst.,Capt. J. W. Mathews, to Miss Mollie A. Johnson.

By the same, at the residence of Mrs. Hiley, on the 10th inst., Mr. B. F. Griffin, to Miss Mary E. Mock.

By the same, at Fort Valley, on the 22d March, Mr. C. R. Fogg to Miss Mary A. Royal.

By Rev. F. Milton Kennedy, May 2, 1866, Dr. D. A. Parker to Miss Bettie Kendall, all of Stanley Co., N. C.

By Rev. Jesse Wood, of the Montgomery Conf., on the 22d of May, 1866, Mr. John McBryde, to Miss Narcissa Freeman, of Cotton Valley, Ala.

On April 24th, by Rev. W. S. Baker, at the residence of the bride's mother, Mr. David C. Walker, of Longstreet, to Miss Amelia R. Fisher, of Irwinton, Ga.

Mrs. Mary Willingham died in Fairfield Dist., S. C., Oct. 17, 1864, in the 60th year of her age...bore the death of five children...and left seven more.... Maggie Willingham.

Rev. Daniel Reagan died on 17th Aug., 1865, in Meriwether co., Ga.,left widowed mother and family.

Mrs. Eliza Jane Sturges, died 31st Aug., in Danville, Texas, daughter of the late Major Philip Cook, of Twiggs co., Ga....

Bro. Joseph T. Burditt was born Sept. 10, 1829, married Jan. 16, 1851, and died in the Confederate Hospital, Camden, S. C., May 9, 1865....left widow and children.   J. J. W.

Issue of June 8, 1866

Rev. John S. Dunn died in Lincoln co., Ga., May 4, 1866, in the 55th year of his age..born and reared in Columbia co., within a few miles of where he died....

Rev. Christian V. Barnes was born in Abbeville Dist., S. C., Dec. 8, 1794, and died near Lowndesville, S. C., Feb. 22, 1866. married three times, first to Ann P. Gunnion, by whom he had nine children, then to Mrs. Elizabeth Furr, and last to Miss S. M. Carn, his now bereveaed widow....

Miss Ellen Lipscomb Wier was born in Columbus, Miss., June 15, 1838, and died at Enterprise, Miss., March 2, 1866....

Nancy C. Campbell, youngest daughter of Wm. and Rhoda Campbell, died in Monroe co., Ga., April 27th, 1866, in the 20th year of her age....

James B. Ogletree was born 3d Dec. 1800, and died on 15th April, in Wilkes co., Ga...married Miss Mary A. Martin, daughter of the late Marshall Martin of Merriwether co., Ga. He moved to Maconco., Ala., about 1845...(no date of death given).

Andrew Ralph Jameson was born in Beaufort Dist., S. C., May 28, 1837, and died in Colleton Dist., S. C., at his brother-in-law's, John W. Lemacks, on 26th Jan. 1865...left wife and one child.

Lewis Zeigler died on 9th Feb. 1866, in Orangeburg Dist., S.

C., class-leader in Andrew Chapel Church, upper Orange circuit.

Died, in Atlanta, Ga.,on 7th May 1866, Annie Lee, daughter of F. M. and Sarah E. Richardson, aged 2 years and 7 months.

Married on the 25th May, by the Rev. Jas. Griffith, H. S. Rush, of Marion co., to Miss M. P. Hollis, of Butler, Ga.

On the 29th May, 1866, by Rev. Wm. C. Richardson, Rev. J.P. Bailey, formerly of Ga. Conf. to Miss Augusta Weems, of Cass co., Ga.

By Rev. R. P. Franks, on 3d May, 1866, Mr. Wm. C. Hicklin, to Miss C. L., daughter of Capt. John G. Baxtrom, all of Chester Dist., S. C.

On the 24th May, 1866, by the same, Mr. R. Warren Boyd, to Miss Sarah J., daughter of Capt. John G. Baxtrom, Chester Dist., S. C.

On Wed. morning, 6th inst., at the residence of the bride's father, by Rev. E. W. Warren, Mr. Chas E. Ross to Miss Jennie G. Andrews, all of Macon.

Issue of June 15, 1866

Died, Clifford, infant son of Col. E. B. and Mrs.M. E. Wilkerson of Union Springs, Ala, 1st June, aged 2 years.

Married in Warretnon, Ga.,on the 3d day of May, by Rev. J. M. Dickey, Rev. Josiah Lewis, jr., of Sparta, Ga. to Miss M. Rosie Hubert, daughter of Dr. R. W. Hubert, of the former place.

In Merriwether co., Ga., May 22d, 1866, by Rev. W. Dixon, Mr. James W. Burdett, of Chambers co., Ala., to Miss Clementine A. Lesley, of Merriwether co., Ga.

On the 21st of March, by Rev. B. B. Ross, Mr. John M. Bridges, of New Orleans, to Miss Sallie W. Bailey, of Tuskegee, Ala.

By the same, at the residence of D. McMullen, on the 28th March, 1866, Mr. Pen. S. Lockard to Miss to Sue McMullen, all of Tuskegee, Ala.

By the same, at the residence of Mr. B. K. Motley, on the 15th of May, 1866, Mr. Thos. J. Sinclair to Miss Gennie Gibson, all of Tuskegee, Ala.

By the same, May 16, 1866, Mr. Wiley C. Denson of Montevallo, Ala., to Miss Hattie C. Smith, of Tuskegee.

By the same, May 22, 1866, Mr. J. Benj. Weathers to Miss Georgia V. Wright, all of Macon co., Ala.

By the Rev. C. D. Oliver, on the 29th May, 1866, Capt. Henry C. Armstrong to Miss Mary H. Harris, daughter of Britton Harris, oa Oak Bowery, Ala.

On the 24th May, 1866, by Rev. J. R. Gaines, Capt. Robert N. Reubens, of Mailton co., Ga. to Miss Sarah E. Jones, of Forsyth co., Ga.

Mrs. Caroline Mason Potts, wife of Wm. L. Potts, Esq., and daughter of Franklin M. and Martha A. Stinson, was born in Early co., Ga., Oct. 4, 1838, and died in Montgomery co., Ala., May 15, 1866...left a husband and babe 15 days old.

Mrs. Elizabeth Coker, wife of Hon. James Coker, of Henry co., Ga., died on 6th April....

Mrs. Martha Huling, wife of Mark A. Huling, was born in Wilkes co., Ga., Oct. 28, 1836, and died in Harris co., Ga.,May 16, 1866....

John Edwin, youngest son of DuBose E. and Helen E. Anthony died in LaFayette co., Ark., April 18, 1866...born in Enon, Macon co., Ala, July 27, 1847....

The child of Mr. and Mrs. Emory Winship, of Macon: Sallie Reid was six years of age, her brother only two....

Capt. C. W. Herbert was born 10th June, 1832, in Newberry Dist., S. C.,and departed ths life March 8, 1866....

Tribute of Respect to John M. Giles who departed this life
May 25, 1866.

Issue of June 22, 1866

Adam Clark Howren, son of Rev. R. H. and M. M. Howren of the
Fla. Conf. was born in Columbia co., Fla., April 16, 1840, and
of 5th Fla. Regt....
Miss Sarah A. Chitwood, daughter of James J. and Mary A.
Chitwood, died in Habersham co., Ga.,April 9, 1866....
Capt. N. Wesley Miller, 31st Ga. Regt. was born in Troup
co., Ga., Nov. 24, 1836, and died June 5, 1865....
Rev. Richard Leigh was born in Perquimans co., N. C., March
20, 1809, and died in Floyd co., Ga., March 26, 1866....
Rev. Dr. N. H. Boring died April 24, 1866, from a Railroad
accident, at Chappell Hill, Texas....
Dr. W. C. Cauthen, was born in Lancaster Dist., S. C.,
Dec. 20, 1825, and died May 4, 1865...1852 elected to State
Legislature.
Mary Victoria, only daughter of Dr. John Dolly Grant, and
wife of Mr. P. L. Criamiles, was born in Roane co., Tenn., Sept.
28, 1837, and died June 16, 1865, in Thomas co., Ga....
Zoonomia Darwin Carter, wife of John D.Carter, died at Colum-
bus, Ga., Jan. 19, 1866, inthe 47th year of her age....
George Allen, eldest son of Alexander and Mary Allen, died
on the 4th inst., having just entered his 19th year.
Married in Marion co., East Florida, May 31, 1866, by Rev.
E. S. Tyner, Mr. Geo. W. neitner to Miss Carrie Geiger, all of
Marion co., E. Fla.
Onthe 7th June, 1866, by Rev. R. B. Lester, Mr. W. T. Weaver,
of Thomaston, Ga., to Mrs. Fannie E. Davis, of Talbot co., Ga.
On 29th May 1866, in Coosa co., Ala., by Rev. L. R. Bell,
Mr. R. D. Spivy, to Miss Mary C. Massengale.

Issue of June 29, 1866

Wm. H. Simmons of Pike co., Ga., died 24th April last, in the
72d year of his age.... J. W. Simmons.
Mrs. Charlotte S. Foster, wife of Col. Joel Foster, died at
Spartanburg, S. C.,on 4th June. She was born in Richland Dist.,
May 4, 1821, where her father Capt. Christian Bookter resided.
married on 24th March 1842, and soon removed to Cass co., Ga.,
where they remained until 1859....
J. A. Pennington, son of Rev. Thaddeus and Mary A. Pennington,
was born 25th Oct. 1832, and died April 20, 1866....
Jacob Woodson Andrews, was born in Prince Edward co., Va.,
Oct. 8k 1799, and died in Spalding co., Ga., Feb. 4, 1866....
Mrs. Margaret McBride, relict of the late James F. McBride,
died in Mobile, Ala., March 20, 1866, in his 71st year...born
in New York, Dec. 1795, came to Mobile in 1825....
William Alston Ott, son of Col. Edward S. and Mrs. Amanda A.
Ott, was born in Barbour co., Ala., Nov. 26, 1848, died in
the Chattahoochee river, near Columbus, Ga.,on 13th inst...June
17, 1866.
John T. Carter, Jr., son of John T. Carter of Merriwether
co., died in Memphis, Tenn., on 14th May, in his 25th year....
Married on 16th June, 1866, at the residence of Mr.Joel
Tolbert, by Rev. L. A. Parker, Mr. John B. Parsons, to Miss
Amanda E. Burgess, all of Pike co., Ala.
On the 14th inst., in St. Paul's Church, Columbus, Ga.,by
Rev. Jos. S. Key, vr. Robert C. Pope to Miss Annie A., daughter
of the late Sterling F. Grimes, all of Columbus, Ga.
On the 14th inst., by Rev. H. H. Parks, Mr. C. W. Motes to

Miss Emily White, all of Athens, Ga.

Issue of July 6, 1866

Mrs. Mary H. Davis, wife of Thomas N. Davis, deceased, was born in Elbert co., Ga., and died in Monroe co., Ga., June 11th, 1866, in the 72d year of her age....

Mrs. H. E. Bates was born in Edgefield Dist., S. C.,on 1st March 1798, died March 1, 1866....

Col. Herbert Hammond, died near Anderson, S. C., on 20th May 1866, born in Elbert co., Ga., March 17, 1797, married to Elizabeth Rich, of Elbert, in 1821....

Horace W. Bronson died in Macon on 12th of June, at the advanced age of three score and ten years....

Rev. Jesse Ellis, late of Montgomery Conf., died in Montgomery co., Ala., April 26, 1866, in the 78th year of his age....

Tribute of Respect to Miss Sallie Miller, St. Luke's Sunday School, Columbus, Ga...

Issue of July 13, 1866

Mrs. Susanah McRoy died at the residence of her son-in-law, Mr. J. W. Hudson, in Darlington Dist., S. C., June 20th, 1866, aged about 65 years...Her father was a minister of the Baptist Church and a native of N. C., where she was also born and reared ...the mother of nine children... J. W. McRoy.

Mrs. Elizabeth Dial Thrower, died in Atlanta, Ga., 28th June. She was born in Laurens Dist., S. C.,Oct. 25, 1804, and moved to Walton co., Ga., 1823, and married Mr. Benjamin Thrower...

Queen Isabella Hanson, daughter of Rev. Wesley, and Candace P. Hanson, died at Russellville, Ga., June 8th, 1866, aged five years and two months and 16 days....

Henry Murph died at his brother's in Houston co., Ga., on the 26th ult., at the advanced age of 94 years...a native of Lexington Dist., S. C.,but lived in Ga. about 30 years....

Issue of July 20, 1866

Charles Munnerlyn Edgerton was born in Marion Dist., S. C., and died in Gadsden co., Fla., Dec. 1865....

Mrs. Nancy C. Andrews, wife of J. G. Andrews, died in Lee co., Ga., July 3d, 1866, aged 45 years. Her mother, Mrs. Francis Bonner, of Baldwin co., Ga., was converted under Bishop Asbury....

Comfort S. Bostwick was born July 1, 1844...Her father was early removed to the better land, and Comfort was raised by her father-in-law, Dr. Willoughby Barton....

On the same day, July 1st, Little Minnie Austin, the youngest of Rev. J. M. Austin's two little girls, died, about 5 years old.

Mrs. Louisa Smith, wife of John A.Smith, died on 16th May, 1866, near McDonough, Henry co., Ga., aged 40 years and 6 days.

Martin Linebarger was born Jan. 21,1803, and died at his residence in Catawba co., N. C.,on 14th June 1866....

James D. Lester, Sr. died in Dooly co.,Ga., July 19, 1866, in the 76th year of his age....

Married on the 26th of June, in Chester Dist., S. C., by Rev. C. H. Pritchard, Rev. E. Lemmond of S. C. Conf. to Miss Rebecca Pratt.

Died, Daniel Webster, infant son of Mr. David and Mrs. Sarah P. Beauchamp, of Greenwood, Fla., June 12th, aged 10 months and 8 days.

Rosa Valeria, only child of Dr. J. Dickson and Mrs.Carrie V. Smith, on June ___, in Houston co., aged 2 years and 4 days.

Issue of July 27, 1866

Elbert A. Holt was born in Elberton, Ga., 27th July, 1801 and died in Montgomery, Ala., July 1st, 1866....

Rev. Charles Fisher died in Chattahoochee co., Ga., May 14, 1866, inthe 79th year of his life, and the 60th year of his ministry....

Mrs. Mary Pegram of Dallas, Gaston co., N. C., died in Charlotte, N. C. on 7th July 1866, in her60th year...member of the Presbyterian Church....

Mrs. Sarah A. Brown, relict of Judge Lewis S. Brown, of Washington, Ga., fell asleep in Jesus, July 1, 1866, in her 70th year....

Mrs. M. H. Johnston, wife of the Rev. G. C. S. Johnston, formerly of Tallahassee, Fla., died in Fernandina, Fla.,on 4th June, 1866, aged 52 years....

Miss Catharine Jennett Bethea, daughter of Rev. S. J. Bethea, died July 3, 1866, at Reedy Creek, Marion Dist., S. C., in her 17th year....

Married on 29th May, 1866,by the Rev. W. F. Easterling, Wm. T. Ormond of Apalachicola, Fla., to Miss Annie V. Smith, of Gadsden co., Fla.

On 31st May, 1866, by the same, Lt. Mortimer Bates, of Apalichocola, Fla. to Miss Esther E. Davis, of Gadsden co., Fla.

Issue of August 3, 1866

Abraham Coffin, was born in Nantuckett, Mass., Jan. 15, 1785, and died in Anderson Dist., S. C., March 28, 1866....

Mrs. Martha Alexander, died in Griffin, Ga., on 24th June. She was born in Mecklenburg co., N. C., removed to Jasper co., in 1815, thence to Griffin in 1840...left a widow in 1830...the mother of eight children, all sons. Only three survive.

Milton Wilder died near Forsyth, Ga., on Friday, 6th July... emigrated in early manhood from Massachusetts, to Ga.

Tribute of Respect to Edward J. Tarpley, who died in Irwinton, July 6, 1866...born in Brunswick co., Va.,Jan. 12, 1816, and received the name of his father Edward Jones Tarpley...In Jan. 1841, married to Miss Ann McRaeny, who survives with eight children....

Tribute of Respect to Rev. Charles Fisher by Jamestown ct. Died, in Tuskegee, Ala., on 29th July, 1866, Katie Lou, daughter of Rev. Lewis and Arcadia Dowdell, aged 1 year and 4 days.

Married on 12th July, 1866, by the same Rev. B. Hew, to Miss M. Josephine Hood, all of Gadsden co., Fla.

On 12th July, 1866, by Rev. W. H. Thomas, Wm. J. Clarke, of St. Marys, to Catharine D. Holzendorf, both of Camden co., Ga.

On 24th July, at Asbury Church, Memphis, Tenn., by Rev. D. J. Allen, Rev. S. M. Cherry, of the Tenn. Conf. to Miss Emma Capers, daughter of the late Rev. B. H. Capers, D. D.

On the 18th July, 1866, by Rev. J. H. Lockhart, Mr. Otis D. Smith to Miss Mary A. Howell, both of Russell co., Ala.

On 25th July, by Rev. W. M. Watts, Mr. R. P. Bird, of Liberty co., and Miss Josephine S. Hines, daughter of Judge T. R. Hines, of Effingham co., Ga.

Issue of August 10, 1866

Robert Washington, eldest son of Rev. R. M. Sanders, of Columbus, Ga., was born Jan. 30, 1853, and died in Macon co., Ala., June 30th, 1866....

Edward North Cudworth died in Charleston, S. C., July 24th, 1866, aged 23 years and 4 months.

Mrs. Nancy P. Arnot, wife of Marvin Arnot, and daughter of
John and Susan Glasscock, died in Catoosa co., Ga., June 23,
1866, in her 49th year....

Issue of August 17, 1866

Dr. Thomas P. Frith was born in Abbeville Dist., S. C., 5th
Oct. 1802, and died in Autauga co., Ala., April 12, 1865...(long
account). A. J. Briggs, Prattville, July 27, 1866.
Mrs. Eliza Williams Harris, eldest daughter of Rev. A. R.
Ramey, and granddaughter of Rev. Jordan Ramey, was born in Abbe-
ville Dist., S. C.,Feb. 26, 1844, married in March 1861, and died
at her father's residence in Greene co., Ala., on 22 June 1866.
Miss Emma Fryer, daughter of Judge B. M. And Mrs. E. A. Fryer,
of Blakely, Early co., Ga.,died at Barnesville, Ga.,on 18th of
July, in the 18th year of her age....
James Lovick Carlton, aged 16 years and 6 months, son of J.
M. and M. J. Carlton, died on 29th June in Panola co., Miss....
Married in Troup co., Ga.,Aug. 7, 1866, by Rev. S. W. Dixon,
Mr. Lucius T. C. Lovelace and Miss Amanda J. Davidson, all of
Troup co., Ga.
On the 31st July, at the residence of John W. Fawcett, by Rev.
A. B. Thrasher, Wm. E. Spier to Mrs. Eliza D. Skinner, all of
Columbia co., Ga.
In Butts co., Ga.,on the 15th July, by Rev. W. W. Oslin, Mr.
Charles A. Gaston to Miss Mollie Mackey.
Died, June 25, 1866, little Carly, infant son of J. J. & Kate
Flowers, of Butler co., Ala., aged 5 months and 5 days.

Issue of August 24, 1866

Rev. John David Weaver Crook, of the S. C. Conf. was born in
Orangeburg Dist., S. C.,Oct. 16, 1820, and died May 1, 1866...
Mrs. Ann Worthy was born in Greenville co., Va., Dec. 6, 1781,
moved in early life to Ga. and thence at a later date to Marengo
co., Ala...died at the residence of her son-in-law, Col. Chas.
Walker, near Uniontown, Sept. 9, 1864, in the 83d year of her
age...She leaves four children: Mrs. Jane Ann Walker, of Marengo
co., Ala., at whose house she died; Mrs. Corry of Perry co., Ala.,
mrs. Crocker of Ga., and Mrs. Steele of Ky.
Mrs. Samuel P. Maner died on 26th July 1866, aged 39 years
and 4 months...daughter of Maner Lawton, a steward of Black
swamp (S.C.) ct..
James Florence Ravens, son of W. S. and N. S. Ravens, died at
Bottsford, Sumter co., Ga.,on 7th July, in his 14th year...the
oldest son of his widowed mother....
Mr. John W. Smith died on 13th July, at the residence of his
son-in-law, Mr. Robert Rodd, in Irwin co., Ga., inthe 71st year
of his age...born in Richland Dist., S. C., March 31, 1796....
married in 1824, Miss Sarah R. Hendrix, of Fairfield Dist., S. C.
Judge L. C. Mathews was born in Jefferson co., Ga., and died
in Washington co., Ga., June 16, 1866, in his 52d year....
Mrs. Mary Gamble, widow of Rev. Jas. Gamble, was born in
Scriven co., Ga., Feb. 11, 1796, and died in Dooly co., July 7,
1866....
George P. Parker, my brother, was born in Hancock co., Ga.,
Oct. 3, 1793, and died near Griffin, May 6, 1866, in his 73d
year.... Sm. C. Parker.
Tribute of Respect to John Wesley Miller by Darlington ct.
Married on Monday, 20th inst., by Rev. J. M. Bonnell, Mr. George
W. Scattergood to Mrs. Mary Eggleston, all of Macon, Ga.
At Dover, Russell co., Ala., on 15th Aug., by Rev. A. T.
Holmes, Mr. Bernard R. Herty of Atlanta, to Miss Lou T. Holmes.

Issue of August 31, 1866

Married on August 23d, by Rev. J. H. Lockhart, Col. N. R.
Lewis, to Mrs. Margaret D. Shaw, both of Russell co., Ala.
Amanda J., wife of Joseph Vinson, and daughter of Wm.
Stripling, died on 4th August, in Macon, in the 25th year of her
age....
Mrs. Sarah Holley, relict of Dr. Wade Holley, and daughter
of Josiah and Amelia Holmes, died in Barnesville, June 10th, in
her 44th year....In her 18th year married to Dr. Holley.
Rev. George G.Witherspoon died near Clinton, Jones co., Ga.,
on 11th Aug, 1866, aged 74 years...a native of N. C., and moved
to this State in 1823....
Georgia E. Densler, daughter of Rev. T. L. and Mary Densler,
was born in Baldwin co., Ga., 22 June 1835, and died July 11,
1866, in Autauga co., Ala....
Mrs. Rebecca A. J. Smith, died in Walker co., Ga., June 29,
1866, in the 22nd year of her age....

Issue of September 7, 1866

Miss Victoria M. Bivins, died on 19th July last, aged 16
years and 10 months, and Miss Mary Ward Bivins died on 7th of
August....
Brohter Aaron Cannon was born July 9, 1815, and died in
Spartanburg Dist., S. C., July 24, 1866....
William Wright was born in Georgia, on 17th Oct., 1797, and
died near Greenville, Butler co., Ala., July 23, 1866....
Charles M. and Robert West, sons of Bro. and Sister E. M.
West of Tallahassee, Fla....
Mrs. Keturah Pringle, died at the residence of her son-in-law,
Dr. J. R. Campbell, in Barnesville, Ga., Aug. 16, 1866, born
in Halifax co., Va., Sept. 24, 1793, and about 1800 emigrated with
her parents to Clark co., Ga. Here she married Coleman S.
Pringle, Jany. 3, 1822...resided in Monroe co., and Pike co.,
shere her husband died April 16, 1850....
Rev. Henry C. Hurlong died in Edgefield Dist.,S. C., May 20th,
1866, in his 65th year....
Mrs. Sarah Jane Freeman died in Graniteville, S. C., on 23
July 1866, aged 32 years 7 months....
Married on August 23d, by Rev. C. P. Murdock, Mr. S. T.
Prescott, to Miss Margaret Fagan, in Newnansville, Fla.
On Aug. 23, by Rev. J. A. Wood, Mr. Melville Golightly, to
Miss Margaret T. West, both of Spartanburg Dist., S. C.

Issue of September 14, 1866

Lafayette Snodgrass was born in Spartan, Tenn. 30th Oct. 1827,
and died 24th August 1866, in Houston, Suwanee co., Fla...
Mrs. Nannie E. Chunn, wife of Mr. William Chunn, of Meri-
wether co., Ga., and daughter of Mr. Thomas and Mrs. Sabina
Barron, of Talbot co., was born 4th April 1844, and married
Sept. 1865, and died at her father's residence 5th Aug. 1866.
Rev. John J. Wells, was born in Hanover co., N. C., in 1796.
He removed to Tenn. when quite young and married to Miss Rebecca
A. Blake in Dixon co., in 1823...died 7th June last.
Sister Nancy Phillips was born 28th of March 1828, and died
30th April 1866...
Daniel G. Livingston, was born in Scotland 28th June 1814.
In the 14th year of his age, he landed at Charleston, S. C...
His early manhood was spent in Marlbor Dist., S. C., where in
1841 he joined the M. E. Church, moved to Madison, Fla., in
1845, and where he died July 9, 1866....

212

Tribute of Respect to W. H. Simmons by Zebulon and Barnesville
Ct....
 Married on Aug 16, 1866, by Rev. J. H. C. McKinney, Mr.
Samuel Liles to Miss Louisa Brown, both of Pickens dist., S. C.
 By Rev. M. G. Jenkins, Mr. Barry Miles to Mrs. Susana Brant-
ley, all of Marion co, Fla.

Issue of September 21, 1866

 Mrs. Mariette Hardeman, daughter of Mr. J. Pitts, decd.,was
born Sept. 2, 1839, married to Isaac Hardeman, Esq.,of Clinton,
Ga., 5th Nov 1856, and died 18th June 1866....
 Mrs. Victoria Sullivan, wife of Capt. T. E. Sullivan, and
daughter of James and Ann Shuptrine, decd, of Thomaston, Ga.,
died at Grayson C. H., Va., on 24th July, in the 25th year of
her age....
 Capt. James A. Zitrour, only son of Mrs. Joanna Zitrour,
died in Savannah, Ga.,4th Sept., aged 30 years....
 George W. House was born Dec. 4, 1830, and married to Miss
Amanda Pilly in 1857, and died in DeKalb co., Ga., Sept. 4, 1866.
 Tribute of Respect to Milton Wilder by Forsyth station....
Died in Decatur, Ga., Spet. 10, Julia Bedford, infant and only
daughter of L. B. and Ella Langford, of Atlanta, Ga.,aged 3 months
and 10 days.
 Married in Augusta, Ga., Sept. 12, 1866, by Rev. G. Kramer,
J. M. Martin, to Kate J., daughter of C. Canning.
 On the 4th inst., by the Rev. S. H. J. Sistrunk, Prof. J. J.
Harvey, of Houston co., to Miss C. E. Fudge, of Dooly co., GA.
 On August 15, 1866, by Rev. R. W. Dixon, in Harris co., Ga.,
Benjamin F. Steger, of Madison co., Ala. to Miss Fannie Moss, of
Harris co., Ga.
 In Macon, Ga., on 10th Sept., 1866, by Rev. T. B. Russell,
Mr. John W. Allen to Miss Mary Ann Walker
 On 12th Sept., by Rev. Wesley F. Smith, Mr. B. F. Davis and
Miss Carrie Searcy, all of Monroe co., Ga.
 In Jacksonville, Fla., Sept. 9, 1866, by Rev. W. A. McLean,
Mr. K. S. Waldron, and Mrs. Frances M. Fernansez.
 On Sept.4th, by Rev. A. J. Dean, Lt. Calvin L. Hutcheson,
of Hamilton co., Tenn., to Miss Mary Luttrell, of Harris co., Ga.
 On the 9th Aug.,by Dr. J. R. Thomas, Mr. E. F. Edwards of
Oglethorpe co., to Miss Mollie E. Evans, of Oxford, Ga., daughter
of Rev. W. H. Evans.
 On Aug 23, 1866, by Rev. J. J. Singleton, Mr. Robert E.
Charles, of Vicksburg, Miss., to Miss Sallie E. Wynne, daughter
of R. J. Wynne, Esq., of Putnam co., Ga.

Issue of September 28, 1866

 Mrs. Charlotte J. Gober, daughter of Rev. Walter and Gills
Manning was born in DeKalb co., Nov. 23, 1832, and married to
Marion C. Gober, Dec. 18, 1856, and died at her father's resi-
dence, in Cobb co., Ga., May 11th, 1866....
 Mrs. Sarah Neal Dickson, wife of Capt. Andrew Dickson of
Pickens Dist., S. C., died on 8th of August, 1866, and in her
42d year...left husband and children.
 Mrs. Esther Gable was born in Lexington Dist., .S C., and
died in Marietta, Ga.,7th August 1866, aged 77 years and six
months...Reared by Lutheran parents....
 Robert Baker Grace, the youngest son of Green B. and Ann
Jane Grace, died in Choctaw co., Ala., on 23d August 1866, in his
12th year.... J. J. Grace.
 Mrs. Sarah White, died in Anderson, S. C., Aug. 3, 1866, in
her 27th year...member of the Baptist Church a number of years....

Mrs. Peyton Ann Phillips, daughter of Maj. Peyton Pinckard, decd.,
was born in Randolph co., Ala., 14th March 1844, married in West
Point, Ga., in 1859 to Orion L. Phillips of Mill Town, Ala.,
and died near Girard, Ala., 22d August 1866....
    Sister Elizabeth H. McMichel was born in Greene co., Ga.,
July 30, 1807, died in Marionco., Ga.,Sept. 11th 1866, married
to Seaborn McMichel, her surviving husband, Feb. 22, 1824....
    Tribute of Respect by Anderson Station and Ct. to Herbert
Hammond and P. W. Seyle....
    Married on the 11th Sept., by the Rev. T. J. Rutledge, Mr.
D. V. Glenn to Mrs. C. V. Parker, all of Glennville, Ala.

Issue of October 5, 1866

    Rev. F. M. Wilson of Fla. Conf., was born Dec. 22, 1838,
and died, 9th of June....
    Mrs. Martha A. E. Carter, my step-daughter died at Green
Hill, Stewart co., Ga., 12th August, 1866, in the 30th year of
her age. Two days after her death Isola Maria, her eldest, a
daughter of nine summers.... J. T. Turner.
    Mrs. Mary Joseph Anderson was born 7th April 1845, and died
7th July 1866...Her Uncle William.
    Rev. John F.Berry was born in Twiggs co., Ga., Sept. 8th,
1837, and died in Ellaville, Ga., Sept. 6, 1866...(long eulogy).
    Sister Mary Ann Sample, wife of John B. Sample, and daughter
of John and Harriet Foy, died near Greenwood, Abbeville Dist.,
S. C., Sept. 1, 1866, aged 29 years, wanting 20 days. And on
the same day, her infant daughter...buried in Salem Church yard.
    Tribute of Respect by Sandy Ridge Circuit, Montgomery conf.
to Rev. Robert Thompson.
    Died in Macon co., Ala., on 29th Sept., John Alexander son
of Rev. A. M. and R. M. Gillespie, aged 6 weeks and 3 days.
    Married in Gainesville, Fla., on the 12th Sept., 1866, by
Rev. O. A. Myers, Dr. J. F. McKinstry to Miss Belle F. McCall
and T. R. Kennedy, Esq., to Miss Cornelia E. McCall.
    In Stewart co., Ga., on the 18th inst., by Rev. E. H. Mc-
Gehee, Dr. Newell M. Thornton to Miss Mary C. Turner.
    On August 28th, by Rev. W. C. Dunlap, Mr. George H. Hues
to Miss Lucinda H. Vincent, both of Bartow co., Ga.
    On Sept. 12th, by Rev. W. C. Dunlap, Mr. Wm. Chambers, to
Miss Emily Bryce, both of Carroll co., Ga.

Issue of October 12, 1866

    Pilona F., wife of Walter C. Johnson, and daughter of Judge
Charles R. Simmons, died in Gainesville, Ga., July 29th, 1866,
in the 22d year of her age....
    Sister Penelope Vanlandingham died in Wilkinson co., Ga.,
Aug. 30, 1866, in the 54th year of her age...was twice married.
first Mr. Adkins, then to Jno. Vanlandingham sr. of this county.
a member of the Primitive Baptist Church.
    Mrs. Nancy D. Williams was born 24th April 1800, and died
at Manville, Mobile co., Ala....
    Royal F. Wright the son of the late David Wright, of Colum-
bus, Ga. aged about 17 years, died on 12th Sept....
    Mrs. Margaret Ezell, daughter of Mrs. E. J. Mooney, died in
Montgomery Ala., July 25.
    Sarah E. Lynn of Wilkes co., Ga., died on the 21st August,
1866...born in Columbia co., Ga., leaves two single daughters
and one son.
    R. Thomas Burditt was born June 30, 1829, and joined the M.
E. Church, Laurens ct., S. C., Cofn., married Miss L. C. Peterson, March 27, 1851, and died May 18, 1866....

Married on the 2d of Oct.,by Rev. J. O. A. Cook, Mr. Edmund
W. Rush, and Mary I. Stephens, all of Upson co.
August 16, 1866, by Rev. J. W. Turner, Mr. Wm. A. Cawthon
to Miss Sarah J. Thurmon, both of Henry co., Ga.
Sept. 23d, by Rev. J. W. Turner, Mr. B. M. JAmes to Mrs. M.
A. Weaver, both of Henry co., Ga.
On Sept. 27, by Rev. T. S. L. Harwell, Mr.Thos. H. Pickett,
to Miss Bettie Davenport, all of Webster co., Ga.
On Thurs., 23d Aug., at Ebenezy Church, South Butler Circuit,
Montgomery conf., by the Rev. H. J. Hunter, the Rev. John D.
Clayland of Jackson, Miss., to Miss Julia A. Ansley, of Butler
co., Ala.
On the 2d Oct., 1866, by the Rev. D. W. Calhoun, Mr. Simeon
B. Glaze, to Miss Carrie C. Wilkerson, all of Sumter co., Ga.
In Whitfield co., near Dalton, Sept. 27th, by Rev. J. M.
Richardson, Mr. Henry Conkin, to Miss Mattie Morris.
In Dalton, Ga., Sept. 27,by Rev. J. M. Richardson, Mr. Robert
S. Rushton and Miss C. E. Sims.
On Sept. 13, 1866, by Rev. J. R. Gaines, Mr. Andrew J. Wills
to Miss Mary A. Burgess, all of Milton co., Ga.
By Rev. Geo. C. Clarke, Sept. 9, W. S. Riley and Martha J.
Searcy, both of Carsonville, Ga.
In Talbot co., on Wed., Sept. 26, by Rev. W. Knox, Mr. Thomas
J. Dozier and Miss Alice Beall.
In Talbot co., Ga., Sept. 26th, by Rev. T. A. Brown, A. L.
Brown of fort Valley, Ga. to Miss R. Nettie Sanford, daughter of
Sterling G. Sanford, Esq., of Talbot co., Ga.

Issue of October 19, 1866

Miss Babe Pennington died Oct. 1, 1866, at Newton Factory,
Ga., in the beauty of young womanhood....
Shatteen S. Mitchell died in Griffin, Ga.,on 27th ult., in
the 65th year of his age, leaving a wife and 13 children...a
native of Virginia, but when quite young moved to Laurens Dist.,
S. C. He was married three times, and the father of 22 children.
member of the Baptist Church...
Mrs. Mary Jewett Sharp, wife of A. D. Sharp, and daughter of
Henry L. Jewett, died on the 19th of Sept., inMacon, Ga., in the
20th year of her age....
Tribute of Respect to William Campbell, who died Sept. 21,
1866 by Asbury Sunday school, Augusta, Ga.
Married on Wed. evening, Oct. 3, 1866, by Rev. W. T. Capers,
Rev. E. G. Gage, of the S. C. Conf., to Miss Mary Fleming,
daughter of Capt. Thos. H. Wade of Columbia, S. C.
Died on the 2nd inst., Lizzie, daughter of Wm. C. and Jane
H. Hurt, aged 5 years and 4 months.

Issue of October 26, 1866

Rebecca G.Everett, wife of Thos. H. Everett, was born in
N. C., in 1811, lived in Ga. and West Florida, in Lumpkin,
Stewart co., Ga....
Miss Mollie F. Winfree died in Lenoir, N. C., Sept. 14, 1866,
in her 28th year...born in Anson co., N. C., and lived there the
greater part of her life....
Mrs. Mary Josephine Danielly died in Monroe co., Ga.,on the
8th of October, in the 33d year of her age,leaving a disconsolate
husband and five children....
William Morris Dugger a native of Brunswick co., Va., was
born Oct. 1, 1781, and died in Glennville, Ala., Sept. 26, 1866.
emigrated to Marengo co., Ala., in 1836, to Macon co., in 1849,
and to this place in 1854....Six weeks previous, his daughter,

Mrs. Mary Moore, wife of J. G. Moore, of Cunnenugee, Ala died...
left a husband, four children and two sisters

Sister C. C. Hartwell died in Vineville, Ga. on 5th August,
1866, in the 34th year of her age...daughter of James and Fannie
Solomon, formerly of Tiwggs co. In 1858, her first husband,
Mr. Paul E. Tarver died, leaving her with two small children, a
daughter and a son...In 1862, married to Dr. Hartwell, formerly
of Va, by whom she became the mother of two children....

Jesse Simmons died at the residence of J. W. Simmons, in
Hancock co.,Ga., on the 19th August, 1866, in his 87th year....

Married on Tuesday evening, Oct. 9th, in Trinity Church,
Savannah, by Rev. A. M. Wynn, Col. W. W. Holland, of Monticello,
Ga. and Miss Lille E., daughter of Gen. George Paul Harrison
of Savannah, Ga.

On same evening by the same, Mr. WM. R. Walker and Miss
Fannie R. Thomas, both of Savannah.

In Americus, Ga.,on the 17th inst.,by Rev. Chas. R. Jewett,
Mr. Thomas A. Graham, formerly of Huntsville, Ala., and Miss
Olivia B., daughter of Mr. C. W. Hancock, Editor of the Sumter
Republican.

On 16th Oct., in the M. E. Church, South, at Oaky Streak,
Butler co., Ala., by the Rev. H. J. Hunter, the Rev. James W.
Gelnn of the Montgomery conf., to Miss Fannie Ride, of Oaky
Streak.

By Rev. U. Langford, on the 11th inst., near Warrenton, Mr.
J. B. Willis of Effingham co., to Miss E. A. Barber of Washington,
Wilkes co., Ga.

In Brunswick, Ga., by Rev. B. C. Franklin, on the 9th Sept.,
W. H. Franklin, to Miss R. C. Gardner, both of Brunswick, Ga.

On the evening of 4th Oct., by same, in Anderson Dist., S. C.,
Rev. W. A. Hodges, of the S. C. Conf. and Miss Cornelia Hardy.

Issue of November 2, 1866

Sister Elizabeth Camp was born in Jackson co., Ga., June 27th,
1800, married bro. S. S. Camp, and died Oct. 7, 1866...leaves
husband and five children.

Rev. Eli Williams died in Coosa co., Ala., July 4, 1866...born
in Kershaw Dist., S. C., May 1, 1797....

Mary Elizabeth Williams, daughter of Morris and Susan Cousins,
died July 8th, 1866, in the 17th year of her age...married to
E. F. Williams Dec. 28, 1865....

Sister Martha J. Sharpe died at the residence of her son,
Robt. D. Sharpe, Esq.,near Sylvania, Ga., Sept. 2, 1866, aged
65 years....

Hezekiah W. Strobhart about 43 years of age, died at Bin-
naker's Camp Ground, Barnwell Dist., S. C., June 13, 1865....

Mrs. Frances M. Steagall, wife of Benson Steagall, and daughter of C. F. and Mary A. Maddux, died in Rusk co., Texas, Sept.
15, 1866, in the 34th or 35th year of her age...born in Warren
co., Ga....

Tribute of Respect by Ebenezer Lodge, 210, Cowikee, Ala.,
to A. A. Rivers, who departed this life Aug. 12....

Married on Oct. 18th, by Rev. F. B. Davies, Mr. W. S. Adams,
to Miss E. A. Elliott, both of Pike co., Ga.

'In Charleston, S. C., on 17th Oct., by Rev. E. J. Meynardie,
Henry S. Wimberly of Twiggs co., Ga., to Mrs. Esther L. Wharton,
of the former place.

On the morning of the 8th Sept., 1866,by Rev. Thos. G. Herbert, of Cokesbury, Abbeville Dist.,S. C., James Wightman Herbert, of Newberry Dist., S. C., to Miss Emma Smith, of the former place.

Oct. 10, 1866, by the Rev. J. C. Simmons, Richard F. Watts, Esq., to Miss Virginia T., eldest daughter of F. F. Kirksey, Esq. all of Lumpkin, Ga.

In Stewart co., Ga., on the 18th Oct.,by Rev. R. H. McGehee, Mr. Clement W. Moore, to Miss Mary S. McGinty.

On the evening of the 16th Oct., at the residence of the bride's father, Montgomery co., Ga., by the Rev. John E. Sentell, Mr. Daniel A. McLenna, of Telfair co., to Miss Caroline E. McArthur.

At Decatur, Ga., by the Rev. James E. Godfrey, Oct. 25th, Mr. Robert A. Branson, to Mrs. Harriet E. Quillian, all of Decatur.

In Beallwood, Oct. 19th, at the residence of Mr. James Euniss, by Rev. J. O. A. Clark, Dr. Nanthan S. Black and Miss Mollis E. Ennis.

On the 18th Oct., by Rev. W. M. D. Bond, Rev. Robert Leslie, to Miss Mollie L. Truett, all of Troup co., Ga.

In Macon, on the 25th Oct., by Rev. Jos. S. Key, Mr. E. R. Carr, of Atlanta, to Miss Florida J. Redding.

In Vineville, on the 30th Oct., by Rev. Jos. S. Key, Mr. J. B. Ross, and Mrs. Mary Ann Longstreet.

In Mulberry St. Church, Macon Ga., on the 30th Oct., by Rev. Jos. S. Key, Mr. William C. Lockett to Miss Loula E. Hammond.

Died on 6th July last, near Jefferson, Texas, Eugene Capers Northern, youngest son of Mrs. Martha A. Northern, formerly from Taylor co., Ga.,aged about 16 years.

In Chickawatchee, Terrell co., Ga., Sept. 30th, 1866, Annie Fisher, daughter of Rev. H. D. and Mrs. C. B. Moore, aged 2 years and 8 months.

In Oglethorpe, Macon co., Ga.,on 22nd Sept., Julia Charlotte Greer, in the 5th year of her age, daughter of Mr. John M. and Mrs. Mary Greer.

Issue of November 9, 1866

Hon. Henry J. Robison, of Jackson co., Fla., was born in Houston co., Ga., June 26, 1840, and died in Harris co., Ga., Sept. 5, 1866, in his 26th year...

Mrs. Abi Barnes died Oct. 5, 1866, in Baldwin co., Ga., in her 58th year....

Mrs. Zamaria M. Huntington, daughter of Wm. and Nancy Stembridge, of Baldwin co., Ga., died in Gordon, Wilkinson co., Ga., 6th Oct., 1866, in her 23d year....

John T. Sligh was born in Lexington Dist., S. C., 25th March, 1802, and died in Richland Dist., S. C.,Oct. 7, 1866....

Rev. Samuel Smoke died at the residence of his son-in-law, J. E. Robinson, near Newnansville, East Fla., Aug. 25, 1866... born in Orangeburg Dist., S. C., May 11, 1804....

Cannon Caison formerly of Fayetteville, N. C., died on 16th August, at Lenoir, N. C. in the 60th year of his age...leaves a wife and eigth children.

Married on the 29th Oct., by Rev. R. J. Rutledge, Mr. W. C. Wright of Mobile to Miss Laura Tibbettes of Glennville, Ala.

On the 30th Oct., by Rev. T. J. Rutledge, Mr. J. B. Upshaw to Miss Anna M. Burke, all of Glennville, Ala.

Issue of November 16, 1866

Bro. Thomas H. Capers was born in Sumter Dist., S. C., March 27, 1811, and died in Monticello, Fla., Oct. 15, 1866. son of Rev. Gabriel Capers and nephew of Bishop William Capers.(long account)

Rev. William N. Peavy was born in Conecuh co., Ala., Nov. 18, 1827, and died in Monroe co., Ala., Aug. 16, 1866...
John McLarin was born July 5, 1825, and died Sept. 5, 1864...
Mrs. A. J. Holliday, daughter of the late Wm. L. McKey, of Griffin, and wife of H. B. Holliday, formerly of Griffin, died in Valdosta, 16th Sept. 1866...
Bro. John Larr died in Orangeburg Dist., S. C., in the 66th year of his age...left two daughters, an aged companion.
Mrs. Ann M. Slaughter, died at the residence of her son-in-law (Rev. S. Harwell) in Chambers co., Ala., Sept. 11, 1866, in her 69th year...
Frederick M. Rast died at the residence of his brother, Rev. L. W. Rast, in Lexington Dist., S. C....
Tribute of Respect to Rev. Sylvanus Walker, who was born in Greenbriar co., Va., Oct. 28, 1799, and died in Montgomery co., Ala., Sept. 20, 1866....
Married on 3d Oct., at the Franklin St. M. E. Church in Mobile, Ala., by the Rev. J. J. Grace, Mr. Edward Marshall to Miss Annie E. Cain, both of Mobile, Ala.
On the 18th Oct., by Rev. G. W. Persons, Mr. John H. Pha , of Newton co., to Miss Sallie R. Slappey, daughter of Geo. H. Slappey, of Macon co., Ga.

Issue of November 23, 1866

Mrs. M. A. Rush, daughter of Stephen Pace, was born in Harris co., Ga., Aug. 25, 1832, and died near Tuskegee, Ala., Sept. 20, 1866. (long eulogy).
Rev. Jas. G. Cotton, was born in Green co., Ga., Oct. 18, 1806, and died in Harris co., Ga., Nov. 1, 1866...reared in Putnam co., Ga. In 1830, he married Miss Ann E. Burford. (long account and eulogy)
Benjamin Seckinger died in Lowndes co., Ga., on the 3d Oct., in his 83d year...leaves a wife and two sons.
Bro. George E. McClellan was born in Barnwell Dist., S. C., July 18, 1797, came to Fla. in 1829, and died in Suwanee co., Fla., 18th Oct. 1866...
Susan D. Harper, daughter of Mitchel and Nettie Story, was born Nov. 13, 1841, died Oct. 30, 1866....
Married in Sumter co., Ga., on the 11th inst., by Rev. Charles R. Jewett, Capt. Roderic P. Worrell of Talbotton, Ga., and Miss Sarah E., daughter of the late J. Nicholas Taylor of the former county.
In Cuthbert, Ga., on the 18th inst., by the Rev. Chas. R. Jewett, Mr. P. B. Simes, and Miss Laura L. Anthony, daughter of Rev. Samuel Anthony, all of Americus, Ga.
In Marshalville, Ga., on the 15th inst., by Rev. Jos. S. Key, Mr. W. W. Wrigley, of Macon, and Miss Annie C. Mellard, of the former place.
At the house of Mr. E. Nebbut, on the evening of the 14th inst., by the Rev. William A. Overton, Mr. Thomas M. Bryan, and Miss Sallie F. Morris, all of Union Point, Ga.
Oct. 31, 1866, by the Rev. A. J. Stokes, Mr. F. C. Brabham and Miss Cornelia A. Brabham, all of Barnwell Dist., S. C.
In Madison, Ga., on 7th inst., by Rev. H. J. Adams, Capt. Thos. L. Langston, of Atlanta, and Miss Annie Virginia Wade, of Madison.
Near Madison, on 25th Oct., by the same, Josiah West Patrick, of Oglethorpe co., and Miss Sidney F. Head, of Morgan co., Ga.
Near Madison, on 1st inst., by the same Wm. W. Shouse, to Miss Elizabeth F. Crowley.
On the 24th Oct., by Rev. Wm. Martin, Rev. Wm. Tertius Capers, of the S. C. Conf. to Sallie, daughter of Jacob Bell, Esq., of

Columbia, S. C.

On the 25th Oct., by Rev. J. V. M. Morris, Mr. Wm. M. Williams, of Louisville, Ga., to Miss Laura C. Vinson, daughter of Martha C. Vinson, of Baldwin co., Ga.

On the 4th Oct., by Rev. W. B. Merritt, J. B. McMichael to Miss Ella A. ----, all of Marion co., Ga.

On the 25th Oct., by Rev. W. B. Merritt, at the residence of Stephen Sims, Marion Co., Ga., Co. E. H. Hollis of Alabama, to Miss Carrie H. ----.

On the 23d Oct., by Rev. D. W. Calhoun, Mr. Thomas J. Winn, of Oglethorpe to Miss Sarah A.Thornbury, of Andersonville, Sumter co., Ga.

On the 31st Oct., in Eatonton, Ga.,by Rev. R. W. Bigham, Capt. Morgan L. McNeel of Texas, to Miss Lizzie B. Birch, of Eatonton, Ga.

On the 3d Oct., at the residence of W. B. Ellington, by Rev. B. B. Quillian, Col. James G. Browne, of Murray co., Ga., to Miss Rachel P. Ellington, of Gilmer co., Ga.

On the 31st Oct., in Savannah, Ga., by Rev. Geo. G. N. Mac-Donell, Mr. Richard Fuller Harmon, to Miss F. Eugenia Walker, daughter of Col. Robt. D. and Mrs. Louisa A. Walker, all of Savannah, Ga.

On the 6th of Nov., by the Rev. D. W. Calhoun, Mr. Henry B. Raiford and Miss Esther Kitchens, all of Sumter co., Ga.

In West Point, Ga.,Nov. 8th, by Rev. J. S. Sappington, Mr. J. B. Hogan of Columbus, Ga. to Miss L. G. McMillan of West Point.

On 18th Oct., 1866, by Rev. Samuel Woodbery, Mr. L. Q. C. Lingo, to Miss Gillie G. Taylor, daughter of Mr. Henry L. Taylor, decd., all of Monticello, Fla.

Nov. 7th, 1866, at the residence of the bride's father, by the Rev. J. E. Evans, Mr. Joseph H. Burke of LaGrange, Ga., and Miss Amelia J. Duncan, daughter of Judge Perry E. Duncan, of Dougherty co., Ga.

At Fernandina, Fla., by the Rev. F. A. Branch, on the 3d of Nov., Hon. Charles P. Cooper, formerly of the Ga. Conf., to Miss Julia E., daughter of Col. Leonard Dozier, of Fernandina.

By Rev. R. H. Howren, Oct. 30th, at the residence of Mr. Wm. Collins, Mr.Samuel P. Harden to Miss Camilla. E. Collins, all of Decatur co., Ga.

On the 21st Oct., at the residence of the Rev. J. P. Glover, by the Rev. James Griffith, Mr. J. J. Saylor, and Miss S. Glover, all of Taylor co., Ga.

Also, on the 6th of Nov., by the same, at the residence of V. Montgomery, Esq., Mr. B. B. Lucas and Miss Susan Shine, all of Taylor co., Ga.

By Rev. John Calvin Johnson, on 14th Oct.,1866, Mr. Ambrose W. Leet to Miss Amanda J. Ward.

On 18th Oct., William H. P. Jones to Miss Martha J. Puryear. On 26th Oct., Mr. George W.Cook to Miss Susan F. Elder.

On 1st Nov., 1866, Mr. George C. Williams, to Miss Mary J. Winn, all of Clarke co., Ga.

In Harris co., Ga., Oct. 21, by Rev. R. W. Dixon, Mr. B. B. Baker, and Miss E. R. Delamar, all of Harris co.

In Troup co., Ga. Nov. 1, 1866, by Rev. R. W. Dixon, Mr. David H. Williams, and Miss Georgia A. White, all of Troup co.

In Troup co., Ga., Nov. 6th, by Rev. R. W. Dixon, Mr. Erasmus M. Leslie, of Meriwether co., Ga. and Miss Josephine Wright, of Troup co.

In Lawrenceville, Ga., by Rev. C. A. Mitchell, on the evening of Nov. 15, 1866, Dr. Tandy K. Mitchell and Miss Athella W. Simmons, daughter of Col. James P. Simmons, all of Lawrenceville.

Died, Mattie Lou, infant daughter of Mr. and Mrs. Chambliss, Macon co., Ala., born Sept. 21, 1865, died Sept. 20, 1866.

Issue of November 30, 1866

Mrs. Sallie Clara Glenn, wife of C. L. Redwine, M. D., died
in Atlanta, Ga., Oct. 19, 1866, in her 30th year...left husband
and children.
Joseph Tooke Perkins died in Houston co., Ga., Oct. 12, 1866,
in his 21st year....
Sister Martha Garrison died on 29th Sept., 1866, at the resi-
dence of her son in Anderson, S. C., in her 79th year....
Tribute of Respect by Students of Oak Hill Seminary, to
Young F. Rigner, who died 27th Sept. 1866....
Married in Crawford co., Ga.,by Rev. Wesley F. Smith, Mr.
S. R. Harrison, and Miss Fannie Webb, all of Crawford co.
At Shiloh Church in Houston co., Nov. 29, 1866, by the same,
Mr. B. A. Northern and Miss Emma H. Thompson, daughter of Mr.
Joseph H. Thompson.
On the 25th Oct., 1866, by Rev. J. V. M. Morris, Wm. P.
Williams, of Louisville, Ga. to Miss Laura C. Vinson, of Baldwin
co., Ga.
By the same, on 18th Nov. 1866, C. W. Ennis to Miss S. F.
Barnes, all of Baldwin co., Ga.
In Eufaula, Barboru co., Ala., on the 15th inst., by the Rev.
Wm. Shepherd,Major Edwin R. Patterson, of Charleston, S. C. to
Miss Louis L. Sternes, daughter of A. Sternes, Esq.
In Sumter Dist., S. C., on the evening of the 8th of Nov.,
by Rev. S. J. Hill, Mr. Robt Muldron to Miss Sue Green.
Also, by the same, on the evening of the 15th Nov., Mr. J. J.
Neason, of Savannah, Ga., to Miss Mary Spann, of Sumter dist.,
S. C.
On 1st Nov. 1866, by Rev. R. B. Lester, Mr. Benj. F. Carlisle,
to Miss Sarah Ann Hall, all of Talbot co., Ga.
On 21st Nov., by the same, Mr. Wm. C. Jamison, of Texas and
Miss Mary H. Jackson, of Talbotton, Ga.
On the 20th inst., by Rev. O. L. Smith, Mr. Robert Merritt
of Monroe co., to Miss Mary Gayle Lewis, of Hancock co., Ga.
On 1st Nov., by Rev. J. H. Lockhart,Mr. Wm. H. Dunn, to Miss
Nancy B. Wright, all of Russell co., Ala.
On the 13th Nov., by the same, Mr. Zachariah T. Lane, to
Miss Mollie T. Baker both of Russell co., Ala.
By Rev. J. W. Burke in Houston co., on the 20th Nov., Mr.
W. F. McGEhee to Miss Eliza J., eldest daughter of Major J. W.
Belvin, all of Houston co.
By Dr. W. H. Felton, in Cartersville, Ga., Nov. 6, Dr. David
H. Bamsaur and Miss Cordelia S. Erwin.
In Muscogee co., on the evening of the 20th inst.,by Rev. W.
C. Bass, W. A. Little, Esq.,of Talbotton, to Miss S. Virginia,
second daughter of John B. Dozier, Esq.
In Macon, Ga. on the 22d inst.,by the same Mr. W. E. White,
of Savannah, and Miss Eliza Davis of Macon.
Near Athens, Ga., 30th Oct., by Rev. H. H. Parks, Mr. Chas.
W. Reynolds, of Atlanta, to Miss Susan M. Jennings, of Clark co.
By the same, Nov. 7th, in Lexington, Ga., Mr. R. T. England
of Atlanta, and Miss Kate C. Young, of Lexington.
By the same, Nov. 13, in Athens, Bartow H. Overby and Miss
Josie V. Thrasher, both of Clark co., Ga.

Issue of December 7, 1866

Rial North was born June 2, 1829, in Georgetown Dist., S. C.,
married March 15, 1853, to Miss Mary Susan, only daughter of
the late Rev. Joseph A. and Mrs. Malinda Hines, of Columbia, S.
C., and died Nov. 6, 1866, at his house in the above named city....
The Rev. John F. Berry was killed by lightning on the 5th

inst....by Baptist Church of Christ at Ellaville, Ga., Friday, Sept. 7, 1866.
Tribute of Respect to Mildred Beall....
Mrs. Sarah Harris, wife of L. D. Harris of Forsyth, Ga., died Nov 1st, leaving a disconsolate husband....
Died in Macon Ga., Oct. 28, 1866, Laura Louise, youngest daughter of Mr. and Mrs. Wm. F. Brown, aged 1 year 8 months and 5 days.
Married on the 12th Oct., by Rev. J. W. Mills, Robert E. Ledwith,of Tallahassee, Fla. and Miss Paulina Munnerlyn, of Decatur co., Ga.
By the same, on the 22d Nov. Mr. Wm. Brantley and Miss Martha J. Watson, all of Dougherty co., Ga.
Oct. 17th, by Rev. J. W. Shores, Mr. R. F. Gallaway, of Pine Level, Ala. to Miss Isabella Skinner, of Pike co., Ala.
Nov. 20th, by Rev. J. W. Shores, Mr. Lewis J. Clayton, to Miss Sallie E. Williams, both of Pike co., Ala.
By the Rev. Jesse Wood, at the residence of the bride's father, Nov. 21, Mr. Elkanah Pace of Creek Stand, to Miss Eliza J. fort, of Cotton Valley, Ala.
Nov. 27th, in Pike co, by Rev. R. N. Maddux, Mr. James W. Means, of Atlanta, and Miss Eliza Shehee,daughter of S. B. Shehee, Esq.
On the 27th inst., by Rev. William A.Overton, Mr. Simron Hester, Jr., near Washington, Ga. to Miss Ann E. Tuggle, daughter of Mr. William TUggl,e of Greene co., Ga.
By the Rev. J. J. Morgan, Mr. Russel T. Ayers, to Miss Martha E. Perkins, all of DeKalb co., Ga.
By the Rev. W. G. Allen on the night of the 27th Nov., in Monroe co., Ga., Mr. S. A. Cunningham of Shelbyville, Tenn. to Miss Laura N. Davis, of Monroe co., Ga.
In Cokesbury, S. C., Oct. 30th, 1866,by the Rev. T. E. Wannamaker, Capt. S. J. Corrie to Miss Alice P., daughter of Col. B. Z. Herndon.
On 13th Nov., by Rev. W. A. Dodge, Mr. J. J. Hulsey and Miss Sallie E. Turner, all of DeKalb co., Ga.
In Marion co., Ga., on 22d Nov.,by Rev. J. T. Ainsworth, Mr. Robt A. Smith, of Mt. Lebanon, Louisiana, to Miss Anna G. Dumham.
At the same time and place, by the same, Mr. Solomon M. Cottle, of Schley co., Ga. to Miss Mary E. Dumham.
In Unionville, S. C.,Nov. 15th, by Rev. O. A. Darby, Mr. Geo. W. Hill of Union dist., S. C., to Miss Sallie J. Graham, of Charlotte, N. C.
In Augusta, Ga. on the 20th inst.,by Rev. JOs. S. Key, Major James H. Whitner, of Anderson, S. C., to Miss Ellen M. Stovall, of the former place.

Issue of December 14, 1866

Isaac J. Heath died in Burke co., Ga., Nov. 6, 1866, in the 65th year of his age.
Nancy Heath, wife of Isaac J.Heath, was taken from earth, July 24th, 1866, in the 52d year of her age....
Robert H. Alexander, was born in Va., 16 Nov. 1820, and died in Takulla, Fla. 20th Oct. 1866....
Tribute of Respect by Richmond Circuit, to Benjamin F. Harris. Tribute of Respect by Mt. Meigs Circuit, Montgomery conf., to E. A. Holt.
Tribute of Respect by Decatur ct., to Ebenezer Tilly.
Died in Macon, Ga., on 9th Dec., at the residence of his son-in-law, Dr. E. H. Myers, William Mackie, aged 81, a native of Scotland, but long a residence of Augusta, Ga.

Died in Pontotoc, Miss., Nov. 3, 1866, Simeon Pitchford, aged
9 years and Oscar Dozier, aged one year, only children of Major
D. L. And Ellen N. Hoyle.
Married on Tuesday evening, Nov. 21, by Rev. C. H. Pritchard,
Rev. Thomas J. Clyde of the S. C. Conf. to Miss Mary Frances,
eldest daughter of Mr. Augustus Massebeau, of Camden, S. C.

Issue of December 21, 1866

Dr. Oscar B. Wynne, oldest son of E. and S. M. Wynne of
Putnam co., died 30th Nov. in his 25th year. His sisters, one
at school in N. C., and the other in her new home in Vicksburg....
Mrs. Elizabeth R. Sasseen, daughter of John and Elizabeth
Henderson, and wife of E. R. Sasseen, died in Atlanta, Ga., on
8th of Sept., 1866...born 28th Feb. 1823, in Jefferson, Tenn.,
and at the age of 17 joined the M. E. Church.
Mrs. Cinthia Freeman, wife of Bro. M. Freeman, and daughter
of Thos. and Mary Harmond (deceased) was born in Abbeville Dist.,
S. C., July 13, 1808, and married Nov. 16, 1826, died Nov. 11,
1866.
Alexander McAfee was born in Buncombe co., N. C. 1st March
1797, and died NOv. 25, 1866, in his 70th year....
Mrs. Fredonia Boykin, wife of R. H. Boykin, and daughter of
Mr. and Mrs.W. H. Stafford, died on 12th Oct., 1866, near Tuske-
gee, Ala....
Mrs. Josephine M. L. Hearn died in Putnam co., Ga. at the
residence of her mother, Mrs. Lucretia Edmondson, June 18, 1866.
Charlie Driver, son of Dr. E. J. and Josephine Driver,
Russell co., Ala., born June 25, 1850, and died Nov. 16, 1866.
Mary E. Tucker, wife of Robert F. Tucker, and daughter of
William and Elizabeth H. Patrick, was born in Newton co., 26th
Aug. 1822, and died near Opelika, Ala., 5th Oct., aged 44 years.
Tribute of Respect to Sister Flora Hooks, by M. E. Church
at Magnolia, Macon co., Ala.
Married on the 5th Dec., in the Methodist Church, at Black-
ville, S. C., by Rev. J. W. McRoy, Mr. Jas. P. Bruce, of Branch-
ville, to Miss O. M. Coburn, daughter of Rev. J. R. Coburn, of
the S. C. Conf.
On the 13th in Swallow Savannah Church, by Rev. J. W. McRoy,
Mr. W. K. Darlington to Miss Lcuy Allen, all of Barnwell Dist.,
S. C.
On the evening of the 11th Dec., at the residence of the
bride's father, by the Rev. Dr. A. A. Lipscomb, Dr. H. N. Harris,
to Miss C. B. Yancey, all of Athens, Ga.
On 21st Nov., by Rev. A. J. Haygood, Mr.B. W. Vandike of ·
Atlanta, Ga. to Miss Lizzie Lowrey of Marietta, Ga.
In Floyd co., Ga. on 10th Dec., by Rev. W. H. Hickey, Mr. D.
J. Kinney to Miss V. A. Antoinette, youngest daughter of A. B.
White, formerly of Atlanta, Ga.
On 21st Nov., by Rev. W. H. Thomas, Mr. J. C. Smith, to Miss
Kate Mizell, both of Carlton co., Ga.
On the 17th Dec., by Rev. Wm. W. Mood, Capt. J. H. DuPont,
ot Quincy, Fla. to Miss Martha Martha, daughter of Capt. Wm.
R. Coskrey, of Clarendon Dist., S. C.
Onthe 12th Dec., by Rev. P. P. Kistler, Rev. Allan McCorquo-
dale, of the S. C. Conf. to Mrs. Elenora Rembert, of Bishopville,
S. C.
In Buena Vista, Ga. Dec. 6, by Rev. J. T. Ainsworth, Mr. Benj.
Daughtry to Miss Matt Fulford.
In Buena Vista, Ga., Dec. 9th, by Rev. J. T. Ainsworth, Mr.
Geo. B. Collier, of Albany, Ga. to Miss A. E. Jordan, of Talbot
co., Ga.
By Rev. A. J. Dean, Nov. 25th, J. T. Hines of Miss M. E.

Houghton, all of Harris co., Ga.

By same, Dec. 6th, Mr. Wm. H. Luttrell to Miss R. A. Farley, all of Harris co., Ga.

By same, Dec. 8th, Mr. M. B. Kimbrough of Harris co., Ga. to Miss M. C. Owen of Talbot co., Ga.

By Rev. Jas. M. Wirght, Dec. 5th, Mr. Henry Dawson to Miss M. M. Griffith, both of Glennville, Ala.

In Cobb co., Ga.,onthe 1st of Nov. by the Rev. Wm. S. Foster, Prof. P. D. Wheeler and Mrs. Amanda Chastain, all of Cobb co., Ga.

On 6th Dec., at the residence of the bride's father, by Rev. Dr. W. W. Leake, Dr. J. A. Thomas to Miss Maggie T. W. Marsh, all of Cartersville, Ga.

On the 6th of Nov., at Creek Stand, Macon co., Ala., by the Rev. H. H. Cottrell, Mr. V. H. Williams, to Miss Burnetta Chatham, both of said county.

On the 27th Nov., at Creek Stand, Macon co., Ala., by the same, Mr. Seth Moore of Opelika Ala. to Miss Jane Adams of Macon co., Ala.

By Rev. John Clavin Johnson, on 16th Nov., Mr. Robt B. Harris, to Miss Martha F. Thompson.

By the same, on the 20th Nov., Mr. John T. Turnell to Miss Eliżabeth Anderson.

By the same, Mr. James H. Elder to Miss Blakely C. Elder. By the same, Mr. William B. Langford, to Miss Ellen Elder, all of Clarke co., Ga.

On the 20th of Nov., by Rev. J. G. A. Cook, Edmund J. Ethridge, and Miss Mary A. J. White.

In Marion co., East Fla., Dec. 2nd, by the Rev. John Penny, the Rev. Jas. P. DePass of the S. C. Conf. to Miss Anna M., daughter of Dr. B. M. and J. R. Gunnells, formerly of Laurens Dist., S. C.

In Sumter co., Ga., Dec. 5, 1866, by Rev. J. T. Norris, Mr. R. B. DeJarnette, Jr., of Lee co., Ga., to Miss Gabriella Harrison, of Sumter co., daughter of the late Dr. Harrison of Macon, Ga.

In Eatonton, Ga.,Oct. 31, by Rev. R. W. Bigham, Capt. Morgan L. McNiel, of Texas and Miss Lizzie R. Reid, of Eatonton, Ga.

In Eatonton, Ga., Dec. 5th by the same, Capt. Richmond A. Reid and Miss Leo H. Rodgers, of Eatonton Ga.

In Eatonton, GA., Dec. 9th, by the same, Edward F. Elliott and Mrs. Catharine F. McNatt, of Eatonton, Ga.

In Eatonton, Ga., Dec. 11th, by the same, Wm. T. Pearson and Miss C. Carrie Harwell, of Eatonton, Ga.

(No issue of December 28, 1866)

Issue of January 4, 1867

Married on the 20th Dec., 1866, by Rev. J. M. N. Low, Mr. W. S. Millner, of Randolph co., Ga., to Miss E. H. Gray, the eldest daughter of Mr. Samuel Gray, of Clay co., Ga.

In Barnesville, Ga.,on 20th Dec., 1866, by the Rev. T. A. Brown, J. T. Blalock, Esq., of Upson co., Ga., to Miss Emma D. Tyler, daughter of W. P. Tyler, Esq., of Barnesville, Ga.

By the Rev. G. T. Embry, on 20th Dec., Mr. William H. Smith, and Miss Sarah Elliot, all of Henry co., Ga.

By Rev. W. W. Oslin, Dec. 19th, Mr. Thos. H. Barnes, to Miss Margaret A., daughter of Wm. H. Thompson, Esq., all of Jasper co., Ga.

By by same, Dec. 20th, Henry Mackey of Butts co., Ga., to Miss Mary E., Hall of Monticello, Ga.

On 29th Nov., 1866, by Rev. J. Emory Watson, Mr. Nathaniel Jefferies to Miss Sarah A. White, both of Union Dist., S. C.

In Troup co., Ga., Dec. 19, by Rev. R. W. Dixon, Mr. R. A. White, and Miss Mattie E. Williams, all of Troup co., Ga.

Also, at the same time and place, Mr. Jas. R. Harwell and Mrs. Jennie Hardy, all of Troup co., Ga.

In Troup co., Ga., Dec. 20th, 1866, by Rev.R. W. Dixon, Mr. L. P. Hill and Mattie A. Reid, all of Troup co., Ga.

On 19th Dec., by Rev. D. D. Cox, in Augusta, Ga.,Mr. Richard Summerall and Miss Jane Smith.

By the same on the 20th Dec.,in Columbia co., Ga.,Mr. William Sims, and Miss Sarah McCollough

In Macon co., Ga., Nov. 31th, by Rev. Wesley F. Smith, Mr. Allen M. Walker and Miss Alice Mitchel.

On 20th Dec., by Rev. R. E. Wannamaker, Capt. Edward Holman of Orangeburg, to Miss Mary E., daughter of F. H. Kennedy, Esq. of Sumter, S. C.

On 11th Dec., by Rev. J. R. Gaines, William J. Burlin of Memphis, Tenn., to Miss C. U. Teasley, of Alpharetta, Ga.

By the same on 20th Dec., Reubin S. Manning to Miss Mary Teasley, all of Alpharetta, Ga.

On the 29th Nov., by Rev. John J. Little, Mr. Robert M. Moss, to Miss M. C. Dunlap of Meriwether co., Ga.

By the same on the evening of the 4th Dec., Mr. Benj. F. Hardy, to Miss Mary C. MaGruder, of Meriwether co., Ga.

By the same on the evening of the 6th Dec., Mr. R. G. Hackney, of Newnan, to Miss Hattie A. Douglas, of Muscogee co., Ga.

In Gwinnett co., Ga., on 19th Dec.,by Rev. G. L. W. Anthony, Rev. John M. Lowery of the Ga. Conf. to Miss Sophia A. G. Davis, of the former place.

By the same, on 20th Dec., Dr. Thomas G. Jacobs and Miss Louisa Strickland, all of GWinnet co., Ga.

In Weston, Ga., Dec. 20th, by Rev. L. J. Davies, Mr.James A. Moore, to Miss Emorette C. Chamberlain, both of Weston.

At the M. E. Church, Georgetown, S. C., on Thursday evening, Nov. 22, 1866, by the Rev. Hos. Mitchell, Dr. Thomas P. Bailey to Maria Laval, second daughter of the late Dr. Charles Williams.

By Rev. T. J. Rtuledge, on the 18th Dec., Dr. J. H. Wooldridge, to Miss Madora S. Greene, all of Jameston, Ga.

In Augusta, Ga., Dec. 10, by Rev. D. D. Cox, Mr. Wm. Broad-water to Miss Fanny Robbins.

By the same, Dec. 11, Mr. Wilson L. Fenley and Mrs. Mattie Bettison.

By the samd Dec. 12, Mr. Hardy H. Fulghum and Miss Catherine L.Ballantine.

By the same Dec. 13th, Mr. Thomas Waters and Mrs. Julia Slater.

By Rev. John Calvin Johnston, 13th Dec., Mr. William F. Summers, of Coweta co., Ga., to Miss Allura K. Elder, of Clark co., Ga.

By the same, on 29th Dec., Mr. Thomas J. Poss to Miss Mary A. McLeroy.

By the same on same day, Mr. Francis A. Crow to Miss Milley Louisa Dicken.

By the same on 23d Dec.,Mr. Jonathan Montgomery, to Miss Margaret E. Simonton.

By the same on 25th Dec., Mr. William F. Phillips to Miss Elizabeth Giles, all the parties of Clark co., Ga.

By Rev. Wm. A. McLean, Dec. 18, 1866, Mr. Charles W. Johnson, and Miss Mary A. Latimer, all of Batton Island, E. Fla.

On the 27th Dec., by Rev. S. S. Sweet, Jas. E. Whitehurst, and Miss Eugenia J. Hardie, all of Bibb co.

At Bethany, Jefferson co., Ga.,on the 1st inst.,by the Rev. W. A. Hayes, Prof. Winfield M. Rivers, late of Augusta, Ga., to Mrs. Mary J. Daniel, widow of the late R. W. Daniel, decd. of Bethany, Ga.

On the 18th Dec.,by Rev. W. F. Easterling, Mr. A. W. Whittle,

of Bristol, Liberty co., Fla., to Miss Mattie E. Gregory, of
Gadsden, Fla.

In Macon, Ga.,on 29th Deç., by Rev. J. S. Key, Mr. Chas. P.
Roberts, to Miss M. Florence Snider, all of Macon, Ga.

In Monroe co., Ga., Dec. 23, by Rev. T. G. Scott, Mr. Cornelius McGinty to Miss S. F. Clements.

On 11th Dec., by Rev. John H. Grogan, the residence of Mrs.
Col. McIntosh, Mr. B. C. Wall to Miss Annie McIntosh, all of
Elbert co., Ga.

On 19th Dec.,by the same, at the residence of Dr. A. C.
Mathews, Mr. E. B. Tate to Miss Ella G. Mathews, all of Elbert
co., Ga.

On 16th Dec., by Rev. James Griffith, Mr. Frank Glover to
Miss Pauline, eldest daughter of Dr. W. H. Christopher, Reynolds,
Ga.

By the same, on 20th Dec., Mr. Benjamin Coodyear to Miss
Sarah Dwight, all of Taylor co., Ga.

On the 27th Dec., by Rev. J. B. Wardlaw, Mr. Seaborn
Fountain of Wilkinson co., to Miss Maggie Irvine, of Cuthbert,
Ga.

. Rev. Isaac Gregory died in Pickens co., Ala., June 24,1865.
He was born in Union Dist., S. C., Aug. 6, 1801...leaves seven
children.

Mrs. H. C. Spain, daughter of Rev. Isaac Gregory, deceased,
died near Columbus, Miss., July 17, 1866, aged 31 years and
8 months...married to John H. Spain in June 1852....

Elizabeth Caroline Spain, died near Pickensville, Ala.,
Aug. 17, 1866, aged 12 years.

Elizabeth W., wife of Geo. T. Quillian, and daughter of
James and Ann Bedford, was born in Burke co., N. C., Aug. 11,
1823, removed to Ga. with her parents in 1837, married 19th Nov
1840, and died at Conyers, Ga. Dec. 4, 1866....

Rev. Vardy Woolley died in Brunswick, Ga., Dec. 18, 1866,
aged about 60 years....

Mrs. Ann Hatton, relict of Rev. Lewis Hatton, died in Griffin,
Ga., on 12th Dec. 1866, in the 81st year of her age...born in
Lumberton, N. C., lived some years at Newberry C. H., S. C.

Mrs. Rebecca Cureton, widow of the late Edward Cureton, died
August 16, 1866, in the 76th year of her age, died at the
residence of Mr. Joseph Cunningham, in Pickens co., Ala...born
near Camden, S. C., resided in that State until fall of 1824,
when....husband moved to Alabama....

Wm. M. Gunnels, eldest son of Dr. and Mrs. G. M. Gunnels,
died on 29th Nov. 1866, in Marionco., Fla....

Issue of January 11, 1867

Married in Houston co., Ga., Dec. 26th, 1866, by Rev. E. H.
McGehee, Mr. Henry Clark to Mrs. Betty Chandler.

On the 4th ult., by Rev. R. W. Johnson, Dr. Wm. H. Pughsley,
to Miss Vienna, daughter of Judge A. E. Tarver, all of Jefferson
co, Ga.

By the same at Bartow, Ga.,on the 26th ult., Dr. Beniah Brown
to Miss Savannah E. Palmer.

By the same, on 1st inst., Mr. Jas. E. Kieman, of Washington,
co., Ga. to Miss Mattie C. Brown, of Jefferson co., Ga.

On 20th Dec., at White Oak Church, Camden co., Ga., by Rev.
Jas. G. A. Sparks, Mr. John H. Morrison of Camden, to Miss
Chattie E. Lawrence, daughter of Richard G. Lawrence, formerly
of Barnwell Dist. S. C.

On the same day, by the same, Mr. S. J. McDonald, of McIntosh,
to Miss Chattie G. Morrison, daughter of George Morrison, of
Camden co., Ga.

By Rev. W. S. Black on 23d Nov., Col. J. F. B. Jackson, of Chattanooga, Tenn. to Miss Sallie E. Hoke of Greenville, S. C.

At the residence of the bride's father, in Fauquier co., Va., on the 1st Jan., by the Rev. Dr. Wyer, Mr. Lewis H. Andrews, of Macon, Ga. to Miss Alice B. Royston, of the former place.

Miss Nannie C. Crowder, eldest daughter of Judge R. P. and and L. A. Crowder, was born in Meriwether co., Ga.,Aug. 8, 1844, and died in Spalding co., Ga., Oct. 10, 1866.

Mrs. Nancy O. Houston, was born in DeKalb co., Ga., Oct. 29, 1830, and died Nov. 19, 1866.... When a child, her parents moved to Russell co., Ala...In Oct. 1838, married G. W. Houston of Harris co., Ga....

Mary Howell, daughter of Mr. and Mrs. Singleton G. Howell, died in Milton co., Ga., on 19th Dec., 1866, in the 20th year of her age....

Mrs. Lavinia A. Richardson, died in Rush co., Texas, Oct. 5, 1866. She was the daughter of C. F. and Mary A. Maddux, born in Marion co., Ga., in 1843, married to Edward E. Richardson in Jan. 1866....

Mr. Richmond R. Kendrick died in Calhoun co., Fla., Oct. 23, 1866, aged about 64 years...brought up in Hancock co., Ga.

Andrew Forsyth, was born in York Dist., S. C., Feb. 12, 1795, and died in Girard, Ala., Dec. 15, 1866....

Miss Jane R. Norton, daughter of Rev. J. W. Norton, decd., died in Autaugaville, Ala., Sept. 21, 1866, aged about 36 years.

Issue of January 18, 1867

Married on 20th Dec., by Rev. Dr. McFerrin, Mr. S. H. DeJarnette, of Eatonton, Ga., to Miss Anna Thomas, of Nashville, Tenn.

On the 2d day of Jan., 1867, by the Rev. Wm. S. Foster, Mr. D. M. Saye to Miss M. A. Cook, all of Cherokee co., Ga.

On Dec. 9, by Rev. Wm. H. Fleming, Rev. W. S. Black of the S. C. Conf. to Miss Mary M. Fleming, daughter of the officiating minister.

By Rev. W. F. Cook, in Barnesville, Ga., Nov. 16, 1866, Col. G. G. Flint and Mrs. P. Mays.

By the same, December 15th, 1866, Samuel K. Cook and Miss Sallie Elder.

In Albany, Ga., 8th of Jan., by Rev. Henry D. Moore, M. D. J. Owen, of Albany to Mrs. Susan D. Douglas, of the same place.

Died at Newburn, Ga. Dec. 31, 1866, Luther Smith, infant son of J. F. and George E. Mixon.

Madame Rosalie Gauvain, died in Athens, Ga. Nov. 10, 1866,. bieng about ninety years old..born in France, May 7, 1777, and related to the French nobility. (long account)

Mickleberry Merritt died in Monroe co., Ga., Nov. 24th, 1866, in the 64th year of his age...born in Greene co., partly reared in Morgan, where in 1824 he married Miss June Brown, in 1826 moved to Monroe....

Mrs. Louisa J. Foster, daughter of John and Abi Edward, died in Elmore co., Ala., on 9th Dec, 1866, in her 15th year...married to John E. Foster, in 1859.

Mrs. Sarah M. Cox, wife of William Cox, of Heard co., Ga., died at the residence of her father, Samuel Mafitt, Sr., of Troup co., Ga., in the 30th year of her age, May 11th, 1866. She was preceded by two of her children, Martha S. E. M. Cox, their infant child on 17th April 1866, and Eugenius A. C. Cox, their son died at Montgomery, Ala., while in service of his country, in the 16th year of his age....

Daniel Turnipseed, died on the 4th Jan., 1867, in Henry co., Ga., in his 72d year...about 14 years ago moved from S. C. to Ga.... Henry Turnipseed.

page 46, issue of February 7, 1862, Mrs. <u>Amanda</u> should be Mrs. Anastasia Foster.

Bascom, Cornelia A. 23
Baskin, H.W. Mrs. 2
  James 2, 61
Bass, Amelia M. Mrs. 65
  A.O. Mrs. 168
  A.Q. Mrs. 175
  Henry Rev. 65
  Henry Blake 165
  Ingram 85
  James 86
  James Ogilby 175
  Jennie 194
  John T. Sgt. 111
  Nancy Mrs. 182
  Nathan H. 194
  Waterman Glover 65
  W.C. (Rev.) 54, 165,
    175
  Wm. F. 85
Bassett, Sarah 118
Bates, H.E. Mrs. 209
  Mortimer Lt. 210
Battay, Frances R. Mrs.
  172
Baugh, Georgiana Mrs. 192
  Robert Col. 193
  William 73, 76
Baughn, David 102
  Lucy A.N. Mrs. 102
Baxter, A.C. Mrs. 87
  D.H. 87
  Francis D. 166
  J.F. 26
  Theophilus D.W.
Baxtrom, C.L. 207
  John G. Capt. 207(2)
  Sarah J. 207
Bayne, Adolphes F. 11
  C.T. 161
  Elzb 91
Beall, Albert A. 115
  Alice 215
  Allen A. 25
  Charlotte A.E. Mrs. 202
  Erasmus T. Col. 202
  James 70
  James M. Col. 42
  Jeremiah 47
  Maria S. (nee Moughoh)
    47
  Mark. A. 70
  Martha F. (nee Heard)
    42
  Mary A. 123
  Mary H. Mrs. 52
  Melinda Mrs. 70
  Mildred 221
  Mollie S. 182
  Sarah E. Mrs. 28
  Thomas 28
  William F. 45
  W.T. 168
Beard, W.A. Dr. 186
Beasley, George J. 45
Beaswell, Mary Mrs. 104
  Wesley 104
Beauchamp, Daniel Webster
  209
  David 209
  Sarah P. Mrs. 209
Beauregard Volunteers 35,
  67, 77
Beavers, Mary L. 151
Beazley, Mary R. Mrs. 24
  Phillip F. 24
Beck, Wm. A. Maj. 62
Beckham, A.J. 130
  James 46
  James D. 40
  John T. 167
  Martha Mrs. 46
  Martha F. 46

Beckham Cont.
  Mary A. Mrs. 130
  Simon 178
Bedding Field, Mary Mrs.
  152
Bedell, Fannie 192
  Geo. W. Lt. 164
Bedford, Ann. Mrs. 225
  James 225
Bedgood, Wm H. 167
Bedsole, Catharine Mrs. 9
  John 9
Beekam, Lavonia 148
Beeman, E.O. 50
Belcher, O.R. Jr. 194
Bell, A. 177
  Augustus J. 115
  Dora Alice 94
  Elzb 79
  Elzb (nee Hampton) 139
  Eliza Jane 39
  Emma 197
  G.N. 18
  Green 202, 205
  Homer S. 200
  Jacob 218
  James B. 124
  John F. 177
  Lawrence 168
  Lazarus W. 94
  Margaret 124
  Mary M. Mrs. 94
  M.E. Mrs. 177
  M.J. Mrs. 140
  Narcissa Mrs. 18
  Sallie 218
  Samuel Mr. & Mrs. 168
  Sardenia A. 172
  Wm. 197
  Willie Edward 94
Bellah, Morgan 55
Bellamy, Wm. G. 181
  Willie 194
Bellinger, L. 58
Bellune, Mary E. Mrs. 150
  Wm. S. 150
  William T. Capers 150
Belsell, Alice 204
Belvin, Eliza J. 220
  J.W. Maj. 220
Belvine, Wm. T. Lt. 126
Benbow, Rebecca (nee
  Hilton) 144
  W.W. 144
Benett, S.A.C. (Nee
  Macky) 51
Bennett, W.R. 51
Benford, Mary An 154
Ben Hill Infantry 105
Bennett, A.G. Dr. 121
  Eli, Rev. 147
  John W. Dr. 41
  Levy N. (nee Bowles) 147
  Martha 141
  Nannie Alberta (?) 121
  S.F. Mrs. 121
  S.R. 18
  William 18
Bennick, A.R. 58
Benson, Mattie 139
Bently, John T. 125
  W.D. 99
Berrien, Minute Guards 67
Berry, Ann C. (nee
  Kennedy) 155
  Eliza Mrs. 111
  John B. 155
  John D. 21
  J/John F. (Rev.) 17,
    21, 34, 214, 220
  Mary A. 58
  Nancy H. Mrs. 46

Berry Cont.
  Nathan 111
  Thos. A. 111
  Wm. B. 13
Besser, Margaret G. Mrs. 4
Bethea, Catharine Jennett
  210
  Goodman Rev. 138
  S.J. Rev. 210
Bethaune, Cherry Mrs. 189
Bethune, John 189
  Susan R. 123
Bettison, Mattie Mrs. 224
Betsill, Joel 68
  Lucretia M. (nee
  Pearson) 68
Betts, Isaac Sr. 106
Bevill, Julia A. Mrs. 126
  William B. 126
  William T. 126
Bibb, Greys 67
Biddenback, J. 102
  M. Mrs. 102
  Margaret G. 102
Bigby, G.M. 167
  Nancy M. Mrs. 167
Biggers, Francis M. 90
  Josephine A. 199
  L.M. 199
  M.E. 197
Bilbro, Jas. A. 204
  T.W. Capt. 171
Billingslea, L. Clinton
  198
Billups, John Maj. 162
  Sarah M. (nee Phinizv)
  162
Binsford, Sarah 21
Birch, E.P. 59
  John N. 130
  Lizzie B. 219
  Susan M. 133
Bird, Behethland Mrs. 145
  Daniel Butler 85
  James Capt. 4
  Nancy Mrs. 19
  Pickney B. Maj. 161
  R.P. 210
  S. 143
  Sarah Mrs. 4
  Solomon 19
  T.D. 134
Birdsong, Carrie E. 105
Bivens, George A. 1
  Mary Ward 212
  Mattie N. 3
  Mildred Mrs. 34
  Nancy Mrs. 3
  Roldnd 31, 34
  Shadrach 34
  Victoria M. 212
Bizzell, Bennett 169
  Mary Mrs. 160
Black, Genia (nee Downs)
  195
  E. Mrs. 80
  Goegre A.J. Mrs. 130
  John 13
  John Lt. 170
  John W. 80
  Joshua S.F. 106
  J.W. 80
  Marcellus A. 106
  Mollie S. 89
  M.W. Mrs. 106
  Nathan S. Dr. 217
  R.C. Dr. 130
  Sarah Mrs. 13
  Susan E.P. 106
  William H. 106
  W.S. (Rev.) 17, 226
Blackburn, Rachel Mrs. 47

231

232

Cook Cont.
W.F. Rev. 57
Cooksey, Elzb Mrs. 46
Robert 46
Coombs, John S. 80, 86
Mary L. (nee Myers) 80
William D. 68
Cooper, Anderson W. 127
Anson W. 149
Arabella M. (nee Wood)
127
Chas P. (Rev.) 177, 219
Hessie Mildred (nee
Jackson) 177
James A. Dr. 108
James L. 56
Julis J. Cpl. 123
L.W. Rev. 56
M.C. 199
Micajah F. 149
Mildred Lewis 177
Noah 179
Robert Harrison 177
Sallie A. 39
S.H. 47
T.W. Rev. 108
Wm. Henry 177
William M. 128
Cope, H/Henderson A. 115,
177
John W. 177
Mary J. (nee Smith) 177
Sarah Mrs. 177
Thomas 115, 177
Copeland, James A. 72
Jasper N. 134
Obadiah 49
Sarah Mrs. 49
Sarah R. Mrs. 119
Wm. B. 147
William E. 49
Coper, Joseph B. Jr. 70
Corbett, Eleanora Mood 126
Hampton 126
Julius Clement 126
Corbin, Cicero B. 161
Isabella C. 2
Peter 2, 116
Corbit, H. Fletcher 44
Corby, Orrison 177
Sarah Nelson 177
Corey(?), Eli 50
Corley, Higden 82
Cornley, Frances Elzb 123
Cornutt, John D. 73
Corrie, S.J. Capt. 221
Corry, Mrs. 211
Coskrey, Martha 222
Wm. R. Capt. 222
Cosper, George H. Rev. 62
George Robert Perrin 62
Costine, Henry 153
Cotten, Jas. L. 50
Cotter, Julia 173
R. Mrs. 173
W.J. Rev. 173
Cottingham, Fannie C. 49
Cottle, Solomon M. 221
Cotton, Ann E. Mrs. 102
Jas. G. (Rev.) 102, 218
Wm. C. 174
Cottrell, Thomas Rev. Dr.
165
Cottrill, E.D. Rev. 177
Cousins, Morris 216
Susan Mrs. 216
Covin, Fannie E. 179
Covington, Margaret 91
Seaborn 99
Cowart, Lucy 160
Cowen, S.O. 82

Cowles, Robert S. 124
Cowper, David 88
Cox, Capt. 86
Alex. J. Mrs. 29
D.D. (Rev.) 97, 169
Elenor Motteray 62
Elzb Mrs. 53
E.O. Mrs. 169
E.R. 135
Esther Mrs. 62
Eugenius A.C. 226
G.W. Lt. 135
J.M. 62
John Rev. 146
Martha A. Mrs. 172
Martha G. 79
Martha S.E.M. 226
Mary Julia 169
M.L. Mrs. 29
Oliver P. 158
Salina Jane 29
Sarah M. (nee Mafitt)
226
Thomas C. 18
T.W. 196
W.H. 110
William 226
Coxe, William T. 106
Crag, Ann R. 137
Craig, C. Thomas 95
Emma E. Mrs. 149
John Grisham 170
J.W. 149
Lola Porter 149
Mary 119
Craige, Allen 53
Crain, Rebecca 19
Cramer, Beulah Ann Mrs. 13
Crane, A.B. 125
Crahe, Malissa 3
Robert S. 199
Cranford, Henry Rev. 68
Henry M. 68
Crapps, Wm. Rev. 106
Craven, I.N. Rev. 160
Cravens, H. 168
N.A. Rev. 142
Cravy, Eliza Mrs. 145
Hur Elzb 145
Crawford, Elzb A. (nee
Morgan) 153
George J. 98
George M.T. 191
Hinton 37
Joseph R. 116
Matthew L. 9
Thirza Mrs. 9
Thomas 9, 103
Thos. C. 153
Wm. Newton 157
Crawley, J.A. 37
S.K. 37
Creech, D.B. Col. 117
Crenshaw, David Rev. 54
J lia M. 54
Crews, Arthur 30
Leonidas Dr. 18
Mary Mrs. 30, 164
Thomas 164, 179
Criamiles, Mary (nee
Grant) 208
P.L. 208
Crocker, Mrs. 211
A.H. Mrs. 129
T.B. 129
William Mouzon 129
Cromer, Sallie V. 74
Crook, John David Rev.
211
Wm. 33
Crooks, Cicero 27

Crosby, G.L. Rev. 72
Isham 43
Stephen M. Sgt. 138
Cross, Nathaniel D. Capt.
91
Croute, Sarah C. Mrs. 143
Crow, Francis A. 224
Crowder, L.A. 226
Nannie C. 226
R.P. Judge 226
Crowell, C.A. Rev. 126
Henry Capt. 154
Crowley, Elzb 218
Mary A.E. (nee Smithwick)
104
Seaborn 104
Crum, Amanda 4
J. Wesley 7
Crumley Wm. M 55
W.M. 62
Crump, Elzb A. Mrs. 11
J.L. Dr. 177
Crumpton, J.A. 18
James Whitman 38
Sallie A. 18
Crymes, Thos. P. Rev. 89
Tinsley T. 61
W.M. Rev. 61
Cubbedge, Mary E. 178
S.J.M. 178
Cudworth, Edward North 210
Culbert, Fannie L. 201
Culler, Mrs. Dr. 22
Alice R. 74
Derrille H. 173
Derrill H. 105
H. Melissa Mrs. 173
John 10
Julia H. 53
Mary E. 173
Culpepper, Elzb Mrs. 134
Joel 134
J.W. Lt. 173
Culver, Frances A. Mrs. 52
James F. D. 27
J.G. 27
Levin E. Rev. 52
Cumming, E. 174
M.J. (nee Vinson) 174
Cunningham, Elzb O. Mrs.
86
Izaphiar Clementine 137
Joseph 225
J.R. 137
J.S. 76
M.C. Mrs. 137
Robert 35
S.A. 221
Sarah Mrs. 56
Sarah Ann Mrs. 35
William C. 76
Willy C. Mrs. 76
Cureton, Edward 225
J.S. 154
Rebecca Mrs. 225
Currell, Sarah M. Mrs. 1
Currie, Wm. R. Rev. 2
Curtis, Edward 155
Eliza Mrs. 155
Esther Ratcliff 187
Julius T. Rev. 138
Nannie 155
Susan H. 117
Curtiss, Lou Belle Mrs.
199
Willie Asbury 199
Cuthbertson, Elzb J. 54

Dickens Cont.
Robert D. 140
Dickenson, Wm. C. 56
Dickey, Ann E. (formerly
Evans) 196
John M. Rev. 196(2)
Dickinson, A.S. Rev. 101
Fannie A. 56
Frank J. Lt. 180
H.C. 17
J.J. 199
J.P. Rev. 180
Martha S. (nee Smith)
101
Mary 186
Dickson, A. Capt. 88
Andrew Capt. 213
Elias D. 79
Elzb. Mrs. 168
David 168
Eugene Summerfield 89
Jas. W. Lt. 142
Mary V. 88
Sarah Neal Mrs. 213
Wm. C. 142
William F. 142
W.N. 94
Dill, B. 37
Dillingham, D.S. 126
John W. 126
Dilworth, L.A. Mrs. 105
R. 105
Susan 105
Dimon, Elzb 203
Dingle, Ann Eliza 42
H.Jr. Maj. 87
James Harvey, Maj. 87
J. Harvey 203
J. Henry 42
Dinkins, John L. Dr. 195
Maria J. Mrs. 195
Mary Elzb 195
W. 144
Disher, Malinda 203
Diskey, Jane A. Mrs. 84
Mary Narcissa 84
W.D. 84
Dismuke, James Z. 12
Dismukes, F.B. 66
James Z. 15
Dixon, James P. 44
J/John Lee Rev. 51, 74, 159
Mary A. Mrs. 44
Mary Virginia 159
M.J. Mrs. 159
M. Victoria 164
Rachel Anna (nee Staley)
51
R.H. 104
R.W. 26, 44, 63, 94
Sallie H. 186
Turner B. 44
Wm. James Sgt. 162
Dobbs, C.L. 114
Dodd, J.E. Rev. 188
Dodson, James Rev. 149
Doggett, James R.R. 71
W.A.C. 89
Dolvin, Jas. 181
Donald, Bettie Lou 124
Carrie Mrs. 124
H.H. 124
Wm. J. 86
Donalson, Wm. 106
Donelson, Sallie R. 173
Doolittle, Henry 159
Dorman, Eliza F. Mrs. 139
L.P. 139
Dorough, Sallie 179
Dorris, Elzb Mrs. 81
James 81
James McKinley 81

Dorsett, Cecilia J. 111
Dorsey, Matthew 42
Dossett, John K. 185
Dougherty, Frances 39
Hibernia L. 13
Thomas Rev. 27
Doughty, John Radcliffe
141
Douglas(s), A.H. 89
Douglass, C.C. Mrs. 89
Ella 3
Franky 89
Hattie A. 224
J. 158
Jno. Dr. 184
John C. Dr. 47
Mary 8
Rebecca (nee Tilman)158
Susan D. Mrs. 226
S. Wade Dr. 184
Tilman (Rev.) 19, 30, 31,
112
Douthit, Benj. H. 71
Destimony Mrs. 71
Gambrell McPherson 71
Dove, Emma F. 156
Indiana H. 133
Dowdell, A.R. Mrs. 133
Arcadia Mrs. 210
Elzb Mrs. 104
James 104
Katie Lou 210
Lewis, Rev. 210
L.F. Rev. 133
Richard Venable 133
Dowling, Angus Rev. 198
Downer, C.M. Mrs. 109
Rialdo Sgt. 109
Downey, Stephen 120
Downing, Catharine Mrs. 85
Charles Richards 85
Lydia 16
Thos. 63
William 85
Downs, Rhoda R. Mrs. 145
Shelby 195
Doyal, Elzb Mrs. 36
Dozier, E.A. 43
G.A.B. 85
James Barrow 33
John B. 220
Jno. W. 23, 33
Julia E. 219
Leonard, Col. 219
Lovick P. 80
L.P. Mrs. 33
L.T. Mrs. 43
Mary Mrs. 139
M.S. 195
Palatine L. 23
Richard Rev. 85
Susan H. Mrs. 155
S. Virginia 220
Thomas 120
Thomas H. Lt. 121
Thomas J. 139, 215
Tillman H. 43
Drake, A.E. Magruder 146
Fannie M. 109
John Dr. 109
John C. Dr. 90
Mary A. 138
Mary A. Mrs. 90
Nicholas J. 90
R.M. Rev. 146
Thomas R. 145
Driggers, Elisha 6
Meredith 63
Driscoll, D.O. 42
Driskell, James 109
Driver, Charlie 222
Cynthia E. 145

Driver Cont.
E.J. Dr. 222
Josephine Mrs. 222
Dry, Allison 7
Daniel 90
Mary E. 7
Rachel Mrs. 90
DuBose, Asa 67
Maty R. 11
Samuel 26
Wiley H. 64
Zimmerman J. 70
Dubrier, Jesse 64
Salena Mrs. 64
Dudley, Edward 75, 170
Henry Lewis 75
Jas. J. 170
Mary Mrs. 170
Mary H.F. Mrs. 75
Wm. A. 170
Due, A.J. 112
Isoline Amanda Mrs. 112
Duffey, Jesse Benjamin 65
Robin M. 143
Dugger, William Morris 215
Duke, Benj. 144
Sarah R. Mrs. 144
S.H. Sgt. 143
Dukes. Abram 121
Elzb Mrs. 121
Elzb J. 15
Eliza R. 121
F.E. 204
R.C. Cpl. 112
T.L. 143
Dumas, Col. 13
Fannie E. 155
Jennie E. 13
Dumham, Anna G. 221
Mary E. 221
Dunaway, Thomas Tees 81
Duncan, Amelia J. 219
Benj. C. 105
Courtney W. (nee Walker)
118
Daniel 45
D/Daniel 191
Erastus B. 118
John F. Rev. 180
John P. Lt. 180
J/John P. Rev. 33, 45,
121
Kate 123
Matthew 105
N.A. Lamar 33
Perry E. Judge 219
Rena 191
Sarah H. Mrs. 124
Duncan(?), Nannie B. 118
Dungan, Jesse R. 122
Dunham, M.A. Maj. 157
Dunlap, David Edwin 121
D.M. Dr. 121
D.R. Dr. 45, 49
Geo. 188
Hannah Peninah Mrs. 188
Mary T. Mrs. 121
M.C. 224
M.L. Cpl. 168
T.J. 110
Winey A. 7
Dunn, H.V. 92
John 75
John S. Rev. 206
Laura 92
Lucy J. 51
Mary 75
Mary Mrs. 92
Nehemiah 116
Sarah Ann Mrs. 75
Wm. H. 220

Glover Cont.
 J.P. Rev. 219
 Ruth Talmage (nee
 Bostwick?) 122
 S. 219
 William 115
Glymph, Lemuet 3
 Martha 2
 Sarah Mrs. 82
Gober, ---- 82
 Charlotte J. (nee
 Manning) 213
 Marion C. 213
 Wesley A. Pvt. 72
Godbee, Malissa 56
Godfrey, Elzb Mrs. 163
 Jas. E. 30
 Mary Jane 137
 Richard Rev. 5
 Sophia A. Mrs. 162
 Tesie J. (nee Frink) 8
 T.J. Dr. 8
Godley, J.B. 136
Godwin, Mary E. 174
Golightly, Fletcher 47
 Harriet Mrs. 47, 64
 Jacob Ketle
 Melville 212
 Richard 47, 64
 Zaccheus Downing 64
Golson, Emanuel 150
 Lewis P. 150
 P.G. 176
Goodbread, Jacob T. Capt.
 46
 J.M. (Capt.) 36
 J.N.B. 196
 Mary Hardee 196
Goode, Eugenia H. 186
Goodman, Mary F. 205
Goodrich, E.R. 139
 Ophelia 139
Goodwin, Eleanor Mrs. 66
 Frances 66
 Joseph 66
Goodwyn, L.J. Mrs. 149
Goodyear, Benjamin 225
Gorce, Robert G. 5
Gorden, J.D. 15
Gordon, Ann Mrs. 167
 E. Jennie 167
 James D. 91
 Saml. O. 167
 Sarah Ann 91
Gore, Henry (Jr.) 53
 Lucy A. (nee Scott) 53
Goren, Nathan 43
Gorley, Mary 53
Goss, Jane Mrs. 114
 Wm. 114
Goudelock, Hamlet Dr. 139
 Oliver 174
Gouedy, Lizzie C. 139
Gouedy(?), Elzb Mrs. 61
 James 61
Govenor's Guards, 3rd Ga.
 Regt. 57
Gowdy, James 136
Grace, Ann Jane Mrs. 213
 Green B. 213
 J.J. 213
 Robert Baker 213
Graddick, Milicent Mrs. 16
 Reddick 16
 Sarah Josephine 16
 Fletcher C. 33
Graham, Alexander Rev. 199
 E. Mrs. 177
 Ella Mrs. 199
 F.D. 98
 Isaac W. Dr. 119
 John Christopher 156

Graham Cont.
 Lucretia V. 39
 Martha J. 3
 Mary Frances Mrs. 119
 P.C. Mrs. 98
 R.T. 177
 Sallie J. 221
 Thomas A. 216
 William Edwin 98
 Wm. M. Rev. 177
 Windsor Rev. 195
 W.W. 38
Gramling, Marcus 93
 William John 93
Granbury's Brigade 167
Granniss, B.E. Mrs. 102
 E.C. 102
 Emma A. 102
 Horace M. Dr. 56
Grant, Bettie H. Mrs. 172
 John Dolly Dr. 208
 Margaret J. (nee
 Segrist) 35
 Mary E. 41
 Samuel W. 96
Grantham, A.M. Rev. 153
 N. Wellborn Lt. 174
Grassel, T. 166
Grasser, C.A. 191
Graves, Ephraim H. 10
 Frank N. 194
 Iverson L. 180, 190
Gray, A. 11, 32, 49
 E.H. 223
 Elzb Mrs. 29
 Ella H. 116
 Frances S. 121
 Hannah Altoe(?) 29
 Jas. H. 137
 James T. Capt. 105(2)
 Louis 55
 Martha E. (nee Baskin)2
 Mary A. 142
 Matthew M. 149
 M.W. Dr. 2
 Samuel 223
 William Henry 149
 Z.T. 29
Greaves, Francis 84
 Rebecca 84
Green, Capt. 103
 A.C. 13
 A.J. Rev. 62
 A.V. (nee Purifoy) 13
 Coleman 2
 Daniel 63
 Dora P. Mrs. 53
 Elzb J. Mrs. 184
 Francis Davie 127
 Frederick 175
 H.D. Rev. 47, 93
 Hester Ann 56
 James W. 65
 J.D. 32
 Jennie A. (nee Harris)
 107
 J.T. 127
 L.D. Mrs. 127
 M.A. Mrs. 32, 66
 Mary Mrs. 90
 Mary A. 1
 Mary A. Mrs. 71
 Mary F. 39
 Matilda Mrs. 62
 M.E. 75
 M.L. 28(2), 148
 Nancy C. (nee Henderson)
 2
 N.L. 100
 Rebecca 47
 Robt/Robert T. 95, 143
 Robert W. 53

Green Cont.
 R.P. 66
 Sarah Tillman 184
 Sue 220
 Susannah Miller 32
 T.C. 57
 Thomas F. Dr. 11
 Thos J. 90
 T.J. 71
 Turner L. 79
 W.G. 144
 Wm. J. 175
 William M. 184
 Wm. P. 71
 Co., Ga. Vols. 55
Green(?), Thompson Rev.
 111
Greene, Charles H. 88
 Charles H. Maj. 192
 Elzb M. (nee Perry) 95
 J.M. 62
 Madora S. 224
 Mattie S. (nee Thompson)
 192
 Myles E. 196
 Sallie A.E. 184
Greenlee, Ephraim M. 105
Greenwood, Ann T. Mrs. 49
 J.T. Lt. 73
 Thomas 73
 Thomas B. 49
Greer, Edward H. 116
 John M. 217
 John W. 26
 Julia Charlotte 217
 Lelitia Mrs. 26
 Levi M. 24
 Martha E. Mrs. 44
 Mary Mrs. 217
 Priscilla J. Mrs. 24
 Salina Frances 24
 Wm. B. 44
 W.W. (Sheriff) 47
Gregg, J.J. Capt. 165
 W.W. Sgt. 68
Gregory, Elzb Mrs. 142
 Harriet Florence Rosa
 92
 Isaac Rev. 225
 James Shurper 92
 Jesse 142
 J.T.M. Rev. 92
 Louis 94
 Mary Mrs. 94
 Mattie E. 225
 Priscilla M. (nee Ray) 6
 Sarah H. 144
 Turplin 202
 W.S. 6
Gresham, Amelia W. Mrs.
 198
 G.W. 198
Grier, B.M. 133
 David 109
 Edward Osgood 133
 Elmoe Marion 133
 Isaac Rev. 4
 L.A. Rev. 133
 Margaret Skinner 133
 Martha Ann 4
 Moses 4
 Rebecca Mrs. 109
 Sarah Mrs. 4
Griffin, Ashley H. 89
 B.F. 206
 C.C. Mrs. 89
 E. Mrs. 201
 E.G. Mrs. 97
 Eliza A. 85
 Eugene P. 201
 George A. 97

242

248

Moore Cont.
 T.W. Dr. 106
 T.W. Jr. 106
 William 65(2)
 William Rev. 118
 William James 118
 Winfred 67
Moorer, Henry J. 71
 J.R. 55
 Mary Mrs. 55
 Mary E. 43
 Robert J. 26
Moorman, Robert 15
 Virginia Caroline Mrs.
  15
 Wm. B. Rev. 166(2)
Moosly, Octabia 52
Morehouse, J.H. 200
 Norman D. Rev. 157
Morel, B.J. 160
 James J. Sgt. 160
 Susan Mrs. 160
Moreland, Isaac Tucker Rev.
  95
 Newdaygate Augustus 95
 Penelope Mrs. 95
 R.O. 75
 Robert Fletcher 75
 Sarah E. Mrs. 161
 Tuttie H. 102
 V.D. Mrs. 75
Morgan, Gen. 175
 Annie E. Mrs. 21(2)
 Asbury Rev. 153
 Eliza Jane 2
 F.E. Mrs. 153
 Harriet Mrs. 47
 Hobson 47
 J.B. Capt. 153
 Jesse Rev. 2
 J.H. Lt. 186
 J. Harmon 143
 J.J. 27, 62
 Julia J.B. 94
 Lucretia A. 106
 Mary (nee Kingman) 153
 Matilda B. Mrs. 183
 Nicholas 17
 P.M. Rev. 88
 Randall 47
 Randel Judge 94
 Sallie R. 21(2)
 Thos Asbury 47
 W.T. 21(2)
Morison, Blancky Mrs. 61
Morris, Judge 136
 Agnes Mrs. 44
 Annie E. Mrs. 141
 Elizabeth Mrs. 86
 Isham 79
 James A. 174
 J. S. 126
 Mary Boyce 126
 Mattie 215
 M. J. T. (nee Brockinton)
  147
 Narcissa 94
 Rhoda 98
 Sallie F. 218
 Sallie H. 136
 Sarah E. 197
 Simeon W. 147
 T. J. 112, 113
 W. D. 196
 Wm. H. Rev. 190
 W. W. 86
Morrison, Angus 131
 Chattie G. 225
 George 225
 John H. 225
 John M. 111

Morrison Cont.
 M.M. 47
Morton, Ann M. 114
 Everet 71
 John W. Rev. 122
Mosely, Jas. H.M. 180
Moss, Fannie 213
 John E. 132
 M.E. Mrs. 37
 Robert M. 224
 Sallie Pope 37
 W.H. Rev. 37
Motes, C.W. 208
Motley, B.K. 207
Motley, Mary Caroline
  (nee Hearn) 129
 T.J. 141
Mott, Hiram H. 2
Mott, Mary Ann H. Mrs. 23
 R.L. 23
Moughon, Thomas 47
Mousseau, Catherine A. 1
Mouzon, 31
 L.H. 119
 William P. 125
Moyer, Enos C. Dr. 35
Muldron, Robt. 220
Mullens, G.W. Sgt. 167
 T.J. 167
Mullinix, Thomas P. 59
 Wm. G. Rev. 59
Mullins, Artemesia (nee
  Deberry) 90
 J.C. Dr. 90
 Mc.F. 56
 M.D. 56
Munden, Isaac 45
 Isaac REv. 182
Mundle, Elzb 31
 Samuel 31
Munds, James Theus 111
Munnerlyn, C.J. Col. 119
 Paulina 221
 William H. Lt. 171
Munro, Edward V. Dr. 113
Munroe, George W.C. 127
 Martha Mrs. 127
 Nancy 126
 Rosa Stevens 127
Murchison, Colin 6, 59,
  112
 Ella J. 6
 John 178
 Kenneth Rev. 6
Murdock, Benjamin S. 34
 C/Chas/Charles P. 14,
  34, 42, 62, 104, 112
 James 34
 Sarah Mrs. 34, 84
 William C. 84
 Wm. P. 34, 84
Murger, Susan J. Mrs. 153
Murph, Henry 209
Murphey, John T. Maj. 196
 Wm. J. 137
Murphy, Anna E. 113
 Caroline Mrs. 46
 Henry L. Rev. 187
 John 91, 187
 John Rev. 187
 John J. 62
 John T. 187
 M.A.E. Mrs. 189
 Martha A. Mrs. 150
 Nancy Mrs. 187
 Patrick 150
 S.Z. 189
 W. Rev. 120
 W.H.N. Lt. 189
 Williams 127
 W.L. 29

Murrah, E.G. Rev. 156
Murray, Arnold 95
 A.S.D. Mr. & Mrs. 28
 Elzb Mrs. 179
 Elzb (nee Mallery) 185
 Eugehia E. Mrs. 58
 H. Hamilton 116
 James B.N. 116
 James Wade 149
 Joel Asbury 95
 Julia Elizabeth 179
 J.W. 32
 Landrum 204
 Lora Bird 116
 Lovick P. 179
 Margaret Ann Drusilla 28
 Maria 156
 Middleton J.K. 95
 N.A.M(?).Mrs. 116
 Philemon Rev. 5
 Thomas J. Lt. 77
 Wm. Dr. 5, 58
Murry, Robert R. Dr. 8
Muse, E.H. 189
 Elliott H. Jr. 37
Mustin, Charles E. 62
 Mary Amelia (nee
  Lathrope) 62
Myers, E.H. Dr. 221
 John W. 167(2)
 Lewis 167
 Lewis Rev. 80
 Oscar A. Rev. 186
 Sophia Mrs. 167
Myrick, Benj. H. 144
 Goodwin Sr. 59
 James Dr. 192, 202
 Martha (nee Parham) 57
 Mary Ann (nee Edmondson)
  144
 Matthew 183
 S.W. 97

Nabers, Nannie 205
Nabors, E.T. Rev. 122
Nail, Mollie E. 3
Nall, John P. 137
Nance, Wm. H. 148
Napier, Nathan 166
 Skelton Jr. 118
Nash, Eliza 2
 Henry 149
 J. 67
 John T. 67
 S. 67
Nathans, Isaac Maj. 14
Neal, Casper 128
 Catharine Mrs. 125
 David Wesley 125
 E.A. 186
 Elena Mrs. 152
 Harriet (nee Turnipseed)
  101
 Jas/James B. 157, 186
 James G. 152
 Martha Bertha Rebecca
  157
 Martha M. Mrs. 157
 Mary Elzb 127,128
 M.F. 185
 Patrick S. 125
 P.T. 101
 Samuel.... 197
 Wm. 152
 Wm/William B. 28, 50
 W.K. 40
Nease, Frederick J. 65
 Irenan 65
 Leonard J. 65

Reid Cont.
  Mattie A. 224
  Mollie E. 148
  Richmond A. Capt. 223
  Sarah Freeman (nee
    Blanton) 25
  Sarah Juliet 137
  Talitha 148
Reife(?), Wm. A. 108
Reinhart, George L. Sgt.
    65
  Jane Mrs. 65
  L.W. 65
  N.F. Lt. 65
Rembert, Elenora Mrs. 222
Ren, Sarah M. (Mrs.?) 5
Rentz, Jacob S. 43(2)
Reubens, Robert N. 207
Revill, William T. 118
Reynolds, Chas. W. 220
  Jas. M. 173
  J/John W. 21, 27, 97
  Lemuel 70
  Lucy Mrs. 33, 70
  Newman 70
  Newnum 33
Rhaney, J. Wm. Sgt. 178
Rheney, R---, Mrs. 197
Rhodes, John H. 177, 197
  Julia A. Mrs. 177
  Whitby H. 197
  Wm./William J. 141, 180
Rhodus, Elzb (formerly
    Headwright) 62
Rhudy, Stephen 120
Rice, Asenath 167
  Berrien 118
  Charles J. 17
  Eddie Benjamin 118
  G.D. Judge 206
  George Duffield 206
  James R. Lt. 144
  Mary Mrs. 118
  T.L. 20
Ricer, Elzb 198
Rich, A.K. Malilda 10
  Elizabeth 209
  William B. Dr. 114
Richards, Carrie 166
  J.C. 101
  Robert 119
Richardson, Annie Lee 207
  Edward E. 226
  E.M. Mrs. 173
  F.M. 207
  Jas. 183
  James P. 15
  Lavinia A. (nee Maddux)
    226
  Mary 39
  Mary S. 41
  P. Maj. 39
  R. Maj. 110
  Sarah E. Mrs. 207
  S.P. (Rev.) 103, 168
  W/Wm. F. 100, 173, 183
  William H. 143
Richbourg, Alice C. 96
  Edwin N. 73
  E.H. Mrs. 63, 107
  F.R. 96
  Isaac A. 107
  J.A. 63(2)
  Joseph F.D. 107
  J.S. Rev. 177
  M.A. Mrs. 96
  Martha R. Mrs. 73
  M.R. Mrs. 21
  Nathaniel 141
  Reuben L.F. Capt. 177
  S.C. 21
  Simeon C. 73

Richbourg Cont.
  Susannah Mrs. 141
  W.H.A. 63
  Agustus Baxter 79
Richie, Lovenia N. 167
Ricks, James J. 75
Riddle, Wm. C. 46
Ride, Fannie 216
Ridgeway, Catharine Mrs.
    175
  Drury 175
  Elzb. Mrs. 71
  James E. 71
  Lorenzo Dow 71
Rigner, Young F. 220
Riley, Darley B. 51
  Drusilla Mrs. 54
  Srusilla (nee Felder)
    38
  Eugenia E. 197
  Francis Mrs. 46
  George 34, 51, 54
  Joseph A. 34
  Mary F. 151
  William 65
  W.S. 215
Ring, E.F. 131
  Margaret Mrs. 131
Rinion, William H. 201
Risher, Benjamin 40
  Mary S. 40
  M.E. 40
Ritchie, C.M. 74
Rivers, A.A. 216
  Emma 203
  Harriet C. Mrs. 189
  James H. 189
  Leonora Augusta 59
  R.H. 98
  Robert L. 189
  Sylvester 15
  Winfield M. Prof. 224
Roach, W.J. 127
Robbins, Fanny 224
Roberds, Martha 148
  R. Thomson 155
  T.L. 108
  W.G. 148
Roberson, James W. 57
  Martha R.L. (nee Wilkins)
    57
  Robert 130
Robert Defenders 50
Roberts, B.F. 171
  Chas. P. 225
  Charlotte 163
  D. Rev. 62, 151
  Francis 163
  Hope H. Lt. 66
  Mary E. 151
  M.M. 9
  Nancy Mrs. 141
  N.H. Mrs. 62
  Robert R.E. 62
  Sarah E. (nee Passmore)
    163
  Wm. F. Rev. 159
  W.K. 159
Robertson, Alfred L. Sgt.
    180
  Benjamin Drake Sr. 64
  Hester Ann Mrs. 88
  Jacob 37
  James 88, 112
  Jas. W. 177
  John Rev. 64
  Lizzie C. (nee Tunnel)
    37
  Nathan B. 88
  Sarah Ann C. 5
Robinson, Benjamin Hill
    96

Robinson Cont.
  Elzb C. 112
  Helen T. Mrs. 153
  H/Henry J. 28, 96
  H.H. Dr. 153
  H.W. Dr. 92
  I.B. 9
  J.E. 217
  J.R. Sgt. 187
  Lauranna A. Mrs. 48
  Mag M. 189
  Margaret Jane 134
  Nancy Elzb 134
  Nancy T. Mrs. 134
  N.T.N. Capt. 123
  Philip B. 134
  R. Calvin 183
  S.A. Mrs. 96
  W.C. Rev. 74
  William C. 74
  Wm. P. 189
Robison, Alexander W. 192
  Francis Monroe 138
  Henry J. 217
  Mary Z. 46
  N.A. Mr. & Mrs. 138
  W.W. Rev. 80, 192, 195
Robuck, W.H. 103
Roch, John 48
Rodd, Matilda E. (nee
    Waite) 104
  Robert 211
Rodgers, A.C. Mrs. 134
  J.C. 134
  Leo H. 223
Rogan, Mary A. 195
Rogers, Alex. G. 65
  Amanda M. 194
  Benjamin T. 65
  C. Dr. 38, 58
  C. Fulwood 23
  Daniel D. 33
  Daniel M. Dr. 147
  Henry 65
  James A. Rev. 149
  James G. Capt. 83
  James H. 91
  James M. 76, 172
  John 170
  Josephine R. Mrs. 112
  Josiah 133
  lewis P. 201
  Lydia L. 37
  Maria A. 194
  Mary 140
  M.W. 126
  Rebecca Mrs. 91
  Rufus 65
  Sallie R. 58
  Sarah 23
  Sarah L. 156
  Simon 38
  Thos. 23
  Washington 91
  William 194(2)
  Wm. A. 11
  William Rev. 156
Rogerson, Mysia 126
Roland, Mary (nee Jackson)
    36
Rollins, Green H. 123
  Sallie 123
  William 128
Rome Light Guards 66
Rone, Clementine 50
Roper, Elzb 30
  John 24
  Mary Mrs. 24
  Samuel A. 20
Rorie, Geo. B. 140
Rosamond, Thomas A. Rev. 44

261

Speer, Alexander Rev. 106
  Elzb A. Mrs. 103
  Frances Albert 106
  J/James F. 175(2)
  Joseph 103
  N.C. Mrs. 175
Speight, Maggie Ophelia
  142
Speir, Alzina Mrs. 58
  James 58
Spell, Amanda M. 111
Spence, Mary Fair (nee
  McMullen) 92
Spencer, Emily Amanda Mrs.
  20
  Shepherd 168
  Wm. S. 20
  W.W. 6
Sperry, Anson McCallum 35
Spier, Wm. E. 211
Spigener, Daniel F. 60
  Paul 52
Spigner, Daniel 61
Spillman, W. 103
Spinks, Zachariah 180
Spivy, Aaron 83
  Aaron S. 83
  Elzb Mrs. 83
  R.D. 208
Springer, William 129
Spruill, James 112
  Wm. E.F. 138
Squires, J.B. 93
Stabler, Caroline E. 10
Stackhouse, Lysias 115
  Nancy (nee Roper) 24
Stacy, A.G. 77
  A.G. Rev. 56
  Alice 174
  C.F. Mrs. 56
  Jas/James 24, 26, 45,
    49
  Sallie White 56
Stafford, Alvis 8
  Henrietta F. 8
  O.G. 73
  Robt. H. 188
  W.H. Mr. & Mrs. 222
Staley, John 66
  Margaret Mrs. 66
  Samuel Mr. & Mrs. 51
  Saml. B. 124
Stallings, Alice 23
  C.M. Mrs. 23
  John M. 23
  S. Mrs. 55
  Wm. Judge 55
Standifer, Catherine Mrs.
  170
Standley, Florida A. Mrs.
  16
Stanford, David 64
  D.P. 52
  Jerome T. 64
  Martha H. Mrs. 64
  M.H. 52
  Wm. O. 52
Stanley, J.B.R. Sgt. 113
  Martin B. Pvt. 142
  Rebecca E. Mrs. 182
Stansell, John W. 20
  John Wesley 101
  Levi Rev. 101
  Susan C. (nee Passmoer)
    114
  William A. 114
  Wm. H. 166
Stanton, James N. 185
Starke, Elzb (nee Dozier)
  85
Starr, Benjamin 6

Starr Cont.
  C.A.Y. 94
  Charlotte Mrs. 6
  John H. 157
  Mary L. Mrs. 157
  S.H.S. 95, 98(2)
  Walter Henry Steele 98
  William D. 6
Steagall, Asbury H. 11
  Fannie Adelia 11
  Frances H. Mrs. 11
  Frances M. (nee Maddux)
    216
  Ivey F. Rev. 23
Stearns, John F. 191
  Marg't. 136
  Zachariah Rev. 191
Steedman, Anderson 52
  Lucretia Mrs. 52
Steele, Mrs. 211
  H.P. Mrs. 81
  John Leak 81
  R.L. 81
Steger, Benjamin F. 213
Stein, John F. Capt. 9,
  15
  Mary A. Mrs. 9
Stelling, J.H. 125
  Rebecca C. Mrs. 125
Stembridge, Nancy Mrs.
  217
  Wm. 217
Stephens, A.B. 22(2), 39
  C.G. Dr. 4
  Elzb J. 187
  Henry E. 111
  James Dr. 32
  J.E. 187
  Jesse 196
  "Little Bella" 32
  M.A. Mrs. 187
  Mary Mrs. 32
  Mary I. 215
  Nancy Josephine 24
  Nathan B. 44
  N.P. 196
  Reuben 140
  R.R. 140
  Solomon 27
Stephenson, Vatavia A.P.
  140
Sternes, A. 25, 220
  Louis L. 220
Stevens, Amanda Mrs. 70
  Elijah 23
  Fath A. Mrs. 22
  Henry 83
  John Mr. & Mrs. 18
  Louis 165
  M.A. 93
  Mary T. Mrs. 88
  Matilda Mrs. 83
  Maynie 88
  P.F. 88
  Rolin W. 1, 70
  Susan L. (Formerly
    Cattrell) 165
  Thomas A. 189
  Toliver 8, 80
  William M. 150
Stevenson, Daniel Capt.
  17
  Judith 137
  M.E. 37
  Phebe 104
  Rachel R. Mrs. 17
Stewart, Earley 116
  Eugenia C. 114
  George 146, 192
  Hester A. Mrs. 52
  Jas (Sr.) 44

Stewart Cont.
  Jas. O. Andrew 98
  Jane J. Mrs. 44
  J.D. 80(2), 139
  John L. Rev. 116
  John W. 50
  Joseph 80
  Julia Ann Mrs. 116
  Larkin 195
  L.E.K. 146
  Lucy M. 146
  Marah Antoinette Mrs.
    101
  Martha Ann 101
  Martha Antoinette 116
  Mary Mrs. 80(2), 139
  Mary Ann Mrs. 192
  Matthew 98, 153
  Nancy (nee Dunn) 116
  Nannie 80
  Osborne Rogers 192
  Penelope (nee Sims) 15
  Priscilla Mrs. 98
  R.B. Rev. 101
  Robert 53
  Roxanna Cornelia 53
  William B. 172
  W.R. 15, 45
Stewart's Cavalry 102
Stiles, Clifford A. Dr.
  95
Still, Harriet R. Mrs. 40
  W.T. 40
Stillings, Henry 114
  Maggie Jane 114
  Rebecca Mrs. 114
Stillwell, Mary E. 81
  S.A. Mrs. 168
  W.A. 168
Stinson, Franklin M. 207
  Martha A. Mrs. 207
Stitt, Harriet R. Mrs. 41
  Wm. Capers Sgt. 53
  W.T. 41
Stivender, Jane F.E. (nee
  Whitestone) 59
Stockdale, James S. 195
Stockton, J/Jas. T. (Rev.)
  11, 29
  J.H. Rev. 122
Stokes, A.J. 59
  C.C. 122
  Eliza J. Mrs. 18
  Emma 109
  Esther Josephine Mrs.
    41
  George W. Rev. 63
  Henry Maj. 109
  Jefferson 182
  J.M. (Rev.) 10, 103
  John R. 48
  Julia A. 140
  Laura 9
  Martha A. Mrs. 109
  Mary A. Mrs. 182
  Mary Eliza 18
  M.C. 41
  M.F. Mrs. 122
  Sarah Eleanor 182
  Wm. 18
  W.W. 122
Stoll, J.C. Rev. 39
Stone, Barton W. 172
  Caroline Sophia (nee
    Whetstone) 172
  Cassie M. 8
  Eliza Mrs. 91
  Elzb Mrs. 19, 184
  George Burton 62
  James G. 91
  J.B. 112

269

272

Wilson Cont.
  Josephine C. (nee Kelley)
    163
  Mary A. 122
  Mary E. Mrs. 182
  Mary M. Mrs. 112
  Mary W. (nee Pooser)
    166
  Nancy Mrs. 122
  Nancy L. 8
  Robt. C. 112
  Sallie 186
  Sarah Chandler Mrs. 81
  William 28
  Wm. J. 202
  Wm. M. Rev. 183
Wily, James A. 200
Wimbach, E.S. Dr. 42
Wimberly, Elzb Mrs. 102
  Gussie E. 102
  Hannah L. Mrs. 194
  Henry S. 216
  James Col. 144, 194
  Penelope Mrs. 1
  Robert R. 1
  Wm. C. 102
  William Hinton 1
Wimbish, James William 60
Wimbly, Wm. 96
Wimbush, Louisiana (nee
    Rodgers) 134
  M.M. 134
  W.M. 161
Wimpy, W.S. 49
Winchester, James M. 86
  Thos. 159
Windsor, Jane J. 74
Winfield, Alex J. 109
Winford, William A. 109
Winfree, Mollie F. 215
Wing, A.M. 11
Wingate, Isabella 7
  Wm. T. 21
Winn, Charles S. 45
  Mary J. 219
  Thomas J. 219
Winship, (son) 207
  Emory, Mr. & Mrs. 207
  Sallie 207
Winstell, Wm. Maj. 135
Winston, Thomas Capt. 190
Winter, Charles 20
  Emily Frances 17
  John 133
  John F. 151
  Mary Ann E. 151
  Guards, Co. F. 50
Wise, J. Benson Dr. 115
  Guard 42
Witherington, James W. 117
Witherspoon, David B. 173
  George G. Dr. 212
  Sallie Hane 173
  Samuel 181
  Sophronia 181
Wofford, Harvey Maj. 98
  Wm. B. Sgt. 98
Woldridge, A.T. 12
Wolf, Mary Mrs. 82
  Samson 82
  Samuel C. 56
  Thomas J. 82
Wolfe, John B. 8
  Texas C. 86
Womack, A.S. Lt. 170
Womble, Curran R. Lt. 190
Wood, Arabella M. 127
  Arminda Mrs. 119
  Benjamin P. 119
  J.A. 102
  Jared H. 63

Wood Cont.
  Jesse (Rev.) 5, 30, 46,
    119
  John J. 119
  L/Landy (Rev.) 1(2),
    23, 29
  Martha C. (nee Garling-
    ton) 21
  Wm. 21
Woodall, Frances Mrs. 126
  J.A. 126
  James D. 126
  Robert B. 45
Wooddy, James Rev. 136
  Thomas J. 136
Wooding, Henry W. 201
  John R. 46
  Matt J. 139
Woodman, James 177
Woodruff, Dr. 80
  Anna L. 80
  M. 97
  M. Mrs. 80
  Samuel 97
  Sophronia W. 123
  William W. 14
Woods, Richard Col. 184
  Susan E. Mrs. 184
Woodward, Addie Mrs. 117
  John G. 197
  John L. Col. 117
  Wallie B. 117
Wooldridge, A.J. 14
  J.H. Dr. 224
Wooley, Maj. 30
Woolley, Vardy Rev. 225
Wooten, A.C. 103
  R.H. 191
Workman, J.J. Rev. 138
  Sarah J. (nee Jenkins)
    108
  William C. 15, 108
Worrell, J.D. 35
  John D. 13
  Roderic P. Capt. 218
Worthy, Ann Mrs. 211
Worwick, Mary Ann Mrs.
    120
  W.A. 120
  Wm. W. 120, 125
Wright, Ann Mrs. 89
  Arminius Rev. 26, 89
  C.C. 55
  C.K. Mrs. 109
  David 192, 214
  George R. Rev. 162
  Georgia V. 207
  H.T. 158
  Isabella H. 23
  Jacob 118
  Jas. D. 99
  James Kendall 109
  J.L. Prof. 109
  John C. Rev. 147
  John M. 68
  John Thos. 147
  John W. Dr. 95
  Josephine 219
  J.T. 65
  Julia 193
  J. Wesley 163
  Lizzie 145
  Margaret M. Mrs. 68
  Martha T. Mrs. 10
  Mary Adaline 95
  Nancy 17
  Nancy B. 220
  Rebecca Mrs. 55
  Rebecca P. 11
  Robert B. 55
  Royal F. 214

Wright Cont.
  Sallie Mrs. 95
  Sallie L. (nee Greer) 26
  Sarah H. Mrs. 37
  Sarah S. Mrs. 67
  Stephen Rev. 37, 82
  Virginia L. Mrs. 147
  W.C. 217
  William 212
  William G. 19
  Wingfield 10
Wrigley, W.W. 218
  B.H. 140
Wyatt, Mary Ella 154
Wylie Capt. 41
Wylley, Naomi Mrs. 30
  W.C. 30
Wyly, James A. 201
Wynn, S.H. 144
Wynne, E. 222
  Frances 32
  Oscar B. Dr. 222
  R.J. 213
  Robt. 52
  Sallie E. 213
  S.M. Mrs. 222
  Susan (nee Hinson) 32(2)
  Susan B. Mrs. 52
  William 32(2)

Yancey, C.B. 222
  Maria E. (nee Ellis) 121
  Milton P.S. 121
  Garland M. 42
Yarbrough, Asbury 36
  Fannie E. 4
  George W. Rev. 126
  J.W. Rev. 174
  S.H. 4
  S.K. Mrs. 4
  Wilbur Fisk, Rev. 174
Yeargin, R.H. 205
Young, Ann F. Mrs. 108
  Charles Morton 170
  Daniel M. 201
  Edward B. 108
  Ellen Augusta 104
  Henry Augustus 108
  I.F. Rev. 61
  James 94
  James Col. 10
  James Rev. 170
  James D. Dr. 203
  Jesse Josephine 150
  John 74
  John C. 61
  J. Simpson 112
  Kate C. 220
  Mary A. 189
  Mary A. (nee Bradley)
    197
  Mary Ann Mrs. 169
  Mary L. 25
  Robert 25
  Robert M. Col. 3
  Samuel H. 169
  Sarah Mrs. 201
  Susan 203
  Thos Young 28
  W.H. 104
  Wm. 163
  Wm. E. 180
  Wm. H. 169, 197
  Wm. H. Jr. 169
Young(?), W.J. 79
Youngblood, A. Jackson 37
  George 39
  George H. 166
  L.E. 37